THE DEVIL'S OWN WORK

Well, I thought when I first heard of the riot in New York, I had some feeling for them, but soon as I found what it really was, I felt it was the devil's own work all through. I guess the strong arm will be exhibited this time up to the shoulder.

—Walt Whitman

We're coming, ancient Abraham, several hundred strong
We hadn't no 300 dollars and so we come along
We hadn't no rich parents to pony up the tin
So we went unto the provost and there were mustered in.

—parody of a Civil War recruiting song

CONTENTS

Acknowledgments	ix
Key Dates and Events	xi
Prologue: "We Have Not One Devil, But Many to Contend With"	1
1. "The Rebel Horde Had Invaded Pennsylvania in Force"	9
2. The Battle Lines Are Drawn: Race, Class, and Religion	29
3. Horace Greeley and the Birth of the Republican Party	46
4. Fernando Wood, the "Southern" Mayor of New York	59
5. "Slavery Must Die That the Nation Might Live"	77
6. Emancipation and Its Enemies	96
7. "A Highwayman's Call on Every American Citizen for '$300 or Your Life'"	113
8. "Down with the Rich Men!": The New York City Draft Riots Begin	125
9. "Chased, Stoned, and Beaten": "A Crusade Against Negroes"	143
10. Monday Night: "The Fiery Nucleus of the Entire Riot"	157
11. "Government in the Hands of the White Race Alone"	171
12. "The Police Cannot Much Longer Sustain the Contest"	184

Kenneth Jackson, Lisa Keller, Owen Gutfreund, and Nancy Haekyung Kwak of Columbia University's Seminar on the City, which provides a stimulating forum for urban historians. Many individuals and institutions were helpful with my research. Kenneth Cobb, the director of New York's Municipal Archives made my work with the court records and claims from the draft riots both efficient and enjoyable. Howard Dodson, the director of the Schomburg Center, thoughtfully told me about the Williamson Collection, which includes an abundance of material on the African American experience during the draft riots. Tom Hoffay encouraged me to visit the American Irish Historical Society, where Scott Kelly guided me to valuable material in the collections and introduced me to Charles Laverty, who generously shared his knowledge of Irish American history. My thanks also go to Ann Jacobs of the Women's Prison Association (and to Elena Sigman for introducing us); Jon A. Peterson of Queens College, CUNY; Russell Flinchum, the archivist at the Century Club; and Peter Scarpa of the Bay Ridge Historical Society.

I received expert assistance from the staffs of the Library of Congress, the Museum of the City of New York, the New-York Historical Society, the Brooklyn Historical Society, the Weeksville Society, and the New York Society Library. At the New York Public Library, the librarians in the Milstein Division at the Humanities Library (Ruth Carr, James Falconi, Maira Liriano, Asa Rubenstein, Charles Scala, and Rob Scott) were especially helpful, as was the staff of the Schomburg Center.

My thanks also go to the Sons of Union Veterans of the Civil War, Oliver Tilden Camp, particularly Donald Steinmaker, who gave me a tour of the veterans' grave sites in the Queens cemeteries. Linda Johns exhaustively and enthusiastically researched the illustrations for the book. Michele Amundsen and Krystyna Skalski at Walker & Company, along with Greg Villepique and Amy King at Bloomsbury, also deserve my thanks.

At Yale, Jaroslav Pelikan encouraged me to pursue a life of historical scholarship, and I had the privilege to study with Edmund Morgan and David Brion Davis. A Beinecke Memorial Scholarship for graduate study also supported my last year at Yale. I offer thanks for the support and encouragement of my parents, Jerrold and Leona Schecter, whose explorations of the past and profound understanding of the present are my constant inspiration.

Last, and most of all, I thank my wife, Vanessa Adler Schecter, for her advice and support and for all the joy, laughter, and love we share.

Key Dates and Events

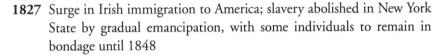

1827 Surge in Irish immigration to America; slavery abolished in New York State by gradual emancipation, with some individuals to remain in bondage until 1848

1828 Competition for jobs leads to recurring race riots in Philadelphia

1829 Race riot in Cincinnati; most of black population flees to Canada

1834 Riots in New York City target growing abolition movement

1837 Economic panic followed by six years of depression

1845 Beginning of Irish Potato Famine (1845–1852) and massive emigration

1846 Mexican War; antislavery Wilmot Proviso reveals split between northern and southern states in U.S. Congress

1848 Famine across northern Europe; rebellions against monarchies

1849 Anti-British, anti-elite riot at Astor Place in New York City

1854 Bloodshed over expansion of slavery into Kansas; Republican party formed; Democrat, Fernando Wood, elected mayor of New York

1857 Republican-backed "Metropolitans" become police force in New York City

1860 Republican president Abraham Lincoln elected; secession begins

1861 Confederacy formed in February; April: the Civil War begins; July: Union defeat at the Battle of Bull Run

1862 April: Battle of Shiloh augurs total war; George B. McClellan begins Peninsular Campaign

June 25–July 1: McClellan driven away from Richmond in Seven Days' Battles

July 17: Militia Draft passed by U.S. Congress (a step toward direct draft)

September 17: Union victory at the Battle of Antietam

September 22: Lincoln's Preliminary Emancipation Proclamation

December 13: Union defeat at the Battle of Fredericksburg

1863 January 1: Emancipation Proclamation declares slaves in Confederacy "forever free"

March 2: First direct federal draft of troops for national army in U.S. history; $300 exemption (commutation clause)

March 6: Race riot in Detroit after announcement of draft law

May: Union defeat at Chancellorsville; draft enrollment begins

June: Robert E. Lee's Confederate army invades Pennsylvania

July 1–3: Union victory at Battle of Gettysburg; Lee retreats

July 4: Confederate surrender of Vicksburg to Ulysses S. Grant

July 13–18: Draft riots in New York City; blacks targeted; violent resistance in Boston and across the North; black troops martyred in Union assault on Fort Wagner, South Carolina

September: Lenient prosecution of rioters; rise of William "Boss" Tweed in New York; Confederate victory at Chickamauga, Tennessee

November: Union victory at Chattanooga, Tennessee

1864 May–August: Grant fights his way toward Petersburg and Richmond

August: Confederate attempt to start riots in Chicago

September: William T. Sherman's Union forces capture Atlanta

November: Lincoln reelected; Confederates try to burn New York

1865 January: Thirteenth Amendment abolishes slavery in the U.S.

April: Grant captures Richmond, war ends; Lincoln assassinated, succeeded by Vice President Andrew Johnson

1866 Riots in Memphis and New Orleans, African Americans massacred; Fourteenth Amendment grants citizenship to African Americans

1867 Reconstruction Act of 1867 puts the South under martial law and helps establish new state governments with participation of blacks

1868 Emergence of Ku Klux Klan; Grant elected president (Republican) over the Democratic candidate, Horatio Seymour, former governor of New York.

1870 Fifteenth Amendment grants voting rights to blacks throughout U.S.

1871 Orange Day riot between Irish Catholics and Irish Protestants in New York City; fall of the corrupt Tweed "Ring"

1872 Grant reelected over the Liberal Republican candidate, and New York *Tribune* editor, Horace Greeley

1873 America's first "Great Depression" begins; massacre of black militia by White League in Colfax, Louisiana

1874 Escalation of anti-black, anti-Republican violence in the South; northern willingness to intervene with federal troops declines

1876 Disputed presidential election between Republican Rutherford B. Hayes and Democrat Samuel Tilden

1877 Hayes wins the White House; withdrawal of federal troops from the South ends Reconstruction; nationwide railroad strike and riots

Prologue: "We Have Not One Devil, But Many to Contend With"

~⌒

ar more important than all military events, & more disastrous, & still more ominous of evil for the North than would be a signal defeat on a battlefield, is the occurrence of a wide-spread & bloody riot in the city of New York," the Virginia secessionist Edmund Ruffin exulted in his diary on July 18, 1863. The nation's first federal conscription, which exempted those who could pay three hundred dollars, triggered the worst riots in American history, which spread from New York to neighboring areas, including Westchester County, Long Island, Staten Island, and Jersey City, as well as Newark and Troy. Violent resistance to the draft had erupted throughout the Union, from the marble quarries of Vermont and the Pennsylvania coalfields to the midwestern states of Ohio, Indiana, Iowa, and Minnesota.[1]

Ruffin, like many southerners, clearly hoped the riots would counteract the stunning Confederate defeat at Gettysburg, which had thwarted General Robert E. Lee's invasion of Pennsylvania two weeks earlier, on July 1–3, 1863. Gettysburg, and the fall of Vicksburg, Mississippi, on July 4, together marked the great turning point of the Civil War, setting the Union on the path to final victory after two years of almost unrelieved failure on the battlefield. The riots were over by the time Ruffin took note of them, but he hoped the forced suspension of the draft in New York City would encourage renewed outbursts across the North.[2]

In his 1860 novel, *Anticipations of the Future,* Ruffin envisioned the destruction of New York by riot and arson, along with

Edmund Ruffin

an alliance between the South and the Midwest, as the keys to victory over the North in a civil war. The slave states would win their independence, Ruffin predicted, because the disruption of trade with the agricultural South would trigger business failures and rampant unemployment in Boston, Philadelphia, New York, and other northern cities.

In the grim certainty of the past tense, Ruffin's narrator described angry workers in New York raiding gun shops and liquor stores, defeating the police and military, and torching buildings all over the city. "A strong wind was blowing, which soon spread the flames faster than did the numerous incendiaries." New York and Brooklyn and their suburbs became "one raging sea of flame . . . rising in billows and breakers above the tops of the houses higher than ever sea was raised by the most violent hurricane," Ruffin wrote. "Many thousands of charred and partly consumed skeletons . . . were afterwards to be seen among the ruins." The South repelled the northern invaders and captured Washington, D.C., which became the seat of the southern federal government; the novel ended with a truce between the two sides, and the prospect of the midwestern states breaking away from the North to ally with the South.[3]

By July 1863, Ruffin seemed clairvoyant. Union forces had suffered so many defeats since the Civil War began in April 1861 that the Confederate States of America seemed on the verge of becoming and remaining a separate, slaveholding republic. New York was burning, and since late June, some 2,500 Confederate cavalrymen led by the bold and reckless John Hunt Morgan had been trying to destabilize the Midwest: Invading from northern Kentucky, the raiders had been tearing through Indiana and Ohio, hoping to spark an insurrection among the disgruntled inhabitants.[4]

Perhaps the Confederate leadership in Richmond was using Ruffin's novel, along with remarks in a similar vein by southern orators and newspaper editors, as a blueprint for its military strategy: Combined with Lee's invasion of Pennsylvania in early July, and with the raid in the Midwest, the riots in New York and other cities struck alarmed northerners as part of a concerted plan. That Lee's invasion had stripped New York of its militia, who were rushed to Pennsylvania two weeks before the riots, likewise fueled this suspicion.

The *New York Times* declared on July 16: "When the plots of the Southern rebels for the overthrow of the Union and the inauguration of war first took form and shape, one of the great elements of power and success upon which they counted was the cooperation of the 'New-York mob,' or the 'Northern mob.' This mob, these masses of the great industrial centres of the North were, in fact, at one time looked upon as the chief tool in the hands of the Secessionists." The *Times* was convinced that "agents direct from Richmond" were in the city "using both energy and money in feeding the flames that for three days have darkened, and for three nights have reddened, the sky of New-York." None of these conspirators had been identified, the *Times* explained: "As a matter of course, they work under false pretexts and with devilish subtlety."[5]

The riots that broke out in New York on July 13, 1863, appeared to be a spontaneous popular uprising against Abraham Lincoln's imposition of the nation's first federal draft and its clause exempting any conscript who could provide a substitute or pay three hundred dollars, which amounted to a year's wages for many workingmen. The *Times* assumed the true "instigators" of the riot were "holding themselves prudently in the background," since "no distinct individual leadership" was discernible among the mobs.[6] Triggered by the sacking and burning of a draft office at Forty-sixth Street and Third Avenue on a Monday morning, the riots quickly escalated into four days of looting, arson, and lynching that left more than one hundred known dead, forced thousands of African Americans to flee the city, and threatened to destroy the Union's commercial and industrial hub.[7]

The strongest evidence against the conspiracy theory is that the Confederates could not re-create the draft riots in the North even though they tried for the rest of the war, using agents based in Canada. The explosive mix of ingredients in 1863 was too complex to replicate at will. Layered with elements of racial, religious, ethnic, and class conflict, the draft riots, as they were known, were about much more than the draft. And the scale of the fighting across the entire metropolitan area—with platoons of troops using live ammunition and artillery rounds—went beyond most riots. In the words of the city's ineffectual mayor, George Opdyke, the draft riots were a "civil war" in which citizen volunteers had to be enlisted against their rioting neighbors because the police and military were overwhelmed.[8]

The rioters took encouragement from earlier speeches by New York's Democratic politicians, including Governor Horatio Seymour and Congressman Fernando Wood, who sympathized with the slaveholding Confederacy and attacked the Lincoln administration for using the war as an excuse to encroach on northerners' civil liberties. Poor, white, and largely Irish Catholic rioters clashed with policemen and soldiers, many of whom were also Irish. The mobs targeted the homes of wealthy, native-born Protestants, who tended to be Republicans, and who appealed to Lincoln for federal troops to crush the immigrant rioters and execute their demagogic leaders. Blacks, resented by poor whites as competitors for jobs and as the favored minority of Republican abolitionists, were attacked wherever they could be found.[9]

Black leaders saw the Democrats and their newspapers as the true culprits. For years, physician James McCune Smith explained, "the press, with but few exceptions, hounded on the increasing hatred of the multitude until it found logical expression in the unspeakable atrocities of the New York riots." Fighting the battle in the press, Manton Marble, editor of the New York *World* and spokesman for the Democrats, defended the rioters and excoriated the Lincoln administration for its military "despotism." Marble also locked horns with Horace Greeley, the Republican editor of the New York *Tribune,* who had pressured Lincoln to abolish slavery and came to be identified with the radical wing of the party during the Civil War, making him and the *Tribune* office prime targets for the mobs.[10]

Indeed, this civil insurrection was a microcosm—within the borders of the supposedly loyal northern states—of the larger Civil War between the North and South. Enmeshed in the fight over the government's new conscription law were the very issues—of slavery versus freedom for African Americans, and the scope of federal power over states and individuals—that had shattered the country and plunged it into years of sectional strife. And the riots themselves prefigured a backlash against the abysmal living and working conditions of America's underclass that turned the rest of the nineteenth century into the most violent period of labor conflict in American history.[11]

• • •

The rioters' rage stemmed as much from the draft as from Republican president Abraham Lincoln's Emancipation Proclamation, which went into effect six months earlier, on January 1, 1863, declaring all slaves in the rebellious states to be "thenceforward and forever free." To fulfill this promise of freedom, Union forces would not only have to win on the battlefield but take over the South and implement a social revolution. Democratic leaders, particularly Fernando Wood, had been telling their working-class constituents for years that free blacks from the South would take their jobs; with the Emancipation Proclamation, they warned, the federal government was sending them to die for the slaves who would replace them on the docks and in the factories.[12]

The Emancipation Proclamation can be seen as the first act in the contentious process of Reconstruction, a struggle to determine not only the proper treatment of the vanquished Confederate states after the war but the legal and social status of African Americans as well. Thus Reconstruction in effect began during the war, even as northerners clashed over how it should end. Radical Republicans wanted to fight on until the South was conquered and slavery was overthrown, after which they intended to raise the former slaves to full equality. Conservatives, mostly Democrats, hoped instead to end the war either by negotiation or by a limited military victory that would reunite the country without reconstructing southern society and leave slavery intact.[13]

New York City, with its strong commercial ties to the South, was a hotbed of sympathy for the Confederates, overrun, according to "loyal" northerners, by traitorous Democratic "Copperheads," named after the poisonous snake, who demanded negotiation, lenient treatment of the Confederates, and preservation of their social structure through whites-only local self-government, referred to as "home rule." New York's radical Republicans—civic leaders like Joseph Choate, George Templeton Strong, and Frederick Law Olmsted—aided the black victims of the draft riots and urged Lincoln to impose martial law as a way to end the violence and purge the city's corrupt, "semi-loyal" officials. By contrast, the Democrats who ran the city—William Tweed, A. Oakey Hall, John Hoffman, and a host of aldermen and state senators—countered that they as local leaders were best suited to calm the mob's fury through negotiation and to cope with the aftermath of the crisis.[14]

Thus not only were the draft riots a microcosm of the Civil War, but the debate over how to end the riots and dispense justice in their wake foreshadowed the national struggle that would develop over Reconstruction. Moreover, the survival and resurgence of the Democratic party in New York City in the dozen years after the riots significantly influenced national events, helping to defeat the radical Republicans' agenda of racial equality.[15]

By 1865, the North had won the Civil War, the country was nominally reunited, and slavery was abolished nationally by the Thirteenth Amendment. The black clergyman Henry Highland Garnet, who had survived the draft riots and ministered to the wounded and homeless in his community, delivered a powerful sermon in the House of Representatives celebrating abolition and laying out the aspirations of African Americans for full citizenship and equal opportunity. However, by 1877 the Democrats, then led by the party organization in New York—most prominently, by the corporate attorney and presidential nominee Samuel Tilden, along with Marble and Wood—were able to undermine this vision and stop radical Reconstruction in its tracks. In the process, they condoned an onslaught of racial violence in the South that echoed the draft riots in its tactics and intent, and perpetuated a caste system in lieu of slavery.[16]

Enflamed by labor competition, the draft rioters' fury against the Emancipation Proclamation was aimed at keeping the majority of African Americans in the South while driving those in the North to the fringes of white society. Once emancipation was a legal reality, the Ku Klux Klan and similar insurgent, terrorist groups in the South sought through murder and intimidation to keep blacks from voting, to counteract the revolution in civil rights that promised to give African Americans full equality under the law.[17]

In this sense, the draft rioters, the Klan, and their Democratic leaders succeeded, at least in their own era. A deal struck in the contested presidential election of 1877 gave the Republican candidate Rutherford B. Hayes the White House in exchange for an end to Reconstruction in the South. Restoration of home rule and the withdrawal of federal troops led to almost a century of Jim Crow, of racial segregation and discrimination that arrested the social and political progress for which the radical Republicans had fought the Civil War.[18]

The draft riots proved to be the first outburst in what became a campaign of anti-Reconstruction racial violence—almost a century of lynching throughout the North and South aimed at suppressing the civil rights of African Americans. Not until the "second Reconstruction" of the 1950s and 1960s, when the federal government once again aggressively enforced the Fourteenth and Fifteenth Amendments to the Constitution, and supplemented them with new laws ensuring voting rights and desegregation of public schools, would the legislation enacted during the Civil War era truly become the basis for full racial equality under the law.[19]

The draft riots were also a preview of the social unrest that would afflict America well into the twentieth century. In New York, Lincoln's decision not to impose martial law left in place the corrupt Democratic machine through which "Boss" Tweed ran the city as a sort of welfare state. This was far more congenial to the poor immigrant seeking medical care or a civil service job than the Republican, Protestant establishment's vision of "scientific charity" and frugal government.* In a larger sense, however, the rioters failed, for the most part, to awaken the conscience of American government and society with regard to the deep-seated grievances of the poor.[20]

Caught in the jaws of an accelerating economy dominated by industrial capitalism, American workers were exploited in the factory system and packed into the festering slums that mushroomed in an era of rapid growth and urbanization. They were free according to Republican free-labor ideology but were "wage slaves" in fact. The class conflict laid bare by the draft riots grew more acute as industrialization advanced and the gulf between rich and poor became wider during the Gilded Age. Americans reluctantly acknowledged that rigid social divisions were as much a fact of life in the United States as in European monarchies.[21]

One legacy of the draft riots was a harsh, repressive response to labor protests by local, state, and federal authorities, spurred by middle- and upperclass anxiety about the "dangerous classes." White workers, like African Americans, faced a long struggle to improve their lot; only gradually would they realize the benefits of joining forces with blacks instead of allowing employers and politicians to pit the two groups against each other on the bottom rung of the economic ladder.[22]

In a letter to his brother, Walt Whitman described the New York draft riots as "the devil's own work" but did not explicitly blame the Irish, as he might have twenty years earlier in newspaper editorials that displayed his extreme nativism, his bigotry against Irish Catholic immigrants.[23] George Templeton Strong's diary, by contrast, openly referred to the rioters as "Celtic devils" and tools of the Democratic party. The Republican press described the rioters as "ferocious fiends" or "human animals possessed by devils."[24]

Democrats, however, regarded the radical Republican agenda of emancipating the slaves, and raising them to full equality, as an infernal evil. After Lincoln issued the Preliminary Emancipation Proclamation in September 1862, conservative diarist Maria Daly declared that between the president and the abolitionists who influenced him, "we have not one devil, but many to contend with." Less than a year later, New York's Democratic press blamed the

---

*The Association for Improving the Condition of the Poor carefully scrutinized poor individuals and families to determine if they "deserved" assistance.

draft riots on the radical Republicans, saying they had provoked the working class by elevating blacks and welcoming them in white society. The New York *Copperhead* called Lincoln the "demon of black Republicanism."[25]

Married to an Irish American judge, Maria Daly voiced the concerns and aspirations of the New York Irish in her diary, revealing their reluctance to fight a war for abolition, and their competition with blacks in the quest for acceptance in American society. Thus, while Walt Whitman was referring to the riots themselves, the phrase "the devil's own work" describes much more: the polarization of the country in the Civil War; the chorus of voices on both sides of the issues within the presumably unified but in fact deeply divided North; the dilemma of how to serve justice after the draft riots and during the remainder of the Reconstruction era.[26]

President Lincoln's decision not to impose martial law in New York and to leave the Democrats in power; President Ulysses S. Grant's similar approach of using the army sparingly in the South to contain Klan violence; and the Compromise of 1877, which left the former slaves to the mercy of white supremacist, "redeemer" governments in the former Confederacy—all were Faustian bargains, exercises in "the art of the possible." The Civil War and Reconstruction laid the groundwork for destroying slavery and the racial caste system in America. However, the compromises in the wake of the draft riots meant the task of exorcising these "demons" from the body politic would continue far into the next century.[27]

For the generation that fought the Civil War, and observed from the home front, the draft riots of 1863 appeared to be an infernal plot, an integral part of Confederate military strategy, coordinated with Lee's invasion of Pennsylvania. Few among New York's blue-blooded families or its hundreds of new millionaires—war profiteers who made up the "shoddy aristocracy"—or its corrupt aldermen heeded the warnings of sanitary reformers that the slums were a volcano ready to erupt. In June of that year, all eyes were on the Potomac River, as Lee's mighty Army of Northern Virginia charged northward, sowing panic and galvanizing the divided people of the North to repel the invaders. In more ways than one, the enemy was already inside the gates.

CHAPTER I

"The Rebel Horde Had Invaded Pennsylvania in Force"

∽

GOD HAS AGAIN CROWNED THE VALOR OF OUR TROOPS WITH SUCCESS," General Robert E. Lee telegraphed Jefferson Davis, president of the Confederacy, on June 15, 1863. Lee's powerful army of seventy-five thousand troops had marched north through the Shenandoah Valley, and the advance corps had overwhelmed the Union defenses at Winchester, in northern Virginia, capturing their artillery, and opening the path to Maryland and Pennsylvania. The Confederate invasion of the North had begun.[1]

The hungry rebel soldiers, no longer able to live off the land in war-torn Virginia, would strip the northern countryside bare in their search for food and supplies, while sending many blacks they captured south into slavery. Panicked northerners knew that if Lee crossed the Potomac River, Washington, D.C., and Baltimore would be exposed to attack, along with Harrisburg, the capital of Pennsylvania. If the rebels pushed on across the Susquehanna River, they would soon be at Philadelphia and then at New York's doorstep, where southern ironclad warships might simultaneously attack the harbor of the Union's commercial and industrial hub.[2]

Horace Greeley's New York *Tribune* claimed to have reliable information that the invasion was "the work of the Copperheads or Peace Democrats," and that "an emissary of this traitorous faction" had visited Jefferson Davis, urging him to "lay waste" Pennsylvania's fields and towns. The term Copperhead referred to a poisonous snake, but southern sympathizers adopted the pejorative label and wore badges made from copper Liberty-head pennies to denounce northern oppression. The *Tribune* also reported that at least one lodge of the Knights of the Golden Circle, a secretive Copperhead organization, was welcoming the rebel army into Pennsylvania.[3]

The success of the invasion was crucial for Lee in part because potential disaster loomed in the western theater of the Civil War. When Lee proposed the invasion in May, he told Davis no reinforcements from Virginia could be spared to save the strategically vital citadel town of Vicksburg, in Davis's home state of Mississippi, which Union general Ulysses S. Grant had besieged. On June 15, Confederate general Joseph E. Johnston told the Confederate secretary of war that Vicksburg could not be saved and refused to attack Grant from the rear.[4]

If Vicksburg fell, along with Port Hudson, Louisiana, to the south, and Grant gained control of the Mississippi River, the Confederates knew he would open it to commerce while stopping the flow of recruits into the rebel army from the western states of the Confederacy: Texas, Louisiana, and Arkansas. Loss of the river would also expose the South to invasion from the west. Lee's invasion of the Northeast was planned to offset that possible loss by securing recognition for the Confederacy from Britain and France, raising a clamor for peace among war-weary northerners, and strengthening the Peace Democrats—Lincoln's most bitter political opponents—perhaps even handing them a victory in the presidential race the following year.[5]

The South did not have the manpower and resources to fight indefinitely, so Lee had recently advised Davis to exploit political divisions in the North by encouraging the "rising peace party" and trying to bring about an armistice. While some Peace Democrats might favor reunification of the North and South—and the Confederacy certainly did not—Lee's main goal was to get the North to sue for peace; the terms could be discussed later.

To take full advantage of the anticipated success of the invasion, Davis also sent Confederate vice president Alexander Stephens on a mission to approach Lincoln and open peace negotiations. While Lee's army moved north, to grab the Union by the throat, Stephens was on a boat headed for the mouth of the Potomac, where he hoped Lincoln would grant him a pass to cross into Union territory and up the river to Washington.[6]

The timing of the invasion was critical in Lee's eyes, because northern newspapers revealed that the terms of enlistment for tens of thousands of Union soldiers were about to expire. With 130 regiments leaving for home in May and June, the War Department needed to bring in 300,000 men to replace them. The new conscription law, passed in March—the first federal draft in U.S. history—was expected to replenish the Union ranks. Lee anticipated this period of transition would cause confusion in the enemy army and saw an opportunity to attack.[7]

No document records that Lee thought his invasion would also coincide with rioting against the draft in northern cities. However, northern Democrats had been marshaling popular opinion against the new law and its clause exempting from the draft anyone who could provide a substitute or pay three hundred dollars—almost a year's salary for the average worker. The habitual violence of urban mobs in the North was viewed by many southerners as an asset to the Confederacy.[8] In 1861, on the eve of the Civil War, South Carolina's *Charleston Mercury* had predicted that lower tariffs in the South would divert European trade away from New York, and that "pauperism and general distress will be so great that uprisings and riots will take place."[9] A year earlier, the *Mercury* had serialized Edmund Ruffin's *Anticipations of the Future*.[10]

Lee's triumphant message of June 15, 1863, to Davis in Richmond, Virginia, the Confederate capital, reflected his faith in the invincibility of his army, seemingly justified by the first two years of the Civil War. Starting with the rebel capture of Fort Sumter in Charleston, South Carolina, in April 1861, the war had gone badly for the North, and the outcome of the struggle remained in doubt. While the initial Union war cry had been "Forward to Richmond," Lee's nimble army and a succession of incompetent, irresolute northern generals had barred the way. Irvin McDowell, George McClellan, John Pope, Ambrose Burnside, and finally Joseph Hooker commanded the federal forces, alternately displaying extreme caution, then fighting and losing tens of thousands of men.[11]

New York City had poured almost fifty thousand men into the field in the heady opening months of the war. A year later, the city's poor who had fled the slums by joining the army quickly discovered that war was a waking nightmare, not an escape or adventure, and their families learned it too. Amputees were seen everywhere in the streets; funerals were frequent. Civic leaders and businessmen who had recruited volunteer units in 1861 were not professional officers and turned out to be incompetent in battle, losing huge numbers of men. New York City's Irish and Italian regiments were being decimated. Irish and Germans captured by the Confederacy were disdained as "Huns" and "barbarians" and treated with special harshness. Newspapers told of the bloodbath, as did illustrated magazines. Deserters fled to the city, where they could disappear in the crowd and avoid prosecution.[12]

The previous six months had been the worst. At Fredericksburg in December 1862, almost thirteen thousand Union troops were killed or wounded. "It was a living hell from which escape seemed scarcely possible," recalled Colonel Robert Nugent of New York's Irish Sixty-ninth Regiment of Volunteers, which was assigned to lead the doomed assault. "By virtue of the commanding position of the enemy no attack could have been successful."[13]

Defeated again at Chancellorsville on May 2–6, 1863, Union forces suffered another seventeen thousand casualties. Lee had gained the confidence to invade the North in June.[14]

By the summer of 1863, Lincoln's three main strategic goals for the year were stalled. One priority was to capture Vicksburg. Grant was on his sixth attempt and remained undaunted as well as unsuccessful. While Lee planned his invasion to precede the North's draft, Grant, with opposite objectives, also felt time pressure because of the upcoming conscription. Grant assumed that if he failed to make progress in his campaign against Vicksburg, "the draft would be resisted, desertions ensue, and the power to capture and punish deserters lost."

Lincoln hoped as well to take Chattanooga and drive the rebels out of central Tennessee, but General William Rosecrans had been bogged down there since an indecisive battle more than six months earlier. Equally discouraging for the North was the inability of the army to advance on Richmond. Adding to Lincoln's frustration in the eastern theater was a failed assault on Fort Sumter in April by eight Union ironclads. The fort, and thus Charleston—capital of the first state to secede and a symbolic prize of great value—remained out of reach.[15]

The capture of Richmond would have put the Confederate government to flight, challenged the South's status as a legitimate, separate nation, and signaled the demise of the rebel war effort. Instead, Lee in June 1863 stood poised to turn the tables on the North, to invade its territory, not to occupy it but to gain European recognition and dictate the terms of peace, thus ensuring the continued existence of the Confederate States of America.

Such a victory over the power of the federal government and vindication of the states' right to secede threatened to dissolve the United States. The Confederacy proclaimed this would be a victory for their independence over a tyrannical central government. Lincoln and his supporters instead viewed the United States as "the last, best hope" for free government on Earth.[16]

"The Pennsylvania Governor, [Andrew] Curtin, cried to us for help; the President called out from the White House that he wanted us to come down to the Border; our Governor, [Horatio] Seymour, said go, and accordingly we hurriedly kissed those we loved best, and started for the wars," recalled John Lockwood, a militiaman in the Twenty-third Regiment, New York State National Guard. While Lee was telegraphing Davis on June 15 about the capture of Winchester, Lincoln issued a call for one hundred thousand state militiamen from the adjacent states—Pennsylvania, Ohio, Maryland, and West Virginia—to assist the army and thwart the invaders.

Doubtful of a full response, Secretary of War Edwin Stanton privately appealed to Governor Horatio Seymour of New York and Major General Charles Sandford, head of the state's militia regiments, for an additional twenty thousand men, to serve for up to six months, until Pennsylvania could muster enough troops to repel the invasion. The states would have to pay the soldiers a bounty but would also have these men deducted from their quota in the upcoming federal draft.

By the following day, June 16, the entire city of New York "moved with a common impulse," Lockwood wrote, as militiamen reported for duty and volunteers hurried to sign up with their favorite regiments. In addition to the regular U.S. Army and the militia, volunteer units comprised a third category of troops in the Union forces.* Uniformed men "were dashing frantically backward and forward through the streets, and in and out of the various armories of the city, in search of essentials," recalled militiaman George Wingate of the Twenty-second Regiment.

On the morning of the seventeenth, "rain fell in torrents" but well-wishers turned out with umbrellas to cheer the city's "gallant" Seventh Regiment, composed of smartly uniformed, well-drilled young men, mostly American-born sons of the upper middle class. The highly disciplined Seventh was the militia unit city fathers habitually relied on to put down the frequent riots that had plagued New York for decades, and it became the first to depart for the front, followed by two other regiments in the evening.

In the emergency of the Confederate invasion, social tensions faded into the background, for the moment. "Martial enthusiasm pervades all classes, welling up from the several armories and overflowing the twin cities" of New York and Brooklyn, Lockwood wrote. The regiments departed, "amid tumultuous cheering, the fluttering of handkerchiefs, the ringing of bells, and the thousand bewildering noises of an enthusiastic crowd," recalled Wingate.

The next day was mercifully overcast for the departing militiamen of the Twenty-third Regiment heading for Fulton Ferry in Brooklyn, sweating under heavy packs filled with equipment and two days' cooked rations. "From the armory all the way down to the river it is a procession of Fairy-Land," Lockwood reported. "The windows flutter with cambric; the streets are thronged with jostling crowds of people, hand-clapping and cheering . . . while up and

---

*When the Civil War began, the regular U.S. Army consisted of fewer than fifteen thousand troops, led by officers drawn from the nation's military academies. However, service in the state militia was compulsory (for men between the ages of eighteen and forty-five), and the president could call on the states to contribute their forces for up to ninety days at a time. In 1862, a new law extended the limit to nine months. Volunteers, who comprised most of the Union army's manpower, and who generally started out with even less training than the militia, were civilians whose patriotism or financial need spurred them to enlist.

down the curving street . . . the gleaming line of bayonets winds through the crowding masses—the men neatly uniformed and stepping steadily as one."[17]

The invasion had stirred a war-weary public in New York, but the rush of patriotism left the city and state virtually defenseless. The Pennsylvania militia had generally failed to muster for the emergency, and in the next two and a half weeks, New York sent almost sixteen thousand men to Pennsylvania—more than any of the neighboring states called on by President Lincoln. Governor Seymour telegraphed Colonel Marshall Lefferts of the Seventh Regiment to assure him the troops would not be kept any longer than necessary: "Will see the regiment is not kept longer than thirty days."[18]

Seymour had reason for concern. The day before Stanton's request for militia regiments, on June 14, Major General John Wool, commander of the U.S. Army's Department of the East, headquartered in New York City, had written to Seymour, warning that the eight forts in New York's harbor were woefully undermanned and the city was vulnerable to attack. Altogether, the forts had only 550 men. After the militia left, Richard Delafield of the U.S. Corps of Engineers also wrote to Seymour, calling for the harbor defenses to be properly garrisoned. "Should the enemy be successful, we are at this moment without any reserve, or, indeed without any force whatever to check an advance on this city."[19]

The Union's first line of defense was the ninety-thousand-man Army of the Potomac, then led by "Fighting Joe" Hooker, who, after Chancellorsville, showed little appetite for another direct clash with Lee's forces.* Encamped on the Rappahannock River in Virginia, Hooker had sent scouts who discovered Lee's march northward in early June, and the Union general proposed an attack on the enemy's rear. Instead, Lincoln told him to confront the rebel intruders head-on. Hooker then suggested a march to Richmond to counter the invasion of the North, at which point Lincoln realized the general would have to be replaced. In the meantime, Lincoln told Hooker to stay on Lee's flank while he moved north toward the Potomac River and attack if possible at a weak point in the long Confederate column that stretched from Fredericksburg to Winchester.[20]

Pressing northward after the capture of Winchester on June 15, Lee's entire army had crossed the Potomac into Maryland by the twenty-seventh, unimpeded by Hooker's forces, which followed too late. Still, Lincoln believed that with Lee cut off from his base in Virginia, Union troops could finally surround

---

*Hooker's nickname resulted from a typo, not his ferocity. A hurried battle dispatch entitled "Fighting—Joe Hooker" was transformed when a typesetter at a New York newspaper left out the dash.

and destroy his army. Hooker, however, immediately offered the same excuses as McClellan had—he needed reinforcements, the politicians in Washington were scheming against him—and Lincoln replaced him with General George Meade on June 28. Though Meade was a corps commander and unknown to the rank and file of the army at large, who adored McClellan, their morale soared after leaving the hostile territory of Virginia to defend northern soil.[21]

Lee's troops had quickly divided, preparing to seize various objectives in Pennsylvania, but news of Meade's forces crossing the Potomac in pursuit prompted Lee to concentrate his strength for a major battle. Union cavalry commander John Buford was also thinking ahead to a decisive clash with the enemy and on June 30 sent two brigades to a hill overlooking Gettysburg, Pennsylvania, a thriving village which he expected the Confederates to enter and try to occupy because of the dozen roads that led in and out of it, and the high ground surrounding it, making it easy to defend. Aside from its strategic value, the town was supposed to have a large supply of shoes, badly needed by many barefoot Confederates. The arrival of a rebel division on the morning of July 1 sparked a three-day battle—the biggest and most pivotal of the Civil War.[22]

Instead of shoes, the Confederates found Buford's cavalrymen dismounted and firing at them rapidly with breech-loading carbines from the cover of fences and trees. While the cavalrymen fended off a much larger Confederate force during the early morning, messengers for both armies quickly spread the word of an impending battle, and infantry were rushed to the scene. Lee's plans had been overtaken by events: With his army still scattered, the Federals had drawn him into a general engagement on ground of their choosing. Meade hadn't planned on a confrontation at Gettysburg either, but Buford could hardly have scouted a better spot.[23]

Union reinforcements arrived two hours later, just in time to halt the rebel advance against the exhausted cavalrymen. By early afternoon, the two sides faced each other along a three-mile arc north of the town, where the nineteen thousand Federals were outnumbered by twenty-four thousand Confederates. Lee arrived from the west and saw his advantage. Without waiting for more troops to arrive, he allowed the commanders present to attack with full force, and with their unnerving rebel yell, the divisions smashed the Union right wing and then drove the tougher left wing off the high ground, ultimately forcing both to retreat through Gettysburg to Cemetery Hill, half a mile south of the town.[24]

Lee's forces had won the first round, but whoever could seize and hold the long ridge and hills south of Gettysburg would ultimately win the battle and control the area. Lee assigned General Richard Ewell to storm Cemetery Hill if possible, but the latter decided against the risky assault, which, had it occurred and succeeded, might well have changed the outcome of the entire battle.

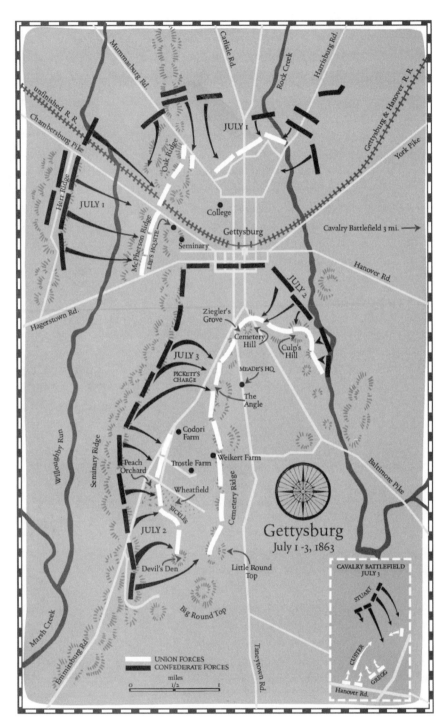

The Battle of Gettysburg, July 1–3, 1863

Instead, by nightfall another corps of Union troops had arrived and extended the defensive line from Cemetery Hill along the entire two-mile ridge and the adjacent hills. Meade arrived that night with more Union forces, further bolstering their natural fortresslike position with artillery, men, and matériel.[25]

General James Longstreet urged Lee to maneuver around the southern end of the Union position, thereby threatening Washington, D.C., and drawing the Federals out into a battlefield of the Confederates' choosing. However, Lee was determined to make a frontal attack the next day, because his men's ardor was at a fever pitch from their repeated successes, and he felt a flanking maneuver would smack of fear and retreat in the face of an inferior foe. Like Lincoln, Lee thirsted for the destruction of the enemy army, which had eluded him despite the big victories in the Seven Days' Battles in 1862, when he had driven McClellan away from the outskirts of Richmond, and at Chancellorsville in May.[26]

"Send forward more troops as rapidly as possible," Governor Curtin of Pennsylvania frantically telegrammed Seymour on July 2. "The battles of yesterday were not decisive, and if Meade should be defeated, unless we have a large army, this State will be overrun by rebels." Seymour responded by sending additional militia regiments, further stripping New York of defenders.[27]

Two days earlier, the Republican mayor of New York City, George Opdyke, had telegraphed Seymour, urging him "as a matter of absolute necessity" to authorize General Sandford to raise twenty or thirty militia regiments in New York City and Brooklyn for home defense. Opdyke estimated that between the militia and U.S. troops, the city had fewer than one thousand men, and told Sandford that at least two or three regiments of militia should be left in the city. Sandford replied that he had to follow Seymour's orders, but assured the mayor that the militia and police could handle any "emergency likely to arise."[28]

Elected mayor in 1861, for decades Opdyke had been manufacturing and selling cheap clothing used for slaves in the South. Like other New York merchants, he profited from slavery but nonetheless became an ardent Republican and a leading war organizer. He found profits there too, supplying thousands of blankets to the Union army. As state clothing inspector, he had recently approved shoddy Union army uniforms from Brooks Brothers.[29]*

---

*In 1864, Opdyke's political nemesis, Thurlow Weed, accused him of having "made more money out of the war by secret partnerships and contracts for army clothing, than any fifty sharpers in New York." A libel trial followed, and Weed's words were borne out. Opdyke had also manufactured guns during his term as mayor, selling them to the army at an exorbitant markup of 66 percent.

Opdyke worried that the city was "filled with Rebel emissaries" spreading "a revolutionary and treasonable spirit among our people," and feared violent resistance to the upcoming draft from New York's poorer citizens, who were clearly angry about the three-hundred-dollar exemption clause. The Lincoln administration viewed that dollar figure as a cap that would help keep the price of a substitute from skyrocketing while raising money to pay bounties to volunteers. As Opdyke explained it, the government was beneficently guaranteeing any draftee a substitute for three hundred dollars instead of leaving him to the mercy of the open market, where the rich would bid up the price. While that amount was equivalent to the average worker's annual salary, factories, workingmen's associations, towns, and cities could raise money for draftees as a group.[30]

For the average worker, however, the exemption seemed a flagrant case of class discrimination, making the conflict "a rich man's war and a poor man's fight." The New York *Evening Post* reported a snippet of conversation on the street in which one man explained

> that the law was intended to provide for the purchase of substitutes and particularly for the support of the families of those who had no $300 and must, therefore, serve. "Tom" seemed convinced that the intent was just, but asked, pertinently:
>
> "Why didn't he say so then?" adding: "[Senator Henry] Wilson is a blockhead to make such a law; he might have known that it would be taken as holding up the rich agin the poor."
>
> "But Wilson was a poor man himself—once a workingman."
>
> "Dunno—if he was, he hasn't a workingman's head." On all of which law makers may do worse than to ponder.[31]

The War Department had begun national enrollment of draft-eligible men between the ages of twenty and forty-five in May and June by sending agents door-to-door in each congressional district. The conscription was intended to spur volunteers to enlist and receive a bounty—instead of taking the chance of being drafted. Any district that did not fill its quota with volunteers would have to make up the deficiency with a draft lottery, the names to be drawn at random from the enrollment lists.[32]

While federal enrollment officers fanned out across the northern states, thousands of potential conscripts fled, many as far as the western territories and to Canada. Others provided incorrect ages, names, and addresses, while the eldest stopped dyeing their hair and let it go gray. Some pooled their money to create draft insurance. Not realizing that firemen were not exempt from military service, as they had been from the National Guard, some men tried to dodge the draft by joining engine companies. Those who preferred arrest for desertion to being drafted began wearing old army uniforms. Still others claimed foreign citizenship. Most resentful of the conscription were recent immigrants who had declared their intention to become U.S. citizens; they had sixty days to leave the country or risk being drafted.[33]

Across the country, almost one hundred enrollment officers were injured and at least two were killed while collecting names door-to-door. Resistance was concentrated in areas where poor immigrants were told by Democratic politicians that the commutation clause was unjust. In the marble quarries of Vermont and the coalfields of Pennsylvania, Irish workers took their cues from party leaders and resisted the machinery of the draft. Opposition sprang up in Ohio, Indiana, Iowa, and to a lesser extent in Minnesota, Wisconsin, Michigan, and Illinois.[34]

In the Midwest, where the Union blockade of the Mississippi River and the loss of trade with the South caused severe economic hardship, resentment of the draft ran high, particularly because the industrial Northeast, aided by high tariffs passed by a mostly Republican Congress, was prospering from the war. Roving mobs in Indiana visited small towns, seizing enrollment lists and intimidating provost marshals. Policemen dispersed a crowd in Milwaukee, Wisconsin, that had attacked an enrollment officer. In Chicago, a marshal was showered with bricks after arresting two men who had failed to cooperate with a draft official. In the coalfields of southwestern Pennsylvania, labor disputes, already bitter, were heightened by the draft. A coal company executive was gunned down after he reportedly provided workers' names to local draft officials.[35]

The first violent resistance in New York City broke out early in July when a laborer on a construction site refused to give his name. Brandishing an iron bar, he threatened the enrolling officer, who fended off the attack by drawing his pistol. When the marshal continued enrolling the names of laborers on the site, the man ran at him, and the two grappled, falling from a plank into the basement. Covered with dirt, the officer crawled up to the street and sent for help, but the military support that had been promised in the event of resistance never arrived. The foreman of the construction site was arrested the following day, but the damage was done: The draft resisters were encouraged, having won the first round.[36]

While Seymour dispatched additional regiments to Pennsylvania on July 2, in response to Governor Curtin's telegram, the battle at Gettysburg entered its second day, which included several hours of the Civil War's most savage combat. Despite Longstreet's vehement objections to the plan for a frontal assault on the Union position, Lee ordered him to lead it, because he had two divisions of fresh troops in his corps. Longstreet was to assault the enemy's left wing at the southern end of Cemetery Ridge, with the expectation that Meade would shift troops from his right wing to fend off the attack. At that point, Ewell was to press forward on the enemy's right at Cemetery and Culp's Hills. Lee envisioned his troops closing in from both flanks and crushing the Union forces once and for all.

The reluctant Longstreet, however, took until 4 p.m. to advance against the enemy's left wing, seriously hampering the coordinated attacks from the start. Two divisions of Union troops had posted themselves half a mile in front of Cemetery Ridge in a line running through a peach orchard, a wheat field, and a group of boulders known by locals as Devil's Den. Longstreet's fifteen thousand howling rebels quickly overwhelmed these Union troops at several points, but Meade and his officers managed to fill the gaps in the line with reinforcements.

When an Alabama brigade did break through and was about to seize Little Round Top—a hill that would have enabled Confederate artillery to dominate Meade's left wing on Cemetery Ridge—a regiment of Union troops from Maine fought them off for two hours. When the Union troops ran out of ammunition, their commander ordered a bayonet charge, down the hill through the smoke-filled woods, and they killed or captured numerous rebels, dumbstruck by the howling bluecoats. Farther north, another Alabama brigade found a gap in the Cemetery Ridge line but was driven back by a regiment of seasoned Minnesota veterans, most of whom were killed in this counterattack. By dusk, the strong defensive line on the Union left was still securely intact. To the north, at Cemetery and Culp's Hills, Ewell's forces had made little headway by nightfall, when Union troops drove them out of some trenches they had gained during the afternoon.

After two days of fighting, almost thirty-five thousand men were killed, wounded, or missing from both armies combined, more than in any other battle of the war up to that time. And the toll would rise: Despite the carnage, and despite the skill displayed by Union officers and troops, Lee believed he was making progress, and the Battle of Gettysburg would resume the following morning.[37]

While Lee invaded Pennsylvania, some 2,500 Confederate troops under General John Hunt Morgan were making a foray into Indiana and Ohio, hoping to stir up a rebellion among the area's prosouthern, Copperhead residents. Having started out from Tennessee in late June, Morgan and his men crossed the Cumberland River into Kentucky on July 2. "The river was out of its banks" because of heavy rains, a commander recalled. Using canoes and small rafts, and making their horses swim, the two brigades hauled four cannon with them across the swift, flooded river.

Confederate general Braxton Bragg had authorized Morgan to raid Kentucky and pin down the Union forces under General Ambrose Burnside, preventing them from reinforcing General Rosecrans in middle Tennessee. However, the maverick Morgan intended to press northward into Indiana and Ohio, pillaging small towns, freeing thousands of rebel prisoners in Indianapolis, and sacking Cincinnati. Morgan's plan would keep him within a day's ride of the Ohio River—the southern border of those two states—should he need to flee in the face of overwhelming Union forces. If he couldn't reach a shallow area to recross the Ohio River, Morgan planned to head east into Pennsylvania and join forces with Lee if he was still there.

In Kentucky, Burnside postponed his march and dispatched cavalry units to hunt down Morgan, who was reported to be attacking everywhere but never materialized. Morgan's telegrapher had tapped into Union army wires on July 2 and sent messages reporting a much larger Confederate force in various places at once all over northern Kentucky. Meanwhile, the rebel horsemen plunged onward toward the Indiana border.[38]

The fighting at Gettysburg resumed at dawn on July 3 with a protracted clash on the Union right, where Federals returning from the left wing retook the few trenches at the base of Culp's Hill that Ewell's men had been able to hold from the previous day. Longstreet meanwhile had again failed to convince Lee that a frontal assault was futile.

Lee's plan, however, was not as impulsive as it seemed. A careful student of military history and an admirer of Napoleon, Lee had thought out a complex scheme in which the frontal assault would mainly be a diversion. While Ewell closed in on the Federals' right wing, providing a second distraction, General J. E. B. Stuart and his six thousand cavalrymen were supposed to hit Cemetery Ridge from the rear like a cleaver, splitting Meade's forces in two. Broken and surrounded, the Union forces would swiftly be destroyed.[39]

Shortly after 1 p.m. Longstreet carried out Lee's order to bombard the Union center in preparation for an assault by three infantry divisions. In the biggest Confederate artillery barrage of the war, Longstreet's 150 guns pounded Cemetery Ridge for two hours, and the Federals, protected by stone walls and breastworks from the balls flying overhead, responded with an equal number of cannon, creating a din that could be heard 150 miles away in Pittsburgh.

When the bombardment stopped around 3 p.m., Longstreet believed the Union artillery had been knocked out and, against his better judgment, ordered the infantry to attack. George Pickett led the charge, as fourteen thousand Confederate troops formed a moving tapestry of gray coats a mile wide, surging forward across open ground to Cemetery Ridge. The Federals had stopped their barrage only to fool the Confederates and save ammunition, and they resumed with a fury, tearing into the enemy ranks with solid shot and exploding shells, followed by canister at closer range. Regiments from Vermont, Ohio, and New York came forward from the ridge and fired on the Confederates' left and right flanks, helping to doom their assault, from which only half the men returned.[40]

Only with the help of the cavalry charge from the east, against the Federals' rear, could Pickett's men have broken through the Union center from the front. Stuart and his formidable horsemen, however, had been cut off by the fearless young commander of the Union cavalry, Brigadier General George Armstrong Custer, and his 2,500 troopers, mostly Michigan "Wolverines," who battled the Confederates to a draw three miles away.[41]

Lee took responsibility for the disaster and quickly formed the retreating men into a defensive line. However, the Union counterattack that Lee expected never arrived. Meade decided that the victory was sufficient, and not knowing how much damage the Federals had inflicted, he did not want to risk an assault that might reverse their gains. In the afternoon of the following day, July 4, Meade was ready to follow up his success, but a heavy rainstorm prevented him from launching an attack.[42]

Nonetheless, the victory as it stood was indeed sufficient to cause jubilation when the news reached Philadelphia, where the *Inquirer* declared, on July 4, "VICTORY! WATERLOO ECLIPSED!" In Washington, Independence Day was celebrated with unprecedented fanfare and excitement. Lincoln bluntly rejected the peace overture from Confederate vice president Stephens by withholding permission for him to proceed up the Potomac. Confederate hopes for British recognition and intervention on their behalf were also dashed by the Union victories. Amazingly, after two years of dispiriting defeats at the hands of Lee's troops, the Union's Army of the Potomac had finally reversed the tide of the war.

The Federals had suffered twenty-three thousand casualties, but the staggering loss was a smaller percentage of the Union's fighting force than were the casualties on the Confederate side. With twenty-eight thousand men—more than a third of his army—killed, wounded, or missing at Gettysburg, Lee began his harrowing retreat in the rain on July 4. For the thousands of wounded, riding in carts that bumped along on uneven dirt roads, the journey was prolonged agony.[43]

·   ·   ·

"A cloudy, muggy, sultry Fourth," New York City attorney George Templeton Strong recorded in his diary. Church bells chimed and cannon fired a "national salute" in Union Square, but the news from Gettysburg arrived in fragments, so the mood in the city was subdued; the public was accustomed to hearing reports of a major battle without details of which side had prevailed—or with exaggerations of Union success—only to be disappointed later, and then devastated by the long casualty lists in the newspapers. Strong, a staunch Republican and founding member of the city's patriotic Union League Club, had slept fitfully the previous night, "tormented by headache," and awakened periodically by bursts of fireworks. "I arose bilious, headachy, backachy, sour, and savage."[44]

The Democrats were not in a festive mood either on July Fourth. At the Academy of Music, Governor Seymour addressed a gathering of the party faithful, which included County Supervisor William Tweed and District Attorney A. Oakey Hall, rising players in Tammany Hall, the dominant Democratic party organization in the city.* Seymour lamented the bitter political division within the northern states—which he blamed on the infringement of civil liberties by the Lincoln administration—and warned of violent consequences. "Let us be admonished now in time," Seymour said, "and take care that this irritation, this feeling which is growing up in our midst shall not also ripen unto civil troubles that shall carry evils of war into our very midst, and about our own homes."[45]

On the same day it passed the new draft law in March, Congress had authorized the suspension of habeas corpus throughout the United States, enabling the administration to detain political prisoners indefinitely without charges or any other due process of law.[46] The draft law also empowered the secretary of war to create a police arm, the office of the provost marshal general, whose assistants scoured the country arresting deserters, spies, traitors, and other people deemed disloyal to the northern war effort.[47†]

When criticized for suspending the writ of habeas corpus, Lincoln replied that the rebels and their agents in the North were violating every other law of the land and using constitutional protections—including freedom of speech and assembly—to shield their destructive, subversive activity. Lincoln

*The Academy of Music, on Fourteenth Street and Irving Place, opened in 1854 and was then the largest opera house in the world.

Tammany Hall, a patriotic society dating back to the American Revolution, was named for Chief Tamanend, a mythic warrior of the Delaware Indians. The club's hierarchy consisted of "sachems," "warriors," and "braves," and the headquarters was dubbed the "wigwam."

†In New York the Lincoln administration's political prisoners were held at Fort Lafayette, which stood close to the Brooklyn shore in the Narrows, where the eastern pier of the Verrazano Bridge now stands.

asked rhetorically, "Are all the laws, but one, to go unexecuted, and the government itself go to pieces, lest that one be violated?"[48]

During the spring of 1863, Democrats had warned that Lincoln was amassing dictatorial powers, and the expanding central government was poised to wipe out what little remained of states' rights. The draft, they said, was the ultimate expression of this arbitrary federal power: The states' role of raising troops had been supplanted, and individuals—those who could not afford a substitute—were to be coerced by the distant bureaucracies in Washington into fighting and dying in an unjust war.[49]

In May and June, during the enrollment, Governor Seymour continued his drive to raise volunteers and forestall the draft, while predicting that it would be overturned in court. He not only asserted that the draft law was unconstitutional, but complained, rightly, that the Republican administration and its newly created Bureau of the Provost Marshal General had set disproportionately high quotas for New York City—which was predominantly Democratic. New York Republicans, including financier John Jay, branded Seymour a traitor and predicted that the governor would refuse to carry out the draft.[50]*

The most prominent civilian arrested by Union military authorities during the war was Ohio congressman Clement Vallandigham, a Peace Democrat running for governor, who denounced the draft, the war, and "King Lincoln" in his campaign across the state in March and April 1863. Arrested for sedition in early May, Vallandigham was denied due process and soon became a martyr for free speech in the Democratic press. Republicans watched nervously as the jailed congressman continued his campaign for both the governor's office and a peace treaty with the South.[51]

Along with Horatio Seymour, Manton Marble's New York *World* had fiercely denounced the arrest and the central government's "despotic power," even praising a mob of Vallandigham's supporters in Columbus, Ohio, who threatened to spring him from the jailhouse. "When free discussion and free voting are allowed, men are not tempted to have recourse to violence and relief of bad rulers," the *World* asserted. "You may stigmatize these irregular avengers as a 'mob,' but there are times when even violence is nobler than cowardly apathy."[52]

Lincoln resolved the immediate political crisis by commuting Vallandigham's prison sentence and banishing him to the South. Union troops turned him over to the Confederates under a flag of truce, and the warm welcome the Copperhead congressman received in the South diminished his standing with the northern public. Lincoln had won a round in convincing

*John Jay II (1817–1894) was the grandson of the founding father.

northerners that the enemies of the Union were cloaking themselves in the banner of civil rights. It was an ongoing struggle, however, since the uproar over Vallandigham's cause continued. In the second half of June, Lincoln issued two letters to the press, defending his vigilance against disloyalty on the home front as well as the battlefield.[53]

Seymour, representing the upstate Democrats known as the Albany Regency, and Marble, speaking for the wealthy urban faction nicknamed the "Swallowtails" after their fancy coats, were both careful to endorse Vallandigham's struggle for free speech but not his opposition to the war. They were not Peace Democrats like Congressman (and former mayor) Fernando Wood, who held a "Mass State Convention for Peace and Reunion" at Cooper Union in New York in June, where speakers lauded Vallandigham while denouncing the war and calling for negotiations to end the hostilities. Not only had Lincoln committed "damnable crimes against the liberty of the citizen," declared Wood, the despotic president had usurped the power of Congress by declaring war.

Wood lashed out at both the Lincoln administration and the Albany Regency, threatening the Democratic party's fragile unity. Marble faced the challenge of trying to marginalize and silence the peace men without splitting the party in two. On behalf of the state party organization, the *World* disavowed Wood's antiwar pronouncements. The policy of the Democratic party, Marble wrote, would be "peace and the Union but, peace or war, the Union."[54]

Unlike the war itself, the draft issue was an opportunity for Democratic party unity, one that had the potential to play well with the public. In the pages of the *World*, Marble articulated the fundamental shift of power that the draft represented in American history and daily life. In an editorial on June 9, he continued to denounce the draft and the administration by linking its infringements of civil rights with the dangers of a standing army controlled by the federal government instead of the states.

> The Constitution, as well as our customs and traditions, have wisely placed the control of the militia in the hands of the local authorities. The founders of our government foresaw that a central power, having command over all the military resources of the nation, would inevitably become a despotism, and hence the people were empowered to bear arms, and the militia was recognized as a state and not a federal organization. We are now asked to give up these safeguards and hand over an unlimited military power to

an administration notoriously incapable and untruthful and which has done all it dare do to subvert our free institutions.

Marble also claimed that the people were unhappy. "Already men are beginning to ask each other, To what use is this new army to be put? Is it to be employed in destroying the armed forces now waging war against the Union and the Constitution, or is it the intention of the administration to use our sons and brothers to take away our civil rights?"

In the same editorial, the *World* declared that "our people have become sick of useless butchery, and dread strengthening a government that is strong only with the weak and unarmed, and nerveless on the battle-field, where alone it should show its power." With this discontent "rife in the community," enforcement of the draft would be met with "manifestations of popular disaffection," Marble wrote. "It is impossible to tell what shape it will assume."[55]

Democratic voices began to meld on the subject of the draft. "The conscription . . . is the all-absorbing topic. Everybody talks of it; fears it as the plague, and thinks it a fraud on the body politic," a column in the *Daily News*—owned by Fernando Wood and edited by his brother Ben—declared in mid-June, under the ominous heading "The Beginning of the End." Noting that a provost marshal had been killed in Indiana, the writer continued: "A free people will not submit to the conscription . . . Justice must mark the course of the Administration, to avoid similar actions to that in Indiana. The life of a Provost Marshal should be respected, yet when citizens will undertake an unholy and unrighteous duty, it is difficult to control the people."[56] What the Copperhead paper claimed were warnings, Republicans denounced as a steady campaign of incitement to riot.

The *Daily News* also introduced the element of class warfare, casting itself as the friend of the workingman, defending the longshoremen—Fernando Wood's political base—who were then on strike for wages that would supply them and their families "with the bare necessaries of life." The paper denounced the merchants who were "growing fat at the expense of their proletarian subjects," and asked, "When, oh when, will these hypocritical pharisees, clothed in purple and fine linen, be stripped of their phylacteries, and taught to respect the honest poverty of those whose distresses cry aloud to heaven against them for vengeance?"[57]

Thus, when Governor Seymour addressed his Fourth of July audience in New York City, he brought to a climax the crescendo of Democratic opposition to the administration that had been building during the spring and early summer. Without mentioning the upcoming draft, Seymour warned the Lincoln administration that its abuses in the name of national security could provoke a popular revolt: "Is it not revolution which you are thus creating when you say that our persons may be rightfully seized, our property confiscated, our homes entered? Are you not exposing yourselves, your own interests to as great a peril as that which you threaten us? Remember this, that the bloody and treasonable and revolutionary doctrine of public necessity can be proclaimed by a mob as well as by a government."[58]

The rainstorm that had prevented Meade's belated counterattack on Independence Day had also swamped the campsite of the New York militia division on its way to assist the Army of the Potomac at Gettysburg. "It was well known by now, that while we were stuck in the mud on the glorious Fourth, the rebels had retreated from Gettysburg, and were now endeavoring to escape through the mountain passes," wrote militiaman George Wingate, "and we were reluctantly compelled to abandon the hopes that had been entertained of earning immortal glory, by coming in at the eleventh hour to turn their defeat into a rout."[59]

By 2 a.m. on July 5, the last of the Confederate troops had left the Gettysburg battlefield and by the following day had reached Hagerstown, Maryland, just six miles north of the Potomac River. The Confederate cavalry under J. E. B. Stuart was in place to protect the retreating army.

The New York militia changed course, hoping to join Meade's forces in pursuing the rebels. "On the 6th day of July, we marched till late at night, expecting to cut off the rebel wagon-train," wrote Wingate. However, the Union troops were too late. "On reaching Newman's Gap, we found that Lee's rear-guard had passed through, about eight hours before we got there."

Wingate kept his sense of humor, noting, "We were compensated by obtaining something to eat; and in addition had the pleasure of having pointed out to us, no less than six houses, in all of which Longstreet had died the previous night, and two others, where he was yet lying mortally wounded." In fact, Longstreet had survived the battle without wounds.

By July 7, Lee's army had reached Williamsport on the Potomac, but the heavy rains had raised the level of the river and the army could not cross. Lee had his troops commandeer every ferryboat in the area and shuttled the wagons of groaning, wounded men across to Virginia, but the bulk of the army was trapped on the Maryland side, waiting for the high water to recede and bracing for an attack by the Federals. Fortunately for Lee, Meade had followed cautiously, taking three days to assess his losses after the battle and treat the tens of thousands of wounded Union troops while waiting for supplies and reinforcements. Provost marshals were also busy trying to apprehend some fifteen thousand deserters who had left the army during the battle and return them to their regiments.

The Army of the Potomac finally set off after the retreating Confederates on July 7. Wingate noted that on that day, "after an unusually fatiguing march over muddy roads, rendered almost impracticable by the passage of Lee's army, the division went into camp at Funkstown." After starving for most of their campaign in Pennsylvania, the militiamen were finally getting fed. "Rations had come up, and though we had to sleep on our arms for fear of attack from Stuart's cavalry, then in our neighborhood, we lay down in first rate spirits and slept the sleep of the just."

Despite the Union delays, Wingate believed that they were "pressing hard upon the heels of Lee's retreating army," but "the main army had a good deal of fight left in it still, and when it turned on its pursuers, as it frequently did, like a stag at bay, it was not to be despised." He added that because of the terrain, "the retreating army derived a great advantage over its pursuers, and were constantly enabled to take positions too strong to be attacked with less than the whole Union army and where a mere show of strength would check our advance; and then before Meade could concentrate his forces, Lee would be off."

However, Wingate also revealed how slowly the Federals moved. On July 8, when the New York militia division was annexed to a brigade of the Army of the Potomac, they were still in Pennsylvania, at Waynesboro. After resting there for three full days, these Union troops finally headed south to Maryland on the afternoon of July 11 to confront Lee's forces, waiting at Williamsport with their backs to the swollen river.

CHAPTER 2

The Battle Lines Are Drawn: Race, Class, and Religion

~つ

While Lee retreated and Meade cautiously pursued in the week following Independence Day, news reports in the Northeast at last confirmed the Union victory at Gettysburg and trumpeted Grant's conquest of Vicksburg, where Confederate general John Pemberton had surrendered the fortified city on July 4. With this double victory, auspiciously occurring on the anniversary of the nation's independence, the North appeared ready to crush the rebellion, and Lincoln seemed well positioned to follow through with the draft. "The events of two days have completely altered the character of the measure and the feeling of the people in regard to it," declared James Gordon Bennett's *New York Herald*. "Of the three hundred thousand new levies it is probable that not one will ever be called into the field."[1]

However, Horace Greeley's *Tribune* warned that the North had to remain vigilant against a Copperhead insurrection, and he reprinted an antiadministration broadside that appeared all over the city on the eve of July 4. Signed "Spirit of '76" and containing thirteen items, the manifesto denounced the federal government as a despotic regime, a "monster smeared with the bloody sacrifice of its own children . . . Should the Confederate army capture Washington and exterminate the herd of thieves, Pharisees, and cutthroats which pasture there, defiling the temple of our liberty, we should regard it as a special interposition of Divine Providence."

Greeley cited the handbill as evidence that local Copperheads "have for months conspired and plotted to bring about a revolution

Republican cartoon: "The Copperhead Party—In Favor of a Vigorous
Prosecution of Peace!"

in the North." Nonetheless, Greeley did not run it as front-page news on July 7
and appears to have concluded that the danger had largely passed; Meade's triumph at Gettysburg, according to Greeley, had prevented an uprising on July 4,
planned to coincide with a successful Confederate invasion of the North.[2]

If the Copperheads had been defanged, class conflict remained a serious
threat. When enrollment was completed and the exact dates of the upcoming
draft lottery in cities and towns across the North remained a secret during the
first half of July, working-class opposition reached a fever pitch. The substitution and commutation clauses of the draft law, by their apparent unfairness,
seemed to strike at the heart of what was unique about America, a society free
from the aristocratic hierarchies and entrenched privilege of Europe's old
regimes. Americans prided themselves on living in a land of equal opportunity, both economic and social, where "every laborer is a possible gentleman."[3]

Republicans seemed hypocritical, denouncing slavery and celebrating the
promise of social mobility in a free-labor system, while enacting the special privilege of the three-hundred-dollar clause, which enabled young entrepreneurs

like J. P. Morgan, Andrew Carnegie, James Mellon, and John D. Rockefeller to procure substitutes, while cutting off the dreams of young workingmen.[4]

During the previous half century, urban growth and a transportation revolution (paved roads, canals, steamships, railroads) along with technological and organizational innovations (the telegraph, interchangeable machine parts, the factory system) had transformed the American economy. At the same time, the switch from preindustrial manufacturing to a capitalist system of mass production undercut the worker in relation to his employer, turning the skilled craftsman into a hired drone and aggravating the relationship between the social classes generally. The draft's exemption clause stirred up the already acute anger and insecurity of the working class, which had been mounting for decades.[5]

At the dawn of the nineteenth century, Thomas Jefferson had warned against the very path the country had taken. Defining freedom as economic independence, Jefferson envisioned an agricultural nation of farmers who owned their land, the source of their livelihoods. Free from the domination of a landlord or factory owner, each would make an ideal citizen in a republic. Let manufacturing and urban slums stay in Europe, Jefferson counseled. "The mobs of great cities add just so much to the support of pure government as sores do to the strength of the human body."

Instead, the United States in the first half of the nineteenth century had realized Alexander Hamilton's dream of an industrial and commercial nation led by a business elite of bankers, merchants, and entrepreneurs. A leader of the Federalist party, which advocated a strong central government, Hamilton also believed that the nation's wealthiest individuals should have the greatest stake in that government in order to secure their loyalty and tap their good judgment.

Indeed, as the new capitalist order emerged, workers' advocates complained that government was creating institutions that bestowed special privileges on the wealthy few: State legislatures controlled the right to form a chartered corporation, enabling influential businessmen and politicians to monopolize various sectors of the economy, from banking and insurance to infrastructure, transportation, and manufacturing. A huge variety of paper money issued by the proliferating state-chartered banks provided a medium of exchange for the growing economy, and to maintain some control over the state banks, in 1816, the federal government chartered a second Bank of the United States; Hamilton had originally conceived of this privately owned entity in which the U.S. Treasury deposited its funds.[6]

By the late 1820s and early 1830s, a bitter backlash against the elite monopolists was spearheaded by Jefferson's political heirs in the Democratic party of President Andrew Jackson. They rallied both urban workers of the Northeast and small farmers from the upper South and lower Midwest—the disaffected fringes of the expanding market economy—to denounce the idle bankers and speculators who grew rich by manipulating the "producing classes," those who created value and wealth through "honest labor." When Jackson vetoed a new charter for the Bank of the United States in 1832, pro-Bank forces called him a tyrant and themselves the Whigs, after the opponents of King George III in the Revolutionary era. The Whigs carried on the traditions of the recently disbanded Federalists in the American two-party system.[7]

Jackson owned slaves, and while he and his followers decried inequality between the rich and poor, they believed that blacks were inherently inferior to whites. Indeed, the enslavement of African Americans was a pillar of the Jacksonians' master race philosophy: All whites, no matter how rich or poor, as citizens of the Republic and members of the master race, were equal. The most humble white was considered superior to any black.

The Democrats' inclusive and unabashed declaration of white supremacy helped to win over unskilled workers in the Northeast, including Irish immigrants, as well as the Butternuts—struggling farmers of southern Ohio, Indiana, and Illinois nicknamed for the butternut tree oil they used to dye their clothing. White supremacy became a consolation in poverty, and a promise of upward mobility for those who would grasp it.[8]

The smoldering political and class conflict of the Jacksonian era—infused with racial, ethnic, and religious hatreds—triggered riots in American cities with grim regularity in the decades before the Civil War, particularly in New York, where the authorities responded with steadily diminishing tolerance and increasing force.

Mayor Opdyke's panic about the absence of the militia during Lee's invasion, and Governor Seymour's resolve to get them back within thirty days, reflected an awareness that these state troops had increasingly become New York City's bulwark against civil disorder when riots raged out of control and overwhelmed the police. During the militiamen's absence in the first half of July 1863, the city faced a more immediate threat from the festering resentments of its own inhabitants than it did from Lee's army.[9]

The three-hundred-dollar exemption clause meant the government "was taking practically the whole number of soldiers called for out of the laboring classes," wrote journalist Joel Tyler Headley. "A great proportion of these being Irish, it naturally became an Irish question . . . It was in their eyes the game of hated England over again—oppression of Irishmen." The British had invaded and colonized Ireland centuries earlier, imposing harsh Protestant rule over the Catholic majority. Immigration to America provided new opportunities for the Irish but not an escape from anti-Catholic hostility.[10]*

Since the American colonies were founded largely by Protestant refugees and explorers, the dominant native culture was Protestant; anti-Catholic sentiment and demonstrations were common. Pope Day celebrations featured effigies of the pope, the devil, and the Pretender, which were linked in an unholy trinity.† Protestants regarded the pope and the entire Catholic Church hierarchy as corrupt and a barrier to the direct experience of faith. While rioting in the colonial era had been confined largely to this kind of ritualistic street theater, as the number of Irish immigrants increased, they added a new twist by responding with violence. On St. Patrick's Day in 1799, teenage boys taunted Irish residents while marching through New York City's slums with grotesque straw-filled effigies of the saint, known as Paddies. The Irish, raised in a culture of constant resistance to the British, attacked the marchers, and one man was killed in the ensuing melee.

Threats against a Catholic church on Christmas Day in 1806 sparked a much larger clash in New York which left one man dead and dozens seriously injured, after Irishmen armed with clubs, rocks, and bricks—along with a bayonet and a stiletto—attacked the city's night watchmen, who had tried to disperse them.

On July 12, 1824, a bloody riot broke out in New York between Catholics and Orangemen—Irish Protestants—who were publicly celebrating the anniversary of the Battle of the Boyne, in which William of Orange defeated Ireland's Catholics in 1690. The watchmen arrested thirty-three Irish Catholics and not a single Orangeman. Thomas Addis Emmet, an Irish émigré and prominent attorney in the city, won the acquittal of the Catholics in a high-profile trial.[11]

Irish American immigrant leaders, both Protestant and Catholic, had been building ties to the Protestant establishment in an attempt to ease the Irish sense of isolation. Emmet and fellow Protestant William Sampson, both leading attorneys in the city, had emigrated after the abortive United Irishmen revolt in 1798. Along with William James MacNeven, a Catholic doctor, they launched the nonsectarian Association of the Friends of Ireland in New-York, which raised money for Daniel O'Connell's nonviolent campaign to abolish anti-Catholic laws in Ireland and the struggle for Catholics' civil rights in England which succeeded in 1829. The *Shamrock, or Hibernian Chronicle,*

*The Irish were New York City's largest immigrant group, numbering more than two hundred thousand in 1860, about a fourth of the population.

†Pope Day was celebrated on November 5, the holiday marking the failed plot of Guy Fawkes to blow up Parliament. The Pretender was Bonnie Prince Charlie, the Scottish Catholic aspirant to the throne of England who was defeated in the Battle of Culloden Moor in 1746.

the city's first Irish American newspaper, was founded in 1810 and gave voice to these exiles' desire to assimilate in New York and unite Catholics and Protestants in a single Irish American community.

However, when Irish immigration increased in the late 1820s and early 1830s, working-class Irish Catholics rejected these efforts. The ties these leaders had fostered within the Irish population—and between the Catholic working class and the city's Protestant establishment—began to fray. Catholic laborers, trapped in the slums and lectured by scornful, Bible-pushing Protestant missionaries, flocked instead to new publications and fraternal organizations that affirmed their ethnic and religious identity. The Catholic archdiocese added new churches across the city to accommodate the influx of immigrants and exuded a new self-confidence in its dealings with the Protestant majority in New York, challenging anti-Catholic language in the public school curriculum and building its own parochial schools.[12]

This strengthening of the Catholic archdiocese coincided with the arrival of numerous Protestant evangelists from New England, including Charles Finney, whose wildly popular revival meetings helped intensify religious divisions in New York. Finney's work was part of the Second Great Awakening, a surge in Protestant revivalism radiating from New England to New York and across northern Ohio, Illinois, and Indiana during the first few decades of the nineteenth century.[13]

Many Protestants viewed the growth of the New York archdiocese, along with the emancipation of Irish and British Catholics in 1829, as a grave threat and launched a frenzy of antipapal activity in both countries in the coming years. British anti-Catholic propaganda arrived in New York, where public meetings, pamphlets, and entire newspapers were devoted to warding off the foreign menace of "Popery." Anxious Protestants declared that since the pope had dictatorial power within the Catholic Church and warm relations with monarchs across Europe, Catholic immigrants must be the entering wedge of a conspiracy to bring down America's democratic government.[14]*

Surrounded by prejudice, most Irish Catholics in America were nonetheless better off economically and politically than they had been in Ireland, where the religious caste system imposed by Britain gave the lowliest Protestant more civil rights than any Catholic. Determined to improve their lot in America, the Irish made the most of the racial caste system they saw all around them, which was buttressed by the Democratic party.

---

*A great promoter of this idea was inventor Samuel F. B. Morse, who wrote two books in the mid-1830s detailing the alleged conspiracy.

In order to distinguish and distance themselves from African Americans at the bottom of the social ladder, Irish craftsmen and longshoremen formed trade unions and welcomed other ethnic groups, but not blacks. Irish workers insisted on segregated workplaces—on the docks and in factories—and threatened to quit as a group if a single black was hired. Having once been the "blacks of Europe," the Irish insisted on their membership in the white race, which at least gave their men the right to vote, ensuring that Democratic politicians would court them with favors.[15]

Blacks had only to meet a minimal property requirement to vote in New York after the Revolution, but when the Democrats came to power in New York State in 1801 with the election of Thomas Jefferson to the White House, they proceeded to contest the qualifications of blacks attempting to vote. In 1821, the Democrats saw to it that the new state constitution eliminated the property requirement for white men while raising it prohibitively—to $250—for blacks.[16*†]

However, statewide emancipation of black slaves in New York in 1827, set in motion earlier by the Federalists, added to white laborers' worries by blurring the distinction they sought to highlight. For the Irish slum dweller in particular, maintaining his whiteness was an uphill battle. Bigots referred to the Irish as "niggers turned inside out" and to blacks as "smoked Irish." In this vein, the Irish were often despised as shiftless loafers and drunks, and the Irish "race" was characterized as *"low-browed, savage, bestial, wild,* and *simian,"* the same terms used to justify the enslavement of blacks as a race, and marshaled by nativists trying to deprive poor white immigrants of their right to vote.[17]

In New York, racial segregation existed in almost every facet of city life, including religion, education, employment, transportation, and politics, but there were no large black ghettoes, and a mixing of the races had been going on for years in the city's poorest neighborhoods. While segregation prevailed in most of the city's public facilities, impoverished tenants, black and white, often lived in the same building or the same apartment because they had no choice.[18‡]

Irishwomen also chose freely to marry black men, and their mulatto children were a common sight in the slums. In New York, racial integration

---

*With Jackson's reelection in 1832, the Democratic-Republican party became the Democratic party.

†In 1826, sixteen blacks in New York County could vote; that number increased only to about three hundred by 1861.

‡Only a few fortunate blacks entered skilled trades, and they were held back within each profession. The *Herald* counted eight black physicians, fourteen clergymen, and seventeen teachers in New York City in the Civil War years. Exceptional black entrepreneurs, who ran successful businesses in white areas, included Thomas Downing, whose famous Oyster House at Broad and Wall streets was a popular meeting place for merchants, financiers, and government officials (Spann, *Gotham at War,* p. 124).

was most evident in Five Points, the city's worst slum, named for the five-cornered intersection of Park, Worth, and Baxter Streets.* The area housed more than half of the city's black residents, along with a heavy concentration of Irish Americans, who, more than any other white group, lived with or right next to blacks. Five Points' bars and brothels offered both black and white prostitutes to customers of all races, and black underworld figures had white wives and girlfriends. Black competition for white women, like black competition in the workplace, tended to stoke the rage of the white male laborer, whose economic power was eroded by industrialization and who found his social and sexual status reduced as well, especially if he could not afford an apartment in which to raise a family.[19]

A dispirited immigrant wrote home to Dublin that the condition of the Irish in America was "one of shame and poverty. They are shunned and despised . . . 'My master is a great tyrant,' said a negro lately, 'he treats me as badly as if I was a *common Irishman.*'"[20]

Blacks, in turn, were furious that recent immigrants could vote as soon as they were naturalized and faced no property requirements. One African American complained that upstanding, educated blacks were "deprived of privileges granted to European *paupers,* blacklegs and burglars!!!"[21] Statewide emancipation on July 4, 1827, did not mean political equality: "Alas! the freedom to which we have attained is defective," declared the Reverend Peter Williams Jr. In New York City, he lamented, it was still true that "the rights of men are decided by the colour of their skin."[22] Williams led a large congregation of free, middle-class blacks, many of whom were active in fighting racial inequality in the North.[23†]

Making ethnic and racial tensions worse, just when New York's newly freed blacks were entering the job market, and when nativist, anti-Catholic sentiment was on the rise, the British government removed all legal barriers to emigration, and more than twenty thousand Irish left for America in 1827. In less than a decade, more than thirty thousand Irish were settling each year in New York City alone. While the city had received Irish immigrants throughout its history, unlike earlier arrivals, these were mostly Catholics. Notably, most were also penniless young men without skills who ended up living in

---

*Formerly, the streets were named Cross Anthony, and Orange. See the Walking Tour in the appendix for the area today.

†The roots of St. Philip's Church, where Williams served as pastor, and of New York City's black middle class, date back to colonial days and the catechism classes led by Elias Neau, an Anglican missionary, beginning in 1705. Originally located on Center Street, St. Philip's Church had moved uptown to Mulberry Street by 1863.

the worst slums, like Five Points. The immigrants were thus poised to clash not only with Protestants but also with blacks in a contest for menial jobs.[24]

Some Protestants advertised jobs with the warning that "Irishmen need not apply" or "any country or color except Irish." Nonetheless, the new waves of Irish immigrants soon displaced blacks from many of the unskilled jobs to which whites had restricted them—as day laborers, dockworkers, domestics, and coachmen. Outside the cities, the Irish were soon mining coal, digging canals, and laying railroad tracks. Blacks in New York City clung to the fringes of the labor market as waiters, barbers, cooks on ships, farmhands, and oystermen.[25]*

However, resentment went both ways: The Irish blamed the presence of blacks in the North for driving down wages. Labor competition soon turned into racial warfare. Beginning in 1828, race riots plagued Philadelphia for twelve years and then continued sporadically until after the Civil War. In Cincinnati, in 1829, a white mob rampaged for three days against black residents and their property, leaving a trail of death and destruction. In the wake of the pogrom, most of the city's two thousand blacks left on foot for Canada.[26]

Racial conflict also accompanied the growth of the abolition movement. Inspired by the Second Great Awakening, New England Protestants were denouncing the sin of slavery. Black leaders were also becoming more outspoken and sending shock waves through New York City. They called for the immediate abolition of slavery—the confiscation of slaves from their owners—not the gradual schemes that had been used in the North.† With their white associates, they began turning New York into a center of the abolition movement.[27]

In 1827, Samuel Cornish, John Russwurm, Peter Williams Jr., and others started *Freedom's Journal,* the nation's first African American newspaper.‡ "African slavery is the deepest darkest crime that ever shaded the character of a nation," an editorial in the paper declared. "Despotic governments blush for its existence—what ought a free people to feel when they look upon the

---

*With European immigration, the proportion of blacks in New York's population fell from 11 percent in the 1790s to 1.5 percent in 1860. The number of black residents peaked at 16,000 in 1840 but fell to 12,500 in 1860 as Irish immigrants drove blacks out of menial jobs.

†Rhode Island, Connecticut, New Jersey, New York, and Pennsylvania enacted gradual emancipation. Vermont, New Hampshire, and Massachusetts provided for immediate abolition with amendments to their state constitutions.

‡Free blacks in Manhattan published fifteen newspapers and three magazines between 1827 and the end of the Civil War.

inhuman traffic in human flesh, which is every day going on in the public markets, in our own country?"[28]

Cornish's editorials and Williams's speeches caught the attention of Arthur Tappan, an affluent silk merchant transplanted from New England in 1815. A white evangelical Protestant, Tappan identified both with these black ministers' religious convictions and with their middle-class message of education and self-help. The advanced abolitionist views of the black clergymen influenced the movement's white leadership.[29]

William Lloyd Garrison, who launched an abolitionist newspaper, the *Liberator,* in Boston in 1831, joined Tappan in withdrawing support for colonization—resettling ex-slaves in Liberia and elsewhere outside the United States. Garrison also condemned the Constitution of the United States for its protection of slavery, calling it a corrupt "bargain and compromise" and a pact with the devil. He publicly burned a copy of the document at a Fourth of July picnic. Charles Finney, the nation's leading Protestant evangelist, regarded slavery as a major obstacle to America's spiritual salvation and encouraged Tappan's abolitionist endeavors.

Tappan enlisted the help of Cornish, Williams, and the black clergyman Theodore Wright, along with white Protestant ministers—some of them outspoken anti-Catholic bigots—to form an interracial organization, the New York Anti-Slavery Society. To emphasize the groundswell of antislavery opinion worldwide, the group timed their first meeting, in October 1833, to coincide with Parliament's abolition of slavery in the British West Indies.[30]*

Colonization advocates warned that freed southern slaves would flood New York, and "amalgamation," the mixing of the races, would pollute the pure blood of America's patrician families. They rallied a large mob to break up the first meeting of the New York Anti-Slavery Society, but its members had already sped through their agenda and escaped out the back of the building.

Not only had the local antislavery forces established themselves in New York, but two months later they made the city a center of the national abolition movement, shifting its focus away from Garrison and his followers in Boston: In December 1833, blacks and whites collaborated to create the American Anti-Slavery Society—a national organization with its headquarters on Nassau Street and its leadership consisting entirely of New York residents, including Arthur Tappan and his brother Lewis, other white merchants, and the black clergymen Cornish, Wright, and Williams.

*Parliament enacted gradual emancipation in 1833 and abolished slavery completely in 1838.

For white merchants who had business dealings with the South, and favored colonization, this was an alarming development. Not only were their trading relationships threatened by the abolitionists' assault on slave owners' property rights, but the new antislavery organizations were chipping away at segregation in New York, placing blacks in leadership roles and welcoming them into white churches. It was little comfort to segregationists that blacks sat in separate pews; they saw their nightmare scenario of racial amalgamation springing to life.[31]

By April 1834, Democratic president Andrew Jackson's war on the Bank of the United States had reinforced his image as the people's champion and polarized the country along class lines. Jackson, a planter from Kentucky, saw the Bank as a dangerous source of special privilege for the Northeast's aristocratic elite.[32]

In New York City, Tammany Hall Democrats supported the president and were joined by labor leaders and workers who wanted to shut down all banks. Laborers bore the brunt of the business cycle's extreme ups and downs. By eliminating the paper money issued by banks and allowing only silver and gold currency—"hard money"—labor groups hoped both to control inflation and to stave off periodic depressions.[33]

New York's mayoral election of April 1834 pitted the "bank aristocracy against the people," declared George Henry Evans, editor of the *Workingman's Advocate*. The working class also received fervent support from William Cullen Bryant, a famous young poet from Massachusetts who had bought the New York *Evening Post* five years earlier; the paper was founded by Alexander Hamilton, but Bryant had strayed from those Federalist roots to become an outspoken Jacksonian Democrat.[34]

The Whig party viewed this local contest, in the midst of the Bank War, as crucial to its eventual success or failure in national politics. Whig merchants and industrialists pressured their workers to vote the party's ticket, using the Hamiltonian argument that the interests of labor and capital were identical, since all the trades, from the merchant down to the carpenter, rigger, and longshoreman, depended on each other. Whigs also turned native-born workmen against the Democratic ticket by pointing to Tammany Hall's successful efforts to attract the threatening new waves of Irish Catholic immigrants as their base of support.[35]

Whig forces taunted the "low Irish" who had turned out to vote for Tammany, and for the three days of the election, thousands of rioters—wealthy merchants and Irish workmen alike—clashed with sticks, clubs, and firearms, many taken by looting gun stores and a state arsenal. The Democratic mayor finally dispatched twelve hundred infantry and cavalrymen, who dispersed the rioters. With public buildings under heavy guard as the votes were counted, the Democrats pulled off a narrow victory.

The Whigs boisterously celebrated their strong showing, but by the summer, the Jacksonians had won the Bank War. Congress voted to deny a new charter and to proceed with removal of funds from the Bank, which was headquartered in Philadelphia. The Bank and the Whigs were fading from the scene in tandem, while New York City emerged as the nation's preeminent financial center. Tammany's alliance with the growing labor movement further consolidated its power.[36]

While the Bank War subsided in the summer of 1834, the furor over abolition burst back on the scene in New York. In June, six months after the founding of the American Anti-Slavery Society, Arthur and Lewis Tappan funded the Female Anti-Slavery Society, bringing upper-class white women into the biracial movement and renewing conservatives' fear of "amalgamation." With the help of procolonization newspapers, unfounded, sensational stories about interracial marriages circulated throughout the city.[37]

Rumor turned to violence in July and escalated into a week of antiabolition rioting—the worst of New York's many riots in the antebellum period. Rioters destroyed numerous homes, stores, and churches of both black and white abolitionists throughout the city. St. Philip's Church and the home of its pastor, Peter Williams Jr., were both destroyed. The humble dwellings of some five hundred poor blacks in Five Points were also ransacked, torched, or demolished, and victims who did not escape were seized and beaten by the mobs.[38]

The Twenty-seventh National Guard regiment and the police were supported by cavalry units and a thousand citizen volunteers in quelling the riots.* Since the rioters appeared to be nativists as well as racists, hundreds of Irish workers signed up to crush them, abandoning their previous neutrality—a rare moment in which immigrant workers briefly acknowledged that they had common interests with blacks. When the riots gradually subsided, the consensus of public opinion pointed the finger at the victims: The antislavery agitators were looking for trouble and had found it.[39]

William Cullen Bryant's *Evening Post* was the lone voice in the city's press condemning the rioters. His Whig rival, Horace Greeley, then editor of the *New-Yorker,* followed the herd.† The antagonism between them grew in

---

*The Twenty-seventh later became the Seventh Regiment.
†Greeley founded the *Tribune* seven years later.

1835 when Bryant again stood alone to defend twenty-one tailors who went on strike, a new tactic for labor, which the employers were quickly able to thwart by having the workers arrested and fined. The *Evening Post* expressed outrage that men could be convicted for refusing "to work for the wages that were offered them . . . If this is not SLAVERY, we have forgotten its definition." The more conservative Greeley denounced "all combinations, either of masters or journeymen . . . Both parties clearly acted wrong." After hungry workers rioted and raided flour warehouses the following winter, Bryant examined their grievances while Greeley chastised them for failing to see the harmony of interests between themselves and "the business community in general."[40]

When New York's abolitionists confronted the wreckage of their homes and institutions, it dampened their ardor and cowed them into retreat. Middle-class blacks like Peter Williams Jr. turned inward to deal with problems of poverty and moral uplift in the black community, while white radicals shifted their attention to the abolition of southern slavery instead of the glaring racial inequality in the North.[41]

In the spring of 1835, after a year of retreat, the Tappan brothers dramatically escalated their antislavery campaign by printing more than a million illustrated pamphlets that detailed the evils of slavery and distributing them throughout the country, both North and South. The American Anti-Slavery Society also deluged the public with abolitionist newspapers, figurines of shackled slaves, handkerchiefs, medallions, and even chocolate wrappers. This merchandising and propaganda effort swelled the ranks of the abolitionists but also alarmed their conservative opponents, who organized riots across the North similar to those in New York a year earlier. The initial abolitionist efforts in Boston had been widely regarded as quixotic and futile, but the Tappans' mass media wizardry—they would soon claim a million members nationwide—was perceived as a grave threat by proslavery groups.

For white southerners, the shift of the abolition movement's base from Boston to New York was particularly galling, since the city already dictated the terms of capital investment and the extension of credit to the South. By late summer, vigilantes in the South were fanning out across harbors and roads and searching slave quarters to intercept and confiscate antislavery tracts. They carried torches in nighttime parades culminating with fiery speeches against the New York abolitionists. Some southerners demanded that the Tappans be turned over to the South for punishment and organized a boycott to ruin their silk-importing firm, the largest in the country. Others suggested that the South stop importing all products from New York, causing distress in the city's Chamber of Commerce.

The American Anti-Slavery Society braced for trouble by barricading its doors, but there was no repetition of the recent riots. Local officials were poised to prevent it, and the federal government willingly appeased slavery proponents by banning the Tappans' tracts from the mail. President Andrew Jackson allowed New York City's postmaster to block delivery of the pamphlets to the South and condemned the abolitionists and their organization in his annual message to Congress.[42]

While the Tappans and Garrisonians shifted their focus to the South after the New York antiabolition riots of 1834, white female charity workers emerged and stepped into the breach to look after the needs of New York's impoverished free blacks, especially the children and the elderly. Some of these women supported the idea of colonizing blacks outside the United States, and their goals for the advancement of blacks in their care were limited for the most part to menial labor rather than higher education. They were steering clear of the abolition controversy, or so they thought.[43]

In 1834, on one of their strolls through a run-down area in Lower Manhattan, Anna Shotwell and her niece, Mary Murray, were inspired by the sight of black orphans sitting on a stoop to establish—with fourteen other women and an advisory board of five men—the Association for the Benefit of Colored Orphans, which they funded with two thousand dollars raised through small subscriptions.[44]

Shotwell and Murray intended to start an orphanage, since none of the three privately funded orphan asylums in the city accepted blacks. In 1837, they started by opening a day school with just five orphans, housed in a small cottage on Twelfth Street. The city later granted some land to the association—twenty lots on Fifth Avenue, between Forty-third and Forty-fourth Streets—where a substantial building was completed in 1843, and twenty more lots were granted the next year.[45]

At first, black leaders did not approve of segregating black children for any reason, even for their supposed benefit. Moreover, with few exceptions, the Colored Orphan Asylum prepared its graduates for the kind of menial labor that blacks saw as a dead end. The children were "bound out" at the age of twelve as indentured servants on farms, "the boys until the age of twenty-one and the girls to age eighteen."[46]* Shotwell argued that without the asylum's intervention these disadvantaged orphans were likely to become "burdens

---

*"At the end of their nine years of service the boys received one hundred dollars with accumulated interest which had been deposited in the bank for them in annual installments; the girls were paid thirty dollars for six years of work" (Freeman, p. 179).

Anna Shotwell, Hannah Shotwell, and Mary Murray, founders of the
Colored Orphan Asylum

on society, and some perhaps would swell the catalogue of its delinquents and convicts." While idealistic charity workers were motivated by the "increasing spirit of compassion and kindness," in America, Shotwell wrote, the asylum also helped reduce "pauperism and crime" and contributed to "public safety."[47]

However, the asylum's work eventually won blacks over, as did the hiring of James McCune Smith, the nation's first accredited black doctor. McCune Smith, who had eagerly celebrated statewide emancipation as a teenager at the African Free School No. 2, continued his education under Peter Williams Jr. and applied to American medical schools but was rejected because he was black. Williams, who led St. Philip's Church for more than twenty years and mentored hundreds of black students, steered McCune Smith to medical school abroad and raised money for his tuition. In 1837, McCune Smith graduated first in his class ahead of hundreds at the University of Glasgow in Scotland. For his colleagues in the Glasgow Emancipation Society, he was a living embodiment of innate racial equality.[48]

He had returned from Scotland and become the attending physician at the asylum in 1843, tending to the health of the eighty-two orphans in the new building on Fifth Avenue.[49] McCune Smith also saw both black and white patients in his thriving private practice on West Broadway. Since his success was so rare, it heightened his frustration with the persistence of racial inequality in the northern states, the "damning thralldom that grinds to dust the colored inhabitants."[50]

For McCune Smith and other black leaders, America's racial caste system not only was wrong but had no basis, since they knew that behind the façade of white supremacy many Americans descended from interracial couples, including mixtures of Dutch, Native American, Spanish, and African blood, and particularly from white masters and their black female slaves in the South.

McCune Smith mocked the pseudoscience of phrenology when he wrote that the black news vendor on the street had facial features common to the "first families" of Virginia and could easily have been sired by Thomas Jefferson, who "contradicted his philosophy of negro hate by seeking the dalliance of black women" and produced numerous children of "mixed blood."[51]* In McCune Smith's literary sketches of the news vendor and other blacks in menial jobs, titled "Heads of Colored People," and in his other writing, he stressed that civilization itself was impossible without a "coming together" of the races, and that the enormous vitality of American society came from the mixture of peoples that had created it.[52]

McCune Smith and other abolitionists were up against the prevailing Jacksonian mind-set of white supremacy. Labor leader and Democratic congressman Ely Moore of New York warned that the Whigs intended to subjugate the working class by freeing the slaves in the South "to compete with the Northern white man in the labor market."

Jacksonian intellectuals declared that charity should "begin at home" in northern states like Massachusetts and New Hampshire. "The abolitionists of the North have mistaken the color of American Slaves," declared Theophilus Fisk, a labor leader and ex-priest based in Boston; "all the real Slaves in the United States have *pale* faces . . . I will venture to affirm that there are more slaves in Lowell and Nashua alone than can be found South

---

*Phrenologists claimed that the intelligence of an individual, and by extension a race, could be definitively measured by the shape and topography of the skull.

James McCune Smith

of the Potomac." Compared to the plight of the northern worker, Fisk claimed, chattel slavery was a benevolent system with a lifelong social safety-net. "Emancipate the slave, and what then! He would fiddle, steal, and then starve."[53]

CHAPTER 3

Horace Greeley and the Birth of the Republican Party

~⌒

ly—scatter through the land—go to the Great West," Horace Greeley exhorted unemployed workers in his weekly paper, the *New-Yorker*. In 1837, the same year that Anna Shotwell and Mary Murray opened their school for black orphans, an economic panic gripped the country. Tens of thousands of New Yorkers were on the verge of starvation, having exhausted their credit with "boarding-houses, landlords, and grocers," Greeley recalled.[1] London's credit markets had contracted suddenly, and southern cotton growers had defaulted on loans to a major New York firm, which had collapsed and set off a domino effect throughout the economy, ruining hundreds of businesses. Banks in every state called in loans and ceased payment in silver and gold, while the country tumbled into six years of economic depression.[2]

Greeley was deeply affected by the sight of workers suffering through no fault of their own and feared widespread misery would lead to riots.

> I saw two families, including six or eight children, burrowing in one cellar under a stable,—a prey to famine on the one hand, and to vermin and cutaneous diseases on the other, with sickness adding its horrors to those of a polluted atmosphere and a wintry temperature. I saw men who each, somehow, supported his family on an income of $5 per week or less, yet who cheerfully gave something to mitigate

the sufferings of those who were *really* poor. I saw three widows, with as many children, living in an attic on the profits of an apple-stand which yielded less than $3 per week, and the landlord came in for a full third of that.[3]

In the coming years Greeley embraced the idea of "Association"; of workers banding together to form cooperative enterprises that would maximize their leverage as both producers and consumers in the new world of unbridled capitalist competition.

This reformulation of French socialist Charles Fourier's far more radical denunciations of capitalism attracted Greeley, then a conservative and a Whig, who hoped to temper the harsh effects of the free market without attacking private property or inciting class warfare. In 1841, Greeley founded the New York *Tribune,* a larger and more influential daily newspaper in which he gave Fourierism ample space on the front page.[4]*

While the Panic of 1837 deepened Greeley's sympathy for the laboring classes and set him on the path of social reform, two other events of that year snapped him out of his complacency about slavery and his acceptance of colonization. One was the campaign of Sam Houston and other "filibusters" to annex the Mexican province of Texas to the United States, "thus expanding the area and enhancing the power of American Slavery." The second event was the murder of Elijah P. Lovejoy, a young abolitionist minister who gained prominence preaching in Missouri, where a mob destroyed the press and type for his newspaper. Lovejoy started over in Ohio, a so-called free state, but he was shot and killed when he refused to stop publishing. Lovejoy's martyrdom for freedom of speech convinced Greeley "that Slavery and true Freedom could not coexist on the same soil," and that slavery's "power in and over the Union" must be combated and contained.[5]

The Panic of 1837 and the ensuing six-year depression exacerbated class and ethnic divisions. Protestant missionaries in the slums felt overwhelmed by the enormity of the economic crisis and began to suspect that poverty—and a foreign, "ignorant" underclass—were becoming a permanent feature of urban life.[6] A combative Irish priest from Philadelphia, "Dagger John" Hughes, who drew a cross resembling a stiletto after his signature, became archbishop of New York in 1841 and took on the Protestant establishment to secure equality for the city's Catholic minority. His flock continued to grow with new waves of Irish immigration, which increased in the late 1830s and 1840s. The

---

*The *Tribune* also had a weekly edition distributed outside of New York City.

depression deterred some would-be refugees, but by 1839, Ireland had suffered sixteen famine winters in a century and a half, the harshest one killing some four hundred thousand people and causing many to flee to America.[7]

Nativist feeling against the Irish surged and then peaked in 1844, with a prolonged street battle in Brooklyn, followed a few days later by massive rioting in Philadelphia. In New York, as the nativists prepared to join forces with their Philadelphia brethren, Hughes posted a thousand defenders around each of the city's eight Catholic churches and warned the nativist mayor, James Harper, that the whole city would burn if any harm came to them.[8]

The most critical aspect of the depression for New York City in the longer term was that the building industry came almost to a standstill. The growing population quickly outstripped the already short housing supply. Working-class neighborhoods became critically overcrowded, approaching the condition of the worst slums.[9]

John H. Griscom, a Quaker doctor, became city inspector in 1842 and launched a detailed study of New York's burgeoning public health crisis. His scathing report asserted that overcrowding and a lack of ventilation in the tenements, particularly in the rear buildings and cellars, were the main causes of the city's needlessly high mortality rate. Griscom also pointed to inadequate, clogged sewers and accumulating solid waste as sources of death and disease. He proposed an extensive new network of drains and sewers, as well as free, clean, running water in every household from the just completed Croton aqueduct and reservoir system.

Griscom called for government intervention to force improvements in the design and construction of housing, bringing in light and fresh air, while capping the number of tenants allowed in a building. To make sure landlords cleaned and maintained their buildings properly, Griscom wanted to assemble a team of impartial medical inspectors empowered to shut down intolerably dirty or overcrowded buildings. The city's aldermen, who appointed the current health wardens, took no action since it would have deprived them of valuable political patronage, and Griscom was not reappointed.

However, with the support of wealthy inventor and industrialist Peter Cooper and other reformers, Griscom's groundbreaking study, *The Sanitary Condition of the Laboring Population of New York,* which described "how the other half lives," was published in 1845. The greatest incentive for the wealthy to clean up the city, Griscom emphasized, was the threat of a violent underclass. The tenements were breeding grounds for people "more difficult to govern, more disposed to robbery, mobs, and other lawless acts, and less accessible to the influence of religious and moral instruction."[10]

·   ·   ·

In the three years between the writing and publication of Griscom's report, the forces of disorder that he identified continued to grow. "Fire rowdies, butcher boys, soap-locks, and all sorts of riotous miscreants" along with the occasional "gang of negroes" were taking over New York's streets, the *Herald* declared hysterically in the summer of 1841.* During the depression that lingered until 1843, dozens of nativist and ethnic street gangs formed. Since industrialization was breaking down the apprentice system and young men had less chance of progressing to journeyman or master craftsman, membership in a uniformed group gave them a sense of power and purpose. Gangs provided members with a new persona and a cushion against the shock of unemployment.[11]

The Forty Thieves, Kerryonians, Shirt Tails, and Plug Uglies were Irish gangs in Five Points, each with a particular grocery-groggery as its den and command center.† The nativist American Guards congregated instead on the Bowery, which was also home to the Bowery B'hoys, O'Connell Guards, and Atlantic Guards. The True Blue Americans were not nativists but Irishmen. More dependable than the names for telling the gangs apart were their uniforms: red stripes, blue-striped pantaloons, black coat and top hat, shirttails out, plug hats stuffed with wool and leather to absorb blows during a riot.

Using a variety of wooden clubs, bricks, and sometimes knives and pistols, each gang defended its turf. Volunteer fire companies, which already consisted of rowdy young men prone to fighting with competitors, had an increasing number of gang members in their ranks, which turned a violent culture even more so. Volunteer fire companies and gangs were also vehicles for entering the world of politics. Tammany ward and district leaders were often saloon owners as well and recruited the Irish toughs who came to their establishments on the Bowery for various assignments, including fraud and intimidation at the polls. The Whigs in turn enlisted nativist thugs, and the gangs clashed in this political capacity as well.[12]

The upsurge in gang activity during the depression coincided with the city authorities' decision to stop tolerating riots and improve the police force. The daytime marshals and constables were prone to corruption as a means of augmenting the fees and rewards from crime victims they received in lieu of salaries. The night watchmen—many of them too old for such work or exhausted from their day jobs—had become a laughingstock. Residents joked that "while the city sleeps, the watchmen do too."[13]

---

*"Soap-locks" were street toughs who stiffened their long hair with soap, much as styling gel is used today.
†A grocery that served liquor was called a grocery-groggery.

In February 1836, a disruptive labor strike had threatened the city's waterfront and trade, spurring business leaders and city officials to action. Overcoming the traditional American abhorrence of standing armies, and empowered by the state legislature to do so, the mayor ordered the elite Twenty-seventh militia regiment to be on call at all times for riot duty. These six hundred "respectable young men of the city"—who had quelled the election and antiabolition riots in 1834—inspired confidence in the city's upper classes and loathing in the crowds they dispersed without remorse.[14]

The regiment had been formed a dozen years earlier and was one of the few, dressed in splendid uniforms, that marked a departure from the "old-time militia," consisting of the city's able-bodied adult males dressed in a motley collection of uniforms, who reported for an occasional day of "drill and parade" and a good deal of drinking. The Twenty-seventh was known as the "foremost in discipline and general excellence," according to one historian. Mostly "young American mechanics of some means," and "firmly fixed in [the city's] social, business and political life," members of the Twenty-seventh generally disdained the immigrant population. Some members had transferred out of the Ninth Regiment "on account of the predominance of the foreign element in that organization."[15]

Hoping to use the military only as a last resort, the city moved tentatively to replace the fragmented, ineffectual police department with a stronger, full-time force. In 1841, the brutal murder of a cigar seller, a beautiful young woman whose battered corpse was found in the Hudson River, created a furor in the press, which spurred the state legislature to establish New York's Municipal Police Department two years later. With each of the city's twelve wards having a station house and nominating officers for mayoral approval, the police—already notoriously corrupt—would be at the beck and call of local politicians. By 1845, the Democrats had won back control of the city government from the Whigs and proceeded to fill the eight-hundred-man police force with party loyalists, including the very gang members the department was meant to curb.[16]

The economic recovery began in 1844 but provided no relief from overcrowding in the slums of American cities, which only grew worse. Immigration to the United States increased fourfold in the mid-1840s, and prosperity widened the gap between rich and poor. In New York, Democrats were extending their grip on the city when a massive influx of Irish immigrants swelled their ranks. British colonial policies over time had forced Irish tenant farmers to subsist mainly on potatoes, and in 1845 a potato blight—exacerbated by British prejudice and mishandling of relief measures—turned into the Great

Famine, one of the worst humanitarian disasters in history. During the next seven years, more than one million died of starvation and more than one million emigrated, crossing the Atlantic on disease-ridden "coffin ships," only to land in the worst slums of America's large cities.[17]

Daniel O'Connell's nonviolent tactics of resistance lost favor during the Great Famine as rage mounted against British rule. However, lacking organization, weapons, and food for the people, the Young Ireland revolt of 1848 immediately collapsed, and the movement's leaders either were exiled to Tasmania or fled to the United States and congregated in New York, where they later founded the Fenian Brotherhood to raise funds for an invasion to liberate their homeland. The Fenians derived their name from Finn MacCool, the mythic leader of a band of Celtic warriors.[18]

Along with famine, violent political upheaval spread throughout Europe in 1848 as popular movements in Italy, France, Germany, and elsewhere launched rebellions against established regimes. During bloody riots in Paris, dubbed the "June Days," ten thousand people were killed or injured when workers clashed with the army in the barricaded streets. European revolutionaries escaped to America, bringing their radicalism to the labor movement, which was still recovering from the depression.[19]

The economic recovery in America was accelerated by the new British and German transatlantic steamships and the products of New York City's thirty East River shipyards: massive square-rigged packet ships, which were soon overtaken by "clippers" bringing tea from China, and, after 1848, infusions of gold from California.[20] Social distinctions became more entrenched as New York earned its name, the Empire City, becoming the hub of far-flung commercial markets and an industrial engine in its own right. New York, like all large cities, "has its poles of social life," one working-class writer noted. "The region which skirts the Wharves with its seething purlieus, dens, and stinking stews, is the antipodes of the flowery land of the Fifth Avenue."[21]

Commerce and bullion in turn spurred New York's emergence in the coming decade as America's foremost industrial city—with a growth rate rivaling that of any manufacturing center on the globe. The development of railroads in the 1830s and steamships in the 1840s had created a demand for the sprawling ironworks along the Hudson and East River waterfronts. The Novelty Works, with some twelve hundred workers, was the nation's biggest metalworking and machine shop, producing enormous ship engines and boilers, along with the "bed-pieces" that supported them.[22]

Other New York foundries fabricated architectural elements and entire cast-iron facades for commercial buildings such as warehouses and stores. Like the manufacturers who were pioneering methods of mass production and prefabricated construction, retailers in the flourishing city were offering their wares in vastly greater quantities and selling them with unprecedented speed. Looking like Renaissance palaces with their tiers of cast-iron classical columns or facades of marble and plate glass, the new luxury hotels and department stores along Fifth Avenue and Broadway drew an endless stream of fashionably dressed window shoppers, turning these arteries into promenades for the city's well-to-do.

Broadway, for all its glittering lights, was the border between two realms and was itself divided between its affluent "dollar side" on the west, and the eastern "shilling side" that touched the slums.[23] The intersection of these two worlds was bitterly evoked in the opening scene of Edward Judson's 1848 novel, *Mysteries and Miseries of New York,* in which a pack of wealthy cads out on the town surrounds a poor young seamstress on a dark street and flips a coin to see who will have her. In the nick of time, a tough old whore comes to her rescue.[24]

Judson was also the right-hand man of Tammany Hall's Isaiah Rynders, a knife-wielding "sportsman" and riverboat captain who specialized in fomenting class warfare to galvanize the Democratic party faithful. In May 1849, Rynders and Judson recruited hundreds of street brawlers from the Bowery—the New York underworld's north-south thoroughfare, synonymous with gambling dens, saloons, gangs, and rowdy firemen—and gave them tickets to a performance at the exclusive Astor Opera House, where they started a riot in the balconies and drowned out the celebrated British actor William Macready. In the midst of the Great Famine and the Young Ireland revolt, which the British had crushed, the genteel Macready had become a symbol of political oppression.

Three days later, after prominent New Yorkers had convinced Macready to continue with his scheduled performances, Rynders again had rioters disrupt the play while ten thousand protesters outside in Astor Place smashed the theater's windows and charged the doors, shouting, "Burn the damned den of the aristocracy!" Overwhelmed, the police called in the militia, mustered in advance by Major General Charles Sandford: cavalry and artillery units, along with two hundred men from the elite Twenty-seventh—recently renamed the Seventh Regiment. They fired into the crowd, ultimately killing 22 people and wounding 150.

Judge Charles Patrick Daly, who handed down harsh sentences for ten of the rioters, was the son of Irish immigrants and a Democrat, but he had little tolerance for machine politics and civil disorder. Judson was identified as a ringleader and spent a year in jail. Greeley's *Tribune* praised the verdict, while the *Herald* and *Irish-American* blamed the Whig merchants and mayor for insisting on Macready's second performance and bringing the military into the fray. Rynders and several followers were tried separately, with Judge John W.

Edmonds presiding. This time, however, Tammany used its political muscle to ensure that Rynders and the others were acquitted. The shattered windows of the Astor Opera House were boarded up, and it never reopened.[25]

The *Nation,* published by Thomas D'Arcy McGee, warned fellow Irishmen to be independent; to avoid "second-rate demagogues" who were exploiting them for votes and creating mob rule: "These men, mostly of Irish origin, flattered them on election days, and despised them all other days; appealed to their passions and bigotries; encouraged their weaknesses and vices. Ward and local meetings were held in taverns . . . political placards were issued with the cross emblazoned on them—the British lion was publicly gored and his 'fangs cut' on innumerable platforms." The *Irish-American* shot back that such charges were "a coarse, vulgar, beastly lie, not having a shadow of truth to bear it out." The *Nation* soon folded, and its editor left town.[26]*

Democratic operatives like Rynders were at work all across America stirring up mobs and trouble, according to Greeley, who remained a staunch law-and-order Whig despite his increasingly liberal and progressive views. A Protestant and a pious temperance man, Greeley despised the Democrats. Moreover, working for the Whigs subsidized his failing *New-Yorker,* and editing their national campaign weekly, the *Log Cabin,* had made him famous while helping William Harrison and John Tyler win the White House in 1840 on the slogan "Tippecanoe and Tyler too."† Greeley stuck with the Whigs, perpetually expecting to be rewarded with a political appointment such as postmaster general or an ambassadorship.[27]

In the early 1840s, sparring factions within the Democratic party lost control to the southern slaveholders. Led by South Carolina senator John C. Calhoun, they had gained strength as slavery expanded westward across the states on the Gulf of Mexico; eventually they aimed to include in their empire not only Texas and the Southwest but all of Mexico and parts of South America and the Caribbean islands.[28] Democrats had roused the people and led America into all its foreign wars, Greeley charged, most recently, under President James Polk, annexing Texas in 1846 and starting the Mexican War in order to conquer the Southwest and extend slavery's reach.[29]

In 1846, Pennsylvania congressman David Wilmot called for the exclusion of slavery from any territories won from Mexico, and his amendment

---

*McGee's newspaper should not be confused with the antislavery magazine *The Nation,* founded in 1865 and still being published today.

†"Tippecanoe" was Harrison's log cabin home that Whig campaign managers invented to give him popular appeal.

was included in a spending bill approved by the House. Northern Democrats, disgruntled with southern domination of their party, had joined forces with northern Whigs to pass the amendment, while southern Whigs had sided with southern Democrats to oppose it. Passage of the Wilmot Proviso signaled a worrisome sectional realignment of the two major political parties. The slavery issue had begun to divide the country, North from South, straining the old two-party system to the breaking point.[30]

When radical abolitionists fused with antislavery Democrats and Whigs to form the Free Soil party in 1848, with a platform of keeping slavery out of the western territories, Greeley "clung fondly" to the Whig party, reluctant to move with the rising tide of change that was reshaping American politics. Greeley insisted that the Whigs—not a fledgling third party—were the best hope for resisting the "aggressions of the Slave Power."[31] However, when the Whig party's power brokers chose a slave owner, General Zachary Taylor, as their candidate and installed him as their puppet in the White House, Greeley's failure to bolt the party smacked of ambition for a political appointment.[32]

With the Compromise of 1850, Congress attempted once again to defuse the time bomb of slavery. The deal excluded slavery from California but not from New Mexico and Utah; the slave trade was abolished in the nation's capital; and slaveholders were granted a harsher fugitive slave law, which committed the federal government to helping owners pursue and recover runaways in the North. Black and white abolitionists joined forces to resist the law, and confrontations on the streets and in courtrooms across the North, particularly in Boston, heightened the sectional animosity that was dividing the country.[33]

Greeley ultimately condoned the territorial compromise as a temporary solution but railed against the fugitive slave law. The *Tribune* continued to crusade for various reforms (better street cleaning, safer immigrant ships, banning child labor and prostitution, and creating more city parks), but Greeley's energies were scattered among numerous causes, fads, and theories, from séances to vegetarianism. He and P. T. Barnum sang hymns together and met near the *Tribune* office for meals of vegetables, unseasoned puddings, and Graham crackers.[34] The time was drawing near, however, when Greeley would have to commit wholeheartedly to opposing slavery.

In the presidential race of 1852, the Whig party self-destructed. The party's northern wing prevailed over southern Whigs to nominate Winfield Scott, an antislavery candidate. The Democrats were similarly divided but found a candidate on whom they could agree: New Hampshire's Franklin Pierce, a Yankee sympathetic to the South. In the general election, many southern Whigs defected, giving the Democrats a huge victory. Greeley, among others, declared that the Whig party was dead.[35]

Horace Greeley

Two years later, the danger that Kansas and Nebraska would be admitted to the Union and quickly become slave states finally focused Greeley's moral fire, while burying the remains of the Whig party. Senator Stephen Douglas, a Democrat from Illinois, spearheaded the effort to organize the territories of Kansas and Nebraska as states; pressured by powerful southern Democrats in the Senate, Douglas called for "popular sovereignty," letting residents decide on slavery by referendum—a violation of the Compromise of 1820, which banned slavery above 36° 30′, the southern border of Missouri.* Greeley unleashed a relentless series of editorials condemning Douglas's bill that helped galvanize antislavery opinion from coast to coast while vastly expanding the *Tribune*'s circulation and influence.

Greeley's talents as a political propagandist had finally crystallized. He branded the passage of the Kansas-Nebraska Act in 1854 "a declaration of war by the slaveholders against the North" and called for the creation of a new national party to unite all free-soil advocates, who were abandoning the Whig and Democratic organizations. Greeley proposed "some simple name

*The compromise designated Missouri a slave state, the only one permitted north of that line.

like *Republican*" to "fitly designate those who had united to restore our Union to its true mission of champion and promulgator of Liberty."[36]

Little by little, the new, all-northern party emerged in the spring and summer of 1854, as antislavery groups prepared for state and congressional elections. Activists gathering at a church in Ripon, Wisconsin, were the first of many groups to declare themselves "Republicans." They were soon followed by thirty antislavery congressmen meeting in Washington and by conventions that proliferated in congressional districts across the North, particularly in the Old Northwest.* The party name was meant to evoke the republican values of the nation's Revolutionary founders in contrast to the slaveholders' tyrannical aristocracy.

Congressman George Julian of Indiana and Senators Salmon Chase of Ohio, William Seward of New York, and Charles Sumner of Massachusetts were a few of the Republican party's leading lights. Newspaper editors, including Greeley's Democratic rival William Cullen Bryant, also joined the new party.[37]

In the harsh, divisive fall campaign, free-soil hecklers in Chicago drowned out a speech by Senator Douglas. Former Illinois congressman Abraham Lincoln, eyeing a future seat in the U.S. Senate, hit the same campaign trail, challenging Douglas and supporting antislavery candidates for the Illinois legislature.† Lincoln remained a Whig in name for another year, even as he voiced the credo of the new Republican party: "Nearly eighty years ago we began by declaring that all men are created equal; but now from that beginning we have run down to the other declaration, that for some men to enslave others is a sacred right of self-government. These principles cannot stand together. They are as opposite as God and Mammon; and whoever holds to the one must despise the other."[38]

Republicans and other antislavery candidates swept the North in 1854, depriving the Democrats of control in the House and in every northern state legislature except Massachusetts and Delaware. Those two states elected majorities from a new and powerful nativist party, dubbed the "Know Nothings" because members claimed to know nothing when asked about their secretive organization. These nativists also attracted a huge number of votes in Pennsylvania, New York, and several other northeastern and border states. Their main goal was to check the growing political power of immigrants by extending the waiting period for naturalization required by federal and state laws.

---

*Before the expansion of the United States from coast to coast, the upper Midwest was known as the Northwest.

†U.S. senators were not yet elected directly by the people, but rather by the state legislature.

After nativism crested and subsided in 1844, the flood of immigration between 1845 and 1854 had packed America's slums even more densely with Irish and German refugees, triggering a fresh wave of xenophobia. Urban crime rates, along with municipal spending on the poor, increased dramatically. Resentment and violence against the new arrivals, particularly against Irish Catholics, were generated as often by more established Protestant immigrants from England, Scotland, and Ireland as by American-born nativists. Targeting Irish and German immigrants, who tended to congregate in groggeries and beer gardens, temperance advocates also provoked ethnic conflict in the early 1850s, with successful campaigns for prohibition in more than a dozen states.[39]

Never one to shrink from confrontation, Archbishop John Hughes of New York gloried in the rapidly increasing number of Catholic churchgoers, which far outstripped the growth of Protestant churches in the previous decade. "The object we hope to accomplish is to convert all Pagan nations, and all Protestant nations," Hughes proclaimed in a widely reprinted speech, *The Decline of Protestantism and Its Causes.* "There is no secrecy in all this . . . Our mission [is] to convert the world—including the inhabitants of the United States—the people of the cities, and the people of the country . . . the Legislatures, the Senate, the Cabinet, the President, and all!" Protestantism was on its deathbed, the archbishopric's newspaper declared, and "its last moment is come when it is fairly set, face to face, with Catholic truth."[40]

Abolitionists, nativists, and prohibitionists had common roots in the evangelical Protestantism of the Second Great Awakening, and members of all three groups tended to oppose both slavery and the Catholic Church. Therefore, when Know Nothings voiced their opposition to the Kansas-Nebraska Act, Republicans took care to distinguish themselves by condemning nativism, just as they did the Democratic party's virulent racism. However, some Republicans also formed alliances with the Know Nothings' American party in an attempt to control and supplant it, as both groups vied to become the main alternative to the Democrats in the mid-1850s.

By 1856, a Republican had been elected Speaker of the U.S. House of Representatives—thanks in part to Greeley's presence in the House cloakroom, where he buttonholed congressmen and wielded the threat of censure in his powerful *Tribune* to enforce party discipline. The Republican party was thus firmly established, while a precipitous decline in immigration after 1854 helped rob the American party of its momentum. More important, most northerners had come to regard anti-Catholic, anti-immigrant hysteria as a sideshow compared to the conflict over slavery's expansion. "Popular sovereignty" had turned Kansas into a savage killing zone.[41]

After the passage of the Kansas-Nebraska Act in 1854, abolitionists and slaveholders both rushed settlers to Kansas, where widespread violence erupted as each side strove to dominate the referendum and determine the fate of slavery in the state. Greeley had never been an abolitionist and publicly denounced the bloodshed, but he also helped send rifles to Kansas for the free-soil forces while using the *Tribune* to encourage settlement and fan the flames of a conflict that, as it grew, helped foster unity under the Republican tent.[42]

"We are playing for a mighty stake," Senator David Atchison of Missouri declared to a colleague. "If we win we carry slavery to the Pacific Ocean, if we fail we lose Missouri Arkansas Texas and all the territories." He told Jefferson Davis, "We will be compelled to shoot, burn & hang" the abolitionists, "but the thing will soon be over." Senator William Seward of New York in turn confronted southern senators: "Since there is no escaping your challenge, I accept it on behalf of the cause of freedom. We will engage in competition for the virgin soil of Kansas, and God give the victory to the side which is stronger in numbers as it is in right."[43]

CHAPTER 4

Fernando Wood, the "Southern" Mayor of New York

~∼

I t is all very well for gentlemen to get up here and clamor about the wrongs and outrages of the southern slaves," declared Mike Walsh on the floor of the House in 1854, "but, sir, even in New York, during the last year, there have been over thirteen hundred people deprived of their liberty without any show or color of offense, but because they were poor, and too honest to commit a crime." Arguing that the "white wages slave of the North" was worse off than the black slave in the South, the Irish American, Democratic congressman from New York continued: "If a dozen of us own a horse in common, we want to ride him as much as possible, and feed him as little as possible. [Laughter] But if you or I own a horse exclusively, we will take good care to feed him well, and not drive him too much to endanger his health."[1]

The North's largely immigrant working class saw no attraction in the new Republican party, in which its Protestant enemies—abolitionists, prohibitionists, nativists, and former Whigs—were mingling. While industrialization threatened to turn workers into "wage slaves," Protestant evangelicals distinguished clearly between chattel slavery and wage work and insisted that the poor were responsible for their own plight; individual integrity and effort, they preached, determined a free laborer's lot in life—not the impersonal forces of the economy or the rapacity of capitalist employers. Thus, to most urban laborers, the abolition of slavery seemed a false and misguided philanthropy which bemoaned the suffering of blacks in the faraway South while neglecting the worker at home, whose job depended on trade with the cotton kingdom.[2]

Moreover, the evil of slavery in the South hardly seemed urgent when, every year, more than half the children in New York City's slums died from disease before the age of five, and the death rate for children younger than two years old stood at 70 percent. Overcrowding had pushed the city's overall mortality rate to a record high of forty deaths per thousand residents in 1845—and it remained at that level nine years later in 1854. Only weeks after the Astor Place riots in 1849, a cholera epidemic wiped out more than five thousand of the city's poorest residents, while the wealthy fled to the suburbs. Cholera afflicted the slums again in 1852, as did an epidemic of typhus. African Americans and immigrants alike suffered huge increases in the number of tuberculosis cases.[3]

In a single year, between 1853 and 1854, inflation drove the cost of living up by almost a third, while wages failed to keep pace. Labor unions, resurgent with the economic boom of the previous ten years, organized frequent strikes when employers did not honor agreements. While the unions strove to smooth over differences between American, Irish, German, French, and workers of other nationalities, they did not welcome African Americans or women into their ranks.

When white male workers representing seventy unions and twenty-eight reform groups had formed the international Industrial Congress in 1850, and formulated the demands that remained central to organized labor's agenda for the rest of the nineteenth century, they focused on "an eight-hour day, a minimum wage on public works projects, and direct city hiring of workers rather than the use of private contractors." They also called for laws to regulate the building and maintenance of tenements, enforcement of public health codes, and public baths and libraries. For those who chose to leave the city, they supported a homestead law to enable workers to settle in the West.

In New York, the groundswell of labor activity in the early 1850s included both the formation of unions and worker cooperatives as well as huge demonstrations, protests at City Hall, and some violent clashes, including a riot at 38th Street and Ninth Avenue, on August 4, 1850, in which hundreds of German tailors confronted subcontractors who were violating the citywide tailors' strike. The police intervened, and two tailors were killed while dozens suffered serious injuries. It was the first fatal clash between striking urban workers and the authorities in U.S. history.

Given the recent flood of immigration, the European upheavals of 1848, and the Astor Place riots of 1849, employers were quick to conclude, as the *Herald* put it, that "vast importations of foreign socialists" had triggered the unrest. German refugees, for example, who had fought in the revolts of 1848, were in fact influential, but they were joining forces with New York's home-grown labor movement, which had simply been dormant until the economy had recovered in the mid-1840s. By 1853, however, the labor movement as a whole remained divided as the new Amalgamated Trades Convention focused on wages and work rules, while turning away from the immigrant revolution-aries' calls for a labor party and sweeping political change.[4]

In 1853, Louis Napoleon, having made himself emperor of France in the wake of the tumultuous uprisings of 1848, commissioned Baron Haussmann to reshape Paris drastically with imperial boulevards too wide for rebel barri-cades. Worried upper-class New Yorkers looked at Manhattan's volatile slums and immigrant enclaves, and despite their democratic ideals, yearned for a forceful leader to clean up the city.[5]

The City Reform League, founded a year earlier by William Dodge, Stephen Whitney, and other wealthy merchants, named industrialist Peter Cooper its president in 1853 and crusaded against high taxes, unbridled spend-ing, and corruption perpetrated by the Tammany-controlled Common Council.* Housed in City Hall, this legislative branch of the city government consisted of a board of aldermen and a board of assistant aldermen elected by each ward.[6]

The municipal government had always been riddled with corruption, but a crop of particularly hungry, lower-middle-class businessmen was elected to the council in 1851. Their rise coincided with the reversal of a long-standing policy regarding street railroads: The council decided to grant fran-chises to railroad companies, allowing them to compete with operators of horse-drawn omnibuses by attaching horses to their trains below Thirty-second Street. This created a bidding war that enriched the aldermen and helped unleash an unprecedented wave of graft. Dubbed the "Forty Thieves," after the street gang, the Common Council embarked on a two-year frenzy of municipal corruption from 1852 to 1853, selling off the city's assets—land, wharves, ferry franchises—or giving them away to cronies, while lining its members' pockets with kickbacks.[7]

Aldermen awarded sanitation contracts to dishonest or inept street-cleaning companies. They also blocked housing codes and labor laws to shield favored businessmen and created or protected monopolies. The sale of franchises to the railroads proceeded without any planning or coordination of the city's transportation system. From 1850 to 1853, taxes had increased 54 percent, while spending by the city had shot up 70 percent in the past two

---

*Established in 1686, today called the City Council.

years. The growing use of revenue anticipation bonds, facilitated by a new law in 1852, was endangering the city's creditworthiness.[8]

Alderman William Tweed typified the parade of loyal small business-men and street toughs—including artisans, grocers, saloon owners, and liquor dealers—with which Tammany had packed the Common Council. The burly, charismatic Tweed had been the foreman of a volunteer fire company when the department's chief engineer terminated him for arming his men with axes and starting a brawl with a competing outfit. Bent on displaying their prowess, young firemen routinely fought with each other; while buildings burned, they insisted on pumping water by hand instead of using modern steam engines.[9]

In defense of the Common Council, Tweed pointed out that the street repairs, police stations, and prisons demanded by the public were expensive. "I ask the people if a city such as ours, daily receiving an immense population of the idle, degenerate, vicious, and good from all parts of the world, could be governed at less expense?" Indeed, reformers were also alarmed by the crime and mayhem spawned by Democratic rule, notably the release of gang members and other rioters from jail in 1852, which coincided with a rash of muggings.[10]

Policemen took bribes and allowed illegal gambling houses to thrive in broad daylight, with firemen, thugs, and gang members as their patrons. Peter Cooper and his allies succeeded in revising the city charter in 1853, weakening the Common Council, strengthening the mayor, and reforming the police. Control of the police department became more centralized with the creation of a board of commissioners, which included the mayor, recorder, and city judges. In an attempt to separate law enforcement from ward politics, the charter specified that councilmen could no longer appoint police officers or preside as judges in municipal courts. With mandatory blue uniforms and job security pegged to performance, the police force became more disciplined and aggressive, collaring 40 percent more criminals the following year.[11]

During the fall elections of 1853, Cooper's league endorsed reform candidates, mostly Whigs, who rode a wave of nativism into office, and drove out the "Forty Thieves" en masse from the Common Council. Tweed had won a seat in Congress while still an alderman, so his career continued. The new aldermen were less corrupt, but they taxed and spent at a rate even higher than their predecessors—especially for the police department and for education—and the City Reform League, in dismay, severed its ties with them. The reform alliance fragmented further in 1854 when longtime Democrats, including Cooper, accepted Tammany's candidate for mayor, Fernando Wood, who promised to be a strong leader and an agent of change: a Napoleon for New York.[12]

•   •   •

"No man ever went into higher office under a deeper cloud of ignominy" than Fernando Wood, declared Horace Greeley's *Tribune* in 1854 when one of the Tammany demagogues he so detested slithered into the mayoralty of New York City. Fernando Wood's opponents had dredged up compelling testimony about dishonesty in his private finances and business dealings, as well as a secret political alliance with the nativists. Nonetheless, Wood's immigrant base of support remained loyal, preferring him to the overtly anti-immigrant candidates. Wood also garnered votes by pitting the working class against the rich, the "producers" against the "nonproducers." This Jacksonian antimonopoly language was borrowed from the Locofocos, a radical Democratic faction Wood helped lead in 1835 in the wake of the Bank War.[13]*

Indeed, for the aristocratic merchants and landowners who had traditionally dominated New York politics, Wood's rise represented a dangerous new phenomenon made possible by the Jacksonian era of universal white male suffrage: the emergence of demagogic, professional politicians, completely lacking in social pedigree, who pandered to the newly enfranchised masses.[14]

The owner of a waterfront grocery-groggery in the 1830s, Fernando Wood rose rapidly within Tammany, and the votes of Irish longshoremen landed him a seat in the U.S. House of Representatives in 1840 at the age of twenty-eight.[15] Wood became part of Senator John Calhoun's inner circle. Opposing tariffs while defending states' rights and slavery, Wood professed to be a champion of the northern worker, protecting him from labor competition and thus from exploitation by employers. Wood also denounced the "slavery and oppression" of the Irish by the British.[16]

Wood lost his House seat in 1842 and resumed life in New York as a shipping merchant on the East River waterfront, trading mostly with the southern states. Calhoun, then secretary of state, gave Wood a federal job in New York with minimal duties that supplemented his income and restored some of his political prestige, while cementing his allegiance to the South Carolinian as well as to southern interests. Wood had generally prospered in the 1840s, remarrying after a bitter divorce and using some of his second wife's money to enter the booming Manhattan real estate market.

---

*At a Tammany Hall meeting in October 1835, conservative Bank Democrats nominated their candidates and then shut the gas to darken the room and prevent dissenters from naming an alternative slate. It was an old trick, and the radicals were ready with "locofocos," slang for friction matches, a new invention, with which they lit fifty candles and finished their business. The conservatives derided the radicals as "Locofocos," and they happily adopted the name.

As a politician-turned-speculator with intimate knowledge of the city's neighborhoods and properties, Wood was well positioned, and he made a fortune.[17]

Once in office as mayor in 1855, Wood saw his popularity soar as he struggled to turn the mayoralty into a bastion for effective, nonpartisan "one-man rule," and bombarded the fiefdoms of the city bureaucracy with imaginative, practical proposals for improving services, sanitation, infrastructure, and parks to meet the needs of the growing city. Dumbfounding his critics, Wood gained a nationwide reputation as the "Model Mayor."[18]

Wood used his momentum to become the first mayor ever to gain control of Tammany Hall, and as New York's apparent Democratic strongman, he backed proslavery candidate James Buchanan for president in 1856, against the Republican candidate, John C. Frémont. A Democratic paper in Ohio warned voters that Republicans would "turn loose . . . millions of Negroes, to elbow you in the workshops, and compete with you in the fields of honest labor." Democrats in Pittsburgh declared that Frémont's party aimed "to elevate the African race in this country to complete equality of political and economic condition with the white man."[19]

The polarization of the country—announced by the House vote on the Wilmot Proviso ten years earlier—had reached a dangerous intensity. Marching by torchlight, Republicans shouted their slogan, "Free Soil, Free Speech, Free Men, Frémont!" Indiana Democrats paraded young girls with banners pleading, "Fathers, save us from nigger husbands!"[20] Buchanan won, and Wood was reelected to a second two-year term as mayor, supported by merchants who had ties to the South.[21]

With Louis Napoleon's assumption of power in France as its subtext, a campaign biography of Wood had stressed the need for more mayoral power over the city's budget and bureaucratic departments.

> Now, how to govern so huge, so densely packed a mass; how to unite or at least keep harmonious, so many, so powerful discordant elements; how to reconcile their antipathies, subdue their jealousies; how to manage the newly-landed hordes of poor; how to please all, or at least keep all quiet—these present a complicated problem, the solution of which requires a wise man . . . A demand for more power would probably be unpopular. Therefore it is a brave thing to demand it, and patiently set to work to prove that it is needed. The man who demands it is brave; the man who obtains it is *capable*, and if capable, a fit ruler for you and for me.[22]

Fernando Wood

If the campaign biography lacked subtlety, so did Wood's use of the Municipal Police to ensure his reelection. During his first term, Wood had shown his reform zeal by strengthening the force and loudly putting criminals on notice that the city's new chief executive stood for law and order; Wood delighted even harsh critics like Horace Greeley by running telegraph wires from every precinct house to the police Central Office, the headquarters on Mulberry Street. With the new "magical" wires, Greeley's *Tribune* envisioned the police swiftly massing officers where they were needed most.[23]

Less visibly, however, Wood had turned the police department into a patronage mill, filling its ranks with immigrant supporters, then systematically levying contributions from the officers to fund his reelection. During the campaign, patrolmen were reassigned or given time off so the gangs of thugs on Wood's payroll could start riots at his opponents' rallies, attacking their speakers with rocks and bricks. At the polls, the mayor's toughs harassed voters, stuffed ballot boxes, and stole returns. While Wood's nativist rivals were also guilty of such violence and traditional Tammany-style intimidation and fraud, the autocratic mayor knew no bounds. Without any legal authority,

Wood suspended the Board of Police Commissioners on which he sat, to silence his outraged colleagues.[24]

"Fernandy Wood!" a crowd of the mayor's supporters chanted on the steps of City Hall. "Down with the Black Republicans!" Wood's mob, sneered Republican attorney George Templeton Strong, was a "miscellaneous assortment of suckers, soap locks, Irishmen, and plug uglies officiating in a guerilla capacity." Also protecting Mayor Wood on June 16, 1857, was a cordon of Municipal policemen surrounding the building.[25]

While the nascent Republican party that Horace Greeley helped create had lost the 1856 presidential election, it won several important northern states and alarmed southern conservatives; in New York, Republicans won the governor's office and control of the state legislature, setting the stage for a showdown with Mayor Wood.

A few months into Wood's second term, in mid-April 1857, the state legislature had passed the blatantly partisan Metropolitan Police Act, replacing New York City's Municipal Police with the "Metropolitans," run by a five-member, state-appointed commission. The metropolitan area was defined as New York, Brooklyn, Staten Island, and Westchester County, and the commission had free rein not only over the police but over the enforcement of election laws, health codes, and Sabbath closings. The two seats on the commission occupied by Mayor Wood and his Brooklyn counterpart were merely honorific, and the three Republican commissioners held all the power.[26]

Coupled with the Liquor Excise Law, which created stringent regulations and costly liquor licenses, the Sunday closings attacked the foundations of Democratic power in the city's wards: The saloons and grocery-groggeries were the local nerve centers of the political machine and sources of revenue from liquor industry lobbyists. The new laws, passed by a coalition of Republicans, nativists, and temperance advocates, also infuriated German and Irish Catholic laborers by policing their leisure time.[27]

Wood had challenged the police bill in court as unconstitutional and in the interim had stubbornly refused to disband his Municipals. He fanned the flames of Democratic resentment toward centralized state authority when he talked of a "subjugated city" in a "feeble state of vassalage" and used Jacksonian rhetoric about "the sovereign people."[28] Meanwhile, New Yorkers had endured a crime spree while the two police forces evicted each other from station houses and freed each other's prisoners.

Wood also asserted the right to name the city's street commissioner, and when the governor's appointee entered City Hall to take office on June 16,

The Metropolitan Police headquarters at 300 Mulberry Street

Wood had him thrown out by the Municipals. When Captain George W. Walling, of the Metropolitan force, tried to arrest Wood—"for blocking the appointment, for assault, and for inciting a riot"—Walling was ejected by the Municipals and thugs guarding the mayor. Walling returned with a phalanx of Metropolitans, and a bloody riot erupted on the front steps. The mob and the Municipals clubbed their opponents relentlessly and gained the upper hand until the city recorder summoned the Seventh Regiment, which happened to be parading on Broadway. Wood was arrested but quickly arranged bail through a friendly judge. On July 2, the courts upheld the Metropolitan Police Act, and the following day Wood finally dissolved his Municipals.[29]

On July 4, the Metropolitans began walking their beats and became embroiled in riots: Street gangs, one of which had campaigned for Wood, targeted them as political enemies, wounding or killing several officers. Rioting continued the following day, and the militia had to be brought in to suppress it. It was the worst riot since Astor Place in 1849, with twelve people killed and thirty-seven wounded. A week later thousands of Germans battled police

and militia regiments in Kleindeutschland to protest the closing of saloons.*
The next day, the funeral for a German blacksmith killed in the riot made its
way up Broadway—ten thousand people and a band of musicians with a banner in German: Victim of the Metropolitan Police. At a rally afterward,
speakers protested the oppressive acts of the Republican legislators.[30]

Broadway, where the angry immigrant workers marched, was the dividing line between New York's rich and poor, marking the chasm between their
customs, values, and politics.[31] Revered by his immigrant constituents, Wood
had come to be associated by the elite with the precariousness of law and order in the growing city. The *New York Times* blamed Wood for opening the
door to mob rule with his "disorganizing and reckless opposition to the laws
of the State."[32]

Observing the situation from the South, planter, writer, and proslavery
propagandist Edmund Ruffin went farther, noting in his diary that "the recent fighting between the separate police forces of the city & the state of New
York . . . seems very much like the beginning of a civil war, which the Federal government may have to interfere [with] to quell." Sizing up New York
City's tendency to support the South, Ruffin continued, "I wish that the city
would secede & form a separate state, with the consent of the Federal government." With two senators in Washington, Ruffin reasoned, New York
City would be an asset to the South.[33]

Less than six months later, in the fall of 1857, a sharp decline in European demand for American wheat drove down farm prices and the value of
railroad stocks. When jittery midwestern businessmen tried to retrieve some
of their capital, their New York bankers were caught short, having recklessly
made dubious loans to other banks and to speculators in the stock market.
The banks called in their matured loans, and the sudden contraction of credit
ruined numerous businesses, setting off another panic, a worldwide financial
crisis resulting in massive unemployment.[34]

Ruffin marveled at "accounts of awful omen, in the city of New York."
Winter had not yet arrived, he noted, and already thousands of hungry laborers, "instigated & led by foreigners," had rallied and were marching through
the city "demanding work & bread." This menacing mob would soon be thirty
thousand strong, Ruffin wrote. "Half that number of desperate villains can
sack & burn the city, & murder its best inhabitants. This fate I predicted for
New York, whenever the dissolution of the union shall remove the conservative
influence of the south & of its institution of slavery. But the fulfillment

---

*Kleindeutschland, or Little Germany, was the predominantly German neighborhood on
Manhattan's Lower East Side, stretching northward from Grand and Division Streets to Six-
teenth Street, and westward from the East River to the Bowery.

seems impending, or openly threatened, sooner than I expected."[35]

When Wood proposed unprecedented public works projects and food distribution to the laborers as part of their pay, he lost whatever remained of his elite support. Then, when Wood could not deliver on his proposals, workers blamed him and marched on City Hall.[36] "Matters look very much like the incidents of the beginnings in Paris of the first French revolution," Ruffin entered in his diary. "The mayor has to be protected by a guard of 50 police-men—& U.S. troops have been sent from the neighboring fort to guard the public treasury in the custom-house. The mayor, [Fernando] Wood, had at first encouraged the kindling of the flame by his own Jacobin declarations."[37]

Expanding their control over city affairs, Republicans in Albany moved the mayoral race to off years to punish Wood, so he faced a run for reelection that fall instead of a year later. Members of Wood's own party fused with Republicans and nativist Know Nothings to defeat him by a narrow margin.[38]

Along with Wood's proposals to relieve the poor, housing regulation was put on hold in 1857. With overcrowding and disease, by 1856 more New Yorkers were dying every year than were being born. Reformers, including John Griscom, had prevailed on the state legislature's Tenement House Committee to address the crisis of the city's slums. In 1857, members of the committee toured the slums and produced a report detailing the abominable conditions.

While they did not consider the deeper causes of poverty—rent increases combined with lower wages—or the proposals of land reformers that the government should create a large volume of public housing, the legislators did call for legal action, and New York State's first housing code was soon put on paper. However, builders and owners protested the new regulations, and they would not be enacted for another decade. Unchecked, the slums continued to deteriorate.[39]

Because they arrived on disease-ridden ships, many immigrants were quarantined on Staten Island before being deported or allowed to proceed to New York City's slums. In September 1858, Edmund Ruffin noted with great interest "the burning, by a mob, of all the quarantine buildings of Staten Island," which "shows a disregard to law which is ominous of much worse results in New York."[40]

With his brother Ben as sole adviser, Fernando Wood resurrected himself, buying the *New York Daily News* as a mouthpiece and later making Ben the editor. Betrayed by Tammany in the last election and unable to take it over, Wood rebelled and created his own organization, Mozart Hall (named after the hotel near Bond Street and Broadway where it met), and announced that he would run for mayor again.[41] Attempting to compete with Tammany for control of the New York State party before the presidential race, Wood arrived early at the state Democratic convention in Syracuse in 1859, and his thugs, in a clash of fists and brandished knives and guns, took control of the proceedings with a shocking display of brute force, solidifying Wood's reputation nationally as a ruthless and lawless villain.[42]

Astonishingly, Wood went on to win his third term as mayor of New York in the fall of 1859, helped by a divided opposition. He also fanned the flames of social, racial, and sectional conflict. The Wood brothers' *Daily News* denounced his wealthy opponents as "a kid-glove, scented, silk stocking, poodle-headed, degenerate aristocracy" that exploited "the hardworking, bone and sinew, hard-fisted, noble, laboring-men of New York" and regarded the working classes as "outside barbarians." Wood used his Locofoco arguments about the "producing class" bearing the tax burden while the idle rich did not pay. Recalling his stand against the Republicans in Albany, Wood cast himself as the "Champion of Municipal Rights."[43]

Most ominously, Wood introduced the national slavery controversy into the mayoral campaign, which coincided with John Brown's abortive raid on a federal installation at Harpers Ferry, West Virginia—an attempt to steal weapons and arm southern slaves for a massive rebellion. The raid had reinforced southern fears of radical antislavery forces in the North and hardened positions on both sides. Wood exploited the event, calling Brown a "bastard of a demagogue" fathered by "Black Republicans" and stressing New York City's reliance on southern trade: "The South is our best customer. She pays the best prices, and pays promptly." The Wood brothers also capitalized on Irish Anglophobia by claiming that Brown was a pawn in an English scheme to divide and defeat the United States.[44]

The *Irish-American* declared that abolitionists were also plotting to incriminate Irish workers and get them fired from their factory jobs. On December 10, 1859, the paper reprinted a notice, purportedly from an anonymous committee of southerners, that had been sent to thousands of Irishmen. It read in part:

TO THE IRISH FRIENDS OF THE SOUTH
IN THE NORTHERN CITIES
(Confidential)

The South looks to its Irish friends in the large free cities to effect a diversion in its favor . . . In the great cities prominent freesoilers and abolitionists own large factories, stores, and granaries, in which vast sums (made out of the South) are invested. This fact furnishes a means of checking their aggressions in the South, and the Irish friends of the South are relied on to make the check effective.—Property is proverbially timid. Whenever a hay stack or cotton gin is burned at the South by freesoil emissaries, let a large factory, or a plethoric store, or an immense granary be given to the flames . . . gather large mobs of your brethren . . . for every dollar's worth of injury to your enemies in the Northern factories, ec.ec., by riot or the torch, the South will amply compensate, and, besides, furnish you a safe refuge and a homestead.

The message was consistent with the predictions and perhaps the hopes of certain southern fire-eaters, especially Edmund Ruffin, but it also bore the hallmarks of a fake, as the *Irish-American* warned. The condescending circular addressed Irish workers as an ignorant and gullible rabble, urging them to use "method, caution," and "double secrecy," while also telling them to ask the foremen at their jobs for specific instructions on carrying out these acts of sabotage. Whoever authored the notice, the idea of deliberate rioting on behalf of the South by immigrant mobs was in the air—a glimmer in the eyes of southern extremists and the nightmare of northern nativists.[45]

A more immediate threat to the country was the collapse of traditional two-party politics. Illinois Democratic senator Stephen Douglas by this time had fallen out with President Buchanan, who insisted on the validity of the infamous Lecompton Constitution for Kansas, a document drawn up by proslavery representatives in the territory who had been elected fraudulently and were bent on excluding free-soil advocates from the government. These strong-arm tactics made a mockery of Douglas's plan for true "popular sovereignty," and he could not abide them. His denunciation of the Lecompton Constitution split the Democratic party, with the slaveholding states damning Douglas as a traitor. Horace Greeley's praise of Douglas for his principled stand intensified the South's anger and rejection of the senator. The Democrats' North-South rupture set the stage for a Republican victory in the presidential election of 1860, which in turn would lead the entire country to break apart along that same sectional divide.[46]

Onetime Illinois congressman Abraham Lincoln had lost the race for the U.S. Senate in 1855 and again in 1859.* However, his political career flourished because of a strong performance in the debates with Douglas in 1858 and

*The state elections took place in 1854 and 1858, and the legislatures chose the U.S. senator in January of 1855 and 1859.

because he stayed busy behind the scenes in the nonelection years helping to turn the Republican party of Illinois into a formidable organization. Part of that work was excluding the radical abolitionist elements from the state party in order to preserve a broad coalition, including moderates and conservatives who opposed the expansion of slavery into the territories but stopped short of calling for the immediate emancipation of slaves in the South. Lincoln had ceased to be a Whig, but he had also toned down his message on slavery since 1854.[47]

In his acceptance speech for the U.S. Senate nomination in 1858, Lincoln had used a familiar biblical quotation: " 'A house divided against itself cannot stand' . . . I believe this government cannot endure, permanently half *slave* and half *free* . . . It will become *all* one thing, or *all* the other." While Lincoln opposed the spread of slavery and hoped it would gradually disappear in the South, the speech was interpreted around the country as a radical declaration, "an implied pledge on behalf of the Republican party to make war upon the institution in the states where it now exists," according to one of his advisers. Lincoln tried to backpedal, denying any such intent.[48]

Lincoln did assert that slavery was morally wrong, but he focused his attacks on Douglas, claiming he was part of a conspiracy to spread slavery throughout the United States, a plot coordinated with President Buchanan and the Supreme Court, which had ruled in the Dred Scott case of 1857 that blacks were not citizens, and slaves could be transported by their owners anywhere in the country, including free states. Chief Justice Roger Taney declared that blacks had "no rights which the white man was bound to respect."[49]

After losing to Douglas in 1859, Lincoln looked ahead to the presidential election of 1860, and while New York's Senator William Seward declared that an "irrepressible conflict" was brewing between the North and South over slavery, Lincoln continued to back away from his "house divided" speech for the sake of party unity. He advised Ohio Republicans not to oppose the infamous fugitive slave law of 1850 lest the party be seen as too radical. Lincoln also admonished Massachusetts Republicans to refrain from nativist legislation in order to secure the Irish and German vote.[50]

In a series of speeches across the Midwest in the second half of 1859 on behalf of candidates in statewide races, Lincoln again went on the attack against Douglas while appealing to the broadest possible constituency of white voters. Lincoln denounced Douglas for claiming that the Declaration of Independence did not include blacks in its statement that all men are created equal. At the same time, Lincoln deflected inflammatory accusations from Democrats that Republicans wanted to intermarry with blacks: The races were equal, Lincoln insisted, only in their right to "life, liberty, and the pursuit of happiness." The evil of slavery spreading into the territories, Lincoln told whites, was its tendency to compete with free labor. The great expanses of the West should be open to homesteaders fleeing the overcrowded cities to make new lives for themselves and their children.[51]

Ironically, while Lincoln cultivated a populist image on the campaign trail, referring to his backwoods roots in Kentucky and his rise by dint of hard work, the reality of his personal story was at odds with free-labor ideology. Lincoln had not simply pulled himself up by his bootstraps but had the help of influential friends in becoming a prominent attorney. His exceptional intellect had enabled him to leave manual labor behind and become an advocate for mammoth railroad corporations; his political sponsors included wealthy farmers and land speculators—individuals owning tens of thousands of acres. In denouncing the world of chattel slavery and idealizing the free-labor economy, Lincoln, like many Republicans, largely ignored the plight of the urban factory worker, whose potential to save, invest, and become an employer himself was almost nonexistent.[52]

Lincoln's tour through Iowa, Ohio, Indiana, Wisconsin, and Kansas prompted newspapers across the country to start mentioning him as a possible presidential candidate. He boosted his chances for the Republican nomination with a brilliant speech at Cooper Union in Manhattan on February 27, 1860. His hosts were Horace Greeley, William Cullen Bryant, and other local Republicans united by their opposition to William Seward, the front-runner. After decades together in the arena of New York politics, each had a particular grudge against the senator. Lincoln spoke before a packed house, surprising many in the audience, who had assumed he was an unsophisticated backwoodsman. Using impressive historical research, Lincoln argued that the intent of the founding fathers in the Constitution was to preserve federal control over slavery in the territories.

Denouncing John Brown's raid, Lincoln called on Republicans to oppose the spread of slavery by every lawful means, while letting it wither gradually in the South. He urged northerners to stand firm in the face of southern threats of secession, triggered by the prospect of a Republican winning the presidency. "Let us have faith that right makes might, and in that faith, let us, to the end, dare to do our duty as we understand it."[53]

Lincoln went on to make almost a dozen speeches in New England. His passionate, morally engaged, but essentially moderate stance on slavery contrasted sharply with Douglas, the presumptive Democratic nominee, and his doctrine of "popular sovereignty." Lincoln also strengthened his position relative to his competitors for the Republican nomination, particularly Seward, whose embrace of the abolitionists' appeal to "a higher law than the Constitution," and predictions of an "irrepressible conflict," stigmatized him as a radical. Moreover, since Douglas and Lincoln were both from Illinois, Lincoln could be expected to counter the senator's popularity in the Midwest.[54]

In April, the Democratic Convention met in Charleston but fell apart after a faction of southern extremists walked out in protest against Douglas, and fifty-seven rounds of voting failed to produce a sufficient majority for any candidate. The Republicans met in Chicago in May, and in a frenzy of excitement, delegates and visitors watched Lincoln come from behind to beat Seward on the third ballot. The Republican platform condemned John Brown's raid but also vowed to oppose the "contemplated treason" of southern secession. The Democrats reconvened in Baltimore in June but split again, the northerners nominating Douglas, and the southerners holding a separate convention to choose Buchanan's vice president, John Breckinridge, as their presidential candidate.

Conservative Whigs formed the Constitutional Union party, fielding a fourth ticket in the presidential race, consisting of Tennessee's John Bell and Edward Everett of Massachusetts as his running mate. Professing neutrality on the slavery issue along with allegiance to the Constitution and the Union, this collection of elite elderly gentlemen hoped to avert national disintegration by drawing votes away from Lincoln and throwing the election into the House of Representatives, where a candidate more sympathetic to the South might rise to the top.[55]

With Lincoln and Douglas vying for the northern states, while Breckinridge fended off Bell's challenge in the South, the sectional divide turned the election of 1860 into a dual race, unlike any other presidential contest in American history. The Democrats stirred up fears of racial amalgamation, especially in New York, where a Republican-sponsored amendment to the state constitution appeared on the ballot, proposing to do away with the $250 property requirement for black voters.

Democratic editorials and campaign speeches accused Republicans of believing "a nigger is better than an Irishman." A parade in New York City included a float bearing effigies of Horace Greeley and a "good looking nigger wench, whom he caressed with all the affection of a true Republican." Nearby, a banner warned that "free love and free niggers will certainly elect Old Abe."[56] Despite Lincoln's failure to oppose the fugitive slave law or call for immediate abolition in the South, the Wood brothers' *Daily News* predicted "negroes among us thicker than blackberries swarming everywhere" if he were elected, while Bennett's *Herald* envisioned labor competition from "four million emancipated negroes."[57]

Fear of slave uprisings spread through the South like wildfire, fanned by pro-Breckenridge newspapers. Vigilantes drove northerners out of their communities, and support for secession grew. John Crittenden, a Democratic senator from Kentucky, condemned the Republicans as fanatics who "think it is their duty to destroy . . . the white man, in order that the black might be free." If Lincoln were elected, he declared, the South "could not submit to the consequences, and therefore, to avoid her fate, will secede from the Union."[58]

The November election confirmed the country's deep sectional divisions. Lincoln won with more than enough electoral votes and 54 percent of the northern popular vote, but Republicans had not even campaigned in the ten most hostile southern and border states, while receiving only 4 percent of the popular vote in the other five. In the country as a whole, Lincoln had been elected with only 40 percent of the popular vote.[59] "A party founded on . . . hatred of African slavery is now the controlling power," seethed the *Richmond Examiner*. The *New Orleans Delta* dismissed Lincoln's moderation as a ruse and declared that the true agenda of the "Black Republicans" was a social revolution leading to racial amalgamation.[60]

Lincoln won New York State but lost in the Democratic stronghold of New York City, where conservative merchants—dreading a disruption of trade and hoping secession would be temporary—urged that the South be allowed to go peacefully if compromise failed. Horace Greeley, for the moment, joined the conciliatory chorus, much to the consternation of fellow Republicans.[61]

"Great distress already reported . . . in the great northern cities," Edmund Ruffin noted at the end of November 1860. Trade with the South had slowed or stopped altogether, and thousands of workers had been laid off. Southern planters repudiated their debts to New York's merchants, taking revenge for charges exacted by them when transferring southern cotton to European buyers. They hated New York's role as middleman, as the country's economic gateway, and predicted the city's demise. A reliable report from New York, Ruffin wrote, estimated "that 25,000 persons in that city have been discharged from employment since the day of the presidential election."[62]

William Russell, a renowned correspondent for the *London Times*, recalled: "As long as there was a chance the struggle might not take place, the merchants of New York were silent, fearful of offending their Southern friends and connections, but inflicting infinite damage on their own government and misleading both sides. Their sentiments, sympathies, and business found them with the South; and indeed . . . the South believed New York was with them, as might be credited from the tone of some organs of the press, and I remember hearing it said by Southerners in Washington, that it was very likely New York would go out of the Union!"[63]

With great fanfare, parades, and mass meetings invoking the spirit of 1776, South Carolina's legislature held a convention to declare its independence and formally secede from the United States on December 20. In the midst of the burgeoning crisis, Mayor Wood used his annual address in January 1861 to sketch a scenario in which New York and other sections of the country would follow South Carolina's example. He suggested that since the state government in Albany deprived New York City of home rule, and since the city had good commercial relationships with all parts of the United States, perhaps it would be best for New York to secede from the Union as well and become a "free city."[64]

Encouraged by South Carolina's example, along with the sympathetic pronouncements of New York Democrats, by the end of January six more states had seceded. Mississippi, Florida, Alabama, Georgia, Louisiana, and Texas joined South Carolina in drafting a constitution and declaring themselves a separate nation, the Confederate States of America.[65]

Some Confederates expounded a vision of the South not merely as a nation but as an empire extending into the tropics of Central America and the Caribbean islands. Through slave labor, the South would control "the two dominant staples of the world's commerce—cotton and sugar," wrote Edward Pollard in his book *Black Diamonds,* published the previous year. The "noble peculiarities of Southern civilization" would be spread southward across the hemisphere.[66]

George Bickley, a Virginian like Pollard, described these dominions as part of a "golden circle" centered on Cuba that would encompass the Gulf of Mexico and the Caribbean Sea. The empire would stretch across the Confederate states, through the American Southwest, and down into Mexico and Central America; it would take in the northern edge of South America, and its eastern border would include the West Indies. Several years earlier, Bickley had established a secret society, the Knights of the Golden Circle, whose members were militant defenders of slaveholders' rights and southern imperialism.[67]

In New York, Ben Wood's *Daily News* loudly supported peaceful secession, and Mayor Wood protested that police superintendent John Kennedy lacked a proper search warrant when he seized the *Monticello,* a steamer headed for Savannah with thirty-eight boxes of muskets and ammunition at the end of January. Wood apologized to Georgia senator Robert Toombs for the "illegal and unjustifiable seizure of public property," but the mayor's conciliatory stance was leaving him increasingly isolated. He was condemned in the New York press for supplying weapons to the "traitors" in the South who were bent on "destroying the unity and peace of the Republic."[68]*

---

*When the governor of Georgia threatened to retaliate in kind against New York's ships in Savannah harbor, the *Monticello* was allowed to depart with its cargo of a thousand muskets.

CHAPTER 5

"Slavery Must Die That the Nation Might Live"

～

The newly elected president visited New York City on his way to Washington in February 1861. Mayor Wood was a gracious host, at first, even though Lincoln had not carried the city in November 1860, and the atmosphere was tense. Wood confronted the president-elect at a formal City Hall reception, saying that the South's separation "sorely afflicted" New York and threatened its "commercial greatness." New York expected from Lincoln "a restoration of fraternal relations between the states—only to be accomplished by peaceful and conciliatory means—aided by the wisdom of God."[1]

The room was aghast at Wood's effrontery, but Lincoln took it in stride, thanking his host and professing to share his feelings. Lincoln said he would work for the good of the city and the country, and then added his own proviso: that the preservation of the Union would overrule all other considerations.[2]

Once in Washington, Lincoln again stood by his principles while letting his adversary be the aggressor. When the Confederacy threatened federal installations in the South, Lincoln insisted on resupplying both Fort Pickens in Pensacola, Florida, and Fort Sumter, in Charleston, South Carolina, thereby asserting federal authority and deftly making the Confederacy draw first blood in the conflict. On April 12, 1861, Edmund Ruffin, as a member of the elite Palmetto Guard, was given the honor of firing the first cannon in the Confederate attack on Fort Sumter, which unleashed the Civil War.[3]

Mobs in New York roughed up Confederate sympathizers,

and the police had to protect Mayor Wood's house as well as the *Daily News* office.[4] George Templeton Strong noted that "the *Herald* office had already been threatened with attack" and, along with the *Express,* had started to waver in its prosouthern pronouncements. Strong expected the less influential *Journal of Commerce* and *Day-Book,* as yet unrepentant, to change their tune shortly, because of the "growing excitement against their treasonable talk."[5] Also under pressure and scrutiny was the leading Irish Catholic newspaper in the city, the *Freeman's Journal,* published by James McMasters, a vocal Peace Democrat. Archbishop John Hughes had founded the paper and retained his influence over it for some time after it changed ownership, but it no longer reflected his views, particularly on the war.[6]

In gratitude to the country that had adopted so many Irish Catholic refugees as citizens, Hughes took a strong pro-Union stand, flying the Stars and Stripes from every steeple in the archdiocese. Like Hughes, the New York Irish community's most influential secular paper, the *Irish-American,* backed the Union cause but opposed the Republican party and abolition with equal vehemence. Similarly, Boston's Irish Catholic *Pilot* exhorted readers to "stand by the Union; fight for the Union; die by the Union."[7]

Along with gratitude was hope that military service and sacrifice would help the Irish assimilate more fully in America and overcome decades if not centuries of nativist discrimination. While native Protestants like George Templeton Strong contended that "our Celtic fellow citizens are almost as remote from us in temperament and constitution as the Chinese," the *Boston Pilot* hoped military service would eventually enable Irish Americans to declare, "We too are Americans, and our fathers bled and died to establish this country."[8]

Anti-British sentiment also spurred Irish support for the Union, since the English appeared to be backing the Confederacy, the major supplier of cotton for their textile industry. Many Irish Americans also blamed British abolitionists for originating the movement, which spread to the United States and sowed discord between the North and South; many saw this as a British plot to divide the Republic—former colonies that had become a competitor on the world stage.[9]

As soon as Fort Sumter fell, Lincoln called on the states to supply seventy-five thousand national guardsmen to the federal government for ninety days of service. Under existing law, this was the longest enlistment the president could require of the militia, but in the heady opening days of the war few northerners believed it would take more than three months to crush the rebellion. New York's merchants dropped their efforts at compromise and rallied behind the war effort in a frenzy of patriotism, hoping a massive show of force would bring the war to a swift conclusion—with prompt national reunification and a resumption of trade. Volunteer regiments formed quickly, including one raised by Mayor Wood, which he managed to make the first from New York City to leave for the front.[10]

"One word to these gentlemen," chided William Russell of the *London Times.* "I am pretty well satisfied that if they had always spoken, written, and acted as they do now, the people of Charleston would not have attacked Sumter so readily."[11]

Eager, not to end slavery, but to preserve the nation that offered them freedom and asylum, Irish Americans volunteered enthusiastically, joining, among others, the Sixty-ninth Regiment of the New York State militia, commanded by Michael Corcoran, an ardent nationalist who had emigrated to New York in the wake of the Young Ireland revolt and had since become a leader of the Fenian Brotherhood. Many of the Irish were already enrolled in smaller all-Irish state militia regiments that had formed in the 1850s for the dual purpose of serving New York State and preparing for the liberation of Ireland. While these units marched in annual St. Patrick's Day parades, Irish nationalists had remained vigilant for opportunities to land troops in Ireland when the British might be distracted by war on other fronts. The Civil War presented a chance to obtain further military training and experience in the service of eventual Irish liberation.[12]

More than 144,000 Irish-born soldiers would fight for the Union in the Civil War, to be joined by at least as many Irish Americans. Thousands were killed, most of them enlisted in regiments with no particular ethnic identity. In order to highlight the Irish Catholic contributions and sacrifices in the war, Corcoran raised the Irish Legion, and fellow Irish nationalist Thomas Francis Meagher commanded another brigade of Irish regiments—recruited from New York, Boston, and Philadelphia—in the Army of the Potomac. In addition to Meagher's command, known as the Irish Brigade, and Corcoran's legion, there were several other Union regiments and brigades composed mostly of Irish soldiers. Eighty-nine Irish-born soldiers earned Congressional Medals of Honor, and officers of Irish descent, including Generals George Meade and Philip Sheridan, played key roles in the war.[13]*

While the pressure of unemployment and the promise of regular pay swept many Irish American volunteers into the Union forces, they were also driven by a desire for acceptance in their adopted country. Charles Halpine, a soldier and journalist, wrote that he and other volunteers thought they were "earning a title, which no foul tongue or niggardly heart would dare to dispute, to the full equality and fraternity of an American citizen."[14]

· · ·

---

*Some thirty thousand Irish fought on the Confederate side. They too saw the war as a training ground for the liberation of Ireland, and believed the Confederacy's struggle for independence was as valid as their own.

Northerners' high hopes for a quick, ninety-day war were dashed with the Union defeat at Bull Run on July 21, 1861. The assumption of many Irish Americans and other conservatives that they were supporting and fighting in a war to preserve the Union—but not for abolition—also came into question. Congress had recently passed resolutions disclaiming any intent to destroy slavery, but after Bull Run the idea of all-out war on the Confederacy gained ground. Republicans began to defend emancipation as a "military necessity." Slaves—who made up more than 50 percent of the South's workforce—not only toiled in fields, mines, and factories but filled numerous noncombat roles in the Confederate army.[15]

"To fight against slaveholders, without fighting against slavery, is but a half-hearted business, and paralyzes the hands engaged in it," declared black abolitionist Frederick Douglass.[16] While the expectations of the Irish community seemed threatened, African Americans were encouraged by the new agenda of emancipation that appeared to be taking hold.[17]

That agenda also began to divide War Democrats from Republicans in Washington, where April's thrilling rush of martial unity had faded. The first piece of northern war legislation that failed to win the support of both parties in Congress was the Confiscation Act of August 6, 1861, which authorized Union forces to seize any property—including slaves—that the rebels were using to wage war. Democrats and border-state representatives voted against the measure in vain. By confiscating the property of individuals as punishment for treason, Republican lawmakers narrowly circumvented the protections for slavery in the Constitution.* While this spelled out a very limited scope for freeing slaves, it was nonetheless a first step that within eighteen months would help shift the goal of the Civil War from a struggle solely to save the Union to a conquest of the South and the destruction of slavery.[18]

John C. Frémont hoped to set that course even sooner. The Republican party's first presidential candidate and a famous explorer, Frémont had recently been appointed commander of the army's Western Department. On August 30, he declared martial law in Missouri and freed all the slaves of Confederate sympathizers. Lincoln, who feared the border states—Maryland, Missouri, and particularly Kentucky—would break away from the Union if their slaveholders were faced with total confiscation, first asked and then ordered Frémont to bring his proclamation in line with the congressional act, freeing only those slaves directly used by the Confederate army.[19]

---

*Without using the word *slave,* the Constitution originally stipulated that three-fifths of each state's slaves would be counted as part of its total population when apportioning representatives; the slave trade was permitted to continue for more than twenty years, until 1808; and fugitive slaves did not become free by escaping to free states. They had to be returned when claimed by their masters.

Lincoln's move against emancipation and his subsequent dismissal of Frémont intensified the debate over slavery in the North and helped drive Republicans into the abolitionist camp.

"Free every slave—slay every traitor—burn every rebel mansion, if these things be necessary to preserve this temple of freedom," thundered radical Republican congressman Thaddeus Stevens of Pennsylvania. Such calls for a "radical revolution" to destroy slavery, along with the largely party-line vote on the Confiscation Act, reinforced Lincoln's fear that his fragile coalition of moderate Republicans, War Democrats, and southern Unionists from the border states would shatter if emancipation became the Union's avowed goal. The Republicans would then have to fight the war alone, Lincoln said, "and the job on our hands is too large for us."[20]

Democrats had their own factional troubles. They had lost the entire southern wing of their party—now absent from Congress, where the all-northern Republican party held sway—and could not afford further divisions within their ranks. Peace Democrats, especially Vallandigham and the Wood brothers, were particularly worrisome to the mainstream party leadership in New York—Samuel Barlow, August Belmont, and Samuel Tilden—because antiwar rhetoric drove patriotic War Democrats out of the party and into the Republican camp. The Copperheads' insistence on a negotiated peace with the Confederacy also enabled the Republicans to label the entire Democracy as disloyal—"to pin the tail of treason on the Democratic donkey."[21]

The peace men continued to draw adherents, dividing the Democrats and thereby boosting the Republicans, whose uniform support for the war helped them win elections across New York State in November 1861, including the three-way mayor's race in New York City, where Republican businessman George Opdyke prevailed and Fernando Wood lost.[22]

Early in 1862, in an effort to resuscitate the party, the War Democrats and Peace Democrats tried to paper over their differences at least in the short term by rallying around their common abhorrence of emancipation.* They calculated that racism could galvanize the party's factions and even lure some conservative, anti-abolition Republicans over to the Democracy. The Republicans faced thorny questions not only about emancipation but about the position blacks should attain in America after they were free—questions which Democrats could try to exploit in order to divide the radicals from the conservatives. Barlow, Belmont, and Tilden remained vigilant for an opportunity to capitalize on public fears about the rising tide of abolitionist sentiment in

---

*The Regency's *Albany Argus,* edited by Dean Richmond, and Tammany Hall's *New York Leader,* edited by John Clancy, were the War Democrats' main newspapers for voicing the party line.

the North. For the moment, however, Lincoln's cautious course on emancipation deprived the Democrats of a unifying issue.[23]

"The bottom is out of the tub. What shall I do?" Lincoln asked one of his generals in January 1862. The Union army had lost several major battles the previous year; the treasury was empty; and George McClellan, commanding the Army of the Potomac, had been incapacitated for almost a month with typhoid fever. Operations were bogged down in the western theater of the war as well.[24]

However, in the next four months, Union forces won a series of victories on the rivers in the West, culminating in early April with the massive Battle of Shiloh in Tennessee, which permanently turned the tide of the war in the Mississippi Valley. At the same time, David Farragut's saltwater fleet captured New Orleans, the South's largest city, and later Baton Rouge and Natchez. However, despite a joint operation by Grant and Farragut, the Confederates refused to surrender Vicksburg, and the effort had to be abandoned for that summer.

Shiloh showed General Grant, and the Union, the tenacity of the rebels in the West and confronted northerners with the fact that they would have to conquer the South, not simply win a decisive battle, to win the war. With about ten thousand killed and wounded on each side, the carnage at Shiloh was a watershed between the smaller battles of the war's first year and the huge ones that followed in the next three years.[25]

By April, McClellan had moved his army down to the Yorktown Peninsula in Virginia and was slowly closing in on Richmond. Seeing progress in both the East and the West—and frustrated with the cumbersome, decentralized system of raising troops—Secretary of War Stanton took the fateful step of shutting down all recruitment for the armed forces in order to come up with a more efficient approach.[26]

In the House of Representatives, radical Republican leader George Julian of Indiana described the emancipation of the slaves as both a military necessity and a moral imperative. Not only would the loss of four million laborers weaken the Confederate war effort, he declared, but a Union victory would be hollow "if slavery be spared to canker the heart of the nation anew, and repeat its diabolical deeds." In the spring of 1862, most conservative and moderate Republicans, who had hoped for a gradual end to slavery followed by colonization, underwent a major shift and began to support the radicals' call for the confiscation of slaves by the Union army.[27]

The realities of the war had pressured Congress to take action. Union forces had captured fifty thousand square miles of territory and were bringing many slaves under their control behind the lines, where they were known as "contrabands" because of their uncertain legal status. In the absence of the Democrats' southern delegations, Congress was dominated by Republicans, and radicals headed key committees in both the House and the Senate. On March 13, Congress forbade Union army officers to return fugitive slaves to their masters. Building on this measure, on April 10 Congress granted Lincoln's request to offer compensation to states willing to enact gradual emancipation.[28]

With this, his first move toward emancipation, Lincoln aimed to split the border states from the Confederacy, but their representatives responded neither to the promise of money nor to the threat of the war's ravages. The war continued to escalate, and support for emancipation increased in the North. Abolitionists, once pariahs, were gaining respectability, and Congress contemplated a second, more sweeping confiscation act, while tens of thousands of fugitive slaves fled to the protection of the invading Union forces.[29]

On May 9, 1862, Union general David Hunter repeated Frémont's action of declaring martial law and freeing the slaves in his military district, the Department of the South, consisting of South Carolina, Georgia, and Florida. Hunter's forces controlled only the coastal islands of South Carolina and Georgia, but the proclamation embraced all of the three states. Once again, Lincoln immediately countermanded the order, saying that such a decisive step was his alone to take. At the same time, however, his language revealed that he was not entirely opposed to Hunter's action—that he believed emancipation might soon "become a necessity indispensable to the maintenance of the government."[30]

In the meantime, Lincoln continued to urge the border states to embrace gradual, compensated emancipation in order to make the transition as smooth as possible. However, representatives of these states and northern Democrats still hoped the war could be ended by McClellan's capture of Richmond, a decisive military victory that would reunite the country with slavery preserved.[31]

Hunter's proclamation was just the opening Barlow, Belmont, and Tilden had been waiting for. Anti-emancipation became the rallying cry to unite the War and Peace factions of the Democratic party. The Albany Regency, the Swallowtails, and Tammany orchestrated a series of mass meetings across New York State to denounce Hunter's actions, and brought the cry of protest to a roar with a huge demonstration in New York City. A Fourth of July celebration sponsored by Tammany welcomed the Peace Democrats back to the fold. Tammany sachem Elijah Purdy made a great show of marching arm in arm with Fernando Wood.[32]

However, Democratic hopes for McClellan's capture of Richmond, a limited war, and the "Union as it was" evaporated further with Union defeat in the Seven Days' Battles of June 25 to July 1, 1862. "I expect to maintain this contest," Lincoln declared, "until successful, or till I die, or am conquered . . . or Congress or the country forsakes me." A manifesto from border-state congressmen on July 13 again rejecting gradual emancipation finally moved Lincoln away from courting the middle to favoring radical action on slavery.[33]

Lincoln had always been morally opposed to slavery, as he made clear throughout the 1850s, especially when campaigning against Stephen Douglas. However, as a pragmatic politician, committed to preserving the Union, he had worked hard to make the Republican party in Illinois a moderate organization and had entered the White House promising to contain slavery, not destroy it. Nonetheless, as Lincoln had told the border-state representatives and senators, public pressure in favor of emancipation was growing: It "is still upon me, and is increasing."[34]

Charles Sumner, the leading radical in the Senate, had been telling Lincoln since the war began that he could and should free the slaves by executive order; the outgoing secretary of war, Simon Cameron, had included the same suggestion in a report in December 1861. The Frémont and Hunter proclamations had also spurred Lincoln. His response to Hunter's declaration in May had been a turning point, signaling that Lincoln had become convinced of his constitutional authority to free the slaves by decree. He had soon reinforced that impression, saying, "As commander in chief of the army and navy, in time of war, I suppose I have a right to take any measure which may best subdue the enemy."[35]

In June, Lincoln secretly began writing a proclamation "giving freedom to the slaves in the South," but publicly continued to express doubts about such a decree, telling Sumner it was "too big a lick"; the proclamation would appear futile and desperate without military successes to back it up. However, by July, McClellan's failure to take Richmond, a morale crisis in the army, and a fall-off in recruitment all impressed on Lincoln the need for drastic action. Riding in a carriage on July 13 with Secretary of State William Seward and navy secretary Gideon Welles, Lincoln revealed that he "had about come to the conclusion that we must free the slaves or be ourselves subdued."[36]

Four days later, Congress heaped more pressure on the president when moderate Republican lawmakers joined the radicals to pass two bills facilitating all-out war against the Confederacy. The Second Confiscation Act, of broader scope than the one passed almost a year earlier, freed not only blacks used by the Confederate army but also those owned by anyone deemed a "traitor." By effectively including southern civilians in this category, Congress was edging closer to an outright abolition of slavery in the South. Since Lincoln believed such a step, in order to conform with the Constitution, had to be taken by the president as part of his "war powers," he could not keep his plans a secret much longer.[37]

With a second bill on July 17, Congress also expanded the North's mobilization of troops. Simply to call upon the states for more troops in the wake of a major defeat might have looked desperate and sown panic across the North. Instead, Secretary of State Seward met with northern governors, who agreed to release a statement—drafted by Seward and backdated to June 28, before McClellan's retreat during the Seven Days' Battles—asking the president to resume recruitment and "follow up" the "recent successes of the Federal arms" and "speedily crush the rebellion." Thus on July 2, when Lincoln called for three hundred thousand additional volunteers to finish off the rebels, he could claim to be satisfying a groundswell of support from the states.[38]

"We are Coming, Father Abraham, Three Hundred Thousand More" was the title of a recruiting poem by James Gibbons, a Quaker abolitionist in New York City. Set to music by Stephen Foster, among others, the verses became popular but failed to bring in volunteers in numbers even approaching the torrent of men the year before. The horrors of war were apparent, and the ranks of the Union army were dwindling. Only one-third of the North's eligible men were under arms, and with plenty of employment available on farms and in factories, few men volunteered. Lincoln's new call required men to commit for three years, which deterred many who were willing to sign up for a shorter term of service.[39]

Under the existing system, the federal government did not draft men directly. The states offered bounty money and recruited volunteers, contributing them to the national force—a standing army of only about sixteen thousand men—according to quotas set by the federal government. The states also required all men between the ages of eighteen and forty-five to perform militia duty and mustered them for federal service in an emergency.[40]

However, on July 17, 1862, Congress passed a militia law authorizing the president to summon state troops for up to nine months of service to the federal government. The president was also empowered to "make all necessary rules and regulations" to enforce the law, indeed to supplant the state governments in raising the militia, particularly in states where enrollment was lax. With this expansion of executive power, Congress laid the groundwork for the federal government to draft men directly. The bill of 1862 also gave the president the option of enrolling blacks in the Union army, paving the way for them, eventually, to serve in combat as well as supporting roles.[41]

A few weeks later, Secretary of War Stanton used the new law to require from the states 300,000 nine-month militiamen above and beyond the 300,000 three-year volunteers Lincoln had called for less than a month earlier. As an incentive for the states to recruit three-year men, Stanton announced that each one raised above a state's quota would count as four men in reducing the militia levy. In the coming months, the states exceeded Stanton's overall goal by raising 421,000 three-year volunteers, with most states, including New York, managing to avoid the 1862 militia draft altogether.[42]

However, a dearth of three-year men in some states triggered the militia draft, which had to be enforced by U.S. troops in areas where resisters attacked enrollment officers. The violence against the militia draft foreshadowed, on a smaller scale, the fierce opposition the federal draft would engender the following year. In 1862, Irish Catholics in the coalfields of eastern Pennsylvania rioted, as did German Catholics in Wisconsin and draftees in southern Ohio and Indiana. Two draft officials were killed by mobs in Indiana, and another was wounded in Wisconsin. Calling for the protection of slaveholders' rights in the Constitution and peaceful reunification of the country, rioters carried banners that read: "The Constitution As It Is, The Union As It Was" and "We won't fight to free the nigger."[43]

Responding to these outbreaks of resistance, in September 1862 Lincoln declared that anyone obstructing recruitment or the draft or aiding the rebel war effort would be subject to martial law and denied a writ of habeas corpus. Stanton carried out Lincoln's proclamation by dispatching deputies to arrest hundreds of draft resisters and peace activists, among them newspaper editors, judges, and politicians, who were jailed without due process or trial. Stanton's use of military police officers for enforcing conscription and punishing dissent would be codified and expanded less than six months later by the passage of a new draft law and the appointment of a provost marshal general at the head of a powerful new bureaucracy within the War Department.[44]

Despite McClellan's failure in the Seven Days' Battles at the end of June 1862, Lincoln resisted Republican pressure to dismiss the general. An outspoken Democrat and opponent of emancipation, McClellan blamed the administration for his defeat in Virginia, claiming he had not received adequate reinforcements—though in fact he vastly outnumbered the rebels. Democrats spread McClellan's complaints among their constituents, and party leaders, including Fernando Wood, had visited the general at his battlefield headquarters asking him to run for president. Many Union soldiers idolized McClellan for whipping the army into shape and shared his opposition to an abolition war. Thus Lincoln hesitated to replace McClellan for fear of mutiny among the troops and Democratic resurgence in the North.[45]

Intent on protecting the Republican majority in Congress from a political backlash in the upcoming fall elections, Lincoln also postponed action on emancipation. On July 22, Lincoln had taken to his cabinet the draft of a proclamation to free the slaves in the Confederacy. Since the measure could only be enforced by taking over the South, Lincoln followed Secretary of State Seward's advice to wait until Union forces were winning, so that the declaration did not appear completely rhetorical and unenforceable.[46]

During the summer, Democrats on the campaign trail stirred up fears of emancipation and labor competition from free blacks flooding the North. Riots against blacks erupted across the country. In Cincinnati, Ohio, where blacks had been brought in as strikebreakers, Irish longshoremen and their supporters launched a series of attacks on black enclaves. Targeting the black women and children working inside, an Irish mob set fire to a tobacco factory in Brooklyn. Despite a shortage of laborers, in southern Illinois rioters drove off black farmhands brought in by the government to help with the harvest.[47]

Confirming Lincoln's worst fears, the threat of emancipation prompted a referendum in his home state of Illinois in which Republicans joined Democrats to bar blacks from the state. When Republicans failed to calm northerners by saying that freed blacks would remain in the South because of the warm climate, Lincoln and others began to promote colonization outside the United States as a solution. While proponents saw this as a concession that would soothe the public and ease the way to emancipation, Frederick Douglass lambasted Lincoln for his racism and "hypocrisy" and predicted the president's support for exiling blacks would provoke "ignorant and base" whites "to commit all kinds of violence and outrage upon the colored people."[48]

Unaware of Lincoln's pending proclamation to free the slaves, radical Republicans also denounced Lincoln for his inaction. Horace Greeley grew increasingly frustrated and by August began pushing hard in the pages of the *Tribune*. For the previous eight months, Greeley had been duped into restraining his criticism of the administration.[49] Greeley had been approached by James Gilmore, a former cotton broker whose travels in the South had turned him completely against slavery. Gilmore had since become a freelance journalist and entrepreneur and had invested in several magazines, including one, yet to be launched, that would press for emancipation. In persuading Greeley to write for the new magazine, Gilmore mentioned that one of its backers was a trusted adviser to Lincoln. Gilmore would thus be privy to "all the inner workings of the administration" and, he implied, could give the *Tribune* a jump on the competition by keeping Greeley informed.

Gilmore also presented the arrangement to Lincoln, who agreed to play along. Lincoln had no intention of releasing advance information, but by allowing Gilmore to relay flattering remarks about Greeley and drawing him into an exclusive back channel of communication, the president managed to rein in the *Tribune*'s attacks on administration policy. By August 1862, however, Greeley realized that Lincoln was not keeping his end of the supposed bargain. Lincoln had neither kept the *Tribune* informed nor listened to its advice about emancipation, and Greeley intended to step up the pressure, he informed Gilmore, who reported back to Lincoln.

"I infer from the recent tone of the *Tribune* that you are not always able to keep Brother Greeley in the traces," Lincoln said to Gilmore. That was true, Gilmore allowed, but he was developing a relationship with the paper's new managing editor, Sidney Gay, who had "softened Mr. Greeley's wrath on several occasions."

"What is he so wrathy about?" Lincoln asked. Gilmore replied that Greeley was particularly agitated about the president's "neglect to make a direct attack upon slavery." Sidney Gay had told him, Gilmore said, that Greeley was "meditating an appeal to the country," which would force Lincoln "to take a decided position."

Greeley turned down an invitation to the White House for a talk with the president, and before Lincoln could dispatch Gilmore to explain his plans for emancipation, a *Tribune* editorial, "The Prayer of Twenty Millions," reverberated across the country and in Europe. Greeley asserted that the great majority of public opinion in the North favored the crushing of the rebellion and dismantling of its "inciting cause"—slavery. Greeley demanded that the president carry out the provisions of the recent Confiscation Act by freeing slaves captured from the rebels and employing them in the Union army.

Lincoln continued to hold his proclamation in reserve. In an open letter to Greeley, the president wrote, "My paramount object is to save the Union, and not either to save or destroy slavery." However, privately, Lincoln had already come to the point, he said, when he felt that "slavery must die that the nation might live."

Despite McClellan's retreat toward the Yorktown Peninsula during the Seven Days' Battles, the main Union army had remained within twenty miles of Richmond in early July. Lincoln appointed Henry Halleck general in chief, expecting "Old Brains" to rally federal forces and keep the pressure on the rebel capital.* Instead, Lee had managed to march his troops northward in July and August, resume the offensive, and shift the war from the outskirts of Richmond to within twenty miles of Washington, D.C. It was an astonishing feat, especially since the combined Union forces under John Pope, north of Richmond, and McClellan to the east, outnumbered the rebels two to one. With the Confederate victory in the Battle of Second Manassas (Bull Run) on August 29–30, 1862, Lee's forces were poised to invade Maryland and descend on Washington. While the wounded Union troops retreated to the defenses around the nation's capital, northern morale plummeted.[50]

Sensing this mood, and emboldened by imminent Confederate offensives in Kentucky and Tennessee, Lee felt compelled to press his advantage instead of retreating to rest his battered and hungry army. With northern congressional elections approaching in the fall, Lee calculated that the presence of his troops at the doorstep of the capital would make voters turn to the Peace Democrats and call for a treaty with the South. The invasion might also win diplomatic recognition for the Confederacy from England and France, further securing the South's independence.

The Confederates, numbering some fifty-five thousand men, crossed the Potomac on September 4, captured Harpers Ferry on the fifteenth, and hunkered down in the village of Sharpsburg, Maryland, to fight the Army of the Potomac under McClellan, ordered by Lincoln "to destroy the rebel army, if possible." As usual, McClellan procrastinated, and Lee's army consolidated its various corps. When Union forces finally crossed Antietam Creek and assaulted the rebels on the seventeenth, the ensuing bloodbath claimed a combined total of twenty-three thousand casualties from both sides—the most in any one day of the Civil War.[51]

While McClellan failed to pursue and crush Lee's retreating army, the repulse of the Confederate invasion at Antietam was enough of a victory to constitute a major turning point in the war. European intervention was forestalled, and Lincoln finally had the military success and momentum that, three months earlier, Secretary of State Seward had convinced him were necessary before declaring the slaves in the Confederate states "forever free." On September 22, 1862, Lincoln issued the Preliminary Emancipation Proclamation, to take effect on January 1, 1863, if the rebellion had not ended by then.[52]

By this proclamation, the war became a struggle to end slavery. Paradoxically, it did not free slaves in the border states—Delaware, Maryland, West

---

*Halleck's nickname reflected his status as a West Point intellectual.

Virginia, Kentucky, and Missouri—for fear of driving them out of the Union. As Seward admitted, "We show our sympathy with slavery by emancipating slaves where we cannot reach them and holding them in bondage where we can set them free."[53]

While it was a political expedient and a tool of war that did not immediately set a single slave free, the proclamation nonetheless put the war on a moral footing, which abolitionists welcomed wholeheartedly. Greeley, who had helped push Lincoln toward this position, rejoiced. "GOD BLESS ABRAHAM LINCOLN . . . It is the beginning of the end of the rebellion . . . it is the beginning of the new life of the nation," the *Tribune* declared.[54]

Indeed, the Emancipation Proclamation effectively marked the beginning of Reconstruction—not the physical rebuilding of a nation ravaged by war, but rather the process of thoroughly revolutionizing American race relations and society. In order to reconstruct America—to fulfill the promise of human equality articulated in the founders' Declaration of Independence and in Lincoln's proclamation—the Civil War generation would first have to begin tearing down a centuries-old slaveholding culture in the South as well as the caste system and residual bigotry where the institution had still existed, only decades earlier, in the North.[55]

Unlike Greeley, more conservative Americans had no desire for what would soon be called Reconstruction, which they saw as an upheaval of the status quo by meddlesome extremists, the destruction of a divinely ordained social structure and racial hierarchy based on the self-evident superiority of whites.[56]

"There is no law but the despotic will of poor Abe Lincoln, who is a worse knave because he is a *cover* for every knave and fanatic who has the address to use him. Therefore we have not one devil, but many to contend with," Maria Daly, wife of the New York Democratic judge Charles Patrick Daly, lamented about the Preliminary Emancipation Proclamation. "Yet he only stands between us and internal revolution. It is terrible. God help our unhappy country!"[57]

By "internal revolution," she meant the Confederate secession. War Democrats like Maria Daly and her husband supported an armed struggle to maintain the integrity of the Union. Charles Daly had been one of the leading proponents of the militia draft in 1862 and an active recruiter, making numerous speeches to spur volunteering in and around New York. However, with mounting losses on the battlefield and a growing sense that the war was being fought not only for the Union but for emancipation, conservatives like the Dalys found themselves in a quandary.[58]

Irish Americans, who had volunteered in great numbers early in the war, became increasingly reluctant to serve in the military. "The government complains that but few Irish, comparatively, volunteer. They have no idea of fighting for the blacks," Maria Daly recorded in her diary. "The abolitionists, [the Irish] say, tell them that soon they will have good, faithful, colored servants, and that these Irish will then have to go back to their poorhouses. The Irish believe the abolitionists hate both Irish and Catholic and want to kill them off. The abolitionists always, the Irish say, put them in front of the battle."[59]

While the Irish community was busy raising money for the numerous widows and orphans of soldiers killed in battle, in the fall of 1862 the Catholic Orphanage in Brooklyn burned down; along with widows and orphans, the number of homeless children was growing at an alarming rate. To keep them out of the clutches of the Protestant-run Children's Aid Society, Archbishop Hughes and other Irish Catholic leaders founded the Catholic Protectory, which opened the following year with room for a thousand homeless children. Charles and Maria Daly led similar relief efforts, including the Working Women's Protective Association, which assisted seamstresses, among other poorly paid workers, and provided day care for working mothers.

City governments had also pledged to support the wives and children of Union army volunteers, but the help was generally less than what had been promised. When public funds were not forthcoming in New York late in 1862, two hundred destitute wives of soldiers rallied in Tompkins Square, where one angry Irishwoman reminded officials, "You have got me men into the souldiers, and now you have to kepe us from starving."[60]

With the Emancipation Proclamation, Lincoln knew he risked alienating the rank and file of the army as well as War Democrats on the home front. He also knew that conservatives within his own party would be unhappy with this expansion of the war's purpose. For Democratic party strategists, headquartered in New York, the militia draft and the Preliminary Emancipation Proclamation provided issues around which to continue the process of Democratic unification and resurgence that had peaked in July 1862 with the statewide anti-emancipation meetings and the rally in Manhattan. The proclamation also drove a wedge between radical and conservative Republicans, even spurring some of the latter to defect to the Democracy.[61]

Among these disgruntled conservative Republicans was twenty-nine-year-old Manton Marble, editor of the struggling New York *World*. The son of an Albany schoolteacher—and a fervent Baptist with rigid ideas about achieving a life of morality, principle, and nobility of spirit—Marble wanted to be "*in* the world, yet not *of* it."[62] However, when he had trouble raising funds to buy a controlling stake in the paper, his ruthless entrepreneurial side had emerged. "I would give my right hand to succeed," Marble wrote to his mentor at the seminary he had attended in Rochester, "but failure stares me in the face." Marble's politics followed his bottom line, and in August 1862, he sought financing from Samuel Barlow, a wealthy corporate lawyer and one of the Swallowtail Democrats who bankrolled the party.[63]

Barlow was allied with Democratic National Committee chairman August Belmont, who represented the Rothschild family and attracted European capital to New York, helping drive the city's growth and industrialization. Samuel Tilden, a powerful corporate lawyer and master political organizer, was also a Swallowtail. They wanted more influence over the party they funded, which was dominated in the city by the scandalously corrupt machine politicians of Tammany and Mozart. With Manton Marble in their camp, the Swallowtails suddenly had a greater voice in the city.[64]

Marble sold large stakes in the *World* to Barlow and three other Democrats—including Fernando Wood and George Barnard, a Tammany judge—which caused many of his employees and friends to accuse him of selling out. The arrangement paid off Marble's debts and gave him a cash cushion, while allowing him to stay on as editor at a handsome salary of $3,500 a year. Former governor Horatio Seymour, along with other party leaders, attended strategy sessions at the *World*'s offices, and Belmont sponsored Marble's application for membership in the elite Century Club. A contemplative, cerebral seminarian who had once seemed destined for a career as a poet and literary scholar, Marble rapidly became a key player in Democratic politics.[65]

Salving his conscience, Marble asserted that he had remained true to his own convictions, and that conservative Republicans like himself would raise the tone of the Democratic party. He played down the fact that he had actively courted the Democrats for an emergency loan and attributed his crossing of party lines to the nomination of an abolitionist for governor at the Republican state convention in the fall of 1862. The appearance of opportunism was merely coincidence, Marble insisted. "The hour struck, the opportunity came. I seized it . . . interest seemed to me for once to coincide with duty."[66]

The Swallowtails' immediate goal was not so much to curb the petty ward politicians they disdained, but to hammer away at the Preliminary Emancipation Proclamation and spur party unity. Democratic newspapers assailed the administration without restraint, saying Lincoln was influenced by "insane radicals," who had once promised they only wanted to stop the spread of slavery. Marble wrote that the president was "fully adrift on the current of radical fanaticism." With Democratic backing and a new, strident message, the *World*'s circulation jumped dramatically.[67]

Manton Marble

Attempting to minimize and suppress the peace faction, Marble proclaimed the Democrats' unity and legitimacy as an opposition party, vital to the two-party system. At the same time, he was developing a refrain he would repeat often in the coming year: If anyone was a danger to the government, it was not the Copperheads and Peace Democrats, but rather the radical Republicans, who were hounding Lincoln to end slavery and overturn white supremacy in America.[68]

At New York's Republican convention that fall, Greeley and his allies had managed to nominate an abolitionist, General James Wadsworth, for governor, but at the cost of further dividing the party, while spurring Democrats to coalesce around Horatio Seymour as the standard-bearer of anti-emancipation and messiah of the northern white workingman. Seymour had been elected governor a decade earlier, but his stand against prohibition in large part had cost him a second term. In 1862, his opposition to temperance became an asset, as did his racism and denunciations of Lincoln's policies. Greeley saw defeat coming and lamented to abolitionist Gerrit Smith that "the Rum-sellers, the Irish and the Slavery idolaters make a big crowd and they are fiendish in their vote against the president's proclamation of freedom."[69]

On Greeley's list of fiends was Fernando Wood, who, after three terms as mayor of New York, was once again running for a seat in Congress.* In a campaign speech that fall, pandering to Irish and German immigrants, Wood crystallized his message of class warfare and racial hatred, claiming that the rich "amassed their wealth from the products of the other classes," and the poor, whose sons were at the front, shouldered the burden of the war while the rich stayed home.

Emancipation, he asserted, was another attempt to exploit poor whites by deluging the North with cheap black laborers, "many of them mechanics," meaning skilled artisans who could compete for good jobs. Whites would no longer be paid "at customary wages," and in their effort to promote "the African" above the white laborer, abolitionists planned to integrate the public schools at taxpayers' expense while putting their own children in private academies.[70]

Frustration with a year and a half of Union losses on the battlefield, opposition to emancipation, and fear of British intervention in the war all fueled conservatism in the North and helped the Democrats. In New York, Tammany and Mozart submerged their differences over the issue of war and peace, which helped send both Ben and Fernando Wood to Congress, and Seymour won the governor's race. Greeley was furious and declared that the state had abandoned the Union cause.[71]

The Democrats also picked up numerous House seats in New Jersey, Pennsylvania, and Ohio, as well as on Lincoln's home turf, Illinois. However, the Republicans still had a majority in the House and an even firmer grip on the Senate. The elections had vented voters' displeasure with Republican handling of the war and the prospect of emancipation, but showed they were willing to stay the course and give Lincoln and his party another chance. Nonetheless, the Democrats had successfully exploited public fear of abolition to unite the party and celebrated their victories across the North. A popular Democratic song declared that abolition "has died before it was weaned, weaned, weaned; it has died before it was weaned."[72]

Virginia's Edmund Ruffin was also encouraged by the election results, particularly in the large and important state of New York. Noting that Democrats had already challenged the federal militia draft of 1862 as unconstitutional, Ruffin hoped further opposition by Wood and Seymour in New York would lead to riots followed by a clash of federal and state authorities that would bring down the government in Washington: "If this [legal challenge to the draft] is made in N.Y. & supported by a triumphant & violent majority

---

*Wood was elected mayor in 1854, 1856, and 1859. The mayoral race was moved to odd years in 1857.

of the people, the Supreme Court of that very corrupt state will readily confirm the popular construction, & so make it the duty of the Governor to prevent the draft. And if the powerful state of New York is placed in full opposition to the Federal Government, the latter will not be able to bear up under such an addition to its previous difficulties."[73]

Elsewhere in the South, the knowledge that the Emancipation Proclamation would probably go into effect in a matter of days triggered not only fear but gruesome retribution. At Christmas, George Templeton Strong heard of nineteen black slaves being hanged in Charleston, presumably because they had grown unmanageable in the expectation of being declared free on New Year's Day. Expressing the polar opposite, antislavery view, Strong asked himself if the president would indeed affirm the proclamation as promised: "Will Lincoln's backbone carry him through the work he is pledged them to do? . . . If he come out fair and square, he will do the 'biggest thing' an Illinois jury-lawyer has ever had a chance of doing, and take high place among the men who have controlled the destinies of nations. If he postpone or dilute his action, his name will be a byword and a hissing till the annals of the nineteenth century are forgotten."[74]

CHAPTER 6

Emancipation and Its Enemies

~⌒

The first indication of ill feeling, on the part of the Irish mob, against us was at the time of the Emancipation Proclamation," on New Year's Day 1863, Lucy Gibbons recalled of her youth. "We were so rejoiced by the proclamation that my sister and I pinned sheets of red, white and blue tissue paper on the second and third story windows, and, in the evening, lit the gas." After festooning and illuminating their house, one in a "long row of houses with pretty courtyards in front" on Manhattan's West Twenty-ninth Street between Eighth and Ninth Avenues, Lucy, then a teenager, and her older sister Julia went out with their father, James. Author of the recruiting poem "We Are Coming, Father Abraham" and a well-known white abolitionist, he and his wife had made their home a haven for runaway slaves on the Underground Railroad.

"When we returned late and entered our courtyard, we trod on something sticky," Lucy recalled. "It was pitch, smeared over the pavement, up the steps and on our front door. Father had the steps and pavement cleaned, but as testimony against the vandals he left the pitch, which nearly covered the door, for several weeks."[1]

A friend wrote to their mother, Abby, from Boston, "The damage, I suppose, is not considerable, and the mortification nothing; but it is a serious thing, considered as revealing the temper of the times." Applying Abraham Lincoln's biblical description of the whole country to the North alone, the friend continued, "There can no longer be any doubt, that what are called the Loyal States make up a house divided against itself."[2]

Quakers from the Philadelphia area, James and Abby Gibbons had moved to New York City in 1836, at the height of the reform movement inspired by the Second Great Awakening. At a time when many middle- and upper-class Protestant families were active in promoting social change through volunteer work, Abby's energy and leadership made her exceptional. She and her colleagues raised money through "Anti-Slavery Fairs"; promoted prison reform and visited inmates at the city jail known as the Tombs; counseled women in a halfway house; and worked with orphans on Blackwell's Island. Abby also started an industrial school for homeless German children and served as headmistress for twelve years. She tirelessly lobbied elected officials to secure support for these charities, including grants of city-owned land.[3]*

Abby adored her only son, Willie, and his teachers predicted greatness in his future. "And my daughters would be his equals, but alas for woman!" she lamented, society deprived them of the same opportunities.[4] Willie received the best education, and Abby fostered his social conscience. "He was in the habit of visiting, with his grandfather or his mother, the cells of the Tombs and other places where were confined the victims of sin and misery, and in this way his sympathy for the poor and suffering was developed," a Harvard classmate wrote of Willie.[5] Willie's sudden death in 1855, after he tripped and fell on his way back to campus on a dark night, had been a severe blow to the entire family, and they kept his possessions along with a sculpted bust of him as a shrine to his memory. Over Willie's coffin Abby had cried, "The light of our home—gone out!"

She kept her grief at bay by plunging deeper into her many charitable activities.[6] When the war broke out, Abby promptly answered the army's plea for nurses in its camps and hospitals, taking her eldest daughter, Sally, with her on a prolonged and dangerous mission to the front.[7]

"Sound the timbrel o'er Egypt's dark sea, Jehova has triumphed, his people are free," sang a black minister and his congregation in Boston's Tremont Temple on January 1, 1863.[8] While African Americans rejoiced over the Emancipation Proclamation, the document promised freedom but not equality. The proclamation allowed blacks to serve in the Union army, but they would be enlisted in separate all-black units under white commanders and would be paid less, often for more dangerous duty.[9]

Nonetheless, in New York, the Reverend Henry Highland Garnet urged black men to enlist, to liberate their own race and disprove the "slanderous

---

*The Women's Prison Association, founded by Abby Hopper Gibbons, still runs transitional housing on Manhattan's Lower East Side for women leaving prison.

Abraham Lincoln

myth" that blacks were cowardly.[10] Garnet had been pastor of Shiloh Presbyterian Church on Prince Street and Broadway for nearly a decade and had made the church a destination for the city's middle-class blacks, who overflowed into the aisles. Garnet's sermons and opinions on events were written up in the African American daily press.[11]

Born a slave in Maryland in 1815, he escaped with his family when they fled north after pretending to attend a funeral at a neighboring estate. In his late teens, Garnet received a classical education at the new High School for Colored Youth in New York and found a mentor in the Reverend Theodore Wright, who groomed him for the ministry. Garnet's extraordinary skill as a debater and orator emerged, and he found heroic role models in Greek and Roman literature that inspired him to lead his people in the fight against slavery.

He was also proud of his own heritage, the Mandingo chiefs and warriors in Africa. Garnet was very dark skinned, defying the stereotype of eloquent blacks needing some white lineage to account for their ability. The warrior ancestry may also have accounted for his defiant attitude and tenacity. At an integrated academy in New Hampshire where Wright had sent him,

Garnet and two black classmates were attacked in their dormitory by a white mob. Garnet, who had been lamed by a knee injury earlier in life, managed to fire several rounds from a double-barreled shotgun as he limped away, saving the lives of his friends along with his own.[12]

Garnet designed recruiting posters full of martial ardor: "Fail Now and Our Race Is Doomed . . . Rather Die Free Men Than Live as Slaves . . . Rise Now and Fly to Arms!" However, his entreaties to "join the armies of John Brown" by "marching through the heart of the rebellion" fell flat, like those of other black leaders in New York, since black men knew the inequality they would face in the army. The militant Garnet thought they should go anyway: Once blacks were armed and trained, the white government would not be able to renege on its promise of freedom—"not without a good fight" at least.[13]

A major obstacle to Garnet's efforts, as well as a discouragement to potential black volunteers, was the fact that the new governor, Horatio Seymour, would not approve the formation of black regiments in New York State, and President Lincoln was unwilling to pressure him on the matter, despite appeals from Garnet, Horace Greeley, and other prominent New Yorkers.[14] In Massachusetts, by contrast, Governor John Andrew was raising the North's first black regiment, the Fifty-fourth Massachusetts, and had enlisted Garnet and other black leaders to recruit African Americans from all over the country to fill its ranks. Even with blacks leaving to enlist in Massachusetts—when they could have helped New York fulfill its quota of volunteers and forestall the militia draft—Seymour would not change his policy.[15]

"We did not cause this war, [but] vast numbers of our people have perished in it," Boston's Irish Catholic *Pilot* lamented. While Republican abolitionists like the Gibbons family celebrated the Emancipation Proclamation along with African Americans, the reaction throughout most Irish American communities was one of anger and dread. Having sacrificed for the Union, the Irish saw that they would now be fighting to liberate blacks, who would compete with them not only for jobs but—once enrolled as soldiers and citizens—for glory on the battlefield and acceptance in American society. The elevation of blacks to equality with whites lowered the status of the Irish worker, New York's *Weekly Day-Book* declared; he was "degraded to a level with negroes."[16]

Reflecting the crisis that Irish Americans had reached by 1863, the *Pilot* announced that "the Irish spirit for the war is dead! . . . Our fighters are dead." With the Irish Brigade's terrible losses, particularly at Fredericksburg in December, nationalists despaired that the army they had hoped to train for Irish liberation was being wiped out instead. While many blamed Thomas

Francis Meagher's recklessness for the decimation of the brigade, he and his defenders pointed out that the War Department would not grant the unit leave so it could recuperate and recruit new members. This deepened Irish suspicion that their men were being used as cannon fodder by the Lincoln administration. The Emancipation Proclamation made the brutal war even more painful. As Archbishop Hughes had warned from the outset, the Irish would lay down their lives for the Union but "turn away in disgust" if asked to fight for abolition.[17]

Hughes had been a strong advocate of the war, serving as Lincoln's unofficial envoy to the Vatican and to France, but the emancipation issue had since created a rift between the administration and the Catholic Church, which viewed abolition as a cause championed by its worst enemies—Protestant Republicans—and a violation of slaveholders' property rights.[18] In January the *Irish-American* responded to a public slur against the Irish poor by a prominent Unitarian minister, calling him a "fanatical vender of the gospel of Abolitionism." Such prejudice and discrimination and "the triumph of Abolition policy" had devalued the Irish-born laborer, making it harder for him to feed and clothe his family, the editorial declared. Denouncing abolitionists as "Nigger propagandists," the paper concluded: "We have no words to express the loathing and contempt we feel for the besotted fanatics."[19]

While Governor Seymour stood firmly against the enlistment of black regiments, in a confrontation with Republicans over New York City's police force, he decided to back down. In 1857, when Republican state legislators replaced Fernando Wood's loyal Municipals with their own Metropolitan police force, they installed a new board of commissioners—Thomas Acton, as president, along with two others. The commissioners in turn appointed John Kennedy as superintendent. The arrival of the Metropolitans had sparked deadly rioting, and tensions in the largely Democratic city had continued to simmer over the next six years.

Most recently, Democrats charged that the Metropolitans had become the instrument of Lincoln's civil rights abuses, arbitrarily arresting political opponents and detaining them without charges in the city's prisons and the dungeons of Fort Lafayette. Moreover, Superintendent Kennedy stood accused of intimidating Democratic voters with the threat of arrest during the fall 1862 elections, for political advantage, not—as he asserted—because they were aliens who had claimed to be exempt from the militia draft.

After Seymour's inauguration on January 1, 1863, his first official act as governor had been to summon the commissioners to Albany for questioning as a prelude to removing them from office. The commissioners,

Horatio Seymour

however, refused to appear, on the grounds that the governor had no jurisdiction over them: He was in Albany County, and they would only submit to questioning by the district attorney of New York County. Seymour—a champion of local control—had seen no choice but to give in and drop the matter.[20]

Even before this showdown, Seymour harbored a deep aversion to New York City, matched by his warm affection for the hinterlands of the state, where he grew up. Seymour was a longtime political ally of the Irish, a friendship sealed by the building of the Erie Canal by Irish laborers in the early 1820s when Seymour was a boy and his father was a state canal commissioner. The father's political connections made for the son's smooth entry into state politics, where his expertise in canal issues kept him at the center of power, leading to his first term as governor.[21]

Guided by sympathy for his Irish constituents, along with his own racism and conservatism, Seymour reaffirmed his opposition to emancipation and the enlistment of black troops in February 1863 when top Democratic leaders met at Delmonico's Restaurant in New York. In this posh setting, the party chieftains and intellectuals formed a propaganda arm called the Society for the Diffusion of Political Knowledge. Hoping to force a reversal of Lincoln's edict, the organization published pamphlets and scholarly articles defending slavery and predicting dire economic consequences for both sides if it were abolished.[22]

Manton Marble attended the summit at Delmonico's, and the *World* continued to be a major part of the anti-emancipation campaign. General George McClellan, dismissed from command a few months earlier, was also on hand. He had moved to New York and was being groomed by Democratic party chairman August Belmont to unseat Lincoln the following year.[23]

A few weeks later, the city's Republican elite responded to the Copperhead challenge—both from the New York Democracy and from midwestern groups like the Knights of the Golden Circle—by establishing the Union League Club. Describing themselves as members of the "intelligent and prosperous classes," three hundred of the city's top business and professional leaders—including George Templeton Strong, Henry Bellows, and Frederick Law Olmsted—banded together to address the burgeoning problem of "disloyalty" and the Union's inability to gain the upper hand in the war, politically and militarily.[24]

Olmsted, the designer, with Calvert Vaux, of New York City's Central Park, and a leader of the U.S. Sanitary Commission, envisioned a club for the "true American aristocracy" that would transform New York politically, socially, and architecturally. Harnessing the power of elite citizens loyal to the national government, the club would win over and pacify the proletariat with recreational facilities like Central Park and various forms of cultural enrichment.[25]

Businessman and philanthropist William Dodge was a member and helped organize the Loyal Publication Society, which churned out almost a million copies of some ninety Unionist pamphlets during the war. The Union League Club also engaged in grassroots political organizing; the magazines *Harper's Weekly* and later the *Nation* became the club's instruments of influence. The enlistment of black soldiers in the Union army would soon become one of the club's priorities.[26]

"Experience has shown that serious defects exist in the militia law, which should be promptly remedied," Stanton had told Congress at the end of 1862. Despite the satisfactory number of men raised, in 1863 the secretary of war remained frustrated by his dependence on the governors and their personnel, their delays, and the overly complicated system with different militia regulations from state to state. Worst of all, from Stanton's perspective, was the nine-month limit on federal service for militia draftees. Keeping the details to himself, while assuring congressional leaders and fellow cabinet members that he would consult with them, Stanton had been developing plans for a uniform, national draft.[27]

To Lincoln and Stanton's chagrin, the Confederacy had resorted to a centralized draft before the Union, in April 1862. The law required every able-bodied, white male citizen, between the ages of eighteen and thirty-five, to serve in the Confederate army for three years. There was no commutation clause, but draftees were allowed to hire substitutes who were not subject to the draft; government officials, workers in essential industries, hospital staff, apothecaries, clergy, and teachers were exempt.

Since the Confederacy was fighting for states' rights, many southerners denounced the national conscription as a violation of their ideals—an abuse of power worthy of the federal government in the North. In some areas, where allegiance to the Confederacy was nil anyway, enrollment officers were forced to retreat, leaving entire counties in the hands of organized draft re-sisters and deserters.[28] Nonetheless, bounties and other incentives for volun-teering, combined with the draft, had built up the Confederate forces in 1862 to some 450,000 troops.[29]

Three times that number—some 1.3 million men—had joined the Union forces between the outbreak of the war and the end of February 1863. However, the army's need for men had increased sharply, while the Lincoln administration's prestige hit a new low. The military setbacks of 1862 made local communities reluctant to provide bounty money, which drove down re-cruitment, while tens of thousands of veterans declined to reenlist. At the same time, the rate of desertion soared: An estimated one hundred thousand men were missing from the Union army at the end of 1862, and by the be-ginning of 1863 several hundred soldiers were leaving every day.

Some were exploiting the bounty system—taking the advance portion of the money and then "skedaddling"—while others left because the army had not paid them for months, the U.S. Treasury being chronically broke from funding the war. Moreover, a private soldier's meager salary of thirteen dol-lars per month didn't compare to potential wages on the home front in an in-flationary economy, and many deserters hurried back to support their impoverished families.[30]

The bigger payday on the home front was often illusory, however. While the war boom in the Northeast had created new jobs, real wages had fallen because of inflation, fueled by the federal government's issuing of paper money, dubbed "greenbacks" for their color, as well as by profiteering and shortages of basic commodities. Unskilled workers—many of them Irish Americans, women, and children—were the most vulnerable to inflation's bite. These economic pressures in turn generated racial conflict as the labor movement revived and organized more strikes—on the basis of white solidarity.[31] In March 1863, the *Irish-American* reported that riots between blacks and whites were breaking out everywhere.[32]

"I seen in the heareld all about the conscripts law," Sergeant Peter Welsh wrote to his wife, Margaret, in New York from an army camp, after reading in the *Herald* about the nation's first federal draft, approved by Congress on March 2, 1863, and signed by the president the following day. Stanton's plans to centralize the process of manning the armed forces, initiated almost a year earlier, had borne fruit in the final days of the Thirty-seventh Congress, when Republican majorities prevailed against Democratic objections, amendments, and delaying tactics, including an attempt, supported by almost a third of House Republicans, to repeal the three-hundred-dollar clause.[33]

Unlike the militia law of 1862, which enabled the federal government to make use of troops drafted by the states, the new "Act for Enrolling and Calling Out the National Forces" empowered the War Department to draft men directly for service in the national army. All "able-bodied male citizens" between the ages of twenty and thirty-five were required to enroll as potential draftees, as were unmarried men from thirty-six to forty-five years old. While blacks enjoyed few if any of the benefits of citizenship, they were subject to the draft. The law also created the Bureau of the Provost Marshal General within the War Department, and Colonel James Fry was placed at the head of it to administer the draft.[34]

"I am very glad it has passed," Welsh wrote. "It will bring the people to their senses and the war will either be settled or the skulking blowers at home will have to come out and do their share of the fighting."[35] Welsh, whose regiment formed part of the Irish Brigade in the Army of the Potomac, was on the front lines in the war's bloodiest battles. Nonetheless, he was one of many Irish Americans whose fierce devotion to the Union cause never wavered, even during the Irish community's crisis of doubt in 1863, brought on by heavy battlefield losses and the North's new abolition agenda.

Like the Irish Catholics described by Maria Daly, and like most Irish American soldiers, Welsh opposed the abolitionists, whom he called "fanatical nigar worshippers."[36] However, in letters to his wife in New York and to his father-in-law in Ireland, Welsh defended his decision to join the army,

Sergeant Peter Welsh

citing St. Paul and Archbishop Hughes as authorities to prove that the Confederate secession was unjustified, despite abolitionist agitation: "This war with all its evils with all its errors and missmanagement is a war in which the people of all nations have a vital interest. this is the first test of a modern free government in the act of sustaining itself against internal enemys and matured rebellion."[37]

Welsh, thirty-three years old, was an Irish Catholic immigrant who had settled in Boston. He and his wife, also Irish, had moved to New York a few years before the war broke out, and he looked for work as a carpenter. When he had trouble getting a job, Welsh went on long drinking binges, the worst of which took place on a visit to Boston, where he had gone by himself to settle a family dispute. Having failed, and incurred his relatives' anger instead, Welsh attempted to drown his frustration in drink over the course of several days. Still in Boston, he awoke penniless and too embarrassed to ask friends or family for help. He ran away to the army on September 3, 1862, enlisting in Company K of the Twenty-eighth Massachusetts Volunteer Infantry, which soon joined the Irish Brigade.[38]

Of those who argued that the draft discriminated against the poor, Peter Welsh told his wife that "they could not labor under a more false impression. no conscription could be fairer then the one which is about to be enforced. it would be impossible to frame it to satisfy everyone." He also thought, rather optimistically, that the draft would crush the will of the Confederacy with a display of Union might "and those drafted men may never have to fight a battle."[39]

In New York, and across the North, fellow Irishmen and the Democratic press were not convinced. New York's *Freeman's Journal,* edited by Peace Democrat James McMasters, was perhaps the most incendiary, calling the federal draft an "outrage" and challenging the citizenry to prove they were not an "enervated, emasculated and slavish people" by resisting the new law.[40] While the *New York Times* and the *Tribune* defended the three-hundred-dollar clause, Manton Marble's *World* declared that "extorted military service" was "repugnant" to a free people, and warned that violent resistance was likely.[41]

In Michigan, the *Detroit Free Press* had also been denouncing the administration for months, frightening white readers with visions of racial amalgamation and labor competition from ex-slaves freed by Lincoln's proclamation. The passage of the federal draft, published in the *Free Press* two days later, on March 5, coincided with labor strikes in Detroit, and the fury of the city's white residents could no longer be contained.[42]

The following day, a mob incited by the *Free Press* rained bricks and paving stones on the soldiers escorting William Faulkner, a prisoner of mixed race, from the courthouse where he had just been convicted on flimsy evidence of raping two nine-year-old girls, one black and one white, at his saloon, described by the newspaper as an "amalgamation den." The mob tried to seize "the black fiend, the monster Faulkner," and the troops opened fire, wounding several people and killing a bystander, before getting the prisoner to his jail cell.

"The mob at this moment became enraged," John Warren, a black clergyman, recalled, "and one man, mounting a stump, cried out, 'Gentlem[e]n, I am for killing all the negroes.' 'Kill the negroes, kill the negroes!' shouted five hundred, at the top of their voices. They came down Benden St., frantic, like so many devils."

The rioters attacked the city's black enclave, burning thirty homes and businesses to the ground and leaving some two hundred black residents without a roof over their heads or a penny to their names. The mob destroyed the thriving cooperage owned by Whitney Reynolds. "This brother has truly distinguished himself by the many hands he employed, and the number of barrels he turned out weekly," Warren wrote. "Brother Reynolds was not home at the time of the riot. His hands fought like heroes to save his property. They never left the building until the house was set on fire."

One employee was an escaped slave who was saving up but would never reach his goal of buying his relatives from their master: A rioter split his head open with an ax. While the Reynolds family fled their home, rioters grabbed an infant and threw it on the pavement. Only two deaths were officially recorded, but scores of blacks were injured. Among them was an "honest and upright old man," eighty years old, who had lived in Detroit half his life; the rioters beat him and left him for dead. At eight o'clock that night, the Twenty-seventh Michigan infantry regiment arrived to put down the riot.*

On that same day, labor competition provided the spark for a clash in New York. "This city was disgraced yesterday by a mob," Greeley's *Tribune* declared on March 6 and quickly revealed the paper's bias. "A few unoffending colored laborers on the wharves were suddenly attacked by two or three hundred vagabond Irishmen." The blacks defended themselves with pistols, wounding some of the Irishmen before the police arrived. According to the *Tribune*, "The rioters made a desperate attack on [the police], endeavoring to seize and lynch a negro who had been arrested for his own safety." The *Tribune* viewed the rioting as "the natural climax" of a campaign in the Democratic press to spread "malignant falsehoods . . . that white men were to be cheated out of work by an immigration of negroes."[43]

In fact, the Irish were again flooding into northern cities, driven from Ireland by a famine comparable to the Great Famine of 1845–52. Irish immigration increased in 1863, to more than three times the average of the previous two years.[44] The poor and working classes plunged into new depths of squalor as homelessness and overcrowding increased, driven by a decline in housing construction. In New York City, the proliferation of industrial and commercial buildings ate up residential space downtown.[45]

During the Civil War, before landfill further expanded its shores, Manhattan had an area of about thirty-four square miles, including its parks. However, unlike large mainland cities such as Philadelphia and London, which had room to expand, New York was confined to the island and concentrated at its southern tip. While businesses and the wealthier workforce of Manhattan could settle on the New Jersey and Long Island shores, working-class New

---

*A week later, Warren could report that "the citizens are making every provision to relieve our suffering people, and our city is again restored to peace." The saloonkeeper's conviction was later overturned when the two girls who had accused him retracted their story. Faulkner started a new business with help from wealthy patrons, but the black victims of the riot never received compensation from the city.

Yorkers had to live right next to the factories and docks that employed them. On an island lacking bridges and tunnels and efficient transit systems, the poor could not afford to commute; moreover, they had to be ready at the factory gates to scramble for work, since employers hired them and laid them off as needed.[46]

Of New York's one million people in the mid-1860s, at least half were poor or working-class. The city, both residential and commercial, was concentrated on the eight square miles of Lower Manhattan—less than a quarter of the island—and the poor, numbering five hundred thousand, were packed into a quarter of that area, about two square miles. The tenements around a single courtyard contained as many as a thousand people, while three city blocks of tenements housed more people than all of Fifth Avenue.[47]

Wealthy New Yorkers moved uptown, where land was selling fast. Immigrants who settled into some of the worst slums on Earth, in Manhattan's lower wards below Canal Street, were moving into the same town houses, mansions, and commercial buildings that the rich had fled, but landlords had subdivided these properties, along with tenements, into dark, airless "suites" in order to maximize occupancy. Five Points was the city's worst slum, where half a dozen people—men, women, and children, both black and white— sometimes lived together in a single dank basement room with inches of dirt on the floor and green slime covering the walls. Walt Whitman called the city's housing conditions a "fertile hotbed for evils the most enormous."[48]

In the absence of zoning, foul-smelling industries were crowded in with the tenement dwellers. Cattle, pigs, and sheep were regularly driven through the streets to the city's two hundred slaughterhouses. In addition to "hundreds of uncleaned stables" and "immense manure heaps," health inspectors told of "fat-boiling, entrails-cleansing, and tripe-curing establishments, which poison the air" for blocks.[49] A tenant in the Fourth Ward* complained that "on a piece of ground 240 feet by 150, there are 20 tenant houses, occupied by 111 families, 5 stables, a large soap and candle factory, and a tan-yard, the receptacle of green hides. The filth and stench of this locality are beyond any power of description."[50]

Waste from these dwellings and factories—including blood and offal from the slaughterhouses—was generally placed in garbage boxes out front or simply dumped in the streets, "covering their surface, filling the gutters [and] obstructing the sewer culverts," wrote one inspector. Children playing in the street floated paper boats on the dark red overflow in the gutters and used it to paint their faces. The stench of butcher shops with barrels of putrefied offal destined to become sausage skins also filled the air.

---

*On the East River below Catherine Street.

"In the winter the filth and garbage, etc., accumulate in the streets, to the depth sometimes of two or three feet," an inspector wrote. Another commented that two streets looked like "dung-hills rather than the thoroughfares of a civilized city."[51]* In the Eleventh Ward,† an inspector reported that "the filth of the streets is composed of house-slops, refuse vegetables, decayed fruit, store and shop sweepings, ashes, dead animals, and even human excrements. These putrifying organic substances are ground together by the constantly passing vehicles. When dried by the summer's heat, they are driven by the wind in every direction in the form of dust." Stirred up into clouds by carriage wheels and horses' hooves, the dust spread across the entire city, another wrote. "No barrier can shut it out, no social distinction can save us from it."[52]

The courtyards and alleys behind the tenements were even filthier than the surrounding streets, because residents threw their household waste into shallow gutters, which tended to clog, overflow, and flood the yards, instead of carrying their contents to the street as intended. Also in the courtyard was "that most pestiferous of all sources of civic uncleanliness and unhealthiness— the privy and cesspool." Most were not connected to the sewers, were rarely emptied, and often overflowed into the yards. The worst privies were built in dark, damp cellars without ventilation and with only four seats for a hundred people. "In some places the foundation of the privies being rotten and broken . . . faecal matter runs into the cellar."[53]

About eighteen thousand of the poorest New Yorkers lived in cellars, "dens of death" where a family of seven could be found in a room eighteen feet square, with a seven-foot ceiling. In the Fourth Ward, where the cellars were dug below sea level, an inspector noted that "at high tide the water often wells up through the floors, submerging them to a considerable depth. In very many cases the vaults of the privies are situated on the same or a higher level, and their contents frequently ooze through the walls into the occupied apartments beside them."[54]

Side by side with this festering subterranean misery, the wartime boom created hundreds of millionaires in New York. When the war broke out, New York City's economy had come to a standstill because of severed ties to the South, but industries supporting the war effort invigorated it within a few months. Great Lakes–Erie Canal traffic increased, and New York surged as the shipping point of the heartland's wheat to Europe and as a manufacturing center for war matériel. Cattle, sugar, and oil poured into the city, to be

---

*Sixth Street between the Bowery and Second Avenue, and Eleventh Street between First and Second Avenues, in today's East Village.
†On the East River above Houston Street.

processed at slaughterhouses and refineries. Ironworks produced naval equipment, guns, and ironclads, including the *Monitor,* launched from Greenpoint, Brooklyn, in January 1862. Federal contracts and protective tariffs created a surge of industrial activity in New York City that rivaled the combined output of all the Confederate states.[55]

The nouveau riche were also labeled the "shoddy aristocracy" for selling defective uniforms, boots, and horses to the government. By 1863, the families constituting the top 1 percent held 61 percent of the city's wealth. On Broadway, the "Republican 'big bugocracy' sports its jewels, silks, and drapery," wrote one working-class diarist, deriding "gold bugs," speculators in gold, which rose in value against government currency with each Union setback on the battlefield.[56] There were conspicuous displays of finery on Fifth Avenue too, carriage rides in the newly opened Central Park, and dinners at Delmonico's—each costing enough to support a soldier and his family for almost a year. A. T. Stewart closed his Marble Palace and opened the largest retail store in the world on Broadway across from Cooper Union.[57]

A three-thousand-dollar shawl Stewart imported for the daughter of Salmon Chase, the secretary of the treasury, caused a sensation, people remarking that it was now worth ten men's lives.[58] The Union defeat at Chancellorsville in May 1863 took another seventeen thousand men out of action and left the Irish Brigade with only a few hundred men. Amid the carnage, some Irish Americans accused the government of deliberately placing these "heroes of the Green" at the front of the battle to spare the lives of others. Still the administration continued to deny Meagher's requests to give the brigade time at home to restore itself, and he finally resigned in protest.[59]

The war boom, profiteering, and conspicuous consumption bred resentment not only among the urban poor in the Northeast, but in the Midwest, where farmers cut off from trade with the South by the Union blockade of the Mississippi were suffering from a severe economic depression. Prices for corn, wheat, pork, and beef had plummeted. Money and jobs were scarce, while businesses and banks failed by the hundreds. Confederate general Braxton Bragg had tried to summon up this resentment in September 1862 when he made a raid into Kentucky, established a provisional government at Frankfort, and issued a proclamation titled "To The People of the Northwest," implying that they should secede from the United States and ally themselves with the South.

Five months later, in February 1863, a baseless report of a secession movement in Kentucky, Ohio, Indiana, and Illinois was splashed all over the newspapers in Richmond, where Confederate officials, with a good deal of

John Hunt Morgan

wishful thinking, discussed how best to exploit the new development. The Copperhead rhetoric of Democratic newspapers in the Midwest also helped convince southern leaders that a breakaway republic like their own was in the making and just needed Confederate encouragement and support.[60]

When John Hunt Morgan and his 2,500 Confederate horsemen invaded Indiana in July, they had hoped to start a Copperhead uprising, since the southern portion of the state was a hotbed of discontent. However, like most of the Confederate leadership, Morgan misjudged antiwar sentiment in the area, where vocal critics of the administration nonetheless remained loyal to the Union. The inhabitants despised Morgan's cavalry as "horse-thieves," "extortionists," and "blackmailers," because they plundered Union army wagons and supply depots along their way. Farmers and villagers expected to be attacked by the marauding Confederate horsemen and were anything but happy to see them.[61]

Those who did not flee the path of the invaders banded together to confront them, and "even the Copperheads and Vallandighamites fought harder than the others," one of Morgan's men reported. On July 9, 1863, armed residents of Corydon, Indiana, surprised Morgan and his men, killing eight and wounding thirty-three before they could regroup and counterattack with swords drawn to disperse the crowd.

Morgan stopped for lunch at the Corydon Hotel, where he learned from the owner of Lee's defeat at Gettysburg and had to scrap his plan to link up with him in Pennsylvania. Having lost that escape route, Morgan nonetheless continued his raid instead of retreating to the Ohio River. Morgan and his men were angry about their casualties at Corydon and pillaged several towns before reaching Salem, Indiana, on July 10. By this time, the Indiana governor was mustering the militia at Indianapolis, and Burnside's cavalrymen were closing in from the south. So, instead of heading north to free the six thousand Confederate prisoners in Indianapolis, Morgan took his men toward the Ohio border, to the northeast, and continued his raid, while Union sailors took gunboats up the Ohio River, hoping to cut off his escape into Kentucky or West Virginia.[62]

CHAPTER 7

"A Highwayman's Call on Every American Citizen for '$300 or Your Life'"

~⊃

Edmund Ruffin was one of the few southerners skeptical about the depth of Copperhead support in the Midwest. He dismissed reports "that many thousands of men in the northwestern states have leagued together, & bound themselves by secret oaths, not to submit to the conscription law, & to resist its being enforced, even by arms & bloodshed." He saw far more potential for a revolt in New York and New Jersey, where both governors were "malcontents" as were many state legislators.[1]

Indeed, in the Northeast there was both leadership and a massive urban constituency for the Copperhead movement. Although Morgan had failed to trigger a popular rebellion by tapping the resentment of midwesterners toward the federal government and the changes the war had wrought in their lives, in the Northeast, competition from black workers, magnified by Democratic politicians, continued to trigger violent retaliation by whites. In one of the deadliest incidents, during the first week of July 1863, jobs as stevedores given to blacks in Buffalo, New York, sparked a riot in which three blacks were killed and twelve severely injured.[2]

Also more forceful than Morgan's cavalry raid in stirring up racial and partisan divisions was the loud resistance to Republican policies by Democratic newspapers, which complained about the secrecy surrounding the federal draft lottery. With its personnel collecting names door-to-door in May and June 1863, the provost marshal general's office had nearly completed the enrollment for the draft at the beginning of July, but the exact date when names were to be drawn in each congressional district had not been made public. In fact, the provost marshal general, James Fry, had decided to begin the lottery on different dates across the North, as soon as the enrollment lists were complete in any given district. By staggering the dates, Fry hoped to expedite the process, while making it easier to quell any resistance, one district at a time.[3]

Manton Marble continued his attacks on the draft and beat the drums of anti-emancipation, stressing the rights of states and slaveholders. On July 8, an editorial in the *World* denounced the notion that the founding fathers were hypocritical in proclaiming all men to be created equal, and that "the United States has been ever since its birth a living lie." Marble cited the seventh article of the final peace treaty between England and the United States, which "stipulates that his Brittanic majesty should evacuate the country with all convenient speed and without causing any destruction or 'carrying away negroes or *other* property of the American inhabitants.'"

For Marble, this was "perfect proof of the status of the Negro in the mind of both England and the United States" at that time. The founders never embraced fraternity and equality, the editorial declared, ideas which led to the excesses of the French Revolution. "Men may prove a hundred times over that slavery is a moral wrong or that it is a political wrong, but they do not thereby prove that it is any man's business" except in his own state.[4]

In less erudite language, Peace Democrats were linking this white supremacist argument with resistance to the draft. "ENTHUSIASTIC PEACE DEMONSTRATION . . . THE DRAFT CONSIDERED," the *Daily News* headlines rang out on July 10. Reporting a speech from the rally by a Mr. Lindley Spring, in column one, the paper clearly espoused its message that military despotism had all but enslaved the North: "When you submit to be seized by Provost Marshals and dragged off to the army, does that vindicate your rights, does it support or relieve the necessities of your wife and children? No; it more firmly rivets your chains."

Spring then linked the draft and abolition. "The [Conscription] act begins with a long and pious preamble, like all those Abolition things which commence with a text of Scripture . . . but it is a clear case of false pretenses." The essential fact, Spring charged, was that the administration believed "the negro is as good as the white man, and they intended to make him legally so." With the draft "they offer to buy up white men for three hundred dollars each, about one third of what a good negro is worth."

Incongruously, after this race-baiting, the speaker dutifully advised his listeners to "resist the draft in a proper and orderly manner, as become good citizens." They should raise money, hire a lawyer, and test the legality of the act in the state courts, thus suspending enforcement of the draft with the jurisdiction of the court. Failing this, they should petition Governor Seymour to defend their rights against "a slavery worse than death" imposed by the "abolition tyranny in Washington."

The next speaker, New Jersey congressman Chauncey Burr, drew laughter and applause when he declared of the draft, "This act is very simple—it is merely a highwayman's call on every American citizen for '$300 or your life.'" Acknowledging that a challenge in the courts would take time, Burr provided specific instructions on how to avoid the draft: "When you are seized, take out a writ of habeas corpus and the action of the United States officers must cease until that is decided. Should the State fail you, you can appeal to the Supreme Court of the United States. Leave no means untried to avoid compliance."

A violent edge then entered the speech. Burr declared he did not mind the term *Copperhead* since it was "a fair, brave snake, never meddling with you without you do with him, and then making himself feared and respected. But the black snake is a mean, sneaking fellow, who never dares to show his head when a Copperhead is around. (Applause.) They say we live by the clemency of the Government. Why, it is by your clemency that Abe Lincoln and all his satraps were not upon the gallows eighteen months ago. (Applause)."[5]

Caught in the awkward position of supporting an unpopular war measure, Greeley's *Tribune* mostly confined itself to publishing factual information about the draft and stressing that the provost marshals were being scrupulous in their collection and recording of names to ensure a fair process.[6]

Bennett's *Herald,* which declared itself independent of both political parties and espoused racist, anti-abolition views, nonetheless asserted that Chauncey Burr's speech went too far. Appealing to the "beastly passions" of the crowd, the speech was "calculated to stir up a moblike spirit in this city," the *Herald* warned. "If Mr. Burr is not careful he will raise a storm that will terminate in insurrection and bloody scenes in this city. When this mob spirit is once started no person can tell where it will end or who will be sacrificed by its vengeance." A "great lack of statesmanship" on the part of Democratic leaders had permitted "blustering revolutionists" like Burr to "lead the masses of the party," the *Herald* charged. Lacking a strong leader who might have "marked out the course for the party," the rank and file "are left to be preyed upon by unprincipled and designing men. Here rests one of the great dangers of the times, and it renders the speeches of such men as Burr all the more dangerous."[7]

"While the militia were thus absent from the city, and its forts and harbor unprotected," Governor Seymour wrote, the draft began on Saturday, July 11. "I was not advised of this step, and I believe the Mayor of the city was equally ignorant of the proceeding."[8] The day for beginning the random drawing of names of actual draftees had not been announced by the administration, and the secrecy surrounding the implementation of the draft aroused suspicion and resentment in Democratic circles, where it was assumed the quotas for New York and other heavily Democratic areas were set too high. The provost marshals, on the other hand, viewed the secrecy as necessary to forestall organized opposition, given New York City's lack of troops.

Not knowing that the draft was to begin that day, on July 11 Seymour sent his adjutant general, Major John Sprague, to Washington to seek an audience with President Lincoln and request that the draft in New York City be postponed until the militia regiments had returned from Pennsylvania. In a gesture of good faith to the administration, Seymour had selected Sprague, a federal officer, and asked Stanton to allow him a leave of absence so he could serve as the chief military aide to the governor. Seymour's attempt at transparency—bringing to his side an officer whose primary allegiance was to the Republican administration—backfired that weekend.[9]

Sprague went to Washington but never made the request of the president or of Stanton because he stopped first to see Provost Marshal General Fry, who ordered him not to make the request. Sprague later told Governor Seymour that he simply had no choice but to obey Fry, who held a higher rank in the U.S. Army. "The Governor simply waved him out of the office accompanied by a look which expressed volumes," recalled Major William Kidd, the governor's military secretary.

From then on, Seymour communicated with Sprague only through an intermediary. The episode, wrote Kidd, confirmed the darkest suspicions in the Democratic camp that Fry pushed ahead with the draft in New York precisely because he wanted to provoke a riot in the defenseless city: The rebellion would provide an excuse to impose martial law and use federal troops both to supervise and to manipulate the upcoming presidential election of 1864, when Lincoln's chances seemed slim.[10]

"There is a lurking mischief in the atmosphere that surrounds this unwelcome stranger," the *Daily News* declared of the draft on the morning of Saturday, July 11, when the drawing of names was scheduled to begin. The *Herald* complained that no information was available about when the draft would begin until the day before, and even then the government did not make a public announcement; the papers learned only that the provost marshal in each congressional district was instructed to begin the lottery "immediately."[11]

Provost Marshal General Fry did not have enough troops to contain rioting if it broke out in several districts at once, so he instructed his assistants

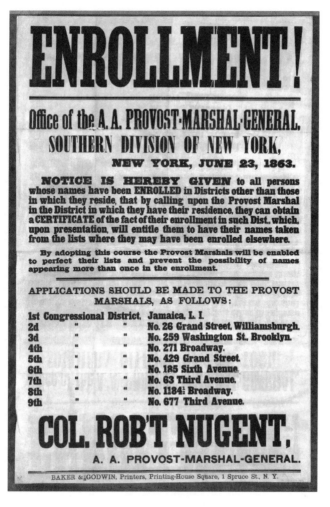

New York City enrollment poster

in various states to "collect what force you can in one designated disaffected district," enforce the draft, and then move the troops to another area of resistance, in the meantime proceeding with the lottery in any districts where there was no disturbance. Optimistically, if not recklessly, Fry's order assumed rebellion would confine itself to individual congressional districts—as drawn on a map—that could be pacified in sequence.[12]

Colonel Robert Nugent, in charge of the draft in New York City, knew as an Irishman the strong resentment that was brewing in the community and planned to start the lottery in the outlying districts of the city on Manhattan, and in Queens and Suffolk Counties on Long Island, to prevent civil disorder from engulfing the whole metropolitan area. While this plan avoided the slums at the lower end of Manhattan and the industrial areas of the East Side, from which protesters might emerge, it placed the first drawing at the

Colonel Robert Nugent

Ninth District draft office on Third Avenue at Forty-sixth Street—a less densely developed area at the northern edge of the city, which nonetheless contained many tenements and shanties full of hostile residents.[13]

The fully settled area of New York City in 1863 extended up to about Forty-seventh Street. Farther north, "the blocks were masses of rocks with squatter shanties perched here and there on the level spots," one resident recalled. "On Fifth Avenue at 45th Street were great cattle yards . . . Only the foundations of the Catholic Cathedral at 50th Street and 5th Avenue had been built . . . Much of Central Park was still unfinished. There were a few lines of street cars, but most of the travelling was done in stages, which started around the city hall and at Union Square turned in different directions."* The northern reaches of Manhattan also contained clusters of development far older than the rapidly expanding street grid, at villages such as Yorkville, on East 86th Street, and Harlem, on East 125th Street.[14]

---

*Stages, or stagecoaches, were horse-drawn conveyances that followed fixed routes. Starting in 1832, they were gradually replaced in New York by streetcars, which used horses to pull railroad coaches on rail tracks, producing a smoother ride and less strain on the horses.

Born in Ireland, Nugent was active in the Fenian Brotherhood, the main Irish nationalist organization formed in the aftermath of the Great Famine. Revolutionaries exiled after the Rising of 1848 established the group in New York City in 1854 and raised money to fulfill their dream of launching an armed rebellion to liberate Ireland from the British. They believed the Civil War would be a good training ground. Nugent had eagerly recruited troops for the Sixty-ninth Regiment of New York Volunteers. "YOUNG AMERICA AND OLD IRELAND ONE AND INSEPARABLE," declared the recruiting posters for the Sixty-ninth. "The COTTON-LORDS and TRAITOR-ALLIES of England Must Be Put Down!"[15]

At Fredricksburg, in December 1862, Nugent had led the Sixty-ninth in the doomed charge against Marye's Heights which decimated the regiment, and he was wounded by a rifle ball in the groin; his pistol shattered from the impact of another ball and saved his life. Transferred back home to recover, Nugent had become acting assistant provost marshal general in April.[16] "Colonel Nugent, the recent idol of the Irish, now Provost-Marshal, was cursed beyond measure," the *Evening Post* reported.[17]

Copperhead resistance could not be discounted either. Saturday began with a report to the police that the Knights of the Golden Circle were plotting to take over one of the arsenals in the city. Since the outbreak of the war, the Knights had been most active in the Midwest, especially Indiana, Illinois, and Iowa, recruiting northerners for the Confederate army, torching the homes of Union volunteers, and smuggling arms into Missouri for the proslavery guerrillas terrorizing that state.[18]

The Knights, a secret organization complete with handshakes and code words for recognizing fellow members, was founded in Cincinnati in 1854 by George Bickley, a quack from Virginia who traveled the country with a suitcase full of paraphernalia for mysterious rituals and established numerous lodges, or "Castles." By 1863, the Knights were said to have some three hundred thousand members, mostly in the Midwest, and it was an open secret that its leaders included outspoken Peace Democrats across the North: James McMasters and Fernando Wood of New York, and Clement Vallandigham and George Pendleton of Ohio.[19]*

Police superintendent John Kennedy sent fifteen men to guard the arsenal at Thirty-fifth Street and Seventh Avenue, but the attack never materialized. "Many stories have been circulated to the effect that bands, gangs and companies have been organized here and there with the intention of resisting the draft, and that the members are armed and drilled, hold secret meetings

---

*Vallandigham, deported to the South in May, had made his way to Canada and remained in contact with his supporters in Ohio and Copperhead groups throughout the Midwest.

and so forth," Greeley's *Tribune* reported calmly on July 11, "but from all that we can learn, no such organizations exist; and even if they did, they will amount to nothing."[20]

A crowd of about 150 people gathered at the Ninth District draft office, and the lottery began at 9 a.m. on Saturday. Superintendent John Kennedy "was on hand and had a large force of police in waiting," even though the department had received no request from Washington to help the provost marshals carry out the draft.[21]

Slips of paper, each "rolled tightly and bound with a ring of India-rubber," were placed in a cylindrical drum, rotated by a handle on the side in order to mix the names randomly. The *Daily News* dubbed it "the wheel of misfortune." A blindfolded clerk pulled the name of the first man "fated to shoulder the musket": William Jones, Forty-ninth Street, near Tenth Avenue. A "suppressed murmur" ran through the crowd inside the office. Then with "considerable merriment" people called out, "How are *you*?" "Poor Jones," and "Good for Jones."

The lottery proceeded peacefully, the *Herald* reported. "The people seemed to take it in more of a jocular than serious mood." When people recognized a name drawn from the wheel, they shouted, "How are you, Brady?" or "How are you, Jones?" followed by "Goodbye, Patrick," or "Goodbye, James." Everything went smoothly, and by 4 p.m. about half of the 2,500-man quota for the district had been drafted. The office closed, and the draft was set to resume on Monday, July 13, at 9 a.m.[22]

The draft had also begun peacefully in Boston, Providence, New Haven, and Pittsburgh, among other cities. The *New Haven Journal* noted that the announcement of the draft and "explanation of the process" had helped relieve much of the public's "rising anxiety." The fact that enrollment officers and provost marshals, blacks and whites, rich and poor, were all "so fortunate as to draw a prize" at the lottery argued for the fairness of the draft and promoted calm among the "very anxious and deeply interested" audience at the draft office, the *Pittsburgh Gazette* reported.

However, the *Providence Journal* pointed out that workingmen who could not afford the three-hundred-dollar exemption would be the ones to actually serve, and their families would immediately become charity cases. "The families of such should be provided for at public expense, and the sooner steps are taken to do this the more cheerfully will men of this class take their places in the ranks, knowing that their wives and little ones will be cared for during their absence," the paper declared. A soldier's pay would "little more than pay the rent of a small tenement."[23]

•   •   •

By Saturday evening, "there was intense excitement in the neighborhood" around the Ninth District draft office in New York, the *Herald* reported. The residents showed a "general determination to resist the law" and viewed anyone who favored the draft as "an enemy of the people." The spirit of defiance "ripened on Sunday," after the *Herald* printed the twelve hundred names drawn in the lottery and people abandoned their churchgoing routines to pore over the list. Angry discussions all over the city focused on "how the rich (made so by a war they sought to make perpetual) were exempted on payment of a nominal amount, which the profits on a roll of shoddy or a few explosive muskets would realize."[24]

According to James Gilmore, Greeley's intermediary with Lincoln in 1862 and now a member of the *Tribune* editorial staff, "throngs of excited men began to crowd the hotels and barrooms" in the area around the Ninth District draft office and were egged on by Copperhead agitators. "Gathering in little knots, they denounced conscription, and openly talked of attacking the draft offices. Mingling among them were men in common, and in some instances shabby, clothing, but whose speech indicated cultivation, and whose hands showed them unused to labor. They advised concert of action, and the gathering of clubs, fence-rails, stones, rusty guns, and every variety of offensive weapon, to be secreted in convenient places, in readiness for a grand outbreak on the morrow."[25]

Like Gilmore, George Templeton Strong was convinced that Copperheads were plotting behind the scenes and fomenting a rebellion. He noted snobbishly in his diary on Sunday that the draft had begun: "*Demos* takes it good-naturedly thus far, but we shall have trouble before we are through . . . That soulless politician, Seymour, will make trouble if he dare. So will F'nandy Wood, Brooks, Marble, and other reptiles. May they only bring their traitorous necks within the cincture of a legal halter! This draft will be the *experimentum crucis* to decide whether we have a government among us."[26]*

The apparent calm of the previous day's lottery had already unraveled, and it dawned on many observers, including journalist Joel Tyler Headley, that starting the draft right before the Sabbath had been a serious mistake. As Headley pointed out, "To have the list of twelve hundred names that had been drawn read over and commented on all day by men who enlivened their discussion with copious draughts of bad whiskey, especially when most of those drawn were laboring-men or poor mechanics, who were unable to hire a substitute, was like applying fire to gunpowder."[27]

Workers gathered in pubs, churches, and on street corners on their one

---

*James Brooks owned the *Express,* which voiced the desire of many New York merchants for an armistice and negotiations to end the war.

day off. Opponents of the draft suddenly had a list of specific draftees around which to rally their disgruntled friends and families. Women too— wives facing imminent widowhood, and poor women generally—spent the day planning resistance for Monday morning and stockpiling a variety of weapons at numerous depots.[28] In a barroom on East Broadway, a former army captain stirred up enthusiastic support when he declared he would rather "blow his own brains out than shoulder the musket in defence of an abolition administration."[29]

Volunteer firemen were particularly angry about being drafted because they had long enjoyed exemption from militia service. In the case of one fire company, drafting its men soon proved to be more trouble than it was worth to the government. Peter Masterson was a building contractor and the foreman of volunteer Fire Engine Company No. 33, which included his brothers, John and William; after one of their men's names was drawn on Saturday, they resolved to do something about it.[30]

Housed near Fifty-eighth Street and Broadway, their engine and company were known as the "Black Joke," after an Albany sloop that saw distinguished service in the War of 1812, and the firemen were dubbed the "Black Jokers."[31] Masterson also started several other firehouses in different parts of the city. In the ten years since he had organized the Black Joke, Masterson had also served in the state legislature for two years, and as an alderman for four years, while rising politically within the citywide fire department, becoming an influential trustee of the Benevolent Fund.[32]

Masterson's was the second company of this name, the first Black Jokers having been disbanded by city authorities in 1843 for violent clashes with other engine companies and breaking department rules by marching in an election parade. This original group of forty firemen was known as "a pretty hard crowd," always ready for a fight. Two "gigantic Negroes," called "Black Jack" and "Black Joe," served as runners for the company and did chores around the firehouse but were not allowed to bunk there. The company described its engine as being painted a "nigger" black with a gold stripe running all the way around.[33]

In 1863, the twenty-four members of the reconstituted Black Joke occupied a spacious three-story brick building with its own telegraph, which made them "the quickest company in the upper districts." They also had the city's first steam-powered fire engine, which the men grudgingly agreed was better than pumping the water by hand.[34] However, they were still "roughs," like their predecessors in the 1840s, ready for a "muss" at the slightest provocation from a rival fire company—or a graver summons from the federal

Peter Masterson

government.[35] They met on Sunday and, with Masterson's approval, vowed to destroy the draft office with the records containing their fellow fireman's name.[36]

On Sunday night, an undercover detective telegraphed the police Central Office that he was tailing a Copperhead soapbox orator named John Andrews who was stirring up crowds on the Lower East Side with denunciations of blacks as well as the draft. A lawyer from Virginia who frequented the haunts of New York's thieves and prostitutes, Andrews had become a familiar figure to the police during his four years in the city. Superintendent Kennedy apparently did not regard Andrews as a serious threat, and the police lost track of him later that night.[37]

The police and federal authorities remained confident that they could handle any eruption of violence. Kennedy was content to assign a sergeant and twelve men to each of the six draft offices for Monday morning, a routine step called for by the expected presence of any crowd.[38] Police captain George W. Walling, who stayed at his Upper West Side station house that night, was the exception: "For my part, I had for several days noticed with great uneasiness the growing discontent among certain classes," he recalled. "Things, I thought, were coming to a head."[39]

Democratic newspapers were busy preparing their Monday morning editorials and going to press Sunday night. These were the editorials Horace Greeley later branded "The Torch that Lit the Flame." Manton Marble's *World* likened Congress to "an oligarchic conspiracy plotting a vast scheme of military servitude" and asserted that the Conscription Act was so oppressive it "could not have been ventured upon in England even in those dark days when the press-gang filled English ships-of-war with slaves, and dimmed the glory of England's noblest naval heroes."[40]

Fernando and Benjamin Wood's *Daily News* denounced "the Inquisition Conscription," charging that the "miscreants at the head of the Government" were using the draft "to kill off" Democratic voters, enfranchise blacks, and remain in power for another four years. "It is a strange perversion of the laws of self-preservation which would compel the white laborer to leave his family destitute and unprotected while he goes forth to free the negro, who, being free, will compete with him in labor . . . Let the laboring population assemble peaceably in mass meeting and express their views upon the subject . . . Let them make it a necessity with the Administration to give up its insane Emancipation scheme. Let them insist that in place of the conscription of white men to serve blacks, we shall have negotiation, compromise, and peace."[41]

Rumors of riot were whispered throughout the city and suburbs. "Hints to be careful had come to various private persons during the previous week from servants and others who had a favor for them," according to the *Evening Post.* "As far off as Yonkers, a gentleman who is connected with the order and law-sustaining wing of the city press, received such an intimation from his Irish cook."[42] At about 3 a.m. on Monday, the *Tribune's* managing editor, Sidney Gay, finished work and left the newspaper's offices at Spruce and Nassau Streets. When he got on the streetcar to head uptown, the driver greeted him: "Stirrin' times, sir. Fa'th an' ye'll have something to talk about to-morrow."

"How so? What do you mean?"

"Nothing; only a mob will resist the draft to-morrow, and New York will see the biggest riot in history."[43]

CHAPTER 8

"Down with the Rich Men!": The New York City Draft Riots Begin

~⟋

Mrs. Hilton said she never saw such creatures, such gaunt-looking savage men and women and even little children armed with brickbats, stones, pokers, shovels and tongs, coal-scuttles, and even tin pans and bits of iron," Maria Daly wrote of her friend, whose husband was also a judge. "They passed her house about four o'clock on Monday morning and continued on in a constant stream until nine o'clock. They looked to her, she said, like Germans, and her first thought was that it was some German festival."[1] Such was the confusion of an upper-class New York woman when the city's mostly Irish poor took the unusual step of leaving the slums and marching northward through the finest neighborhoods, that she mistook them for revelers.

By 6 a.m., when workers usually started their twelve-hour day at factories, shipyards, railroads, and other industries, small groups coming up from the southern end of the island had gathered at several points on the west side and traveled north along Eighth and Ninth Avenues. On the East River waterfront, "some fifty rough and rowdyish-looking fellows were observed . . . prowling along the wharves and picking up recruits," the *Evening Post* reported. From the squatters' shacks crowding the city's open lots, and the slums the police called "Mackerelville," new marchers quickly swelled their ranks, and crowds of women trailed behind them.*

"They went on gaining insolence by increase of numbers,

---

*Mackerelville stretched from Tenth to Fourteenth Street between Second Avenue and the East River.

until they began to enter the iron-foundries and other places of manual labor," the *Evening Post* recalled disapprovingly, "and by persuasion and threats, induced the workmen to join them. So they swelled and rolled on."[2] The crowds that gathered to protest the draft on Monday morning were imposing their own form of conscription.[3] They soon enforced a work stoppage—a citywide labor strike that included street crews and other laborers on public works.[4] Some rioters would later plead innocence on the grounds that they had been coerced.[5]

James Jackson was standing in the yard of his iron foundry on the corner of Second Avenue and Twenty-eighth Street, when an employee alerted him to the mob of a hundred men and boys, armed with stones, sticks, and clubs, "hallowing and hooting and making a noise" in front of the factory. Jackson allowed four or five men, including cartman Thomas Fitzsimmons, into the lobby of the building, where they said they "did not wish to injure Mr. Jackson," but demanded that he close the shop until the next day so the workers could help protest the draft. The men "intimated that unless he did so his men would be forced to stop work," one of Jackson's clerks recalled. Some of the employees stopped working immediately, the mob moved on to another factory, and Jackson closed the ironworks within a few hours.[6]

The crowds of striking workers mingled with the unemployed and converged on a large vacant lot just east of Central Park and north of Fifty-ninth Street, pouring into it like "living streams," journalist Joel Tyler Headley wrote.[7] A motley crew of leaders emerged to direct the crowds. Among them were John Andrews, the lawyer from Virginia tailed by the police the previous night; Francis Cusick, an Irish-born stage driver and former policeman; James Whitten, a barber at the Astor House hotel; and Irish workingmen like Patrick Merry, a cellar digger, Patrick Canary, a stonemason, and Henry Wade, a boilermaker. Some Germans were in the crowds too, led by Adam Chairman, an escaped convict, and Andrew Smith, among others. Henry Tilton, an English-born grocer and gardener, was also identified by witnesses as a "ringleader."[8]

After listening to several speeches, many marchers, like Thomas Fitzsimmons and his group, who wanted a one-day strike, not a crime spree, broke away from the mob.[9] The leaders conferred momentarily at 8 a.m., and then the mob, carrying placards painted simply with the words *NO DRAFT,* set off down Fifth and Sixth Avenues in two columns, which joined after both turned east onto Forty-seventh Street and "heaved tumultuously toward Third Avenue," Headley wrote. The mob consisted of perhaps ten thousand people, he calculated, given that "it filled the broad street from curbstone to curbstone and was moving rapidly" but still "took between twenty and twenty-five minutes . . . to pass a single point."[10]

The mob's target was the Ninth District draft office, a four-story brick building at Forty-sixth and Third, but some men stopped to cut down telegraph poles with axes stolen from a hardware store, while women pulled up the Fourth Avenue railroad tracks with crowbars. The loss of the poles and tracks threatened to cut off not only the links between the police Central Office and the precincts, established by Mayor Wood in the mid-1850s, but the city's communication with its suburbs and the rest of the country.[11]

Throughout the morning, the mayor and police reacted with a series of small deployments that were rapidly swept aside by the gathering mobs. Robert Nugent, the federal official in charge of the draft in the city, had only seventy soldiers attached to his office, and his attempt to coordinate with the police and military came too late to be effective.

At about 7:30 a.m. on Monday, Nugent "received intelligence that opposition was to be made" to the draft in the Ninth District. He sent twenty-five troops there and twenty-five more to the state arsenal at Seventh Avenue and Thirty-fifth Street, in case of trouble at the nearby Eighth District draft office. The remaining twenty men at Nugent's disposal from the army's Invalid Corps—a unit composed of convalescents like himself who were unfit for much more than garrison duty—stood by in their barracks as reinforcements.

According to Nugent, he then went in person to the heads of the police, the army, and the state militia in the city, who promised to send reinforcements to the draft offices and to Nugent's headquarters. On second thought, the commanders, along with Nugent, agreed that both state and federal troops should be sent to the state arsenal. From there, Nugent wrote, "they might be dispatched to any section where they would be most needed, besides protecting the large amount of arms . . . which, once in the hands of the mob, would have rendered them perfectly uncontrollable."[12]

As law and order broke down, between 8 and 9 a.m., James Crowley, the superintendent of the police telegraph system, began to convey the magnitude of the problem to headquarters. He was on his way downtown when the mob stopped the Third Avenue streetcar he was riding, forced the passengers out, and pushed the car off the track. Crowley noticed the severed telegraph wires in the gutter and gathered them up.

"He is one of the damned operators," the rioters shouted, while Crowley proceeded to coil the wires around a lamppost and ground them, keeping them functional. "Smash him, kill him!" the rioters chanted as they closed in. "Only getting the wires out of your way, boys," Crowley answered, as he slipped away and hurried to a station house at Thirty-fifth Street, where he telegraphed the Central Office.[13]

With Crowley's alarm, the seriousness of the situation began to dawn on Superintendent Kennedy, but he still did not send enough men. A detail of about sixty Metropolitans was dispatched from the East Fifty-ninth Street station house, and they joined the dozen officers inside the draft office on Third Avenue at Forty-sixth Street. Kennedy also dispatched almost seventy men to the draft office on Broadway at Twenty-ninth Street, where another mob had gathered.[14]

At 9 a.m., deluged with telegrams warning of trouble around the city, Kennedy telegraphed all of his police stations, including those in Brooklyn, ordering them to call in their reserves and stand by. Thanks to Crowley's efforts, Kennedy had just enough time to contact Manhattan's upper precincts before rioters knocked out the lines.[15]

Later, Kennedy ordered other detachments to converge on the draft office at Forty-sixth and Third, including the squad at Broadway and Twenty-ninth, which had scattered the mob there, allowing the draft to proceed. Then, out of uniform, and armed only with a bamboo cane, Kennedy set off from headquarters in a buggy to inspect the scene himself. After visiting the arsenal on Thirty-fifth Street and Seventh Avenue, he had his driver take him close enough to Forty-sixth and Third that he could approach the draft office on foot.[16]

The weather that morning was a "deadly muggy sort with a muddy sky and lifeless air," wrote George Templeton Strong, who went up to the Ninth District draft office to see the disturbance.[17] Third Avenue for several blocks north and south of Forty-sixth Street was a scene of mounting chaos, fueled by alcohol from nearby bars, which did a brisk business.[18] The core of the mob "was concealed by an outside layer of ordinary peaceable lookers-on," but Strong, with unabashed bigotry, calculated that inside there were between five hundred and a thousand of "the lowest Irish day laborers . . . Every brute in the drove was pure Celtic—hod-carrier or loafer."[19]

"Let's go in boys, stick together and we can lick all the damn police in the city," declared Francis Cusick. Then he recognized the superintendent. "Here comes the son of a bitch Kennedy, let's finish him," shouted Cusick, who struck the superintendent on the chest and shoulder with a large wooden club, knocking him to the sidewalk. Turning to Kennedy's driver, Cusick shouted, "You son of a bitch, I've got you now, and I'll finish you," before beating him unconscious and stealing his coat, pants, pistol, and cash. A third officer, a clerk from headquarters, was also attacked when the mob closed in.

Only of medium height and slim except for his broad shoulders, the sixty-year-old Kennedy was quickly dragged to an embankment and thrown over the side into muddy water on a vacant lot below. He managed to rise, only to be struck down again, kicked, and pummeled. Then he recognized an old acquaintance in the crowd, a Democratic politician from that ward. "John Eagan, save my life!" Kennedy cried out. Eagan stepped in and convinced the mob that Kennedy was dead or would be soon. Kennedy's clerk and driver had recovered enough to flag down a wagon, stretch their chief out in it, and head down to the police Central Office, at 300 Mulberry Street, near Bleecker.[20]*

According to the disdainful *Evening Post*, the rioters became ecstatic as rumor spread that the hated Republican superintendent of the Metropolitans was dead. "A sort of war-dance was improvised on the spot and cudgels and curses and heels flew in an ungovernable 'shindig.'"[21]

Mayor George Opdyke arrived at his City Hall office at 9:45 and proceeded to duplicate Nugent's efforts, but with far greater hesitation. Opdyke soon received a report which convinced him that "a serious riot was in progress." However, the state's Metropolitan Police Act of 1857 had deprived the mayor of control over the police. That power, along with the authority to call out the militia, had been transferred to the five-member Metropolitan Police Commission—appointed by the state—which in turn appointed the police superintendent. Since the mayors of New York and Brooklyn were given merely ceremonial roles, the commission was dominated by Thomas Acton, the president, and his two Republican colleagues. So at 10 a.m. Opdyke sent a note to Acton.

Opdyke also contacted Major General Charles Sandford of the state militia and Major General John Wool of the U.S. Army. Apparently hoping that the police would get the riot under control by themselves, the mayor merely asked Wool to hold federal troops "in readiness" and described the developments uptown as "demonstrations" that might get out of hand. However, Sandford arrived at the mayor's office at 10:15 with a report that the police uptown were overwhelmed by the size of the mobs. Opdyke had not yet heard from Commissioner Acton but learned from Sandford that the State Militia Act empowered the mayor to "order out the military" in the event of a riot. Opdyke immediately gave Sandford an order declaring that "a riot exists" and telling him to "suppress it without delay."

---

*Kennedy was born and raised in Maryland, a slave state, and was "an old-fashioned Jacksonian Democrat," according to Thomas Acton, so he knew Eagan and other Tammany figures personally. However, Kennedy publicly opposed slavery and the extreme views on states' rights espoused by Senator John Calhoun of South Carolina.

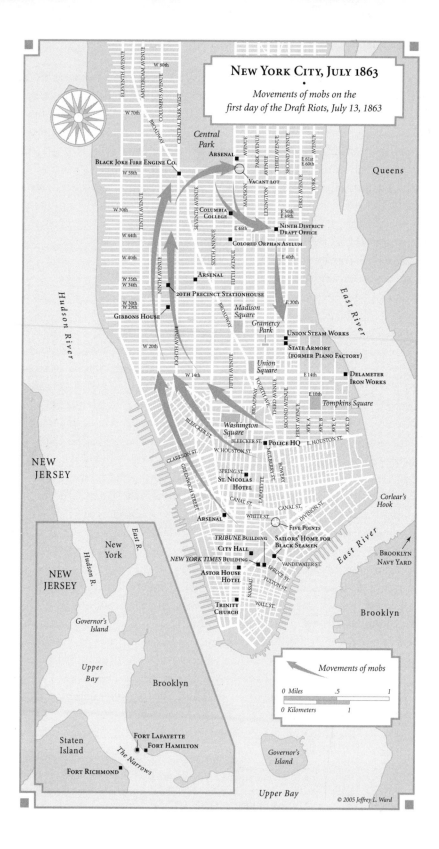

NEW YORK CITY, JULY 1863

•

*Movements of mobs on the
first day of the Draft Riots, July 13, 1863*

Even this was too little, too late. Half the morning had slipped away, and Sandford had a relatively small force at his disposal. Opdyke also worried that some of those militiamen "might, from the semi-political character of the riot, sympathize with the mob," leaving the city with "military strength altogether inadequate for the emergency."[22] As a Republican, Opdyke was particularly anxious to avoid inflaming the situation with a harsh response, since he had to work with the leaders of the city's Democratic majority every day.[23] Like many Republicans, Joseph Choate, a lawyer and a cousin of the Gibbons family, was disgusted by the mayor's handling of the crisis. "We were in a very bad way at the outset," Choate scoffed. "Mayor Opdyke has no power and no pluck to use it if he had."[24]

With an orderly crowd filling the draft office, Provost Marshal Charles Jenkins had set the lottery wheel in motion at the Forty-sixth Street draft office at 10 a.m., and in the next half hour a blindfolded clerk pulled about seventy-five names, which Jenkins read aloud. He recalled, "Everything went on quietly, and I began to hope that no attack would be made." Then Peter Masterson's Black Joke Engine Company arrived with its steam engine and the men dressed in their firefighting gear. A pistol shot rang out like a starting gun, a hail of paving stones crashed through the draft office windows, and the firemen, supported by the crowd, surged forward.

Shouting "Down with the rich men!" the crowd stormed the draft office, setting it on fire and severely injuring several enrolling officers with clubs. "I stepped forward," Jenkins reported, "but was borne back by the mass, and pushed through the back door into the back yard, and took refuge in the next building." Without resorting to their guns, the Metropolitans fought off the rioters, enabling a federal marshal to lock the enrollment records in an iron safe that the rioters were unable to open or remove from the burning building.[25]

While the bruised and battered policemen escaped from the burning draft office, and the fire spread to other buildings on that block, the mob outside hurled rocks and paving stones at Nugent's fifty convalescent soldiers from the Invalid Corps who had belatedly converged on the scene. A round of blank cartridges did nothing to frighten the mob, so some of the soldiers, panicked and without orders, fired musket balls, which killed or wounded several rioters. Without time to reload, the soldiers were quickly disarmed by the enraged mob, which clubbed two of them to death with their own guns and chased a third to a rocky ledge near the East River and threw him off before dropping boulders on his lifeless body. These first casualties of the draft riots had barely survived the carnage of Civil War battlefields, only to meet their deaths on the Union home front.[26]

Most of the Invalid Corps troops, however, escaped with varying degrees of injury. John Alcock was chased along Fortieth Street toward Second

Avenue, where the mob "took his musket from his hands, and struck him with their fists, with stones, and with sticks, knocking him down, fracturing his skull, and breaking his left arm, and bruising his left side." Prone on the sidewalk, Alcock was kicked by Daniel Conroy, a forty-six-year-old laborer, and Thomas Kiernan, forty, a contractor, both Irish-born residents of the immediate area, who left him bleeding on the sidewalk.

Thomas Maguire, another Irish American, had Alcock carried into his store until the soldier could be evacuated to a hospital. When a few relentless rioters entered and clubbed Alcock on the head, Maguire hid him in the basement, covered in hay, and brought in a doctor to dress his wounds, which had "bled profusely." The police later rescued Alcock with a carriage.[27]

Soon a second phase of the riots began to unfold, as political protest combined with sabotage of government targets gave way to street crime and looting; attacks on individuals and private property were suddenly tempting in the chaotic atmosphere. On Lexington Avenue just below Forty-fifth Street, the rioters had set their sights on several three-story houses and were throwing cobblestones through the front windows while women and children fled out the back doors. "Then men and small boys appeared at rear windows and began smashing the sashes and blinds and shied out light articles, such as books and crockery, and dropped chairs and mirrors into the back yard," Strong wrote. "The rear fence was demolished and the loafers were seen marching off with portable articles of furniture. And at last a light smoke began to float out of the windows . . . The fury of the low Irish women in that region was noteworthy. Stalwart young vixens and withered old hags were swarming everywhere, all cursing the 'bloody draft' and egging on their men to mischief."[28]

At 11:30 the six draft offices around the city received orders from Nugent to suspend work and transfer their records to Governors Island to keep them out of the clutches of the mob. Nugent also emptied his headquarters of all papers, weapons, and equipment, he wrote, "as the mob had threatened not only to hang me but destroy the building also."[29]

Most of the mob surged down Third Avenue, preventing the various reinforcements sent by Kennedy from ever reaching the draft office at Forty-sixth Street. The Metropolitans coming up from the Broadway draft office clashed with the mob at Forty-fourth Street but were outnumbered and forced to retreat. Two more police detachments were similarly beaten in rapid succession and fell back, dragging their fallen comrades with them.

Sergeant Robert McCredie, known as "Fighting Mac," arrived with a fourth squad and was soon joined by a fifth. With fewer than fifty men—those

from all five squads who had not yet been wounded—McCredie turned the
tide and drove the rioters up to Forty-fifth Street. However, they turned out
to be just the vanguard of the mob, and its full weight suddenly pressed forward down Third Avenue while more rioters poured in from the side streets,
engulfing the police and scattering them southward again.

All of them were injured; McCredie was chased up the stoop of a building and, in the process of being beaten, rammed through the wooden panels
of the front door. He managed to reach the second floor, where a German
woman concealed him under a mattress and told his pursuers that he had fled
through the window. When the mob torched the building, the woman carried McCredie on her back all the way to Lexington Avenue, where a cab
took him to a police station. She had saved his life, but the mob had disabled
one of the department's most effective officers.[30]

While the police were battling the rioters on Third Avenue, clusters of
men, women, and children from the city's slums filtered northward and
looted hungrily, with few policemen to stop them.[31] Set in motion by the
draft and Democratic denunciations of excessive federal and state power, the
metaphor of class warfare—exploited for decades by Democrats like Fernando Wood and Isaiah Rynders to garner immigrant votes—had become a
literal, violent eruption, far bigger than any they had provoked before.

When the feed wagon carrying Superintendent Kennedy arrived at the Central Office, Thomas Acton, president of the police commission, happened to
be out front. "Around to the station," he ordered the driver, assuming the
bruised and mud-covered figure under the burlap sacks was a rioter and
should be locked up. When the driver told him it was Kennedy, Acton
seethed with anger. Kennedy was brought inside, where a surgeon determined that no bones were broken, and that he could recover at a friend's
home instead of in the hospital.[32]

Following the law, the Metropolitan police commissioners, who had
originally appointed Kennedy, stepped in to do his job. One of the three Republican commissioners had gone to the front as a brigadier general of volunteers, and the second, who lived in Brooklyn, managed the riots there and
on Staten Island, while Acton took charge in Manhattan.[33] "Of a nervous
temperament, he was quick and prompt, yet cool and decided, and relentless
as death in the discharge of his duty," Headley wrote reverently of Acton.
"Holding the views of the first Napoleon respecting mobs, he did not believe
in speechmaking to them. His addresses were to be locust clubs and grapeshot."[34] A stockbroker, prominent Republican, and founding member of
the city's Union League Club, Acton was an unconditional supporter of the

Lincoln administration's policies aimed at suppressing dissent and winning the war.[35]

Most immediate was the problem of the mob's growing strength and cohesion, and apparent intent to cripple if not destroy the city, starting with the communications and transportation infrastructure. Instead of confronting the rioters wherever they roamed and spreading his forces thin, Acton decided to concentrate his reserves—about a thousand men, he hoped—and deploy them rapidly to critical flash points.

Before any telegraph lines were cut, Kennedy had ordered off-duty policemen in all thirty-two precincts to muster at their station houses, so Acton, after dispatching available officers to trouble spots, telegraphed the precincts below Sixtieth Street that could still be reached by wire, summoning their reserves to the Central Office on Mulberry Street.[36] Of the department's sixteen hundred patrolmen, almost half were left to protect Brooklyn, Westchester, and Staten Island, while others were unreachable, and a few were kept on guard at each of the station houses. Thus Acton could deploy no more than about eight hundred men at a time, including some fifty officers already at headquarters and in the adjacent precincts.[37]

Acton knew he would have to leave large areas of the city without protection, a risk he deemed necessary. At the same time, he asked Mayor Opdyke to request the mobilization of the state militia and have federal troops brought in from the harbor forts. Acton also sent plainclothes detectives to mix with the crowds and predict their movements.[38]

Around the city, scenes unfolded that revealed the chasm between New York's social classes—and how deeply the antidraft rioters craved equal treatment at a time when the poor lacked the most basic amenities. "Turn out; turn out by six o'clock, or we'll burn you in your beds!" a rioter shouted from the basement of St. Luke's Hospital at Fifth Avenue and Fifty-fifth Street, threatening some one hundred sick and wounded soldiers. The "huge, hatless laborer, with his sleeves rolled up to the armpits, bare-breasted, red with liquor and rage, strode up and down the hall," according to Eliza Woolsey Howland, who served beside her sisters as a nurse caring for Union troops.

"But a wounded rioter (shot, with a brick-bat in his hand), was about this time brought by a crowd to the hospital door, promptly admitted, and kindly cared for" by the Reverend Dr. William Muhlenberg, the founder and director of the charitable hospital. An "elderly man . . . with a noble face, white hair and wonderful dark eyes," Muhlenberg then left the rioter's bedside and went outside to speak with the mob. Explaining that his hospital was open to anyone who needed treatment, he asked if they would still "threaten this house with fire and storm."

The crowd responded with shouts of "No, no; long live St. Luke's," and established a "vigilance committee" to defend the hospital. "As he braved alone that howling mob of men and women, and by his personal magnetism quieted their rage," Howland wrote, "it was like the picture of the working of a miracle by a mediaeval saint."[39]

"It was now noon, but the hot July sun was obscured by heavy clouds, that hung in ominous shadows over the city," Headley wrote, "while from near Cooper Institute to Forty-Sixth Street, or about thirty blocks, [Third Avenue] was black with human beings,—house-tops, windows, and stoops all filled with rioters or spectators. Dividing it like a stream, horse-cars arrested in their course lay strung along as far as the eye could reach. As the glance ran along this mighty mass of men and women north, it rested at length on huge columns of smoke rolling heavenward from burning buildings."[40] Of the estimated fifty thousand people on Third Avenue, most were spectators, but about ten thousand were actively rioting. Of the latter, several thousand prevented the fire department's chief engineer, John Decker, and his men from getting near the draft office with their equipment, despite the fact that poor, mostly German families lived in the upper stories and adjacent buildings.[41]

While these women and children fled the blaze and lost their belongings, John Andrews, the Copperhead lawyer from Virginia briefly tailed by the police the night before, kept the crowd stirred up with a harangue against the draft.[42] " 'You must organize, boys.' (Cries of 'That's the talk,' 'You're the boy, my chicken,' &c.) 'You must organize and keep together, and appoint leaders, and crush this damned abolition draft into the dust.' (Tremendous cheering.) . . . 'If you don't find any one to lead you, by Heaven! I will do it myself.' (Great sensation and applause.)" Many in the crowd wondered who the speaker was, and when someone said it was Ben Wood, Andrews was cheered even more enthusiastically.[43]

At about 12:30, when chief engineer Decker managed to address the rioters, he expressed sympathy with their objections to the draft but pleaded with them to step aside and let him save the property of residents who had nothing to do with it. Hoping to contain the mayhem he had sparked, Black Joke foreman Peter Masterson supported Decker's appeal, and the cheering crowd parted momentarily, but a more aggressive mob returned to the scene and kept the firefighters back.[44] When the crowd shifted its attention to plundering stores and homes, the fire engines were put to use, but almost the entire block was consumed.[45]

While Decker was trying to soothe the mob uptown, James Whitten, a barber at the Astor House hotel downtown, spent his lunch break stirring up a crowd of almost five hundred people armed with clubs and stones gathered in front of the *Tribune* building on Printing House Square, across Park Row from City Hall. A *Tribune* employee peering from a second-floor window said Whitten was dressed in a Panama hat and light-colored coat and "called for Horace Greeley to show himself; that he was a G[o]d d[amne]d scoundrel, a d[amne]d Abolitionist, and that if he would come down he would take his life, or take his heart out." Led by Whitten, the crowd alternated cheers for the *Caucasian* (a Copperhead paper with offices nearby), groans for the *Tribune*, cheers for McClellan, and groans for the *Times*.

At the Astor House, Whitten's coworkers and customers were used to hearing him "talk treason in the barber-shop." In early July, when the Confederates were at Gettysburg, a soldier being shaved in the next chair had heard Whitten declare "he was in hopes he would shave Jeff. Davis in New-York within 60 days; also, that Harrisburg would be taken, Baltimore next; that the railroad would be torn up by Lee's cavalry at Annapolis Junction, at the Relay House; that a corps of the Rebel army was going to cross Virginia by way of the Occoquan, to blockade the Potomac River; that Washington would surrender without a battle, and that peace would be dictated to the North in two months."

After an hour of rallying the mob in Printing House Square, Whitten returned to work at the Astor House, where he denounced the draft's three-hundred-dollar exemption clause and tried to enlist all the waiters for a planned attack on the *Tribune* that evening. "Whitten came to me and seemed to be well posted on the movements of the mob," one of the headwaiters recalled. Whitten told him that if the waiters "did not turn out and help they would get their own heads broke, as the mob would be the strongest party." The newspaper dealer at the hotel's front entrance also received a warning from Whitten "to shut up, as the mob would very soon be down and it would not be safe to keep open."[46]

The uptown mob had continued to grow as it surged southward on Third Avenue from Forty-sixth Street, picking up new members from smaller groups that had been dispersed by the police in other parts of the city. Clusters of people from the various slums "where the low Irish dwelt," according to Headley, continued to appear on almost every street corner, lured by the news of looting.[47] Having routed five squads of Metropolitans, the main mass of about ten thousand rioters had continued south to Thirty-fifth Street, where smaller groups pillaged the side streets while the mob paused and selected its next major target. "To the armory! To the armory," shouted the rioters.[48]

It was widely known that Mayor Opdyke and his son-in-law owned a warehouse on the northeast corner of Second Avenue and Twenty-first Street, a former piano factory, of which the top three floors contained the state armory.[49] The local precinct commander had already sent some policemen to guard the five hundred guns and stores of ammunition.[50] Just one block north stood the Union Steam Works, which had been converted to manufacture army carbines and contained more than four thousand of the short rifles.[51] A small police guard had arrived there too.

When an attack on the state armory appeared imminent, thirty-two men from the elite "Broadway Squad" were assigned there and equipped with carbines as well as their pistols and locust clubs. The squad was based in the Central Office precinct, and its men were picked for their height and strength.[52] Aware of the policemen inside, the crowd of several thousand rioters hesitated at the doors of the armory. Then, just after 1 p.m., having failed to set fire to the large brick building, the rioters pelted the windows and doors with rocks and gunfire. When several rioters charged and began breaking down the doors, the policemen shot them dead with their revolvers. As the standoff continued, the sergeant in charge succeeded in calling for reinforcements, but the precinct commander had none to send.[53]

The mob seemed to be steadily gaining the upper hand. Several thousand more rioters, who had stayed behind at Forty-sixth and Third to listen to Andrews, then swept down to Allerton's Bull's Head Hotel on Forty-third Street near Lexington Avenue, where the American Telegraph Company kept an office. Apparently targeting the city's communications nodes, a few leaders chopped their way into the hotel lobby with axes, enabling the mob to sack the interior, douse it with turpentine, and set it on fire. While the hotel burned, other rioters were tearing up the tracks of the New Haven Railroad on Fourth Avenue from Forty-second to Forty-sixth Street.[54]

At City Hall, Mayor Opdyke attempted to confer with the Board of Aldermen on a plan to restore order in the city, but only six of the twenty-four members arrived for the meeting. The Tammany politicians were reluctant to crack down on their riotous constituents, some of whom were demonstrating noisily right outside. Former alderman William Tweed, now a county supervisor, took it upon himself to locate other members of the Board of Aldermen and get them to cooperate with the mayor.

After his stint as one of the Common Council's "Forty Thieves" in 1852–53, Tweed had spent a term in the House of Representatives but then decided local politics was far more exciting—and lucrative. He was elected to the twelve-man New York County Board of Supervisors in 1858 and within a year had bribed enough of the six Republican members to keep the Democrats in control.* He divided the remaining profits from padded contracts approved by the board with cooperative colleagues. In 1861, Tweed also became the deputy street commissioner, which enabled him to dispense hundreds of jobs to his constituents. Six months before the draft riots, in January 1863, Tammany Hall had acknowledged Tweed's growing power by electing him chairman of its general committee.[55]

Despite Tweed's help, Opdyke had made little progress with the aldermen and adjourned the meeting at 1:30 p.m.[56] The Board of Aldermen then met for a special session but, lacking a quorum, could do little but listen to a speech by Alderman Terence Farley, a Democrat, who lamented that the riot would "affect the reputation of the city, and possibly be a pretext for the declaration of martial law here. It affords the excuse probably desired by the [Lincoln] Administration, for supplanting the civil by the military law in this Democratic City."[57]

At about 2 p.m., Mayor Opdyke telegrammed Secretary of War Stanton in Washington but did not yet ask for intervention by federal troops beyond those already in the city and the harbor forts. Similarly, in a message to Governor Seymour, he merely asked for state troops from the surrounding areas, not as many as had been sent to Gettysburg. With the help of General Wool, he deployed the available U.S. Army troops to protect federal offices like the Customs House and the Post Office as well as state arsenals. For the moment, the mayor was operating on the model of deadly, smaller disturbances in the past, like the Astor Place riot of 1849 and labor protests during the Panic of 1857.[58]

The mayor's caution was compounded by General Sandford's inaction. Opdyke and Acton had asked Sandford to call out the state militia in the city, and the troops were mustered early Monday morning in the arsenals at Seventh Avenue and Thirty-fifth Street, in Central Park at Sixty-first Street and Fifth Avenue, and downtown at White and Elm Streets.† However, Sandford,

---

*The Board of Supervisors was a legislative body for the county and city, with functions that overlapped those of city officials. The supervisors, who were supposed to discourage graft among the oldermen, indulged in corruption themselves.

†The arsenal in Central Park is now the headquarters of the Parks Department. See the Walking Tour in the appendix.

George Opdyke

who had handled the mob so aggressively at Astor Place some fifteen years earlier, remained almost oblivious to the events unfolding outside, dismissing every report of rioting as exaggeration—while overestimating the danger to the arsenals and fussing over their defenses.

Sandford, after nearly thirty years as commander, displayed a bureaucratic circumspection, exacerbated by telegrams from the state adjutant general, John Sprague, warning him to guard the arsenals.[59] Moreover, since Sandford commanded state troops, he technically reported to the governor, and his reluctance to move forcefully against the rioters suggested a desire to keep in step with Seymour and other Democratic politicians.[60]

By about 2 p.m., as the situation deteriorated, Opdyke's requests for military aid became increasingly urgent. General Wool responded by calling in marines from the navy yard in Brooklyn along with troops and artillery from the forts and vessels in the harbor, collecting them on a gunboat dispatched from Governors Island. Using his authority as commander of the army's Department of the East, Wool also helped the mayor appeal for aid to the governors of New Jersey, Connecticut, and Rhode Island in addition to local officials in cities across New York State.[61]

Seventy-five years old, Wool had served competently in three wars but, like Sandford, had outlived his usefulness as a commander, and his battlefield experience helped little in the unfamiliar arena of urban crowd control. In poor health and overwhelmed, Wool declared Sandford to be in charge of all the forces—both state and federal—available to put down the riot. This placed Wool's deputy, Brigadier General Harvey Brown, commander of the military post of the city and harbor of New York, under Sandford's command.

Brown, however, took matters into his own hands. A graduate of West Point and a veteran of the Mexican War, Brown had been put in charge of Fort Pickens, Florida, in 1861 and prevented the Confederates from capturing the island. When he learned that Wool had ordered Lieutenant T. P. McElrath at Fort Hamilton to dispatch a mere eighty men from the harbor forts, Brown, his immediate superior, told McElrath instead to have all of the roughly three hundred troops "at Fort Hamilton, Fort Lafayette, and Fort Richmond" ready "to move at a moment's notice."[62]*

Brown then defied Sandford's order to report for duty at the arsenal at Thirty-fifth Street and Seventh Avenue, which would have left the police and military forces dangerously divided. Instead, he took the small force under his immediate command to the police Central Office and put himself under Acton's orders.[63]

In disobeying Wool's order to serve under Sandford, Brown had not simply insisted on his proper rank as an officer of the regular army, in which a militia general had no rank at all. More important, by putting himself at Acton's disposal, Brown was restricting himself to the proper role of federal forces in a situation where martial law had not been proclaimed. "I never for a moment forgot that to the police was confided the conservation of the peace of the city," Brown later wrote, "and that only in conjunction with the city authorities, and on their requisition, could the United States forces be lawfully and properly employed in suppressing the riots."[64]

Acton was in the process of drawing his forces down from the upper reaches of the city and concentrating them at 300 Mulberry Street. By 3 p.m., he was beginning for the first time to assemble a body of men large enough for rapid deployment against the toughest nodes of the mob.[65] However, the rioters soon took advantage of the fact that the city above Seventy-sixth Street was protected only by skeleton crews at the police stations, police telegrapher Charles Loring Chapin recalled, and the officers "in the more densely

---

*Fort Hamilton overlooks the Narrows from the Brooklyn shore, as does Fort Richmond (now Fort Wadsworth) from the Staten Island side. Fort Lafayette stood in the Narrows, where the eastern pier of the Verrazano Bridge now stands.

populated and more important portions of the city were left at the Station-Houses under call by telegraph."[66] At headquarters, Acton still needed some time to organize this large force so it was ready for action.

While Acton pulled his Metropolitans in from around the city, the men of the Broadway Squad, besieged in the state armory on Second Avenue and Twenty-first Street, gave up waiting for reinforcements: They wriggled through a hole in the back wall and clung to a drainpipe to reach the ground eighteen feet below, before fleeing through backyards and fighting their way to the nearest station house. Attacked there, the squad finally escaped back to its own precinct.

The rioters burst through the front doors of the state armory and began seizing weapons, particularly on the third floor, which was used for military training drills. While the distracted mob packed into the armory, about one hundred of the Metropolitans who had been beaten on Third Avenue regrouped and marched down Second Avenue, where they dispersed the crowd out front. Then, at the door the police formed two lines, facing each other, and clubbed down every rioter who came out laden with guns and other loot.

Fearing the police would pursue them on the third floor, the rioters in the drill room barricaded the doors from inside. Others, on the lower floors, decided to set fire to the building rather than turn it over to the police. While flames raced through the dry wooden interior and shot up the stairwells, rioters leaped from the windows and stumbled out the doors. Trapped in the drill room, at least ten victims suddenly plunged to their deaths when the floor collapsed and crashed down into the cauldron of fire below.[67]

While Acton gathered his forces and the state armory burned on Monday afternoon, the lower wards of the city belatedly erupted in violence, directed mainly at blacks, many of whom, like the men of the Broadway Squad but with far fewer resources, found themselves abandoned to the onslaught of the mob. The police were overwhelmed, and General Sandford, who could have dispatched militiamen from the White Street arsenal to the Fourth and Sixth Wards and Greenwich Village, did nothing.[68]

Smaller mobs broke off from the main one and roamed the entire width of the island, starting to focus their attacks on blacks wherever they could be found: individuals on the street, waiters in restaurants, families in mostly black tenement houses, seamen in boardinghouses, and prostitutes in brothels. Blacks did not live in a distinct, large ghetto where they might have rallied to defend their turf and defeat the rioters, but rather were concentrated in individual buildings and streets throughout the city, which left them easy prey to the roving mobs.[69]

"I don't know that the niggers themselves is responsible for this here trouble, but by God there is a war about 'm, damn 'm, and we'll pound 'm," a rioter told a reporter from the *World*. "It's the abolitionists that have been pushing matters eternally, and we won't stop it. We'll pound the God damn abolitionists as well as the niggers."[70]

A British visitor to the city was astounded. "Never having been in New York before, and being totally ignorant of the state of feeling with regard to Negroes, I inquired of a bystander what the Negroes had done that they should want to kill them? He replied civilly enough—'Oh sir, they hate them here; they are the innocent cause of all these troubles.' "[71]

CHAPTER 9

"Chased, Stoned, and Beaten": "A Crusade Against Negroes"

~⊃

The Seamen's Home for black seamen on Vandewater Street was owned by Albro Lyons, who lived there with his wife and children and had made the large brick building a station of the Underground Railroad. Over the years, the Lyons family "fed and furnished new disguises to upwards of a thousand fugitive slaves."[1] Lyons also owned an outfitting store for seamen, which served as an employment agency too, finding jobs and collecting wages for black sailors, while providing captains and shipowners with "good Stewards, Stewardesses, Cooks & Seamen at the shortest notice."[2]

Like his friend James McCune Smith, the best man at his wedding and godfather to his children, Albro Lyons saw the vitality and strength of the American people stemming from a rich amalgam of races: His fair-haired, blue-eyed mother had Dutch and Native American blood, while his wife Mary's mother "was distinctly a poor white of English descent."[3]

Albro's daughter, Maritcha Lyons, then a teenager, recalled that on Monday afternoon "a rabble attacked our house, breaking window panes, smashing shutters, and partially demolishing the main front door. Had not the mob's attention been suddenly diverted, further damage would certainly have ensued." Her parents' determination and resourcefulness also fended off the rioters. "The stones thrown in were utilized as material to form a barricade for the otherwise unprotected main front doorway," Maritcha Lyons wrote, and her parents braced themselves for the next assault.[4]

Because of his religious convictions, fellow abolitionist

Albro Lyons

William Powell was unwilling to shed blood to defend his business and personal property, the Colored Sailors' Home nearby on Dover Street. He had founded it almost twenty-five years earlier "on the strict principles of temperance, and the moral and religious elevation of my brethren of the sea" to protect them from the "snares and temptations which unhappily beset them on shore." Along with Cornish, Wright, Williams, and the Tappans, Powell had been a founding member of the American Anti-Slavery Society thirty years earlier, and his sea-men's home, aside from being a profitable enterprise, served as a distribution center for abolitionist literature—making it a prime target for the rioters.

Writing to William Lloyd Garrison, Powell recalled an anniversary meeting of the American Anti-Slavery Society years earlier that was "mobbed, and driven out of the Broadway Tabernacle and other public buildings by the notorious Capt. [Isaiah] Rynders and his hellish crew." Powell hoped that such outrages were a thing of the past. Instead, he told Garrison: "From 2 p.m. till 8 p.m. myself and family were prisoners in my own house to *king mob*, from which there was no escape but over the roofs of adjoining houses. About 4 p.m., I sent a note to Superintendent Kennedy for protection, but received

Mary Lyons

none, from the fact that he had been seriously injured by the mob in another part of the city. Well, the mob commenced throwing stones at the lower windows until they had succeeded in making an opening." Powell sent his wife, Mercy, and their children, including an invalid daughter Sarah, to wait on the next-door neighbor's roof while he remained in the house, "determined not to leave until driven from the premises."[5]

Like Albro and Mary Lyons, eight African American women on Thompson Street were prepared to fight back. They had filled large tin containers with water, soap, and ashes and heated the mixture they called "the King of Pain" on a massive antique stove. When the prominent black abolitionist William Wells Brown entered the room, it was filled with a "dense fog" from the steaming pots, and the "octet of Amazons" stood by, "armed with dippers."

"How will you manage if they attempt to come into this room?" asked Brown.

"We'll fling hot water on them, and scald their very hearts out."

"Can you all throw water without injuring each other?"

"O yes, Honey, we've been practicing all day."[6]

•   •   •

Anna Shotwell, founder and director of the Colored Orphan Asylum on Fifth Avenue, reflected on its progress shortly before the riots and how its fortunes had stabilized over the years. "No debts tarnished the records of the Society, and a small balance was found on hand—an unusual occurrence in its history." The house was well supplied with food, clothing, linens, and furniture, including new carpeting in some of the rooms. Most of the managers had left for the summer, while a few who lived nearby tried to make weekly visits.[7]

Shotwell proudly described the spacious, healthful building, prominently placed on Fifth Avenue not far from the city's opulent marble mansions, the antithesis of the fetid slums of lower Manhattan.

> It is situated on the very eligible piece of ground . . . near the Croton Reservoir, at Forty-second street. The building is one hundred and forty feet in front, varying from forty-two to fifty feet in depth. The cellar or basement, which, at the north end is level with the ground, has two fine play rooms, beside ample space for coal, vegetables, &c. On the first floor are the kitchen, laundry, dining-room, bathing-room, and two infirmaries: the latter may be entirely cut off from communication with the rest of the house. The second story has a large, airy and cheerful school-room in each wing, beside an infant school-room in the main building.

On the third floor, one wing served as the girls' dormitory, and the other the boys'. Shotwell noted that "ventilation has been very carefully and successfully studied," and that "the dining-room, one of the infirmaries, and the school-rooms now in use, are heated by the circulation of hot water in iron pipes."[8]

Its very success in the past twenty years had made the asylum a highly visible symbol of white philanthropy toward blacks. Funds from the city and state and private donations from whites all supported the asylum.[9] The asylum was also an example of blacks helping themselves, since the city's black elite contributed significantly. A year earlier, for example, the Ladies' Union of Brooklyn and New York held a bazaar as part of a broader effort that resulted in a donation of almost $1,500 from African American women.[10]

"At 4 p.m., the children, numbering 233, were quietly seated in their school-rooms, playing in the nursery, or reclining on a sick bed in the hospital," Anna Shotwell wrote about the first day of the riots.[11] "The physician in

Schoolyard of the Colored Orphan Asylum

attendance, Dr. [James] Barnett, had through the day of the mob felt great anxiety as to the safety of the Institution. He was carefully watching and gave the first alarm."*

From the mass of several thousand men, women, and children, some five hundred armed rioters surged forward, broke down the front door with an ax, and entered the orphanage, shouting, "Burn the niggers' nest!"[12] The staff hurried from room to room, gathering the children in one place, and one of the teachers rallied them. "Children, do you believe that Almighty God can deliver you from a mob?" The children all said they did. "Then I wish you now to pray silently to God to protect you from this mob; I believe that he is able, and that He will do it. Pray earnestly to Him and when I give the signal, go in order, without noise, to the dining-room." When the teacher rang a bell and the children raised their heads, tears were streaming down their cheeks, but they made no noise. As they proceeded down the stairs and through the halls, "the yells and horrible sounds" from the front of the building grew louder.

At this point, John Decker, the chief engineer of the fire department who had tried to save the Third Avenue draft office that morning, arrived with only a dozen men and two fire hoses, since his main force, with two

*James McCune Smith was away from the asylum due to illness.

steam engines, was fighting a large fire on Broadway and Twenty-ninth Street. The Eighth District draft office was consumed in that fire, and the rioters there moved on to loot the houses of blacks in the West Thirties; General Sandford and his troops were a few blocks away at the Thirty-fifth Street arsenal but did nothing.[13]

"Will you stick by me?" Decker asked his men, and they promised to as they entered the asylum and began putting out some fifteen fires, set by the rioters all over the building. "This was of little avail, for the mob had decreed its destruction, and had saturated the floors with inflammable substances to facilitate their infamous design," Shotwell wrote, "and Decker was told if he repeated this act, he should be killed. His men replied: 'In that attempt you will have to pass over our dead bodies.'"

While the flames spread through the building, the mob plundered the "furniture, bedding, clothing, dry goods, etc., etc.," Shotwell recalled. Decker then saw fire coming out of the roof, where the "straw beds in the garret had been heaped together and set fire to, as well as the desks, books, maps, etc., in the school-rooms, and, having no apparatus at hand capable of reaching the roof, he was finally obliged to consign to the flames this work of faith and love, and prayer and praise." Within twenty minutes the orphanage was consumed. The staff had gathered the children and marched them out the north end of the building into Forty-fourth Street, which was nearly filled with rioters.

According to Shotwell, an Irishman standing in the street sacrificed himself by shouting, "If there's a man among you, with a heart within him, come and help these poor children." The mob "laid hold of him, and appeared ready to tear him to pieces," while the children and their caretakers proceeded unharmed, "leaving this generous-spirited man in the hands of the ruffians," Shotwell wrote. The children and their teachers headed down Seventh Avenue, not knowing where they would find safety. The superintendent, William Davis, decided the group should go to the Twentieth Precinct station house on Thirty-fourth Street near Ninth Avenue.

About twenty of the children who had been separated from the group and surrounded by the mob were rescued by "a young Irishman, named Paddy M'Caffrey, with four stage-drivers of the Forty-second Street line and the members of Engine Company No. 18," the *Times* reported. Ignoring threats from dozens of "fiends," who shouted, "Murder the d[amne]d monkeys," and "Wring the necks of the d[amne]d Lincolnites," they brought the orphans to the Twentieth Precinct station house.[14]

A six-year-old boy wandered from the group between the asylum and the police station and tried to hide in a nearby house. "The poor lady of the dwelling was greatly alarmed," thinking the mob would attack her home

THE RIOTS IN NEW YORK: DESTRUCTION OF THE COLOURED ORPHAN ASYLUM.

The burning of the Colored Orphan Asylum

because of the boy, "and wringing her hands in agony, she appealed to an Irishman passing by for redress," Shotwell reported. Fortunately for the boy, the man happened to be a mason who had worked for the asylum for more than a decade. "He wrapped [the boy] in a cloth and carried him like a bundle to his own home." From there, his daughter carried the boy safely to Allen Griffin, "a faithful colored officer of the Asylum." Shotwell also mentioned that "a little girl, who in crossing 7th Avenue was lost in the crowd, was kindly protected by a Mr. Osborn who took her to his own house."

At the police station, "the children were at first stowed compactly together into a tier of cells. But when a large number of rioters were brought in, some of whom were covered with blood, they were turned out, and stood (for there was not room to lie down,) in the passageway. The captain, on taking a survey of them, sat down and burst into tears." When the captain barked orders for the officers to form ranks and return to the streets, the children all screamed and crowded toward the wall, afraid they were being turned out.

The asylum's superintendent was deputized as a provost marshal and put in charge of not only the children but also the many blacks who took refuge in the crowded station house and were fed with the ample provisions from friends of the asylum who lived nearby. Caps, bonnets, and shoes were also supplied by a concerned woman, since the children had fled without them. Only a sergeant, two doormen, and a few partly disabled officers drawn from the sick list were left to guard the station.[15]

While the Colored Orphan Asylum burned, Alderman Jacob Long tried to flee uptown in a wagon, presumably toward his home at 110th Street and First Avenue, or simply to safety outside the city. Wealthy New Yorkers who were fortunate enough to find a hack driver were paying one hundred dollars or more for a ride to Westchester County, where trains were still in service. Long had just gotten north of the asylum when Richard Lynch, a twenty-one-year-old laborer and volunteer fireman, accosted him.

"Hold up Colonel Long, give me a couple of dollars, or else by Jesus, I'll upset your waggon," shouted Lynch, who was wearing his fireman's hat.

"This is all wrong for a fire laddie to do this kind of business," the alderman replied.

"Give us a couple of dollars anyhow, I want to get something to drink."

By this time, the mob had gathered around the wagon, and Long gave Lynch the two dollars in order to extricate himself from the situation. It was not the last robbery Lynch committed that day.[16] Nor would it be the last dollar extracted by the mob from the city's Democratic politicians.

Rioters on the west side continued their search for weapons, attacking gun shops and private homes, carrying off firearms, furniture, and silverware, while women, children, and servants escaped from burning wreckage or fled before they were attacked.[17] On Brevoort Place in Greenwich Village, socialite Caroline Woolsey quickly left a note that captured the chaotic atmosphere as she prepared to flee the city.

> The city is in a tumult and Uncle Edward wishes us to go out to Astoria in the 6 o'clock boat. The regulars are all out and the streets are full of rioters. The gas house on Twenty-third Street is blown up and Tenth Street full of black ashes—our doorsteps

covered. They say they will blow up the powder mill in Twenty-eighth Street where the Gilmans live and we have told them (if they will) to come all here. Hatty G. was in a minute ago, and Mr. Prentiss. There has been a great noise in town all day. The carriage is waiting, but I was afraid you would feel anxious. We would like very much to stay, but Uncle E. insists.[18]

A family friend of the Woolseys, Lucy Gibbons tried her best to remain unperturbed by the upheaval outside her parents' home on West Twenty-ninth Street. Her mother and eldest sister, Sally, had been away for most of the previous two years, tending to soldiers at the front, and her father had gone, late that morning, to the Fifth Avenue Hotel "to get news about the condition of things in the city," Lucy remembered. He had come home and gone out again in the afternoon to take a houseguest to the train, when "Aunt Sue came in to see me in great trouble and alarm. She told me that the mob was burning the Colored Orphan Asylum and that the colored children were being carried out in people's arms. The horror of this news made us quiet for a minute."

Lucy recalled that her more practical sister, Julia, was away in the country: "In her absence I could think of nothing to do but wander about the house, setting things right and trying to make the rooms look neat against her return. Father did not come home until late in the afternoon, and then said little of his anxiety, not wanting to alarm me . . . He need not have worried . . . I had the feeling that the trouble was only temporary and would quiet down very soon."[19]

Unfortunately for the Colored Orphan Asylum, it was attacked around 4 p.m., just when reports came in to Acton that a mob was threatening what was to him a higher-priority target: the home of the city's top elected official, Mayor George Opdyke, on Fifth Avenue at Fourteenth Street. As a Republican, Opdyke symbolized both the oppression of the state legislature and the Lincoln administration, while his wealth and business dealings marked him as a profiteer, benefiting from the protracted war in which the poor were dying on the front lines.

An armed civilian patrol organized by a neighbor had occupied Opdyke's house and fended off another mob earlier in the day, with help from Tammany judge George Barnard, who lived nearby. Greeted warmly by the rioters and invited to speak, Barnard had denounced the draft but urged the crowd to obey the law and trust the courts to protect their rights. A squad of Metropolitans arrived later to drive off a second mob, and by the time the third and largest mob appeared, an artillery unit of eighty-eight U.S. troops from Governors Island had taken up positions in front of the house.[20]

Having started to gather his forces around 3 p.m., Acton was ready an hour later to dispatch Inspector Daniel Carpenter with two hundred men to protect the mayor's house. Unbeknownst to Acton, the latest mass of five to ten thousand rioters had already been deterred by the sight of the U.S. troops and was headed down Broadway for an assault on police headquarters.[21] Detectives mingling with the mobs had learned that the next targets were the financial district, the banks, and the U.S. Sub-Treasury in Lower Manhattan—where the federal government stored its gold in the city.[22]*

Acton gave Carpenter his final instructions for rescuing the mayor's house and said quietly, "Sergeant, make no arrests."[23]

Outside on Mulberry Street, Carpenter quickly formed his men in ranks and repeated Acton's orders. "We are to meet and put down a mob. We are to take no prisoners. We must strike quick and strike hard."[24] Carpenter then gave the signal to march, Headley reported. "Solid, and silent save their heavy, measured tread on the pavement, they moved down Bleecker Street towards Broadway."[25]

Fortunately for Acton, Carpenter's route immediately brought him face-to-face with the throng. When the police turned onto lower Broadway, the sea of rioters "armed with clubs, pitchforks, iron bars, and some with guns and pistols" was only a block away and filled the avenue, "far as the eye could reach," Headley wrote. The marchers in front carried a huge board bearing the words *NO DRAFT*. The sky was darkened by black smoke from the numerous houses they had torched along their route. "Pedestrians fled down the side streets, stores were hastily closed, stages vanished, and [the rioters] had the street to themselves," according to Headley.[26] The marchers stopped in front of Lafarge House, but the police did not give the rioters time to attack the many black waiters employed there.[27]

Carpenter quickly realized that he could not allow the battle to take place on the narrow side streets, where the police would be penned in and trampled by the mob. He sent a flanking party of fifty men up each of the parallel side streets on the left and right of the mob as far as Seventh Street. When they were in place, he shouted, "By the right flank Company front, double-quick, CHARGE!" With his remaining men, Carpenter pressed forward, exhorting them to take no prisoners. After he felled a gigantic rioter at the head of the procession in single combat, the well-disciplined policemen

*At Wall and Broad Streets, today the building is the Federal Hall National Memorial.

closing in from three sides were able to disperse the mob by clubbing them relentlessly with sometimes lethal blows, Headley wrote. "For a few minutes nothing was heard but the heavy thud of clubs falling on human skulls, thick and fast as hail stones upon a window pane."[28]

As the rioters in front tried to turn and flee, they were trapped by the crowd behind them which still pressed forward, until the police attacked from the sides. The sea of rioters heaved back and forth up and down Broadway and against the buildings that hemmed it in. As the marchers tried to escape through the side streets, the police were waiting to strike them down. When it was all over, "Broadway looked like a field of battle, for the pavement was strewn thick with bleeding, prostrate forms," Headley wrote. Carpenter left the rioters to care for their wounded and withdrew to assist his own. He then proceeded up Broadway toward the mayor's house on Fourteenth Street.[29]

Strolling along Fourteenth Street at that moment were Horace Greeley's friend and biographer, James Parton, and his wife, who had just reached Fifth Avenue when they were nearly struck by a large stone hurled at a black man galloping by on horseback.[30] It had been thrown by one of about two hundred rioters "streaming down Fifth Avenue," a loose column, about a quarter of a mile long, of "ill-dressed and ill-favored men and boys, each carrying a long stick or piece of board, and one or two of them a rusty musket," Parton recalled. On seeing him, one of the rioters shouted, "There's a three-hundred-dollar fellow," but did not attack.

"I had lived in New York from childhood, and supposed myself acquainted with the various classes of inhabitants," Parton noted. "But I did not recognize that crowd." They were not dressed like "laborers or mechanics," and he guessed they might be "dock-thieves, plunderers of shipyards, and stealers of old iron and copper." Fury at class discrimination, coupled with the anarchy of the riots, had brought into broad daylight the scavengers, the deepest layer of the city's underclass that normally scrambled for survival invisibly, in the slums and in the dark of night.

Parton waited for the column to pass before asking a straggler where the mob was headed. "To the *Tribune* office," he replied. Indeed, the mob soon began singing, "We'll hang old Greeley to a sour apple tree!"—to the tune of the abolitionist song "John Brown's Body."[31] Parton and his wife were then about a mile and a half from the *Tribune* building on Printing House Square, opposite City Hall Park, and hoped he could get there before the mob by catching an omnibus down Broadway, just a block or two away.

However, "the omnibuses being full," Parton wrote, "I strode on at a great pace down-town, and thus had the exquisite satisfaction of seeing that crew of villains put to flight near the corner of Tenth Street." The Fifth Avenue mob that had passed Parton and his wife on their way to the *Tribune* had turned onto Broadway and run head-on into Carpenter's patrolmen, fresh from their victory at Bleecker Street and on their way uptown to Opdyke's house. A minute later the mob had scattered, leaving only one wounded man on Broadway. Parton recalled: "[The rioter] staggered into a drug store as I got into an omnibus. He was evidently in a damaged condition about the head, and his face was covered with blood."

Carpenter found no disturbance at the mayor's house and marched his men back to headquarters. However, between 4 and 5 p.m., roughly from the time Carpenter left the Central Office until he returned, clashes had broken out all over the city, with indications that the campaign against blacks had grown to include all prominent abolitionists.

The Reverend Henry Highland Garnet, being both black and a radical abolitionist, was a particular target, and rioters charged down Thirteenth Street, where he lived, calling his name. However, his daughter had cut down the nameplate on the door with an ax.[32] The Reverend James Massie, a British abolitionist touring the United States, was scheduled to give a lecture to hundreds of parishioners at Garnet's church on Monday evening. Unable to find a streetcar, Massie and his companion walked down Broadway to Shiloh Presbyterian Church, only to find the premises in total darkness, "an instance of forethought which greatly relieved us," Massie recalled. "We ultimately found the sexton, who did not at first recognize us, and with great reluctance he informed us where Mr. Garnet could be seen." Massie found Garnet sitting in the darkened parlor of his home with four friends, one of whom had barely escaped the mobs. They braced themselves for "the events of the evening," Massie wrote, "dreading every falling footstep which seemed to approach the door."[33]

The leader of a large congregation, and of the black community nationally, Garnet chose not to surrender his life by defending Shiloh Church with a shotgun as he would have in his youth. Someone, he knew, would have to care for the thousands of black victims in the riots' aftermath, and to answer the call of Lord Byron's poem *Childe Harold's Pilgrimage,* which Garnet often quoted to African Americans: "Hereditary bondsmen, know ye not / Who would be free, themselves must strike the blow?"[34]

•   •   •

While James Parton was rushing down to the *Tribune* building, John An-drews, the lawyer from Virginia, had taken James Whitten's place at the head of the mob there and was giving another rousing speech while shaking his fists at the newspaper's staff looking down from the windows of the editorial of-fices on the fourth floor. "Down with the *Tribune!*" the crowd responded. "Down with the old white coat that thinks a naygar as good as an Irishman!"[35]

Greeley's trademark coat, a bleached white duster, was left over from the country preacher persona he had cultivated earlier in his career. Amid the well-dressed urban gentlemen of Park Row, he had shuffled along in farmer's boots and a hat with a wide, floppy brim, sometimes carrying a basket to do his marketing, his pockets always stuffed with articles, correspondence, and other papers. The disheveled, absentminded look, the necktie askew, eye-glasses slipping down his nose, piqued readers' curiosity about the eccentric editor and promoted the unpretentious, straight-talking style to be found in his *Tribune*.

Sidney Gay, the *Tribune's* managing editor, who had risen at nine that morning and returned to the offices, confronted Greeley, who could usually be found in his cluttered, musty office on the third floor, bent myopically over his work, Graham crackers and milk at his elbow. "The authorities have taken no steps for our defence," Gay exclaimed. "The *Evening Post* has armed its build-ing; we must do the same if it is to be saved. This is not a riot, but a revolution."

"It looks like it," Greeley replied. "It is just what I have expected, and I have no doubt they will hang *me*; but I want no arms brought into the building."

Editorial writer Charles Congdon joined Gay in urging Greeley to leave the building quietly by a back door and flee the city. Instead, Greeley insisted on going out the front and sticking to his daily routine. "If I can't eat my din-ner when I'm hungry, my life isn't worth anything to me," he declared. Putting on his hat, Greeley walked out into the street, accompanied by a col-league from another newspaper who had stopped in to see him. Arm in arm, the two men made their way calmly through the mass of rioters and into Windust's Restaurant on the corner of Park Row and Ann Street. After din-ner, according to the *Tribune,* Greeley "at once took a carriage thence to his lodging in broad daylight and with no sort of concealment or disguise."[36]

A little after 5 p.m., Sidney Gay set off in search of Mayor Opdyke and a promise of police protection for the *Tribune,* and James Parton arrived to find the five-story building completely defenseless. All the windows and doors were open, and the offices empty, since both editors and reporters had fanned out across the city to cover the riot. James Gilmore arrived at the same time, and both men went in to see the publisher, Samuel Sinclair, who informed them of Greeley's instruction that no firearms be brought into the building.

Gilmore recalled that he and Parton decided to "arm the building on our own responsibility," since "a blow aimed at the *Tribune* was aimed equally at free speech."[37]

Their first stop was the police Central Office, where they were promised a squad of one hundred men to guard the *Tribune* building. Next they proceeded to General Wool's headquarters at the St. Nicholas Hotel on Broadway at Spring Street. There they found the general and his staff, along with Mayor Opdyke, and Gilmore persuaded them to issue an order for one hundred muskets and a supply of ammunition that he could present at Governors Island.[38]

"I had mounted the top of an omnibus, and made my way with all possible speed to the Battery," Gilmore recalled. "The route was obstructed with vehicles, and it was past seven o'clock before I reached the South Ferry." He could not get across the channel to Governors Island, however, because all of the boatmen had left the waterfront, "probably to reinforce the mob." Gilmore searched the docks and finally found a pilot, "an old longshoreman, in a ragged tarpaulin and greasy trousers, quietly smoking a pipe" and leaning against the rail of a schooner.

"Old man," Gilmore said, "I have a ten-dollar greenback in my pocket that is yours, if you will jump into that boat and row me at once to Governor's Island."

"Can't do it sir," the man replied. "The captain is away. Couldn't do it for ten times the money; but you can get a boat at the Battery."

"Well, come along and show me where. I'll pay you well for your trouble."

Gilmore struggled to keep up with the spry old man, who led him to the Battery, where they found several boats docked and not a soul in sight. "In a very few minutes," Gilmore wrote, "I was seated in the stern of a boat, with my feet ankle-deep in water, and the old man was pushing the leaky craft out into the river."[39]

CHAPTER 10

Monday Night: "The Fiery Nucleus of the Entire Riot"

∼⟩

William Jones, a black cartman, went out to buy a loaf of bread in the wrong place at the wrong time: Clarkson Street on Manhattan's Lower West Side, Monday evening, a little after 6 p.m. He found himself in the middle of a wild, hideous chase. Three black men walking home from work along Varick Street had been set upon by an Irish bricklayer and two accomplices lurking in a liquor store. Two of the blacks managed to escape, while the attackers and a growing mob of men and boys closed in on the third man, chanting, "Kill the nigger!" and "Kill the black son of a bitch!" They overtook their quarry a few times, kicking and beating him, but each time he rose and fled, making his final escape at Clarkson Street by shooting the bricklayer with a pistol. The enraged mob grabbed William Jones, who was heading home with his bread.[1]

They beat him unconscious and then "hung him from one of the trees that shade the sidewalk by St. John's Cemetery," *Harper's Weekly* reported. "The fiends did not stop there, however. Procuring long sticks, they tied rags and straw to the ends of them, and with these torches they danced around their victim, setting fire to his clothes, and burning him almost to a cinder." The atrocity took place "within ten feet of consecrated ground," *Harper's* lamented, "where the white headstones of the cemetery are seen gleaming through the wooden railing."[2]

The rioters' effort to purge the city of its black residents continued into the evening and soon overwhelmed the police. "Can't you send five or ten men here?" the Eighth Precinct telegraphed the Central Office at 6 p.m.* "They are driving all the niggers out of the ward, as soon as they show on the street." A little before 7 p.m., the Eighteenth Precinct station house at Third Avenue and Twenty-second Street reported that the mob controlled the surrounding streets. The Fourth Precinct wrote: "Station house being stoned. Muskets in use."† An hour later, it warned that "colored" boardinghouses were being robbed and burned, and that the police "have not force enough to prevent it." Suddenly, the telegraph line was cut.[3]

After Gilmore headed down to South Ferry, James Parton had gone back to the *Tribune* office, arriving there at about 7 p.m. "The appearance of the neighborhood had changed," Parton recalled.[4] "The office was closed, and the shutters were up. A large number of people were in the open space in front of it, talking in groups, but not in a loud or excited manner. Not a policeman was to be seen." Only two or three employees were in the building, and they had heard nothing about a squad of patrolmen or any other steps taken to protect the newspaper and its staff.

Parton walked across Park Row to the small police station inside City Hall and learned from the officer on duty that the promised squad of more than one hundred men had been there briefly, before they were dispatched to quell rioting that had broken out suddenly in the First Ward. Calculating that Gilmore would need at least two more hours to get back from Governors Island, Parton mingled with the crowd in front of the *Tribune*, trying to overhear their plans. A police sergeant, in plain clothes, was also circulating through the crowd. At dusk, when he learned that the rioters planned to set the building on fire, the officer dashed back to the station house nearby on Beekman Street to get help.[5]

To Parton, the crowd seemed to be composed of rather harmless, curious bystanders, including newsboys no more than twelve years old. However, Parton wrote, "one good-natured-looking bull of a man was declaiming a little, 'What's the use of killing the niggers?' said he. 'The niggers haven't done nothing. They didn't bring themselves here, did they? They are peaceable enough! They don't interfere with nobody!' Then, pointing to the editorial rooms of the *Tribune*, he exclaimed, '*Them* are the niggers up there.' Others were holding forth in a similar strain."

Gradually the crowd pressed forward and besieged the building, "which loomed up in the dusk of the evening, unlighted, and apparently unoccupied,"

---

*The Eighth Precinct was at the heart of today's SoHo district, south of Houston Street.
†The Fourth Precinct was near today's Brooklyn Bridge.

Parton recalled. The crowd remained quiet until a gang of toughs similar to the one Parton had seen on Fifth Avenue that afternoon arrived and mingled with the crowd, eliciting "laughter and cheers which appeared to work the mob up to the point of committing violence." Someone threw a stone, which hit one of the shutters on the building and provoked "a perfect yell of applause." At that moment Parton felt certain for the first time that "the office was in danger."

Parton hurried back to the police station in City Hall. "The mob are beginning to throw stones at the *Tribune* office," he told the six patrolmen on duty. "Five men can stop the mischief now; in ten minutes, a hundred cannot." Five of the officers came with Parton and found the mob breaking the *Tribune*'s windows and howling with delight while the young boys ran back and forth, retrieving stones that had bounced off the shutters and fallen in front of the building. Brandishing their locust wood clubs, the patrolmen interposed themselves between the crowd and the entrance.

The stone-throwing stopped for a few minutes as the rioters shrank back, but resumed as soon as they realized the officers were alone and had no revolvers. The mob pressed forward and swept the policemen aside. "Amid the frantic yells of the multitude, the main door was forced, and the mob poured into the building," Parton reported. "I supposed then that the *Tribune* was gone."

Just then, however, a pistol shot rang out, and the panicked mob not only evacuated the building but crossed the street and tried to flee through the gates of City Hall Park, which quickly became congested by the stampede. In the next moment, the promised squad of one hundred patrolmen suddenly arrived, Parton recalled, and "in the dim light of the evening it seemed as if Nassau Street was a rushing torrent of dark blue cloth and brass buttons."

In a few minutes, the police had cleared Printing House Square of several thousand rioters and disrupted "whatever of organization they had in the lower part of the city," one officer concluded. By saving the *Tribune*, they had also saved the *Times* and *Post* buildings, as well as the "massed and hoarded wealth collected below Canal Street."

The *Tribune*'s managing editor, Sidney Gay, had set out from the office at 5 p.m. to find the mayor, who had left City Hall and joined General Wool at the St. Nicholas Hotel.[6] By the time Gay arrived at Wool's suite, Gilmore and Parton had already come and gone, and the managing editor was neither well received nor impressed by what he found: "A secretary, in a captain's uniform, was writing orders at a tall desk perched against the wall, and a score or more of army officers and civilians were talking together in low tones in various parts of the room. Anxiety and irresolution were depicted on every countenance; and even the scarred veteran [General Wool] who had ridden through a score of battles, seemed, for the moment, mastered by the occasion." Having already released one hundred muskets to "some importunate gentlemen"—whom the confused general remembered as being from the racist *Herald* instead of the abolitionist *Tribune*—Wool declined to help Gay, saying that the guns would end up in the mob's hands anyway.

Gay was heading back to the office at about 8 p.m. when he heard rumors that the *Tribune* building had been "sacked and burned." He proceeded down Broadway and arrived "just as the police were driving off the rear-guard of the rioters." Gay found the reports had been exaggerated, but the first floor was indeed ransacked. "Gas burners were twisted off, counters and desks were overturned, and, in the centre of the room, two charred pots, littered over with paper cinders, showed where fire had been kindled to reduce the building to ashes."

Of the *Tribune*'s 150 employees, Gay found only seven in the building, and he had to produce and distribute forty thousand copies of the newspaper by sunrise. Seeing from his office that the mob had fled, Gay ventured into the street and persuaded a dozen more printers to come back inside. Once they had set to work, others followed, and "in half an hour the types were clicking, and the monstrous press was rumbling."

As soon as the police moved on to other flash points, however, Printing House Square began to fill once again with thousands of rioters intent on destroying the *Tribune* building. By 9 p.m., the whole area "had become one swaying sea of battered hats, lit by the flaring glare of the street lamps, and flecked with the foam of perhaps ten thousand human faces." A half hour later, a reporter who had been mingling with the crowd burst into Gay's office to announce that the rioters would attack at 11 p.m. Gay tucked a pen behind his ear, looked down at the growing crowd, and kept working.

The financial district, home to the banks and the U.S. Sub-Treasury, had been spared by the police victory at the *Tribune,* and by the heavy defenses at financial institutions. However, the boardinghouses where black sailors, cooks, and waiters lived were also concentrated in Lower Manhattan, particularly near the East River waterfront, and they were attacked ferociously.

One of the "colored" boardinghouses that the Fourth Precinct had reported were under attack earlier that evening was the Seamen's Home owned and occupied by the Lyons family, where Albro and his wife, Mary, continued to stand guard. "Before dusk arrangements had been effected to secure the safety of the two children of the family who were at home," Maritcha Lyons recalled. "As the evening drew on, a resolute man and a courageous woman quietly seated themselves in the exposed hall, determined to protect their property, to sell their lives as dearly as maybe the need should arise."[7]

On Dover Street, William Powell finally had to cede his house to the mob. "I remained till the mob broke in, and then narrowly escaped." He joined his family and boarders on the roof of the adjacent building. "This was about 8:30 p.m. We remained on the roof for an hour; still I hoped relief would come." Powell's neighbors, expecting the mob to burn his house down, were in a flurry of activity, pulling their own furniture and possessions out of their homes to protect them from fire. However, the mob was so busy plundering Powell's home that they did not torch it.

"How to escape from the roof of a five-story building with four females—and one a cripple—besides eight men, without a ladder, or any assistance from outside," Powell declared, was simply beyond him. Help came from the Jewish neighbor next door.

> But God that succored Hagar in her flight came to my relief in the person of a little, deformed, despised Israelite—who, Samaritan-like, took my poor helpless daughter under his protection in his house . . . He also supplied me with a long rope . . . and though pitchy dark, I took *soundings* with the rope, to see if it would touch the next roof, after which I took a clove hitch around the clothesline which was fastened to the wall by pulleys, and which led from one roof to the other over a space of about one hundred feet. In this manner I managed to lower my family down to the next roof, and from one roof to another, until I landed them in a neighbor's yard.[8]

Through tireless effort, the police downtown did manage to rescue many blacks from attack, but far more might have been saved if General Sandford had not held the militia in reserve all day while waiting for retired officers and veterans actively recruiting volunteer regiments to respond to a printed announcement summoning them to the Seventh Avenue arsenal that evening. Starting at 8 p.m., Sandford met with two hundred of these "gentlemen," and "measures were adopted for the enrollment and organization of volunteers in various parts of the city, and suitable commanders were designated," wrote William Stoddard, an adviser to President Lincoln who happened to be in New York that week. "The commanding general was thereby relieved of a mass of work and responsibility."[9]

Sandford had also kept some federal troops under his immediate command out of the action and had protested to General Wool that General Brown was not following his orders with regard to the other federal forces. When Wool reprimanded Brown and reminded him that Sandford was in charge, Brown's patience finally snapped. At 9 p.m., he burst into Wool's suite at the St. Nicholas Hotel, where he denounced Sandford for failing to go on the offensive against the rioters. Brown insisted on an independent command putting him in charge of all federal troops in the city. Wool, who had never liked Brown, instead replaced him with Colonel Nugent, again specifying that Sandford was in overall command.[10]

By 9 p.m., the Fourth Precinct had repaired its telegraph lines and told the Central Office: "Things awful bad here. Inspector D.C. [Daniel Carpenter] here with big force, but excitement increases. Two colored men brought in almost dead." The adjacent Sixth Precinct reported "a large crowd tearing down colored dwellings in Park Street." Farther south the First Precinct station house was "taking in a good many colored lodgers for protection."

Once black refugees were inside, the station houses became targets, and the few officers left to guard them had to bluff their way through when mobs threatened to attack. A sergeant at the Second Precinct station guarding dozens of blacks brandished his revolver and cowed the mob while he and one patrolman waited for reinforcements. At the Fourth Precinct station, eight officers used their revolvers and two empty muskets to scatter a mob. Acton granted the besieged officers of the Eighteenth Precinct permission to "shut up shop" and flee at 9 p.m., and their station house was later burned to the ground.[11]*

"The drinking shops down town are all closed, nominally at least, doing business only with closed doors," the *World* reported. "The proprietors of eating-houses where colored waiters are employed were closed during the day, and few will be open [tomorrow]. Some have discharged their colored waiters, and will employ others."[12]

The city was essentially controlled by the rioters at dusk; the night was hot, and columns of black smoke rose from burning structures all over town.[13] At General Wool's headquarters, confusion reigned. Lieutenant T. P. McElrath arrived in Manhattan from Fort Hamilton and reported for duty at the St. Nicholas Hotel. The lieutenant recalled: "Approaching Major [Christian] Christensen, General Wool's Adjutant-General, I enquired what had been

*At Third Avenue and Twenty-second Street.

going on in the city that day, for as yet I was ignorant of the details. Major Christensen's reply was characteristic: 'Good God, McElrath, this is the one spot in New York where the least is known of what is taking place!' "[14] When McElrath learned that General Brown had been relieved of duty, he reported to General Wool, who sent him to the Seventh Avenue arsenal, where General Sandford simply assigned him and his men to quarters inside.[15]

Back at the hotel, civic leaders of both parties had started to arrive, anxious to consult with the mayor and General Wool about putting down the riots. The violent demonstration of that morning had escalated far beyond the expectations of even the most determined antidraft Democrats. However, the means of stopping the riots quickly became a new source of dispute.

George Templeton Strong and other members of the Union League Club called for the immediate imposition of martial law and occupation of the city by federal troops for as long as it might take to silence all opposition to the draft and ensure that the lottery was completed without further interruption.[16] According to Strong, Opdyke and Wool each claimed that the other had sole authority to declare martial law in the city, and both refused to take action.

"Then, Mr. Mayor, issue a proclamation calling on all loyal and law-abiding citizens to enroll themselves as a volunteer force for defense of life and property," Strong suggested.

"Why, that is *civil war* at once," Opdyke replied.

Strong had a long talk with Colonel Thomas Cram, Wool's chief of staff, who said all was well, and they had plenty of troops to handle the situation. "Don't believe it," Strong wrote.[17]

Also vying for Mayor Opdyke's attention that night were Tammany Democrats—including William Tweed, District Attorney A. Oakey Hall, and Isaiah Rynders—who felt martial law would further enrage the rioters and result in even more widespread destruction and loss of life. They hoped to combine limited military force with the kind of persuasion Judge Barnard had used in front of Opdyke's house that day: a sympathetic but firm voice urging obedience to the law and redress through the courts.

Opdyke believed that the worst of the rioting was over, and, swayed by the Democrats, chose not to request a federal imposition of martial law.[18] According to Opdyke, both he and General Wool believed

> nothing could have been more suicidal. That extreme measure, in the absence of military strength to inforce it, would have savored of the folly of flaunting scarlet cloth in the face of a mad bull in the absence of means of defence or escape. It would have exasperated

the rioters, increased their numbers, and those in sympathy with them, for the Democratic party were, to a man, opposed to the measure. The probable result would have been the sacking and burning of the city, and the massacre of many of its inhabitants.[19]

Opdyke promised the Union League Club representatives that he would keep the military option open and use it if the situation did not improve in the next few days. The staunch Republicans telegraphed President Lincoln from Wool's suite, pleading for "instant help in troops and an officer to command them and to declare martial law."[20] Then they left the hotel in disgust. The culprits, they believed, were not only the agitators in the streets—but Democratic politicians and editors. The rioters, Strong wrote in his diary, "will either destroy the city or damage the Copperhead cause fatally. Could we but catch the scoundrels who have stirred them up, what a blessing it would be!"[21]

Lucy Gibbons continued to believe the rioting would soon be over, but for the city and for her family in particular, the onslaught had just begun.

> As the evening approached, Aunt Rachel sent one of her servants to get a loaf of bread at the baker's shop around the corner; the girl came back without the bread, and crying. She said that while she was in the baker's shop, a man had come in and announced, "We are going to burn Gibbonses and Sinclair's tonight."*
>
> I asked father if it was a threat important enough to make it wise for us to carry into Uncle Samuel's—two doors away—some of the things which money could not replace. He answered quickly: "Decidedly yes!" and as soon as it was dark enough in the street for us probably to escape observation, he carried over the heavy marble bust of our beloved Willie, who had died a few years before, at Harvard.[22]

Lucy took down every picture of Willie in the house, while James also carried two drawers full of Willie's possessions and keepsakes associated with him. His room had been kept vacant as a shrine to him. James also carried his youngest son's baby clothes. With her aunt Rachel's help, Lucy also took her mother's dresses, jewelry, silver, and letters.[23]

---

*Samuel Sinclair was a relative of Greeley and the publisher of the *Tribune*. Greeley was a friend of the Gibbons family and stayed at their home often, once when he was ill, so some of the rioters mistakenly believed that he was a boarder there.

. . .

Rowing vigorously against the strong current of the East River, the long-shoreman had reached Governors Island in fifteen minutes. James Gilmore had paid and dismissed the old sailor and set off to find the commander of the garrison, but soon discovered that the island was nearly deserted.[24] Gilmore's shouts finally roused a young officer with his arm in a sling, who summoned the commandant and twelve privates forming the skeleton crew left to defend the island's vast supply of guns and ammunition while the rest of the garrison fought the rioters on Manhattan. It took almost an hour to load the heavy boxes of muskets and cartridges onto a small steamboat in which Gilmore set off for the Battery. "The moon was down," he recalled, "and a thick veil of clouds muffled the stars; but a deep glow lit up the whole northern horizon. Here and there great banks of lurid light were rising in the night,—the reflection of half a hundred conflagrations. Evidently the upper part of the city was in a blaze."

A little before 10 p.m., the steamer landed at the Battery. "I saw the boat a-coming and came down to warn you," said the old longshoreman who had rowed Gilmore to the island. "The *Trybune* is burned to the ground, and a mob of ten thousand is emptin' all the banks in Wall Street. If ye go up, every musket'll be taken." The captain of the steamer agreed, and Gilmore hesitated. However, looking north, he saw no signs of a fire around City Hall Park and offered the old man more money to find a wagon. "I've had pay enough," the longshoreman replied. "I'm at your orders the rest of to-night free gratis."

Within ten minutes, he had found an Irish drayman, who agreed, for a price, to transport the boxes of guns and ammunition on his cart. Then Gilmore confided in the longshoreman: "Old man, I can trust you, or I'm no judge of faces. These are muskets to arm the *Tribune* building. I must go ahead to see that the coast is clear, and I want you to take this revolver and ride along with the drayman. See that he goes directly up Pearl Street, and stops at the corner of Franklin Square, and does not exchange a word with anyone." Gilmore recalled that the man's eyes were "glowing like coals in the gaslight" when he replied: "Ay, ay, sir. I'll stand by ye, sir, if you *are* a black Republican."

Not knowing if the *Tribune* building had been gutted by fire, Gilmore "mounted to the top of an omnibus" at about 10 p.m. and went ahead of the cart loaded with muskets. "My way was slow," Gilmore remembered, "for the street was a turbulent river of men and wagons; but at last I came abreast of the Park, and saw the well-known [*Tribune*] sign and a flame of gaslight streaming down from the upper windows. A dense mass of men, hooting, shouting, and yelling, filled every open space around the building."

Gilmore went around to the Spruce Street entrance, which the staff un-bolted to let him in. He informed Gay that he had one hundred muskets nearby and asked him to send as many patrolmen as possible to protect the cart during the final few blocks of the trip. Then Gilmore went to Franklin Square, where the cart had just arrived, and replaced the Irishman at the reins. "Soon after we turned into Spruce Street," according to Gilmore, "some thirty policemen emerged from the shadow of the opposite warehouses, and quietly formed a cordon around the slow-moving vehicle." The sight of the police-men's clubs was enough to part the crowd, and ten minutes later, "the huge boxes were hoisted into the second story of the *Tribune* building."

By this time, about 125 staff members were on hand, some having re-turned with their own firearms to defend the offices. Nonetheless, Gilmore wondered how they would hold off the mob that was "surging in black waves all around the building" and envisioned himself "being roasted like a live eel upon a gridiron." For Gilmore, the view of the street from the fourth-floor windows was a literal vision of hell: "total depravity, and the devil and his an-gels, shouting, and hooting, and yelling, in living reality on the pavement. A hundred muskets discharged among the rioters would have no more effect than a bundle of firecrackers." He urged the longshoreman to go home, but the old man insisted on keeping his promise to be available for the rest of the night.

At that moment, a reporter quietly summoned Gilmore into Gay's office, where he explained what he had told the managing editor and no one else: After the muskets from Governors Island were taken out of the crates and spread out on a long table in the library, he had tried to load several of them and discovered that the ammunition did not fit. Gilmore decided they would have to bluff their way through until morning. The massive crates filled with guns and forty rounds of ammunition for each must have looked "like a com-plete arsenal" to the rioters who watched them brought into the building. He sent the old longshoreman across to the police station in City Hall to tell them that the mob planned to attack at 11 p.m. and request that a few plain-clothesmen spread the word among the crowd that the newspapermen were "loaded up to the muzzle."

Fifteen minutes later, the longshoreman had completed his mission, and the mob "seemed to sway to and fro, as if moved by some invisible force," Gilmore wrote; its "more savage-looking" members were conferring in small groups. While the mob hesitated, the staff continued to produce the next morning's paper: reporters writing stories, printers setting type, and Gay com-posing an editorial "that branded the mob as the rear-guard of Lee's army."

As 11 p.m. approached, however, "a long yell echoed through every cor-ner of the building, coming up as if from the very bowels of the earth,"

The attack on the Tribune Building

Gilmore wrote. Thinking it was the signal for the attack, every man grabbed his weapon and rushed to the windows. "Streaming from Broadway into the Park was a gang of about three hundred ruffians, mostly in red shirts, shouting and yelling like fiends," according to Gilmore. By the "flaring light of the Park lamps," it was clear that they were armed and moving swiftly, with military precision. "They were the fiery nucleus of the entire riot," according to Gilmore. "It was for them that the mob below had waited, and the long yell they had sent up was a shout of welcome."

As it headed straight for the *Tribune* building, the phalanx picked up speed, "and clear and loud their tread sounded, like blow after blow on the cover of a coffin," Gilmore wrote. However, just as they were coming out of City Hall Park, Inspector Carpenter "sprang from the shadow of the high iron fence" and gave the order "Up, boys, and at them!" His squad of 110 patrolmen aimed their clubs at the rioters' temples, and one *Tribune* editor recalled hearing "the tap, tap, of the police clubs on the heads of the fugitives."[25]

Within a few minutes, "those of the three hundred who were not on the ground dead or helpless, were fleeing wildly in all directions," according to Gilmore. Carpenter then formed his men in tight ranks, "about twenty men front and five or six deep," and plowed through the sea of remaining rioters, dispersing "the crowd of probably ten thousand like frightened deer."

Even more decisive than the empty muskets and the police, Gilmore wrote, was a heavy rainstorm "from the merciful heavens" at 11 p.m., which finished the job of "driving the ruffians to their holes" and tamed the fires raging all over lower Manhattan.

Acton sent two telegraphers out in the storm to make temporary repairs, and they restored most of the system over the next two days.[26] Dressed like workmen, they melted into the mobs before splitting off to recover downed wires, threading them through alleys, over rooftops, and onto clotheslines to put them back in service. One of the men had "his boots burned off in tramping through the burning ruins of a building after the wires," and the other was nearly killed by the police, who thought he was a looter in the ruins of a building, until a captain identified him in the nick of time.

The pair also posed as hack drivers in order to get around the city quickly and penetrate areas controlled by the rioters without attracting attention. Again, the ruse worked too well, and some pistol-waving rioters hailed the carriage, insisting on a ride downtown. The telegraphers slyly tried to take their passengers to police headquarters and have them arrested but were soon told to turn around and head in a different direction. When the rioters got out at an alehouse that apparently served as their headquarters, they gave the telegraphers a drink and fifty cents before bidding them farewell.

These encounters and escapes were not always so amicable. Driving a wagon, the pair was surrounded by a mob and saved themselves only by claiming to be farmers from Westchester County. In another instance, one of the telegraphers tried to avoid a mob by flagging down the carriage of a Catholic priest. The crowd mistook the passengers for journalists and stopped the carriage, shouting, "Down with the d[amne]d reporters." Only when they recognized the priest did the rioters back off.

Along with the telegraphers, fifteen police detectives had spread out across the city, blending in with the rioters and relaying information about their intentions to headquarters. The detectives were sometimes suspected, and a shout would go up, "There goes Kennedy's spies," but skillful acting would convince the rioters they were mistaken. In the case of Detective Slowey, however, he was recognized in a crowd, apparently by a man he had once arrested, who pointed and yelled, "Detective!" Thrown to the ground and beaten by the mob, the detective struggled to his feet and reached the top of a nearby stoop, where a woman put her house at risk by letting him inside. After many loud threats, however, the rioters moved on to easier prey.[27]

Less reliable than the telegraphers and detectives were some of the city's volunteer fire companies, which were also helping the authorities on Monday night. Peter Masterson and his Black Jokers, having unleashed the riots, tried to get the genie back in the bottle. Beginning on Monday night, he and his men performed heroically in the upper reaches of the city, patrolling the area from Fiftieth to Sixty-second Street, between Sixth Avenue and the Hudson River, and saving the property of grateful residents.[28]

Other fire companies took similar action in various wards across the city starting on Monday night, fighting off mobs and saving property, including a police station, a lumberyard, and the grounds of Columbia College. However, some firemen made it clear that they continued to oppose the draft and were merely carrying out their civic duty. One engine company went so far as to print a public notice explaining its position and denouncing the conscription as "unnecessary and illegal."[29]

Like the firemen, many of the workers who led the strike that morning reversed course and joined the effort to restore order. These protesters tended to be skilled artisans in the building trades, not industrial workers and unskilled laborers—from the city's docks, quarries, road crews, and factories—who generally continued to riot. The journeymen in the more established trades were perhaps restrained to some degree by the clear hierarchies in their professions—by the system of apprenticeship to more experienced craftsmen.[30]

Longshoremen and other manual laborers, by contrast, had more autonomy in negotiating the terms of their employment, though without more leverage and with far less job security. As a cartman, Thomas Fitzsimmons might have been expected to fall into this category. Instead, after leading the group that pressured James Jackson to shut down his foundry in the morning, Fitzsimmons returned home to Twenty-eighth Street and patrolled the area with a group of neighbors around the clock starting on Monday night. In addition to protecting their homes, they were able to fend off a mob trying to lynch a black man.[31]

· · ·

When Commissioner Acton learned just before midnight that the charred body of William Jones still hung from the tree on Clarkson Street, he ordered the closest precinct, "Take it down forthwith; and if you can't, let me know." Half an hour later, the precinct reported, "The mob won't let us have the body." Only after a second attempt—this time with one hundred patrolmen—was the body finally recovered.[32]

Acton had not taken a break since the riots began and had no plans to do so. General Sandford, by contrast, "who for some reason did not wear his uniform at any time during the riot, put on his hat, and bidding us good-evening, took his departure for his private residence" around midnight, Lieutenant McElrath recalled, "leaving two of his staff to act during his absence." At the Thirty-fifth Street arsenal, "there appeared to be constant uncertainty throughout the night as to which of these officers was really in command."[33]

Captain Walter Franklin, another regular army officer dispatched to the city from the harbor forts by General Brown on Monday, later reported to McElrath: "On arriving at the arsenal, I found everything in a great state of confusion. No one seemed to know who was in command; some said Colonel Nugent, and others, some colonel whose name I do not recollect. There was no officer of the day on guard, and no guard stationed, except one at the arsenal door."[34] Colonel Nugent took Franklin's suggestion that the immediate area be cleared of rioters and guards posted at all four streets leading to the arsenal. With the help of the marines, these basic steps were taken, and toward midnight they and Franklin's men marched through the rain to 300 Mulberry Street, as ordered.

Franklin then proceeded to the St. Nicholas Hotel and reported to General Wool. "The room at this time was full of gentlemen, and the general seemed to be very much confused . . . and worn out, and I should judge unable to perform any duty." Sometime after midnight, Wool, like Sandford, retired for the night, but instead of going home, dismissed his visitors and staff. "I think only one orderly remained with him" at the hotel suite, Franklin wrote, "and he on the outside of the door."

At 2 a.m., when additional federal troops arrived at the Thirty-fifth Street arsenal with some of Lieutenant McElrath's artillery, he asked one of Sandford's staff officers if he could place the cannon outside, since there were no openings to fire through, and the general "already had too much ordnance hidden in the building." Permission granted, McElrath positioned the guns at the street corners so they dominated the approaches to the building. "One hundred infantry and those two guns," McElrath reported to Brown, "could have defended the arsenal against any mob that was concentrated in the city during the riot."[35]

CHAPTER II

"Government in the Hands of the White Race Alone"

~⌒

At the Seaman's Home, Albro and Mary Lyons continued to guard their own property on Monday night. "Lights having been extinguished, a lonely vigil of hours passed in mingled darkness, indignation, uncertainty, and dread," Maritcha Lyons wrote.

> Just after midnight, a yell announced that a second mob was gathering to attempt assault. As one of the foremost rioters attempted [to] ascend the front steps, father advanced into the doorway and fired point blank into the crowd. Not knowing what might be concealed in the darkened interior, the fickle mob more disorganized than reckless, retreated out of sight hastily and no further demonstration was made that night.[1]

At daybreak on Tuesday, the couple heard footsteps of a single person approaching the doorway, and a voice cried out: "Don't shoot, Al. It's only me." An Irish policeman, Officer Kelly of the local precinct, had heard reports of the attack on their home and had come to check on them. "This kind hearted man sat on our steps and sobbed like a child," Maritcha Lyons recalled.[2]

Blacks were mostly left to fend for themselves again on Tuesday, with the added element of neighbors looking on without helping or calling the police. "On Tuesday, the second day of the riot, I was at Cavanagh's liquor store in Leroy Street corner of Washington at about six o'clock in the morning," Edward Ray, a local schoolboy, testified.* I was standing in front of the store when a colored man came to me and asked me where a grocery store was. I told him." The black man had just come ashore at the foot of Leroy Street from a vessel in the Hudson River where he undoubtedly served as a cook or in some other menial job; he carried a bag and a basket on one arm.[3]

"A man named Edward Canfield came out of Jones's liquor store and asked the colored man what he wanted," Ray continued. Several other white laborers and boys had gathered around. "He answered that he wanted a grocery store." Without another word, Canfield hit the man and knocked him down. He then kicked the man, jumped on him, and "kicked his eyes out" while leaning on the shoulder of another man for support, Ray said. "Go into him! Let him have it!" a passing neighbor heard the men shout, but he was too frightened to do more than go home and watch through the windows with his family.

Yet another tormenter came up and stuck a knife in the black man's chest. "He could not get it in," Ray noticed. "He threw it into the street. I ran and got it, and some big boys took it away from me." From the stoop where he stood with two of his sisters, Ray saw a next-door neighbor, James Lamb, throw some small stones, before dropping a chunk of flagstone the size of a man's head on the victim's chest several times and declaring that "he would like to kill some white niggers." Three of the men then took turns jumping on the prone man's chest, before they all retired to Jones's liquor store, cheering and swearing "vengeance on every nigger in New-York." Canfield, drunk and with "blood on the front of his pants," later walked to a nearby stable and warned the owner "not to put any niggers to work."

Several other residents and shopkeepers witnessed the attack or saw the man lying on the pavement but did nothing to report it. One resident said that a group of firemen came by, looked at the victim, who was still alive, and then left the scene, where a crowd of women and children had gathered around the body.[4] Finally, two passersby asked the same resident for directions to the precinct station house, and the police soon arrived to put the injured man in a wagon and send him to the hospital, where he died two hours later having answered almost inaudibly that his name was "William" or "Williams."[5]

Like "Williams," the rest of the city's black residents had been targeted by the rioters since Monday, "and today it became a regular hunt for them," wrote

*Leroy Street is on Manhattan's Lower West Side.

journalist Joel Tyler Headley, whose sympathy for blacks was enhanced by his long-standing hatred of the Irish. "A sight of one in the streets would call forth a halloo, as when a fox breaks cover, and away would dash half a dozen men in pursuit. Sometimes a whole crowd streamed after with shouts and curses . . . If overtaken, he was pounded to death at once; if he escaped into a negro house for safety, it was set on fire . . . If he could reach a police station he felt safe; but, alas! If the force happened to be away on duty, he could not stay even there." Headley described the corpse of a black man at Seventh Avenue and Twenty-seventh Street, "stripped nearly naked, and around it a collection of Irishmen, absolutely dancing or shouting like wild Indians."

The pillaging of entire black neighborhoods that had begun the previous night continued on Tuesday. On Sullivan and Roosevelt Streets, where blacks lived in great numbers, boardinghouses, a grocery, and a barbershop were burned down since they either were owned by blacks or catered to them.* Station houses soon overflowed, and hundreds of refugees had to be sheltered and fed at the arsenal and police headquarters, where they slept on the floors.[6]

Some blacks were chased all the way to the rivers and off the ends of piers. If they did not drown or swim out to a ship, they clung to the pilings under the piers until the mob had left. Occasionally they were rescued by whites. The workers at a brickyard on the Hudson shore at Thirtieth Street put a black refugee into a rowboat on Tuesday morning, enabling him to escape to New Jersey.

Another black man, pursued by a mob, ran down Washington Street toward the Canal Street ferry, where a white man shouted for him to get on board, which he did. The ferry pilot then shut the gates and pulled away, leaving the noisy band of rioters on the dock. At Hoboken, the white man took up a collection so the refugee could reach the home of friends in Paterson, New Jersey.[7] Since Monday the ferries had been packed with black refugees escaping Manhattan to Brooklyn, Staten Island, and New Jersey, but those who were too old, infirm, or poor to make the trip remained within reach of the rioters.[8]

Blacks in Brooklyn were also vulnerable, because the draft had been carried out successfully there and one hundred policemen had been sent over to Manhattan. "The riot in New-York created an intense excitement in Brooklyn, and large numbers of persons crossed the river to see what was going on," the *World* reported. "The colored people are having a hard time of it.

*Sullivan Street straddles today's SoHo and Greenwich Village neighborhoods; Roosevelt Street lay due east of City Hall, just north of the Brooklyn Bridge, which in 1863 had not yet been built.

They are attacked everywhere and beaten. They crowded about the police stations . . . asking for protection, being prevented from going to their homes or even walking the streets."

Authorities in Brooklyn put more effort into protecting the navy yard, which buzzed with activity. "The walls were manned and mounted with guns—thirteen 18-pounders are mounted on the Flushing Avenue side so as to sweep everything, two 32-pounders command the main entrance, and all the vessels have been hauled into the stream, the guns shotted, and everything ready for any emergency," according to the *World*.

Heavily armed marines were sent over to Manhattan, and the gunboats that carried them were equipped with antipersonnel ammunition for their cannon—"boxes loaded with percussion cap shells, shrapnel, canister, and grape shot," the *World* reported. "The marines were accompanied by 300 sailors, armed with cutlasses and revolvers."[9]

Many blacks, including a fair number of seamen, left the city on foot, walking along the Hudson River railroad tracks on Manhattan's West Side, heading north toward Westchester and Albany. The rioters had torn up portions of the track and threatened to burn the bridge over Spuyten Duyvil Creek to further disrupt the trains and prevent soldiers from reaching the city.[10]

In the midst of this acute crisis, and despite the atrocities committed, the *World* continued to add fuel to the fire on Tuesday, ostensibly through the voice of the people. Its editor, Manton Marble, wrote that "although the community generally condemns the plundering and cruelty perpetrated by some hangers-on of the mob, yet there is an astonishing deal of public and private sympathy expressed in public places with the one idea of resistance to the draft. The laboring classes say that they are confident that it will never be enforced in the city, and that any new attempt will meet with still more serious opposition. They believe that no force, military or civil, will be able to enforce this unpopular measure."[11]

After going through the motions of denouncing the violence, Marble quickly escalated his attacks on the administration's infringement of civil rights and blamed Lincoln for the riots: "Will the insensate men at Washington now at length listen to our voice? Will they now give ear to our warnings and adjurations? Will they now believe that Defiance of Law in rulers breeds Defiance of Law in the people? Does the doctrine proclaimed from the Capitol that in war laws are silent please them [when] put in practice in the streets of New York?"

The *World* insisted that the people wanted a war for "the Union and the Constitution"—not for abolition—and that Lincoln had ignored them.

Thousands of men had thronged Union Square two years earlier in support of the war effort, Marble wrote. "These are the very men whom his imbecility, his wanton exercise of arbitrary power, his stretches of ungranted authority have transformed into a mob."[12]

"Does any man wonder that poor men refuse to be forced into a war mismanaged almost into hopelessness, perverted almost into partisanship?" the *World* asked. "Did the President and his cabinet imagine that their lawlessness could conquer, or their folly seduce a free people?" Appearing at the height of mob rule, Marble's words struck his rivals as irresponsible. Bryant's *Evening Post* charged that the *World* had been "for weeks endeavoring to arouse the mob spirit in this city" and was now determined to "inflame the passions of ignorant readers, and incite such to violence."[13]

In two more editorials on Tuesday, Marble criticized the *Times* and expanded his attack both on the draft and on abolition. Surveying the country's eighty-year history, the *World* pointed out that Americans had prevailed in two wars—in 1812 and 1846—without resorting to a federal draft. In the war with Mexico over Texas in 1846, President Polk rejected the idea of annexing Mexico too, according to Marble, because "the addition of a mongrel race, part Indian, part negro, and part Spanish, would, it was thought, be a fatal error, as it was not fitted for, nor capable of self-government." The blacks of the South, the *World* declared, were no more competent than Mexicans, and the American people wanted their government "in the hands of the white race alone."[14]

The suppression of the riot, meanwhile, remained in the feeble hands of Major General Wool, who relied on Sandford and Nugent, while the energetic General Brown had been out of the picture since nine o'clock the previous night. Early on Tuesday morning, however, Brown arrived at Wool's suite, admitting his error and requesting to resume command of the federal troops. Mayor Opdyke and prominent Republicans had put him up to it. When Wool restored Brown to his command, he immediately returned to the police Central Office and continued to coordinate with Commissioner Acton while ignoring General Sandford. When Sandford again called for all troops to muster at the Thirty-fifth Street arsenal—which had no telegraph link to the police Central Office—Brown declared that the order applied only to militia.[15]

Leaving men to guard the station houses and other public buildings, Acton had gathered the bulk of his force at the Central Office on Mulberry Street, where more than seven hundred troops under General Brown stood ready to reinforce them. Some four hundred civilian "Volunteer Specials" had been sworn in and equipped with clubs and badges; they were expected to do guard duty for the most part and free up the police and soldiers to do the heavy fighting.[16]

Many shopkeepers and factory owners were optimistic. Not seeing any mobs downtown and thinking the worst was over, they opened for business.[17] However, looks were deceptive, and calm prevailed only in certain areas. Headley recalled that "from Sixth Avenue in the west nearly to Second Avenue in the east, and down almost to Broome Street, the streets were black with excited men." Workers from empty stores and factories had joined the crowds either by choice or by coercion, and as they ruled the streets in various wards, Acton realized he would have to strike back in several places at once. "Indeed, the air was charged with electricity," Headley wrote, "but the commissioners now felt ready to meet the storm whenever and wherever it should burst."[18]

At 9:15 a.m., Acton received an urgent telegram from the Twenty-first Precinct that the mob was burning buildings at Thirty-fourth Street and Second Avenue. He dispatched Inspector Carpenter from Mulberry Street with three hundred men, and they boarded the Third Avenue streetcars to speed their trip.[19] Many of the rioters were just curious onlookers, and "a Catholic priest, who harangued them, urging them to maintain peace," had a temporary effect on those within earshot, Headley wrote. However, the mob, some ten thousand strong, was immediately galvanized by the arrival of Carpenter's force, which they met "with an ominous silence," according to the *Tribune.*[20]

In addition to the crowds jamming the avenue and closing in from in front and behind, on both sides rioters had ascended to the rooftops, from which they hurled "a thick shower" of paving stones and bricks at Carpenter's column, inflicting serious head injuries on two Metropolitans. The police seemed on the verge of being overwhelmed in this trap, but their officers rallied them, and a hail of gunfire from their revolvers drove the rioters back from their perches at the windows and on the rooftops. Carpenter detached fifty men to clear the rioters from the houses, while the others charged forward and dispersed the crowd in the street. Then they turned and charged the crowd that had closed in from the rear, "scattering it and filling the gutters with disabled ruffians," William Stoddard wrote.

Breaking down barricaded doors and fighting their way through narrow scuttles to reach the roofs, the police inside the houses clubbed the rioters mercilessly. An hour later Second Avenue was littered with bodies of men and women who had either fallen or jumped from the roofs or been clubbed as they came out the doors. At Riley's porterhouse on the corner, the rioters were "literally tossed down stairs," while "other policemen caught them as they rolled or tumbled out of the doors and administered a second dose of the locust," the *Tribune* reported.[21]

During the struggle, one of the two officers Sandford had placed in command of the arsenal on Monday night sent a detachment of 150 soldiers under Colonel H. T. O'Brien along with Lieutenant McElrath's artillery unit of twenty-five men and two cannons to support Carpenter. O'Brien, an Irish American who lived in the neighborhood, was in the process of recruiting a volunteer regiment for the war and was well known to the crowd, but not liked. Earlier in the day, the colonel had left his home "in full uniform with his sword in his hand" and lectured the mob nearby "in the most intemperate language," which the *Tribune* felt was not fit to print. The rioters, who expected Irishmen like O'Brien to assist them or at least remain neutral in the uprising, for the moment had "only replied with muttered threats."[22]

O'Brien's men joined forces with the police and marched down the avenue, but the mob had regrouped and blocked their way. Hoping to frighten the rioters away, O'Brien had the artillerists load the two cannons with blanks. He ordered his own men to fire real bullets from their muskets but to aim over the rioters' heads. The bullets "whistled through the air in every direction, shattering shutters and doors," and killing seven people, including two children who were watching from windows. The unexpected use of artillery and ammunition set off a stampede as the rioters fled, leaving only the wounded and dead and those who remained to care for them.[23]

"Who is responsible for this injudicious proceeding, I do not know," fumed Lieutenant McElrath to General Brown. McElrath's artillery company had been temporarily taken away from him that morning, and he knew the results were dangerous. By using blank artillery shells and having the troops aim high with their muskets, O'Brien had spared the hard-core rioters and killed bystanders, enflaming rather than suppressing the mob.[24]

While the police and military had temporarily cleared Second Avenue between Thirty-fourth and Thirty-fifth Streets at 10 a.m., resistance was breaking out elsewhere. In the industrial slums of Corlear's Hook on the Lower East Side, 130 federal troops dispatched by General Brown under Lieutenant Thomas Wood confronted five thousand rioters on Pitt Street who refused to disperse. When the mob attacked with "clubs, stones, and other missiles," the soldiers opened fire, killing fourteen and wounding seventeen, by the lieutenant's count. The soldiers reloaded and scattered the rest of the mob with a bayonet charge. One private proclaimed victory by bayoneting a rioter and capturing his flag, before returning to the safety of the soldier's ranks. At the corner of Division and Grand Streets, another mob confronted these troops, but the threat of opening fire, followed up by "the point of the bayonet," was enough to clear the streets.[25]

Despite Lieutenant Wood's apparent success, the rioters were becoming increasingly determined and organized in this industrial zone bordering the East River, with its acres of sprawling metal shops and adjacent slums. The Delameter Iron Works on Fourteenth Street, which produced ironclad ships for the navy, had a mob at its gates, and the local precinct was urgently calling for help from the Central Office. Since Acton had no telegraphic link to Sandford at the Seventh Avenue arsenal, he sent requests for troops via the nearby Twentieth Precinct—requests that went unanswered. Acton and Brown sent some federal troops to patrol Grand Street, where the rioters waited quietly until the troops had passed before looting a gun store. In the Eleventh Precinct, just north of Grand Street on the river, the mob would not give way even after troops opened fire on them, and the military retreated. Sandford was no more cooperative on the West Side, where he could easily have dispatched troops to support the police.[26]

At the *Tribune,* James Gilmore and Sidney Gay had gone to sleep at 4 a.m. on a pair of couches and were awakened several hours later when breakfast arrived from the nearby Astor House hotel. Having learned from reporters in the field that the mob still intended "to raze the *Tribune* building to the ground," the two men resolved over coffee that the newspaper "must set up as an independent nationality, with war-making powers," Gilmore wrote. "It must arm itself to the very teeth, and, looking for no outside aid, resist the rioters to the last extremity."[27]

Gilmore proceeded to the Brooklyn Navy Yard, where he asked Admiral Hiram Paulding what weapons would be best. Gilmore recalled that "there was a pleasurable gleam in the old veteran's eyes, as he said: 'It's bombshells, young man,—bombshells and hand-grenades,—and I'll give you enough of both to send ten thousand of those rascals to the devil to-night." Paulding ordered up two wagonloads of the grenades and shells, personally adjusting the fuses on the latter so they would explode immediately upon hitting the pavement. Gilmore was both impressed and amused by the "belligerent zeal" of the "white-haired admiral" and said he hoped the bombs would not have to be used. Paulding replied that Gilmore must "plant every one of them in Printing House Square to-night. If you do there never will be another riot in New York."

Returning to the *Tribune* with the wagons, Gilmore found the staff, directed by an army colonel, busily preparing for an attack. The broken doors and windows on the ground floor had been "barricaded with bales of printing-paper, thoroughly saturated with water, and a hose was attached to the huge boiler below, so that the whole floor could be deluged with scalding steam in an instant." On both the second and third floors, a cannon loaded with grapeshot and canister stood at one window, while large mounds of Admiral Paulding's hand grenades were soon arranged in front of the others.

In the editorial offices on the fourth floor, Gilmore took charge of the bombshells. Paulding had supplied him with a long wooden trough, which, projected out the window and over the street, would land the bombs on the rioters, not against the front of the building. The muskets had since been loaded with appropriate ammunition and placed at every window, while a friend of Greeley's, the abolitionist preacher Henry Ward Beecher, had sent a Sharps revolving rifle along with his "compliments to the rioters." The nearby *Times* building was similarly equipped, and the release of a bombshell by Gilmore was agreed upon as the signal for the staff at both newspapers to open fire with everything they had.

Greeley had taken a streetcar downtown from his house on Nineteenth Street past barricades and plumes of smoke from burning buildings. Insisting on his routine, he walked from the streetcar through the mobs to his office.[28] He was dismayed to find that the *Tribune* building had become an arsenal.

"What are these, Mr. Gilmore?" he asked, pointing to the bombshells by the window.

"Brimstone pills for those red ragamuffins down there on the sidewalk," Gilmore replied.

"But I wanted no arms brought into the building."

"Oh, yes; but that was yesterday. Now this building is under martial law."

"Take 'em away, take 'em away!" Greeley ordered in his high-pitched, squeaky voice. "I don't want to kill anybody, and besides they're a damn sight more likely to go off and kill some of us!"

Greeley went to his office and immersed himself in writing editorials while the mob outside continued to swell.[29]

He soon declared he could not concentrate surrounded by guns and ammunition and left the editorial offices for the city room, where he sat and composed his daily editorial, surrounded by jittery young reporters.[30] Periodically, friends went in and pleaded with him to leave the building, and he repeatedly put them off by promising he would go as soon as he finished what he was working on. The army colonel who had organized the building's defenses warned Gilmore and Gay: "Mr. Greeley ought to go. The mob knows he is here, and if he stays it is likely they will attack us. The consequence will be a good deal of useless slaughter." Nonetheless, as the afternoon wore on and the crowd grew, Greeley remained in the city room.[31]

The charred ruins of the armory on Second Avenue and Twenty-first Street were still smoking at noon on Tuesday when the mob attacked the Union

Steam Works one block to the north, which contained some four thousand carbines. The willingness of the police and military to use firearms in battle-field formations had made the rioters' quest for guns all the more urgent. Since factories and stores had been forced shut, the streets for ten blocks around the Union Steam Works "swarmed with infuriated men," while "all the women and children of the neighborhood seemed to be either mingling with the men in the streets, standing in doorways, or looking out through the windows."[32]

Encouraged by several leaders, including Francis Cusick, who had clubbed Superintendent Kennedy, the rioters drove off the police guard, poured into the Union Steam Works, and began distributing the rifles, while preparing to turn the large brick building into a stronghold.[33] At 2 p.m., Inspector George Dilks and two hundred Metropolitans dispatched from the Central Office ar-rived to recapture the building and the arms, sparking the most intense fight-ing of the entire week. First they had to clear a thousand rioters from the street in front of the building, which they did by closing ranks tightly and charging into the mob like a flying wedge, clubbing men to the ground, and retrieving stolen guns.[34]

One of the leaders was clubbed so hard that he staggered and fell for-ward against an iron gate, one of the pickets entering under his chin as far as the roof of his mouth. When the police later removed the hanging body, the cashmere pants, linen shirt, and costly vest under his workman's clothing, along with his "delicate features" and "white, fair skin," fueled suspicion that wealthy Copperheads were behind the riots. The man's body, like those of so many rioters, was reportedly carried off by his friends during the week of mayhem, leaving his identity a mystery. The *World* also noted that one or two people in each crowd "of better appearance and apparel than the rest" were seen inciting others to violence but disappeared when the time came to follow through.[35]

Inspector Dilks, having sown panic among the rioters and cleared the street, proceeded to send a detachment inside the Union Steam Works to se-cure the carbines. The Metropolitans fought their way up the stairs of the factory and into the main room on the second floor where the rioters had holed up. Many rioters were injured or killed after leaping from the windows, and any who escaped through the doors were clubbed down by the police waiting in the street.[36]

"While this was going on, a large number of women excitedly rushed forward with bricks and stones which they hurled at the police, fiercely swearing the while," the *World* reported. "The women manifested much more pluck and courage than the men, resolutely standing their ground

Soldiers firing on rioters at the Union Steam Works

when ordered to disperse by the officers." However, the attack prompted the police to start using their revolvers, and they quickly killed more than a dozen rioters. "A scene, which defies all powers of description then followed," according to the *Times*. "Men, women, and children rushed through the streets in the most frantic state of mind, and as the dead and wounded were borne from the place, the wild howlings of the bereaved, were truly sad to hear."[37]

Dilks and his men piled as many of the carbines as they could on a large wagon, carried some in their arms, and left the rest in the Union Steam Works with a small contingent of patrolmen to guard them. On their march back to Mulberry Street "the people poured out of the houses along the way to cheer the triumphal procession," Stoddard wrote. "Dilks and his men and their trophies were a sort of sunshine in a great darkness."[38]

Across the North in communities where the draft lottery had not yet begun, provost marshals were hoping New York's authorities would put down the mob aggressively and set an example. In Detroit, a district provost marshal telegraphed his superior that anger over conscription "has become intensified to an alarming degree by the successful violence in the city of New York, compelling the draft to be deferred. A spark here would explode the whole and bring it into the most violent action."

The captain also underscored Detroit's recent history: "We have had a Negro riot here within the last few months that controlled the city fully, burning some thirty houses, and finally was quelled by the arrival of the Twenty-seventh Michigan Infantry. That mob violence is here now, but intensified a thousand fold . . . The condition of things is more critical than they have been at any time during the war . . . A strong force should be ordered to this city at once." The substance of this report was forwarded to

Washington with the warning that parts of Detroit harbored "a most bitter opposition to the Government, and it extends to other portions of the State . . . unless the present mob is put down most summarily in New York the attempt to execute the draft here will lead to similar violence unless supported by a strong military force."

Closer to New York, in Newark, New Jersey, rioters had already smashed the windows of a district provost marshal's home and those of the *Daily Mercury,* which he owned. "The city authorities did nothing to prevent these outrages," a resident telegraphed Secretary of State Seward. "The citizens are at the mercy of ruffians."

Farther up the Hudson, at Kingston, New York, a district provost marshal reported that "a large meeting was held at [the village of] Rondout last evening, mostly made up of the Irish" who adopted resolutions "to resist the draft at all and any hazard, and to-day men are seen at various places in small groups making threats of resistance, &c . . . Again, we have no arms in this district and are wholly unprotected except my deputy and two special officers." At both Rondout and Saugerties, the meetings were said to have "hurrahed for Jeff. Davis and Lee."

As in Kingston, the military in Elmira, New York, expected a riot and requested five hundred "well-disciplined" troops if the draft was to be enforced. With his resources stretched thin and a flurry of such messages from across the state, Provost Marshal General James Fry ordered the draft suspended in Buffalo on Tuesday.

At the same time, he pushed forward with the drawing of names in some parts of Philadelphia, despite an appeal from the mayor to postpone the draft for a week. The army commander there was confident he could maintain order if the lottery were held in one district at a time, at least to start. Fry adopted the same strategy for Harrisburg and other parts of Pennsylvania, instructing his deputies to call on the military to "employ the necessary force to carry out the law."

From Iowa City, a telegram to Secretary of War Stanton spoke for all the rest: "The enforcement of the draft throughout the country depends upon its enforcement in New York City. If it can be successfully resisted there, it cannot be enforced elsewhere. For God's sake let there be no compromising or half-way measures."[39]

Following events from the South, Edmund Ruffin came to a similar conclusion from opposite motives, writing hopefully in his diary that "the timidity & forbearance" of the authorities in New York would trigger rioting all over the North. Ruffin predicted that the damage from the New York riot to "Lincoln's government, & Yankeedom" would be greater than the ravages of one hundred thousand Confederate troops; far worse would be the impact on the Union's reputation and moral standing in the eyes of the world. Ruffin wrote, "I shall await the consummation most anxiously—& earnestly," "though but faintly hoping that the atrocity & rage of the mob may be so extended, & unrestrained, as [to] lay in ashes the whole of the great city of New York, with all its appendages & wealth, as just retribution for its share of the outrages perpetrated on the people of the South."[40]

CHAPTER 12

"The Police Cannot Much Longer Sustain the Contest"

~

While the New York rioters tried to burn the bridge that linked Manhattan to the mainland on Monday night, Robert E. Lee's forces were at the Maryland border, stealthily building a pontoon bridge they hoped would be the army's lifeline, securing its escape to Virginia.

New York militiaman George Wingate recalled the mood in camp. "All were in high spirits. It was universally supposed that the rains had made the Potomac unfordable, 'and that Lee was a goner this time sure'; but as hour after hour passed without a sound of the heavy cannonading which marks 'the battle's opening roar,' and rumor after rumor filled the air, the talk, as time lengthened, grew less and less hopeful." While the militiamen waited in vain for the order to attack the trapped enemy backed up against the swollen river, the Confederates had begun to cross over to Virginia.[1]

By 11 a.m. on Tuesday, July 14, Lee's entire army, except a five-hundred-man rear guard, had escaped across the Potomac into Virginia, and the pontoon bridge was destroyed. During the afternoon, Wingate wrote, "we learned definitely that 'the play was played out.' Lee was gone, boots and baggage, and our hopes of taking a hand in the contest which would probably have decided the war, were gone with him."[2]

Lincoln was irate and ready to fire Meade but decided to check his anger and give the victor of Gettysburg another chance. The militia units still supporting Meade in Maryland "chafed" to go home and put down the riots, which they had just learned about from the Baltimore papers on Tuesday morning. John Lockwood of the Twenty-third Regiment wrote that the news "created somewhat of a stir in camp as may be imagined," the men thinking of their homes "exposed to the tender mercies of mob law, and we, to whom the city was accustomed to look for protection against such violence, unable to defend them."

Having patriotically marched to destroy the invading rebels, Lockwood wrote, "and now to be assailed by this dastardly fire in the rear made us turn with even sharper vengeance against the insurgents at home." The men were eager "to be seen marching up Broadway with firm step to the rescue of our dishonored metropolis."[3]

Similarly, Wingate wrote that the day they learned of the riots "was the first, and we hope the only time in our lives, that anyone was heard to say that he felt ashamed to think that he had been born in the city of New York." Having read about the riots in the *Herald*, which complained that the "military fired on the *people*," Wingate wrote, the militiamen were ready to gun down the editors, "for a more angry set of men" than this division "was never seen."[4]

The army, however, was only willing to send five regiments of militia back to New York right away, the elite Seventh, and four others that did not include Lockwood's or Wingate's. The news of Lee's escape would not reach New York until Tuesday night, and the first of the returning troops, traveling by train and boat, would not arrive until Wednesday night. In the interim, the mayor, the governor, the police, and the military had to cope—in their various ways—with the escalating violence in the streets.[5]

"Just as the City Hall clock struck twelve," at noon on Tuesday, the *World* reported, "a large crowd, composed mainly of mechanics, gathered about the *Tribune* office, apparently as if by previous arrangement. A man mounted the door step of the office and began haranguing the assemblage in favor of sacking the establishment, when the cry was raised, 'Governor Seymour,' 'Governor Seymour,' and away ran the crowd to the park."[6]

Governor Seymour, who was traveling to see relatives in New Jersey when the riots broke out and had to be contacted on the road, did not arrive in the city until Tuesday morning. He might have arrived almost a day earlier if he had taken a direct route and not chosen to spend Monday night in New Jersey. Republicans quickly seized on his tardiness as evidence of his sympathy for the rioters, while the *World* countered that he had spent the previous week in the city tending to the harbor defenses and had left on Friday, July 10, without any warning from federal authorities that they were about to implement the draft.[7]

William Tweed, who had been out on the streets since the riots began, trying to calm his constituents and keep abreast of events, met the governor at the ferry and escorted him to the St. Nicholas Hotel, where he joined Mayor Opdyke for a closed-door meeting. Just before noon, Seymour walked down Broadway without a guard or police escort to City Hall. Along with the mayor and a few other officials, including Tweed and District Attorney A. Oakey Hall, Seymour mounted the front steps. Mayor Opdyke looked "ghastly white," and his hands trembled, according to one reporter. "In his person he symbolized the fear that possessed the town." Seymour, by contrast, appeared calm. He addressed the cheering throng as "My friends" and launched into a speech.[8]*

"I call on the people to maintain law and order . . . for your salvation depends on this. Anarchy will be ruin," Seymour declared. "If the conscription law will not bear the test of the courts and the Constitution, it will not be enforced," Seymour promised his listeners, "but if upheld by the courts, then the state and city authorities will combine for the purpose of equalizing the tax and making it bear proportionately on the rich and the poor." The crowd cheered loudly.[9]

After the speech, Seymour conferred with Mayor Opdyke, military leaders, and other local officials, telling them he deemed martial law a last resort, and Opdyke still shared the governor's conciliatory approach. Intent on forestalling federal intervention and keeping the city in Democratic hands, the governor then issued a proclamation that placed him in command of enforcing law and order in the city, the local authorities being overwhelmed.

It urged the rioters and all citizens to return to their homes and jobs on pain of full prosecution under the law, but also promised that the rights of every draftee would be protected by the courts of New York State. For residents willing to serve on civilian patrols and volunteer military regiments, Seymour announced meeting places where they would be deputized. Seymour also sent a message to Archbishop John Hughes entreating him, as a leader of the Irish Catholic community, to call on the rioters to desist.[10]

Seymour got into a carriage with Tweed, and "amid the cheers of the multitude that thronged about the vehicle," they set off on a tour of the city, accompanied by other Democratic officials. The governor was cheered throughout the excursion and gave two more speeches, one on Wall Street, and the other to workers uptown on the West Side. Aside from President

---

*Republicans claimed that Seymour addressed the crowd as "My friends," and seized on the phrase to condemn him for fomenting the riots and sympathizing with the violent mob. Some of Seymour's defenders asserted that he never used those words, and press reports varied on the issue, offering different transcriptions of the speech.

THE MEETING OF THE FRIENDS,
CITY HALL PARK.

Republican cartoon of Governor Seymour addressing
a crowd during the draft riots

Lincoln and federal officials, Seymour had the greatest power to determine the government's handling of the draft riots, and by his words and actions, he endorsed the conciliatory approach of men like Judge Barnard and others who had addressed the crowds on Monday.[11]

Seymour set up his own headquarters at the Saint Nicholas Hotel on Tuesday, where he conferred with Samuel Barlow, General George McClellan, and other prominent Democrats, many of whom he sent as his emissaries to flash points across the city, where they persuaded mobs to disperse. Uptown, small-business and property owners along with clergymen also addressed the mobs, offering help in opposing the draft's three-hundred-dollar clause in exchange for an end to the violence. One such meeting drew up a petition to the city government calling for a suspension of the draft and an appropriation from the Common Council to pay the commutation fees of workers if the courts ultimately declared the conscription law to be constitutional.[12]

Catholic priests also intervened successfully at Columbia College on East Forty-ninth Street, where botany professor John Torrey reported, "The mob had been in the College Grounds, & came to our house—wishing to know if a republican lived there, & what the College building was used for."* The rioters declared they would burn President Charles King's house "as he was rich, & a decided republican." However, "the rioters were induced to go away by one or two Catholic priests, who made pacific speeches to them."[13]

Maria Daly concluded that "Catholic priests have done their duty as Christian ministers in denouncing these riotous proceedings. One of them remonstrated with a woman in the crowd who wanted to cut off the ears of a Negro [who] was hung. The priest told her that Negroes had souls. 'Sure, your reverence,' said she, 'I thought they only had gizzards.'"[14]

Despite the occasional successes of Democratic leaders and Catholic priests in mollifying the rioters, on the whole, the violence continued to escalate. At about the time that Seymour addressed the crowd at City Hall, rioters across the city stepped up their quest for firearms by raiding gun retailers' shops. Gun stores had sprung up all over the city during the war and carried large inventories to meet the growing demand. Fortunately for the city, the stores did not keep much ammunition or gunpowder on hand, and the biggest gun dealers were in the Wall Street area—the best-defended in the city.[15] By noon, heavy defenses were in place at government facilities. A navy gunboat in the East River at the foot of Wall Street stood ready to mow down any rioters that crossed its path, while marines equipped with artillery protected the government's gold in the U.S. Sub-Treasury at Wall and Broad Streets.[16]†

Unlike the saloonkeepers and small-property owners uptown, who negotiated with the rioters, wealthy Republican merchants and financiers on Wall Street banded together to form civilian patrols. William Dodge, vice president of the Chamber of Commerce and a member of the Union League Club, and his allies dominated the meeting at the Merchants' Exchange on Broadway but could not get a unanimous vote in favor of federal intervention. Over cries of "no" from their more conservative colleagues, the merchants resolved to "recommend to the proper authorities the consideration and the propriety of declaring martial law in this city."[17]

---

*Today the site of Rockefeller Center. The college moved to West 116th Street in 1897.
†Today the Federal Hall National Monument. See the Walking Tour in the appendix.

Dodge and several other prominent businessmen also addressed a crowd from the steps of the U.S. Sub-Treasury, denouncing the rioters and rallying support for the Union cause. By publicly calling for a swift, forceful response to the mobs, and having their words reported in the newspapers, the speakers risked reprisals against their homes and businesses. Many wealthy men chose instead to leave the city or remain hidden until the riots were over.[18]

Colonel O'Brien's cursing of the mob, followed by his orders to open fire on Second Avenue that morning, had marked him for revenge. When he recklessly returned to his neighborhood alone at about 2 p.m., he may have intended to check on his family, unaware that they had escaped to Brooklyn that morning after the mob sacked his house. Coming out of a drugstore, O'Brien cocked his pistol to intimidate the crowd that had gathered around the door. When a woman threw a stone at him, he fired low and the bullet ricocheted off the ground into her knee.

"She instantly fell, and from that moment the Colonel's fate was sealed," according to the *Tribune*. The mob knocked O'Brien to the ground and beat him unconscious with bricks and clubs. "Yelling like so many devils, three or four men seized the Colonel by his hair and dragged him into the street," the *Evening Post* reported. When the druggist tried to intervene and give O'Brien some water, the mob ransacked his store. After torturing the colonel's body for several hours, they dragged him into an alley and stood guard over their prize, smashing his head on the pavement when periodic groans indicated he was still alive.

Father Clowry, an Irish Catholic priest, also tried to stop the murder, but his pleas were ignored, and the mutilation continued for a few more hours. Clowry knelt down in the street and administered the last rites to O'Brien just before he died. When the mob was distracted by a commotion elsewhere, Clowry and another priest, with the help of some neighbors, hefted the enormous corpse onto a handcart and wheeled it to the morgue at Bellevue hospital. "He was terribly mangled," the *Tribune* reported after talking to Clowry, "and his body was almost naked and covered with gore."[19]

O'Brien's murder was one of many fierce encounters unfolding across the city. Also at about 2 p.m., rioters on Sixth and Second Avenues coalesced into one enormous mob around several opulent Fifth Avenue mansions in the area of Forty-sixth Street that they believed were owned by prominent Republicans. "On my reporting to General Brown, I was ordered to proceed with my company to Forty-sixth Street, where the mob was burning buildings," Captain H. R. Putnam of the Twelfth U.S. Infantry recalled. He and his eighty-two men had arrived in the city Monday night, only to be sent by

General Wool on a pointless march from the St. Nicholas Hotel to City Hall, back to the hotel, and finally to 300 Mulberry Street. They would march some twelve miles on Tuesday fighting the rioters.[20]

A rising star in the military, Putnam was in charge of the fort at Sandy Hook, the gateway to New York's waters from the Atlantic Ocean. The captain exhibited the best qualities of his legendary ancestor, Major General Israel Putnam, the fearless Revolutionary War hero. Wounded during the Battle of Bull Run, Captain Putnam had nonetheless dragged others to safety.[21]

At Forty-sixth Street, Putnam's troops "found the mob in strong force, burning and destroying property," he reported. He was joined by sixty patrolmen under Captain George Walling, who estimated the crowd at more than two thousand people. "I shouted at the top of my voice," Walling recalled, "so that the rioters could hear me: 'Kill every man who has a club! Double quick! Charge!'" The police and soldiers plowed into the crowd, while women at the edges of the melee yelled at the rioters to "stand up and give the police hell!" According to Putnam, the mob "fought desperately for about five minutes, when they broke in all directions . . . Their loss in killed and wounded would not fall short of forty."[22]

One newspaper reported that "in every street they might be seen reeling to and fro, their faces covered with clotted blood, their clothes torn, and everything about their appearance disgusting and absolutely sickening to behold." Several soldiers were injured by stones, and two "who had stumbled in the charge were set upon and badly beaten before they could be rescued." One of them was sent to the nearby Jews' Hospital because his wounds were so severe.[23]*

The mob had reassembled and taken back the Union Steam Works not long after Dilks and his men departed, easily overwhelming the small garrison he had left behind.[24] The rioters also fended off an assault on the factory by policemen of the local precinct. At 2:30 p.m., a large force of police and volunteer specials followed by some regular troops converged on the factory "and found the building in possession of the rioters, who crowded the windows" and showered them with "brick-bats and stones and shot," the *Tribune* reported.

Captain John Helme and his patrolmen had just thwarted an attack on the mayor's house and were the first on the scene. Wielding their clubs, they

---

*Founded in 1852, the Jews' Hospital, on West Twenty-eighth Street, was later renamed Mount Sinai Hospital and moved to its present location at Fifth Avenue and 100th Street.

charged, battling the rioters outside and inside the building for a full ten minutes and seizing the remaining carbines while rescuing the few men Dilks had left behind to guard them. "The policemen also made liberal use of their revolvers," according to the *World.* The rioters were seen "throwing away their guns and making the best use of their legs to get away, screaming and howling with pain, as the clubs were playing with terrible force upon them."

Their mission accomplished, the police piled nearly a thousand carbines on a wagon commandeered from its angry owner, and prepared to leave. David Barnes of the *Times* reported: "By the time the wagon was loaded and the force in line, they were completely surrounded by an overwhelming and infuriated mob; not a man flinched; all felt their critical situation, but were determined to fight their way out. Just at this juncture, when they were showered with stone and shot, and when the mob, reinforced by that which had murdered Col. O'Brien, were about rallying for an attack, Inspector Dilks, with his command of police and military, wheeled into the avenue from Twenty-first Street."

Helme's men cheered loudly, while Dilks and his 150 patrolmen, supported by more than 100 U.S. infantrymen under Captain Walter Franklin, plowed into the rioters from behind. The mob retreated but kept "firing stones and muskets continually" at the soldiers, Franklin recalled. "The crowd grew more insolent, and increased the firing as we advanced," so he fought them like an enemy in a pitched battle. "I halted the company, and fired by sections, allowing each section to fall to the rear to load as fast as it had fired."

These tactics cleared the streets and drove the rioters into houses and onto rooftops from which they fired on the troops until Franklin's men made it "dangerous to show a head anywhere." The police and soldiers then marched away, but the angry mob closed in behind them on Second Avenue. "They were allowed to get quite close to us, when I faced the rear section about, and fired one or two volleys," Franklin reported, "which must have been very effective, as they dispersed, and did not give us any further trouble."

As the police left with the carbines, crowds filled the streets again "and from every window women again looked out," the *World* reported.[25] "The dead bodies of the killed were to be seen being borne away by their friends, the blood trickling on the pavement. Pools of blood would be met at frequent intervals, and in a large number of houses lay the wounded writhing in pain." Many were killed and wounded, according to the *World,* including innocent bystanders, some of them women and children struck by bullets "half a mile away." On the street corners clusters of people swore vengeance and called for coordinated action against the police.

A "middle-aged Irish woman" addressed one of the larger crowds in the area, "expressing in strong terms her contempt of the behavior of the mob when attacked by the police," the *World* reported. "After such an exhibition of cowardliness, they ought to be ashamed ever again to show their heads. There were as many of them with carbines in their hands as there were of the police, she said, but instead of bravely defending themselves they threw down their weapons and with abject whines allowed themselves to be pummeled and struck to the ground."

One man got the attention of the crowd by shouting, "All we want is a leader, and then we will go to victory or the devil!" He drew loud cheers, but when he tried to lead them west along Twenty-second Street to "punish the aristocrats of Fifth Avenue," he had trouble gathering more than a few dozen boys and men, and a general consensus was reached that they should meet that night to make further plans.

Throughout the day, the rioters had systematically stopped streetcars and stages to deprive the police of vehicles they needed to reach the mobs all over the city. Anticipating this tactic, Acton had already gathered enough street-cars from Third and Sixth Avenues, and stages from the Bowery and Broadway, to form a long line in front of police headquarters on Mulberry Street, and had thrown at least one uncooperative driver into a holding cell.[26]

Captain Franklin and his men had rested for an hour or two after their return from the Union Steam Works when Acton put them in stages and sent them to Eighth Avenue and Twenty-ninth Street, where trouble had been brewing all afternoon. At 2 p.m., half a dozen drunken rioters, including a bugle-blowing Irish peddler named John Corrigan, had each taken a horse from the stables of the Red Bird stage line on West Thirty-fifth Street and joined the "riotous and disorderly men and boys" looting stores up and down the West Side "armed with clubs sticks and other missels," a witness reported. The horsemen named Patrick Burke their "colonel," but Corrigan, sounding his brass horn, at times appeared to be the "ringleader," as when he rode his mount into a corner saloon and the mob burst in after him to drink the place dry.[27]

Nearby, on Twenty-ninth Street, Lucy Gibbons and her sister Julia continued to prepare for the worst.[28] Going through the house, Lucy recalled, "[we were] trying to think of things my mother and sister Sally,—who were nursing the soldiers down South,—would like saved; but it was very hard to think." Their father had told them that the whole row of houses was threatened, and not to bother shifting their possessions from one house to another. They did not attempt to move the family's library of some two thousand books, even though, according to Lucy, it was "very dear" to them.

Nonetheless, they did take baskets of clothing and some documents. A cousin, Sarah Powell, came in to help them. "[We] carried all the things we had packed up to our attic and over the roof, down into Uncle Samuel's house . . . We worked hard until we dropped everything on the floor of Uncle Samuel's attic," Lucy remembered. "In fact, we were busy all day, but so little alarmed, that, at about 5 o'clock, when we were going into Aunt R's, I proposed taking a bath."

However, they were not to have the leisure of a good soak. Indeed they were lucky to have left their own house in the nick of time. "We heard a sudden uproar in the street," Lucy wrote. "We ran to the window and looked out through the shutters, and saw two men on horse-back galloping down the sidewalk, waving swords and shouting 'Greeley! Greeley!' A crowd of men and women that seemed to fill the middle of the street followed the horsemen past our house to Ninth Avenue, then turned back, shouting 'Greeley! Gibbons! Greeley! Gibbons! Gibbons!' "

Mounted on the horses from the Red Bird stables, two of the rioters stopped at the Gibbonses' courtyard gate and faced the mob. They selected about a dozen men with pickaxes, who entered the yard and climbed onto the balcony, broke through the parlor windows, and disappeared into the house. While the crowd waited and chafed, the axmen ransacked the interior and tossed valuables out the windows, Lucy recalled. "In front of the house all was noise, confusion, and quarreling."

The sisters were afraid their father might return at any moment and try to drive the looters out with his pistol, since he had sworn to defend the house. "We dared not open the shutters and saw things imperfectly, now looking, now drawing back. There was fighting. I saw one man drop like lead, drew back, looked again and saw the books falling like rain until they were heaped up and hid the fence."

James Gibbons, like his daughters, had fortunately left the house, to get a newspaper, just before the mob attacked. He had also left his revolver in his desk drawer. Returning to find the house full of rioters, James wrote, "I went in among them and up to my desk, making room, as I entered towards the library, for the villain who had our mattress; but seeing that the place was fully in possession of the mob, with my pistol in hand, I could go no further. They did not know me as the owner of the house, and I passed, unharmed, down the stairs again."[29]

At this point the police arrived and charged into the house, clubbing the rioters and driving them out into the courtyard, where additional officers stood ready to strike them. Captain Franklin and his troops arrived at the same time, and in the confusion, some of them fired without orders, wounding half a dozen policemen, one of them fatally.[30] The soldiers drove the rioters away, Lucy recalled, and "returned and drove away the mob a second time, and then marched away. As they disappeared one way, the mob returned in full force by another and the looting went on."

Lucy watched as a man carried off the keyboard of her piano, and "sheets of music seemed to be flying in every direction." She also observed: "On the sidewalk some women, laden with spoils, were leaning against the courtyard railing; one had a pot and was fanning herself with the lid. I know the police were doing what they could, but I did not see them. Suddenly smoke poured in clouds out of the windows. We learned later that neighbors, alarmed lest the fire should spread to their own houses, carried water over the roofs and down into our house and put out the fires; and I think some of our cousins worked at that."[31]

Ironically, in venting their fury at Horace Greeley, radical Republicanism, and abolition, these poor, mostly Irish, whites were laying waste the home of a woman who had devoted her life to lifting up New York's underclass, and caring for their sick or wounded sons and husbands in the army. "In the midst of the riot," one eyewitness reported, "a voice in the crowd was heard crying 'Shame! Don't you know what Mrs. Gibbons did for the 69th Regiment?' But nothing could restrain them."[32]

Fortunately for Julia and Lucy, their cousin Joseph Choate had canceled a trip to Salem, Massachusetts, and at his wife Carrie's urging had searched until he found the sisters at the Browns' two doors down. Lucy recalled that Choate "had been all through our house looking for us in the mob which filled it. He said there must have been two hundred of them there. I said, 'Don't leave us,' and he answered, 'I will only do so while I get a carriage and take you to our house.'"[33]

A fervent anti-Irish Republican, a lawyer, and later a prominent judge, Choate was filled more with indignation than fear by the riot. "We cannot even think of leaving until it is over," he had written to his mother that afternoon, after sheltering four black refugees in his home. "The accounts in the papers do not tell the half of the brutality of the human beasts who for the moment have control. Yesterday morning when the riot commenced in the 22nd Ward, it was headed by the Alderman of that Ward." The riots and violence against blacks, he wrote, were "the natural fruits of the doctrines of Seymour, Wood, Vallandigham, etc."[34]

Toward evening, the rioters became even better organized and took the alarming step of barricading avenues and streets on both sides of the city. Starting with wagons and carts, felled telegraph poles and lampposts, they added furniture, barrels, and crates, "the vehicles being lashed together with telegraph wires, or anything else that came to hand," Captain Walling recalled. "My orders were simply to 'clear the streets.'" The mobs' shift from roving vandalism to stationary defenses signaled an intent to seal off and control discrete areas of the city over an extended time period. Police telegrapher Charles Loring Chapin, who had stood behind the barricades in Berlin during the revolts of 1848, saw this as an ominous escalation, from riot to insurrection: "The mob were introducing the revolutionary methods of Europe."[35]

The police had to act quickly, before they lost the daylight needed to break up the barricades and before the rioters could strengthen these improvised ramparts any further. Walling had been battling the mob all afternoon, and as he prepared his men to storm and dismantle the barricades along six blocks of Ninth Avenue between Thirty-sixth and Forty-second Streets, he requested military reinforcements from General Brown at the Central Office and from General Sandford at the arsenal. Brown's U.S. infantrymen arrived at Walling's station house on Twenty-fourth Street near Ninth Avenue at 6 p.m. At 7:40, Brown made a final attempt to stir Sandford by sending a telegram to Walling's precinct for delivery by messenger to the arsenal but received no answer. When the sun began to set and General Sandford's promised troops had still not arrived, the police, supported by the regulars, began their assault without them.[36]

"Many of the rioters had fire-arms" and were posted "not only behind the barricades, but on the house-tops," Walling observed. "We advanced towards the first barricade on the 'double-quick,' with the soldiers in our rear." A hail of bullets met the police. "Fortunately most of the balls passed over our heads, but it was warm work." The patrolmen stepped aside, allowing the soldiers to aim round after round of musket fire at the rioters.

When the mob finally retreated to the next barricade, one block north, the police broke up the first barrier, "which of course occupied time, and exposed them to the missiles of the mob," the infantry captain, John Wilkins, reported. The soldiers started to pick off the snipers from the rooftops, including a rioter who kept "dodging behind one of the chimneys," Walling recalled. "He tried this once too often. Suddenly, while I was watching him, he threw up his arms and fell headlong to the street with a rifle ball through the very centre of his forehead."[37]

Another relentless stream of gunfire from the troops dislodged the rioters from the second barricade, and the combined force advanced until it had eliminated every obstruction from the avenue. Defenseless, the rioters scattered, and the soldiers broke ranks to pursue and shoot them on the side streets.[38] More rioters remained on the rooftops, however, and the infantry found themselves "suddenly assailed with a terrific shower of brick-bats, thrown by unseen hands," Wilkins wrote. The soldiers fought back briefly, and then proceeded to the station house since it was by then "almost too dark to operate with any success."[39]

"A carriage will be here instantly," Gilmore told Greeley at 8 p.m. "We want you to leave the office." When Greeley insisted on staying, Gilmore became adamant. "A hundred and fifty of us are risking our lives to defend this building, and you have no right to add to our danger." Greeley finally gave in, saying he would take a streetcar home instead of a private carriage. Pointing to the mob outside, Gilmore informed Greeley that he would never make it to a streetcar, and the reluctant editor allowed himself to be spirited out the back door and into a shuttered carriage on Spruce Street.

When Gilmore turned to go back inside, the longshoreman who had rowed him to Governors Island tapped his arm and asked to join him: "I told ye I'd see the dance out, and ye'll have warm work before morning." Gilmore brought the old sailor into the building, but the arsenal being fully manned, asked him instead to repeat his mission of the night before. It would be "a Christian deed" and save many lives, Gilmore told him, if he would spread the word throughout the mob that Greeley had departed and the building was "so thoroughly armed that the first discharge from it would slay a thousand of the rioters." The night wore on, and the warning appeared to have worked. The mob "surged and howled around the building," Gilmore recalled, but they did not attack.[40]

Elsewhere around the city, however, in their continued campaign to terrorize and expel the black population, the rioters pursued more vulnerable targets. On Roosevelt Street, where the many black residents had fled their homes, mobs burned two black tenements to the ground and pulled down three wooden buildings which were then made into a bonfire. In Greenwich Village, a gang on a looting spree tried to burn "the Arch," a row of tenements full of black families. The rioters ignited a barrel full of straw and wood shavings treated with camphene and placed it in the open archway under the buildings. The block was saved only because a fire company responding to a call uptown happened to be passing by and smothered the flames.[41]

Not as fortunate were the Derricksons—a black man with a white wife and two children—who were viciously attacked in their cellar apartment on Worth Street that night. When the mob announced they would lynch Derrickson and broke down his door, he fled out the rear window, thinking black men were the rioters' targets and that his wife and children would be safe. Instead, the intruders beat Derrickson's young son with an ax and with a spoke from a cart wheel. "For God's sake, kill me and save my boy," his mother shrieked, while covering her son's body with her own and absorbing most of the blows, but the assailants hauled him into the street and stripped him as he lay unconscious.

Mrs. Derrickson again tried to shield her son, but the men continued to beat both of them. While the rioters considered whether to lynch the boy or set him on fire, the grocer from next door intervened, saying, "It was a shame for you to hit that boy, you great big men to come here and attack a boy, why don't you hit men, if you want to fight." The rioters threatened to hang the grocer, but, armed with a pistol, he roused the German residents on the block to reinforce him. One of the mob's leaders said, "Come on boys there is no use in standing here any longer—there is another nest of niggers round in Leonard Street—let's clear them out." Mrs. Derrickson had indeed given her life to save her son: He survived the beating, and she died a month later from her injuries.[42]

The rioters' anger and cries for vengeance after the second battle at the Union Steam Works had continued to build all afternoon and evening; by 10:30 p.m., the surrounding ward had erupted with arson. Thwarted in their attempt to turn the Union Steam Works into an armed fortress, the frustrated rioters set fire to the five-story brick factory. They also attacked the police station on Twenty-second Street near First Avenue, where the four officers on duty barely escaped by knocking out the bars in a cell window and climbing through before the building went up in a tall plume of smoke and flames.[43]

"The flames soon wreathed the tower and rose in majestic columns," wrote Ellen Leonard, a young woman visiting relatives in the city. "The whole neighborhood was flooded with light. Thousands of spectators gazed upon the scene, crowning the house-tops as with statues of living fire."[44]

In his house nearby at Gramercy Park, George Templeton Strong stopped writing in his diary and went outside to see the blaze. He chose not to get close, however, because he found himself "in a crowd of Celtic spectators" from the surrounding tenements who "were exulting over the damage to 'them bloody police,' and so on." Strong had no sympathy for the grievances of the Irish laborer who had escaped famine in Ireland only to encounter prejudice and exploitation in America. "Paddy has left his Egypt—Connaught— and reigns in his promised land of milk and honey and perfect freedom. Hurrah, there goes a strong squad of police marching eastward down this street, followed by a company of infantry with gleaming bayonets."[45]

William Powell and his family, after escaping from their roof using the rope and clothesline, spent a full twenty-four hours locked up in the police station, while every last piece of their personal property was "scattered to the four winds." Late on Tuesday night, the police took them to a boat leaving for New Haven, and they continued on to New Bedford, Massachusetts, temporarily leaving their invalid daughter with friends in New York.

"As a devoted loyal Unionist, I have done all I could do to perpetuate and uphold the integrity of this free government," Powell told William Lloyd Garrison. "My oldest son is now serving my country as a surgeon in the United States army, and myself had just received a commission in the naval service. What more could I do? What further evidence was wanting to prove my allegiance in the exigencies of our unfortunate country? I am now an old man, stripped of everything which I once possessed, of all the comforts of life; but I thank God that He has yet spared my life, which I am ready to yield in the defence of my country."[46]

Powell was grateful that he and his family had at least survived, and as cramped as they were in the station house, they were more fortunate than many blacks who found no room at the local precinct. Shortly before midnight, Captain Walling's station house on Twenty-fourth Street off Ninth Avenue was filled to capacity, and he had to send a group of black refugees from nearby tenements to Twentieth Street and Seventh Avenue to find shelter.

At midnight, Walling responded to a report that rioters had attacked an African American church on Thirtieth Street between Seventh and Eighth Avenues, intending to chop it apart with axes instead of burning it so their friends in adjacent houses would not be harmed. "It happened that several fire-engines were passing through the street at the time," Walling recalled, "and mixing with the party of firemen we approached close to the church without attracting much attention." The vandals were surprised and met the police with a barrage of gunfire from "the street, alleys, and doorways," David Barnes reported. Walling noted that his men used their pistols for the first time that day and with a single shot killed a rioter on the roof who was "hacking away at the timbers with an axe." The police also used their clubs. "Scores of heads were cracked," wrote Barnes, the church was saved, and the area was cleared.[47]

"All this time," Headley wrote, the arsenal at Thirty-fifth Street and Seventh Avenue "wore the look of a besieged fortress," since Sandford "evidently thought he had as much as he could do to hold that building, without doing anything to quell the riot in the city." Some of General Brown's men "were there cooped up as useless as in garrison—for if seven hundred men with cannon sweeping every approach could not hold it, seven thousand could not."[48]

Late on Tuesday night, Governor Seymour's declaration of "a state of insurrection" in the city seemed to augur more aggressive action. However, the effect was to forestall federal intervention and martial law by putting Seymour in charge of restoring order—and thus to endorse the Democrats' more conciliatory approach toward the rioters.[49] Seymour's strained relationship with Acton and the other police commissioners, resulting from his attempt six months earlier to remove them, also compromised the effort to put down the riots.

With Seymour and Acton not speaking to each other, and General Brown still hoping to extricate his remaining troops from Sandford's grip at the arsenal, the clerk of the police commission, Seth Hawley, who knew the governor, was sent to enlist his help. Hawley arrived at the St. Nicholas Hotel, where Seymour professed total ignorance of what was transpiring at the arsenal, since Sandford had not kept him informed. When Hawley asked the governor to send a messenger there with an order to release Brown's troops, Seymour remained aloof, saying he could not spare one, but finally relented and agreed to send Hawley, who was careful to deliver the order not to Sandford but to his adjutant.[50]

Worried that the rioters would "attack a Negro tenement house some blocks below us, as they had attacked others, I ordered the doors to be shut and no gas to be lighted in front of the house," Maria Daly wrote. The Dalys lived just west of Washington Square. "I was afraid people would come to visit Judge Daly, ask questions, etc. I did not wonder at the spirit in which the poor resented the three-hundred-dollar clause . . . This is exceedingly unjust. The laboring classes say that they are sold for three hundred dollars, whilst they pay one thousand dollars for Negroes."[51]

While Maria Daly's political sympathies and opinions led her to view the violence against blacks in terms of her own safety, abolitionists and others took some grave risks. From the Jewish family's house at the end of the street, Joseph Choate had bundled Lucy and Julia Gibbons into the carriage he had waiting on Eighth Avenue and had taken them to his parents' home on Twenty-first Street, where Lucy learned that her aunt and uncle's "warmest sympathy and kindness" also extended to "five colored refugees in the kitchen."[52]

John Torrey, the botany professor at Columbia College, was about to leave for the country when the riots broke out. He had planned to go directly to the train from his second job, at the government assay office downtown, but a colleague "came in & said he saw a mob stop two 3rd Avenue cars to take out some negroes & maltreat them," Torrey wrote. "This decided me to return home, so as to protect my colored servants."

Torrey boarded a Fourth Avenue streetcar, heading for his house on the Columbia campus at Fifth Avenue and Forty-ninth Street, but the car went no farther than Thirty-fourth Street. "I found the whole road way & sidewalks filled with rough fellows (& some equally rough women) who were tearing up rails, cutting down telegraph poles, & setting fire to buildings," he reported. "I walked quietly along through the midst of them, without being molested. In 49 st. they were numerous, & made, as I was passing near the College, an attack upon one of a row of new houses in our street."

At home, Torrey found his two grown daughters "a little alarmed, but not frightened." Later in the week he noted that the police stations were overflowing with black refugees and hundreds had fled to Central Park, where they huddled without any shelter from the heavy rains. Expecting an assault on his own household, Torrey wrote, "We are all quite calm & are chiefly concerned about our servants."[53]

Republicans like the Choates and Torreys were not the only ones who took in blacks. An elderly woman from Cannon Street later reported that she and her husband, along with about a dozen other blacks, were sheltered and fed in the home of an Irish Catholic family for two days before a police escort was arranged to conduct them to the station house.[54]

Safe at the Choates' house, Lucy Gibbons and her sister nonetheless passed a fitful night on Tuesday: "Julia and I had a room together, but of course we could not sleep, and after a few hours we got up and stood at the open window. The dead silence of the night was dreadful. Once we heard a faint cry, three times repeated, far away: 'Murder! Murder! Murder!' "[55]

Tuesday had been far worse than Monday in the sheer scale of the violence—in lives lost and buildings destroyed. "Excuse me for saying that this mob is testing the Government nearly as strongly as the Southern rebellion," a War Department telegrapher in New York warned Stanton on Tuesday. "We are expecting momentarily that our Southern wires will be cut, as the rioters are at work in their immediate neighborhood," he wrote that evening. "The police so far report themselves as having been successful in every fight, of which they have had many, but they say they are exhausted, and cannot much longer sustain the unequal contest."[56]

CHAPTER 13

Doom or Deliverance: Wednesday, July 15—Day Three

~⁀

Mayor Opdyke was unaware of Lee's escape across the Potomac on Tuesday morning when he finally telegraphed a direct appeal to Stanton that afternoon for troops to put down the riot. Stanton replied from Washington that the Seventh Regiment and four other militia units were on their way: "Five regiments are under orders to return to New York. The retreat of Lee having now become a rout, with his army broken and much heavier loss of killed and wounded than was supposed, will relieve a large force for the restoration of order in New York."

The secretary of war added more good news, that operations against Charleston, South Carolina—the cockpit of the Confederacy—had begun well: "All but one fort on Morris Island have been captured, and that will be speedily reduced, after which Sumter must follow."[1] Putting a good spin on the news from the Potomac, Stanton did not mention that Meade's hesitation had allowed Lee to escape at the very moment when the rebel Army of Northern Virginia lay in tatters after the defeat at Gettysburg and might have been crushed once and for all.

At the same time, New York's newspapers chided midwesterners for failing to repel the comparatively tiny invasion by John Hunt Morgan and his rampaging Confederate horsemen, who were still at large. Just when it seemed Morgan was retreating toward the Ohio River, the *Times* wrote, "the dispatches tell us that Cincinnati is in high excitement, that martial law is proclaimed, and every preparation making to repel an expected attack on that city!" Frustrated and disgusted with the authorities in the Midwest, the *Times* noted that no one was really sure where Morgan would strike next. "Thus three great States—Ohio, Indiana and Kentucky—are prodigiously agitated, and their military leaders apparently nonplussed by a raid of about 4,000 rebels, and four guns, through their borders."[2]

Morgan's force was even smaller than the *Times* estimated and was getting smaller every day. Forgoing the temptation to free the rebel prisoners at Indianapolis, Morgan's cavalry had proceeded northeastward and crossed the border into Ohio on July 13, aiming instead for Cincinnati. However, having lost 20 percent of his force, and exhausted the remaining two thousand men by constant riding, Morgan reluctantly decided to bypass Cincinnati and finally paused at Williamsburg, Ohio, at dusk on the fourteenth.

With federal troops drawing closer every hour, Morgan planned to rest briefly, then continue east 120 miles to Buffington Ford, where the shallow water would enable his troopers to cross the Ohio River into West Virginia. Next they would veer to the southwest into Kentucky and head for points south. Given that they had just ridden almost one hundred miles in a day and a half, and their horses were badly in need of rest, Morgan's officers were dubious, but there was no alternative. Some seven thousand Union cavalry and infantry had joined the hunt, while residents along the rebels' path took shots at them and felled trees as roadblocks. The raid had become a retreat, and they had to keep moving.[3]

"If Lee had been annihilated, Richmond was a ripe apple waiting to drop into our hands," the *Tribune* lamented on Wednesday morning. Perhaps it was not too late to catch Lee's army if a "vigorous pursuit" into the Shenandoah Valley was launched, the paper suggested, withholding judgment against Meade and blasting General in Chief Halleck for "the imbecile strategy which kept the forces of Gen. [John] Dix promenading on the Peninsula, while a decisive struggle was pending in Pennsylvania," where he might have cut off Lee's retreat by moving north from Virginia. In any event, Greeley's paper concluded, the Confederate army had "seen the Northern elephant and felt his tusks . . . we have doubtless seen the last serious invasion of the North by the Rebels."[4]

The fire continued to rage in the rear, however. "Albany, Troy, Yonkers, Hartford, Boston, and other cities have each their Irish anti-conscription Nigger-murdering mob, of the same type as ours," wrote George Templeton Strong. "It is a grave business, a *jacquerie* that must be put down by heroic doses of lead and steel."[5]

In Boston's North End on Tuesday night, a mob of almost a thousand people attacked an armory on Cooper Street. Ignoring warnings from the soldiers inside, the crowd smashed the windows with bricks and rocks and forced open the door. On the verge of losing all to the rioters, the defenders fired a cannon loaded with canister, an exploding container of shot, killing four or five people and wounding about a dozen others, some seriously. One of the dead had eleven pieces of shot in his head and body and his arm was nearly taken off. When the rioters persisted, the soldiers scattered them with a bayonet charge.[6]

Smaller mobs of "several hundred persons" raided gun shops in Dock Square and Faneuil Hall Square, stealing dozens of muskets, pistols, and knives, before the police and militia descended on them. The mayor, along with the police chief and his deputy, arrived promptly and stationed troops and officers, including cavalry and artillery units, at strategic points throughout the city to forestall any further rioting. The *New York Times* praised Boston's handling of the outbreak as "The Way to Deal With the Mob" and urged more aggressive measures in Manhattan.[7]

However, no militia or regiments from the Army of the Potomac had arrived yet, and the military forces in the city were exhausted. Draft riots had also broken out in Newark, Jersey City, Hastings, Tarrytown, Rye, New Rochelle, Jamaica, and on Staten Island.[8] Wednesday thus became a turning point at which the city had to be saved or fall to the mob completely.[9]

The hottest day of the year dawned with black smoke from sixty charred buildings filling the air. The roads in Westchester County were jammed with refugees, as were the docks and railroad stations. People fled on the assumption that New York City would soon be completely destroyed. Many others could not flee because the rioters had torn up the railroad tracks. For those who remained in the city, especially blacks, danger lurked around every corner, particularly if they dared to show themselves in the street. The rioters continued to purge the black neighborhoods.[10]

After long marches, policemen returned to Mulberry Street for brief rest breaks in the predawn darkness and were sent out again across the city. Acton stood in front of the Central Office and shouted encouragement. "Go on boys! Go on! Give it to them now! Quail on toast for every man of you, as soon as the mob is put down. Quail on toast, boys!"[11]

Like the day before, Wednesday began with the grisly murder of a black man who had the gall to defend himself. At about 6 a.m., James Costello, a black shoemaker, was chased down West Thirty-second Street by William Mealy, a volunteer fireman. Costello was known as "an active man in his business—industrious and sober," and Mealy, also a shoemaker, may have resented the incursion of a black man into the trade. When Costello turned and shot Mealy in the head with a pistol, his mother and brother arrived on the scene with at least a dozen others, "howling and yelling." They quickly attracted a mob of two or three hundred rioters, who chased Costello and grabbed him before he could enter a nearby house.

"Dragging him into the middle of the street they jumped upon him and pounded him with their fists and with stones until life was extinct," the *Tribune* reported. A fourteen-year-old butcher's boy named Jacob Long threw several stones at the body. "Hang him—hang him," the mob chanted. The owner of a nearby stable provided a rope, and they hanged Costello from a tree. Soon, "his fingers and toes had been sliced off, and there was scarcely an inch of his flesh which was not gashed."[12]

Thinking the house they had pulled Costello from was his own, the mob gutted and burned it, then moved on to a row of tenements behind it, which a local woman had informed them were full of black families. Warned by a neighbor of the impending attack, the tenants had fled, and the mob burned the buildings. At other black homes in the neighborhood, the rioters carted away furniture, bedding, clothes, and other humble possessions, before torching the buildings. Two young black children had their clothes stolen straight off their bodies.

James Cassidy, an Irish laborer at the head of one mob, was more intent on ridding the area of blacks than on looting. Before burning their house, he gave his black neighbors five minutes to clear out, calling them "damned niggers," and warning one woman, "Don't never show your face in this street again."[13]

General Brown ordered troops to the scene, including an artillery unit under Lieutenant B. Franklin Ryer, who "marched there through a heavy rain" with one hundred men and reported seeing the rioters disperse "without having to fire a shot." Costello's body was cut down from the tree, and the troops proceeded to the arsenal on Seventh Avenue at about 8 a.m. When Ryer asked where he should go next to confront the mob, Sandford ordered him to stay inside the heavily guarded perimeter around the arsenal.

However, Ryer was soon sent back down to Thirty-second Street, where the mob had reappeared and was attacking a house in which several black families had tried to hide. Ryer's men scattered the rioters and brought some fourteen blacks to safety in the arsenal. The rain had put the cannons out of commission, but Ryer had one platoon fan out across Seventh Avenue at Thirty-second Street and block the rioters' charge up the avenue with two rounds of musket fire. The mob fell back with "considerable loss," Ryer reported. "Soon after, one of the rioters endeavored to wrest the musket from the hands of one of my sentries, but received the contents instead."

With at least twenty-three people, including women and children, killed or wounded in the barrage from Ryer's troops, the neighborhood was in shock, "the women and children filling the air with their cries and lamentations," the

Times reported, while the men who had lost friends "sat mournful and sullen."

At the same time, Lieutenant Robert Joyce, in command of the second platoon at the arsenal, had received a tip that rioters had a large cache of weapons in a house on Thirty-second Street and Broadway. He set off with fifteen men and stormed the house, capturing seventy-three Enfield rifles and bringing them back to the arsenal on a wagon despite the menacing crowds along his route.[14]

Less fortunate was the foray by a cavalry troop into Thirty-third Street, where a gang of thugs had beaten and was chasing a black man, Augustus Stuart, who panicked and fired a pistol at the soldiers, mistaking them for rioters. Drawing his sword, one of the mounted soldiers slashed Stuart, who later died from the wound. When the various contingents of soldiers returned to the arsenal and to police headquarters, the defiant mob reassembled on Thirty-second Street, hanged Costello's body again, and searched for new victims.[15]

Like the city's entire black population, Henry Highland Garnet had been forced to stay indoors for almost three days, but on Wednesday he ventured out of his house and found the structure of Shiloh Church on Prince Street intact; the interior, however, was thoroughly ransacked. Risking his life, he walked through the streets, where he found "marauding bands dancing and howling around the red flames of the burning buildings."[16]

A black man named Charles Jackson left the hotel where he was a waiter, hoping to reach Pier Number 3 on the Hudson River and a boat to take him off Manhattan before the mobs closed in. Half a block from the river's edge Jackson counted about a dozen men grabbing and surrounding him. A blow on the head from a brick knocked him down, and "someone kicked me in the eye with the heel of his boot," Jackson recalled. He passed out and the men threw him in the river. He awoke naked, under the wharf, where he crawled up on the rocks between the pilings and waited until his pursuers lost interest.[17]

At about the same time, Abraham Franklin, a twenty-three-year-old black coachman, stopped in to see his mother at Seventh Avenue and Twenty-eighth Street when "the mob broke down the door, seized him, beat him over the head and face with fists and clubs," and dragged him into the street. An Irish laborer who lived nearby shouted, "Hang the damned negro!" The crowd set Franklin's mother's house on fire before they kicked and beat him nearly to death and hanged him from a lamppost while his mother watched helplessly. When soldiers scattered the crowd and cut Franklin down, he "raised his arm once slightly and gave a few signs of life." He was left on the street after the troops moved on, however, and the mob suspended

Franklin's body again, "cutting out pieces of flesh and otherwise mutilating it." A sixteen-year-old butcher's apprentice "took hold of the private parts . . . on several occasions and dragged the body" through the streets.[18]

"Wednesday begins with heavy showers, and now (ten a.m.) cloudy, hot, and steaming," George Templeton Strong noted in his diary. "Morning papers report nothing specially grave as occurring since midnight. But there will be much trouble today. Rabbledom is not yet dethroned any more than its ally and instigator, Rebeldom."

However, news of the war effort was encouraging. "Port Hudson surrendered. Sherman said to have beaten Johnston somewhere near Vicksburg. Operations commencing against Charleston. Bragg seems to be abandoning Chattanooga and retiring on Atlanta. *Per contra,* Lee has got safely off. I thought he would."

Strong visited the U.S. Sub-Treasury on Wall Street and found it "in military occupation—sentinels pacing, windows barricaded, and so on." He was shown a "live shell ready to throw out of the window and the 'battery' to project Assay Office oil-of-vitriol and the like." The Custom House was also well supplied with "shells, grenades, muskets, and men," but Strong was disappointed to find the collector of the port "doubtful about his right to fire on the mob, and generally flaccid and tremulous—poor devil!"

At the Union League Club, however, Strong learned that the police were unable to spare a squad to protect the premises. One alarmed club member was predicting disaster: that the Croton water mains would be cut and gasworks destroyed that evening along with the houses of prominent club members. Strong dismissed this as "the loudest and most emphatic jawing" but was glad to have taken the precaution, nonetheless, of having "the bathtubs filled, and also all the pots, kettles, and pails in the house."[19]

In response to Governor Seymour's request, on Tuesday afternoon, that Archbishop Hughes exert his "powerful influence" to help quell the riots, an appeal from the prelate appeared in the *Herald* on Wednesday morning. Republican critics noted that if Hughes had taken the initiative to denounce the riots on Monday, he might have forestalled much of the violence that ensued on Tuesday and Wednesday. Hughes, however, had always promoted and defended the rights of Catholics in absolute terms, provoking rather than avoiding controversy. He had never been one to scold his own flock publicly, and the message in the *Herald* hardly seemed calculated to pacify the city's Irish Catholic working class.[20]

George Templeton Strong

On the contrary, the one-paragraph call for peace was tacked on to an open letter defending the Irish and attacking Horace Greeley—a lengthy rebuttal to comments about Hughes that appeared in Tuesday's *Tribune*. Greeley had pointed out that the archbishop was one of the first to support a draft as a way of equalizing the burden of the war, since reliance on volunteering drew a large proportion of the poor into the army. With the passage of the exemption clause, and the shift to a war of conquest and emancipation, Hughes no longer wanted to be associated with a prodraft stance and tried clumsily to distance himself from it. Greeley mocked Hughes's statement that he favored conscription, but not a "coercive conscription." Was there any other kind? Greeley asked.[21]

In order to explain his initial support for conscription, Hughes revisited the same fear of labor competition that had helped generate the riots in the first place. Pointing to the heavy casualties suffered by patriotic Irish American regiments, he asserted that when the war broke out, devious factory owners had temporarily shut down in order "to compel these Irish and Catholic operatives to enlist, in order that their families might not starve." Once these nativist employers had driven the immigrants out, they promptly replaced them with American-born workers, according to Hughes.

Meanwhile, he noted, "such manufacturers and traffickers upon the public calamities of civil war have been vastly more prosperous than ever before." The butchery of the Civil War, prolonged for the sake of such profiteers, must be brought to an end as quickly as possible, Hughes declared. As for the riots, he urged any Catholics who might have been involved to "retire to their homes" and to "dissolve their bad associations with reckless men, who have little regard either for Divine or human laws."[22]

As if to further embolden the mob, the notoriously corrupt Tammany judge John H. McCunn's ruling that the draft was unconstitutional also appeared in the morning papers. The case, decided the day before, involved a man who had refused to give his name to an enrollment officer. McCunn asserted that withholding one's name was not a crime under the draft law, and the officer had no right to make the arrest. McCunn's convoluted opinion then invalidated the entire draft law by arguing that the conscripted men constituted neither a standing army nor a militia force, and therefore fell outside the authority of Congress to "raise and support armies." The administration would soon have the flimsy ruling overturned on appeal; the real danger lay in McCunn's ability to foment more violence, even as he professed dismay that people were not seeking redress through legal channels.[23]

"I think things begin to look better now," Joseph Choate wrote tentatively on Wednesday morning to his mother in Salem, Massachusetts. "Powder and ball are beginning to tell . . . but the riot is yet to be suppressed. This morning before breakfast I walked over to the 5th Ave. Hotel, and met a man who had just seen a negro hung by the Irish on the corner of 32nd St. & 6th Avenue. There has been nothing like this I think since the French Revolution. The barbarity and the extent of the mob you have no idea of. But we shall get the upper hand. Carrie and the girls are very brave and fear no danger."[24]

Lucy and Julia Gibbons wanted to return to their uncle Samuel's to get some clothes, but Choate gave them strict orders not to answer the door and with a male friend went to run the errand for them.[25] James Gibbons went to report the attack on his house and remained upbeat. "You will see by the papers that our house has been sacked," he wrote to a friend on Wednesday. "Our daughters saved most of their best clothing by previous removal. Everything taken. If you have any means of communication with Mrs. Gibbons, please say we are all well and in jovial spirits. It is our contribution to the war."[26]

Knowing that despite the sabotage of the railroads her mother would try to come back from the front, Julia wrote to her that day: "Now about thy coming home! Thee had *very decidedly,* better *not* come." Emphasizing she could do nothing even if she managed to return, Julia continued: "Uncle Samuel is this morning having the windows indoors boarded up so that we may have an opportunity of going down through the roof and seeing if there is anything left . . . We are so glad to get off with our lives and dearest possessions, that we can only be satisfied with the result. Many lives have been endangered, and our just having left the house, and father having been out of the neighborhood, are such fortunate circumstances that we can regret nothing . . . and the only thing left for us to do is *wait.*"[27]

Choate and his friend "returned each with a pillow-case full of things they had picked from the floor of Uncle Samuel's attic," Lucy Gibbons recalled.

> They had seen a doctor's gig before the house of our next door neighbor, Mr. Wilson, and asked if they might borrow it to carry some things to us; but Mr. Wilson refused to do anything for people "who had brought so much trouble into the neighborhood." So Mr. Choate and Mr. Carter walked back to us with stuffed pillow-cases under their arms.
>
> This Mr. Wilson was so bitter against the abolitionists that he was called an "iron head" instead of a "copper head," and during the riot, when there was danger of his house catching fire from ours, he had gone out on his doorstep and tried to address the mob. The mob thought he was Horace Greeley, and beat him badly.[28]

Between 10 and 11 a.m., Josiah Porter looked out the front windows of his house at Fifth Avenue and Sixty-first Street and saw four armed men approaching. They were all young, unskilled laborers, Irish like himself, and he knew them by name: Patrick Kiernan, Barney Fagan, Frederick Hammens, and Michael Dunn. They began shouting when they saw him: "You damned old black republican Orange Son of a bitch. We'll burn your house down and murder you this day."[29] They started to throw rocks at the house.

The attack was planned by a laborer named Doherty, employed in Central Park, who had wanted to build a shanty on Porter's property. When Porter turned him down, Doherty convinced his fellow Irish Catholic laborers that Porter was an enemy on two counts: He was both an Orangeman (an Irish Protestant) and a Republican.[30] Doherty exploited the nexus of the current political crisis, and the centuries-old hatred between Irish Catholics and Protestants, a perennial source of friction that sparked riots on ethnic and national holidays, particularly the anniversary of the Battle of the Boyne.*

When Ellen Porter boldly strode outside to see who was threatening her husband, Fagan aimed his gun at her, saying, "Hold on till I shoot the damned Orange bitch." He did not shoot, but the men threw stones at her, before going to the corner to add two more men to their group. Shouting that they would cut Josiah Porter "in four quarters and throw him in the flames," they entered the house through the back door, while he slipped out the front and entered the basement through an exterior door. Porter holed up in the cellar with an old musket and listened to their footsteps above him as they searched the house.

They told Mrs. Porter they did not want to harm her or her children and to clear out her possessions because they would set fire to the house that evening. When the men left, they stole an ax from the house, and Mrs. Porter followed them down to Sixtieth Street, where she overheard them making plans to burn the house that afternoon instead.

They fulfilled their threat to return and burn the house, but with a different leader. Matthew Powers, a twenty-four-year-old brass finisher from Ireland who lived a dozen blocks to the south, came to search the house in the afternoon with six or seven men. He warned Ellen Porter that she had two hours to clear out, and returned in the early evening, this time with a bundle of papers and a box of matches.

Anxious neighbors had joined Ellen Porter in the house, and one pleaded with Powers "in the name of God and in honor of the blessed Virgin Mary not to burn the house," but he refused. Another neighbor warned that they "were laying themselves liable to the law," to which Powers retorted that "there was no law in New York," and chased him out the door. Powers and one accomplice then set the house on fire.

While the lynching and looting continued that morning, the Common Council focused on creating a $2.5-million fund to pay for any drafted New Yorker who could not afford the three-hundred-dollar commutation fee. The aldermen instructed the city's corporation counsel to challenge the constitutionality of the draft law in the hope that the courts would strike it down; if they did not, the fund would provide relief. The money was to be raised with bonds paying up to 7 percent interest and maturing in 1880. Direct aid to

---

*In 1690, William of Orange defeated Ireland's Catholics in the Battle of the Boyne. The Orangemen's celebration of the anniversary on July 12 was the occasion of several bloody riots in New York during the nineteenth century.

the poor at public expense—using charity to solidify political power—was a classic Tammany-style maneuver. Moreover, debt financing—to pay for soldiers' bounties at the beginning of the war, and for labor-intensive infrastructure projects in the growing city—was rapidly becoming the Democrats' preferred method of greasing the political machine.[31]

"The city gover[n]ment has by this action completely submitted to the mob," Edmund Ruffin rejoiced when he read about the appropriation in the southern press. He called it "a signal victory for the rioters . . . as the payment for their exemption is fixed in advance, & at the expense of other people—of the class whose goods they have been plundering & destroying, & whose houses they have been burning." It was like "offering a reward of $300 . . . to every rioter who would have been liable to conscription. This is enough to induce like riots in every Yankee town."[32]

For that very reason, Mayor Opdyke opposed the measure. "I was strongly urged by many leading citizens to give it my official sanction at once as a means of pacifying the rioters," Opdyke wrote of the proposed fund, but he refused to sign the bill—to "bow to the dictation of the mob, and in effect nullify the draft." Opdyke also insisted that the mob was "under our control."[33]

By proposing the fund while the riots still raged instead of quelling them first, Republicans charged, the Democrats were rewarding violent behavior. "It was plain that if the draft was the cause of the continued riot, it would now cease," Headley wrote. However, despite the public announcement of the Common Council's appropriation, reports of rioting continued to come in from all over the city.[34] The *Times* declared that "the whole thing, if it continues, bids fair to become a gigantic mob of plunderers, with no more reference to the Conscription than to the Koran."[35]

Beyond plunder, the final stages of the riots became a territorial struggle. The barricades on Ninth Avenue had been cleared, but on the East Side rioters had built others to cordon off three separate tenement and factory districts where they lived and worked. The women urged their men to resist the draft and "die at home" fighting the authorities. To assert their sole possession of these areas, the mobs patrolled the streets and began house-to-house searches, hunting down wounded policemen or soldiers.[36]

The Wednesday headlines of Marble's *World* carried Governor Seymour's proclamation of the night before declaring New York City to be "in a state of insurrection." Under state law, those words empowered the governor to take charge of the crisis. The next headline read: "Law to be Maintained in New-York by the Governor of New-York," a clear message to Republicans that

Democrats intended to keep the reins of power by preventing the federal imposition of martial law.[37]

Some staunch Republicans not only wanted martial law but appealed to President Lincoln and members of his cabinet on Wednesday morning to send General Benjamin Butler to run the occupation and enforce the draft. Butler was known in the South as "the Beast" because of his ruthless tactics while military governor of New Orleans the previous year. Not all Republicans favored the appointment of Butler. Greeley, for example, considered General Brown to be a suitable choice.

However, nearly all agreed that General Wool was incompetent and a stronger officer was needed to win a battle against the rioters, on one hand, and the disloyal Democratic leadership, on the other. The belief had begun to spread among Republicans that the protest against the draft was "not simply a riot but the commencement of a revolution, organized by sympathizers in the North with the Southern Rebellion."[38]

The Confederacy had hoped, according to the *Times,* that "as soon as the Government was weakened by the secession of the Southern States, and business was destroyed by the withdrawal of Southern trade," northern mobs would "rush into scenes of violence, blood and anarchy." From the beginning of the war, the rebels, "knowing the immense value to their cause of a Northern diversion or defection, have never ceased since then to labor assiduously for that end." However, the *Times* confidently predicted that " 'the left wing of Lee's army,' as the mob has been so aptly styled, will come to as disastrous and infamous an end as has just befallen the centre of that army on the Potomac."[39]

Perhaps the strongest advocate of martial law was Frederick Law Olmsted, a founder of the Union League Club. The club's members identified the "semi-loyalty" of New York's Democratic leadership as the pernicious influence that had led the working classes astray, and planned to root it out by persuading the Lincoln administration to conduct a full investigation of the riots' causes and instigators. "Let Barlow and Brooks and Belmont and Barnard and the Woods and Andrews and Clancy be hung if possible. Stir the govt up to it," Olmsted wrote to a friend. "I did not mean to omit Seymour."[40]*

Talk of executing political opponents as traitors, in the private letters and diaries of Olmsted and Strong, may have constituted a serious policy goal or may have simply been a venting of anger. What is clear is that Union League Club members eventually hoped to reconstruct New York City much as radical Republicans in Congress would try to reconstruct the rebellious

---

*James Brooks was the editor of the *Express;* John Andrews was the agitator and lawyer from Virginia; John Clancy was the editor of Tammany's newspaper, the *Leader.*

southern states. For the moment, the club's top priority was to restore order in the city—with an unambiguous show of force.[41]

Anything less, they warned, would send a dangerous message to the rest of the country and to European powers, whose eyes were all fixed on New York. "The whole country is observing with interest the course of the Administration in dealing with the New York Conscription," a prominent Philadelphia Republican wrote to President Lincoln. "If not proceeded with, say, by an officer of known determination such as General Butler with military and naval forces to support him, the Union goes up in a blaze of States Rights. An exhibition of resolution will insure Seymour's submission, the execution of the draft elsewhere and avoidance of foreign intervention."[42]

CHAPTER 14

"Hellish Passions Culminating in Riots, Arson, and Murder"

~⁀

In the absence of martial law, on Wednesday Acton and Brown changed their strategy. Instead of using the Central Office as the sole launching point for their forces, they carved up the city into four zones and massed their men at a staging area in each: two uptown on the East Side, one downtown at City Hall, and a fourth at the northern tip of Manhattan. This, and the redeployment of men who had been concentrated at government buildings, made it easier to respond to the emerging pattern of more sporadic surprise attacks by smaller bands at widely distant points.

However, Acton and Brown also faced the opposite problem of "the plague spots," as Brown dubbed them: three factory and tenement areas on the East Side where rioters had concentrated their strength behind barricades. To secure the areas they controlled, the rioters had also placed guards on street corners and made sure that no soldiers or policemen remained hidden in the buildings. In this case, the decision not to impose martial law proved helpful to Acton and Brown. Taking a conciliatory approach, Tammany officials had restored some measure of quiet in many neighborhoods, which civilian volunteers and policemen could patrol adequately, enabling the military to focus on the areas of strongest resistance.[1]

While the radical Republicans sought to influence President Lincoln and vilified the Democrats, Manton Marble continued his campaign for Democratic party unity by shifting the blame for the riots and lynching onto the Republicans. "There, of course, can be no excuse for the maltreatment and murder of these unfortunate people; but the hatred of the negroes has been mainly caused by the attempt of the radicals to force them into a position they never can attain in this country," the *World* declared. "The *Tribune,* whose course for the last ten years has done more than any other agency to incite the antipathy to the negro race which is working out such terrible results in the streets of New-York today, which is responsible, with the *Evening Post,* above all other agencies for bringing on this war, which has not omitted a single day since this war began to incite the hellish passions which are now culminating in riots, arson, and murder, quotes from our city report as follows, and dares to utter these infamous lies regarding it."[2]

The *World*'s description of white mobs pulling blacks off of streetcars right in front of its offices on Fourth Avenue and beating them to death had "not a word of rebuke for this infernal exhibition of cowardly ruffianism," according to Greeley's *Tribune.* By this third day of the riots, the newspaper battle was also in full swing, with Democratic and Republican editors quoting from each other at length to damn the opposition with his own words and blame him for starting the riots.

Sounding much like Marble's *World,* Peace Democrat Ben Wood's *Daily News* struck back at William Cullen Bryant's *Evening Post* under the heading "REPUBLICAN PARTY RESPONSIBLE": "The Black Republican journals, with an unparalleled effrontery, are endeavoring to fix upon the Democracy the responsibility of the present disturbances in this city." Calling this accusation "the antipodes of truth," the *Daily News* went on to assert that the *Evening Post* was to blame for the "exasperation of the populace," because it favored policies "peculiarly distasteful to the masses of the North." While shamelessly dodging its share of guilt, the paper neatly summed up the political and social context of the riots.

> [The *Evening Post*] has been the avowed champion of the doctrine of augmenting Union authority, and has invariably inclined toward a centralization of power and an abrogation of State Sovereignty. It has earnestly advocated the incorporation of the black element into our armies, and has at all times demonstrated such intense sympathy with the negro, at the expense of white men, that the Northern sentiment has been naturally embittered toward the unfortunate race, which is thus being accursed by the guardianship of fanaticism. And lastly, when the odious Conscription act was broached in Congress, *The Evening Post* was its zealous supporter and has been indefatigable in its attempts to bring about its enforcement.[3]

Such editorials had already marked the office buildings of Republican newspapers as targets for attack. "We were under marching orders nearly the entire night, patrolling various streets, cleaning out the rioters," wrote Major H. E. Richmond, who commanded an artillery detail from Fort Hamilton. "Our special attention was directed to the safety of the *Times* and *Tribune* buildings."[4]

The *Tribune* announced in an editorial on Wednesday that it was armed and would slaughter the rioters if attacked.[5] Horace Greeley refused to alter his schedule and had come to work as usual for the third day in a row, taking a private carriage on Wednesday, however, since there was no longer any public transportation, and remained until the late afternoon.[6] Taking heed of the attempt to burn the *Tribune* on Monday, the *Times* had not only fortified its offices but "established a regular garrison inside, while it brilliantly illuminated the open space all around it, in the circle of which the rioters did not dare come," Headley wrote.[7] "Give them grape, and a plenty of it," *Times* editor Henry Raymond declared.[8]

While the Democratic papers expressed their racism, the Republicans were unabashed, at least privately, about their disdain for the Irish and for immigrants in general. Gilmore declared: "We did not observe a single native-born workingman among the rioters. The mob consisted in about equal proportions of the more ignorant of our foreign-born population, and of the criminal class that lives by plunder, and has a hand against every man's person and property."[9]

On Wednesday afternoon, Mayor Opdyke issued a proclamation, addressed "to the citizens of New York," in which he blamed the chaos of the previous two days on the "temporary absence" of the local militia units but declared nonetheless that the riot was largely under control. "What now remains of the mob are fragments prowling about for plunder," the mayor claimed, but in the next line admitted that the police and military were on the point of "exhaustion from continued movements" and asked residents to form "voluntary associations" to protect their own neighborhoods. He also urged people to go back to their jobs and ordered the "various lines of omnibuses, railways, and telegraphs" to resume full service right away, while promising them military protection.[10]

Opdyke, along with Seymour, hoped that an announcement of the draft being suspended would also help bring order to the city. They summoned Colonel Nugent to the St. Nicholas Hotel on Wednesday and asked what orders he had received. Fry had telegraphed Nugent from Washington on Tuesday, telling him to "suspend the draft in New York City and Brooklyn," but had also forbade him to publish the order, which could be interpreted as a retreat by the government in the face of the mob. Opdyke and Seymour urged Nugent to publish the telegram, but he refused, insisting that he needed Fry's permission. However, Nugent agreed to sign his own name, not Fry's, to an informal bulletin for the following day's newspapers, declaring, "The draft has been suspended in New York City and Brooklyn."[11]

Clearly frustrated by Fry's orders from Washington and a lack of military support, Nugent offered his superior some advice. "I would suggest that when an adequate force is sent here, the draft should be resumed in one district at a time, and rigidly enforced there . . . I trust the Government will see the necessity of instructing the major-general commanding in this department to give me all the assistance he possibly can to sustain its authority," Nugent wrote on Wednesday. "The mob spirit must be put down by the strong arm of the military power. There is no use in trying to conciliate or reason with it. It has now assumed the character of an organized mass of plunderers, and the public generally have lost all sympathy for it; so that now is the time to crush out rebellion. This can be easily done, if the proper force is placed at our disposal."

Nugent added a bitter postscript: "I inclose you an extract from the *World*—Copperhead—by which you will see that the mob have paid their respects to my residence."[12]

Despite advice like Nugent's, and appeals from Republican leaders, martial law was never declared in the city. Opdyke's fear, shared by other local leaders and the administration, was that such a step would alienate Democratic leaders, who may have led the working classes into disloyalty, but who could also bring them back into line again, as they were demonstrating through their speeches to the mobs across the city. Without their influence and cooperation, Opdyke felt, the city might descend even farther into chaos, and the military would be spread thin trying to subdue the entire metropolis, not just discrete affected areas.[13]

At last, around 4 p.m., General Sandford went on the offensive for the first time, sending Lieutenant Ryer out from the arsenal to help the police fight a mob, some two thousand strong, that was reportedly setting fire to buildings near Forty-second Street and Tenth Avenue.[14] Arriving at the scene, Ryer recalled, he and his fifty men were "saluted with groans, hisses, etc." and "received a storm of bricks, and missiles of every description, and shots from the roof and windows of the buildings."

When the rioters ignored Ryer's warning to disperse, he ordered his riflemen to pour one volley after another into the crowd. After five or more volleys the mob finally broke and fled, but the soldiers were still under attack from gunmen inside and on top of buildings, so Ryer detached a lieutenant and ten men, who cleared the houses. When they returned with two prisoners, Ryer decided his job was done and started marching his unit back to the arsenal. The rioters, however, had been reinforced by a second mob and charged the soldiers from behind. Ryer "faced the second platoon to the rear, and fired two more volleys into them."

Ryer noted proudly, "[It was the rioters'] last gathering in that locality. There were at least fifty killed, and a large number wounded, and I marched off with my command, without hardly a scratch." The accounts of participants and witnesses like Ryer, taken together, suggest that the actual death toll for the riots was much higher than the official count of 105. Even allowing for some overstatement of casualties, Ryer's action on Forty-second Street by itself accounts for a large percentage of the total.

Soon after Ryer returned to the arsenal, Tammany police court judge Michael Connolly came in to complain that the troops had killed women and children on Tenth Avenue, and to arrest the officer who led the attack. Sandford claimed he did not know who had been in charge. Connolly insisted that he could maintain order in the Twenty-second Ward and that sending more troops would only inflame the situation, but Sandford uncharacteristically refused such an arrangement.[15]

At 6 p.m., a militia officer reported to Sandford that a large mob had gathered on First Avenue between Eighteenth and Nineteenth Streets and seemed to be organizing for a rampage. For a second and last time, Sandford responded with vigor, sending 150 volunteers under Colonel Cleveland Winslow and others commanded by Colonel Edward Jardine equipped with two howitzers. Neither U.S. infantry nor state militia, these troops were citizens who had joined the volunteer regiments that sprang up in the surge of enthusiasm at the beginning of the war. Thus while some were two-year veterans, they were not professional soldiers.[16]*

To make matters worse, they hurried to First Avenue without support from the police or regular troops and soon found themselves in a deadly trap of tenement-lined streets. Ellen Leonard was visiting from out of town and staying with relatives nearby. She recalled someone in the excited mob shouting, "They are coming!" when the soldiers appeared. Upon hearing that, "the mob seemed to swell into vast dimensions, and densely filled the whole street before them. Hundreds hurried out on the house-tops, tore up brickbats, and hurled them with savage howls at the approaching soldiers. Shots were fired

*The men under Winslow were drawn from the Duryea Zouaves, and those under Jardine from the Hawkins Zouaves. The Zouaves dressed in colorful North African–style uniforms.

from secret ambushes, and soldiers fell before they had fired. Then they charged bravely into the mob, but their force was wholly inadequate."[17]

Jardine's artillerymen "raked the avenue up and down" with ten rounds of canister, killing some thirty rioters and bystanders with these exploding containers of shot, the *Times* reported. This tactic only scattered the crowd, however, while "the more bold among them lurked behind the corners of the buildings" and darted out to fire at the troops each time they reloaded the howitzers. Winslow did not have enough men to dispatch a portion of them into the houses and onto the rooftops, and after twenty minutes of punishing fire, ten soldiers had been killed or wounded. The mob seemed "remarkably well organized, firing at the word of command," according to the *Times*. Ryer's estimate of casualties on Forty-second Street and this *Times* account strongly contradict the official death toll for the riots by suggesting that some ninety people were killed in these two incidents alone.

Winslow ordered a retreat, and the soldiers "were followed at some distance by the howling mob, who were left masters of the field," the *Times* reported.[18] The dead soldiers fell into "the hands of the frenzied mob," while the wounded were brought into the middle-class neighborhood west of the tenement area, near Second Avenue. Colonel Jardine, whose thighbone had been fractured by a bullet made from lead pipe, was taken in by the Leonards, along with a few of his wounded men.[19]

Sandford's dispatch of troops had been a fiasco. When Winslow appeared at the St. Nicholas Hotel to tell Horatio Seymour the state of affairs, the governor dispensed with political jealousies and immediately sent the colonel to General Brown on Mulberry Street to get help. At 9 p.m., Brown sent Captain H. R. Putnam with 150 U.S. troops and an artillery piece to escort Colonel Jardine and his wounded men out of the besieged neighborhood.[20]

"Doors and windows were at once closed, and the house became a hospital," Ellen Leonard recalled. "We flew for fans, ice water and bandages."[21] One of Jardine's men was a surgeon and dressed the soldiers' wounds. "Already [the rioters] were clamoring for the wounded soldiers who had escaped them," Leonard wrote. "We thought of Colonel O'Brien's fate, and could not suppress the thought that our own house might be made the scene of a like tragedy."

Jardine dismissed the idea of defending themselves; even if they fought off the rioters, the house could easily be set on fire. Instead, Jardine and another severely injured soldier were to pose as civilian bystanders accidentally caught up in the riot, while the walking wounded were to escape over the rooftops and get help. "Arms, military apparel, and bloody clothing were accordingly concealed," Leonard wrote. "The Colonel was conveyed to the cellar and placed on a mattress," accompanied by the surgeon. The other badly wounded soldier was hidden in the "rear apartment on the upper floor" under the care of Leonard and her mother.

Leonard's brother, "with his bandaged head and disabled arm" from a beating at the hands of rioters earlier in the week, joined a soldier with a bad foot wound who could still walk, and they set out over the rooftops. Along with Leonard and her mother, her brother's wife and her sister stayed behind. "The two heroic women, H. and her sister, remained below to confront the mob."

Having posted guards on both avenues, the rioters controlled the street and were conducting a house-to-house search. They finally arrived at the Leonards' and pounded on door, shouting, "The soldiers! the soldiers!" "Bring out the soldiers!" One of the women went out and tried to convince them that the soldiers had come and gone.

"We know the men are here, and if you give them up to us, you shall not be harmed," the mob's leader said. "But if you do not, and we find them . . . your house will be burned over your heads, and I will not guarantee your lives for five minutes."

"You will not do that," she replied. "We are not the kind of people whose houses you wish to burn. My only son works as you do, and perhaps in the same shop with some of you, for seventy cents a day." Ellen Leonard noted that this shrewd response was only partly true: "She did not tell them that her amateur apprentice boy had left his place to go to Pennsylvania and fight their friends the rebels."

The woman agreed to let half a dozen men search the house, but most of the mob pushed their way inside. While one woman led the rioters from room to room, the other befriended the sentinel they had posted at the front door. The search party discovered the surgeon in the cellar, beat him, and took him outside to be lynched. They did not believe Jardine was a civilian either and aimed four muskets at his head. Before they could fire, however, he asked for a priest, and they were stunned.

"What, are you a Catholic?"

"Yes," Jardine replied.

The rioters hesitated, and the woman upstairs, hearing the commotion in the cellar, appealed to the sentinel to save the colonel's life. He went down below and pretended to recognize Jardine. "I used to go to school with him. He is no soldier." That was enough to convince the leaders of the mob, who called off their reluctant followers, and even offered to place a sentinel in front of the house "to prevent the annoyance of any further search."

As the hours passed, Jardine's condition grew worse, and there was no sign of a rescue party. In hiding Jardine from the mob, the Leonards had also concealed him from Putnam and his troops, who had been dispatched to battle the rioters and search the area. The women had no means of transporting Jardine to a safer location. Finally, sometime after midnight, Leonard heard "the distant clank of a horse's hoof on the pavement" and "the steady, resolute tramp of a trained and disciplined body. No music was ever half so beautiful!" When she saw "a long line of muskets gleam out from the darkness," and Putnam's men stopped outside, she rushed downstairs and out the front door. Standing there, "pale and exhausted," was her brother, who had brought the soldiers to the house.

After scattering the mob at the end of the street, the soldiers evacuated the wounded men and the women to the police Central Office. "With much state and ceremony," the heroic women were "presented to the chieftains of civic power" and then escorted to more comfortable rooms at the St. Nicholas Hotel, where they arrived at 2:30 a.m., exhausted but unable to sleep, Leonard recalled. "The exciting scenes of the night, and the incessant roar and rumble of Broadway, kept all awake."

To workingmen, the draft's exemption clause was one more example of "special privilege" conferred by government on wealthy capitalists and a confirmation of the hardworking laborer's declining status in the new industrial order. Underlining their resentment, just after 11 p.m. on Wednesday, two hundred former grain shovelers descended on the Atlantic Dock Basin in Brooklyn and took revenge on the owners for hiring strikebreakers the previous summer. The mob drove off the few workers on duty with a hail of stones and, by igniting a barrel of pitch, set fire to a pair of enormous grain elevators that had eliminated hundreds of jobs when they were built two years earlier. While the rioters disappeared into the night, threatening similar action against the Erie Basin, the towering elevators and a scow were "burned to the water's edge," the *Times* reported, at a cost of more than one hundred thousand dollars to the owners.[22]

Earlier in the week, rioters in Manhattan had destroyed two newly patented street-sweeping machines owned by the city, denouncing them and the grain elevators as "laborsaving machines" that cost workingmen their jobs.[23]

By improvising solutions, and concealing their repair work from the mobs, the telegraphers who had set out in the storm on Monday night had made a good deal of progress. Carrying lines over the tops of houses, or around them through backyards, and supporting the wires on clothesline poles, by Wednesday evening they had fully restored the system in Lower Manhattan.

Union soldiers in New York City during the riots

Farther north, they had reconnected most of the precincts to police headquarters.[24]

"We are overrun with Negroes," the station houses telegraphed to the Central Office. "Give all people protection," came the reply.[25] By 10 p.m. on Wednesday, Acton had been at police headquarters for three days and nights, never stopping to sleep or change his clothes, while he fired off and received some four thousand telegrams.[26] "The police and the military here have been very effective," Mayor Opdyke telegraphed Stanton, "but their duties have been so arduous that they are greatly exhausted."[27]

Just when the police and soldiers were succumbing to fatigue, reinforcements began to arrive. The Seventy-fourth Regiment of the New York State National Guard arrived in the city at about 10 p.m., followed, before midnight, by the Sixty-fifth Regiment. The 152nd New York Volunteers as well as the 26th Michigan Volunteers would soon follow, a total of more than four thousand troops. At about 4:30 a.m., Acton received a telegram from the Twenty-eighth Precinct: The Seventh Regiment, some six hundred strong and the city's mainstay in the recent decades of rioting, had arrived from Pennsylvania and disembarked at the foot of Canal Street.[28]

In the gray, predawn light, "the steady ranks were seen marching along Canal Street towards Broadway, and soon drew up in front of the St. Nicholas

Hotel," Headley reported. "It was the beginning of the end, to the minds of many thousands who speedily heard of their arrival," Stoddard wrote. "Loud cheers brought us to the window to see the glorious returning 'Seventh' marshaled before us," Ellen Leonard recalled, "and with all our hearts and voices we joined in the welcome which greeted them."[29]

CHAPTER 15

The Final Days: Thursday and Friday

∼⁀

The heavy military presence came too late for Albro and Mary Lyons. Having failed on Monday and Tuesday, on Wednesday night the rioters managed to storm their house. "This sent father over the back fence to the Oak Street station, while mother took refuge on the premises of a neighbor," Maritcha Lyons wrote. "This was a friendly German who in the morning had loosened boards of intervening fences in anticipation of an emergency. This charitable man, some weeks after, was waylaid and severely beaten by 'parties unknown.'" Maritcha's parents were safe, but their home, and the business that had brought Albro and his family to the verge of middle-class affluence, had essentially been destroyed.

Not until after the rioters had entered the house did the police take action against them, Maritcha Lyons recalled bitterly.

> In one short hour the police had cleared the premises and both parents were at home after the ravages. What a home! Its interior was dismantled, furniture was missing or broken. From basement to attic evidences of the worst vandalism prevailed. A fire, kindled in one of the upper rooms was discovered in time to prevent a conflagration. The dismayed parents had to submit to the indignity of taking refuge in the police station house. A three days' reign of terror disgraced a city unable to protect its inhabitants.[1]

Despite the arrival of four thousand troops, reports to the Central Office from various precincts early Thursday morning "indicated another sharp day's work," Stoddard noted. On the East Side, fifty rioters had chased a black man named Samuel Johnson to the Thirty-fourth Street ferry, "beat him very badly," and then pitched him into the East River, where he drowned. Blacks were hiding "in cellars and garrets, hardly daring to venture out for food," Stoddard wrote. Then they fled to the nearest police station as soon as the mobs passed on. "Receive colored people as long as you can" was Acton's consistent message, telegraphed again on Thursday to all station houses, many of which overflowed with refugees. "Refuse nobody."

Fear continued to grip the city. The gas companies were under heavy military guard to prevent sabotage. The huge Delameter Iron Works, which produced ironclads for the navy, refused to start up again without similar protection. Through another announcement in the papers, Mayor Opdyke called on residents to return to work, and some streetcar and omnibus lines reopened, but a mob of one hundred men "stopped the Second Avenue cars on the corner of Twenty-third Street, and made them turn back," the precinct reported. Two other lines were also targeted by rioters. On Fourth Avenue, the conductor and passengers were robbed of their valuables; on First Avenue, the mob decided to let the car proceed when someone shouted that the owner was a staunch Democrat, unlike the abolitionists who operated the Third Avenue line.[2]

Like the many underutilized officers and men stationed at the arsenal on Seventh Avenue, Horatio Seymour had lost confidence in General Sandford's leadership. The governor had sent the panicked Colonel Winslow to the police Central Office the night before, and on Thursday he also instructed the New York State regiments, just back from Pennsylvania, to report to General Brown.[3]

By 8 a.m., Brown had dispatched Colonel William Berens with three companies of New York militia to guard three foundries on the East Side that produced guns and ammunition, including James Jackson's foundry, which rioters had threatened and forced to close on Monday morning. While Berens stationed about twenty men with a cannon at each of two bombshell factories, menacing crowds began milling around his column. With one company left, Berens was heading up First Avenue toward Jackson's foundry on Twenty-eighth Street at about 1 p.m., when rioters attacked.

Berens's men swung from a column of march into a line of fire and blasted away, accompanied by their howitzer, which quickly cleared the avenue. However, when the troops advanced from Twenty-second to Twenty-third Street, they came under fire from two sides. Berens kept his men moving forward and firing at the same time, while he sent one man to the Central Office to request help.

At Twenty-eighth Street, the militiamen charged through the dense mob around Jackson's foundry only to find that the doors were locked. They broke in and stationed themselves inside, fending off the mob with a steady barrage of gunfire and a charge into the street until Berens's messenger returned with two more companies to help guard the foundry.

Displaying their intense hatred of the Metropolitans, several rioters came forward to demand that the four policemen inside the foundry with the soldiers be turned over to the mob. Only if the patrolmen were "delivered up" would the mob disperse. "The committee stood at a respectful distance while delivering their message, and took to their heels, on an intimation to do so or they would be shot," David Barnes reported. The policemen exchanged their uniforms for workmen's clothes discovered in the foundry and slowly made their escape through the crowds in the street. The rioters had not given up, however, and as the day wore on, they hovered nearby, waiting for a chance to attack.[4]

Even though such skirmishing continued, and entire areas of the city remained under the mobs' control, in the early afternoon Mayor Opdyke telegraphed Stanton that the riot was over "for the present," and "Andrews, one of the chief leaders, is arrested."[5] John Andrews had egged on the mobs throughout the week with his speeches, most visibly at the Ninth District draft office where the riots began on Monday. Four detectives entered a house on Eleventh Street and approached Andrews while he was in bed with his mistress, a black madam who had been a prostitute for a dozen years. The plainclothesmen duped Andrews into leaving with them, and after a brief stop at the police Central Office, he was shackled and transferred to Fort Lafayette, off the Brooklyn shore. Thus he became a political prisoner—the only rioter in federal custody—awaiting trial for conspiracy.

As the most clearly identifiable leader of the riots, Andrews became the focus of public anger, even though he appears to have been an associate of small-time criminals, not grand Copperhead conspirators. True to its white supremacist credo, the *World* was more dismayed that Andrews was a "practical amalgamationist," consorting with a black woman, than that he had fomented so much violence and destruction. The *Tribune,* by contrast, condemned Andrews as one who had "roused the fierce passions of the mob, and turned men into incarnate devils."[6]

Mayor Opdyke believed the arrival of the regiments on Thursday "removed all doubt as to our ability to promptly quell the riots and restore the supremacy of law." Indeed, people began to resume business as usual, open-ing stores that had been shuttered for two days and braving the streets to buy fresh milk and ice.[7] Joseph Choate wrote to his mother: "Law and order ap-pear to be getting the upper hand again, although up to day-break there was not much to reassure us . . . The cruelty which has for these three days been perpetrated on the blacks is without a parallel in history . . . Several of our city regiments have now actually arrived and retribution awaits the ri-oters."[8]

Colonel Robert Nugent was not convinced. "Apparently everything is quiet, but it is the opinion of well-informed persons that this state of things will not last long," he reported to Fry, the provost marshal general. "It is well, also, that you should be aware that so far as the protection of the public prop-erty in my possession, and of my own life and the lives of those attached to my office, I am utterly powerless."

Wool had given Brown "command of all the United States forces, in-cluding the Invalid Corps," Nugent complained, while Sandford and Acton were, of course, in charge of the militia and police, respectively. "Though it is a well-known fact that the hostility of the mob has been directed against me personally, and against this office, though threats of the most diabolical kind have been made against my life, I am unable at this moment to procure a guard for the protection of this office against even ordinary danger." Nu-gent went on to deliver a verdict on the incompetence of the military in han-dling the riots.

> It is a very delicate matter to complain of officers intrusted by the authorities with high responsibility, but I cannot help saying that the confusion, vacillation, and conflict of orders which exist among the general officers of the regular, volunteer, and militia force at present in this city, have the effect of encouraging the rioters and lessening the confidence of the public in the Adminis-tration . . . Subordinate officers . . . have been so annoyed and perplexed by conflicting orders that half of their efficiency is destroyed. To enforce the draft properly . . . we must have a force of at least 15,000 men, under the command of some deci-sive, energetic officer, who is neither afraid nor ashamed to exe-cute it.[9]

The riots were not over, and the war of words in the press still flared as well. Marble's editorials in the *World* on Thursday continued to blame the Repub-licans while pursuing his political agenda of portraying the Democracy as united in favor of the war. "Negroes are cruelly beaten in New-York because mock philanthropists have made them odious by parading them and their emancipation as the object to which peace first and the Union afterward, with the lives of myriads of Northern men, are to be sacrificed. Upon this the abolitionists of the *Post* and *Tribune* call out to all mankind that the overwhelming majority of people of New-York are in sympathy with secession! If this be not practical treason, what shall be so styled?"[10]

Henry Raymond of the *New York Times* had a reply. The *World* did not name the *Times* along with the *Tribune* and *Evening Post* because Raymond's paper was more conservative and downplayed the issues of slavery and abolition, but he took up the challenge nonetheless.[11]

"The *World*, with an eager ferocity which finds its proper counterpart in the ranks of the mob, seizes the opportunity to denounce those journals which support the Government as responsible for the riot, and to point them out to the mob as proper objects of its vengeance," Raymond declared in an editorial on Thursday. The charge that the city's radical Republican newspapers had precipitated the riots was ludicrous, Raymond replied: "The *World* knows better."

If the motive for the riots was opposition to the draft, the *Times* asked, "Who stimulated that opposition? Who has day after day devoted time and talent and strength to denunciations of the law—long after it had been placed upon the statute-book, and when criticism had thus become utterly unavailing for any purpose consistent with the public good? Who has filled column after column with incendiary appeals to the poorer classes, and with utterly false and mischievous statements as to the object and effect of the national conscription?" Clearly, Raymond implied, it was the Democratic, not the Republican, press that had incited the riots.

"The *World* permits itself to read a lecture to the 'radical journals' for not having heeded its warnings of the 'rude vengeance' of which it gave them notice, and, with an apparent consciousness of temporary power, it deals lavishly in threats of still further punishment at the hands of the mob," Raymond asserted. Nonetheless, the *Times* always had and always would follow its own conscience and freedom of speech "without regard to the warnings of the *World* or the menaces of the mob," Raymond declared.

In the same issue the *Times* also noted that financial confidence had not been shaken and the price of gold had gone down instead of up. This was due to a sense that mob rule could not last long, and to the string of Union victories in the past two weeks, the paper said. "Within a fortnight Lee has been beaten back into Virginia with a loss of two-fifths of his army—Vicksburg and Port Hudson have fallen, which gives the Government complete command of the Southwest—Bragg has been forced well down into Georgia, which secures entire Tennessee—and Charleston, which has so often baffled our efforts, has been approached so successfully that its speedy fall is probable."

While the political battle raged in the press, Democratic and Republican officials continued to exert pressure on each other face-to-face, vying to shape the course and the outcome of the riots. On Thursday afternoon, Judge Michael Connolly, still dissatisfied after his meeting with General Sandford the day before, joined forces with state senator John Bradley and called on Governor Seymour. This time they wanted to clear the Eighteenth Ward of troops and let the respectable middle-class families there use their influence to restore order. Since this plan fit with Seymour's own approach of touring the city and appealing firmly but sympathetically to the rioters, he wrote a letter of support for Connolly and Bradley, which they presented when they made their request to Acton.

"I naturally felt very indignant," Acton recalled. "It can't be done," he told them. "I would not do it to save your lives. We have been fighting a week, and are going to keep on until every man, white or black, can go anywhere on this island in perfect safety." General Brown concurred. "There's been too much tampering with rebels already," he told the two Tammany officials, "and I'll not move a man unless Mr. Acton tells me to."[12]

Brown was equally adamant in refusing to negotiate with rioters that afternoon at Jackson's foundry. At 5 p.m., while some four thousand rioters continued to surround Berens and his company of militiamen inside the factory, a Catholic priest relayed a message from the mob threatening to burn the building if the troops did not leave, and promising a truce while they withdrew. The building's owners, who initially wanted military protection, were suddenly eager to have the troops leave. However, when Berens requested guidance from the Central Office, Brown instructed him to stand his ground. The rioters started to assault the foundry that evening, but a fusillade from the militiamen drove them back and discouraged any further attacks.[13]

Captain Putnam had rescued Colonel Jardine and his men on Wednesday night and performed ably throughout the week, so General Brown naturally turned to him on Thursday evening at about 6 p.m. to redeem a dangerous mess—a reprise of the previous night—that had unfolded earlier in the day near Gramercy Park.

A colonel stationed there with his cavalry unit had taken eighty of his men on foot to reconnoiter east of the park on Twenty-second Street when they were ambushed between Second and Third Avenues by snipers firing from the roofs and windows of barricaded houses and by rioters in the street. In their chaotic retreat, the troops left behind the body of a sergeant, while their colonel fled to police headquarters and reported the rout to General Brown. "What are you doing here, sir?" Brown shouted at the colonel. "Go, sir. Your place is with your men."[14]

Brown sent Captain Putnam, leading 160 infantry and artillerymen and some Metropolitans, to recover the sergeant's body and flush the rioters from the buildings.[15] At Gramercy Park, Putnam's men stormed a house from which rioters were firing on the cavalrymen, but the snipers escaped out the back. Leaving the women in the house with a warning that it would be leveled by artillery if they allowed it to be used as a snipers' nest again, Putnam and his force proceeded east on Twenty-second Street, where they found the body of the slain cavalry sergeant. Putnam recalled: "I ordered a livery-stable keeper to put his horses to a carriage, and accompany me, for the purpose of carrying the dead and wounded. He replied that the mob would kill him if he did, and that he dare not do it. He was informed that he would be protected if he went, but if he refused he would be instantly shot. The horses were speedily harnessed and the body put into the carriage."

Suddenly, the mob began firing from the houses, but Putnam did not retreat. "If they had been cool and steady, they might have done us great harm," Putnam wrote. "As it was, they fired wildly, running to a window and firing, and then retreating back out of danger." While Putnam's skirmishers in the street fired at the windows and rooftops to drive the snipers back, the rest of his men stormed the houses and searched them from top to bottom, killing most of the rioters in close combat and taking a few prisoners.

When every house was cleared, Putnam's force marched east to Second Avenue and drove the mob up as far as Thirty-first Street, where it was reinforced, and snipers again opened fire. Putnam had his artillerymen reply with canister, which cleared the street of rioters, except for the dozen or more who lay dead or dying. Putnam's skirmishers brought down others from the rooftops and windows, and his men once again searched the houses, flushing rioters from under beds and out of closets, chasing them down dark halls and on narrow stairways. "Some of them fought like incarnate fiends, and would not surrender," Putnam reported. "All such were shot on the spot."

Along with several prisoners, Putnam's men captured many large revolvers, which he allowed the troops to keep as trophies. The rioters had an impressive but motley arsenal, Putnam recalled, including "one blunderbuss which they fired on us," possibly a relic of the press-gang riots a century earlier. Forming a tight column with their prisoners, the troops marched back to the Central Office, where Putnam received a hero's welcome. "The loss of the rioters was great," Acton noted, "and seemed for the first time to break down the desperate spirit of the mob." As events transpired, Putnam's men had fought the last major battle of the riots.

The vast mobs that had ruled the city all week gradually and grudgingly dispersed, while those with guns made their final stand in sporadic fighting that continued into the night on Thursday. The last of the rioters—determined to hold the areas they had cordoned off with barricades and sniper nests— had to be flushed out one at a time. The Seventh Regiment pacified the East Side between Fourteenth and Thirty-fifth Streets, the last of the "plague spots," where rioters shot at them from windows and rooftops.

"One of the most determined rioters, who deliberately loaded and fired from behind a woman, was finally brought down by two of our men who are stationed on top of a house and has since died," militiaman Henry Congdon wrote. Another sniper, named Martin Moran, was one of the few suspected "ringleaders" identified by name in the newspapers. He had been trying to decapitate the militia units by firing at their officers when he was captured and nearly hanged by soldiers on Thursday night; the officers restrained their men, and Moran was taken into custody by the police. "About 10 p.m.," Congdon reported, "we formed a strong force and with a howitzer in front patrolled the neighborhood and met with no resistance." The city quieted down after midnight, and at 2 a.m., Commissioner Acton, who had not slept for four days, finally closed his eyes.[16]

"I suppose Abby and Sally may conclude to come home—that is, if we can be said to have a home—to N.Y., at all events," James Gibbons wrote to a relative on Thursday. "If any opportunity occur to advise them to come to our friends, the Choate's, No. 93 West 21st St., please do so. The first information they get will be by the papers, and they may leave before receiving my letters, written on the 14th and 15th, in which case, their movements will be entirely unknown to me." He continued: "The girls bear up wonderfully. Julia, at times, in her intensity, comes to a breakdown point . . . That is the whole. It is already over. Those grand widowed mothers, Dwight, Sedgwick, Putnam, Lowell, who sent their only, or *all* their sons, to the war, have mortal and incurable wounds—we, only a scratch. I am ashamed to have deserved no more."[17]

Despite his initial euphoria at being unhurt after their house was sacked, Gibbons was beginning to feel the pain of the family's losses. However, he reassured himself that they could start over—that the life of a family was above all its shared memories, not the objects that were invested with them. One object, however, was missed in particular. It was, Sally wrote, "an India china bird, given by a freed slave to Abby, when she was nine or ten years old, as a token of gratitude for the little girl's kindness and sympathy. This was carefully treasured through her childhood, becoming, in after years, a sacred plaything to her own children . . . During Friend [John] Hopper's last illness (which he passed at his daughter's house) this bird was kept on the mantelpiece in his room; he said 'I like to look at it.' "[18]

Word of the Gibbons family's losses spread rapidly as stories of the riot were reported in the newspapers of other cities. The family received numerous offers of help from their friends, one of them writing that they had clearly been "the victims of the senseless rage, and love of plunder, of the crew whom the Devil, with Governor Seymour for his Prime Minister, seems to have let loose in New-York. For mercy's sake, write a line and let us know how it is with you all."[19]

From Boston, where the mayor had put down the riot quickly on Tuesday night, a friend wrote to James Gibbons that the country had now "learned how to deal with mobs": "In this matter, I cannot help thinking that our example will have precedence. In mercy to the rabble, bullets and canister first, blank cartridges afterwards."[20]

Another friend, writing to James Gibbons from Washington, agreed: "But what is to be said of the miserable authorities of your city? All the alleged imbecility, tenderness for rebels, and mismanagement of the United States Government and Generals, sink out of sight compared with that of New-York officials. Five hundred men, armed with rifles, could have prevented all this disgrace. We are all very much cast down by the event—the glorious successes of Vicksburg &c. &c., do not relish, with such a bitter draught as New-York sends us."[21]

Both friends voiced a widespread Republican view that the New York riots could have been prevented if authorities had responded decisively and with overwhelming force. George Smalley, a veteran of the battle of Antietam and a member of the *Tribune* editorial staff, who remained at his post throughout the week, considered the riots "the flank movement of the Rebellion; an attempt not only to prevent the enforcement of the draft, which President Lincoln had too long delayed, but to compel the Unionist forces to return northward for the defense of their homes. A mad scheme, yet for near four days New York was in possession of the mob. I never understood why, since a couple of good regiments would at any moment have restored order, as the event showed. For want of them New York had to defend itself, and did it rather clumsily, enduring needless disasters and losses both of property and life."[22]

The riots also inflicted diplomatic damage on the North, boosting not only the South's morale but its status among supporters in France and England, who assumed that an apparently divided North could neither enforce the draft nor subdue the Confederacy. Reacting to news of the riots, one

French newspaper called for an armistice and southern independence. Another characterized the riots as a "revolution" which would lead inevitably to chaos across the North and Lincoln's resignation or ouster. Two other papers declared that the North was on the verge of its own civil war.[23]

"Everything is quiet this morning and the city has generally resumed its normal appearance," Joseph Choate wrote to his mother on Friday. "General Brown now has about 12,000 troops and police under his command and some five thousand more are expected before tomorrow. General [Hugh] Kilpatrick, also, has arrived and is organizing a strong cavalry force. The disturbance yesterday was confined to the East Side of the city but it ended last night in a very desperate conflict in which a large number of rioters were killed & wounded and some thirty were taken prisoners."[24] Despite further small clashes on Friday, Mayor Opdyke announced in the papers that the city was under control and had enough troops to meet any contingency.

Governor Seymour had asked Archbishop Hughes on Tuesday to intercede, but aside from his appeal in the newspapers on Wednesday, he did not do so until 2 p.m. on Friday. Drawn by announcements in the press and flyers, some six thousand people gathered under the balcony of Hughes's residence at Madison Avenue and Thirty-sixth Street. Too feeble to stand, the archbishop, accompanied by a dozen Catholic priests, remained seated during his hour-long speech. Republican critics felt his belated call for peace, restraint, and order might have saved lives had it been delivered several days earlier.[25] However, the archbishop had clearly been reluctant to address his flock about the riots, since the very act could have been construed as a validation of bigoted claims that the rioters were all Irish Catholics, and all Irish Catholics were brutes who needed to be reprimanded by their own ethnic and religious leader.

"Men of New York," Hughes began. "They call you rioters, but I cannot see a rioter's face among you (applause)."[26] The archbishop then stoked his listeners' Anglophobia, saying that "if the city were invaded by the British or any other foreign power," he knew they would behave like real men. The remark also served notice that Catholics were loyal American citizens, despite the long-standing nativist claim that they were subversive agents of European despotism, beholden to the pope.

Before an appreciative, vocal crowd, Hughes continued to extol the good character of the Irish people and recalled his unstinting service to them. He denounced the "wretched tyranny" of the British that had destroyed their homeland, but urged them to value the relative freedom and opportunity to be

Archbishop John Hughes

found in America. Then, after another denial that the rioters were Irishmen, the archbishop gradually and gently admonished the crowd to bear their troubles patiently. "In this country the Constitution has made it the right of the people to make a revolution quietly every four years" with "ballots not bullets."

Hughes praised the American form of government while pointedly refraining from comment on the current leaders, which provoked a cry from someone in the crowd: "Let the nigger stay South," followed by shouts of "order." As the speech continued, Hughes repeatedly denied that his listeners were rioters but also became increasingly direct in advising them to refrain from violence. "At least let such of you as love God and revere the laws of the country, of which not a single statute has been enacted against you either as Irish or as Catholics, withdraw from crowds; because you have, as well as others, suffered enough already."

Hughes also appealed to the audience to live up to the proud history of the Irish people, who resorted to arms only in self-defense. He asked:

> That if, when the smoke clears away, the responsibility of these so-called rioters shall be thrown upon Catholics, especially Irish Catholics, and centred upon my heart, I wish you would tell me in what country I should claim to have been born (voices, "Ireland"). Yes but what do you say if these stories are true? What do you say? Ireland! That never committed by her own sons, or on her own soil, until she was oppressed, a single act of cruelty. Ireland, that has been the mother of heroes and poets, but never the mother of a coward (applause). Perhaps you will think that this is blarney . . . it is a fact . . . [W]hen St. Patrick came, he spoke to the multitude, and they listened to him; to the doctrines of Christianity, just as you have been patient enough to listen to me to-day.

The military acknowledged the power of Hughes's leadership by keeping troops nearby but out of sight during the address, ready to contain violence but not be accused of provoking it. The archbishop's address capped the process that began with Seymour's City Hall speech on Tuesday: Republican officials gave Catholic and Democratic leaders some room to carry out their policy of conciliation on the assumption that it would make their own job of putting down the riots a little easier.[27]

Radical Republicans, however, were furious and still hoped for martial law. "Archbishop Hughes has behaved like the Devil during all this, and Gov. Seymour not much better," Joseph Choate complained in a letter to his mother. "Witness their public acts and proceedings. The only hope for the redemption of this City is for Mr. Lincoln to come to our aid and declare martial law. That alone will displace Seymour. Then by a summary trial the ring leaders of this riot can be punished. By the ordinary courts nothing effective will be done. They are all in the hands of the Irish."[28]

Republican denunciations of "the Irish" notwithstanding, rioters and corrupt politicians were distinctly a minority of the two hundred thousand Irish Americans who comprised nearly a quarter of the city's population. Indeed, Irish Americans were among those most angered by the riots and most adamant about punishing the mobs' leaders. Sergeant Peter Welsh, at the front with Meagher's Irish Brigade, wrote to his wife, Margaret, from the front: "I am sorry to hear that there is such disgracefull riots in New York. i hope it will not get near to you nor anoy you . . . i see they tried the virtue of grape and canister on them and it had a very good efect. the originaters of those riots should be hung like dogs. they are the agents of jef davis and had their plans laid [to] start those riots simultanesly with Lees raid into Pensilvenia. i hope the authorutys will use canister freely. it will bring the bloody cutthroats to their censes."[29]

Welsh emphasized that the majority of rioters must have been misled by Confederate agitators, but the Union victories at Gettysburg, Vicksburg, and Port Hudson would at last convince New Yorkers of dubious loyalty that the North had the upper hand: "A pretty time they are getting up mob riots when one unanimous efort might finish up this acursed war in a few weeks. jeffs agents have been working very slyly and cuning but they will be foiled in all their skemes. every leader and instigator of those riots should be made an example of. there was hundreds no doubt mixed into them that did not know what they were doing caried away by excitement and under the influence of traitorous cut throats who made them believe they were resisting a great wrong."[30]

Welsh also told his wife he was "very sorry that the Irish men of New York took so large a part in them disgracefull riots. God help the Irish. They are to easily led into such snares which gives their enemys an oppertunity to malighn and abuse them."[31]

In a letter to the *Times* on July 29 another Irish American, A. F. Warburton, declared that "for the honor of Old Ireland," New York's Irish community, not the Common Council, should raise the funds to rebuild the Colored Orphan Asylum. He hoped the "smoking ruins of passion, prejudice and crime may be converted, by Ireland's sons, into a noble monument of liberal reparation and justice." Since its destruction, he wrote, "my blood has tingled with shame to know that this deed of fiendish atrocity was perpetrated mainly by parties (I cannot dignify them with the name of men) who claim to have come from that dear old Isle, which has given birth to those whose names are loved and honored in every land, and whose gallant sons are even now showing their devotion to the country of their adoption by shedding their blood bravely for her defense."

Warburton evidently feared a nativist backlash against the Irish in the wake of the riots. He pledged as much as five hundred dollars and suggested that "our honored fellow-citizen Charles O'Conor—whom no one will accuse of being an Abolitionist, but whose generosity and love of justice we all admire—be made Treasurer" of the fund in order to "put the matter beyond reach of any political imputation."

Indeed, the selection of O'Conor—one of the city's leading attorneys and a defender of the Confederacy—would have expressed a universal condemnation of the attack on the orphanage. Warburton also mentioned the city's preeminent Irish businessman, John Devlin, and two Tammany politicians, James Brady and Richard O'Gorman, as likely leaders for an effort to raise $50,000 to $100,000. Ultimately, however, funds to rebuild the Colored Orphan Asylum came primarily from the city.[32]

Some habitual critics of the working-class Irish came to their defense. Orestes Brownson, dubbed a "Catholic Know-Nothing" because of his disdain for immigrants, blamed conservative Catholic leaders as well as demagogic American politicians for leading the Irish rioters astray. A Protestant minister and prominent intellectual who had shocked his Yankee peers by converting to Catholicism twenty years earlier, Brownson was a latecomer to the antislavery cause in 1857, a switch that also put him at odds with the Catholic establishment.

He calculated that "nearly nine-tenths of the active rioters were Irishmen and Catholics," and almost all were "from the lowest and most degraded social class, even when instigated by men of high social standing." He condemned "the general tone of the clergy and respectable Catholics of the city; and especially of the Catholic press," which was lukewarm in its support for the Union cause and thereby influenced the rioters. "Yet the riot was not a Catholic riot," Brownson declared. "These things they did not as Catholics or Irishmen, but as adherents of the DEMOCRATIC PARTY, as partisans of Horatio Seymour, Fernando Wood, James Brooks, Clement L. Vallandigham, and others . . . who had worked them up to uncontrollable fury."[33]

While George Templeton Strong was willing to "see war made on Irish scum as in 1688," after the riots, Greeley and other Republicans admitted that the mobs were a minority of the Irish community, and that the mostly Irish residents of the crime-ridden Sixth and Fourteenth Wards, which included the Five Points slum, had been peaceful, even toward their black neighbors. "This is due in great measure to the personal influence of Controller M. T. Brennan and Police Justice Dowling," the *Tribune* declared.* "Both these gentlemen have been unremitting in their exertions to dissuade their friends from giving way to overt acts, which could only result in calling down upon them the penalties of the law." In these famously violent wards, the Democrats' conciliatory approach had been applied preemptively to keep the peace.[34]

Even *Harper's Weekly,* the highly partisan Republican journal—which regularly printed Thomas Nast's anti-Tammany, anti-Catholic, anti-Irish cartoons—called for tolerance. The Irish had rioted not as Irishmen but as part

---

*Comptroller Matthew Brennan and Police Justice Joseph Dowling were both Irish Americans who had risen from humble beginnings in the Sixth Ward to prominence in the Tammany hierarchy.

of the city's working class, in which they happened to be the largest ethnic group, *Harper's* later asserted. Americans should bear in mind that

> in many wards of the city, the Irish were during the late riot staunch friends of law and order; that Irishmen helped to rescue the colored orphans in the asylum . . . that a large proportion of the police, who behaved throughout the riot with the most exemplary gallantry, are Irishmen; that the Roman Catholic priesthood to a man used their influence on the side of the law; and that perhaps the most scathing rebuke administered to the riot was written by an Irishman—James T. Brady. It is important that this riot should teach us something more useful than a revival of Know-Nothing prejudices.[35]

However, *Harper's* also stated that the ignorance and impulsiveness of the Irish had led them to riot: A revival of nativism was precisely what the *Irish-American* feared. Its editors saw Republican attempts in other newspapers to blame the riots on the Irish as a political maneuver to bolster the party's ranks by creating a frenzy of Know-Nothingism. Irish volunteers in the army had hoped to overcome nativist discrimination, and the stigma of the draft riots seemed poised to wipe out whatever progress they had made. Trying to stem the tide, the *Irish-American* maintained that New York would continue to provide plenty of volunteers and that the draft was unnecessary. The paper blamed radical abolitionist journals for insulting Irish Catholics and generating the hostility that fueled the riots.[36]

The slowness with which federal authorities had responded to the riots, and President Lincoln's choice of a Democrat, General John A. Dix, to replace General Wool on Friday, clearly disgusted those New Yorkers who had hoped for General Butler and a declaration of martial law. "The folk at Washington have, I perceive, with their usual promptitude, dispatched Gen. Dix, who with Gens. Wool and Sanford are to *'cooperate'* with our city fathers and 'take measures' to quell the riots," photographer Clarence Eytinge wrote sarcastically to a friend. "If they could make it convenient to send to Holland for my Paternal Grandmother to consult with our Generals we would then have *four* old women equal to the Emergency, and no more negro children would be necessarily thrown out of 3 story windows as a pleasing amusement for the juvenile portion of the mob. (vide *Herald.*)"[37]

However, while Dix's appointment signaled that Lincoln was willing to work with the War Democrats of Tammany Hall instead of sweeping them aside, the president also intended to put a stop to the rioting and enforce the draft in New York—and the Democrats would have to cooperate. As commander of the Maryland Department, Dix had tolerated no disloyalty, a fact which recommended him for his new post.[38] Maria Daly reported in her diary that some of Judge Daly's colleagues had gone to Washington "to see what can be done," and the prognosis was not good. "New York, being a Democratic city, may expect little indulgence from the Administration," she wrote. "The Judge went up to see General Dix, now in command here, who says that government is determined to carry the draft measure through at all costs."[39]

Dix, a New Yorker, had the confidence of the city's financial leaders, since he was himself an attorney and financier to whom they had turned before in moments of crisis. They had gotten him appointed secretary of the treasury in 1861 to help the feckless lame-duck president, James Buchanan, as he stumbled through the secession crisis. At that time, Dix had also persuaded eastern capitalists to lend the federal government five million dollars to shore up its finances. The choice of a conservative War Democrat with a national reputation for integrity, nonpartisan leadership, and toughness as a military commander seemed to confirm President Lincoln's mastery of political compromise.[40]

By appointing Dix, Lincoln kept conservative, loyal Democrats in his war coalition and also pleased many ardent Republicans. "The announcement that General Dix has been ordered to take command here . . . gives us all great confidence," Joseph Choate reported to his mother, "and the fact that the power is to be transferred from Governor Seymour to him is encouraging."[41]

While the retirement of General Wool was expected and hoped for, the War Department's replacement of General Brown, despite his central role in rescuing the city, seemed gratuitous, insulting, and unjust. General E. R. S. Canby, also an aggressive officer, who had prevented a confederate invasion of the New Mexico territory, took charge of federal troops in New York City and the harbor forts.

Headley noted that Stanton's order for Brown's removal was issued before Washington had news that the rioting was over: "Why General Brown should have been removed at this critical moment, when he and the Police Commissioners were performing their herculean task so faithfully and well, is not so plain; unless it was the result of one of those freaks of passion or despotic impulse, for which the Secretary of War was so ignobly distinguished."

Given Wool's abiding dislike of Brown, and the fact that he dismissed him once during the riots, Brown's removal may have been a concession to Wool to help him save face as he left the service. Whatever the true reason, when the riots were over, only the least effective and most counterproductive of the three generals in charge—General Sandford—had retained his post.[42]

CHAPTER 16

A Plot to "Make the Northern States a Battle-Field"

~

R iot, murder, and conflagration have begun in New York," the *Richmond Enquirer* rejoiced on Saturday, July 18, under the optimistic heading "BEGINNING OF CHAOS." The Confederate paper considered it "a world's wonder that this good work did not commence long ago; and this excellent outbreak may be the opening scene of the inevitable revolution which is to tear to pieces that most rotten society, and leave the Northern half of the old American Union a desert of blood-soaked ashes. We bid it good speed." The paper predicted that the riots would be "the parent of other and still worse convulsions."[1]

Edmund Ruffin also looked forward to further rioting and used a grand historical analogy to pronounce the imminent demise of the North. Noting that Philadelphia was considering a commutation fund like the $2.5-million appropriation in New York, Ruffin wrote:

> I hope that the measure may be adopted there & in other cities. For instead of allaying the disposition for mob violence, it must greatly stimulate its action. It will operate like the policy of the sinking western Roman empire in buying the mercy, & the retreat, of the invading hosts of barbarians, when threatening to enter & to sack & burn the city of Rome. Temporary relief would . . . thus be dearly purchased, only to invite other hordes, or the same, to come

again in search of the like payments for forbearance, or to merely divert the destruction to other localities.[2]

In fact, the riots in New York were the culmination, not the beginning, of resistance to the draft, as the South hoped. By Saturday, the city was largely quiet. No great Copperhead uprising had materialized in the Midwest, where John Hunt Morgan's raid through southern Indiana and Ohio was in its third week. Instead, the rebel horsemen had all they could do to escape across the Ohio River into West Virginia. They approached Buffington Ford on Saturday, July 18, but three hundred Federals patrolled the crossing, so the horsemen rested overnight before advancing again at sunrise. The Union infantry had moved on, so the Confederates began crossing the river, only to fall into a trap.

Two gunboats suddenly appeared, blasting the rebel column with their artillery, while five thousand Union cavalry moved in for the kill. Morgan managed to escape northward with a thousand men after ordering one of the brigades to stay back and protect his retreat. The Federals killed 120 Confederates and took 700 prisoners, nearly half of Morgan's command. Attempting to cross the river at a different ford later that day, Morgan was separated from three hundred more of his men, who made it across despite another ambush by Union gunboats. Morgan was halfway across the river but turned back to rejoin the seven hundred men stuck on the Ohio side.

After fleeing to the north and east for an entire week, the rebel horsemen were finally surrounded and captured by Union troops near the Pennsylvania state line. They had covered more than a thousand miles in three and a half weeks, only to land in the state prison at Columbus, Ohio. General Burnside and Ohio's governor refused to treat them as prisoners of war, subject to parole and exchange. Instead they were jailed as criminals, deprived not only of their uniforms, their hair, and their beards but of visitors of any kind, including Morgan's mother, who made the trip from Kentucky in vain.[3]

George Wingate of the Twenty-second militia regiment recalled that "on the 18th day of July we found ourselves swinging up Broadway, glad to be home once more, but sorry enough to think that we were denied the pleasure of a shot at the rioters in general, and our worthy ex-mayor [Fernando Wood] in particular."

While the militia had been criticized as "Broadway troops, good for playing soldier" but unfit for the hardships of the real army, Wingate wrote, their campaign around Gettysburg had proven the critics wrong. "Marching one hundred and seventy miles in less than three weeks, in the most inclement weather, through mountain passes and over abominable roads, on ten days rations, without a change of clothing, in expectation of an attack at any moment (our regiment alone forming line of battle over nineteen times), they point with pride to the thanks tendered to them by General Meade in his official report, and claim that they have done all that could be expected of them—if not more."[4]

Despite Meade's victory at Gettysburg, and the patriotism of the militia, Lincoln was furious about Lee's escape across the Potomac on July 14—at the very moment when Union forces were gaining ground elsewhere. Port Hudson, Louisiana, had fallen five days after Vicksburg, giving the Union control of the Mississippi and dividing the Confederacy. In middle Tennessee, Rosecrans had finally moved against the rebels, who fell back to Chattanooga. Seizing Chattanooga would place a strategic rail hub in Union hands and leave Georgia open to invasion, presenting another chance to split the Confederate states, east from west. Together, these advances suggested to Lincoln that destroying Lee's army right after Gettysburg would have ended the war. Instead, Lee continued to block the road to Richmond.[5]

Also frustrating the North was the lack of progress in capturing Charleston, where the Union navy attacked the forts at the mouth of the harbor with little result except casualties. Sergeant Robert Simmons, a black New Yorker in the Fifty-fourth Massachusetts Regiment, died in the Union assault on Fort Wagner on Saturday, July 18. Earlier in the week, the draft rioters had destroyed his family's home and killed his nephew.[6]

Harper's Weekly praised the brave black troops and condemned the Irish rioters. "It was at the very hour when negroes were pouring out their blood for the stars and stripes on the slopes of Fort Wagner that naturalized foreigners, who hauled down the Stars and Stripes whenever they saw them, tried to exterminate the negro race in New York."[7] Because of such Republican outrage, the blacks at Fort Wagner did not die in vain: The juxtaposition of their contribution with the horror of the riots did much to win support for black regiments and to transform public opinion in the North in the coming months in favor of emancipation and against the Democrats' racism.[8]

Southerners, by contrast, were enraged by the use of black troops. On July 20, Edmund Ruffin learned of a raid in South Carolina carried out by black troops backed up by Union gunboats in which thirty-four country estates and their groves of stately oak trees—worth two million dollars—were burned to the ground. "Is it carrying too far the desire for retribution and vengeance," he fumed in his diary, "to rejoice at the sacking & burning in New York, & to wish that the same calamities, carried out fully, & the destruction made complete, may attend every Yankee city?"[9]

·   ·   ·

"We are once more at peace in New York," Joseph Choate wrote to his mother on Saturday, July 18, "and as the government are concentrating a large military force here, we are not likely to be again disturbed. It has been a bloody enough week though. I think as many as five hundred, all told, must have been killed. The negroes have fled in all directions as from a slaughter-house."[10]

Many fled for safety to free-black communities beyond Brooklyn on Long Island. As far east as Quogue, blacks took up weapons or hid wherever they could, in barns and other buildings. At Weeksville, Carsville, New Brooklyn, Flatbush, and Flatlands, armed blacks patrolled the edges of the settlements, keeping rioters away and creating havens for hundreds of refugees from New York City and Brooklyn.* Refugees overflowed from these small villages and hid in the woods for days on end without food or shelter. They also fled to the swamps along the New Jersey shore near Bergen, and north of Manhattan, to Morrisania.† A charitable organization concluded that "at these places were scattered some five thousand homeless and helpless men, women, and children."[11]

A black woman, her two children, and the Choates' housekeeper's brother had found shelter with them for the week. When the four ventured out, they found that the buildings where they lived and all of their belongings had been destroyed; the landlord of the man's boardinghouse, unable to flee on his crutches, had been lynched. "What is to be done for these helpless victims, I do not know," Choate continued. "We shall keep our quota for the present, and do what we can to meet their most urgent wants, but the general distress among them must be very great."[12]

By contrast, Maria Daly continued to rely on an instinct for self-preservation. "Father came into the city on Friday, being warned about his house, and found fifteen Negroes secreted in it by [his housekeeper] Rachel. They came from York Street, which the mob had attacked, with all their goods and chattels. Father had to order them out. We feared for our own block on account of the Negro tenements below MacDougal Street, where the Negroes were on the roof, singing psalms and having firearms."[13]

Maria Daly, like other New Yorkers, began to piece together fragments of information and rumors that suggested the riots were a conspiracy. She also heard that "among those killed or wounded have been found men with delicate hands and feet, and under their outward laborers' clothes were fine cambric shirts and costly underclothing. A dressmaker says she saw from her

---

*Today, four restored houses of the Weeksville settlement are open to visitors in the Crown Heights section of Brooklyn. See the Walking Tour in the appendix.

†Morrisania, once the estate of the Morris family, today is part of the Bronx.

window a gentleman whom she knows and has seen with young ladies, but whose name she could not remember, disguised in this way in the mob on Sixth Avenue."[14]

She also heard from friends in Westchester that "there was a secessionist plot to burn all the houses in the neighborhood on Thursday night . . . and that the principal instigator and mover in it was one of the richest and most influential men in the neighborhood. The purpose of the plot was to intimidate the government and prevent conscription."[15]

Similarly, John Jay, grandson of the founding father and president of the Union League Club, wrote Stanton on July 18: "Apart from the Irish the copperhead element in the rural districts is ready to co-operate with them. In the usually quiet neighborhood where I live, in Westchester County, some forty miles from town, threats of murder and arson are openly made."[16] This was part of a larger conspiracy that had gotten out of control, Jay insisted; Governor Seymour, Judge McCunn, and Archbishop Hughes were helping to restore order in New York with the approval of the Copperhead plotters, who intended to make another attempt.

> An armed revolution in New York has been resolved on by the rebel sympathizers almost from the commencement [of the war]. Before the fall of Sumter, Fernando Wood, in a message to the Common Council, announced that by the secession of South Carolina the Union was dissolved, and it becomes every city and every community to take care of itself, and suggested that New York become a free city, like Frankfort-on-the-Main.
>
> A secret organization was set on foot for this purpose, and I was told by a Democrat now in the service of the Government that 5,000 names were pledged to the movement almost from the beginning.
>
> This organization, as I believe, has been long perfected in the different wards, and a movement for the last 4th of July was averted by the news of national victories. The existing riots were not contemplated in the shape they took and have interfered with the original plan.

Jay offered no names or documentation, but concluded "from various suggestions let drop by newspapers and individuals" that the Copperheads' new plan was to instigate an "armed conflict between the National Government and the State government." First the plotters hoped to have the state courts rule against the constitutionality of the draft. Then Lincoln's expected refusal to "obey the mandate of the State courts" would cause Seymour to call out the militia, followed by a popular uprising against federal tyranny, that would "make the Northern States a battle-field."

This scenario matched the one described by Edmund Ruffin in his diary after Seymour was elected governor in 1862, but Ruffin was never implicated in a conspiracy; he was merely expressing his hopes, not his plans. Nonetheless, Jay saw the plot as an extension of Confederate strategy. "This is the last great card, I think, of the rebellion, and demands careful play on the part of the Government," to avoid such a confrontation without backing down on the draft. Jay suggested that the government preempt the conspirators by taking the draft law to the courts and obtaining a quick, favorable ruling; the recent victories at Gettysburg, Vicksburg, and Port Hudson gave the administration enough of an advantage to postpone the draft for a few weeks.

Colonel Robert Nugent, in charge of restarting the draft lottery, impressed on Fry that the riots were fomented by Lincoln's political opponents, but counseled a show of force instead of avoiding confrontation.

> There is no doubt that most, if not all, of the Democratic politicians are at the bottom of this riot, and that the rioters themselves include not only the thieves and gamblers that infest this metropolis, but nearly every one of the vast Democratic majority, which has so constantly been thrown at every election against the Administration . . . Should any conflict between the Federal and State authorities occur, and it is not unlikely that it should, Seymour will most certainly side with the State, and would bring with him most of the militia . . . I would advise the proclamation of martial law, and the presence of an adequate [federal] force here, before any steps are taken to enforce the draft.[17]

Completely absorbed with his work, and committed to taking a stand against the rioters, Horace Greeley did not leave the city until Saturday to join his wife and children, who were alone at the family's farm in Chappaqua, New York. Greeley, whose paper reported on the full scope of the rioting in the suburbs, might well have known that his wife, Mary, and daughters, Ida and Gabrielle, were in danger.

He soon learned that a drunken mob from Sing Sing, nearby on the Hudson River, had threatened the farm but was stopped at the gates by a neighbor, who declared that the property was protected by a trail of gunpowder, easily ignited if they came any closer. "Heed my warning, my brethren," the Quaker farmer reportedly said, "Horace Greeley is a man of peace, but Mary Greeley will fight to the last." The crowd moved off, while

Mary, isolated on the farm and suffering from chronic mental illness, closed all the shutters and kept a lonely vigil until her husband's return.[18]

Greeley did not remain with her long, however. He headed back to the city the following day. *Tribune* editorials denounced Irish immigrants as infidels for not observing the Lord's Sabbath, but the paper's founder stuck to his habit of working on Sundays. On that day, Unitarian minister Octavius B. Frothingham, a friend of Greeley's for twenty-five years, told his congregation, "The one man who, before and above all others, was a mark for the rage of the populace . . . the one man who was hunted for his blood as by wolves . . . was a man who had been the steadfast friend of these very people who hungered for his blood."[19]

The effort to help the city's black victims began with individuals like Joseph Choate and his wife bravely providing shelter to their own servants and the servants' relatives. Henry Raymond of the *Times* spurred the effort to the next level with an editorial on Friday, and by Saturday businessmen including William Dodge had set up the Committee of Merchants for the Relief of Colored People Suffering from the Late Riots and eventually received contributions of more than forty thousand dollars. Like Dodge, who had courageously spoken out against the rioting earlier in the week, they all risked retaliation by publishing their names as benefactors of the black community.

Blacks were cautious at first, the committee observed in its final report, but soon the streets outside the relief office on Fourth Street near Broadway "were literally filled with applicants," men, women, and children, showing signs of starvation after a week of hiding, and some with wounds from the riots. They applied for emergency aid and received small cash payments, usually no more than five dollars; they were allowed to apply repeatedly if necessary in the coming weeks. The office was not far from the police Central Office, so help could be dispatched in case of a disturbance.

The committee also made additional payments after Henry Highland Garnet, Charles Ray, and other black clergymen reviewed cases, made home visits, and sought out black refugees hiding in the suburbs to determine their level of need. Because the clergymen were trusted to evaluate the validity of claims, many blacks and their families received aid in the next month, a total of almost thirteen thousand people. At the Fourth Street office, lawyers also volunteered their services to help applicants file claims against the city.[20]

An office was also set up in Brooklyn, where the committee helped more than two thousand blacks and employed four black ministers to make home visits and verify need. The committee noted that an Irish American named Edgar McMullen had been helping the refugees who were still scattered in the woods near Weeksville and other free-black communities. With his help the committee supplied them with "Bread, Hams, Flour, Rice, Sugar, and Tea, and in some few cases of great need small sums of money." While most blacks promptly returned to work in Brooklyn, according to the committee, the two hundred who worked in the tobacco factories remained unemployed because the owners feared more violence.[21]

"Those who know the colored people of this city, can testify to their being a peaceable, industrious people, having their own churches, Sunday-schools and charitable Societies; and that, as a class they seldom depend on charity," the committee declared. Spurred by altruism—and the fear that blacks, who had been relatively self-sufficient, would suddenly become a class of paupers "dependent on the charity of the city"—the committee reassured white employers that the military would protect them while blacks resumed their former jobs.[22]

In a message to racist employers and white workers, the committee appealed to their conservatism and self-interest, asking them to "restore the colored laborer to his customary place" and to "restore the old order of things." The committee also pointed out that if white workers drove blacks out of the city, rural white workers would come in to take their place in the most menial jobs, enlarging the supply of white laborers and depressing wages. Blacks, rather than posing a competitive threat, in fact occupied a lowly niche that kept the Irish on a slightly higher rung of the economic ladder.[23]

Implicit in the praise of blacks' industriousness was the committee's disdain for the Irish Catholic poor as "loafers." Union League Club members on the committee were mostly Protestants and nativists whose efforts to cultivate the loyalty of the city's immigrant population through charitable moral reform crusades before the war had been rebuffed. In the wake of the riots, helping responsive blacks and gaining their loyalty also provided an opportunity for Republicans to rehabilitate New York's reputation, badly tarnished as a hotbed of Copperhead disloyalty and racial violence. In that vein, the Union League Club also resolved that week to raise a black regiment from New York for the Union army.[24] It would be a direct challenge to Governor Seymour's long-standing refusal to authorize such regiments.

Lucy and Julia Gibbons left for the country with Abby's father, John Hopper, while their father waited for Abby and Sally to return to the city from the military hospital. Joseph Choate predicted that the Gibbons family would not suffer financially. "The Legislature of New York in 1855 passed a law making the City or the County liable for all property destroyed or injured in consequence of a riot or mob, and I do not think that the authorities of the City or County will be slow to make just amends for the losses. At any rate if there is any hesitation . . . we shall sue them."[25]

Choate correctly calculated that blacks would suffer immeasurably more than white victims. For Albro and Mary Lyons, the bitterly ironic finale of the riots was that they—the city's peaceful, responsible residents—had to sneak out of New York like thieves. "Under the cover of darkness the police conveyed our parents to the Williamsburg ferry," Maritcha Lyons wrote. "There steamboats were kept in readiness to either transport fugitives or to outwit rioters by pulling out into midstream. To such humiliations, to such outrages, were law abiding citizens exposed and that in a city where they were domiciled tax payers. Is it any wonder that for them New York was never after to be considered home. From one end of Long Island to the other, mother with her children undertook the hazardous journey of getting to New England by crossing the Long Island Sound."[26]

While Albro stayed in New York to salvage their property and document their losses, Mary Lyons took her children to New London, Connecticut, where friends put them up briefly before they moved on to Salem, Massachusetts. "Even there one was not safe from the onslaughts of an irrepressible mob," Maritcha Lyons noted, "but the authorities were prepared to forestall any suspicion of lawlessness," and rioting never materialized. Maritcha Lyons was not alone in her belief that the catastrophe in New York could similarly have been prevented if authorities had taken more precautions. "We reached Salem tired, travel stained, with only the garments we had on. Mother's fortitude never relaxed nor did her courage fail."[27]

However, their psychological needs were as great as their physical ones. "The Remond family, with whom we took refuge, outdid themselves in showering upon us kind attentions, anxious to cheer and to incite hope to replace despair," Maritcha Lyons recalled.

> Before her marriage, mother had been closely associated with this family, as clerk in their confectionery store in the summer, and instructor of the daughters in the various branches of hair work during the winter, for she had been a pupil of Martel, a noted New York French hairdresser. Maritcha Remond was mother's bridesmaid and I am named for her.
>
> Mother had always been treated by them as a daughter of the house and their tender regard did much to arouse her from a state of apathy which threatened to overwhelm her upon her arrival at a place of refuge with the termination of her untoward journey.[28]

Maritcha Remond Lyons

The children from the Colored Orphan Asylum fared somewhat better than most blacks, since they had white managers to represent them. Nonetheless, they too were in miserable shape, still wearing the dirty and disheveled clothing from the night they fled to the police station, as Samuel Denison from the Committee of Merchants for the Relief of Colored People discovered when he visited the refugees on Blackwell's Island on July 22. The secretary and the manager of the asylum sent a note with Denison, and the merchants' committee responded with a grant of a thousand dollars. "Most of the Officers and domestics of the Institution lost all their clothing and other effects, so intent were they in saving the children," Anna Shotwell wrote.[29]

By the weekend, the city was comparatively peaceful, but the trauma of the riots persisted. The merchants' committee reported that "some four or five white women, wives of colored men . . . had been severely dealt with by the mob. One Irish woman, Mrs. C. was so persecuted and shunned by every one, that when she called for aid, she was nearly insane . . . Several cases of insanity among the colored people appear, as directly traceable to the riots."[30]

·   ·   ·

The financial cost of the draft riots has been calculated both officially and unofficially. By law, the city was responsible, in the event of a riot, for the damage or loss of private property, and eventually paid out $1.5 million to settle claims, including a negligible amount to blacks. Given that more than one hundred buildings were burned and two hundred others looted or damaged, various accounts estimate the actual property loss as high as $3 million and even $5 million—equivalent to $60 million or $100 million in today's dollars. The economic loss from the disruption of business and the flight of residents was never calculated in a dollar amount.[31]

While the committee evaluating the riot claims was part of the Tweed-dominated New York County Board of Supervisors, it does not appear to have taken the tragedy as one more chance to raid public funds and reward cronies. This uncharacteristic restraint had its downside, however, in that the claims of blacks in particular were scrutinized, reduced, and often denied, both by the committee and by the comptroller, Matthew Brennan, who made the final determination in each case.

Altogether, the claims put forward by African Americans amounted to only about $17,500, far less than their true needs, yet the Democratic city government treated these cases with suspicion and dismissed many as fraudulent. The examiners also invented an excuse to deprive blacks of compensation: If they fled their homes before an actual attack and their possessions were carried off, the loss was considered an ordinary robbery—by neighbors or thieves—and the city denied responsibility.

The Committee of Merchants for the Relief of Colored People, which had raised some forty thousand dollars through private donations for black riot victims, demanded of Brennan that "in cases where the Comptroller calls for a deduction," from "the amount awarded by the Board of Supervisors," he "is requested to furnish a copy of the evidence upon which such deduction is claimed." The merchants' committee was a watchdog with no teeth, however, and many blacks were left destitute by the riots.[32]

Many poor whites, who had rioted against the draft's three-hundred-dollar clause—which aggravated their already miserable poverty—remained no better off, save for a few items they may have looted. Colonel Nugent's ceremonial sword, which disappeared when his home was ransacked on Monday night, turned up in the hands of a street urchin on Manhattan's East Side, the blade ruined and the jewel encrusted handle stripped bare. Tapestries, oil paintings, silk fabric, and sacks full of stolen gloves or shoes hung incongruously in hovels around the city, announcing the growing gap of wealth and privilege in an increasingly industrial and urban society. The deeper causes of the draft riot continued to fester, setting the stage for future strikes and riots in the decades ahead.[33]

The tragic depth of poverty in the nation's commercial center was underscored a week after the draft riots. The looting was over, so hungry women and children picked through the rubble of the charred Eighteenth Precinct station house, hunting for chunks of wood and coal to sell or to warm themselves through the fall and winter. The wall of the building collapsed on the scavengers, and two boys were killed.[34]

Once the police turned to the military for help in New York City, blank cartridges had proved counterproductive and put the soldiers in danger. However, while Protestant Republicans urged a shoot-first-and-ask-questions-later approach to the largely Irish Catholic mobs, more effective methods of crowd control that reduced casualties were already being used successfully in England. By deploying officers mounted on horseback to dominate and corral large groups of rioters, the police might well have controlled the disturbances in the early stages, instead of stoking the fury of the mobs with direct attacks.[35]

In the absence of cavalry, the police had to rely on their locust-wood clubs, the military used live ammunition, and the draft riots in New York City became the deadliest in American history. Official documents confirm 105 deaths directly attributable to the riots, a figure that includes six soldiers and three policemen. The toll rises to 119 if deaths from wounds, falls, and the collapse of charred buildings shortly after the riots are included.[36] These conservative, documented figures are two to four times the number of confirmed deaths in other major American riots, and the true toll, suggested by contemporary accounts, was almost certainly much higher.*

Documents record that eighteen blacks were lynched, five drowned in the rivers, and seventy were reported missing. However, a week after the riots, the *Christian Recorder,* the official newspaper of the African Methodist Episcopal Church, published in Philadelphia, contained an estimate that "175 persons of color lost their lives." Black clergyman Charles Ray, who visited New York's black refugees to assess their damage claims, wrote that "it is a wonder, exposed and hunted as they were, that more lives were not taken."[37]

While a few contemporary estimates claimed as many as 1,200 deaths, those that put the toll at 500 were probably more accurate. Since most of the dead were the rioters themselves, not their intended victims, the estimate of 1,200 may have stemmed in part from an exaggeration of the number of

---

*In the Tulsa, Oklahoma, riot of 1921, according to an official estimate, 10 whites and 26 blacks were killed, while later reports, never verified, raised the number of dead to 300. In the 1992 Los Angeles riots, during which violence broke out in other cities around the country, and military forces were called in, an estimated 50 to 60 people were killed.

active participants in the mobs. While there may have been fifty thousand people filling the length of Third Avenue on the morning of July 13, as Headley calculated, the vast majority were spectators. A few roving bands, each consisting of several thousand people, terrorized the city throughout the week. However, each band typically had a core of one to three hundred leaders who took the brunt of the clubbing from the police and absorbed the volleys of gunfire from the military. Most of the gangs or mobs were far smaller, numbering between twenty and fifty people.[38]

Thus the targets for the police and military were far fewer than many imagined, and most of the gunfire came from notoriously inaccurate muskets, aimed in the general direction of the mobs, and far less from rifles, possessed by only the best-equipped regiments. Even when artillery was brought in, the number of dead did not soar. After Captain Putnam's fiercest clash with the mobs, on Thursday night, he reported thirteen rioters killed and twenty-four wounded.[39]

While one account of the fire in the Second Avenue armory claimed that "more than fifty baskets and barrels of human bones were carted from the ruins and buried in Potter's Field," a more likely version had thirteen rioters killed at the armory, ten of them in the fire.[40] The most exaggerated figures also reflected the political agendas of those who calculated them. The Republicans wanted to bring in federal troops, while the Democrats quoted high figures to show the excessive force and brutality wielded against their constituents by their political opponents.[41]

Nonetheless, the official count of 105 is almost certainly low, given that a mere handful of the skirmishes between the rioters and the military resulted in at least that many deaths, according to the reports of participants. The true death toll probably lies somewhere between the documented figure and the sober contemporary estimate of 500.

Official reports showed 73 soldiers injured in the riots, along with 105 policemen. While 128 civilians were recorded as injured, the true number was much larger. Only the more severely wounded went to hospitals, where they entered the official record, while many others were treated by doctors and pharmacists. Thousands of blacks—many with untreated injuries—went into hiding or fled the city altogether.[42]

Beyond these physical injuries, the legacy of the draft riots—the deeper and more long-lasting damage to the fabric of American society—would become evident in the coming decades. The rioters had succeeded in scattering free blacks to the edges of white society, a prelude to the formation of large black ghettoes in New York and other cities. Moreover, the terror campaign by hooded horsemen in the South, aimed at segregating and disfranchising blacks after emancipation and destroying their schools, would bear a striking resemblance to the racial pogrom in the streets of New York.[43]

CHAPTER 17

Aftermath: Sitting on Two Volcanoes

~

When the riots were over, James Gilmore took a train up to Lake George to spend a few days in the country at the estate of his father-in-law, Judge John W. Edmonds, who had presided at the trial of Isaiah Rynders and other leaders of the Astor Place riots a dozen years earlier. As usual, Gilmore was a man with a mission. He and Sidney Gay had already written to President Lincoln, asking if he would appoint Judge Edmonds as "a special commissioner to investigate the origin of the riots," with the aim of exposing the high-level Copperheads the *Tribune* men believed were "the secret instigators and directors" of the revolt. Gilmore asked his father-in-law to take on the task.

"Do you know, my dear boy, what you are asking of me?" the judge replied. "If I should undertake that work my life wouldn't be worth a bad half-dollar. There's not a rough in New York who wouldn't shoot me on sight; but my time is about up, and it may serve the country. You can tell Mr. Lincoln that I will accept the appointment." However, Lincoln's reply about launching an investigation was equivocal, so Gilmore brought up the subject when he went to see the president in Washington.

"Well, you see if I had said no," Lincoln said to Gilmore, "I should have admitted that I dare not enforce the laws, and consequently have no business to be President of the United States. If I had said yes, and had appointed the judge, I should—as he would have done his duty—have simply touched a match to a barrel of gunpowder." Lincoln calculated that martial law in the city, and a full investigation of the riots, would provoke still more violence.

"You have heard of sitting on a volcano. We are sitting upon two; one is blazing away already, and the other will blaze away the moment we scrape a little loose dirt from the top of the crater. Better let the dirt alone,—at least for the present. One rebellion at a time is about as much as we can conveniently handle."

For Lincoln, the blazing volcano was the war as a whole, and the smoldering one was the seismic headache presented by New York's Democratic politicians and seething mobs. Gilmore undoubtedly left the meeting dissatisfied but later concluded that "Mr. Lincoln was right," when the president told him the hidden meaning of the second volcano: Federal agents had detected an active conspiracy to trigger riots and free Confederate prisoners in the Midwest, where discontent had been rumbling throughout the war but had yet to erupt on a large scale. The trouble seemed to have passed in New York, and the president was focused on disrupting the threat that loomed in Chicago. While many criticized Lincoln for moving too slowly, Gilmore came to believe that Lincoln's deliberative style saved the Union from defeat at more than one juncture during the war.

In the case of the New York draft riots, Lincoln chose to overlook Gilmore's conspiracy theory. Gilmore reported that Sidney Gay had a friend and informant—"a prominent Copperhead politician"—who was privy to the plot but mortified by the violence once it had been unleashed. This man, according to Gilmore, had come to the managing editor on the first day of the riots, warning him to flee the uprising, which was "a revolution intended to further the cause of Southern independence." Each day that week, he had visited Gay to ease his conscience and provided, without naming names, enough information "to identify and single out the secret leaders of the riots from among the prominent men of the Copperhead party." If Gilmore provided the president with any names or proof of these assertions, they have never come to light.[1]

The invitation for Lincoln to prosecute and overthrow the Democratic machine in New York, tempting as it may have seemed, was unrealistic for other reasons aside from a lack of evidence. By doing so, he would have surpassed all of his previous extensions of federal authority over the states and individuals and threatened the very fabric of the nation's federal system, already strained by the war and his earlier edicts. No matter how corruptly the Democrats had been elected and retained power, the use of martial law not simply to maintain order but to unseat them from the local government would also have been a subjugation of the civil to the military authority, a violation of the defining tenets of republican government that distinguished it from dictatorship.[2]

While Republicans still hoped for martial law, Seymour, Tilden, and other powerful upstate Democrats continued to believe the courts might declare the draft unconstitutional. Seymour spent several weeks after the riots trying to convince Lincoln that the quotas for New York State were too high, the draft law was illegal, and that New York City would never tolerate it.

When General Dix wrote to Seymour at the end of July, saying the draft would soon resume and asking for New York State militia to enforce it—preferring them to federal troops whose presence might spark more rioting—Seymour said he would talk to Lincoln before deciding. The president told the governor he would address the glaring disparities between quotas for certain districts and allow Seymour's representatives to observe the reenrollment process. Lincoln also agreed to have the Supreme Court consider the constitutionality of the draft law but insisted the draft must continue while the decision was pending.[3]

With the lottery looming, the aldermen's hope of preventing more violence with a commutation fund seemed stalled. At the height of the riots, Mayor Opdyke had condemned the Common Council's hurried approval of a $2.5-million bond issue to give poor draftees the three-hundred-dollar exemption fee. Ten days later, he had formally vetoed the bill on the grounds that it would "nullify the draft"—even as his own son bought his way out of military service. The Democrats, however, would not be denied and took the issue to the twelve-man New York County Board of Supervisors, which was essentially run by Tweed.

In mid-August, Tweed conferred with Orison Blunt, a Republican supervisor whose gun factories had been damaged in the riots, and with Mayor Opdyke, to work out a deal that would appease the public and avoid another riot without depriving the army of conscripts. They agreed that the Board of Supervisors should appropriate three million dollars to purchase substitutes for police, firemen, and militia who were drafted as well as for New Yorkers who could demonstrate that their absence would impoverish their families. If these draftees decided to serve, they would receive a three-hundred-dollar bounty, just as if they had volunteered.[4]

Governor Seymour issued a proclamation on August 18, advising New Yorkers to accept the draft, and warned there would be no tolerance of riots. Seymour had persuaded Lincoln to reduce New York's quota and was still negotiating to get credit for volunteers up to the day before the lottery. The draft resumed on August 19, with ten thousand federal troops camped in New York City. Kennedy had resumed his post as police superintendent and had "scant mercy" for mobs, police telegrapher Charles Loring Chapin wrote: "Clubs were trumps."[5]

The draft went off peacefully, in part because of the federal troops at the provost marshals' offices, and in part because Tammany officials were on hand too, reassuring their constituents that the county supervisors would take care of any conscript who needed relief. When Tweed himself was drafted, the drawing of his name from a wheel in the Seventh Ward drew much appreciative cheering for the Tammany chieftain in the crowded office.[6]

"The draft in the state of N.Y., as in other northern states, is progressing quietly," Edmund Ruffin noted with disappointment in his diary. "No violent resistance now seems probable anywhere. Much has been done by Lincoln, & also by the city authorities, to smooth down the opposition spirit in New York—which measures have been so much yielding to the popular discontents."[7]

Tweed, Blunt, and Opdyke had taken their plan for a three-million-dollar fund to the full Board of Supervisors and won approval. Then Tweed and Blunt traveled to Washington, where they secured Lincoln's and Stanton's agreement. In September, the County Substitute and Relief Committee, consisting of two Democrats and two Republicans, including Tweed and Blunt, questioned some one thousand draftees applying for relief and procured substitutes for virtually all of them. Because of the fund, substitutes entering the army from New York City soon outnumbered draftees two to one. The city of Brooklyn adopted a similar plan.[8]

Republicans, who had equal representation on the Board of Supervisors, hoped to bask in the public gratitude for this protection against the draft along with the Democrats, particularly since the bond issue avoided a tax increase. Ultimately, however, the Democrats were associated with relief from the draft, and the county committee that furnished substitutes and fees for drafted men helped the Democrats consolidate their power in the wake of the riots. At the top of the Democratic hierarchy, County Supervisor and Deputy Street Commissioner William Tweed was well on his way to becoming the most legendary of urban machine "bosses."[9]

Because the public money attracted men to volunteer as substitutes, the County Substitute and Relief Committee that administered the fund effectively became a recruiting agency for the army and was aptly renamed the Volunteer Committee. The Board of Supervisors took credit for helping to fill the city's federal quota of volunteers and sounded the Democratic refrain that a draft was unnecessary.

However, the pool of money was also a magnet for unscrupulous bounty brokers who set themselves up as middlemen between the recruits and the committee, collecting the substitution fees and disbursing only a small portion to the men they deceived and presented for enlistment.

The county funds in New York exacerbated a problem that existed across the North, where brokers swarmed around army recruitment offices, filling the entrances and hallways, and making it virtually impossible for a man to enlist and collect his bounty money directly. The ability of these brokers to control the supply of substitutes and volunteers—by getting them drunk, drugging or beating them, or making false promises—became a nationwide scourge, which also spilled over into Canada, where agents, particularly from nearby Detroit, sent their runners to round up men. While Manton Marble's *World* had compared the federal conscription to the British press-gangs of colonial times, in fact the violent bounty brokers most deserved that charge.

Transporting their victims to towns and cities that paid the highest bounties, for the rest of the war the brokers created a vast intra- and interstate traffic in men, who were "sold like mules," while various communities vainly protested that they were being robbed of the local men to fill their federal quota of volunteers. Brokers also used the threat of transporting men to squelch attempts by conscientious local officials to create new rules allowing for the payment of bounties only to the principals themselves. In New York, much of the eight million dollars the county borrowed to pay bounties in 1863–65 went into the pockets of brokers. Colluding with them were corrupt provost marshals and examining surgeons who enlisted physically and mentally unfit substitutes, thus diluting the army's strength.[10]

Bounty "jumpers" also abused the system by fleeing the draft at home in order to enlist, desert, and reenlist in several other locations, collecting multiple bounties. In late August 1863, Sergeant Peter Welsh wrote to his wife: "We got a lot of conscripts last sunday. they are nearly [all] New Yorkers who went to Boston and came out as substitutes. a great many of them have been out before in two year regiments. there was about two hundred came altogether. They are a wild lot of fellows with plenty of mony. some of them got four to five hundred dollars for coming . . . My dear wife i hope you are getting better health. i wish this war was over so that i could go home to you and nothing but death should separate us again."[11]

Tammany Hall officials sensed the public mood of outrage in the wake of the draft riots and, as loyal War Democrats, were well positioned to take advantage of it. Not only did they cooperate with General Dix in keeping the peace across the city and enforcing the draft, but they set about prosecuting the rioters at the end of July and kept on for two more months, with City Recorder John Hoffman overseeing the tribunal and District Attorney A. Oakey Hall representing the state.* However, the Tammany-run trials were more show than substance. Hall was a less-than-zealous, often incompetent, prosecutor, and various other Democratic politicians used their influence with judges to

*The recorder was the presiding judge of New York's Court of General Sessions.

see that the rioters, for the most part, went free. Nonetheless, the sight of New York's hardened criminals being manacled and marched through the courthouse, and the reports of their testimony in the daily press, won Hoffman and Hall plaudits from a grateful city, and they went on to seemingly brilliant careers as governor and mayor.[12]

Some 450 suspects were detained, but charges were brought only against half that number. Despite a five-hundred-dollar reward offered by Mayor Opdyke, evidence was hard to come by, especially since some rioters intimidated potential witnesses. Charges against ten suspects were dismissed for lack of evidence; the grand jury declined to indict in another three dozen cases; and a handful of men fled after posting bail, only one of them getting caught. Some seventy-five others were indicted, but their cases were eventually dropped. Ultimately, sixty-seven people were found guilty. Twenty-five of them were given six months or less in the city jail, while plea bargains ensured light sentences for many of the rest.[13]

Incongruously, under the existing laws, the punishment of thieves was equal to or greater than that of murderers. One of the men who attacked Charles Jackson and threw him into the river was put away for ten years in state prison mainly because he had stolen Jackson's valuables at the same time. This was the only harsh sentence against anyone who had beaten or killed blacks during the riot. The man who led the attack on the Derrickson family, beating the son and killing the mother, was sentenced to two years in the state prison at Sing Sing. The same sentence was given to a woman for stealing 120 pairs of gloves, while two men received ten years each for equally minor thefts. The most severe punishments—fifteen years at hard labor in state prison—came down on two Irishmen who stole a three-dollar hat.[14]

Edmund Ruffin noted with satisfaction that "the very mild punishments of the convicts indicate the timidity of the government. 30 days and 60 days were the penalties stated—the heavier punishment being for an Irishman who was the leader of the rioters in the attack on the *Tribune* office."[15]

Matthew Powers was one of about a dozen rioters who were permitted to join the army and had the charges against them dismissed. Indicted for arson after burning the home of Josiah and Ellen Porter, he incurred a political debt to jump from the proverbial frying pan into the fire: He wrote to Comptroller Brennan, asking to be transferred from the Tombs to the battlefront.

Unlike many of the most violent rioters, Powers was literate and a skilled craftsman. "Sir, I have made up my mind to Enlist if you will be so Kind as to Arrange it So I am not under the Impression that I will be Convicted. But laying in here another month I do not like. I Can get a number of Respectable Citizens to give me a character [reference]."

Powers understood the give-and-take that greased the wheels of the political machine. "I would Rather Stand on the Battle field Any time than in Court," he wrote to Brennan. "By complying with The above you will Confer a favor that will Never be forgot on your humble Servant." Ironically, his participation in riots aimed at disrupting the draft had brought him to the extremity of choosing enlistment as the lesser of two evils.[16]

Peter Masterson—the fireman whose company attacked the Ninth District draft office and ignited the riots before trying to contain them—far from being prosecuted, emerged as a hero, at least to those whose lives and property he saved. Residents on the West Side presented him with "a case of beautiful pistols, and the company with a large purse of money."[17]

Apparently under some sort of pressure or intimidation, the *Commercial Advertiser* retracted an earlier statement that Masterson had helped spark the riots and declared that he had been out of town on July 13. The paper also heaped praise on the Black Joke for its efforts to contain the rioting on the West Side.[18]

The *Times,* however, denounced Masterson for acting on his "party prejudices instead of his public duties" during the riots. "He favors burning down a Provost-Marshal's office because he does not like the draft, and he opposes burning other buildings because he can make a little political capital by so doing."[19] Nonetheless, the Masterson brothers—Peter, William, and John—all remained active and influential in the Tammany political hierarchy for years to come.[20]

While the draft resumed in New York and the rioters were prosecuted, Lincoln had pressured Rosecrans to move forward again in middle Tennessee. He had driven the rebels eighty miles south toward Chattanooga in early July but then stopped to repair bridges and amass supplies for his next march. In mid-August, Rosecrans advanced in league with Burnside, and by early September, they had outflanked the Confederates under Braxton Bragg, causing them to evacuate both Knoxville and Chattanooga without a battle. With these twin disasters, morale in the South hit a new low, similar to the despondency after Union successes in the first half of 1862. Confederate desertions were rampant.

While Edmund Ruffin anxiously studied news reports about the intensified Union bombardment of Charleston's forts in early September, he also noted that "the draft throughout the state of N.Y. has been carried out, quietly, & without resistance . . . All Gov. Seymour's pledges & threats have come to nothing. It is very likely that the bad condition & prospects of the [Confederate states], indeed their desperate condition . . . has served as the main inducement to mollify the opposition. For if persuaded to believe in the early &

certain subjugation or submission of the South, the democratic party will be as ready to support the war as the abolitionists."[21]

Remembering how Lee and Stonewall Jackson had turned the tide by attacking McClellan in 1862, Jefferson Davis reinforced Bragg and urged him to strike back. Davis sent two divisions to Bragg from Johnston's force in Mississippi and brought Longstreet and his corps over from Lee's Army of Northern Virginia. On September 19 and 20, the Confederates whipped Rosecrans at the Battle of Chickamauga, sending the Union general fleeing to the fortifications in nearby Chattanooga, while his subordinate, George Thomas, "the Rock of Chickamauga," took charge on the field to protect the retreat.

Reeling from heavy Confederate losses, Bragg failed to follow up his victory, and the Federals remained in control of the strategically vital ground at Chattanooga. However, Rosecrans seemed "confused and stunned like a duck hit on the head," according to Lincoln, and the Federals soon found themselves not only bereft of leadership but besieged by Bragg's forces and running out of food. From the west, General William Sherman at Vicksburg was ordered to bring four divisions to Chattanooga, and from the east, the War Department transferred Hooker and twenty thousand troops by rail from Meade's Army of the Potomac, which for the moment seemed unlikely to bestir itself and attack Lee's forces in Virginia. Despite the reinforcements, as September turned to October, the Confederate siege of Chattanooga continued.[22]

With Bragg bottling up the Union forces in Chattanooga and choking off their supplies, in the middle of October Lincoln moved decisively to shake up the command structure. He created a vast, new military department, stretching from the Mississippi River to the Appalachian Mountains, and put the conqueror of Vicksburg, Ulysses Grant, in charge. The president also issued a call for three hundred thousand more troops on October 17. This was the first draft under the conscription law since its enforcement was resumed in August. Again, the call was made to spur volunteering, with the draft to follow if quotas were not met.[23]

Grant arrived at Chattanooga on October 23, replaced Rosecrans with Thomas, and a week later had beaten back the rebels far enough to establish a new supply line and start feeding the troops. Two weeks later, Sherman arrived with seventeen thousand troops, and the Federals were ready to start turning the tables on Bragg. On November 24 and 25, Grant's forces defeated the Confederates at the Battle of Chattanooga, driving them out of the path to Georgia. Four days later, Union forces hurled back Longstreet's attempt to seize Knoxville. To complete the grim outlook for the Confederacy, Meade had thwarted an attempt by Lee to move against Washington in October and inflicted heavy casualties on the Army of Northern Virginia during a clash in November.[24]

Confederate attempts to have a British firm build naval attack-vessels also collapsed in the fall of 1863. The vaunted "Laird rams"—ironclads armed with seven-foot spikes to tear apart the wooden hulls of the Union's blockade fleet—were supposed to hold New York City at their mercy until the North sued for peace. However, intense diplomatic pressure from the American ambassador, Charles Francis Adams, persuaded the British government not to let the ships leave Liverpool. His son, and secretary, Henry Adams, called the diplomatic victory "a second Vicksburg."[25]

A slender reed of cheer for the Confederates in the late fall of 1863 was the stunning escape of John Hunt Morgan and half a dozen of his men from their prison cells in Columbus, Ohio, on November 27, after just four months behind bars. Following a plan hatched by one of Morgan's aides, Captain Thomas Hines, the men used knives from the prison cafeteria to chip a hole through the six-inch concrete floor, crawl through a ventilation shaft into the prison yard, and scale the wall with an improvised grappling hook at the end of a rope made of bedsheets.

Having checked the rail schedule in a newspaper, Morgan and Hines caught a 1 a.m. train to Cincinnati, while the others took different routes to foil the ensuing manhunt. After crossing the Ohio in a small boat and mounting a friend's horses on the Kentucky side, Morgan and Hines were more than one hundred miles away before prison officials noticed they were gone. Two escapees were captured in Kentucky, but Morgan and Hines eluded the Union cavalry long enough to get beyond their reach, in North Carolina. The two men would soon be back in action with the Confederate forces.[26]

As the November elections approached in 1863, Republican strategists capitalized on Union battlefield victories and public outrage over the draft riots, which focused on Fernando Wood and the Peace Democrats. While Wood claimed he was not even in the city during that bloody week, New Yorkers remembered the police riot of 1857 and associated his name with attempts to manipulate urban violence for political ends. Given his prosouthern remarks during the secession crisis and at the beginning of the war, many believed Wood and the Peace Democrats had plotted with the Confederacy to spark the insurrection during Lee's invasion of the North. Irish and German workers, once Wood's core constituency, abandoned the Peace Democrats in order to cast off the stigma of treason left by the riots.[27]

Across the North, the Peace Democrats struggled to regain lost ground by protesting, as they had successfully a year earlier, the administration's civil rights abuses, the war for abolition, and the draft's exemption clause. In Ohio and Pennsylvania, the stakes were high, since the Democratic nominees for governor—Clement Vallandigham and George Woodward—were both Copperheads. Lincoln "had more anxiety in regard to [them] than he had in 1860 when he was chosen," according to Secretary of the Navy Gideon Welles. If either were successful, this would encourage the Confederacy, damage northern unity, and prolong the war. Exiled from the northern states by Lincoln in May, Vallandigham at the time of the draft riots had been making his way from the South up to Windsor, Ontario, where he carried on a long-distance campaign for the Ohio governor's office. Woodward, a state supreme court judge in Pennsylvania, was less vocal in his prosouthern sympathies than Vallandigham, but equally fervent.[28]

No longer able to denounce the Republicans' incompetent prosecution of the war, Ohio Democrats instead played the race card, fanning the same flames of resentment and fear that had led to the draft riots and to earlier riots in the Midwest. Whereas William Seward, as a senator before the war, had famously called the slavery issue an "irrepressible conflict" between the states, Ohio Democrats called the struggle an " 'irrepressible conflict' between white and black laborers." They urged supporters to vote for "the *white* man, and against the Abolition hordes, who would place negro children in your schools, negro jurors in your jury boxes, and negro votes in your ballot boxes!" Pennsylvania Democrats also campaigned against emancipation and equal rights for blacks.[29]

However, voters across the North were also disgusted by the lynching of blacks and the burning of the Colored Orphan Asylum during the draft riots—and favorably impressed at the same time by the valor of black troops at Fort Wagner, Milliken's Bend, Port Hudson, and other battles. Their bravery was a strong argument for emancipation, and both Lincoln and the Republican press drove home the point: To favor the Copperheads and deny the aspirations of loyal soldiers fighting for the Union was tantamount to treason.

In an open letter to Democrats, Lincoln warned that the Union—helped by emancipation and the enlistment of black troops—would ultimately win the war, and "there will be some black men who can remember that, with silent tongue, and clenched teeth, and steady eye, and well-poised bayonet, they have helped mankind on to this great consummation; while, I fear, there will be some white ones, unable to forget that, with malignant heart, and deceitful speech, they have strove to hinder it." Lincoln's leadership helped Republican candidates switch from an uneasy embrace of the Emancipation Proclamation to a proud, offensive strategy that turned the tables on the Democrats, questioning their patriotism and deflating their calls for white supremacy.[30]

Republicans trounced the Democrats across the North in the November elections of 1863, including the races for governor in Pennsylvania and Ohio, the New York State legislature, and local contests in New York City.[31]

The Democratic party nationally, despite its surge the previous fall, was once again in dire straits, as it had been, essentially, since it split apart on the eve of the Civil War. "The old Democratic party is dead as the old Whig party," the *Herald* declared.[32]

Fernando Wood, however, was still in Congress, which convened in early December, and he remained unrepentant. On the floor of the House, he asserted that he was not in New York City when the riots broke out, and loudly continued his opposition to the war and the draft, which he said discriminated against working-class Democrats. He blamed the riots on the Lincoln administration or its radical Republican agents who wanted an excuse to declare martial law and urged federal troops to fire indiscriminately into the crowds.

Wood and his third wife, an heiress he married in 1860 when she was sixteen and he was forty-eight, held numerous lavish dinner parties at their elegant Washington home, winning new friends for the embattled congressman and polishing his image among colleagues as a gracious host instead of a "vulgar, treacherous New York politico in hot pursuit of graft and patronage." Nonetheless, the draft riots were a watershed for Wood, signaling the decline of his power in New York politics. He remained on the national stage but was confined, for the moment, to the role of vocal dissenter in the minority party, denouncing the fact that "any man who speaks of peace is called a traitor."[33]

In an effort to salvage the fortunes of the Democratic party, Manton Marble—who played a growing role in plotting strategy with Barlow and Belmont—wooed ousted Union general George B. McClellan to run against Lincoln in 1864. The great issue of the day, as the *Herald* put it, was "war for the Union or peace at the price of dissolution," and Marble calculated that in order to survive and rebound, the Democrats had to divorce themselves completely from the peace men.[34]

Tweed came to the same realization and opposed the Wood brothers by forging an alliance with Tammany War Democrats. By rewarding them with appointments to the committees he and his right-hand man Peter B. Sweeny chaired, and purging longtime rivals while retaining key decision-making powers, Tweed solidified his grip on the city Democracy, setting the stage for his rise as "Boss" Tweed in the coming years. In the words of one historian, Tweed had taken the first step by creating "the possibility of bossism; he could discipline Tammany, but Tammany could not discipline him."[35]

While Tweed identified himself with the War Democrats inside Tammany, he courted the Irish vote outside the organization that had defected from Fernando Wood in the wake of the draft riots. Tammany could point to a number of prominent Irish Americans in its ranks: Comptroller Matthew Brennan; County Clerk John Clancy, who also edited the organization's newspaper, the *Leader*; and John Kelly, who had served both as sheriff and as a congressman.[36]

William "Boss" Tweed

In appealing to the immigrant community, Tweed also had the benefit of two Irish American lieutenants, Richard Connolly and Peter B. Sweeny. Some said the *B* stood not for Barr but for "Brains" since Sweeny was the intellectual of Tweed's inner circle—a friend of Baron Haussmann and Victor Hugo—and the mastermind of Tweed's political machinations. The son of an Irish saloonkeeper, a lawyer, and former district attorney, Sweeny was born in New York and had succeeded in the arena of Democratic politics while downplaying his ethnic origins.[37]

Connolly, by contrast, was born in Ireland and had come up through the rough-and-tumble world of New York's Democratic ward politics in the 1830s, where he served as one of the "Hooray Boys," stirring up the enthusiasm of the newly enfranchised immigrant population and delivering the Irish Catholic vote for Tammany. Connolly's marriage into an established, Protestant, New York family did not diminish his standing with immigrant voters and furthered his career by introducing him to the city's bankers and financiers. Both Connolly and Sweeny would soon share in Tweed's rise to power.[38]

Nonetheless, securing the Irish vote for Tammany remained a challenge in the wake of the draft riots. Having distanced themselves from Fernando Wood's Peace Democracy and the stigma of disloyalty, the Irish were wary of being labeled an "ignorant," monolithic voting bloc and resisted control by any Democratic organization. Tammany would not be able to take the Irish vote for granted. In the fall of 1863, C. Godfrey Gunther, a German merchant, became the mayor of New York, supported by both German and Irish Democrats, the latter forming a movement behind the Irish attorney John McKeon and John Kelly, who had defected from Tweed's Tammany Hall. Like the McKeonites, Gunther and his German supporters—largely middle-class merchants—rejected both the growing power of the federal government under the Republicans and Tammany rule in New York, with its corruption and high taxes.[39]

While Tweed and the Tammany Democrats worked to stage a political comeback by highlighting their patriotism, and Irish Americans flexed their political muscles, many blacks, both poor and middle-class, were deciding to leave New York for good. Within two years, the city's black population had dropped below 10,000—a 20 percent decline from more than 12,500 in 1860.[40] The draft riots inaugurated an exodus of African Americans from New York City that lasted for seven years.[41]

"When the late autumn arrived," Maritcha Lyons wrote, "we left our hospitable refuge to reluctantly take the trip back to New York, the house having been temporarily arranged for our accommodation. We were to remain only till plans could be made for a permanent removal." Mary and the children moved to Providence, Rhode Island, where the schools had a reputation for excellence.

Taking on the school board over segregation, Mary Lyons won, and by an act of the state legislature, Maritcha became the first black student to enter Providence High School, where she graduated in 1869. While ensuring a better future for her daughter in the wake of the riots, Mary Lyons was thrown back in time to the trades she had given up twenty-five years earlier when she got married: working as a clerk in a candy store and as a hairdresser.

Because of the $250 property requirement for black voters in New York, they sought to enter the middle class for political as well as economic reasons. The riots were a setback on both levels for the city's black community, and Albro Lyons, like his wife, saw his own hopes for advancement shattered. "Father lingered in the city till the last vestige vanished concerning the possibility of reviving his business there," Maritcha wrote. "Dismissing what to him was a veritable 'lost cause,' he emulated the example of his wife and took up again in exile—for it was never anything else to him—the trade he had learned in his you[th], the manufacture of ice cream." Unlike William Powell, who eventually reopened his boardinghouse for black sailors, Albro and Mary Lyons never made Manhattan their home again.[42]

For blacks who remained in New York or were scattered to its suburbs, their suffering from the riots did not end with the quelling of the mobs in July. The process of expelling blacks from the city continued, taking different forms. Blacks had trouble getting their old jobs back, particularly on the docks, where white longshoremen drove them away. Blacks could not get to jobs that were available, because conductors and passengers on street railroads, both from prejudice and fear of renewed attacks by white mobs, refused to let them onto the cars. Blacks also continued to be assaulted sporadically by bands of white youths.

The Common Council, meanwhile, had come to the rescue of poor white conscripts with millions of dollars before the riots were even over, and done nothing to help the black community.[43] The winter of 1863–64 fell hardest on the many blacks who had been left destitute by the destruction of their homes and property during the riots—and to whom the city failed to pay damages. "Nearly one thousand persons, most of them the heads of families, lost all they had, excepting what they took with them in their flight, or had deposited elsewhere," according to Henry Highland Garnet's colleague, the Reverend Charles Ray of the Bethesda Congregationalist Church.

Ray called the city's failure disgraceful and unjust: "Could they have witnessed the sufferings I have witnessed . . . for the want of this act of justice toward them, they must have had hearts of stone not to award to them the amount to make good their losses." Ray, who had worked extensively with the black victims of the riots, stressed that their claims were modest and reasonable, "the value of articles lost laid at about half the cost of new, and much below their worth to them."[44]

Ray had arrived in New York from New England more than thirty years earlier, proud of his mixed-race ancestry dating back four generations: aboriginal Indian, English white settler, and the first black in New England. Ray started at the Crosby Street Congregational Church, remaining there for a dozen years, and joined the New York Committee of Vigilance (the Committee of Thirteen) composed of black and white men, which was formed in 1835 to launch legal investigations into the arrests of blacks said to be escaped slaves. Ray also edited the *Colored American* for several years.[45]

The riots affected Ray's work as a pastor and missionary, as it did the work of all of the city's black clergymen. The riots "broke up the homes of our people for a time, and scattered them indiscriminately and closed our schools, so it also closed our churches and for several weeks they were not opened," Ray noted. "This week of terror increased rather than diminished our missionary work, not only to hunt up our flock and bring them together again, but to look after the people generally. Many of them were not only broken up in their homes and despoiled of their goods, but deprived, for a time, of their usual employment and reduced to want."

After traveling "to all parts of the city and among all classes of the people" so that claims could be verified and the merchants' committee funds disbursed, the black ministers' work in many cases "had just begun," since people sought them out for help during the winter, for advice in resolving their claims.

Ray assailed the rioters as "fiends in human shape" and asserted that the week of pandemonium "scarcely has a parallel in this or any other country, unless it were in the Sepoy massacre in India.* It was for a brief time the reign of an infatuated mob—the Reign of Terror."[46]

As they had done after the assault on Fort Wagner on July 18, 1863, Republican journals like *Harper's Weekly* and the New York *Tribune,* along with black voices in the *Christian Recorder,* continued to contrast the disgraceful draft riots with the heroism of black regiments in the Union army.[47] At the same time, desertions and massive Union losses on the battlefield increased the demand for black troops, and opposition to their enlistment melted away.[48] By January 1864, Secretary of War Edwin Stanton had finally listened to the appeals of Garnet and a committee of sixty other prominent New Yorkers and overridden Governor Seymour to approve the formation of a black regiment from New York. The Union League Club helped raise the funds as it had sworn to do during the draft riots.

Between two and three thousand African American soldiers were billeted on Rikers Island, where Garnet was their chaplain. He had urged blacks to enlist at the outbreak of the war and was instrumental in keeping them coming by listening to their grievances and protesting abuses against them to General Dix.[49†]

On the raw, cold afternoon of March 5, 1864, New York State's first black regiment marched off to war, and the cheers in the streets of New York were a miraculous change from the riots seven months earlier, when they had

---

*The sepoys were Indian troops serving in the army of the British East India Company. They mutinied in 1857, sparking a widespread revolt. After numerous atrocities by both sides, the insurrection was brutally crushed by British forces.

†Tragically, Rikers Island today is a prison, and the quest for equality launched by these first African American troops remains incomplete. For various reasons, including limited educational and economic opportunities, young black men make up a disproportionate number of Americans behind bars.

been "mobbed, hunted down, and beaten," James McCune Smith observed. From Rikers Island, a ferry brought the thousand troops to the Thirty-sixth Street Pier on Manhattan's East Side, and they marched down to Union Square, arriving in front of the Union League Club at 1 p.m. Henry Highland Garnet mused that the glorious reception of the troops put "ordinary miracles in the shade."[50]

For Garnet and his wife, Julia, and for the other dignitaries on the platform in Union Square, the presentation of flags by the club to the regiment was an impressive sight. President Charles King of Columbia University addressed the black troops, saying they were "emancipated, regenerated—and disenthralled—the peer of the proudest soldier in the land."[51]

With a band playing military tunes, the regiment marched down Broadway to South Ferry accompanied by one hundred policemen and members of the Union League Club. Garnet shook hands with each soldier at the dock as the regiment embarked for New Orleans on the USS *Ericsson*.[52]

The *New York Herald* spoke for the many New Yorkers who remained unreconstructed racists, denouncing the ceremonies as a display of "miscegenation," because the presentation of flags by white women to black men constituted a "marriage ceremony."[53] The Workingmen's United Political Association also reacted negatively, declaring that "the very object of arming the Negroes is based on the instinctive idea of using them to put down the white laboring classes."[54] Charles Halpine composed a song for his fictional Private Miles O'Reilly, titled "Sambo's Right to Be Kilt," suggesting that the Irish only welcomed black troops in the army because they would be used as cannon fodder instead.[55]

Many New Yorkers, even conservatives, however, were stirred by the scene in Union Square, which signaled a repudiation of the draft riots and of Governor Seymour by the people of New York, as well as progress, however provisional and gradual, for African Americans. Maria Daly recalled:

> It was a very interesting and a very touching sight to see the first colored regiment from this city march down the street for the front. They were a fine body of men and had a look of satisfaction in their faces, as though they felt they had gained a right to be more respected. Many old, respectable darkies stood at the street corners, men and women with tears in their eyes as if they saw the redemption of their race afar off but still the beginning of a better state of affairs for them. Though I am little Negrophilish and would always prefer the commonest white that lives to a Negro, still I could not but feel moved.[56]

CHAPTER 18

"Our Bleeding, Bankrupt, Almost Dying Country"

~)

r. Brennan, I Expect to hold a pretty Honorable position in this Service before my Term of Service is Expired, that is if I do not get killed very Soon. I am very ambitious in that Respect." Matthew Powers, the Irish brass finisher, rioter, and arsonist, had seen mostly guard duty in the Union ranks and wrote to Comptroller Brennan again on Christmas Day 1863 from Beaufort, South Carolina, to thank him for getting him out of jail and into the army, where he was enjoying the strict discipline and hoping to make something of himself. His letter implied that he had political ambitions too: If he made it back to New York, he would become a loyal lieutenant for the Democrats.[1]*

While the political culture of the Democratic machine continued uninterrupted in New York, the president and Congress focused their attention on the South. The capture of Port Hudson, Louisiana, on the Mississippi, Bragg's defeat at Chattanooga and retreat from Tennessee, and the Union occupation of Little Rock, Arkansas—along with growing evidence of demoralization and dissension in the Confederacy—all emboldened Lincoln to look ahead and plan for the return of rebel states into the Union. In December 1863, the president continued the process

---

*Unlike Powers, most Irish American soldiers did more than guard duty, bearing the brunt of the war's bloodiest battles. On January 2, 1864, the shattered Irish Brigade returned to New York City, and only a few hundred relatives and friends greeted them, not the cheering throng that had sent them off. The following day, Archbishop Hughes died, which was another blow to the Irish community's morale (Spann, *Gotham at War*, p. 117).

of Reconstruction by declaring that all rebels—except Confederate government officials and high-ranking military officers—would be pardoned and granted amnesty if they took an oath of allegiance to the United States.

In order to speed the process of restoring loyal state governments, Lincoln promised to grant them official recognition when these oaths of allegiance amounted to a mere 10 percent of the voters in that state in 1860. Lincoln's lenient terms were designed to rally the submerged minority of southern Whigs and Unionists who were never die-hard secessionists and provide them with a simple procedure for getting civil government up and running again. In the meantime, military governors appointed by Lincoln were overseeing this process in the areas of Tennessee, Louisiana, and Arkansas that had come under Union control.

Lincoln had stretched his constitutional authority as president to the limit and soon ran up against the powers of Congress, whose members wanted to exert their legitimate influence over Reconstruction. Once new state governments were formed, Congress asserted its sole right to decide if a state's senators and representatives should be recognized and seated at the Capitol in Washington. Congressional leaders were concerned that unrepentant rebels could submit to the loyalty oath falsely and regain power at the expense of true Unionists. Many Republicans in Congress also favored giving ex-slaves the right to vote as a check on the political power of secessionists. Lincoln, as he had with emancipation, moved more slowly than many Republicans on the issue of black suffrage, but he looked forward to giving blacks the right to vote, he said, "at least . . . on the basis of intelligence and military service."[2]

While Lincoln and congressional Republicans debated the fine points of the rebel states' legal status and competed to define and control Reconstruction, they left the rebellious city of New York out of their plans. Strong, Olmsted, and Gilmore, among others, had asked Lincoln to impose a military regime and in effect to reconstruct the city just as he was doing in parts of Texas, Louisiana, and Arkansas. Like the oaths of allegiance Lincoln proposed, the investigation of the draft riots requested by these staunch Republicans was intended to isolate disloyal Copperheads and ensconce Unionists as the loyal core around which New York City could rally to create a new political culture. Instead, a Democratic, white supremacist resurgence was taking hold in New York City, which in the next dozen years helped to undermine Republican plans for national Reconstruction.

"The plan for creating a Revolution in the West by the release of prisoners was first presented by me to the authorities at Richmond in the month of

February, 1864," recalled Captain Thomas Hines, the guerrilla raider and mastermind of Morgan's recent prison break in Ohio.[3] This "Revolution," known as the "Northwest Conspiracy," promised to free some fifty thousand Confederate prisoners of war held in various camps in the Midwest, including Camp Douglas outside Chicago; Rock Island, on the Illinois side of the Mississippi River; Johnson's Island near Sandusky, Ohio; and a facility in Indianapolis that held many of Morgan's cavalrymen.[4]

The freed prisoners were to join forces with the secretive Sons of Liberty—previously known as the Order of American Knights, and before that as the Knights of the Golden Circle—who, according to Confederate spies, had almost five hundred thousand armed members ready to overthrow local and state governments in the Midwest. While taking the entire region out of the Union so it could resume friendly relations with the South, the Sons of Liberty also hoped to drive free blacks and abolitionists from their states or murder them if they resisted. The plan called for Morgan to support the uprising with an even larger raid than he had launched in 1863, and for teams of arsonists to burn Chicago and New York to the ground.[5]

A Missourian known to history only as Captain Longuemare was actually the first to lay the plan before Jefferson Davis, two years earlier, and described the president of the Confederacy "jumping to his feet with the quick nervous motion peculiar to him." Pacing the floor, Davis declared: "It is a great plan. In the West you have men, in the East only mannequins. You show me that this conspiracy is engineered and led by good men. I want military men: men that were connected with West Point. Give me some, even if only one or two, and I will have confidence in it."[6]

Clement Vallandigham was the "Grand Commander," the titular head of the Sons of Liberty, but they lacked military leadership. Longuemare's plan was shelved until the Confederacy grew more desperate to recover its prisoners, and Hines, basking in the glow of his raids and his escape from prison with Morgan, stepped forward. Hines urged the Confederate government to send agents to Canada, which, like England, was officially neutral, but in practice supported the Confederacy. By rallying escaped rebel prisoners there, Hines could more easily launch forays into the United States and mobilize the midwestern Copperheads.[7]

In March, Hines received written orders from Confederate secretary of war James Seddon, which allocated funds from the sale of two hundred bales of cotton—about one hundred thousand dollars—for the mission. As the Northwest Conspiracy unfolded, the Confederacy apparently spent ten times that amount on its various operations.[8] Unlike civilian agents sent to Canada by ship through the Union naval blockade of the South, Hines was instructed to make his way overland through the northern states, stopping to meet with Peace Democrats and other sympathetic leaders and involve them in his plans.[9]

Jacob Thompson, former U.S. secretary of the interior under Buchanan, and Clement Clay, a former U.S. senator from Alabama, were among the civilian agents in Canada, where they disbursed funds to Peace Democrats— to subsidize their newspapers, political campaigns, and rallies. Thompson funneled twenty-five thousand dollars to Fernando and Ben Wood's *Daily News* in New York, to cultivate and sustain the paper as an outlet for Copperhead propaganda. The agents in Canada also purchased arms and supplies for arsonists. By not only selecting military targets but robbing banks and burning the property of wealthy northerners, Thompson hoped to make them "feel their insecurity and tire them out with the war."[10]

While the draft riots were apparently a popular revolt, not a Confederate conspiracy, the bloody week in New York had displayed the potential for disruption behind Union lines that Edmund Ruffin and others had pointed out on the eve of the Civil War. Fernando Wood had spoken of New York and other parts of the Union breaking away, and Ruffin had envisioned an alliance of the Midwest and the South against the North. In April 1864, Hines arrived in Toronto determined to make these Confederate dreams a reality.[11]

Lincoln needed generals who could win the war before northerners grew tired of it, and in the spring of 1864, the cream of Union military leadership finally rose to the top. Lincoln promoted Grant to general in chief of all Union forces, demoting Halleck to chief of staff. Sherman took charge of the armies west of the Appalachians, while Grant established his headquarters with the Army of the Potomac. Meade kept his command, but Grant would dictate the strategy, and he brought Philip Sheridan east to lead the cavalry.

The Confederacy had weathered a desperate winter in 1863–64 with barely enough to eat. Having instituted the draft before the Union, the Confederate Congress now did away with substitution—retroactively and going forward—and in mid-February refused to honor the upcoming expiration of three-year enlistments. The range of draft age was lowered to seventeen and raised to fifty. With families starving at home, soldiers deserted to support them despite the new restrictions, and Union forces poised for a spring offensive in Virginia and Georgia soon outnumbered the rebels more than two to one.

However, occupation of one hundred thousand square miles of territory already captured by Union armies and the job of maintaining order in the border slave states drained considerable manpower from Grant's combat forces. When the Federals penetrated deep into the South, they also expected to leave many troops in the rear to protect their supply lines, again deducting from their principal fighting force. Moreover, the remaining rebel forces were in high spirits, despite the hardships; many of the veterans had decided to stay on before the order came from the government. Inspired by the example of Robert E. Lee, they were ready to fight with the tenacity of men who have everything to gain and nothing to lose.[12]

In the North, the Union's three-year men who had signed up at the beginning of the war received incentives, not orders, to stay on. These included a four-hundred-dollar federal bounty in addition to state and local money. "They use a man here just the same as they do a turkey at a shooting match, fire at it all day and if they don't kill it raffle it off in the evening," wrote one veteran, "so with us, if they can't kill you in three years they want you for three more—but I will stay." He was one of about 136,000 who reenlisted.[13]

Conscripts, substitutes, and bounty-hungry volunteers brought in by the first draft in 1863 were supposed to replace the wounded and the dead in the hard-hit Army of the Potomac, as well as the one hundred thousand veterans who chose not to stay on.[14] However, most of these replacements made poor, unreliable soldiers. Many were career criminals who added bounty jumping to their repertoire, collecting multiple bounties by enlisting, deserting, and reenlisting in new locations under different names.

Some had rioted against the draft and then avoided prison by temporarily joining the army. A captain in the Eighty-third Pennsylvania Regiment complained that a mob of New Yorkers was ruining the unit.

> These were the cream and flower, the very head and front of the New York rioters, gamblers, thieves, pickpockets and blacklegs, many of whom, it was said, had fled to escape punishment for the crimes of arson, robbery, and homicide . . . They fought, gambled and stole after they got to the regiment. The company streets of the once-peaceful Eighty-third became uproarious at times with their midnight broils and battles. They were always spoiling for a fight except when in the presence of the enemy. One would have supposed that when men would wake up at midnight and fall to pummeling each other in bed, as they often did, they would have become transported at the prospect of battle; but it was at such times that they skulked and seized the opportunity to desert. They would get each other drunk and pick each other's pockets while asleep. They would decoy each other out of camp after dark, on pretense of going out to get something good to drink, and then knock their deluded victims down and rob them of their money. In short, the men would have disgraced the

regiment beyond all recovery had they remained three months in it; but thanks to a kind Providence, or to some other invisible power of redemption, they kept deserting, a dozen at a time, until they were nearly all gone.[15]

Grant calculated that a staggering 80 percent of these new recruits deserted, leaving the Union forces with much less of an advantage over the rebels in 1864 than the War Department had expected.

Lee had factored in the potentially disruptive effect of expiring enlistments and the Union's first draft before invading the North less than a year before; in early 1864, he hoped to exploit Grant's manpower shortage in the service of a defensive strategy. If the Confederate armies could simply stand their ground until the northern presidential election in the fall, conquest of the South would appear increasingly futile, Lee hoped, and Democrats might well elect the next president—someone amenable to a negotiated settlement of the war and Confederate independence. Grant was determined to capture Richmond before that scenario could unfold.[16]

Grant hoped to stretch the rebel armies thin and isolate them from each other by launching attacks in several places at once. Meade was ordered to pursue Lee and his Army of Northern Virginia, keeping him busy while Sherman advanced into Georgia, attacking Johnston's army and destroying Confederate infrastructure and supplies. Three other generals, Benjamin Butler on the Peninsula in Virginia, Franz Sigel in West Virginia and the Shenandoah Valley, and Nathaniel Banks in Louisiana, were to play supporting roles, moving against strategic railroads and cities to engage secondary rebel forces and prevent them from reinforcing Lee and Johnston. When told of the co-ordinated plan, Lincoln summed it up enthusiastically, like a hunter who has bagged a deer: "Those not skinning can hold a leg."[17]

Sergeant Peter Welsh was delighted in April by news that his wife's brother Francis had arrived in New York from Ireland and that she would at last have some companionship in her husband's absence. Liquor had changed the course of Welsh's life, and he offered his young brother-in-law some advice "from dearly bought experiance and with sincere brotherly afection." Welsh had an immigrant's love of New York as a place of boundless opportunity but hinted at the city's dangers: its dives, saloons, and street gangs.

> Shun the wine cup and company keeping. shun the use of intoxicating drink as you would a foul and venomous serpent . . . The man who will shun those two vices and atend regularly to the

dutys of his relegion will be prosperous and happy no matter what his profession or abiliys may be. One thing more. never for heavens sake let a thought of enlisting in this army cross your mind. it is right and the duty of citizens and those who have lived long enough in this country to become citizens to fight for the maintainence of law and order and nationality. but the country has no claim on you and never bring upon yourself the dangers and hardships of a soldiers life where the country nor cause has no claim on your service.[18]

The following month, Welsh was with Grant's forces when they crossed the Rapidan River to do battle with Lee's troops. Both Grant and Lee were keenly aware of the Union defeat a year earlier on this same ground, and while Grant hoped to get beyond the Wilderness, the dense forest around Chancellorsville, and engage Lee's troops in the open, Lee intended to strike the Federals in the tangled woods, which would neutralize their numerical superiority. On May 5, 1864, the two armies collided in the Wilderness, sparking two days of slaughter that cost Grant 17,500 casualties to the rebels' 10,000.

Having told Lincoln that "there will be no turning back," Grant then astonished both the enemy and his own troops on May 7 by pressing forward instead of retreating, as all of his predecessors had done after clashing with Lee. Union morale soared that night as Grant struck southward around Lee's right and headed for the village of Spotsylvania, a crossroads that would place the Federals between Lee and Richmond. Lee was forced to drop back to an entrenched position just north of Spotsylvania, where the two armies battered each other for the next five days. Despite fierce, close combat, Grant failed to break decisively through the rebel lines, and by May 12, Union casualties at the Wilderness and Spotsylvania had mounted to 32,000, more than in any single week since the war began three years earlier.[19]

Sergeant Peter Welsh was wounded that day at Spotsylvania. He was part of a successful thrust by the Federals and reported to his wife: "we licked saucepans out of them. My dear wife i think i can get sent to new york to hospital. if not I will get a sick furlow to go home." However, the supposedly minor wound that had been wrongly diagnosed at the field hospital proved far more serious when examined at the Carver Hospital in Washington, and blood poisoning set in after surgery on his arm, leading to a slow and ghastly death.

Whether his distraught wife, Margaret, reached his side before he died, about ten days later, is not known. She collected his few belongings and telegrammed her uncle, "HE IS DEAD AND WILL BE IN NEW YORK IN

MORNING." Welsh was buried in Calvary Cemetery in Woodside, New York. Chiseled in the granite monument at Welsh's grave are words that express the pride of an immigrant at home in his adopted land: "Peter Welsh. Color Sargeant, Co. K 29th Mass. Vol's., Irish Brigade."*

As color sergeant, Welsh had carried the Irish flag into battle as a rallying point for his unit. Welsh had written to his wife: "When we are fighting for America we are fighting in the interest of Irland striking a double blow cutting with a two edged sword . . . striking a blow at Irlands enemy and opressor England hates this country because of its growing power and greatness. She hates it for its republican liberty and she hates it because Irishmen have a home and a government here and a voice in the counsels of the nation that is growing stronger every day."[20]

Welsh's vision of Irish Americans overcoming nativist prejudice and rising to positions of power and influence in America would soon be realized, particularly in the arena of Democratic politics.

With the number of Union soldiers killed, wounded, and missing after Spotsylvania double that of the Confederates, "the land was thus in mourning under God's chastisement," Maria Daly wrote of the North. Grant spent the next week making further fruitless attacks at Spotsylvania. "Eight days of fighting in Virginia have been without any definite result, except that of driving Lee nearer Richmond," Daly wrote on May 18. Her brother reported from the front that he was unhurt, but that Union prospects were "far from brilliant," Daly noted. "Grant seems confident of final success, but says he may have to fight all summer."[21]

Pressure mounted on Grant to achieve a breakthrough, to prevent Lee's strategy of swaying public opinion in the North against the Lincoln administration before the election from gaining momentum.[22] In New York, Democratic power broker Samuel Barlow had already declared, "We shall nominate McClellan . . . and unless there are greater successes in the field than now seem probable we shall win." If Grant failed, Barlow reasoned, no one would forgive Lincoln for the "monstrous crime" of having dismissed McClellan.[23]

Time was on Lee's side, so Grant allowed no pause in the fighting, making another trek southward, skirting Lee's right flank and forcing him to follow, first to the North Anna River, and then to Cold Harbor, a crossroads some ten miles northeast of Richmond where both armies dug in on June 1.

*Calvary Cemetery in Woodside, Queens, and its Civil War grave sites are part of the Walking Tour; see the appendix.

The Federals had suffered forty-four thousand casualties in the relentless campaign thus far, but Grant concluded that the rebels were even more shell-shocked and exhausted than his own troops. Moreover, he would lose another twelve regiments in July when their enlistments expired, and needed a decisive victory. On June 3, he ordered an ill-fated assault on the complex network of enemy trenches and suffered seven thousand casualties to the rebels' fifteen hundred. Grant regretted the attack, and Meade, denounced by many for not pouncing on Lee's cornered army after Gettysburg, felt his caution had been vindicated by the disaster.[24]

"We have lost some of our best generals," Maria Daly noted, "and thousands of heroes whose names are known but to their sorrowing families." She described a rally at Union Square in New York, where her husband, Judge Charles Patrick Daly, "took a prominent part to thank and encourage our soldiers." Northern leaders struggled to maintain both the public's morale and their own faith in the restoration of the Union: "Our nationality will be born anew in blood and tears," Maria Daly wrote, "but we trust it will rise purified and ennobled."[25]

On the night of June 12, Grant put in motion a new plan, a longer and wider march southward around Lee's right flank, this time across the James River to Petersburg, an important railroad junction south of Richmond. However, when the Union forces arrived, the soldiers—still traumatized by the carnage at Cold Harbor—were intimidated by the elaborate fortifications around Petersburg, and their corps commanders hesitated, squandering the opportunity to storm the lightly defended breastworks and trenches. By the time they had forced the rebels back to a tighter perimeter around Petersburg on June 18, Lee had arrived with the bulk of his army. Further Union attacks were repulsed with heavy losses, so Grant decided to entrench his own lines and give his troops a rest from combat.[26]

The bloodiest seven weeks of the war came to a close with sixty-five thousand Union casualties. The psychological toll on the northern home front was also debilitating. As Lee had hoped, Union battlefield losses translated into civilian disillusionment and calls for peace. Even the wife of radical Republican general Benjamin Butler questioned the purpose of "all this struggling and fighting . . . This ruin and death of thousands of families . . . What advancement of mankind to compensate for the present horrible calamities?" The army had also lost thousands of troops as their enlistments expired, and recruiters faced a colossal challenge to replace them. Democrats labeled Grant a "butcher" who was throwing away the lives of white soldiers to free black slaves, while bringing ruin on the country.[27]

However, as both Lee and Lincoln could see, Grant had made tremendous progress at a proportionately high cost to the Confederacy. Lee's much smaller army had lost at least thirty-five thousand men killed, wounded, or missing, while Grant had pressed forward eighty miles to the outskirts of Petersburg and Richmond. By starting to cut off Lee's communications and supply lines to the rest of the South, Grant was turning the nimble Confederate general's game of cat-and-mouse into a siege of the rebel capital.[28]

With the presidential election just four months away, however, Lincoln could not afford to strangle the Confederacy slowly; he needed his armies to deliver a crushing blow. Sherman had also gained eighty miles in Georgia during May and June, repeatedly skirting Johnston's left flank, forcing him to fight or fall back. The armies clashed very little, since Johnston stayed on the defensive, depressing southern morale with each retreat. However, on June 27, when Sherman attacked the rebels at Kennesaw Mountain in their heavily fortified position straddling the railroad line twenty miles north of Atlanta, the Federals were thrown back with heavy losses, and the Confederacy rejoiced. Union forces had suffered ninety thousand casualties in two months, and both Grant's and Sherman's campaigns seemed to have petered out just short of their objectives.[29]

Moreover, Grant's strength in Virginia was diluted by the hurried transfer of his finest troops to Washington in the first half of July to fend off a Confederate raid—a reprise on a smaller scale of Lee's invasion exactly a year earlier. Confederate commander Jubal Early's fifteen thousand troops had bested the Federals at Lynchburg, Virginia, before proceeding through the Shenandoah Valley and across the Potomac. The invaders then routed hastily gathered Union troops near Frederick, Maryland, clearing the path to Washington, where they arrived on July 11. Astonishingly, like Lee before him, Early seemed to have turned the tide of the war, shifting the focus from the outskirts of Richmond to the northern capital, where only the city's fortifications stood between the White House and the rebels.

Grant's Sixth Corps arrived in time to forestall an attack, but federal troops in the path of Early's retreat failed to capture him or destroy his forces. After the marauding Confederates had made their way south, burning houses and gathering loot—including huge sums of money from terrified townspeople in Pennsylvania and Maryland—a furious Ulysses Grant promoted cavalry commander Philip Sheridan and ordered him to hunt down Early. Grant encountered further setbacks in his siege of Petersburg, and while Sherman continued to press forward toward Atlanta in July and August, his progress was slow. European confidence in the Confederacy rose once again.[30]

"I see no bright spot anywhere," lamented George Templeton Strong. "Rebeldom is beginning to bother Sherman's long line of communications. We may expect to hear any day that he is fighting his way back to Chattanooga and that Grant has bid Richmond good-bye. I fear the blood and treasure spent on this summer's campaign have done little for the country." With the election approaching, Strong worried that Lincoln might be defeated, and that "the people may be deluded into electing some so-called War Democrat who will betray the country."[31]

"Our bleeding, bankrupt, almost dying country . . . longs for peace—shudders at the prospect of fresh conscriptions, of further wholesale devastations, and of new rivers of human blood," Horace Greeley wrote to Lincoln in July 1864.[32] Discouraged like many northerners, the formerly hawkish Greeley wanted the president to negotiate with Jefferson Davis, who had sent two representatives, Clement Clay and James Holcomb, to Niagara Falls, Canada.

Lincoln permitted Greeley to meet with the rebel envoys and agreed to consider any written proposal for peace that included emancipation and national reunification. Such conditions were, of course, a nonstarter, but Lincoln knew the rebel agents were not there to negotiate in good faith either. They were part of Hines's network of spies and saboteurs plotting to stir up a massive riot and rebellion on Union soil.[33]

The spark this time was to have been the return of Clement Vallandigham to Ohio in June, which the plotters assumed would prompt Lincoln to rearrest him for violating his banishment and would provoke rioting.[34] Vallandigham met with Hines and Thompson before leaving Canada and expressed reservations about a full-blown insurrection. However, soon after his return to Ohio, on June 15, Vallandigham had encouraged the Confederates with a speech in which he warned "the men in power" that "there is a vast multitude, a host whom they cannot number, bound together by the strongest and holiest of ties, to defend by whatever means the exigencies of the times demand, their natural and constitutional rights as free men, at all hazard and to the last extremity."[35] Despite the provocation, Lincoln decided not to jail the Copperhead leader, believing martyrdom would only play into his hands. Hines and Thompson were deprived of their riots.[36]

The conspirators shifted their plans to coincide with the opening of the Democratic national convention in Chicago on July 4, where Vallandigham's popularity and his ability to divide the party were expected to give him leverage at least over the platform if not the selection of the nominee and his running mate. If the government or Republican protesters tried to disrupt the coppery convention, Hines and his allies were ready to turn the rioting into a full-blown insurrection.[37] Hines's key ally in Chicago was Charles Walsh, the Irish American boss of the Cook County Democratic machine, who claimed

Clement Vallandigham

to have two thousand armed men ready for action. Hines's accounts show that he budgeted two thousand dollars for "raising the Irish in Chicago."[38]

However, because developments on the southern battlefields were in limbo, the Democratic leadership delayed the convention until August 29. Not wanting to wait that long, the Confederate agents reset the date to July 20 since Lincoln was expected to announce a third round of the draft in July and they hoped to take advantage of resentment against the ongoing conscription. Hines and his veterans were to make a disturbance, signaling the various groups of armed Copperheads to join the fray.[39]

Lincoln called for more troops on July 18, a half million volunteers, with any shortfall in each state's quota to be made up by the draft.[40]* However, the promised uprising fizzled two days later, when the Copperheads informed Hines that their preparations were not complete and asked for a postponement. Military leadership was not enough to mobilize untrained civilians, and

*Following on a troop call in March, this was the third round of the draft after its resumption in August 1863.

Hines began to have doubts about the Copperheads. "There was a reluctance on their part to sacrifice life for a cause," he wrote. "Some sort of violence was needed to make them act . . . We were determined to bring that about."[41]

The frustrated southerners retreated to their base in Canada, where Hines, Thompson, and Clay met with Vallandigham and agreed that another attempt was to be made on August 29, the first day of the Democratic convention. Hines envisioned the streets packed with crowds of visitors that he could provoke into rioting, and while the authorities were distracted by the chaos, Copperheads were to attack Camp Douglas, outside of Chicago, and free its five thousand inmates. Arming them from caches of weapons in and around Chicago, including one in Walsh's house, the growing force was to take over the city before proceeding by train and on horseback to liberate Camp Morton at Indianapolis and two other prison compounds.[42]

For his part, Lincoln's call for more troops on July 18—and announcement of another round of the draft—seemed to seal his political doom. The Republicans had renominated Lincoln unanimously a month earlier, with Andrew Johnson, a War Democrat from Tennessee, as his running mate. Calling themselves the "Union party," the Republicans hoped to expand their base of support with the new ticket. However, many in the party were still considering alternatives, though like Greeley and William Cullen Bryant, who were no longer on speaking terms, they had trouble agreeing on a candidate. New York City's mercantile community, led by William Dodge, wavered in its support for Lincoln's reelection and still wanted a compromise to preserve slavery and bring the South back into the Union.[43] Lincoln's decision to let Greeley meet with Confederate envoys at Niagara Falls, Canada, only made matters worse.

On the day Lincoln announced the new draft call, Greeley and John Hay, the president's private secretary, met with Confederate agents Clay and Holcomb. On behalf of the president, Hay offered them safe conduct to Washington for peace negotiations, but only based on the terms Lincoln had already spelled out to Greeley: reunion of the North and South, and abolition of slavery. Predictably, the conference ended abruptly. Lincoln had hoped to achieve a propaganda coup by getting the rebel agents to counter his conditions with two of their own, namely that Confederate independence and the continuation of slavery must be the starting point for negotiations.

Lincoln hoped this would deal a heavy blow to the Democrats by showing northerners that the South had no intention of coming back into the Union, even while Lee and his agents encouraged that hope among the peace faction. Lincoln's message to the North was that only a vigorous prosecution of the war would preserve the Union. Instead of countering the president's terms, however, the rebel agents cleverly fed news of the meeting to the Associated Press, and newspapers in both the North and South soon carried reports that made Lincoln appear intransigent. Democrats attacked him for undermining peace efforts and prolonging the war, while Republicans questioned his judgment in handling the affair.[44]

Coincidentally, Lincoln had also authorized his own peace mission, sending the *Tribune*'s James Gilmore, recently become a freelance journalist, and James Jaquess, colonel of an Illinois regiment and a Methodist clergyman, south to make a peace proposal to Jefferson Davis. The two men were not official envoys, but Davis and Confederate secretary of state Judah Benjamin met with them anyway, having to please peace advocates in the Confederacy.

However, when Gilmore and Jaquess put forward Lincoln's terms, including restoration of the Union, emancipation, and the amnesty he had offered in December 1863, Davis launched into a tirade about fighting to the death for Confederate independence. Gilmore's report and Greeley's Niagara meeting appeared in the northern press at the same time, and Davis's inflexibility helped blunt the outcry against Lincoln. It also undermined the Copperheads' calls for reunification through a peace treaty instead of by military victory. Lee's divide-and-conquer strategy of bolstering the northern peace faction by falsely holding out the possibility of reunion had been thwarted by Davis's impassioned rhetoric.[45]

Nonetheless, Lincoln's prospects for reelection remained dim in August. "Mr. Lincoln is already beaten. He cannot be elected. And we must have another ticket to save us from utter overthrow," Horace Greeley lamented to former New York mayor George Opdyke on August 18.[46] Democrats brushed aside Davis's unwillingness to negotiate and focused instead on Lincoln's demand for abolition as a precondition for peace talks. They denounced the war as sacrificing white soldiers to the president's "negro mania." Republicans, too, faulted Lincoln for committing to emancipation and handing the opposition a powerful rallying cry. In the absence of decisive progress on the battlefield, the administration and the party were losing popular support.

Many northerners still held out the hope, however misguided, that if Lincoln made reunion his absolute priority and dropped emancipation, the country could be brought back together peacefully. However, Lincoln replied to their entreaties that the value of emancipation was both practical and moral. To crush the rebellion, the Union had 130,000 black soldiers and sailors on its side, and if he broke his promise of freedom and they left, the war effort would break down in a few weeks. Moreover, Lincoln said, if he allowed the blacks who fought at Port Hudson and other battles to be reenslaved, "I should be damned in time & in eternity for doing so. The world shall know that I will keep my faith to friends and enemies, come what will."[47]

·   ·   ·

In Toronto, Hines put together a squad of seventy men, supplying each of them with a new pistol and ammunition, one hundred dollars, and a round-trip train ticket to Chicago. In pairs, they started leaving for Chicago on August 10, about three weeks before the Democratic convention. Hines and his top associates took a suite at the Richmond House, where a banner announcing them as the "Missouri Delegation" disguised their meetings with local Copperheads.

The streets and hotels were soon overrun with delegates and other visitors arriving by train, horse, wagon, and on foot. Some slept on the sidewalks after a long night of drinking, because they could not get rooms. Some were armed with revolvers. The crowds and the chaotic atmosphere reassured Hines that the materials of a great riot were at hand, waiting for him to strike the match.[48]

However, when Walsh and the other Copperheads arrived at the Richmond House the night before the convention, Hines could see that they had lost their nerve. Walsh explained that their chain of command had broken down: The Sons of Liberty in Ohio and Indiana would not be coming to Chicago for the uprising the following day, since their instructions were never delivered. Hines and his lieutenants were furious, especially since the manpower they needed to conquer all of Illinois was in the city, but they lacked the military organization to harness its strength.[49]

Walsh promised to try again, and the meeting was adjourned until the next day, August 29. Hines was beginning to give up hope that night as he watched the torchlight convention parade from his hotel window. His spirits quickly rose, however, when three thousand federal troops came marching into Chicago, providing what he hoped would be the spark for the uprising. Hines spread the word among the Copperheads that the soldiers had come to harass law-abiding Democrats at their convention. In fact, the troops had been sent to secure the city and reinforce the guards at Camp Douglas, where the commandant had discovered the conspiracy by deciphering the prisoners' mail.[50]

"We emphasized that any arrest would mean violent interference with the rights of the people," wrote Captain John Castleman, a close friend and trusted subordinate of Hines. "We knew that an arrest by the troops was our best hope and it mattered little who was arrested. In other words an inflammable mob might thus be led beyond retreat."[51]

Angry, drunken men taunted the soldiers throughout the night as they patrolled the city, but no violence erupted. By daybreak, Hines could see that the conspiracy had unraveled. Nonetheless, in the afternoon and evening he called two more meetings, hoping to rally five hundred Copperheads, and failing that, just two hundred. Pounding his fist on a map of Chicago spread out in front of him, Hines described how teams of ten men could fan out across the city, sever its telegraph lines, burn the bridges, and break open the Federal arsenal. They would use the last remaining telegraph wire to trumpet their success across the entire Midwest and all the way back to New York City, before setting off to conquer Springfield, Illinois, the state capital.[52]

Hines's vision stirred the Copperhead leaders, but they could muster no more than twenty-five men. Hines and his squad of seventy left the city the next day, putting little faith in the Copperheads' declarations that they were going to impose military discipline within the Sons of Liberty and be ready for action by Election Day in November.[53]

The failed plot revealed that the ranks of the Sons of Liberty were not nearly as numerous as the organization and its promoters claimed. Copperhead resistance in the Midwest proved to be confined to a relatively few zealots, while most Peace Democrats lost their taste for revolution when the moment of truth arrived, preferring to act through the political process, since prospects for success looked good in the late summer of 1864.[54]

The Democrats in Chicago nominated McClellan, but because his contradictory statements about peace negotiations implied that he might continue the war if elected, and Vallandigham's peace faction threatened the party's fragile unity, the convention compromised and named Congressman George Pendleton of Ohio, a peace man, for vice president. The platform endorsed slavery, condemned Lincoln's civil rights abuses, and included Vallandigham's call for an armistice to be followed by a convention at a later date to discuss reunion. Confederate leaders and newspaper editors saw their dreams coming true. If they could hold out on the battlefield until November, McClellan's election and the Democratic platform would end the war and guarantee their independence.[55]

Yet, as the Democrats prepared to celebrate, events in the South overtook their plans. "Atlanta is ours, and fairly won," Sherman telegraphed Lincoln on September 1. When the news spread across the North, there was wild rejoicing. "Glorious news this morning—*Atlanta taken at last!!!*" wrote George Templeton Strong. "If it be true, it is (coming at this political crisis) the greatest event of the war."[56] Lincoln's political fortunes were reversed just in time, and the Democrats were thrown on the defensive.[57]

In Virginia, Edmund Ruffin recorded the casualty figures of the latest battles in his diary, while downplaying the significance of the northern victories and clinging to reports of continued popular discontent and official lenience about enforcing the draft: "The Yankee government was evidently afraid to enforce the ordered draft, (which was to have been on the 5th,) fully & strictly. First, by order from the War Department, the whole requisition was reduced from 500,000 to 300,000 men. Next, [in] the city of N.Y. and Brooklyn (where armed resistance was expected, & was threatened in the speeches at a public meeting . . .) the draft was ordered to be omitted entirely, on the ground just assumed, that these cities had furnished their quota of men, in recruits supplied to the navy."

Finally, the draft all over the North was to be delayed for several weeks, with the excuse that officials needed more time to prepare the necessary paperwork, Ruffin noted: "I doubt whether it was not bad policy to postpone the draft. The splendor of the glory acquired by the capture of the Mobile forts, & of Atlanta, will have greatly faded in a few weeks, & the greatly exaggerated importance of these successes will be reduced to something like truth."[58]

Instead, those victories began to look more and more like the beginning of the Confederacy's ultimate defeat. By late September, General Philip Sheridan had defeated Jubal Early, his nemesis in the Shenandoah Valley, which throughout the war had served the Confederacy both as a breadbasket for the army and as an invasion route to the North. Under orders from Grant, in October Sheridan began a ruthless campaign to destroy the area's crops, farms, and villages—and to smoke out the guerrillas who harassed his army.[59]

Enraged, Ruffin wrote in his diary: "Would that our government had the boldness & vigor, (which would be useful even at this late time,) to order the shooting & hanging of all officers captured of these marauding & destroying forces, & all privates belonging to bodies that had engaged actively in such services! Thus treating them, not as soldiers, nor even as Yankee invaders, but as robbers, house-burners, destroyers & murderers."[60]

CHAPTER 19

"Villainous Threats of Laying Northern Cities in Ashes"

~⌒

espite Union victories and the president's unswerving commitment to the Emancipation Proclamation, the prospect of freedom and equality for African Americans remained dim in the fall of 1864. A little more than a year after the draft riots in New York, the city's black population was shrinking, and those who remained were struggling. The finances of black churches suffered from the steep decline in their membership.[1]

The interior of St. Philip's Church, on Mulberry Street across from police headquarters, was nearly wrecked during the riots, not by a mob but by the police. "Without anyone's permission, the police had broken open the door, taken possession of the building, and occupied it as a barracks for policemen and out-of-town soldiers." To the congregation, the police had behaved like looters instead of protecting their property. Extensive repairs eventually amounted to almost $2,500, of which the city, after years of delay, paid only a fraction.[2]

While the orphans themselves were unharmed, the Colored Orphan Asylum was in financial distress. The orphanage had moved into a new temporary home rented by the Association for the Benefit of Colored Orphans in lower Westchester along the Hudson River.* The orphans enjoyed roaming free on the property, gathering nuts and playing in the woods, with panoramic views of the Hudson and plenty of fresh air—a healthful envi-

---

*Today's Riverdale, in the Bronx.

ronment compared to the neighborhoods they might have encountered in the city itself. James McCune Smith, back with the orphans after a long illness, described most of the children as being in "hilarious out-door health in the pleasant abode which has been fortunately secured for them."[3]*

However, 1864 was a difficult year for the Colored Orphan Asylum, since the children had been deprived, "by the malice of a mob, of the home which for twenty years had sheltered them," Anna Shotwell wrote. In their new home in Carmansville, the need for clothing, bedding, and furniture created an emergency since the treasury was exhausted. "It is true that with diminished means we have been obliged to curtail expenses; several domestics have been discharged, and four teachers are performing the duties of six," Shotwell reported. "But adversity has stimulated exertion, and many who in prosperity were indifferent, have been induced to extend to us a generous support." They were rescued by private donations, including an individual gift of twenty thousand dollars.[4]

The city also paid seventy-three thousand dollars in damages from the riots, which was set aside for a building fund. A smaller building was erected that year on the grounds of the old asylum, and served as an "office and depot of material for the Institution" while plans for the reconstruction of the main building moved forward; a leading New York architect was approached to submit drawings.[5]

However, property owners in the adjacent blocks had urged the Colored Orphan Asylum to move elsewhere, and the institution gradually became another example of the increased racial segregation in New York after the draft riots. Unable to sell off the city-owned parcels "held under perpetual grant from the Corporation" and use the proceeds to buy other property, the managers forfeited the land and moved the asylum to Fifty-first Street. Four years later, it was moved again, to 143rd Street between Amsterdam and Broadway. This outlying area of the city would later become the famed black enclave of Harlem.[6]†

The finances of Henry Highland Garnet's Shiloh Church, like those of the city's other black churches, were in a dismal state. Garnet had wanted to accompany New York's black troops to war, but the army would not accept him as a chaplain, because the job came with an officer's commission. So Garnet

---

*McCune Smith's health problems forced him to retire after serving the Colored Orphan Asylum for twenty-two years, but he remained a consulting physician.
†St. Philip's Church eventually moved to Harlem too. After moving to West Twenty-fifth Street in 1889, the church finally settled on West 134th Street in 1910. See the Walking Tour in the appendix.

had accepted an invitation to lead a church in Washington, D.C., where he hoped to lend his support to the national government.

However, despite several visits to the White House and requests to see the president, Garnet never met Lincoln. Frustrated, Garnet rationalized that the president was simply weary of numerous petitions from blacks that he could not satisfy. Accustomed to being received in Europe by "nobility and royalty," Garnet noted: "I have never seen people harder to reach than the leader of government in Washington."[7]

With the abolition of slavery and the status of African Americans in the United States beset by so much uncertainty, Garnet urged the National Convention of Colored Men to meet for the first time in more than ten years, which it did in Syracuse, New York, on October 4, 1864. The black convention movement had begun in 1830 with a meeting in Philadelphia dominated by local delegates, "the first attempt by blacks to achieve an organized national presence." The following year, and at subsequent meetings, attendance grew to include delegates from all over the Northeast as well as Ohio, Delaware, Maryland, and Virginia. The debates centered on the educational, economic, and political advancement of free blacks, as well as emancipation in the South and emigration. In the 1840s, Garnet was also a driving force in the state convention movement organized by blacks in New York, and spearheaded its campaign for voting rights. Until the 1850s, black women were generally excluded from public speaking, except in separate charitable and literary societies.[8]

Because Garnet had collaborated with affluent whites in 1858 to establish the African Civilization Society and promote black emigration to Africa and the West Indies, the convention of 1864 isolated him and made Frederick Douglass its permanent president. Black nationalists like Garnet and his friend Alexander Crummell envisioned African Americans starting over in independent black countries, where the products of their free labor would undermine slavery around the globe. Douglass, like most of the delegates, asserted instead that blacks must struggle for progress and an equal stake in America; that their destiny lay in the land of their birth—the United States—not in the home of their ancestors.[9]

"How come you take money from white men, Mr. Garnet?" one delegate asked, referring to the fact that the African Civilization Society was expanding its influence by funding schools for blacks in the South. Garnet, it seemed to his critics, had made a deal with the devil.

"If Jeff Davis would send an amount to educate colored children," Garnet replied, "I would gladly receive it and say at least that's one good thing you have done." The convention proceeded to pass a resolution condemning the African Civilization Society.

Henry Highland Garnet

Stung by rejection, Garnet was walking alone that evening when a group of Irishmen leaving a tavern attacked him and stole both the wooden stump for his missing leg and his silver-plated cane, forcing him to crawl on the muddy ground. The next morning, the delegates rallied around Garnet and contributed the funds to replace his lost cane and stump.[10]

Garnet's searing remarks to the convention made clear that, more than a year later, blacks still relived the horror of the draft riots and needed to exorcise it from their minds.

> Mr. Garnet drew a picture of the shadows which fell upon New-York city in July 1863, where demoniac hate culminated in that memorable mob. He told us of how one man was hung upon a tree; and that then a demon in human form, taking a sharp knife, cut out pieces of the quivering flesh, and offered it to the greedy, blood-thirsty mob, saying, "Who wants some nigger meat?" and then the reply, "I!" "I!" "I!" as if they were scrambling for pieces of gold.[11]

Possibly the most disturbing recollection of the draft riots ever recorded, Garnet's comparison of black flesh with gold identified both the white mob's hatred and its hunger; demagogues had preyed on the poverty of whites to convince them that blacks posed both a social and economic threat.

At the convention, blacks also took stock of their relationship to the Irish. The minutes of the Syracuse convention reveal that black leaders did not regard the Irish people per se as their enemies. On the contrary, they saw them as fellow sufferers of prejudice. Calling the lynch mob's leader a "demon in human form" implied that he was possessed and manipulated by a third party.

> Mr. Garnet referred to the nationality of those composing the mob, and said he could not tell how it was that men crossing the ocean only should change as much as they. He had traveled from Belfast to Cork, and from Dublin to the Giant's Causeway, and the treatment he received was uniformly that of kindness. He had stood in public beside the great O'Connell; and we know what his hatred of oppression was. He attributed the change in the Irish people to the debasing influence of unprincipled American politicians. The name of O'Connell was received with great applause. Mr. Garnet was heartily cheered during his speech.[12]

Daniel O'Connell, the legendary Irish political leader, active from the 1820s until 1845, was committed to nonviolence and had warned Americans that slaveholding was a sin that would come back to haunt the United States. However, when he tried to support the antislavery movement in America, many Irish Americans withdrew financial support for his movement to abolish anti-Catholic laws in Ireland.[13]

With an awareness that the Civil War had yet to be won and its goals secured, the Syracuse convention issued an address to the American people, urging them not to take the demise of slavery for granted, as their forefathers had, but instead to work actively for its destruction.

> Why would you let slavery continue? . . . Do you answer, that you no longer have anything to fear? That slavery has already received its death-blow? That it can only have transient existence, even if permitted to live beyond the war? We answer, So thought your Revolutionary fathers when they framed the Federal Constitution; and to-day, the bloody fruits of their mistake are all around us. Shall we avoid or shall we repeat their stupendous error?[14]

Garnet had envisioned the convention as a means of building unity and had opened the first session by exhorting the delegates to resume regular meetings until "complete freedom is ours." However, the divisiveness that prevailed, exemplified by the challenges to Garnet by Douglass and others, produced bitter feelings and little agreement on concrete recommendations to the black community. Like emancipation itself, the black convention movement was beset by uncertainty.[15]*

Ultimately, the promise of the Emancipation Proclamation could only be guaranteed by an amendment to the Constitution; first, however, it would have to be secured by Union victory on the battlefield. Jubal Early's forces made one more attempt to retake the Shenandoah Valley but were soundly beaten by Philip Sheridan at Cedar Creek on October 19, 1864. Grant, meanwhile, had kept up the pressure on the Confederate forces around Petersburg, forcing them to stretch their lines thin. Lee sensed that disaster was imminent. Northern soldiers saw victory on the horizon and reenlisted; the draft proceeded without major problems, and Grant's forces were replenished with far better troops than the draftees, substitutes, rioters, and bounty jumpers that had weakened the army during the previous year. Republicans on the campaign trail pointed to military successes in order to reelect Lincoln.[16]

Enraged by military defeats, the destruction of huge swaths of the South, and the likelihood of a second term for Lincoln, the Confederates had revived their plans for sabotage in the North, despite their failed insurrection in Chicago. In September 1864, twenty rebel agents operating out of Windsor, Canada, had tried to capture a Union gunboat on Lake Erie and liberate Confederate prisoners of war on Johnson's Island, but a War Department detective posing as a sympathizer uncovered and foiled the plot. In October, leading figures in the Sons of Liberty were arrested in southern Indiana, after provost marshals discovered caches of weapons linked to the group.[17]

Accused of conspiring to help the enemy and foment an uprising, the defendants were tried in a military court where Union agents on the case testified that leading Democrats, particularly Vallandigham, were involved in the Sons' schemes to bring down the federal government. During the trials, the U.S. judge-advocate general issued a report describing the Sons of Liberty as a formidable, well-armed group, supported by the Confederacy, that posed a

---

*James McCune Smith noted that the draft riots destroyed nearly all the minutes of the convention movement, "our Alexandrine Library—from which some of the noblest pages in the history of our people could have been selected."

grave threat to the North. With the presidential election just weeks away, Republicans made the most of these charges. "REBELLION IN THE NORTH!! Extraordinary Disclosure! Val's Plan to Overthrow the Government! Peace Party Plot!" blared Republican newspapers. Four men were condemned to death by the military tribunal.[18]

While Vallandigham was indeed the titular head of the Sons of Liberty, his direct involvement in the organization's plots, like that of other top Democrats, was probably exaggerated by the Republicans. As the failed uprising at the Democratic convention had demonstrated, the rebel spymasters in Canada—Thomas Hines and Jacob Thompson—were perpetually frustrated by the lack of cooperation from professed allies in the North and their wishful, unrealistic claims about the number of members in the Sons. Nonetheless, the organization and others like it were real, and Thompson, who had conferred with some of their leaders in Canada, claimed he had enough documentation to prove the membership included "very many of the prominent men in the North."[19]

Like the Sons of Liberty in the Midwest, the organization in neighboring Missouri—which still called itself the Order of American Knights—consisted of some die-hard leaders with very little dependable grassroots membership. However, it wreaked far more havoc, particularly by forging an alliance with Confederate general Sterling Price, naming him the order's "military commander," and inviting his forces to come north from Arkansas to invade the state.

Price in turn wooed the leaders of guerrilla bands that had been terrorizing Missouri residents for years in the worst violence of the Civil War by forces outside the regular military. Ever since the struggle over "popular sovereignty" in 1854, the border between Kansas and Missouri had been the scene of savage attacks and reprisals between proslavery and antislavery guerrillas, which grew far worse after the war broke out. The pro-Confederate fighters, in league with the Order of American Knights, also encouraged Price to invade Missouri, promising that his arrival would spark a massive insurrection to shake off Union control of the state.

Launching a coordinated assault, Price crossed the border into Missouri with twelve thousand cavalry in September 1864. The guerrillas operated behind Union lines, ahead of Price in the center of the state, attacking trains, wagons, and boats, and putting the Federals in the jaws of a pincer movement. The Order of American Knights, meanwhile, was supposed to rouse the inhabitants and turn the invasion into a popular rebellion. Once the Copperhead leaders had been arrested by Union forces, however, it quickly became clear that they had no base of support.

By contrast, the proslavery guerrillas flocked to Price's side as he moved toward the state capital, Jefferson City, intent on installing the Confederate governor he had brought with him. However, Union forces along with militia from both Missouri and Kansas closed in from all sides. In late October, they clashed repeatedly with Price and his auxiliaries southeast of Kansas City, forcing the general to retreat back to Arkansas, killing many guerrilla leaders, and ending their reign of terror in Missouri.[20]

As they had with the conspiracy trials in southern Indiana, Republicans used the reports of Copperhead resistance in Missouri to accuse Democrats of disloyalty and bolster Lincoln's campaign to stay in the White House. Thrown on the defensive, Democrats resorted to the same tactics they had used in the fall of 1862: shrill appeals to the racism of northern whites and to their fear of black emancipation.[21] As it had before and during the draft riots a year earlier, Manton Marble's *World* played a conspicuous role in articulating the Democratic doctrine of white supremacy and stirring up racial antagonism.

Two members of the *World*'s staff produced an anonymous pamphlet titled *Miscegenation: The Theory of the Blending of the Races.* In it they posed, not very convincingly, as Republicans and advocated interracial marriage or "miscegenation." The pamphleteers also appealed to immigrant hatred of Republican nativists when they wrote that blending with blacks would "be of infinite service to the Irish." The clear message of this pamphlet and many others was that Lincoln's reelection and a war for abolition would culminate in racial amalgamation. A flood of such racially and sexually charged propaganda issued from the Democratic camp.[22]

Democrats once again linked abolition and the draft, denouncing both Lincoln the emancipator and "Abe the Widowmaker," who sent hundreds of thousands of white men to die in battle because, they said, he "loves his country less, and the negro more." Supporting petitions to suspend the draft, one newspaper called on the people to "suspend Old Abe—by the neck if necessary to stop the accursed slaughter of our citizens." In Wisconsin, a parody of "When Johnny Comes Marching Home" appeared in a Copperhead newspaper supporting McClellan:

> The widow-maker soon must cave,
> Hurrah, Hurrah,
> We'll plant him in some nigger's grave,
> Hurrah, Hurrah.

> Torn from your farm, your ship, your raft,
> Conscript. How do you like the draft,
> And we'll stop that too,
> When little Mac takes the helm.[23]

For several weeks before the November election in 1864, Thomas Hines moved about undetected through the midwestern states, rallying the Sons of Liberty and trying to organize them into commando squads with military discipline. The saboteurs were trained to cut telegraph wires, blow up prison gates, and start fires in government buildings. On Election Day, November 8, Hines planned to wreak havoc throughout the North, from New York City to rural Iowa.[24]

Charles Walsh, the Chicago political boss, was one of the few key leaders in the Sons of Liberty who had not been imprisoned during the arrests and trials in October, and he promised Hines there would be no repeat of the fiasco at the Democratic convention. He had hundreds of weapons stashed beneath the floorboards in his house, a stone's throw from the entrance to Camp Douglas, and his Copperhead followers were now "ready to shed blood."[25]

Hines's agent in Missouri had armed three hundred guerrillas for raids into Iowa, instructing them to put every town and village in their path to the torch. Chicago, Cincinnati, New York, and Boston were also marked for destruction by arsonists. In Toronto, Jacob Thompson doled out generous amounts of cash to fund the dozens of Copperheads and Confederate agents who pledged to set the fires and spark massive riots on election day.[26]

In New York, James McMasters, the Peace Democrat whose *Freeman's Journal* had urged violent resistance to the conscription before the draft riots in 1863, now promised the Confederate agents a Copperhead uprising and takeover of the city. All government buildings, including the U.S. Sub-Treasury, police headquarters, and even Fort Lafayette in the Narrows, were to be seized. Liberated Confederates and political prisoners would join in the sacking and burning of New York, while General John Dix, who had enforced the resumption of the draft after the riots a year earlier, was to be taken hostage and held in the government's own prison.[27]

The anti-Lincoln atmosphere in New York during the final days of the election campaign further encouraged the Confederates, a team led by Colonel Robert Martin that included Lieutenant John Headley and Robert Cobb Kennedy; Martin and Headley had both participated in John Hunt Morgan's cavalry raid in the summer of 1863. Tammany Hall held various rallies that seemed to verge on riots, and when the Democrats marched up Broadway to

Madison Square by torchlight on November 5 for fireworks and a speech by McClellan from the balcony of the Fifth Avenue Hotel, effigies of Lincoln drew hisses and groans from the crowds, which dwarfed the Republican rally of the previous night.[28]

However, federal authorities had infiltrated the Sons of Liberty, and by November 7, the plots across the country were exposed. Republicans who were disappointed that General Benjamin Butler had not been sent to New York to enforce martial law after the draft riots at least had the satisfaction of seeing him arrive little more than a year later with some five thousand troops to preserve order during the election. The *Times* declared that Butler would foil the rebel agents sent to carry out the "villainous threats, made by Richmond papers, of laying New York, Buffalo, and northern cities in ashes."[29]

In Chicago, Hines barely escaped, while federal agents rounded up more than one hundred Copperheads and Confederates, including Walsh and his cache of weapons.[30] In New York, the news from Chicago and the arrival of Butler and his troops prompted McMasters and the Sons of Liberty to call for a delay of the rebellion. "The more we insisted on the attempt to burn New York City, the weaker Mr. McMasters became," wrote Headley. After numerous meetings with the Copperheads, the attack was rescheduled for November 25, Thanksgiving Day. Soon, the Sons of Liberty pulled out altogether: "We have decided to withdraw from any further connection with the proposed revolution," McMasters informed Martin.[31]

With most of Butler's troops discreetly out of sight but ready to intervene, Election Day passed peacefully. Lincoln won every state exccept Kentucky, Delaware, and New Jersey, giving him a margin of half a million in the popular vote and 212 to 21 in the electoral college. With only the northern and border states voting in 1864, the results replicated the pattern of Republican support for Lincoln in 1860. In every state where Lincoln won, the Republicans also took or retained control of the governor's mansion and the statehouse. In New York, Seymour lost the governor's race to a radical Republican, Reuben Fenton. Ben and Fernando Wood both lost their seats in Congress, where the Republicans amassed a three-fourths majority.[32]

To no one's surprise, Lincoln lost in New York City, where McClellan won with Irish support. The city's Irish voters appeared to be out of step with the rest of the North, but their alliance with the city's Democratic party supported its resurgence and would help turn the tide in national politics over the next dozen years.[33]

New York Democrats accused the Republicans of foul play at the voting booth and of irregularities in counting the absentee votes of enlisted men. Lincoln had not imposed martial law, but the presence of the army to supervise the draft in August and the elections in November created a grievance—justified in some cases—and an excuse for Democratic failures. Democrats like Governor Seymour's military secretary, William Kidd—who believed the Republicans had carried out the draft lottery in July 1863 when the militia were off in Pennsylvania in order to precipitate riots, have an excuse for martial law, and manipulate elections—undoubtedly saw their fears realized in the election of 1864.

Another challenge for Tammany Democrats, in local elections, was the loss of their traditionally solid support from labor. In the fall of 1864, the labor movement in New York began fielding independent candidates. Accustomed to working from dawn until dusk, if not longer, workers demanded legislation and enforcement of an eight-hour workday. The movement called for reduced hours to secure "the independence of the working class" and create a more perfect democracy by allowing time for educational pursuits and political action. The formula of eight hours' work, eight hours' rest, and eight hours of "moral cultivation" proclaimed the "respectability" of the worker, who was disciplined and productive enough to put in a full day's labor in this reduced span of time. In the wake of the draft riots, which had buttressed the stereotype of the hard-drinking, brawling worker, the eight-hour movement sought to cast its members in a more favorable light.[34]

Beyond the threats from Republicans and the defection of labor in New York, the Democratic party faced the fundamental problem that began with its internal split in the 1850s and continued with the war: the need to offer a vision for the future; to unite and rebuild the party by adapting traditional Jacksonian principles of small government, individual freedom, and states' rights to the realities of the war and the forces of change it had unleashed.[35]

The demands of fighting a war against rebellion and supplying a vast army had transformed the federal government, increasing its size and turning it into a truly national power. Though they could not turn back the clock, the Democrats, over the next dozen years, would do all they could to preserve their conservative vision and stalemate the causes for which the war was fought. Locked in a struggle with a Republican Congress during Reconstruction, they would soon pay lip service to black equality in order to neutralize it as a political issue. At the same time, they would demand "home rule" in the South in order to keep blacks in a subservient role, socially, economically, and politically despite the abolition of outright slavery.[36]

Despite the fall of Atlanta and Lincoln's reelection, the Confederacy remained defiant and determined to keep fighting for its independence. Jefferson Davis toured the South making speeches that rallied the people and the military. General John Bell Hood, who had succeeded Johnston as commander of the Army of Tennessee, continued to prey on Sherman's supply line, which stretched all the way back from Atlanta to Tennessee. Frustrated by having to backtrack and defend territory he had just covered, Sherman came up with an unorthodox and risky plan to press forward from Atlanta.

Instead of maintaining a supply line by rail behind him, which he would constantly have to protect, he asked Grant and Lincoln for permission to plunge deeper into enemy territory and live off the land. After his reluctant superiors agreed, Sherman spent the second week of November preparing to set off on a scorched-earth campaign, a 285-mile march to Savannah and the sea. From Savannah, Sherman planned to march north through the Carolinas to Virginia and attack Lee from the behind while Grant pressed forward from the north.

Instead of pursuing Sherman, Hood took his army in the opposite direction, north into Tennessee, where General Thomas with sixty thousand Federals was expecting him. Hood had already burned much of Atlanta before he fled, and on November 15 as Sherman's troops departed, they set fire to any remaining structures that might have been of use to the rebels. Heading for Savannah, the Union troops pillaged every farm and town in their path, deliberately terrorizing the inhabitants and breaking the Confederate spirit of resistance.[37]

CHAPTER 20

War's End: Slavery Is Dead, the "Demon of Caste" Lives On

~

The day Sherman left Atlanta, General Butler left New York City, well satisfied by the peaceful election and the gratitude of prominent Republicans who had lavishly feted and honored him for a week. Ten days later, however, on November 25, Martin and his squad of Confederates sprang into action, having decided to proceed without the help of the Sons of Liberty.

The Confederate cause appeared increasingly hopeless, but the saboteurs were intent on revenge for Sherman's and Sheridan's scorched-earth campaigns. From a chemist on the west side of Washington Square, Headley had procured a suitcase containing twelve dozen four-ounce bottles of "Greek fire." A combination of phosphorus and bisulfide of carbon, the clear liquid would ignite when exposed to the air: Each jar was a firebomb ready to be smashed against a wall or floor.[1]

That evening, each of the half-dozen arsonists took a supply of Greek fire and checked into several of the city's best hotels, which included the Astor House, the Fifth Avenue Hotel, the St. Nicholas, and the Hoffman House, where General Butler had stayed—a new building off Madison Square that replaced burned-out stores torched during the draft riots. After piling all the flammable material in his room on the bed, each arsonist threw a firebomb on the floor to ignite the pyre, locked the door, and left the key at the front desk before moving on, without appearing rushed, to the next hotel.[2]

Between them, the Confederates checked into nineteen hotels, and the streets were soon filled with angry crowds watching the flames pour out the windows and vowing to hang the rebels. Firemen raced up and down Broadway with bells clanging and black smoke pouring from their steam engines. Barnum's Museum was also on fire, and the caged circus animals in the basement were bellowing in terror. The firemen rescued a woman from the second floor with a ladder but were unable to calm Barnum's panicked giantess, a woman seven feet tall who charged through the crowd howling and knocking aside anyone who tried to help her. Five firemen, a few bystanders, and a doctor finally subdued and sedated her, putting her in a room at a nearby hotel.[3]

In the mayhem, the Confederates moved through the streets unnoticed. Headley's mission included a trip to the Hudson River piers, where he fire-bombed several vessels, including a hay barge that exploded, shooting flames into the night sky. The other saboteurs struck theaters, stores, factories, and lumberyards in an effort to burn the whole city. The plot failed, for the most part, but the city suffered more than four hundred thousand dollars' worth of damage. It might have been worse if the conspirators had opened the windows in the hotel rooms, giving the flames enough oxygen to increase and spread. Several hotels, including the St. Nicholas—headquarters for General Dix, and for General Wool before him, during the draft riots—were largely destroyed nonetheless.[4]

Within hours, police superintendent John Kennedy had made two arrests and declared, "There will be many more before long." After finishing their tasks, the saboteurs regrouped briefly, and Martin had them divide up into pairs to avoid detection. Another blaze the following night, probably set by local Copperheads, triggered mass arrests throughout the city. McMasters and other members of the Sons of Liberty were seized by federal detectives, but Martin and his squad boarded a train the next night, hid in the berths of the sleeper compartments, and escaped back to Canada.[5]*

While the fires in New York made front-page news across the globe, in the South, Sherman's juggernaut rolled on. By mid-December, his forces were approaching Savannah when the Confederates evacuated, allowing the Federals to march in unopposed and enabling Sherman to present the city to President Lincoln as a Christmas gift. At the same time, General Thomas smashed Hood's army at Nashville, leading the Confederate general to resign less than a month later.[6]

On December 19, 1864, Lincoln issued a call for 500,000 more troops—the fourth and final call after the resumption of the draft in August 1863. By this time Lee's forces were nearly surrounded, and another round of

*Four months later, Robert Cobb Kennedy was captured on American soil, convicted of espionage, and hanged at Fort Lafayette.

the draft seemed unlikely. After tens of thousands of men claimed to be exempt from military service, paid their three hundred dollars, furnished substitutes, or failed to report when drafted, of the 1.2 million men who entered the Union army between 1863 and 1865, only 46,000 were conscripts and 118,000 were substitutes. While the draft thus accounted for only 13 percent of the men raised in this period, it served its purpose by prodding many more to join the Union ranks as volunteers.[7]*

Having given up on capturing Charleston, on January 15, 1865, Union forces aboard the largest fleet assembled during the war bombarded and seized Fort Fisher at the mouth of the Cape Fear River in North Carolina. Nearby Wilmington was thus blockaded and soon surrendered, depriving Confederate soldiers of badly needed supplies of food and putting most of the state's coastline under Union control. On February 1, Sherman left Savannah and marched into South Carolina, on his way north to Virginia. With Union forces advancing on all fronts, General Winfield Scott's Anaconda Plan to strangle the Confederacy, laid out at the beginning of the war, was nearly complete.[8]

Legislative triumphs went hand in hand with Union military successes. Preferring not to wait for the Thirty-eighth Congress to end in March and for lame-duck Democrats to be swept out of the House, Lincoln appealed to them for help in approving the Thirteenth Amendment, abolishing slavery in the United States. The Senate had passed the amendment in 1864, and it needed House approval before going on to the state legislatures; once ratified by three-fourths of the states, the amendment would protect the Emancipation Proclamation against judicial or presidential attempts to repeal it in years to come.[9]

All but four of the eighty House Democrats had helped defeat the amendment in the previous session, but Lincoln's reelection, along with other Republican victories in November and Union momentum on the battlefields, helped mute criticism of the president's agenda. Moreover, a few Democrats blamed the election results on the party's failure to "cut loose from the dead carcass of negro slavery." Both in his annual message and in face-to-face meetings at the White House, Lincoln asked wavering Democratic and border-state congressmen for their votes, telling them, "[The amendment] will bring the war, I have no doubt, rapidly to a close."[10]

Rumors abounded that the president engaged in corrupt horse-trading to win support, promising federal jobs, relief from railroad regulation, and other

*New York City provided 26,000 substitutes and fewer than 10,000 conscripts.

favors, none of which was ever documented. In any event, enough Democrats were swayed, and the House approved the Thirteenth Amendment on January 31, 1865.[11]

Sixteen Democrats voted "Aye," and the final tally prompted an outburst of cheering from spectators in the gallery unlike any the House had ever seen. "Members joined in the shouting and kept it up for some minutes," George Julian of Indiana recalled. "Some embraced one another, others wept like children." The roar of a hundred-gun salute filled the air in Washington, and the House declared the rest of the day a holiday, to celebrate "this immortal and sublime event." Julian, a longtime abolitionist, wrote in his diary, "I have felt, ever since the vote, as if I were in a new country."[12]

While African Americans celebrated the passage of the Thirteenth Amendment, their leaders began to set forth the definition of full equality under the law that they argued had to accompany the liberation of the slaves. Henry Highland Garnet, who had escaped slavery as a boy of nine and had labored as an advocate for blacks for more than twenty-five years, was recognized as "the most eloquent black man in the land" by the chaplain of the House of Representatives, the Reverend William Henry Channing, who invited him, with the approval of Lincoln and his cabinet, to deliver a sermon celebrating the Thirteenth Amendment.

At the special Sunday morning service in the House chambers on February 12, 1865, which also happened to be the president's birthday, Garnet became the first African American to deliver a sermon there. The sight of a black choir, from Garnet's church, was also unprecedented. At 11 a.m., every seat on the House floor was filled, and the galleries overflowed with guests, both black and white. For an hour, beginning at noon, Garnet held the breathless attention of the audience. The sermon, and the setting—with a full-length portrait of Washington on Garnet's right and one of Lafayette on his left—recalled the American Revolution and celebrated the completion of the task the founders had left unfinished.

"These worthies," Garnet said, "if they looked down on the scene which transpired in this hall a few days since, when the great National Work was consummated, they must have responded with the angel choir, an hearty amen!" Since applause was not appropriate during a sermon, the audience voiced its approval periodically with a passionate "amen."[13]

Garnet began by denouncing slavery, "this demon, which people have worshipped as a God." He defined it as "the highly concentrated essence of all conceivable wickedness. Theft, robbery, pollution, incest, cruelty, coldblooded murder, blasphemy, and the defiance of the laws of God." He described the terrible toll slavery had taken on the country.

It has divided our national councils. It has engendered deadly strife between brethren. It has wasted the treasure of the Commonwealth, and the lives of thousands of brave men, and driven troops of helpless men and women into yawning tombs. It has caused the bloodiest Civil War ever recorded in the book of time. It has shorn this nation of its locks of strength that was rising as a young lion in the western world.[14]

Garnet acknowledged that many people wanted to know at what point abolitionists would be satisfied in their demands for reform, and he answered:

When emancipation shall be followed by enfranchisement, and all men holding allegiance to the government shall enjoy right of American citizenship. When our brave and gallant soldiers shall have justice done unto them. When the men who endure the sufferings and perils of the battle-field in the defense of their country and in order to keep our rulers in their places, shall enjoy the well-earned privilege of voting for them. When in the army and navy, and in every legitimate and honorable occupation, promotion shall smile upon merit without the slightest regard to the complexion of a man's face. When there shall be no more class-legislation, and no more trouble concerning the black man and his rights, than there is in regard to other American citizens. When in every respect, he shall be equal before the law, and shall be left to make his own way in the social walks of life.[15]

Garnet's "Memorial Discourse" was widely acclaimed, and his church had the sermon published with an introduction by James McCune Smith, who described Garnet as the nation's most influential black leader.[16]

Garnet's hour of glory and hope would be short-lived, however. The postwar phase of Reconstruction would bring a new onslaught of murder and intimidation, aimed at depriving blacks of their basic civil rights. In his sermon, Garnet had singled out Fernando Wood as an enemy of African Americans by condemning the Copperhead congressman's recent declaration in the House that *the best possible condition of the negro is slavery.*[17] Despite the triumph of the Thirteenth Amendment, in the next dozen years Wood's vision, not Garnet's, would prevail. Blacks would not be returned to slavery as such, but the Democratic resurgence, combined with the northern public's desire to put the war in the past, would make it almost impossible to enforce subsequent amendments protecting blacks' rights. As the North and South drew closer together, blacks and whites would be driven farther apart.[18]

Republican senator Charles Sumner lamented in 1865 that the "demon of Caste" had yet to be vanquished. "The same national authority that destroyed slavery must see that this other pretension is not permitted to survive."[19] However, the use of federal troops to enforce civil rights and quell racial violence in the South would be hampered by cries of military despotism—by the same qualms that had kept Lincoln from imposing martial law in New York City and bringing the draft rioters to justice.

While the New York rioters effectively prevailed in their attack on racial equality, their demand for justice as exploited workers in an urban, industrial environment met with considerably less relief and sympathy from the managerial classes. Horace Greeley had championed the cause of the American worker since 1837 in editorials, essays, and speeches about "Association" and worker cooperatives. As a Whig and then a Republican, he had also favored protective tariffs for American industry, believing, idealistically, that as the nation prospered and expanded, fair-minded employers, negotiating with labor unions and cooperatives, would raise wages accordingly and all classes would benefit. Greeley had hoped the Homestead Act, offering public land at $1.25 per acre to settlers in the West, would be an antidote to urban slums.[20]

However, Greeley became disillusioned when he realized that prices had risen 100 percent between 1860 and 1865 but wages had hardly budged. An unskilled man brought home only three to five dollars a week, while a female garment worker typically earned half that amount, the *Tribune* reported. Buffeted by declining real wages and waves of immigration, labor unions collapsed during the war, as they had after the Panic of 1837. On the other side of the growing chasm between the rich and poor, William B. Astor had a revenue stream of a million dollars a year from his investments and properties, which included blocks of tenements where entire immigrant families were packed into airless single-room apartments and basements.[21]

As for homesteading in the West, big timber, cattle, railroad, and mining companies were gobbling up the land, which Congress served to them on a silver platter. Even such moral crusaders of radical Republicanism as Thaddeus Stevens and Ben Wade had soiled their hands by promoting legislation that gave away land to a mining company in which they had invested. New England's textile industry and other northeastern manufacturers also enjoyed favors delivered by their Republican representatives, in the form of tariff increases, while more and more craftsmen were drawn into the expanding factory system.[22]

"Congress has been voting away the richest lands on earth," the *Tribune* declared, "and the wise and necessary prize of a railroad to the Pacific has been made to cover the most shameless legislation that ever disgraced Congress."[23] Ultimately of less concern to Greeley were the government's broken promises about redistributing land in the South to former slaves. While Congress "appropriated land by the million acres to pet railroad schemes," one freedman protested, his people were "starving and in rags."[24]

In the North, urban slums continued to be a source of working-class resentment as well as middle- and upper-class anxiety, which was heightened by memories of the draft riots. Six months after the riots, a few medical reformers in New York, including Elisha Harris and Stephen Smith, with support from the new Democratic mayor Godfrey Gunther, had formed the nonpartisan Citizens' Association, with more than one hundred prominent New Yorkers such as Peter Cooper, Hamilton Fish, August Belmont, William Astor, John Jacob Astor Jr., and the highly respected Irish American attorney Charles O'Conor. Through hundreds of public meetings and millions of pamphlets, the elite Citizens' Association signaled a belief that American cities, especially New York, were in dire need of reform. Wealthy industrialist Peter Cooper attacked the county Board of Supervisors with allegations of bribery on a massive scale.[25]

In 1865, the Citizens' Association published a detailed study of sanitary conditions in Manhattan. In addition to linking dirty, diseased areas with vice and crime, the association's inspectors remarked on a consequence of the draft riots: the decline of New York's black population ward by ward throughout the city. The black neighborhood on Sullivan Street had been replaced by Germans, they reported, and across the city "the colored population formerly so numerous have almost entirely disappeared."[26]

The day after Garnet delivered his sermon in Washington, in February 1865, the state senate met in Albany for hearings on public hygiene in New York City. The association's report conveyed to lawmakers the horrors of the slums through the perspective of upper-middle-class volunteer inspectors.[27]

"Like the fabled vampires . . . diseases here hover about the pillow of childhood, sipping from the dewy springs of life till life itself is gone," one inspector wrote of New York City's overcrowded tenements. "On the walls of these living tombs DEATH hastens to inscribe the names of more than half of those whose hapless fate it is to be born within their dismal precincts." The tone of the report was calculated to inspire disgust and fear more than sympathy.

Adolescent and adult survivors in the city's filthy slums faced a complex of premature "physical, mental, and moral decline" known colloquially among health professionals as "TENANT-HOUSE ROT," the inspector wrote.

"The eye becomes bleared, the senses blunted, the limbs shrunken and tremulous, the secretions exceedingly offensive." Unable to care for their children, the adults watch impassively as the family deteriorates, the inspector declared, and to all of this "may be plainly traced much of the immorality and crime which prevail among us."

Referring to the explosive draft riots, the inspector warned that the "terrible elements of society we saw brought to the surface" still lurked in the city's slums and were growing every year. "The tocsin which next summons them from their dark and noisome haunts may be the prelude to a scene of universal pillage, slaughter and destruction."

The voluminous report, and fear of a cholera epidemic, led to the establishment of the city's Metropolitan Board of Health the following year. The first such body in the nation, it had extraordinary powers insulating it from judicial interference and enabling it to enforce sanitary measures it deemed necessary. Acting on nearly thirty thousand complaints in its first six months, the board removed more than a hundred dead horses from the streets, along with some four thousand dead dogs and cats and almost one hundred thousand barrels of offal. Inspectors also intercepted and destroyed almost two hundred thousand pounds of tainted veal and fish on its way to market.[28]

After two decades of delay since Griscom's report, *The Sanitary Condition of the Laboring Population of New York,* the state also passed the first housing regulations to combat overcrowding in New York's tenements. The Tenement House Law of 1867 required adequate ventilation, fire escapes, and a privy stall for every twenty residents, instead of the usual one-per-hundred. While landlords took advantage of loopholes in the law to avoid compliance, the Metropolitan Board of Health struck back with a wave of lawsuits targeting thousands of violations. In the coming years, conditions began to improve as brick tenements conforming to new standards replaced the older wooden housing in New York's slums.[29]

During the two terms of radical Republican governor Reuben Fenton, from 1864 to 1868, the state of New York passed the most extensive series of reform laws in the North. Many of these laws addressed problems highlighted by the draft riots, according to Republicans, who also sought to dismantle the Democratic machine. Empowering the new Board of Health with control over liquor licenses and Sunday closings, Republicans took aim at the grocery-groggeries that made up the Democrats' grassroots network, as they had with the Liquor Act of 1857.

New York City's volunteer "fire laddies" also constituted a reservoir of Democratic loyalists, and they were placed under the grip of a centralized, professional fire department. At the hearings in Albany, police commissioner

Thomas Acton undercut possible opposition from the old volunteer department by making clear that he had the names of firemen who had taken the side of the rioters in July 1863.[30]

While Governor Fenton and Horace Greeley backed an effort to repeal the state's $250 property requirement that kept most blacks from voting, the essentially conservative Citizens' Association had no desire to go that far in reconstructing New York's political culture; indeed, many of its members hoped to restrict the suffrage of whites to protect middle- and upper-class "taxpayers" from the masses of workingmen and the Democratic leaders who bought their votes with wasteful municipal construction projects and government jobs. Reacting against the antebellum mass culture that was a powerful ingredient of the draft riots, the association added to the growing class tensions in the city.

A strike by the city's street cleaners early in 1865 signaled that a backlash against the association had begun. Over the next decade, while the city's labor movement insisted on workers' rights, the Citizens' Association countered with its own philosophy of taxpayers' privileges. In harmony with E. L. Godkin's influential magazine, the *Nation,* Republican reformers attacked Democratic corruption and proposed efficient government in the hands of elite, disinterested men who were supposedly above the fray of partisan politics. The emergence of this brand of reform, whose leaders called themselves the "best men," would have a decisive impact on the fate of both African Americans and working-class whites in the postwar period.[31]

On March 6, 1865, a huge procession in New York City celebrated Lincoln's second inaugural, and a few weeks later news of Union victories poured into the North. Sherman had reached North Carolina in late March, Grant had stormed the Petersburg lines, and Lee was forced to abandon Richmond, which fell on April 3.[32]

At his home in Virginia, within earshot of the Petersburg battlefield, Edmund Ruffin noted that a messenger had arrived with "the worst of news. Lee's army has been defeated, & Richmond evacuated!"

Ruffin braced himself for the arrival of "the vindictive & atrocious enemy," and for "robbery and destitution." Moreover, he believed his notoriety made him a particular target. "I have long been marked, & anxiously wished for, as a victim of malignant hatred & vengeance—& if captured, & recognized as the long-continued enemy and opposer of Yankee oppression, & the man who fired the first gun against Fort Sumter, I should be subjected to treatment compared to which the infliction of immediate death, by shot or halter, would be merciful."[33]

On April 7, 1865, Grant called on Lee to surrender, and the message was carried through the lines by Colonel Robert Nugent of the Irish Sixty-ninth Regiment. Nugent had ended his term as acting assistant provost marshal general a few months after the draft riots and soon left the army. He was recommissioned a year later and served through the Petersburg campaign, in which the regiment was again decimated.

The Irish Sixty-ninth, along with other Irish regiments, had played a conspicuous role on the front lines throughout the four-year struggle.[34] Nugent wrote of the Sixty-ninth that "the same old spirit prevailed that characterized the Irish soldier the world over—full of fun, full of frolic and full of fight . . . It was ever cheerful and brave, ready to respond to the bugle call." This "noble brigade," he wrote, deserved "a place upon the enduring escutcheon of fame along with the Light Brigade at Balaklava."[35]

With Lee's surrender at Appomattox on April 9, the war came to an end. The following day, Maria Daly wrote in her diary: "Last night at midnight, we heard an extra called. The Judge rushed to the door, 'Surrender of Lee's army, ten cents and no mistake,' said the boy all in one breath (a true young American). It was Palm Sunday, and hosanna may we well cry! Glory be to God on high; the rebellion is ended!"[36]

The war was over, but amid the celebration, northern leaders set a tone that would have grave consequences for black Americans. Like Grant, many northerners of various political stripes were determined to treat the defeated enemy generously. Indeed, Greeley headlined his editorial on April 10 "MAGNANIMITY IN TRIUMPH" and urged that all the rebels, including those deemed leaders, be granted clemency. Maria Daly noted approvingly that Grant had allowed Confederate officers and privates "to go to their homes on their parole, not to be disturbed by the U.S. government so long as they keep the peace and behave as loyal citizens. I hope the animosity that has so long reigned will now pass away." A friend told her the North "must give a general amnesty—even let Jeff Davis go. If we execute him, we should make him a martyr. Let him go and he is only a miserable failure whom no one will care for, from whom we shall have nothing to fear."[37]

Only five days later, Maria Daly wrote: "What dreadful news! President Lincoln assassinated; Secretary Seward's throat cut . . . Poor Lincoln . . . God save us all. What may not a day bring forth!"[38] On April 14, the president was watching a play at Ford's Theater in Washington when he was shot in the back of the head by John Wilkes Booth, a well-known actor enraged by Lincoln's elevation of blacks to freedom and citizenship.

With nine other conspirators, Booth had set out to decapitate the federal government, but the planned attacks on Vice President Andrew Johnson and other officials went awry. Several people in Seward's house were slashed when they tried to apprehend his attacker, but none was killed and Seward survived. The president died on April 15, Good Friday. Booth fled to Virginia and died in a shoot-out with federal troops who surrounded the barn where he was hiding. Four of Booth's accomplices were hanged, four were jailed, and one was acquitted. For the moment, the conciliatory northern mood had been dealt a heavy blow.[39]

Without any evidence, Jefferson Davis was charged as an accomplice in the assassination and captured in Georgia by federal cavalrymen, who put him in irons and deposited him in Fort Monroe at the tip of Virginia's Yorktown Peninsula. However, federal prosecutors soon had trouble building a case against Davis, and the government considered releasing him but dreaded the political fallout. Davis became a political prisoner, trapped in jail without the prospect of a day in court.[40]

In the coming months, Greeley continued to argue for "Universal Amnesty" for the rebels even when, as a *Tribune* pamphlet put it, "the assassination of Mr. Lincoln had wrought the North into a frenzy of grief and wrath which would hardly tolerate suggestions of forbearance and mercy." Greeley believed that punishing the rebels would not advance the rights of blacks in the South, but rather perpetuate a vicious cycle by giving whites a justification for oppressing them. However, Greeley did not explain how giving ex-Confederates political power would protect blacks. Indeed, there could be no explanation. Despite his best intentions, Greeley's proposals were a recipe for white supremacy in the South.[41]

In May 1865, the Army of the Potomac paraded in front of the Capitol in Washington, with Robert Nugent leading what was left of the Irish Brigade, its flags in tatters. The brigade returned to New York early in the summer, some seven hundred men, for a final parade. They were soon followed by the similarly diminished Irish Legion. "The men looked strong and hardy," one observer recalled, "their faces, bronzed by the exposure of years, were wreathed with smiles and bestowed with tears as cheer upon cheer rent the air."[42]

While the North rejoiced, the defeated Confederacy slid into despair. Edmund Ruffin sat down to write the defiant last entry in his diary on June 17, 1865: "I hereby declare my unmitigated hatred to Yankee rule . . . & to the Yankee race. Would that I could impress these sentiments, in their full force, on every living southerner, & bequeath them to every one yet to be born! May such sentiments be held universally in the outraged & downtrodden South, though in silence & in stillness, until the now far distant day shall arrive for just retribution for Yankee usurpation, oppression, & atrocious outrages—& for deliverance & vengeance for the now ruined, subjugated, & enslaved Southern States!"

Ironically, the visionary secessionist regarded the sacking and burning of northern cities as the South's most potent weapon but was most outraged by attacks on southern civilians—by "the invading forces who perpetrated, & their leaders & higher authorities who encouraged, directed, or permitted . . . robbery, rapine & destruction, & house-burning, all committed contrary to the laws of war on non-combatant residents, & still worse on aged men & helpless women!"

Ruffin had been struggling with the religious taboo against suicide but gradually, through close scrutiny of the Bible, had overcome his qualms. After writing these final words and leaving instructions for his family, Ruffin, still seated, put the muzzle of a musket in his mouth and pulled the trigger. The gun misfired, and the exploding cap frightened the women in the house but left Ruffin unharmed. While the women ran to get his son from the cornfield, Ruffin made a second attempt and took his own life.[43] His final written words not only expressed bitter enmity toward the North but signaled that the Confederacy would continue to resist even in defeat. The spirit of Edmund Ruffin would live on in the fight for "home rule"—and against Reconstruction.

CHAPTER 21

"Condemnation and Reversal of Negro Suffrage"

~⌒

Some day I will show the stuck-up aristocrats who is running the country," President Andrew Johnson had sworn as a young man in Tennessee. "A cheap purse-proud set they are, not half as good as the man who earns his bread by the sweat of his brow." The vice president who succeeded Lincoln was a Jacksonian Democrat through and through; having grown up poor, Johnson held a grudge against the wealthy planter class that had led the rebellion in the South, and seemed at first to take a hard line against the defeated Confederates. Much to the liking of radical Republicans in Congress, Johnson declared that the rebels "must not only be punished" but "impoverished," and "their social power must be destroyed."[1]

However, Johnson also distrusted the northeastern elite, the "bloated, corrupt aristocracy" that controlled so much of the nation's industrial and commercial wealth. Moreover, far from sharing the Republicans' abolitionist views, the new president—a former slave owner himself—believed in the supremacy of the white race and referred to blacks, in private, as "niggers." When a delegation led by Frederick Douglass met with Johnson at the White House, he rebuffed their appeals for black suffrage.[2] At this critical juncture, when blacks needed a defender and a champion, they were confronted instead with a man of uncertain loyalties.

Ultimately Johnson's prejudices would shape his approach to Reconstruction, which he tellingly called "Restoration."

Like Lincoln, Johnson believed that while individual secessionists might be punished for treason, the southern states could not and should not be deprived of their rights or treated as conquered territories. Johnson also shared Lincoln's assumption that the president, not Congress, was entitled to play the leading role in the process of Reconstruction. Thus, despite the impression of northern solidarity in the wake of Lincoln's assassination, the new president was on a collision course with radical Republican lawmakers.[3]

After six weeks in office, Johnson issued a proclamation that essentially reaffirmed the conditions for amnesty set forth by Lincoln on December 8, 1863: All rebels taking an oath of allegiance to the United States—except several categories of Confederate officials—would have their political rights and their property, excluding slaves, fully restored. Proscribed individuals could apply for presidential pardons. Johnson also began appointing provisional governors for the southern states and having them convene delegates to write new state constitutions nullifying secession and abolishing slavery. By empowering southern moderates who had been swept along in the tide of secession, Johnson attempted to foster a new political and social order in the South, but one that still excluded blacks from the voting booth.[4]

Most Republicans in Congress were willing to give Johnson's "experiment" a chance and to enfranchise southern blacks at some point in the future. However, radical Republicans, led by Charles Sumner and Thaddeus Stevens, loudly denounced Johnson's approach to Reconstruction, warning that without the right to vote, former slaves would be subject to the whim of white governments and little better off than they were before the war. The radicals found themselves in an awkward position, however, since only six northern states allowed blacks to vote and imposed prohibitive property requirements.[5] This hypocrisy would prove to be a fatal weakness of Reconstruction.

Instead of voluntarily enfranchising blacks, as some Republicans had hoped they would, ex-Confederates and their new whites-only state governments became openly defiant, insisting on their sovereignty and autonomy in terms that echoed the secession crisis on the eve of the war. Numerous ex-Confederate civilian and military leaders, including former Confederate vice president Alexander Stephens, were soon elected to the U.S. Congress and to state offices.[6]

The Thirteenth Amendment, abolishing slavery, was ratified in December 1865, but at the same time southern states were enacting "black codes," discriminatory laws that threatened to keep blacks in de facto enslavement

Andrew Johnson

even if they were legally free.[7]* Johnson's rhetoric indicated that he opposed such measures in principle, but in practice he failed to support vigorous action against them.[8] "It looks as though the President has made up his mind to go whole hog with those who predicted that 'the blacks cannot live among us except as slaves,' and are striving to make good their prophecy," Greeley complained in the pages of the *Tribune*.[9] A chorus of Republican criticism and southern flattery inspired Johnson with visions of returning to his Democratic roots and leading the party—reunited across the sectional divide—to victory in the next presidential race.[10]

---

*The Thirteenth Amendment was ratified by every northern state legislature except New Jersey within a few months of its approval by Congress in January 1865. Three border states—Maryland, West Virginia, and Missouri—also ratified the amendment, along with Louisiana and Tennessee, ex-Confederate states with new legislatures dominated by Unionists. The remaining southern states followed suit in the final months of 1865 under the terms of President Johnson's plan for restoring them to the Union. Two border states—Delaware and Kentucky—joined New Jersey in rejecting the amendment. These were the three states where McClellan won in 1864.

Blacks and white Unionists in the South, bereft of presidential support, also became the target of deadly attacks. In May 1866, a traffic accident in Memphis, Tennessee, sparked an orgy of racial violence. After a collision involving two horse-drawn hacks, the police arrested the black driver and let the white one go free. When several black Union veterans stepped in to prevent the arrest, white residents flocked to the scene. The confrontation escalated into three days of rioting, with white mobs, including many Irish policemen and firemen, tearing through black neighborhoods. At least forty-six blacks were killed, five black women were raped, and hundreds of structures—black homes, churches, and schools—were sacked or burned.[11]

In New Orleans, President Johnson had pardoned the ex-Confederate who became mayor and approved his order forbidding a black suffrage convention which attempted to meet on July 30. Ignoring the president, the commander of federal troops in the city tried to protect the convention delegates, but white rioters, including policemen, arrived first and massacred thirty-seven blacks along with three of their white colleagues. More than one hundred were injured.[12]

A week later, a remorseless President Johnson declared in a speech that Republicans were responsible for the incident, because their policies antagonized whites and led to mob violence.[13] This refrain, heard after the 1834 antiabolition riots in New York and again during the Civil War draft riots, was also becoming the standard Democratic justification for white violence against the campaign for black civil rights during Reconstruction.[14]

"No matter what the cost," wrote Greeley in the *Tribune,* "we of the North must take care that Southern Blacks are not left at the mercy of that diabolic spirit which manifested itself through the late massacres of Memphis and New-Orleans."[15]

Spurred by the recent violence, moderate Republicans in Congress—including Senators William Fessenden of Maine and Lyman Trumbull of Illinois—joined the radicals, led by Sumner, Julian, and Stevens, in refusing to seat the newly elected southern members and passing legislation to protect blacks physically from assault while guaranteeing their civil rights. However, President Johnson vetoed both a civil rights bill and a bill expanding the Freedmen's Bureau, which was established in March 1865 to assist the former slaves. The new bill authorized the bureau to provide schools for the freedmen. The president insisted that laws targeted at the southern states but passed without their participation were not valid.[16]

Congressional Republicans redrafted, negotiated, and revised their legislation throughout the winter and spring; by the summer of 1866, they had managed to override Johnson's vetoes and frame the Fourteenth Amendment, which was approved by the necessary two-thirds majority in both houses on June 13, after prolonged debate. The amendment granted the "privileges and immunities" of citizenship to blacks, and the "equal protection of the laws," which did not include a guarantee of the right to vote.[17]

Instead, the amendment penalized any state that prevented a group of its adult male citizens from voting by reducing the size of the state's congressional delegation. That reduction would be in the same proportion that the number of disfranchised men "shall bear to the whole number of male citizens twenty-one years of age in such State." Since the northern states had minuscule black populations compared to the South, the penalty would have no effect and they could blithely continue to disfranchise blacks, Chinese immigrants, and white minorities despised by nativists, including Germans and Irish Catholics. Southern whites, by contrast, would see their political strength diluted either by black suffrage or by a reduced "basis of representation."[18]

Abolitionists were outraged and denounced this portion of the amendment as a "swindle," a "wanton betrayal of justice and humanity" that protected "the North and the white race, while it leaves the Negro to his fate."[19] Congressional Republicans had stopped short of imposing black suffrage on the South; they also softened the blow in the section of the amendment that disqualified ex-Confederates from voting or holding office, scrapping a provision that affected all who had willingly rebelled for the next four years and narrowing its scope considerably. From the perspective of the Republicans who framed it, the amendment was lenient, but if southern states were sensible and ratified it, they deserved to be readmitted to the Union.[20]

Despite its shortcomings, moderate and radical Republicans rallied around the Fourteenth Amendment during the congressional elections in the fall of 1866, while President Johnson, along with a coalition of Democrats and conservative Republicans, campaigned against it and called for an immediate restoration of the southern states to the Union. The Republicans were victorious throughout the North, as well as in West Virginia, Missouri, and Tennessee, largely because the Democratic party still bore the stigma of having sided with rebellion during the war.[21]

Republicans exploited this association in voters' minds by "waving the bloody shirt," which included referring to the draft riots as the ultimate badge of dishonor. A speech in 1866 by Indiana's Republican governor, Oliver Morton, was a prime example.

> Every bounty jumper, every deserter, every sneak who ran away
> from the draft calls himself a Democrat . . . Every man who

labored for the rebellion in the field, who murdered Union prisoners by cruelty and starvation, who conspired to bring about civil war in the loyal states . . . calls himself a Democrat. Every New York rioter in 1863 who burned up little children in colored asylums, who robbed, ravished and murdered indiscriminately . . . called himself a Democrat. In short, the Democratic party may be described as a common sewer and loathsome receptacle, into which is emptied every element of treason North and South, every element of inhumanity and barbarism which has dishonored the age.[22]

Despite Republican electoral victories and the inevitability of harsher measures if they rejected the Fourteenth Amendment, southern states, encouraged by President Johnson, refused to ratify it. Provoked by southern stubbornness over what they viewed as lenient terms, in February and March 1867 congressional Republicans shifted to a more aggressive program of Reconstruction. Tennessee having been readmitted to the Union after ratifying the Fourteenth Amendment, Congress treated the remaining ten states of the Confederacy as territories, dividing them into five military districts under martial law. These former Confederate states' civil governments were accorded only temporary status: They had to create new constitutions and ratify the Fourteenth Amendment in order to regain their place in the Union, including their seats in Congress.[23]

Many southern legislators and voters declared that they would rather remain outside the Union and refused to form new state constitutions with black voters. Republicans in Washington then passed a second Reconstruction act by which federal occupation troops were to register voters in the South and set in motion the process of forming new state governments. Blacks registered to vote, as did northern transplants to the South, derided as "carpetbaggers," and their southern allies, despised as "scalawags" by resentful ex-Confederates. Together, these three groups formed the southern Republican party.[24]

After the war, the Union League clubs of the North had spread their operations to the South to organize blacks politically, and the clubs played a prominent role in forming the new constitutions and Reconstruction governments. Having been thwarted in their attempt to dismantle Democratic power in New York City by Lincoln's decision not to investigate the draft riots, Union League members seized the opportunity in the South. Blacks were attracted to the party of Lincoln and the Emancipation Proclamation, and the black vote would give Republicans a majority in at least half of the southern states.[25]

Greeley, who presided at the birth of the Republican party in the 1850s and pushed relentlessly for emancipation, had cast off from his moorings into treacherous waters. Once again reveling in the role of the maverick, he was prepared to sacrifice the rights of African Americans on the altar of national reunification. Greeley had warned that as long as high-ranking Confederates remained barred from political life in the South, they would be resentful and would try to prevent blacks from voting. Jefferson Davis should be released, Greeley argued, since he had been imprisoned since 1865 and putting him on trial for treason at this late date would "rekindle passions that have nearly burned out" and "arrest the progress of reconciliation."

Ideally, clemency for all rebels should go hand in hand with black suffrage, Greeley argued, but if black suffrage had to be deferred, so be it. Even if "the North were able to force Impartial Suffrage on the South it would prove of little value while resisted by a strong majority of the dominant caste there," Greeley wrote in the *Tribune.* "But let the North and South strike hands on the basis of Universal Amnesty with Impartial Suffrage, and the resulting peace will be perfect, all-embracing, and enduring."[26]

In May 1867, Greeley even went to Richmond and posted part of the one-hundred-thousand-dollar bail for Jefferson Davis, and the U.S. Circuit Court there released him from prison. "So long as any man was seeking to overthrow our government, he was my enemy," Greeley explained, but "from the hour in which he laid down his arms, he was my formerly erring countryman." A storm of controversy greeted Greeley in New York, where thousands of readers canceled their subscriptions to the *Tribune,* and the officers of the Union League Club prepared to expel him but summoned him to a special meeting first.

In a long letter, Greeley wrote back that he would not attend and blasted the Union League men for their vindictiveness toward the South.

> You evidently regard me as a weak sentimentalist, misled by a maudlin philanthropy. I arraign you as narrow-minded blockheads, who would like to be useful to a great and good cause, but don't know how. Your attempt to base a great, enduring party on the hate and wrath necessarily engendered by a bloody Civil War, is as though you should plant a colony on an iceberg which had somehow drifted into a tropical ocean. I tell you here that, out of a life earnestly devoted to the good of human kind, your children will select my going to Richmond and signing that bail-bond as the wisest act, and will feel that it did more for Freedom and Humanity than all of you were competent to do, though you had lived to the age of Methusaleh.[27]

In fact, the Republican experiment in the South showed more promise of advancing "Freedom and Humanity" than Greeley's vision of amnesty for the ex-Confederate elite, which claimed to move the country forward but instead harkened back to the prewar hierarchy in the South, ruled by wealthy white planters.

Congressional Republicans went ahead with their plans, and by September, voter registration was complete in the ten southern states in question; during the winter of 1867–68, conventions composed of both black and white delegates drew up new state constitutions establishing the right to vote for all men in these states. Denounced by whites who had chosen not to attend, the conventions were unprecedented both because of black participation and because of the constitutions that were created, enfranchising blacks, expanding social services, reforming the states' penal systems, and creating public schools for both races. In 1868 the first blacks were elected to local and statewide office, as high as lieutenant governor, and to the U.S. House and Senate.[28]

The new constitutions were more progressive than those of most northern states, where black suffrage was still restricted or nonexistent. The hypocrisy and the political calculation behind the Fourteenth Amendment were made all the more glaring by this spectacle of black political participation in the South, imposed more for the benefit of the Republican party than for the blacks themselves, by northerners who were loath to accept the same developments in their own states.[29]

The same leading New York Democrats who had raised the banner of white supremacy in reaction to the Emancipation Proclamation in 1863 and helped precipitate the draft riots, used strikingly similar language to oppose the Republican governments in the South—and fueled the new wave of racial violence that began in Memphis and New Orleans in 1866. Manton Marble and Samuel Tilden had used racism and the draft to unite War and Peace Democrats across the North in 1863; five years later, they made New York City the pulpit of white supremacy in a bid to reunite the northern and southern wings of the Democratic party.[30]

Fernando Wood, who had encouraged Confederate intransigence with his talk of New York City seceding on the eve of the war in 1861, and with calls for an armistice in 1863, again took the stage to endorse the South's culture of racism. Having lost his House seat in 1864, Wood was reelected two years later with Irish support in New York's Ninth District—where the draft riots began. Wood, a pariah after the riots, regained the Irish vote when he loudly defended the Fenian Brotherhood after its ill-conceived attempt to invade Canada—and thereby force the British out of Ireland—collapsed in February 1866. Tammany supported him in exchange for bringing in the Irish vote.[31]

In a speech on the House floor in January 1868, Wood denounced the imposition of martial law in the South, warning that "the cord which binds this people together under one fundamental form of government has been strained to its utmost tension. But a little more pressure would be required to break that tie and involve us in anarchy, revolution, and annihilation." He flayed a Reconstruction bill under consideration as "a monstrosity, a measure the most infamous of the many infamous acts of this infamous Congress." At that point, Wood was silenced by the Speaker of the House and formally censured.

In the suppressed speech, which Wood soon published as a pamphlet, he declared that the Civil War ruined the South and "destroyed the distinctions which culture, refinement, and virtue necessarily create, by elevating the degraded and ignorant to its social and political level" and "obliterated for a time the differences which the Almighty has established between the races . . . Are not these results a sufficient punishment?" The Republicans wanted to go farther, Wood charged, and "place over them a permanent negro government for all time to come, and to force that degradation upon them by military authority."

The Republicans were doing this not only to punish the South, Wood asserted, but for partisan advantage. "By creating negro State governments it is also supposed negro representation to Congress and to the electoral colleges for the election of the next President will be secured. Thus we have a combination of motives and influences which may be properly summed up as fanatical, devilish, and dishonest, and which must result in anarchy and national disruption."

Near the end of the speech, Wood warned of impending violence—the righteous wrath of the people—in language reminiscent of *Daily News* editorials on the eve of the draft riots; the blame for the violence would rest on the Republicans because their elevation of blacks betrayed the natural order: "Is it not infamous to erect a military despotism over them . . . to take advantage of the wrong thus committed to make that people the serfs and dependents of a degraded and barbarous race, who disregard any restraint in the indulgence of its brutal instincts? And is it not doubly infamous to perpetrate all these outrages for no other motive than to obtain partisan power and to continue it indefinitely in their own hands as against the coming popular retribution now threatening to overwhelm them?"

Having accused the Republicans of "devilish" motives, Wood concluded that "if these acts, already partly performed and the remainder provided for in this bill, are not 'infamous' and do not consign their authors to eternal infamy there is no hell and no punishment, either here or elsewhere, for the crimes of men."[32]

In the *World,* Manton Marble quoted Samuel Tilden as saying that in government, as in the family, Americans had always refused to "enter into partnership . . . with inferior or mixed races." Marble pointed to the exclusion of blacks from the earliest days of the Republic, citing the first constitution framed by Massachusetts patriots in 1780. "The children of the Pilgrims who had mercilessly exterminated the race of red men had no intention of contaminating their stock with the blacks."

Marble labeled Greeley's *Tribune* the "organ of the hybridizing Radicals" and denounced "the miscegenation which the *Tribune* upholds and which the American people by a righteous instinct of self-preservation abhor." Marble concluded his editorial with a challenge to Greeley: "March up to the issue, Mr. *Tribune,* and meet us . . . Go before the country like a man with your flag. Proclaim your purpose to bring the negro into the State and into the Family, and let the American people pass upon you in the daylight, not in the dark!"[33]

During the vote to ratify the new state constitutions in the South, whites who felt threatened by black suffrage labeled it "negro rule" and either stayed away from the polls or tried to keep blacks away by violent means. The Ku Klux Klan, a secret order of mounted terrorists founded by former Confederate cavalry commander Nathan Bedford Forrest, had existed for two years but now emerged and became active, striking at night against blacks and white Republicans. A *Tribune* article described how the Klansmen dressed up as devils to frighten their victims.

> The costume consists of red flannel trowsers, black blouse, trimmed with red and gathered at the waist, and a black cowl covering the face and falling down to the breast, with a cape behind. The holes cut for the eyes are bordered with white, and from the mouth protrudes a piece of red flannel representing a long tongue. For a headpiece real horns are sometimes worn . . . It is easy to imagine with what terror they inspire the poor, ignorant negroes on the plantations, who know that their errand is always violence, and often murder.

According to the *Tribune,* "The real leaders of the Ku-Klux are the Court-House and tavern politicians, and the rank and file is composed of the idle, ignorant and worthless poor white element." The paper noted that "in addition to the political animosity entertained toward the Negroes," there was "a desire among the poor whites to drive them away, so that they shall not come into competition with them as laborers."[34]

While Greeley's *Tribune* regularly reported on the "outrages" perpetrated by the Klan, Marble's *World* claimed to "know nothing of this society except from the wild stories put afloat in the newspapers." If the Klan did exist, its acts were the responsibility of the Republicans, the *World* asserted; such violence was "the natural fruit of the policy pursued towards the South."[35]

For the moment, with twenty thousand federal troops occupying the South, Klan attacks, while intimidating, were not enough to derail the process of approving new state constitutions. Ten states did so by May 1868 and elected Republicans to state offices and legislatures, which quickly led to ratification of the Fourteenth Amendment, establishing citizenship for blacks.

In June, seven states that had taken these steps—North and South Carolina, Florida, Georgia, Alabama, Louisiana, and Arkansas—were readmitted to the Union, despite the fears of many Republicans in Washington that Democrats would regain control in the South if the process of Reconstruction proceeded too quickly and federal troops were withdrawn. Republicans were under political pressure from northern constituents not to carry on "bayonet rule" indefinitely; with the 1868 presidential election approaching, Republicans felt constrained to reestablish civil law and follow through with restoration of the southern states as promised.

Problems persisted in Texas, Virginia, and Mississippi, and they were not readmitted to the Union for another six months. In Mississippi, two thousand federal troops could not prevent whites from defeating the new constitution by threats and assaults that drove twenty thousand Republicans away from the polls.[36]

"I have forwarded to you the call of the Democratic National Committee for the holding of the next National Convention in the City of New York on the 4th of July next," DNC chairman August Belmont had written in an open letter to committee members. The choice of Tammany Hall's clubhouse on Fourteenth Street as the site for the convention in the 1868 presidential race signaled that William Tweed's powerful local organization would be the engine behind a revival of the Democratic party nationally.

Belmont instructed party leaders to target "the conservative element throughout the Union which has not heretofore acted with the Democratic party," and he urged every voter, "Unite with us in our efforts to save our free institutions from the lawless despotism which now threatens the very foundation of our Government." The radical Republicans had to be driven from power, Belmont wrote. The *World,* which reprinted the letter, summed up the Democratic position as "Opposition to Congressional usurpation," "Opposition to negro supremacy," and "Immediate restoration of the unity and peace of the nation."[37]

The resurgence of the Democratic party was to be based on a platform of fierce opposition to the advancement of African Americans, along with the restoration of "home rule," meaning white supremacy, in the South. The re-union of northern and southern Democrats was crucial to restoring the party's lock on the White House.[38]

Opposition to Republican policies had drawn the Irish deeply into Democratic politics, which in turn became a route to power in the postwar years.[39] Nowhere was this truer than in New York. There, the presidential election of 1868—pitting Republican nominee Ulysses S. Grant against Horatio Seymour—solidified Irish support for Tammany and increased Tweed's power, while continuing the process of assimilation which the Irish had begun through politics and with their battlefield sacrifices during the war. The antagonisms of the war were still fresh in the campaign, the racial issues unresolved and still threatening to the Democrats.[40]

Grant, the victorious general who promised the country peace, had been nominated unanimously by the Republican convention. Seymour was also nominated unanimously, at Tammany Hall—but on the twenty-second ballot. Emphasizing his lack of desire for the nomination, Seymour had become a delegate and was then elected permanent chairman of the convention, a post he assumed would take him out of the running, since candidates were expected to absent themselves from the proceedings. He opened the convention by denouncing Grant as a "military chieftain" and a threat to the values of the founding fathers, who insisted "the military should ever be subordinate to the civil authority." Under the Republicans, Seymour charged, dissenters were "tried and punished by military tribunal" and "dragged to prison."[41]

The convention also listened to two petitions, the first from the National Labor Union, a coalition formed in 1866 to lobby for the eight-hour day without wage reductions. The message to the convention also stressed that public lands should be given to "actual settlers," not corporations. The oppressive hours and wages for "working girls and women" were a "standing reproach to civilization," the petition declared, as it attempted to win promises of concrete action from candidates.[42]

The second petition, from the Women's Suffrage Association of America, was signed by a central committee consisting of Elizabeth Cady Stanton, Mary Greeley (Horace's wife), Susan B. Anthony, and Abby Hopper Gibbons.

The women condemned the Republicans for ignoring their "innumerable petitions"—for enfranchising two million black men and leaving fifteen million white women "dethroned." They urged the Democrats to move with the "tide of progress" and support "universal suffrage."[43]

The balloting began on July 7 and soon became deadlocked, as eastern and midwestern, radical and conservative candidates canceled each other out; President Andrew Johnson, nominated for vice president by the Republicans in 1864, had returned to his Democratic roots but garnered little support. Two days later, after the twenty-first round, the Ohio delegation suddenly threw its support behind Seymour, setting off a stampede in his favor.

Seymour gave a speech refusing the nomination, which only bolstered his popularity among the cheering delegates. As Seymour "fled from the platform in dismay" and left the building, Clement Vallandigham took the floor to declare that "the safety of the people is the supreme law, and the safety of the American Republic demands the nomination of Horatio Seymour, of New York." Tilden courteously allowed the other thirty-six states to precede him and then cast New York's ballots for Seymour. Francis Blair of Missouri, a Union general, was unanimously nominated as Seymour's running mate.

An extreme conservative, Blair had declared that the "real and only issue in this contest is the overthrow of reconstruction."[44] The Democrats denounced the Reconstruction Acts and called for white supremacy—for the dismantling of the "carpet-bag State Governments," as Blair called them, and for "the white people to reorganize their own governments." Republicans "waved the bloody shirt"—reminding voters of the carnage of the Civil War and Democratic sympathy for the rebels—and made the draft riots of 1863 a prominent motif in the campaign.[45]

William Cullen Bryant's accusation in the *Evening Post* five years earlier that Seymour addressed the mob at City Hall as "My friends" had sparked a furor, which Republicans revived as grist for their propaganda mill. Cartoons in various newspapers contrasted Grant demanding the surrender of Vicksburg with Seymour appeasing the rioters. Seymour appeared unfazed by the *Tribune*'s shrill attacks, remarking blandly to a friend that "Mr. Greeley is mad."[46]

A Republican pamphlet titled *Seymour, Vallandigham, and the Riots of 1863* declared that the riots were a conspiracy, and quoted as evidence Seymour's Fourth of July speech at the Academy of Music in 1863, in which he had warned the Lincoln administration that "PUBLIC NECESSITY CAN BE PROCLAIMED BY A **MOB** AS WELL AS BY A GOVERNMENT." The pamphlet continued:

> Little did the Loyal people of our country know what this short, yet pregnant sentence meant; little did they think that the Governor

of a Loyal State could be in league with the enemies of the Government . . . could be familiar with the plans of the Rebels . . . to INAUGURATE CIVIL WAR AT THE NORTH . . . TO CAUSE RIOTS IN ALL THE NORTHERN CITIES, and yet it is beyond a doubt that HORATIO SEYMOUR DID KNOW ALL OF THIS, AND HELPED TO INCITE THE GREAT JULY RIOTS, in 1863, by the speech from which we have quoted.

The pamphlet then reprinted an affidavit from a ship captain who claimed to have transported Vallandigham and some thirty Confederate officers from Bermuda to Halifax at the end of June 1863, enabling them to evade the Union blockade and reach Boston and New York to start the riots. The captain, Francis Johns, testified that the Confederate agent who hired his vessel, Major Norman S. Walker,

> stated definitely and positively that it was a secret mission organized at Richmond, which Vallandigham was the head of; that they were TO HAVE MOB MEETINGS IN THE CITIES OF BOSTON AND NEW YORK, TO CREATE A DIVERSION IN FAVOR OF GEN. LEE AND THE SOUTHERN ARMY, THEN ABOUT TO INVADE THE NORTH. I was expressly directed by Major Walker to proceed without a moment's delay, as Mr. Vallandigham and others were bound to be in Boston and New York before the Fourth of July, THE DAY ON WHICH THE MOB MEETINGS WERE TO TAKE PLACE IN THOSE CITIES.

The captain swore further that in "several private chats" Vallandigham not only confirmed what Walker had told him about the mission, but showed him the "letter of authority under which he was acting . . . signed by Mr. Mallory."* However, according to the captain, when a Union frigate stopped the ship, he hid the conspirators belowdecks and, at Vallandigham's request, burned all of his documents, including the instructions from Richmond, in the ship's furnace.

The captain's deposition was the only evidence of a conspiracy the Republicans could muster. Nonetheless, the pamphlet proclaimed that Seymour was in contact with Vallandigham, knew of his movements, and was part of the plot. The pamphlet also accused Seymour of influencing "the merciful

---

*Stephen Mallory, the Confederate secretary of the navy.

Lincoln (afterward murdered by one of Vallandigham's friends)" to commute Vallandigham's death sentence to banishment in May 1863. "CAN SUCH MEN BE TRUSTED WITH THE AFFAIRS OF THE NATION!"[47]

Thomas Nast's political cartoons likened the torching of schools for free blacks by the Ku Klux Klan in the South to the New York rioters' burning of the Colored Orphan Asylum. In one such drawing in *Harper's Weekly*, Nast placed a black Union veteran atop a tall granite monument with the Emancipation Proclamation in his lap, yet helpless to protect the slain figures at the base of the monument, including a black woman and two children. The Colored Orphan Asylum burns in the background, a rioter threatens the veteran with a club, and a Klansman aims a pistol at the veteran while a schoolhouse for freedmen is consumed by flames. Contrasting the heroism of black soldiers and the horrors of the draft riots, as *Harper's* and other Republican papers had done since the assault on Fort Wagner in 1863, Nast updated this theme by adding the Klan to the equation. He inscribed the monument with a chronological list of African American suffering at the hands of whites, including slavery, riots, and other massacres. The last items included Klan violence and discriminatory laws in the South depriving blacks of civil rights. Summing up these 250 years of oppression, Nast included a quote attributed to Manton Marble's New York *World:* "WE DESPISE THE NEGRO."[48]

In a cartoon with a similar background—the burning orphan asylum and freedmen's school—Nast took aim at the Democratic party platform, which declared the Reconstruction Acts "unconstitutional, revolutionary, and void." Proclaiming "THIS IS A WHITE MAN'S GOVERNMENT," an Irishman from New York's Five Points slum joins hands with former Confederate cavalry commander and Ku Klux Klan founder Nathan Bedford Forrest and Democratic financier August Belmont. The trio steps on a fallen black veteran. Displaying his long-standing nativism and bigotry against Irish Catholics, Nast evinced the Republicans' newly kindled fear of a Democratic party reunited across the North-South divide.[49]

Nast's prejudices aside, these cartoons reflected an alarming reality in the South, where the Klan and similar groups had become an unofficial military arm of the Democratic party, carrying out a terrorist onslaught between April and November of 1868 that killed hundreds of people. In the seven states readmitted to the Union in June, federally imposed martial law had ceased, and the national armed forces could only be deployed at the request of local authorities. One thousand Republicans, mostly blacks, died in Klan attacks and riots in Louisiana, while more than two hundred potential Grant supporters were killed in Arkansas and in Georgia, where assaults and intimidation had a similar effect. Across the South, tens of thousands of Republicans stayed away from the polls.[50]

Thomas Nast cartoon drawing a parallel between the draft riots and
Ku Klux Klan violence

Congressional Republicans who had warned against restoring southern states prematurely and tying the hands of federal troops saw their worst fears realized during the 1868 election. With federal military rule replaced by civil self-government, the state governors had to scrape together regiments of inexperienced militiamen, who were no match for the ex-Confederate horsemen of the Klan.[51]

Nast's cartoons suggested that Klan attacks echoed the pattern of the draft riots, when the mobs targeted white Republican leaders and institutions that assisted blacks, as well as blacks themselves. Indeed, in 1868, New York's Democratic press justified Klan violence in terms analogous to those used to defend the rioters five years earlier: The Union League was organizing black voters in the South—elevating and integrating them in white society—which left whites no choice but to strike back. Klansmen were cast as defenders of the social order, resisting the military despotism of the federal government.[52] Marble wrote that Congress was trying to put the South "into the hands of the most ignorant and incapable part of their population, and to conduct that section through negro insolence into anarchy."[53]

"Our position must be *condemnation and reversal of negro suffrage in the states*," Samuel Tilden told party leaders in 1868. This political strategy, Tilden explained, would galvanize party loyalists and swing voters while hurting the Republicans. It would also be attractive "to the adopted citizens—whether Irish or German; to all the workingmen; to the young men just becoming voters." Tilden had no qualms about exploiting the same racial and class divisions that had erupted in New York City only five years earlier. Marble's *World* and other Democratic newspapers echoed Tilden and denounced Republican hypocrisy in not enfranchising northern blacks.[54]

Campaigning for Grant, Republicans labeled the Democrats "Rebels" and "Copperheads" who were attempting, through violence and intimidation, to roll back the nation's progress won through four years of war. The Klan attacks gave the Democrats gains in some areas of the South, but generally bolstered Republican accusations, and Grant beat Seymour nationally by a substantial margin. Seymour amassed only eighty electoral votes—from Oregon, New Jersey, and New York in the North, three border states, and two southern states. Without Tammany's corrupt inflation of the Democratic vote in New York City, Seymour might well have lost his home state too.[55]

Nonetheless, Tammany Democrats had plenty to celebrate at the end of 1868. Seymour had carried New York State, where the Democrats defeated the radical Republican governor, Reuben Fenton. William Tweed had been elected a state senator the previous year, and his power in New York—both

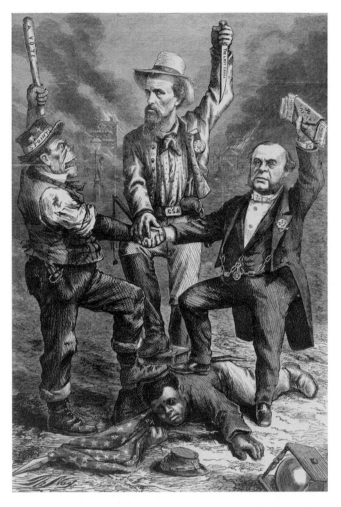

Thomas Nast cartoon denouncing the Democratic platform of 1868:
"This Is A White Man's Government"

city and state—was growing rapidly as his pawns moved into high office.
John Hoffman, the magistrate who had overseen the prosecution of the draft
rioters and was elected mayor in 1867, now became the governor. The district
attorney, A. Oakey Hall, who had also become popular in the wake of the
draft riots, was elected in December to fill out the remaining year of Hoffman's term as mayor.[56]

In addition to Hoffman and Hall, Tweed counted on his two Irish American lieutenants, Richard Connolly, who had become the city's comptroller,
and Peter Sweeny, now the city chamberlain, another key financial post.*

As the dominant power broker in the city, county, and state of New York,

*The chamberlain was in charge of depositing the city's funds into bank accounts.

Tweed was well positioned to control the revival of the Democratic party nationally. With Seymour, the Albany Regency's candidate, out of the picture, Tweed believed he had a fair chance of putting Hoffman in the White House in the next election.[57] By defeating Fenton, New York's Democrats had used their formidable party organization to deliver "New York from the thralldom of Radical tyranny," Tammany's house organ, the *Leader,* declared, and advised the rest of the northern Democracy to follow this example in regaining its former strength. By championing home rule against Republican "tyranny" in New York City, Tammany Democrats implicitly denounced Reconstruction and reached out to the southern wing of the party.[58]

Thus, five years after the draft riots, many of the same Tammany officials who had established an atmosphere of resistance to the federal conscription had since reaped the full benefit of Lincoln's forbearance in the aftermath of that bloody week. Having been allowed to remain in office and advance their careers, they conciliated the rioters, prosecuted them halfheartedly, and provided three million dollars in public relief for them while ignoring the suffering of the black community. These officials had become instrumental in the entrenchment and expansion of Democratic power, which would ultimately have a decisive impact on the fate of Reconstruction.

While not part of the Tammany organization, Manton Marble had also emerged unscathed from the draft riots, and in 1868 he was riding high on the same racist message he had formulated in July 1863. Black businesses and churches had been destroyed and continued to falter while the city's black population declined, but Marble enjoyed his most profitable year at the *World.* He was happily married, with two children and a four-story brownstone mansion on upper Fifth Avenue. Marble's neighbors were financiers and industrialists, the Gilded Age "robber barons," and he vacationed with them in Newport, Rhode Island. At the age of thirty-four, the once-struggling editor had truly arrived.[59]*

Even the Republicans' exposure of Tammany's voter registration fraud right after the 1868 election did not hamper the Democratic resurgence. Judge Barnard and Judge McCunn, who had played conspicuous roles in the draft riots—negotiating with the rioters in the street and declaring the draft unconstitutional—were found to be at the center of the scandal, having turned their courtrooms into naturalization mills where some sixty thousand new immigrants were briskly turned into citizens. A. Oakey Hall,

---

*The late nineteenth century was dubbed the Gilded Age after the title of Mark Twain and Charles Dudley Warner's 1873 novel, in which they satirized American materialism.

as district attorney, played a crucial role in the fraud by directing party operatives in how to count votes and to honor the naturalization papers at the polls.

Unable to get Lincoln to declare martial law in 1863, this time the Union League Club prevailed on Congress to launch an investigation into the naturalization scheme, resulting one year later in laws that provided for extensive federal supervision of elections in northern cities, especially New York. During the federal inquiry, Tammany struck back with all its muscle, and the *Irish-American* denounced Republican investigators as nativists.[60]

Horace Greeley had written an open letter to Samuel Tilden in the wake of the naturalization frauds in 1868, charging him as equally guilty as Tweed or Mayor Hall in the workings of the Democratic machine and challenging him to stop the corruption.[61] Instead, the years of reform activity at the state level, spearheaded by Governor Fenton and by Greeley, came to a halt. Their effort in 1867 to amend the state constitution and enfranchise black men without a property requirement had provoked the backlash that helped Hoffman beat Fenton in 1868 and gave Democrats control of the state legislature in 1869. That same year, the constitutional amendment on black suffrage was voted down in a statewide referendum.[62]

In February 1869, Congress took the first step toward overriding that referendum by approving the Fifteenth Amendment. Whereas the Thirteenth had ended slavery and the Fourteenth granted citizenship to blacks, the Fifteenth was aimed at securing their right to vote. The Fifteenth would be ratified the following year, resulting in the first election in New York State under universal male suffrage. The amendment did nothing to enfranchise women and drove a wedge between the feminist and abolitionist movements, which had until then worked in tandem.[63]

In the year between approval and ratification, New York's Democrats furiously denounced the Fifteenth Amendment. Tilden's keynote address at the state convention in Syracuse in September 1869 was full of race-baiting—warnings that the transfer of control over suffrage from the states to Congress would allow hordes of Chinese and blacks to flood the state and vote there.[64] Governor Hoffman also devoted considerable energy to opposing the amendment.[65]

However, more farsighted Democrats, strategists like Manton Marble of the Swallowtails, and Tammany's Peter Sweeny, realized that Democratic opposition to universal male suffrage would alienate immigrants, particularly the many working-class German voters who were wary of nativist attempts, successful in some states, to disfranchise them using residency, literacy, and property requirements. Indeed, Tammany viewed with growing alarm the independent labor candidates running in the fall elections of 1869 and the large number of Germans supporting them.[66]

Debt financing had created growth and jobs, but the unbridled pace of the city's expansion had degraded conditions for workers in the building trades and on public works, forcing them to work long hours and live in squalid conditions near job sites at the fringes of town. Richard Matthews, who helped lead a bricklayers' strike in 1868, denounced the idea that "William M. Tweed had a right to choose politicians to represent the cause of the workingmen."[67]

While Congress had passed an eight-hour law for federal employees in 1868, state laws, regulating hours in the private sector, contained loopholes that made them unenforceable. In New York, Governor Hoffman, Tweed's pawn in Albany, had signed an eight-hour law, but as elsewhere, freedom-of-contract clauses left employers at liberty to set longer hours.[68]

On October 13, the German "Association of United Workingmen" held a mass meeting at Cooper Institute, where it endorsed the principles of the National Labor Union in Washington, D.C., including the eight-hour day and the repeal of state conspiracy laws designed to break up unions. The meeting also denounced both major political parties as "corrupt, serving capital instead of labor."[69]

German and Irish working-class discontent had won C. Godfrey Gunther the mayor's race in 1863 and brought forth independent labor candidates campaigning for the eight-hour day the following year. That ferment now came to a head: Whereas the labor movement had been divided in the 1850s between those who favored political action and those who wanted to focus on regulating the workplace, in 1869 the two sides came together. English-speaking and German trade unionists formed a "Joint-Committee" which made workplace concerns—enforcement of the state's eight-hour law and repeal of the conspiracy law—the labor candidates' top priorities.[70]

Soon the German labor paper *Die Arbeiter Union* came out in favor of the Fifteenth Amendment, arguing that the abolition of chattel slavery in 1865 and the progress of African Americans should be regarded as a hopeful sign that white workers could someday liberate themselves from wage slavery. New York's German workers, sympathetic to abolition in the 1830s and alienated from the Republican party in the 1850s and 1860s, were taking the first steps to distance themselves from the racial violence of the draft riots and to accept blacks as fellow workers and citizens.[71]

The black vote in New York would be extremely small, in any case, Sweeny reasoned. "We ought to get rid of the negro question," he declared. "It hurts us more than the negro vote could injure us." By giving blacks the vote and removing their grievance from the political arena, Sweeny argued, the country could move on to more important things.[72] At the top of Tammany's agenda was the Democratic party's quest for the White House.

In October during his reelection campaign for the state senate, Tweed addressed an enormous nighttime rally in New York City, telling the party faithful that they—"the true democracy"—must take back the national government from the Republicans. Parades from several wards featuring horse-drawn fire engines, including Tweed's "Big Six" Engine Company, had converged at the torchlight gathering, along with a volunteer artillery unit complete with cannon, a contingent dressed as Indians, and various other displays of Tammany hoopla. "The Red Men of the Wigwam on the War Path," the *Herald* reported.

The erudite Mayor Hall gave a lengthy speech, as did Congressman Fernando Wood, elected in 1866 and again in 1868 after regaining his Irish base and with it the leverage to attract Tammany's support. "THE TAMMANY REGENCY," blared the *Herald*'s headline, suggesting that the power within the Democracy had shifted from the effete elders in Albany to the "fierce democracy" of New York City.[73]

After the Tammany victories in November 1869, Sweeny declared, "It gives us a great opportunity for a long lease of power in the State, and to lay a substantial foundation for the democratic party of the country."[74]

CHAPTER 22

Strange Bedfellows: Greeley and the Liberal Republicans

~⁀

lysses S. Grant was inaugurated in March 1869, having campaigned on the slogan "Let Us Have Peace." As commander of the army under Johnson, Grant had simply carried out the president's orders and assigned troops to trouble spots across the South, but he took no personal initiative and avoided the sphere of politics. As president, Grant continued to use the army conservatively, letting Congress and his cabinet shape policy, and confining himself to the narrowest interpretation of his powers as chief executive. Not only was Grant a neophyte in politics, but as a commanding general assuming the helm of a free nation, he was determined not to be labeled a military despot—a Caesar, Cromwell, or Napoleon—and to preserve the supremacy of civilian authority.[1]

Grant's administration did supply the state militias of North and South Carolina with arms and ammunition, but on the whole, as Klan violence continued in 1868 and 1869, state governors in the South found themselves hampered by a lack of cavalry, while the end of federally imposed martial law meant the six thousand troops still in the region could intervene only when local authorities called on them. Moreover, the reopening of civil courts made army commanders reluctant to set up military tribunals. Texas, Arkansas, and Tennessee were the exceptions: Their governors declared martial law and fought back aggressively, disrupting Klan activity, making arrests, and even executing some terrorists by firing squad. In most of the South, however, the presence of federal troops merely propped up the

Republican governments and prevented some rioting but could do little more to curb the Klan.[2]

By March 1870, the Fifteenth Amendment was ratified, purportedly guaranteeing black suffrage throughout the country, including the North. In Virginia, Mississippi, Texas, and Georgia, where Reconstruction had been delayed by violence or flagrant political maneuvering against black legislators, Congress required ratification of both the Fifteenth and Fourteenth Amendments before readmission to the Union. With a total of thirty-seven states, these four, combined with twenty-five others, where Republicans controlled the legislature, produced the three-fourths majority required for ratification.[3]

Manton Marble's *World* encouraged the southern states to circumvent the Fifteenth Amendment—and the penalty of losing some of their congressional seats, as stipulated in the Fourteenth Amendment—by using nonracial criteria such as poll taxes, literacy tests, and property requirements to deny blacks the vote. Many followed this advice to "accomplish *nearly* all they desire without raising any question under the XIVth or XVth amendment."[4]

The loopholes in the amendments allowing for such hurdles reflected the glaring hypocrisy of northern Republicans, who had long been excluding Chinese immigrants and poor whites, especially Germans and Irish Catholics, from the polls. Ironically, Republican determination to keep these exclusions against the Chinese and certain whites in the North had compromised the advancement of voting rights for blacks in the Fourteenth Amendment and led to a weakened Fifteenth Amendment as well.[5]

Despite the defects of the Fifteenth Amendment, with all states readmitted to the Union, many Republicans felt Reconstruction was complete and former slaves should no longer be supported as "wards of the nation." Congressman and future president James Garfield asserted that the amendment "confers upon the African race the care of its own destiny. It places their fortunes in their own hands." A newspaper in Illinois declared that "the negro is now a voter and a citizen. Let him hereafter take his chances in the battle of life."[6]

However, hundreds of murders were still being committed by Klansmen intent on toppling the carpetbagger governments in the South and driving blacks from the polls. Moderate Republicans in Congress found themselves in a dilemma not unlike Lincoln's in the wake of the draft riots when he chose not to impose martial law and bring the rioters before military tribunals. Joseph Choate had complained in 1863 that New York City's civil courts were in the hands of corrupt Democratic judges; in 1870, southern Republicans also wanted an alternative to the local courts, where blacks were kept off juries and many jurors were Klansmen. However, the prosecution of crimes committed by individuals—like assault, murder, and arson—had traditionally been left to the states, and some congressional leaders worried that more federal innovations and intervention would threaten the very fabric of the nation's constitutional system.

Looking for some constitutional justification for intervention, Congress found it in the clauses of the Fourteenth and Fifteenth Amendments that allowed lawmakers to create legislation for the enforcement of the amendments. With the passage of the first enforcement act on May 31, 1870, any assault on a person's civil and political rights, including voting rights, became a felony. Klansmen became vulnerable to prosecution in federal courts, and the president could use the army to capture them.

Nonetheless, Klan violence increased during the next twelve months, leading Grant to abandon some of his political caution. Aided by two new enforcement laws, Grant and his attorney general, Amos Akerman, took tougher steps against the terrorists. The law of February 1871 set up federal oversight for registration and voting, while another bill in April, dubbed the Ku Klux Act, gave the president more power, just short of complete martial law, to go after the Klan. The president could dispatch federal troops to troublesome counties and, declaring them to be in a state of insurrection, suspend the writ of habeas corpus. Trials would continue to take place in civil courts, but jurors would have to swear under oath that they were not Klansmen and face severe legal consequences if caught perjuring themselves.[7]

Angry Democrats in Congress branded the Republican bill a "crowning act of centralization and consolidation." Fernando Wood and other Democrats in Congress denounced the law as a usurpation of states' rights and a tool of military dictatorship. Fellow New York congressman S. S. Cox even praised the Klansmen as freedom fighters, like those of Italy, France, and Ireland. The *Jackson* (Mississippi) *Clarion* decried the "unconstitutional and hideously despotic" law, intended "to supercede State authority with the government of the bayonet and of marshal law." In North Carolina, Raleigh's *Sentinel* called the Ku Klux Act an attempt by Grant to "declare the State in insurrection and, by military terror, carry the [1872] election."[8]

In the *Tribune*, Horace Greeley continued to lobby for "Universal Amnesty" for ex-Confederates, which he felt would help in "disarming and dissolving the Ku-Klux," but he defended the new enforcement act as "a very different thing from proclaiming martial law, which is the supremacy of the will of the military commander to all civil law. The Ku-Klux act simply provides for the arrest, legal trial, and punishment of the masquerading villains."[9]

A few prominent Republicans in Congress, including Lyman Trumbull and Carl Schurz, joined the Democrats in blasting the Ku Klux Act's expansion of federal authority and calling for reconciliation with the South.

Ulysses S. Grant

Thus, despite the surge in public support for federal action against the Klan, the new law clearly had the potential to become a political liability for the administration.

In May 1871, after much hesitation, the War and Justice Departments, with Grant's reluctant approval, started gathering evidence against the Klan and launching prosecutions in the South. At the same time, Congress began holding hearings in what became an exhaustive investigation of the Klan lasting some nine months.[10] Republicans seemed poised to bring the Klan to justice—with precisely the means Lincoln had refrained from using against the draft rioters and New York's Democratic machine.

In 1871 and 1872, federal marshals and troops arrested thousands of Klansmen in the Carolinas and Mississippi, as well as in other states. However, acutely sensitive to charges of despotism, the Grant administration focused primarily on breaking up the Klan and pacifying the South—not on locking up thousands of prisoners. Reluctant to further inflame Democratic resentment against bayonet rule, Grant used the military only in the most afflicted areas and later dispensed numerous pardons to convicted Klansmen.[11]

Like Lincoln in 1863, Grant evidently calculated that overplaying the hand of federal power would be counterproductive.

The results, therefore, were similar to those at the end of the draft riots. In 1871–72, federal grand juries indicted more than 3,000 Klansmen, but plea bargaining won suspended sentences for hundreds of them. The government dismissed about 2,000 cases in order to home in on the ringleaders. Some 350 of them were convicted, but most served little or no jail time. The harshest sentences, given to 65 Klansmen, were for five years or less. Not surprisingly, the respite from racial and political violence in the South that followed Grant's crackdown did not last for long.[12]

The New York lynch mobs of July 1863 and the Klan were both elements of an ongoing counterrevolution against Reconstruction. The extreme alternative to Lincoln's and Grant's measured response to these threats was presented to Americans by the gruesome events unfolding in Paris during the spring and summer of 1871. After the Paris Commune, a failed communist uprising, French authorities executed many of the revolutionaries by firing squad, stacking their corpses like so much cordwood, hundreds side by side and three layers deep in the public squares of the city. Between the violent insurrection and its aftermath, some twenty thousand French citizens were killed.[13]

The *New York Times* compared the Paris Commune to the draft riots, grudgingly admitting that America, though a free country, was not free from the same elements of class conflict that plagued autocratic European regimes. An editorial in June 1871 declared that

> only once in the history of the city did this terrible *proletaire* class show its revolutionary head. For a few days in 1863, New York seemed like Paris, under the Reds . . . The cruelties inflicted by our "Reds" on the unhappy Negroes quite equaled in atrocity anything that the French Reds perpetrated on their priests. Our "communists" had already begun to move toward the houses of the rich, and the cry of war to property was already heard, when the spirited assistance of the United States soldiery enabled the better classes to put down the disturbance. But had the rioters been able to hold their own a week longer, had they plundered the banks and begun to enjoy the luxuries of the rich, and been permitted to arm and organize themselves, we should have seen a communistic explosion in New York which would probably have

left the city in ashes and blood. Every great city has within it the communistic elements of a revolution.

The *Times* revealed the heightened middle- and upper-class fear of mob rule, along with the hardening of class divisions, that were important legacies of the draft riots. The feeling that only the "United States soldiery" stood between the propertied classes and the volcanic forces of proletarian discontent became a constant of the Gilded Age, when American cities were growing rapidly and the gap between rich and poor became even wider than it had been in 1863.

The *Times* struck an optimistic note by commending "the industrial school and the children's charity" along with individual effort as the best routes out of poverty. Nonetheless, Republican, free-labor ideology with its vision of every worker as a potential capitalist was beginning to wear thin against a backdrop of revived union-building and simmering labor unrest in the early 1870s.[14]

Right after the draft riots, and in the nearly eight years since then, Tweed's Tammany Hall, unlike the Republican party, seemed to have found a formula that defused class conflict and maintained urban harmony without resorting to the gallows, the firing squad, or coercive legislation to punish the underclass and the demagogues who provoked it to violence.[15]

Named the grand sachem of Tammany Hall after his handpicked candidate, Hoffman, became governor, and reelected to the state senate in 1869, Tweed had amassed enough power to encompass both New York City and Albany, where in 1870 he pushed through the state legislature a new charter for the city that simplified the municipal bureaucracy and strengthened the mayor. These changes promised to create more efficient, effective governance of the growing metropolis and to reduce taxes while overturning the state-imposed, Republican-dominated commissions of 1857 and restoring local control, or "home rule." Wealthy property owners hailed Tweed's plans with little scrutiny of his motives or of the city's finances.[16]

Ever since a law allowing assessment bonds was passed in 1852, New York's aldermen had been fueling the city's growth with the same financing methods used by the big railroad corporations in Wall Street's thriving securities market. By issuing municipal bonds, the city was able to pay contractors for public works before revenue came in from increased tax assessments in improved areas of Manhattan. Since contractors did not have to wait long periods for payment, more companies, including those without cash cushions, were able to work for the city. By providing the infrastructure—streets, sewers, transportation—for new upscale neighborhoods and commercial districts and increasing the pace of northward expansion on Manhattan, politicians kept wealthy developers, investors, and real estate owners happy while providing hundreds of jobs for constituents in the building trades and on public works.[17]

August Belmont, chairman of the Democratic National Committee and American agent for the Rothschild family, had taken the whole process a step farther by attracting European investors and creating a transatlantic market for the city's bonds in the late 1860s and 1870s. In a similar way, nationally he had helped provide European capital for American railroad expansion in the 1850s and early 1860s. During the Civil War, New York's aldermen had first used debt financing in the heady months after Fort Sumter fell to raise money for soldiers' bounties. Two years later, the New York County Board of Supervisors, dominated by Tweed, issued its first bonds to pay damage claims after the draft riots. Next came the supervisors' three-million-dollar bond issue to pay for exemptions under the draft's three-hundred-dollar clause. Thus, by the time Tweed had reached the full height of his power in 1869–71, debt financing had become the currency of his political machine, both its fuel and the lubricant that kept its constituent parts from clashing and throwing off sparks.[18]

While the city's black population played a negligible role in Tweed's version of democracy, Tammany officials reached out to the Irish, and the attraction was mutual. The Irish constituted a major voting bloc, and Tammany offered a path to mainstream acceptance in America: In the wake of the draft riots, Tammany officials stressed that they had always been War Democrats, opposed to Wood's Peace Democracy, and they had a long tradition of frenzied flag-waving on the Fourth of July to prove their undying patriotism.[19]

Remarkably, of Tweed's closest associates, Mayor A. Oakey Hall—not the two Irishmen, Connolly and Sweeny—made the most public display of admiration for all things Celtic. The mayor insisted humorously that his initials, A. O. H., stood for the Ancient Order of Hibernians. On Saint Patrick's Day in 1870, Hall mounted a platform to review the parade dressed "in the supposed regalia of an Irish Prince," noted an appreciative observer. "It was not enough for him to put a shamrock on the lapel of his coat . . . to adequately typify his consuming love for the 'Exiles of Erin,' he wore a coat of green material and a flourishing cravat of the same inspiring color."[20]

A wealthy Harvard graduate, Hall conveyed an aura of literary sophistication but also tried his best to connect with the public, dispensing with the formal greeting, "Your Honor," enjoyed by previous mayors. The sight of an establishment figure reaching out and putting his stamp of approval on Irish American culture helped an embattled minority feel all the more at home in its adopted land.[21]

As the Democratic resurgence continued in New York, and as Tweed groomed Governor Hoffman to run for the White House in 1872, Mayor Hall became his heir apparent. During the first half of 1871, both Hoffman and Hall focused on building records of achievement they could campaign on, while trying to project at least the impression of their independence from Tweed. Mayor Hall won praise from both parties for taking on the Herculean task of implementing the new charter and demonstrating its advantages over the state commissions that once controlled the city's affairs.[22]

However, Tweed had duped reformers, led by the venerable Peter Cooper, into supporting a new charter that was in fact designed to facilitate the theft of money from the public treasury. As the city's mercantile elite welcomed the charter and signed new contracts with the city, Tweed drew them into his web. By July 1871, Tweed's unprecedented personal power over the city and state had reached its apex.[23]

Building on the corrupt system put in place by Fernando Wood during his mayoralty in the 1850s, four men—Tweed, Sweeny, Connolly, and Hall—comprised a "Ring," which divided the kickbacks from padded city contracts. What began as a 10 percent levy on all city and county contracts eventually reached 65 percent in 1869. Some bills sent to Comptroller Connolly's office were not merely padded but entirely invented; others were for work that was never completed, or contracting jobs for the mansions of the Ring members that were billed to the city at exorbitant rates.[24]

Tweed's share of the total intake of cash reached 25 percent, Connolly's 20, Sweeny's 10, and Hall's 5 percent, with another 5 percent for the bagmen, and the rest for bribing members of the legislatures in the city and at Albany.[25] In all, an estimated forty-five million dollars was stolen, making the principals extremely wealthy.[26]*

On July 8, 1871, the *Times* began publishing extensive revelations of Tweed's corruption, backed up with proof in the form of comptroller's records turned over by an unhappy insider, former sheriff James O'Brien. While the Ring members stonewalled, conferred, and plotted how to betray each other and save themselves, the banks on both sides of the Atlantic that had nourished Tweed's reign soon cut off the city's credit.[27]

While New York's skyrocketing bonded debt was one vulnerability, the identification of Tammany in the public mind with the Irish and with urban violence, which Tweed's organization had tried to transform ever since July 1863, soon proved to be another key to his downfall. Just four days after the first revelations in the *Times,* and exactly eight years after the draft riots, on July 12, 1871, rioting between Irish Catholics and Protestant during a parade

---

*The amount stolen was the equivalent of almost one billion dollars today.

helped set in motion the end of Tweed's reign and the final phase of the Democracy's resurgence as a national party.[28]

The city's Orangemen wanted a permit to march on the anniversary of the Battle of the Boyne, but they had clashed with Catholics at previous celebrations, including the last parade, in 1870, so Mayor Hall denied the permit to forestall any violence. When the Orangemen orchestrated a public outcry for their right to march and accused the mayor of caving in to Catholic threats, Governor Hoffman intervened, and the parade took place under heavy militia protection. Angry Catholics massed along the parade route, a shot rang out, and the militia fired into the crowd. When the conflict was over, more than a hundred people lay dead or wounded. It was the worst violence the city had seen since the draft riots.[29]

Coming on the heels of the revolutionary Paris Commune that spring, after which many radicals had fled to New York City, the Orange riot brought class tension and fear of communism to a fever pitch.[30] The Orange riot, blamed by many on the alliance of Tammany and the city's Irish Catholics, revived memories of the draft riots and triggered a strong response from conservative elites—a fear of mob rule and a decisive law-and-order approach to handling the urban poor—which further exacerbated class tensions.[31]

Journalist Joel Tyler Headley linked the Orange riot and the Paris Commune, lumping the Irish and French radicals together as a threat from overseas, and helping to spark a fresh wave of nativism. Protestant leaders denounced the "supremacy of political Irish Catholics." An influential anti-Tammany pamphlet, with illustrations by Thomas Nast, labeled the "Hibernian Riot" as "communism, Murder, Socialism, Robbery, Arson."[32]

The pamphlet also signaled that the riot of 1871 had unleashed "the Insurrection of the Capitalists," a backlash that was gathering momentum and would eventually manifest itself in antidemocratic efforts by affluent New Yorkers to restrict suffrage by instituting property requirements for whites as well as blacks. The elite hoped to focus public attention on the rights of the "better classes"—the city's taxpayers—who deserved to be free from mob rule and the wasteful corruption of Tammany Hall.[33]

The elite saw themselves as crusaders against the excesses of Jacksonian democracy, the new laws of the 1820s and 1830s that created a horde of working-class, foreign-born voters, providing a power base for a new breed of demagogic, professional politician, exemplified by Fernando Wood, William Tweed, and others who had risen from humble origins to positions of great power. The reformers declared that the absence of elite, disinterested men, who had turned away from politics in disgust during the middle decades of the nineteenth century, left a vacuum that was filled by demagogues, who set the stage for the draft riots and the Orange riot and posed a continuing threat to society.[34]

While the prosecution of the draft rioters in 1863 had helped Hall rise from district attorney to mayor, and Hoffman from city recorder to governor, the Orange riot unraveled their promising careers. The *Irish-American* excused Hall while pinning the blame on Hoffman for the bloodbath because he had allowed the Protestants to have their anti-Catholic parade. Hall broke off his close working relationship with the governor but could not escape some share of responsibility for the event, and Tammany as a whole suffered, drawing the wrath of both Catholics and nativists. Upstate and city Democrats took sides with the governor and mayor respectively, while Republicans linked Tammany with riots and mayhem. Tweed's machine would come crashing down in part because it failed to keep the fragile peace it had engineered in the wake of the draft riots.[35]

The Orange riot, however, was only half of Tweed's catastrophic troubles. Because Peter Cooper's Citizens' Association had been discredited by its approval of Tweed's charter, Samuel Tilden and William Havemeyer called a meeting at Cooper Union on September 4, 1871, to launch the Council for Political Reform. Havemeyer, scion of an old New York family, who won the mayoral race twice in the 1840s, represented the breed of elite politician that had been largely absent from city politics in recent decades. Tilden had long been in competition with Tammany for control of the party in the city and state. He welcomed the opportunity to bring down Tweed and his circle—without destroying the Democratic party.[36]

The merchants and financiers at the meeting—including Belmont, Opdyke, and real estate developer Samuel Ruggles—decried the Ring's frauds as an assault on the rights of taxpayers and property owners like themselves. They also agreed to appoint a committee, called the Committee of Seventy, to investigate the accusations in the *Times* and bring charges against the Ring members. The bipartisan committee would include Havemeyer, a Democrat, as its chairman; Republican Union League members Joseph Choate and Robert Roosevelt;* Democrat-turned-Republican John Dix, picked by Lincoln in 1863 to supervise the resumption of the draft; and wealthy merchants from both parties, such as Theodore Steinway, the piano manufacturer.[37]

Tilden, while not a member of the Committee of Seventy, as chairman of the state Democratic organization led the party in calling for a full disclosure of the facts. Careful and methodical, Tilden gradually emerged as the party's guiding light. Clearly referring to Tweed in a major speech, Tilden declared, "It is time now to proclaim and to enforce the doctrine that whoever plunders the people, though he steals the livery of Heaven to serve the devil . . . is no Democrat."[38]

---

*Father of the future U.S. president Theodore Roosevelt.

The New York Irish were both the devils and the white knights of the Tweed Ring's demise, which, like the draft riots, exposed the fallacy of anti-Irish stereotypes. The reformers turned to Charles O'Conor, the respected Irish Catholic lawyer whose father, Thomas, had edited the *Shamrock,* New York's first Irish newspaper. O'Conor was appointed special state attorney general to trace the public funds embezzled by the Ring. Tilden's choice to replace Tweed at the head of Tammany was "Honest" John Kelly, a devout Irish Catholic and untainted former city sheriff.[39]

A week after the reformers gathered at Cooper Union, the foursome that comprised the Ring met to plot damage control. Mayor Hall suggested that if Comptroller Connolly stepped down, the whole scandal might blow over. Sweeny concurred, while Tweed hung back, appearing to side with Connolly against those who would make him take the fall for the Ring. In a city abuzz with rumor, where little remained secret, or even out of the press, George Templeton Strong caught wind of the meeting. "It is understood," he wrote in his diary, "that Hall and Sweeny are in alliance, offensive and defensive, against Tweed and Conn[olly]—skunk vs. rattlesnake."[40]

On top of the Orange riot and the investigation of fraud, Tweed's Tammany Hall faced a continuing challenge from New York's labor unions, which were fielding independent candidates and fighting for enforcement of the state's eight-hour law. Despite the rain on September 13, some eight thousand workers marched down Broadway to City Hall, denouncing Tammany and declaring their solidarity with the city's stonecutters, who were striking for an eight-hour day.

Along with American-born, Irish, French, and German workers, a group of African American trade unionists joined the procession, which culminated in a mass meeting at Cooper Union and a resolution to "throw off all allegiance to the Democratic party in the Fall elections." The presence of blacks signaled that the working class had slowly begun, in the wake of the Fifteenth Amendment, to reject Tammany's vision of a whites-only society and to disavow the racial violence of the draft riots.[41]

The pressures mounted within the Ring and from the investigators. Connolly became the first Ring member to defect and put his fate in the reformers' hands: He contacted Havemeyer, once his boss in the private sector, to ask for a meeting with Tilden. On September 15, Tilden informed Connolly that his political career was over, but also instructed him to remain in office and appoint Andrew Haswell Green as his temporary deputy and successor, as permitted by Tweed's new charter. Ironically, a loophole created to maintain the Ring's hold on the comptroller's office became Tilden's tool for putting his own man in place and bringing the records of the city treasury to light.[42]

Connolly's supporters, the rank-and-file Irish Democrats of the Twenty-first Ward, believed the comptroller had been forced to take the fall for the rest of the Ring because he was Irish, and they gathered near City Hall on September 16 to protest his treatment. However, once it became clear that Connolly had betrayed the other three men—and effectively abandoned the constituents who depended on him for jobs and promotion—his life was in danger, and a police guard was stationed at his office, where he continued to go every day, as instructed by Tilden. "I should not care to insure his life," wrote George Templeton Strong.[43]

The reformers also feared the Ring members might incite the masses on their behalf, producing violence on a scale similar to that of the draft riots. By the end of September, stewardship of the city treasury had been turned over to Green, payments had been frozen, and five thousand angry Parks Department laborers had gone without pay for weeks. Under the heading "LET US HAVE NO RIOT," Greeley's *Tribune* chastised Hall, Tweed, and Sweeny for not cooperating with Green to resolve the crisis and for blaming it on the reformers in order to enrage the workers.

> There is to be tonight, at the main entrance of the Central Park, a mass-meeting of these men—men who recognize only that they are about to be dismissed from work. They will not stop to think that they are to be thrown out of employment because the Ring has robbed the treasurer and now refuses to aid the acting treasury of the City in providing new resources . . . We have been told that men prominent in the riots of 1863 will appear at this meeting to-night, and that a man named Burke, the leader of the rioters of that year, will seek to incite like disturbances to-night.

Greeley declared that a "large force of policemen should be in attendance," to "protect these men from the dangerous influence of the leaders of the mob by suppressing every riotous indication on their part."[44] In the end, the fifty thousand dollars for the city employees' back pay came from Tweed's pocket, but Green, the acting comptroller, never reimbursed him, on the assumption that the money had been stolen from the city in the first place.[45]

Having angered both the elite and the working class, Tammany lost badly in city elections that fall, and reformers won control of the state legislature.[46] At the end of November, Tilden moved in for the kill by having Connolly arrested in his own office and held for bail of one million dollars. The press initially sympathized with Connolly since he had been cooperating when Tilden betrayed him. The notorious Judge George Barnard, who had used writs of habeas corpus to free prisoners at the height of the draft riots, did the same for Connolly.[47]

When Tilden produced further evidence against Tweed, the state supreme court issued a warrant for his arrest. Tweed easily posted the million-dollar bond, but his political power, like that of Connolly, Hall, and Sweeny, had been destroyed. On December 30, Tammany Hall voted to expel all four members of the Ring and began a new era under "Honest" John Kelly. Two days later, on January 1, 1872, Connolly and his wife escaped to Europe, reportedly with six million dollars. Sweeny settled the claim of the city against him, and Mayor Hall was acquitted in two separate trials. Tweed, after several trials, an escape from prison, and recapture in Spain, became the only Ring member to end his life behind bars.[48]

Having purged Tweed from the Democratic party, Tilden gained a national reputation for integrity. Even as he helped complete the revitalization of the party and carried it into the future, his message was still based on traditional Jacksonian principles of local control and limited government. It was a conservative message in the guise of reform: that honest, efficient government should allow free trade but serve the needs of the business community. The hostility to Republican activist government—and the rights of blacks—remained strong.[49]

When the Tweed Ring began to collapse in the summer of 1871, Greeley had just returned to New York from a tour of the South and continued his campaign for "Universal Amnesty." He saw "the policy of excluding from office the leading men of the South as a very great mistake and a very great injury to the National cause and to the Republican party." During congressional reconstruction, Greeley argued, the military governor of South Carolina

> was crippled and enfeebled in his effort to govern that State well by the fact that her best men, her most intelligent men, her most considerate and conservative men, were not available to him as magistrates because of an exclusion whereof Andrew Johnson was the author. He said, "I cannot govern South Carolina as well as I could if I were able to choose the best men to help me, instead of the second-best." I am entirely of that conviction. I believe it was a mistake, when you allowed a million Confederates to vote for Members of Congress, to deny them the right to vote for just such men as they preferred.[50]

With this elitist emphasis on the "best men" as the appropriate leaders of society, Greeley's ideas and rhetoric were beginning to converge with those of a small but influential group of reformers in the North that included editors, economists, businessmen, and political figures, who shared a dogmatic belief in the tenets of classical British liberalism: faith in the free market and sound money based on the gold standard. In politics as in economics, reform ideology insisted on a minimal role for government.

For liberal reformers, the Tweed Ring and other political machines, both Democratic and Republican, embodied the dangers of big government, namely wasteful tax-and-spend policies and rampant corruption. Members of the Citizens' Association in New York embodied this reform impulse, but its leaders and adherents could be found in both the Northeast and the Midwest—in Boston, Cincinnati, and Chicago—while the movement's doctrines were taking root in colleges across the North. E. L. Godkin of the *Nation* was a chief exponent of liberal reform, as were the politicians Carl Schurz and James Garfield, both outspoken critics of Reconstruction, and of federal intervention in the South during Grant's first term.[51]

Counting the presidents of Harvard and Yale among their members, these prominent and highly educated urban intellectuals described themselves as the "best men" and denounced northern workers, Tammany-style demagogues, and railroad speculators as an "ignorant proletariat and a half-taught plutocracy." The liberal reformers also turned their verbal arsenal against Republican corruption in the South, where they found a parallel situation: the votes of a black underclass marshaled by "thieving carpetbaggers" who had taken over the state governments and were exploiting the South for financial gain.[52]

"They are fellows who crawled down South in the track of our armies, generally at a very safe distance in the rear," Greeley explained in a speech. "They got into the Legislatures; they went into issuing State bonds; they pretended to use them in aid of railroads and other improvements. But the improvements were not made, and the bonds stuck in the issuers' pockets. That is the pity of it." Most of the carpetbaggers were admirable, Greeley acknowledged, and risked their lives to help the former slaves and rebuild the South. The corrupt few, however, were enough to sow hatred against the Republican party.[53]

It was time for amnesty, said the liberal reformers, for their counterparts in the South—the "best men," as Greeley had pointedly called them—to resume their role as the "natural leaders" of the shattered region. This return to home rule would amount to white supremacy, but Greeley and Schurz both argued that blacks would be better off. Greeley envisioned an atmosphere of reconciliation in which moderate whites, former Whigs like himself, would join the southern Republican party, and the Klan would fade away.[54]

.   .   .

By 1871, the liberal reformers were looking to the following year's election and were using the term *Grantism* to pin a host of problems on the president. In the South, he was using "bayonet rule" to sustain corrupt "carpetbag-negro government." In the North, Grant took the blame for presiding over a Republican party that had once been animated by radical idealism and had devolved after the Civil War into a collection of state-party machines that existed for the purpose of funneling federal patronage jobs—the spoils of office—to their constituents.[55]

Grant's cabinet consisted of loyal cronies instead of experienced, influential political figures, and the administration had become mired in one scandal or debacle after another. The president's own political naïveté led him to socialize with Jay Gould and Jim Fisk, notorious speculators in gold and railroads who brought on the market crash of 1869 known as Black Friday. Grant also lent his support to land speculators lobbying for the annexation of Santo Domingo (today's Dominican Republic), and he allowed opponents in Congress to sabotage civil service reform, the introduction of a merit-based program of competitive exams intended to replace the spoils system.[56]

The liberal reformers initially hoped to take hold of the Republican party machinery and run their own presidential candidate in 1872, but recognizing Grant's strength and resilience, they made plans instead to splinter off and create a new party.[57] Greeley took note of the state races in Virginia, Tennessee, and Missouri, where fusion tickets of reform Republicans and Democrats had won upset victories in 1870, and began to consider joining in the liberals' revolt.

In the *Tribune*, Greeley ran exposés of Grantism, from embezzlement at the New York Customs House to carpetbagger corruption, and exhorted regular Republicans to embrace reform before the scandals emanating from Washington ruined the party. At the same time, he struggled with the decision to bolt the party he had helped create and whose new breed of spoilsmen, the "Stalwarts," increasingly returned his scorn. In April 1871, Greeley finally cut the cord: The *Tribune* came out against Grant's reelection.[58]

In September, Carl Schurz made a speech in Nashville that marked the Liberal Republicans' entry into the presidential race as a full-fledged third party and announced their program of hard money, lower tariffs and taxes, civil service reform, ending land grants to railroads, and, above all, replacing Reconstruction in the South with "local self-government."* The party would

---

*"Hard money" advocates favored a conservative monetary policy. They wanted to limit the supply of paper currency in order to control inflation, a gold standard, and the repayment of war debts in silver or gold as opposed to "greenbacks" issued by the government. Debtors, both public and private, by contrast, preferred to pay back their obligations in paper currency.

hold its convention in Cincinnati the following May to choose a candidate. "Reconstruction and slavery we have done with;" wrote E. L. Godkin in the *Nation,* "for administrative and revenue reform we are eager."[59]

Tweed's downfall and the Orange riot had taken Governor Hoffman out of the running, and the New York Democrats lacked a presidential contender. Schurz, who could not be president because he was born abroad, contacted Democratic National Committee chairman August Belmont and secretly sounded him out on his party's support for a ticket consisting of the frosty and aristocratic diplomat Charles Francis Adams and the more fiery Senator Lyman Trumbull. However, by May 1872, when the Liberal Republicans convened in Cincinnati, various disgruntled founders of the regular party, including radicals like George Julian and Reuben Fenton as well as Lincoln's confidant, Judge David Davis, had joined the revolt, creating a long list of potential nominees.[60]

Greeley, who had been waiting decades for a political appointment and had served just one term in the House during his long career, also declared his availability in the customary way—by loudly denying any interest in the nomination. The daily and weekly editions of the *Tribune,* his speaking tours, and his antislavery activism made Greeley both well known and popular around the country; his support for protective tariffs, however, and his eccentric persona made him an unlikely pick for the genteel free-traders of the Liberal Republican party, who favored Adams. Nonetheless, Greeley's protégé at the *Tribune,* Whitelaw Reid, went to Cincinnati and managed to get his boss's name in the running.

When the convention got under way, the prime contenders, Adams and Davis, reached a stalemate after five ballots; in the frenzied realignment of votes for the sixth round, Reid and his team worked the convention floor and gathered enough support to win Greeley the nomination, with Governor B. Gratz Brown of Missouri as his running mate. The news caused a stir in New York. A reporter from the *Sun* was interviewing Greeley in his office when the sound of cannon fire from City Hall Park thundered through the *Tribune* building. From his window, Greeley looked down at the smoke from the guns and the enormous crowd in front of the building. The sights and sounds were reminiscent of the draft riots, but now the guns were an official salute, and the people were cheering and shouting, "Go it, Uncle Horace!"[61]

Like other leaders of the Liberal movement, Schurz was shocked and disgusted by the outcome and asked Greeley to withdraw, but he refused. "That Grant is an Ass, no man can deny, but better an Ass than a mischievous Idiot," an Ohio Liberal complained of Greeley. William Cullen Bryant, Greeley's longtime competitor at the New York *Evening Post,* called the nomination "sheer insanity." Nonetheless, most Liberal Republicans reluctantly rallied behind him with a slogan that captured both their fervor and their ambivalence: "Anything to beat Grant !"[62]

When word of Greeley's nomination in Cincinnati reached Washington, Fernando Wood shared in the "loud and general guffaw" that "broke out all over the [House] floor." It was hard to take Old White Coat seriously—with all his faddish enthusiasms and eccentricities—but even harder for Wood to support the man who had been his archenemy for the past forty years, opposing and harassing him on every issue: slavery, tariffs, the draft riots, the Irish, temperance, and Sabbath laws, among others.[63]

Nonetheless, Wood, like the rest of the northern Democratic party, saw no choice but to endorse him and ally with the Liberal Republicans, for lack of an alternative candidate, and because Greeley supported the working man, advocated a general amnesty for Confederates, and pushed for an end to military intervention in the South with federal troops. Thus developed the astonishing spectacle of Greeley also being nominated by the Democrats at their convention in July, after which the party took up the Liberals' slogan, "Anything to beat Grant." Northern Democrats tried to rally behind Greeley, who had once embodied wartime radical Republicanism and denounced them as treasonous Copperheads.[64]

Democratic politicians who wanted to move the party forward saw his former radicalism as an asset that would help them shed the stigma of disloyalty. Although Marble detested Greeley personally, and would not support him, the *World* asserted that Greeley's nomination "cut the party loose from the dead issues of an effete past." Ever since their failure to block ratification of the Fifteenth Amendment, the Democrats had been toning down their overt racist rhetoric and focusing on their traditional message of fiscal conservatism and small government. Arch-Copperhead Clement Vallandigham's surprising conversion to the new party line made sense because the Democrats, despite their professions about accepting the consequences of the Civil War, remained firm in their opposition to federal enforcement of the Reconstruction amendments. Their "New Departure" rang hollow.[65]

Scouting the Democrats' motives, the pioneering abolitionist William Lloyd Garrison condemned the Liberal Republican party as "simply a stool pigeon for the Democracy to capture the Presidency." Making a similar point, a Thomas Nast cartoon depicted Greeley as the captain of a pirate ship, concealing heavily armed Confederates belowdecks, ready to capture another vessel, the American government.[66] The prominent feminist and abolitionist Lydia Maria Child declared she would prefer "the Devil himself" to the Democrats "at the helm of the ship of state."[67]

Indeed, since Greeley was at odds with Liberal Republicans on free trade, his campaign ended up focusing on the two issues that united the reformers

July 20, 1872, *Vanity Fair* cartoon of Greeley as a presidential
candidate: "Anything to beat Grant."

and were also the Democrats' priorities: a general amnesty and home rule in
the South. Since very few Confederate officials were still banned from voting
and holding office, Republicans in Congress sought to eliminate the largely
symbolic issue by immediately passing an amnesty law that embraced all but
the most hard-core ex-rebels. However, black congressmen were outraged.
Elected in the South after the new state constitutions of 1867–68 gave blacks
the vote, they saw the bill as a harbinger of Reconstruction's total demise.[68]*

Greeley provoked a storm of controversy when he declared his "confident trust that the masses of our countrymen . . . are eager to clasp hands

---

*Blacks in Congress included Congressmen Benjamin Turner of Alabama, Robert Smalls and
Robert Elliot of South Carolina, and Senator Blanche Bruce of Mississippi.

across the bloody chasm which has too long divided them." The campaign degenerated into one of the most vicious presidential contests in American history. Nast lambasted Greeley with a series of cartoons that showed him shaking hands with rebels over the dead body of a Union soldier, across the Andersonville prison, over a black Klan victim, and even with John Wilkes Booth across Lincoln's grave.[69]

Even before the campaign, Greeley had shifted from a long career of speaking out for African Americans to criticizing them in the same harsh terms used by Democrats. In letters and speeches, Greeley declared that the former slaves should not be coddled by welfare agencies but left to their own devices; otherwise the innate laziness and weakness of their race would be encouraged. In 1872, the *Tribune* declared that the biracial Reconstruction governments, rife with "ignorance and degradation," should be supplanted by "local self-government."[70]

Greeley also became estranged at this time from the working class, for which he had such long-standing sympathy. In the spring and summer of 1872, an estimated one hundred thousand workers in New York launched a massive strike for the eight-hour day. Labor's growing organizational efforts frightened the managerial classes—sensitized by the draft riots, the Paris Commune, and the Orange riot—and they ultimately rejected this powerful bid for greater respect and more control in the workplace. After six tense weeks, employers closed ranks, and the strike finally collapsed. Greeley's absence from labor's side, on the campaign trail, was a symptom of the growing elitism, articulated by the Liberals, that would curb the aspirations of workers in the Gilded Age.[71]

Instead of sitting on the porch of his house in Chappaqua and playing the reluctant candidate, as the tradition of American presidential campaigns dictated and his doctor advised, Greeley embarked on a relentless whistle-stop tour across the country. In Indiana, he explained his abolitionist past as part of his struggle for the American worker: "I was in the days of slavery an enemy of slavery, because I thought slavery inconsistent with the rights, dignity and highest well-being of free labor . . . I was anxious first of all for labor—that the laboring class should everywhere be free men." He also spoke about the need for Americans to come together again as "one people." In Ohio, he asked farmers, "Shall ours be a Union cemented only by bayonets, or shall it be a Union of hearts and hopes and hands?"[72]

Blacks in the South stood by Grant, as did most northern Republicans, who, for the moment, were still more outraged by Klan violence than by Grant's exercise of bayonet rule.[73] Grant's political organization also wielded huge amounts of campaign money, much of it from railroad magnates and other corporate donors anxious to stop the liberal reformers in their tracks. Despite Greeley's strenuous efforts, his chances dwindled rapidly.[74]

Greeley was also worn out from years of overexertion on the lecture circuit and at the *Tribune* office. The punishing campaign schedule sapped his last reserves of strength. On the campaign trail in October, he received jolting news from his daughter Ida that his wife, Mary, already chronically ill with rheumatism and other complaints, was in failing health. Having neglected to stop at the farm in Chappaqua to check on her a month earlier, and perceiving the political defeat that loomed in November, Greeley was overcome with regret and canceled his tour. He brought Mary into the city, where she could receive the best medical care, but she died at the end of October.[75]

A week later, Grant beat Greeley in a landslide victory. Winning thirty-one of the thirty-seven states, Grant had lost only three southern states (Georgia, Tennessee, and Texas) and three border states (Kentucky, Maryland, and Missouri). The Republicans also retained control of the House and Senate. Grant's crackdown on the Klan had produced a relatively peaceful day of voting across the South, marred only by violence in Georgia, where Democratic officials failed to protect blacks and other Republicans from attack. Despite narrow margins of victory in some states, Republicans hailed the overall result as proof that "home rule" in the South did not mean Democratic, white supremacy—if the whole population was permitted to vote without coercion and fear.

The Liberal Republican ticket suffered in part because many Democrats simply could not bring themselves to vote for Greeley and stayed away from the polls.[76] Having lost his political career and his wife, Greeley not only was in mourning but soon suffered a nervous breakdown. He clung vainly to the *Tribune,* in which he had failed to amass a controlling share, being disorganized with his finances, overly generous, and chronically in debt.

The *Tribune's* publisher and business manager, Samuel Sinclair, owned 20 percent of its shares. He was corralling the other owners and scheming to sell off the *Tribune* to William Orton, president of the Western Union Telegraph Company, who planned to install Greeley's nemesis from the regular Republican machine, Grant's conniving and corrupt former vice president, Schuyler ("Smiler") Colfax, as editor in chief. The infamous Jay Gould, who embodied the venality of the Gilded Age, also formed part of the wolf pack around the ailing Greeley, ready to buy out the troublesome, reformist newspaper. Greeley's handpicked successor, Whitelaw Reid, was to be ousted, but Greeley suspected him of treachery too and plunged into depression and a not unwarranted paranoia.[77]

Greeley took to his bed, where he scribbled hysterically, trying to write a will and to call in outstanding loans for the sake of his two daughters' inheritance. "Having done wrong to millions, while intending only good to hundreds, I pray God that he may quickly take me from a world where all I have done seems to have turned to evil," Greeley scrawled on *Tribune* notepaper. Rushed to a private mental hospital a few miles from Chappaqua, he was examined by renowned doctors, who diagnosed "nervous prostration," the *Tribune* reported. Greeley had bouts of delirium and soon slipped into a coma. He died on November 29 at the age of sixty-one.

"Plant me in my favorite pumpkin arbor, with a gooseberry bush for a footstone," Uncle Horace, the Sage of Chappaqua, had written, but his friends and colleagues would not hear of it. Clergymen, governors, and editors of all political stripes attended his stately funeral on Fifth Avenue, where even Greeley's various adversaries, including William Cullen Bryant and Manton Marble, delivered decorous eulogies. Across the country, and across the Atlantic, newspapers carried obituaries full of praise for Greeley and expressions of the public's "profound sorrow." Crowds of New Yorkers lined the avenue, church bells chimed, and the city stood still while the procession—with President Grant in a carriage near the front—took Greeley to Brooklyn's Green-Wood Cemetery.[78]*

Marble's *World* described Greeley as "a great light of American journalism and perhaps the most remarkable American of his period." Bryant's *Evening Post* declared that in the fight to end slavery, "we doubt whether any single instrument used against the gigantic wrong was more effective in the work of its gradual overthrow than the press which [Greeley] managed with so much courage and determination." When Greeley began denouncing slavery, the paper reminded readers, "the prejudices of the public mind were so fierce that it was as much as one's life was worth to speak even timidly against the horrible wrong. The most gentle hint, the softest whisper of persuasion, was likely to provoke a mob."[79]

Summing up Greeley's rise from obscurity, the *Evening Post* concluded: "Mr. Greeley won his place of influence and distinction by the sheer force of his intellectual ability and the determination of his character. By good natural abilities, by industry, by temperance, by sympathy with what is noblest and best in human nature, and by earnest purpose, the ignorant, friendless, unknown printer's boy of a few years since became the powerful and famous journalist, whose words went to the ends of the earth, affecting the destinies of all mankind."[80]

*See the Walking Tour in the appendix.

CHAPTER 23

A Final Devil's Bargain: The End of Reconstruction

~◯

With Grant's reelection in 1872, one Republican newspaper declared it was "scarcely possible to doubt that this will be the death of the Democratic party."[1] Manton Marble read the future differently—and more accurately. As he explained in the *World* on November 15, the election was instead the death knell of the radical Republican movement. In order to oppose Grant's political organization, which had excluded them, Charles Sumner and other aging founders of the Republican party had supported Greeley's anti-Reconstruction candidacy, confirming that radicalism as a set of principles had disintegrated. With the retirement of these erstwhile giants, Marble declared, regular Republicans would have to draw candidates from the mediocre Stalwarts who now ran the party machinery.[2]

Pushing the northern Democracy's deceptive "New Departure" strategy—of accepting the Reconstruction amendments but opposing their enforcement by insisting on home rule in the South—Marble declared that the "Negro question" was resolved at last, and the two major parties should go head-to-head on economic policy. In a bid to absorb the Liberal Republican movement, Marble called on Democrats to embrace a free-trade philosophy, as expounded by the leading liberal reformers. Marble declared that the immediate task was to "reunite all who held Democratic doctrines before the Republican party was formed, and to reinforce them by the numerous recent converts to the same order of economic and political ideas."[3]

Marble's wish would be fulfilled in the course of the next

few years: While Schurz went back to the regular Republican party, many important Liberal Republicans, including Trumbull, Julian, and Adams, allied themselves with the Democrats. William Lloyd Garrison's warning in 1872—that the Democrats were using the Liberal Republican party as a stalking horse to retake the White House—continued to be valid; the Democrats were borrowing the prestige of the Liberals to burnish a new, more respectable image.[4]

The Democrats were also helped along in their struggle for survival and resurgence by the Panic of 1873 and the ensuing Great Depression, which reached its nadir five years later but lasted, with ups and downs, for about a quarter of a century.* The feverish expansion of the railroads and the overextension of credit that fueled the booming economy in the decade after the Civil War created a bubble that was bound to burst.[5]

Like the fifty years before the Civil War, the Reconstruction era was one of bewildering national growth and change. Within a mere eight years after the war, the industrial output of the United States had grown by 75 percent, while the North and West had absorbed three million new immigrants. Outside of farming, the railroads employed more workers than any other sector of the economy. The railroads in turn spawned new industries and technologies, including the use of coal instead of wood to produce steam, the refrigerated railroad car, and, as a result, meat processing and packing. Coal and pig iron production grew by more than 100 percent, and the Bessemer process for making steel became more widespread in the decade after the war. Between 1866 and 1873, the railroads added thirty-five thousand miles of new track, matching the entire amount laid down in the previous thirty-five years. In 1869, the completion of the transcontinental railroad, largely by Irish and Chinese laborers, thrilled the nation and the world.[6]

This westward growth had its darker side. Grant's campaign call for "Peace" did not include the Plains Indians, who clashed with federal troops and were driven from their ancestral homelands. Railroads and large farms destroyed the buffalo herds which the Native Americans depended on for survival, and their territory shrank to the reservations allotted by the federal government. The Indians were rarely replaced by settlers working small family plots, as envisioned by free-labor ideology: Slavery in the South had been destroyed, but in the West indentured Chinese and Mexican workers labored on immense commercial farms served by the new railroads. And while the

---

*Until the stock market crash of 1929 and the ensuing depression of the 1930s, the economic contraction following the Panic of 1873 was known as the Great Depression.

railroads reduced freight costs and turned the country into a single sprawling marketplace, the exuberant capital investment on Wall Street, across the North, and in the West largely bypassed the former Confederacy, stifling its postwar recovery and progress—economic, political, and social.[7]

Moreover, the fast pace of railroad expansion, made possible by government land grants and loans, led to poor-quality tracks, corruption, and precarious financing schemes.[8] After failing to sell a multimillion-dollar bond issue for the Northern Pacific Railroad in September 1873, Jay Cooke and Company of Philadelphia, one of the country's major banks, collapsed, triggering the Panic, which shut down the supply of credit throughout the financial system, ruined businesses, and created massive unemployment.[9]

In the depths of the depression, most of the country's railroads stopped laying track and went bankrupt, which hurt iron producers and other related industries, destroying companies by the thousands. Whereas the American economy before the Civil War had been in transition from preindustrial manufacturing to mechanized production, by 1873, that transformation was all but complete, and the United States was rapidly eclipsing England as the world's largest manufacturer; the depression, which also afflicted western Europe, marked the "first great crisis of industrial capitalism."[10]

Democrats benefited in various ways from the crisis. Because of anxiety about militant labor protests and violent strikes sparked by wage cuts and unemployment, "the labor question" would soon overshadow "the Negro question" as northerners' chief concern. Northern apathy about the plight of blacks would help pave the way for "home rule" in the South and the demise of Reconstruction.[11]

Moreover, with northerners struggling to make ends meet, Democrats succeeded in blaming the depression on the party in power, the Republicans. In the wake of the Crédit Mobilier scandal—involving the cozy, profitable relationship between directors of the Union Pacific Railroad and certain members of Congress—economic distress enabled the Democrats to call for reform and to sharpen their attacks on bloated and corrupt government, both in Washington and under the carpetbaggers in the South.* After a trail of scandals in the Grant administration, northerners began to listen more closely to Democrats' often exaggerated charges of corruption in the carpetbagger governments.[12]

---

*Crédit Mobilier was the name of a construction company created by Union Pacific's stockholders. The directors of the combined companies profited by awarding padded railroad construction contracts to Crédit Mobilier. To deflect government scrutiny, several congressmen were drawn into the arrangement with gifts of stock. After the scandal broke in 1872, Americans no longer accepted elected officials' conflicts of interest as an innocuous part of business as usual.

•   •   •

Louisiana's Reconstruction government was an egregious example of that corruption, and even Republicans in Washington admitted it: The carpetbag governor, William Kellogg, was a scoundrel, and his administration would fall unless backed by federal force. Disputed gubernatorial and legislative election results in Louisiana in 1872 had led to the formation of two competing state governments. A federal district court ruled in favor of the Republicans, but instead of backing down, the Democrats organized armed bands, called the White League, that controlled the rural areas covering most of the state.[13]

Attacking white and black Republicans, the white guerrilla government encountered little effective resistance from the police, the state's mostly black militia, or federal troops stationed primarily in New Orleans. At Colfax, Louisiana, on April 13, 1873, the White League massacred the militia, killing some seventy black men, many of whom had already surrendered. More than one hundred of the White Leaguers were arrested and indicted by federal authorities. The following year, in the run-up to the fall elections, six Republican officials were murdered near Shreveport, and a massive riot broke out in New Orleans two weeks later, leaving thirty dead and one hundred wounded. The police and militia had failed to subdue the White League, and Grant sent more troops to the state.[14]

Federal troops restored relative calm to Louisiana during the 1874 midterm elections, but they had scant effect in rural areas, where blacks were generally coerced to vote the Democratic ticket. When Republican election officials invalidated the returns from several parishes, the status of five Democratic candidates was thrown into doubt. After the elections, Democrats attempted forcibly to seat the five legislators, and Governor Kellogg called in federal troops, who removed them from the statehouse.[15]

This display of military force against civil authority shocked the nation, and many Republicans joined the Democratic outcry. Such a dangerous precedent threatened the very foundations of free government, warned Carl Schurz. "If this can be done in Louisiana," he asked, "how long will it be before it can be done in Massachusetts and Ohio? . . . How long before a soldier may stalk into the national House of Representatives, and, pointing to the Speaker's mace, say, 'Take away that bauble!'"[16]

In Boston, a cockpit of the American Revolution, outraged residents held a public meeting at Faneuil Hall, where they denounced General Philip Sheridan, whose forces had entered the state capitol in New Orleans, while likening the White League and its struggle for freedom to that of the founding fathers. When the renowned abolitionist Wendell Phillips rose to declare the necessity of protecting freedmen in the South, he was heckled by the gathering and drowned out. The New York Times observed that Phillips and

William Lloyd Garrison were all but "extinct from American politics," especially in their "ideas in regard to the South."[17]

In New York, Cincinnati, and other cities, sympathetic Republican leaders addressed rallies organized by Democrats, whose newspapers called for Grant's impeachment and new legal restrictions on presidential use of the military. "Tyranny!" howled Manton Marble's *World.* "A Sovereign State Murdered." The removal of the Democratic legislators, declared the *New Orleans Daily Picayune,* proved that Kellogg's carpetbagger government, "brought forth by bayonets" and "nursed by bayonets," could not function without them.[18]

However, Sheridan called the White Leaguers "banditti" and urged that they be prosecuted in military courts. A majority of radical Republicans, and even some moderates, agreed. One radical Republican paper declared, "Better military rule for forty years than the South be given over to lawlessness and blood for a day."[19]

This was, in essence, the same advice the Union League gave Lincoln regarding New York after the draft riots. Tragically, the situation in the South echoed Lincoln's very real dilemma over launching an investigation and imposing martial law eleven years earlier. Ultimately, Americans in both the North and South were more upset by the spectacle of federal troops intervening to eject Democratic legislators from a statehouse than they were by the Klan violence that put them in office.[20]

Undoubtedly, the inherent constraints of republican government—the principle of civil over military rule, and its political impact on northern public opinion—shaped Lincoln's decision not to impose martial law in New York City. Union League men viewed the token prosecution of the draft rioters as a shameful miscarriage of justice, but Lincoln believed a military crackdown on the Democratic machine in New York would have backfired and undermined federal authority while sparking further violence.[21]

Judging from the results in the South eleven years later, Lincoln may well have been right. The best solution, as the governors of Texas, Arkansas, and Tennessee had demonstrated, was for state authorities to clamp down on local political violence without federal help. However, these governors remained the exceptions. Where such vigorous state action was not forthcoming, the best practical solution was a truce by which local Democrats were allowed to keep whatever political offices and power they had attained but were put on notice that the president would not tolerate outbreaks of violence, and federal troops would be used to enforce his will.[22]

This was Lincoln's approach in 1863 when he refrained from declaring martial law in New York City but sent ten thousand troops to enforce the resumption of the draft. Grant walked a similar fine line in his cautious prosecution of the Klan. He sought to disrupt Klan activity without creating grounds for political grievances against the federal government as an occupying power.

The problem in Louisiana was that the military had gotten out ahead of Grant and crossed that fine line: Colonel Phillippe de Trobriand had responded to Governor Kellogg's request, with Sheridan's subsequent approval, but as Grant later told Congress, he was not notified of the action until it was over. Struggling to contain the political fallout, Grant disavowed but half-heartedly defended the military intervention. By removing Democrats from office, rather than confining itself to quelling violence, the military had entered politics and undermined vital northern support for Reconstruction, even as it tried to uphold it.[23]

To restore order in Louisiana, Grant, like Lincoln in New York, opted for compromise. He accepted a deal, worked out by a congressional committee, giving Democrats in Louisiana the contested seats and with them control of the legislature's lower house; in exchange, they allowed the carpetbag governor to finish the last two years of his term in peace.[24]

Violence was rampant in other states across the South during the 1874 midterm elections, helping to break down the local Republican organizations and deliver Democratic victories. In Arkansas, South Carolina, and Florida, Republicans began splitting into contending groups, giving the Democrats an advantage. At the beginning of 1873, Republicans had firmly controlled only four southern states—Arkansas, Louisiana, Mississippi, and South Carolina—while keeping a tenuous grip on several others. By the end of 1874, Arkansas, Alabama, and Texas had been added to the list of state governments being run entirely by Democrats.[25]

The Democrats' electoral gains in 1874 were not confined to the southern states, and they took control of the House of Representatives for the first time since 1856. The depression fueled the Democratic resurgence, but Republicans also suspected that their support for carpetbagger governments was a liability. With the presidential election of 1876 approaching, northern Republicans were ready to cut loose from their sinking southern party members and to end Reconstruction.[26]

That southern Republicans were on their own became abundantly clear when Democratic "rifle clubs" in Mississippi systematically started riots at Republican gatherings across the state. In a single incident at Vicksburg in December 1874, thirty-five blacks were killed. The attacks continued, and nine months later Ohio Republicans, after taking the pulse of their constituents during the fall elections, persuaded the Grant administration not to send federal troops to Mississippi despite an appeal from the carpetbag governor, a decorated Union veteran and distinguished public servant.[27]

Thus Reconstruction, which seemed to have gotten a solid endorsement with Grant's victory some two years earlier, remained under vigorous attack, while support for it in the North proved shallow and soon evaporated.[28] Federal arrests and prosecutions of Klansmen had declined in 1873, and by 1874 northerners were more concerned with leaving the war in the past than with the protection of blacks' civil rights. The South was no longer the enemy, and the "military necessity" that motivated the Emancipation Proclamation was gone, along with the veneer of idealism possessed by all but the most radical of Republicans.[29]

In the South, Klan violence resumed as federal arrests declined. The survival of the Democratic party meant that Marble's and Wood's version of settling the "Negro question" would soon prevail over Garnet's definition of racial equality. The lynch-mob aspect of the draft riots—the outcry against the Emancipation Proclamation and black equality at the dawn of the Reconstruction era in 1863—would continue to shape its course until the end.[30]

In New York, the 1874 elections solidified Manton Marble's allegiance to Samuel Tilden, the "Sage of Gramercy Park," also hailed since Tweed's demise as "the Hercules who slew the Tammany Hydra." Tilden was pitted by the Democrats against the incumbent, John Dix, in the governor's race. Dix was assailed as a creature of Grantism, since he was president of the Union Pacific Railroad during the Crédit Mobilier scandal. Marble's *World* decried the monopolistic power of the railroads for crushing competition and free trade. Grant himself was accused of sustaining Reconstruction policies that were "crimes against the social order and human honesty." As for the president's handling of the depression, the *World* declared, "Every vote for Dix is a vote for Grant and Hard Times."[31]

Tilden won the governorship by a large margin, and Marble more than ever became the spokesman of the rising Democratic tide. He spelled out the Democrats' party line—hard money, free trade, and home rule—and their ambition to win control of the Senate and retake the White House. In Tilden, the crusading new governor of the wealthiest and most populous state, the party at last had a viable presidential candidate, just in time for the nation's centennial election in 1876.[32]

At the same time, the *World*'s circulation and advertising revenue, on the decline for several years, began to plummet. While 1868 had been Marble's most profitable year, he had bucked the party line on various occasions since then and alienated Democratic readers. His opposition to the Seymour-Blair ticket in 1868 had angered the Albany Regency and its constituents, much as criticism of Tweed and his new charter upset Tammany loyalists in 1870. Marble's failure to rally behind Greeley in 1872 also counted against him with party leaders intent on beating Grant. Starting in 1873, the depression accelerated the *World*'s failure, and by September 1875 it was losing money so quickly that Marble had to put it up for sale. The sale was "a very serious sacrifice of my own personal interests and ambitions," he said.[33]

It also proved to be a major compromise of his political principles. Marble, the apostle of laissez-faire economics, who had fervently denounced railroad monopolies and government handouts that enabled them to grow, ended up selling his cherished newspaper to Thomas Scott, president of the Pennsylvania Railroad. In desperate financial straits, Marble was determined to sell to the highest bidder. His reluctance to part with the *World* and his distrust of Scott led to protracted negotiations.

A clause in the sale agreement guaranteed Marble an additional one hundred thousand dollars if Congress endorsed the bonds of Scott's Texas and Pacific Railroad or approved any other guarantees to subsidize the notorious scheme. Since Democrats now controlled the House and generally opposed government subsidies, Scott needed to change their minds. By purchasing Marble's paper and his political influence, Scott clearly hoped to neutralize potential opponents, particularly Tilden.[34]

With the loss of the *World* and the editorial pulpit which had given Marble some measure of independence within the Democracy when there were disagreements over policy, he increasingly became a mere party functionary, his identity enmeshed with that of the presidential contender. "You are Tilden, and he is Marble," Samuel Barlow declared to him. "This is recognized everywhere."[35] The paper was sold in May 1876, and in June Marble became a delegate to the Democratic convention. He drafted the platform the New York delegation brought with it to St. Louis, confident of Tilden's nomination.[36]

The document declared "the Administration of the Federal Gov't to be in urgent need of Reform" and listed at length the "abuses, wrongs, and crimes" committed during Grant's tenure. Relegating the complex issues of Reconstruction to the past, the platform pledged to the American taxpayer a new dawn of pure government, which meant minimal government achieved through cuts in spending.[37]

The Democrats had made the strategic decision to refrain from overt racial politics, but their program continued to undermine African Americans. Economy in government translated into slashing funds for the deployment of federal troops in the South, ending aid to former slaves through the Freedmen's

Bureau, and imposing civil service reform, which would deprive blacks of government employment by mandating exams that amounted to literacy tests—even for jobs that required no such skills.[38]

The Democrats' "Mississippi Plan" of murder and intimidation gave them control of the state in the elections of 1875, and as the country headed into the presidential race of 1876 only South Carolina, Louisiana, and Florida still had Reconstruction governments. Democrats controlled the House of Representatives, where they reduced the Justice Department's budget to hinder its enforcement of the Reconstruction amendments. Two Supreme Court rulings in 1876 had a similar impact by declaring that the enforcement provisions of the Fourteenth and Fifteenth Amendments did not give Congress authority to pass laws "for the suppression of ordinary crime within the States." The culprits in the Colfax, Louisiana, massacre of 1873 went free.[39]

Further revelations of scandalous corruption in the Grant administration eroded Republican prestige and power in the North, while undercutting the few Reconstruction governments that hung on precariously in the South. Already tarred with the brush of corruption, whether they deserved it or not, the carpetbaggers would soon be swept away by an election in which *reform* was the Democratic buzzword. The presidential race of 1876 pitted Tilden against the Republican candidate, three-time Ohio governor and Civil War general Rutherford B. Hayes.[40]

A Harvard-educated lawyer, Hayes volunteered for the army in 1861 and was appointed a major in the Twenty-third Ohio Regiment. His unit fought guerrillas in West Virginia, took part in the campaign leading up to Antietam, and helped capture John Hunt Morgan and his raiders in Ohio in July 1863. Wounded four times, Hayes had proved a fearless leader in battle, helping Sheridan rally his forces at Cedar Creek in 1864. Before Hayes left the army in 1865, he was promoted to the rank of major general in the U.S. Volunteers. Elected to Congress, the moderate Hayes found himself captivated by the forceful oratory of Thaddeus Stevens and supported the radical Republicans' Reconstruction program.

Radicals in Ohio repaid him with the nomination for governor in 1867, and in his first two terms he led the fight to ratify the Fourteenth and Fifteenth Amendments in his state. Pressured by his party to run again after a hiatus of four years, he was narrowly elected governor for the third time in 1875. Hayes's victory with a strident nativist message and hard-money platform signaled that the electorate was more concerned with currency, inflation, and other economic issues than with Reconstruction. Hayes reassured a friend in the South that northerners supported a "let alone policy" and felt "nothing but good will" toward the former Confederacy. Dismissed by one prominent critic as a "third-rate nonentity," Hayes had nonetheless emerged in 1876 as a moderate candidate acceptable to various Republican factions.[41]

The contradictory Republican platform was deliberately vague, calling for both an end to bloodshed in the South and the enforcement of equal rights. While Hayes did not say so publicly, he intended to pursue a conciliatory policy toward moderate southern Democrats—former Whigs like himself—and bring them into the Republican party. It was the same approach another former Whig, Abraham Lincoln, had taken a dozen years earlier when he first launched the process of Reconstruction in 1863. Given the problems of "bayonet rule," Hayes viewed a coalition with moderates, and thorough reform of the corrupt Reconstruction governments, as the best hope for ending racial violence.[42]

However, because of continued rioting and murders of blacks during the campaign, particularly in South Carolina, where Democrats and their "Red Shirt" paramilitary groups were pushing hard to topple the carpetbag government, northern outrage was rekindled briefly, and President Grant sent federal troops at the governor's request. Republicans, prompted by party leaders including Hayes, resorted to "waving the bloody shirt," which also served to distract voters from the depressed economy.[43]

With most of the former slave states firmly in Democratic hands— "redeemed," according to white supremacists—and the remaining three overrun by the party's armed auxiliaries, the Tilden campaign looked forward to carrying the entire South. Tilden would then need only forty-seven electoral votes from the North to reach a total of 185 and win the election. Northern fatigue with "the everlasting Negro question" and the ongoing depression both worked in Tilden's favor. Moreover, despite federal protection and supervision of polling sites, rampant violence and intimidation cost the Republicans roughly a quarter of a million votes across the South. The Republican leadership quietly braced itself for defeat as the returns came in on November 7.[44]

Tilden won New York, Connecticut, New Jersey, and Indiana, giving him far more than the forty-seven electoral votes he needed from the North. He almost swept the South, where Hayes won South Carolina by a slim margin, but the Democrats claimed victory there in the race for the governorship and control of the legislature. In the three states with Republican governments— Louisiana, Florida, and South Carolina—the returning boards that supervised the elections were controlled by carpetbaggers, and they challenged the grossly lopsided totals from areas where Democrats had evidently driven their opponents from the polls by threats and violence. Tilden, with 184 electoral votes, needed only one of the nineteen votes from the three disputed states to win. Hayes needed all of them.[45]

Samuel Tilden

Calling them "visiting statesmen," northern Democrats rushed delegations to the contested states to spread money around and prevent the Republican election officials from tampering with the ballots. Violence and intimidation by both sides during the campaign left Democrats and Republicans alike feeling justified in the extreme measures they were taking, particularly the Republicans, who denounced the Mississippi Plan used by the Democrats to keep blacks from voting. Florida's Republican governor received four companies of federal troops to maintain order.[46]

Manton Marble arrived in Tallahassee, Florida, on November 15 and took charge of Democratic operatives, sending them around the state to prevent Republican fraud while appealing to state election officials to move ahead with the vote count. Marble also filed reports to northern newspapers detailing Republican abuses. Telegrams between Marble and Tilden's nephew in New York reveal that Marble also planned to bribe election officials to ensure a Democratic victory. On December 2, Marble wrote that he had "just received a proposition to hand over at any hour required Tilden decision of Board and certificate for Governor for 200,000."[47]

If Marble did proceed in this attempt, he failed, and on December 6, Florida's Board of Canvassers declared that all the Republican candidates had won. With similar results in the other two undecided southern states, Congress stepped in to count the electoral votes. The Democrats declared that the House, which they controlled, had the authority to discard the votes from the contested states and decide the election. The Republicans, on the other hand, asserted that the votes should be counted by the president of the Senate, the chamber which they controlled.[48]

Democrats, including Fernando Wood, talked of using force to seat Tilden as president, creating fear that the country would be plunged back into civil war. Rumors spread that Copperhead rifle clubs were springing up in the North to join forces with southern paramilitary groups. Wood plotted legislative measures—including impeachment of President Grant for misuse of the army during the election—and the calling of new elections altogether in the disputed states. Grant in turn had the army discreetly deploy additional troops to Washington to maintain order.[49]

However, Democratic businessmen, buffeted by the depression, favored a peaceful resolution of the crisis. Southern Democrats, distrustful of the party's northern wing—which had betrayed them by favoring peaceful secession and then joining the Union war effort in 1861—left it to the northerners to challenge the Republican election fraud. Fernando Wood and others like him were "invincible in peace and invisible in war," declared Congressman Benjamin Hill of Georgia.[50]

Republicans exploited these divisions, and Democrats, including Tilden and Wood, acquiesced on January 18, 1877, when special House and Senate committees proposed the creation of an electoral commission to determine the outcome of the election, composed of eight Republicans and seven Democrats drawn from the three branches of government. Congress voted the commission into law. Congress was to meet in joint session, count the electoral returns from the states in alphabetical order, and the Electoral Commission was to rule on disputed returns.[51]*

Much to the dismay of the Democrats, however, it soon became clear that the commission was voting along partisan lines to give Hayes the disputed states. Fernando Wood made a speech on the House floor upbraiding the commission. Working himself into a frenzy, he asked: "Why have they done this? This House demands to know why; the American people demand to know why; and history will ask, with wonder and amazement, why?" His venting did nothing to stop the Republicans, who proceeded with the vote count.[52]

*The Electoral Commission's rulings could be overturned only by a vote of both the House and Senate.

In the midst of these and other futile delaying tactics, the Democratic Speaker of the House, Samuel Randall of Pennsylvania, held a private conference at his home, after which he and Wood announced an astonishing reversal of their position: They would work to prevent any Democratic filibustering. Both men were aware that Hayes had opened channels to southern Democrats and was promising railroad subsidies and other funds for restoring and developing the South's infrastructure. Wood and Randall could see that their obstructionism was doomed and self-defeating. Their careers and ambitions would be better served by playing the role of statesmen instead of an embittered opposition. Moreover, Wood and Randall knew that Hayes favored home rule in the South.[53]

The Republicans proceeded to give Hayes the presidency by a single electoral vote. In Washington, the electoral crisis ended not in an explosive, tragic confrontation but in farce on the House floor. When a Democratic representative from Maryland denounced Wood as "the high priest of the Republican party" for his treachery, "Mr. Wood raised his hands over Mr. O'Brien's head as if in the act of conferring a blessing," a reporter wrote. "The scene was so funny that the entire House broke out in loud roars of laughter."[54]

Praised for his high-minded leadership by newspapers across the political spectrum, Wood had managed to pull off another unlikely political rebirth. Riding the Speaker's coattails, he had left the stain of his Civil War reputation in the past. In exchange for his support, which helped the Speaker retain his post, Wood was rewarded with the chairmanship of the powerful House Ways and Means Committee.[55] Southern Democrats soon got over their anger at Wood, whose racism reassured them that the caste system and home rule would be preserved in the former slave states. Hayes's conciliatory tone also suggested that blacks would be left to fend for themselves in a solidly Democratic South.[56]

In the end, the unofficial agreement that came to be called the Compromise of 1877 had just that result. In April, the new Republican administration recognized the Democratic governors of Louisiana and South Carolina, in exchange for promises that they would protect the civil rights of blacks. Hayes then removed federal troops from New Orleans and Charleston, triggering the fall of the last carpetbag governments. Many northern Republicans decried the abandonment of southern blacks and predicted correctly that assurances of fairness from Democrats would soon be violated.[57] "The whole South—every state in the South," declared one black southerner, "had got into the hands of the very men that held us as slaves." Another was dismayed to think "that Hayes could go back on us, when we had to wade through blood to help place him where he is now."[58]

However, most of the country was content to have passed through the electoral deadlock peacefully and happy to see the end of bayonet rule imposed by the federal government on the states. Some black leaders, including Frederick Douglass, while unhappy with Hayes's action, at least refrained from criticizing the president. Reviewing the events of the previous two years, they concluded that Hayes had no alternative.[59] As the *Herald* put it, Hayes was constrained to follow through with "what in the course of years has been done by his predecessor or by Congress."[60]

Grant had begun the process of retreat from the South in 1875 when he declined to send troops to Mississippi and told the governor to make do with state militia. The Supreme Court rulings the following year had gutted the enforcement acts. Now, having already chopped the attorney general's budget to curtail enforcement of the Reconstruction amendments, House Democrats were vowing to cut military spending if Hayes dispatched troops to the South. "What is called the President's policy," said Douglass in May 1877, "might rather be considered the President's necessity . . . Statesmen often are compelled to act upon facts as they are, and not as they would like to have them."[61]

Ironically, while northerners denounced the use of federal troops to protect blacks in the South as bayonet rule, they were eager for the army to put down labor unrest in their own states, which was coming to a head after ten years of union-building and four years of economic hard times since the Panic of 1873.[62] The era of Reconstruction, which effectively began with the Emancipation Proclamation and the suppression of the draft riots in 1863, ended fourteen years later with a reversal of fortune for blacks, and military action against another massive working-class protest: a nationwide railroad strike. Thus, 1877 appeared to be a year of ultimate defeat for the goals of both the draft rioters and their black victims. This time, however, while the railroad strike reinforced class antagonisms, it engendered solidarity between black and white workers, sowing the seeds for broader cooperation in the future.[63]

Only ten nationwide labor unions had emerged intact from the Civil War, but within a decade there were more than thirty. Inflation eased after the war, while economic expansion increased the demand for workers. Their bargaining power grew, as did the number of strikes for higher wages and shorter hours.[64] As it had before and during the Civil War, the northern labor movement called for equal rights but remained hostile to black workers, Chinese immigrants, and women, who formed their own unions.[65]

Whites continued to fear black labor competition, even though the threatened influx of former slaves to urban centers in the North would not occur until early in the next century, since freedmen in the South, accustomed to agriculture, not factory work, migrated mainly to the West, settling in Arkansas and Oklahoma.[66] Black workers remained loyal to the Republican party and pinned their hopes on Reconstruction, while white labor leaders denounced the carpetbaggers and the Freedmen's Bureau and called for reconciliation with the South in order to spur cotton production and create related jobs in the North.[67]

With the panic and depression in 1873, wages fell along with prices, and unemployment became rampant, leading to the collapse of labor unions, cooperatives, and the few local laws ensuring an eight-hour day. Chanting "Work or Bread," the jobless staged huge protests in cities across the North in the winter of 1873–74 to demand public works projects—on streets, parks, and urban transit systems—or simply public relief. On January 13, 1874, some seven thousand workers rallied at Tompkins Square in New York, where club-wielding policemen, some on horseback, attacked and scattered the protesters while making numerous arrests. New York's harsh response to the demonstration crushed the campaign for public works and spawned a crackdown on labor rallies in cities across the North.[68]

Organized labor began to fragment, with many German immigrants looking toward socialist solutions, including nationalization of the railroads and other industries. Skilled American craftsmen, particularly those in Pittsburgh's iron and steel industry, distanced themselves from the growing public perception of organized labor as a collection of violent communists and anarchists. Avoiding clashes with employers and the police, they focused instead on the survival of their unions and preserving decent wages and working conditions. Closing ranks, skilled workers shunned the unemployed, who were often used as strikebreakers, and severed ties with unions of unskilled laborers.[69]

Nonetheless, in the midwestern mining industry and on the railroads, falling wages in 1874 prompted strikes and deadly clashes. In 1875, a strike by some fifteen thousand textile workers in the Northeast dragged on for two months before it finally collapsed.[70] A protracted strike in the coal fields of eastern Pennsylvania that year also failed after the governor secured legal injunctions against the miners and called out the militia.[71]

By 1877, some of the striking Pennsylvania miners—from the same community of unskilled Irish Catholics that had rebelled against the Republican draft fourteen years earlier—had been exposed as members of the secretive Molly Maguires and were tried and convicted for assassinations and other acts of revenge against Protestant mine owners, foremen, and skilled workers. Twenty of the Mollies were convicted of murder and hanged, paving the way for a broad crackdown by mine owners on all the workmen's groups they had wanted to crush, including those that were moderate and nonviolent.[72]

Railroad workers, too, were unable to prevent deep wage cuts, and on July 16, 1877, a strike in Martinsburg, West Virginia, quickly spread across the country and reached massive proportions, uniting labor groups that had become estranged during the depression. Steel workers and some forty thousand miners in Pennsylvania joined the work stoppage, along with sympathetic citizens. They held protests and took over railroad switches, shutting down the major lines serving every region except New England and the Deep South.[73]

In Chicago and St. Louis, the Great Strike brought all business to a halt and revived calls for an eight-hour day, along with adequate wages, a ban on child labor, public ownership of the railroads, and an end to the vagrancy laws that enabled local authorities to arrest the many unemployed workers who were crisscrossing the country in search of jobs. In St. Louis, Louisville, and elsewhere, blacks and whites joined forces, as did workers of every ethnic background. San Francisco was the exception: Strikers ended up attacking Chinese laborers, who made up about 25 percent of the city's workforce and, like blacks in the Northeast, were deemed a competitive threat.[74]

While local militias tended to side with their neighbors, ten governors mustered state troops willing to fire on the crowds, and President Hayes sent federal forces—some of them redeployed from Louisiana and other parts of the South—to six major cities and several smaller ones across the North to break the Great Strike.[75]* The harbor forts around New York City were emptied of federal troops to meet the emergency, leading Assistant Secretary of the Treasury Thomas Hillhouse to fear a repetition of the Civil War draft riots.

The government had one hundred million dollars stored in the Custom House and Sub-Treasury, he warned, and "the city is filled with the most inflammable materials for a riot, if an opportunity should occur." Some troops were brought back to New York, and Secretary of the Navy Richard Thompson sent an ironclad to "clear the streets around the Custom House." The curving streets of Lower Manhattan did not lend themselves to such tactics, but Secretary of State William Evarts declared: "The big guns will straighten them."[76]

Working-class solidarity was matched by that of middle- and upper-class groups in the large cities. They joined local officials and veterans' associations to form heavily armed "citizens' militias" to defend their property and disperse the strikers. In St. Louis, the Committee of Public Safety mustered a large civilian force commanded by two retired generals—one Union, and the other Confederate. The leading citizens of Louisville volunteered to supplement the police force and were issued weapons at City Hall, which was used as an arms depot during the insurrection.[77]

The Great Strike of 1877 lasted for almost two weeks, leaving one hundred people dead and hundreds of others wounded. After the violence subsided on July 29, President Hayes wrote emphatically in his diary, "The strikers have been put down by *force*."[78] The wrath of the hungry, exploited American worker, paired with the anxiety of the middle and upper classes,

---

*Buffalo, Pittsburgh, Baltimore, St. Louis, Louisville, and Chicago.

The Great Strike of 1877: Soldiers fire on strikers at the Halsted
Street viaduct in Chicago

turned the rest of the nineteenth century into the most violent period of labor protest in American history.[79] In the space of twenty-five years, governors called out the National Guard more than one hundred times to deal with confrontations between workers and management. Federal troops were sent, not to enforce the Fourteenth and Fifteenth Amendments in the South—where the rights and lives of African Americans were still under attack—but to industrial trouble spots, easily reachable from new fortresslike armories constructed in large cities across the North.[80]

During the draft riots in 1863, Mayor George Opdyke could still proclaim that, unlike other countries, American society had no "ruling class," and that "here, where the suffrage is universal," all protest should be made through the ballot box.[81] With industrial capitalism still in its infancy, Republicans could deny that class conflict was an American phenomenon and confidently expound the tenets of free-labor ideology, which envisioned the United States as a land of equal opportunity and upward mobility.[82]

Of the rioters, presidential adviser William Stoddard could declare that "these fiends in human form are in no wise to be confounded with 'American working-men.' This conduct left no stain upon us, for they were not and are not of us. Whether born on the soil or born elsewhere, they were foreigners to every idea and hope and instinct which at all belongs to this free country. In shooting them down, afterwards, the police and military were destroying a hellish raid from the slums of Europe."[83]

After the Great Strike of 1877, Americans fearfully began to view class conflict as a fact of life. Industrial capitalism had perpetuated in the United States what the *Nation* called "the great curse of the Old World—the division of society into classes." Few Americans continued to insist on a harmony of interests between labor and capital. "The days are over in which this country could rejoice in its freedom from the elements of social strife which have long abounded in the old countries," the *New York Times* declared in July 1877. "We cannot too soon face the fact that we have dangerous social elements to contend with."[84]

The rags-to-riches Horatio Alger stories, and Herbert Spencer's theory of "social Darwinism," applying the evolutionary principle of the survival-of-the-fittest to human society, were put forward to deny any fixed hierarchy in America; nonetheless, for many people, the vision of nineteenth-century America as a fluid, classless society had been challenged by the draft riots and was exploded by the Gilded Age with its undeniable and ever-widening chasm between rich and poor.[85]

The draft riots were, in part, a labor protest—demanding economic justice for working-class men, women, and children—but the white perpetrators of violence in July 1863 fared little better than their black victims in the decades after the Civil War. With the end of Reconstruction, African Americans would have to struggle for almost a century to gain effective legal protection of their civil rights, while enduring, through the 1930s, waves of reactionary violence of a type that began in 1863 in response to the first momentous act of Reconstruction, the Emancipation Proclamation. For the white northern worker, what began as an outcry against the three-hundred-dollar commutation clause would continue into the next century as a crusade against class discrimination, a quest for fair wages and safety of life and limb on the job. In that quest would come the slow, painfully belated recognition that racial harmony could mean strength in numbers and progress for all.[86]

Appendix: A Walking Tour
of Civil War New York

~⁂

The following is a partial list of the sights included in the complete Walking Tour, available at http://www.walkerbooks.com. The Web site provides detailed directions, phone numbers, and other information for this self-guided tour.

MANHATTAN

LOWER MANHATTAN: In Battery Park, at the southern tip of the Manhattan,[1] the **Castle Clinton National Monument** is a circular stone fort from the War of 1812 that served as New York State's immigrant landing depot from 1855 to 1890, receiving more than eight million people before it was replaced by the federal facility at Ellis Island. The Great Famine of 1845–52, the potato blight that spurred more than a million Irish émigrés to leave for America, is commemorated by the **Irish Hunger Memorial,** at 290 Vesey Street, one block west of the former World Trade Center site. **Federal Hall National Memorial,** at Broad and Wall Streets, was a branch of the U.S. Treasury during the Civil War, and its stores of gold were a target of the draft rioters. The **New York City Police Museum,** at 100 Old Slip Street (between Water and South Streets), chronicles the service of "New York's Finest" while also displaying tools and weapons used by the city's nineteenth-century gangs and criminals.

The collection at the **New York City Fire Museum,** located in **SoHo,** at 278 Spring Street (between Varick and Hudson Streets), includes nineteenth-century firefighting equipment. A large portion of the original **St. Nicholas Hotel,** destroyed by Confederate arsonists in 1864, still stands at 521–523 Broadway, near Spring Street, in SoHo. Archbishop Hughes's church, the **former St. Patrick's Cathedral,** still stands at 260–264 Mulberry Street, near Prince Street, in SoHo.

The nearby **South Street Seaport Historic District** is an eleven-square-block area of Federal-style brick buildings and Belgian-block streets that preserves part of what was once New York's commercial center. This waterfront, where Irish longshoremen and African American workers clashed over jobs, was an important source of Mayor and Congressman Fernando Wood's political power. Guided tours are available through the **South Street Seaport Museum.** For tours of **Governors Island,** information is available from the Pier 17 ticket booth at South Street Seaport. During the Civil War, the forts on Governors Island held Confederate prisoners, and the supplies of arms and ammunition on the island were distributed to both soldiers and civilian volunteers who battled the draft rioters in 1863.

Horace Greeley, editor of the *New York Tribune,* and one of Fernando Wood's harshest critics, is commemorated by a **statue next to the east wing of City Hall.** The seated figure of Greeley is just across Park Row from Pace University. One block south stands the **former *New York Times* building,** which bears a plaque explaining that the *Tribune* was around the corner at Spruce and Nassau Streets. The *Evening Post, Herald,* and *World* were also nearby. This concentration of newspaper offices across from City Hall was known as Printing House Square. Directly behind City Hall, to the north, stands the **"Tweed Courthouse."** Built by the Tweed Ring at an exorbitant cost to taxpayers, it is now occupied by the city's Department of Education. North and west of City Hall, on Duane Street between Church and West Broadway, is a steak and seafood **restaurant named City Hall in a building that dates from 1863.**

The **African Burial Ground Interpretive Center,** at 290 Broadway (between Reade and Duane Streets), is adjacent to the **African Burial Ground site.** One of the most significant archaeological finds in U.S. history, the burial ground covered the equivalent of five city blocks. During the seventeenth and eighteenth centuries, some twenty thousand enslaved and free African Americans were buried in the cemetery. The site attests to the important role of African Americans in the founding and growth of New York City, and to the widespread use of slave labor in the northern colonies and states.

North and east of the City Hall area, court buildings and Chinatown have transformed the notorious slum called **Five Points,** where the poorest immigrants, especially Irish Americans, and blacks lived together during the Civil War era. The New York County Supreme Court building at 60 Center Street, built in 1913, stands on the site of the Old Brewery, a crowded rookery that reformers turned into the Five Points Mission. Directly across Center Street stood the saloon of Tammany comptroller and sheriff Matthew Brennan, one of the first Irish Americans to rise through the ranks of New York City's Democratic political machine. Three blocks north, on Center Street between Leonard and Franklin Streets, stood the city jail called the "Tombs."

Five Points was named for the five-cornered intersection of Worth, Baxter, and Park Streets, which today is partially covered by the **southwestern corner of Columbus Park.** What remains of Park Street is now Mosco Street, a single block between Mulberry and Mott Streets, east of the park. Some of the buildings on Mulberry Street date from the nineteenth century, as does the **Roman Catholic Church of the Transfiguration,** a block farther east at Mott and Mosco Streets, which the Dead Rabbits gang defended as part of their turf when the arrival of the new Metropolitan police force sparked deadly riots in 1857. A plaque on **St. James's Church,** on St. James Place just south of Chatham Square, tells that the church blessed the colors of the "Fighting Irish" Sixty-ninth Regiment of Volunteers and served the poor Irish community during the Civil War.

The draft riots were, in part, a product of the festering slums in New York's immigrant neighborhoods. North and east of Chinatown, the **Lower East Side Tenement Museum,** at 90 Orchard Street, provides tours of a historic tenement building, opened in 1863 by a German immigrant. The **Tenement Theatre,** at 97 Orchard Street, is in **an 1863 pub, formerly Scheider's Saloon.** On East Seventh Street, just east of Third Avenue, stands **McSorley's Old Ale House.** Established by an Irish immigrant, John

McSorley, in 1854, it is New York's oldest and most famous saloon. Farther east, between Avenue A and Avenue B, and extending north from Seventh to Tenth Street, **Tompkins Square Park** was the site of frequent political protests, especially by Irish and German immigrants from the surrounding neighborhoods. The Tompkins Square neighborhood was part of Kleindeutschland, Little Germany. Impoverished wives of volunteer soldiers protested here in 1862 to demand overdue relief payments, and unemployed laborers demanding "Work or Bread" were dispersed by police in 1874, signaling that class conflict in America, laid bare by the draft riots, would dominate the Gilded Age. Most recently, rioting between the police and residents flared up in 1988, during the gentrification of the area and the city's removal of a homeless encampment from the park.

A few blocks west of Tompkins Square Park, on West Eighth Street between Third and Fourth Avenues, stands **Cooper Union,** the institute founded by industrialist and civic reformer Peter Cooper to educate the sons of the working class on full scholarships. The institute's Great Hall was the site of momentous public meetings in the Civil War era, ranging from rallies of the Peace Democrats addressed by Fernando Wood, to Lincoln's famed "right makes might" speech in 1860, to the gathering of irate citizens who formed the Committee of Seventy to investigate the Tweed Ring in 1871. Here at **Astor Place,** the thoroughfares of the rich and the poor—Broadway and the Bowery (here called Fourth Avenue)—came within a block of each other, creating a friction point. The Astor Place Opera House was the focus of deadly riots in 1849.

Six blocks north of Astor Place lies **Union Square,** the neighborhood and park named for the convergence of the Bloomingdale Road (now Broadway) and the Bowery (here called Park Avenue South). Starting in the Civil War era, frequent rallies and demonstrations were held in the park, including patriotic outpourings like the massive rally in support of the war in April 1861, and various labor protests. The **bronze statue of Abraham Lincoln** by Henry Kirke Brown was installed in 1868. Along the perimeter of the southern half of the park, **a series of bronze tablets based on period prints and photographs** is embedded in the pavement. The plaques depict Union Square in various stages of its development during the nineteenth century and major events in the neighborhood, including the flag ceremony for New York's first African American regiment in March 1864, and Lincoln's funeral in April 1865. **Madison Square Park,** at Broadway and Twenty-third Street, was also the site of political rallies, including Tammany's parade for McClellan in the election of 1864. At the southwestern entrance to the park sits a **bronze statue of William Seward,** a governor of New York, a senator, and Lincoln's secretary of state.

MIDTOWN: During the Civil War, the site of the New York Public Library at Fifth Avenue and Forty-second Street was occupied by the Croton Reservoir. Two blocks north stood the Colored Orphan Asylum. **Bryant Park,** behind the library, is named for William Cullen Bryant, editor of the New York *Evening Post* and Horace Greeley's main Republican rival. A **bronze statue of Bryant, set in a monument to him,** dominates the eastern end of the park. In the middle of the park's north side stands a **bronze statue of William E. Dodge,** a prominent businessman who led New York's Chamber of Commerce during the Civil War. Active in his support of the Union cause and heedless of his personal safety when helping to quell the draft riots, Dodge nonetheless embodied the ambivalence of New York's merchants toward the war and their desire to compromise with the South for the sake of trade.

UPPER EAST SIDE: The **Arsenal in Central Park,** at Fifth Avenue and Sixty-third Street, now the headquarters of the Parks Department, was built in 1847–51 as a state arsenal. Today the Arsenal hosts art exhibits and public forums in its third-floor gallery. At Park Avenue and Sixty-eighth Street, the **Seventh Regiment Armory,** built in 1880, is a brick fortress typical of the armories constructed during the Gilded Age throughout the northern states in response to the draft riots, immigration, and labor unrest during the Great Depression that began in 1873, particularly the Great Strike of 1877. **The Museum of the City of New York,** on Fifth Avenue at 103rd Street, has a permanent **exhibit on "Firefighters,"** which includes an ornament from the Black Joke engine and the engine from the volunteer company that launched "Boss" Tweed's political career—and was the source of Tammany Hall's tiger logo.

UPPER WEST SIDE/HARLEM/WASHINGTON HEIGHTS: On Central Park West at Seventy-seventh Street, the **New-York Historical Society's Henry Luce III Center for the Study of American Culture** displays **artifacts from the Civil War era, including a draft wheel,** from which names of conscripts were drawn during the lottery. **Civil War monuments in or near Riverside Park** include the **Soldiers' and Sailors' Monument** at 89th Street; an **equestrian statue of the German American general Franz Sigel** at 106th Street and Riverside Drive; and the **General Grant National Memorial** at 120th Street, the largest mausoleum in North America, which contains the tomb of Ulysses S. Grant and his wife, Julia. On the edge of Morningside Park at Morningside Drive and 116th Street, **a small monument honors Carl Schurz,** a German American, senator, and leader of the Liberal Republican revolt against Grant in the election of 1872. (He is also commemorated by **Carl Schurz Park** at the foot of East 89th Street, the site of Gracie Mansion). **St. Philip's Church** now stands at 204 West 134th Street. **Fernando Wood's grave** is in the **uptown Trinity Cemetery** at 153rd Street and Broadway. **Bennett Park,** on Fort Washington Avenue and 183rd Street, was named for James Gordon Bennett, the founder and editor of the *New York Herald.*

BROOKLYN

Points of interest include the **Harbor Defense Museum** at Fort Hamilton and **Civil War–era cannons** on the grounds; the **Monitor Museum** in Greenpoint, commemorating the ironclad that was built and launched here; the Domino **sugar plant from the 1850s** in Williamsburg; **nineteenth-century industrial buildings** on Water Street in DUMBO, Down Under the Manhattan Bridge Overpass; **Civil War–era factory buildings** in Red Hook, now converted into art galleries; the remains of the **Atlantic and Erie Basins,** where draft rioters burned the grain elevators; **houses from the 1830s and 1840s** and a **firehouse from 1855** in the **Vinegar Hill neighborhood ("Irish Town")** next to the **Brooklyn Navy Yard.**[2]

The **Historic Hunterfly Road Houses** in Crown Heights were once part of **Weeksville,** a settlement of free blacks founded by James Weeks in 1838. In 1863, Weeksville became a haven for black refugees fleeing the draft riots in Manhattan. **Green-Wood Cemetery** contains the graves of some four thousand Civil War soldiers and sailors from both sides of the conflict, including monuments to sixteen Union generals and two Confederate generals. Also in these 478 acres are the grave sites of prominent New Yorkers of the period, including Horace Greeley, Henry Raymond (founder and editor of the *New York Times*), the abolitionists James and Abby Gibbons, and several people killed in the draft riots.

THE BRONX

Among the grave sites in **Woodlawn Cemetery** are those of **William E. Dodge, William Havemeyer,** and other prominent New Yorkers of the period.[3]

STATEN ISLAND

Points of interest include the **graveyard at Sandy Ground, a free-black settlement,** and **Historic Richmond Town,** which hosts an annual reenactment of incidents from the draft riots that occurred on Staten Island.[4]

QUEENS

A **church in a parking lot in downtown Flushing** is the remnant of a free-black settlement.[5] **Cypress Hills Cemetery** contains the **graves of numerous Confederate prisoners** who were buried alongside Union veterans. **Calvary Cemetery** has a **monument to the Irish Sixty-ninth Regiment,** and the **grave sites of General Michael Corcoran and Sergeant Peter Welsh,** as well as other Irish American veterans. **Lutheran All Faiths Cemetery,** among others, also has Civil War veterans' graves.

NASSAU COUNTY

Old Bethpage Village Restoration, near Farmingdale, Long Island, has an annual reenactment of the draft riots that took place in the town of Jamaica.

Notes

ABBREVIATIONS

MACNY   Municipal Archives of the City of New York
N-YHS   New-York Historical Society
NYPL   New York Public Library

PROLOGUE: "WE HAVE NOT ONE DEVIL, BUT MANY TO CONTEND WITH"

1. Ruffin, *Diary*, 3:70; Geary, *We Need Men*, p. 105; New York *Tribune*, July 14–18, 1863.
2. Ruffin, *Diary*, 3:71; McPherson, *Battle Cry*, p. 665.
3. Ruffin, *Diary*, 3:71 and 1:xxxix–xl; *Anticipations of the Future*, pp. 285–312, 327–42.
4. Cook, *Armies of the Streets*, p. xi; Burrows and Wallace, *Gotham*, p. 866; Kinchen, *Confederate Operations*, pp. 20–21.
5. *Times*, July 16, 1863.
6. Ibid.
7. Official death toll: Cook, pp. 193–95, 213–18; *Report of the Committee of Merchants*, p. 7.
8. Strong, *Diary of the Civil War*, p. 337. According to Strong, he suggested to Mayor Opdyke that citizen volunteers be enlisted, and the mayor replied that such a step would turn the riots into a "civil war."
9. *New York Daily News*, July 6, 1863; Mushkat, *Fernando Wood*, p. 138; *Harper's Weekly*, August 1, 1863; Strong, pp. 333, 337; Bernstein, *Draft Riots*, pp. 8–11, 56–57.
10. Introduction by McCune Smith in Garnet, *A Memorial Discourse*, p. 56; New York *World*, July 8, 1863; Hale, *Horace Greeley*, pp. 257–61, 271–74.
11. Emerson, *Abby Gibbons*, 1:385; Foner, *Reconstruction*, p. 585; Quigley, *Second Founding*, p. xiv.
12. Bernstein, p. 3; McPherson, *Battle Cry*, pp. 500, 558–59; *Daily News*, July 13, 1863.

13. Foner, pp. xxv, 585; McPherson, *Battle Cry,* pp. 559–60 and *Ordeal,* p. 497; Mushkat, *The Reconstruction,* pp. 27–28.

14. Harris, *In the Shadow of Slavery,* pp. 189–90; Mushkat, *The Reconstruction,* p. 28; Bernstein, p. 56; Ackerman, *Boss Tweed,* pp. 11–30.

15. Quigley, pp. xii, 50; Mushkat, *The Reconstruction,* pp. 10, 12; Foner, pp. 575–83.

16. Garnet, *A Memorial Discourse,* pp. 69–91; Mushkat, *The Reconstruction,* pp. 130, 236; Nast, cartoons in *Harper's Weekly,* Sept. 5 and Oct. 10, 1868.

17. Du Bois, *Black Reconstruction,* p. 18; Trelease, *White Terror,* p. 419.

18. Morris, *Fraud,* p. 3; Foner, pp. 575–83; Woodward, *Reunion and Reaction,* pp. xi, xii, 12.

19. Woodward, pp. xi, xii; *Slavery and the Making of America: The Challenge of Freedom,* PBS film; "A Lynching Memorial Unveiled in Duluth," *New York Times* editorial, Dec. 5, 2003.

20. Allen, *The Tiger,* pp. x–xi; "scientific charity," including footnote: Bernstein, pp. 68–69.

21. Schlesinger, *Jackson,* pp. 490–91; Foner, pp. 28–29, 156–57, 585.

22. Stoddard, *Volcano,* pp. 4, 316–33; Foner, pp. 514, 583–86; Homberger, *Life of a City,* p. 196; Ottley and Weatherby, eds., *The Negro in New York,* p. xvi (preface by James Baldwin).

23. Lowenfels, ed., *Walt Whitman's Civil War,* p. 141; Anbinder, *Five Points,* p. 155.

24. "Celtic devils" quoted in Spann, "Union Green," p. 205; *Tribune,* July 14, 1863.

25. Daly, *Diary,* p. 179; Lee, *Discontent in New York,* p. 102.

26. Daly, pp. 182–83; Emerson, *Abby Gibbons,* 1:385.

27. Garnet, p. 73; Foner, p. 232. Next paragraph: Burrows and Wallace, pp. 785, 877.

I. "THE REBEL HORDE HAD INVADED PENNSYLVANIA IN FORCE"

1. Lee, *The Wartime Papers of Robert E. Lee,* p. 515; McPherson, *Battle Cry,* p. 648; Swinton, *Seventh Regiment,* pp. 292–93; Sears, *Gettysburg,* pp. 12, 13, 15.

2. McPherson, *Battle Cry,* pp. 647, 649; Swinton, p. 293; *Herald,* July 10, 1863; Delafield, Letterpress Copybook, pp. 375–80.

3. *Tribune,* June 30 and July 7, 1863; McPherson, *Battle Cry,* p. 494n.

4. McPherson, *Battle Cry,* pp. 646–47, 635.

5. Sears, pp. xiii, 2, 15; McPherson, *Battle Cry,* p. 647.

6. Lee, *Papers,* pp. 507–9; Sears, pp. 76–77; Stevens, *1863,* p. 231; *Herald,* July 10, 1863; McPherson, *Battle Cry,* p. 650.

7. Sears, p. 14; Lee, *Papers,* pp. 434–35; Stevens, p. 107.

8. Geary, pp. 103–5; Bernstein, pp. 8–9; Burrows and Wallace, pp. 865–66; Ruffin, *Diary,* 1:222, 229 and 3:71.

9. Quoted in Spann, *Gotham at War,* p. 10.

10. Ruffin, *Diary,* 1:xl.

11. Sears, p. 51; McPherson, *Battle Cry,* p. 645; Hale, pp. 243–44; Swinton, p. 292.

12. Spann, *Gotham at War,* p. 60; Burrows and Wallace, pp. 881–82.

13. Nugent, "The Sixty-ninth Regiment at Fredericksburg," p. 198.

14. McPherson, *Battle Cry,* pp. 572 and 645–47.

15. Stevens, p. 9; Swinton, p. 292; Grant quoted in Stevens, p. 94; McPherson, *Battle Cry*, pp. 645–46.
16. Swinton, p. 293; McPherson, *Battle Cry*, pp. vii and 647.
17. Lockwood, *Our Campaign*, pp. 15–18; Wingate, *Last Campaign*, p. 3; Swinton, pp. 292–93; Wall, *Horatio Seymour*, p. 33; Spann, *Gotham at War*, p. 97.
18. Wall, pp. 33–34; Swinton, pp. 294–98.
19. Wall, p. 33; Delafield, pp. 375–80.
20. McPherson, *Battle Cry*, pp. 651–52; Stevens, p. 218; footnote: Stevens, p. 174.
21. McPherson, *Battle Cry*, p. 652; *Stevens*, pp. 234–35.
22. McPherson, *Battle Cry*, pp. 653–54; Stevens, pp. 236–37 and 255; Catton, *Never Call Retreat*, pp. 178–79.
23. McPherson, *Battle Cry*, pp. 653–55; Stevens, pp. 255–64; Catton, pp. 180–81.
24. McPherson, *Battle Cry*, pp. 653–55; Stevens, pp. 255–64; Catton, pp. 181–83.
25. McPherson, *Battle Cry*, pp. 653–55; Stevens, pp. 255–64; Catton, pp. 183–84.
26. McPherson, *Battle Cry*, pp. 653–55; Stevens, pp. 255–64; Catton, p. 184.
27. Quoted in Governor Seymour's "Second Annual Message," Fairchild Collection, N-YHS, typescript.
28. Opdyke, *Documents*, p. 264; Spann, *Gotham at War*, p. 97.
29. This paragraph and footnote: Spann, *Gotham at War*, p. 49.
30. Opdyke, pp. 264 and 292; Geary, pp. 20–21, 104–5; Bernstein, p. 9.
31. Sandburg, *Lincoln: The War Years*, 2:362; *Evening Post*, July 23, 1863.
32. Wall, p. 31; Stevens, p. 301; Geary, p. 65.
33. Stevens, p. 301; Spann, *Gotham at War*, p. 62; McPherson, *Battle Cry*, p. 818; Yacovone, *Freedom's Journey*, p. 79.
34. Geary, pp. 103–5; Bernstein, p. 9.
35. Kinchen, pp. 15–16; Stevens, p. 301; Catton, p. 170.
36. Kirk, *Heavy Guns and Light*, pp. 104–5; Asbury, *Gangs of New York*, pp. 113–14.
37. McPherson, *Battle Cry*, pp. 656–60; Stevens, pp. 266–76; Catton, pp. 185–86.
38. Stevens, p. 299; Kinchen, pp. 20–21; quote and details of crossing river: Headley, *Confederate Operations*, p. 133; Stern, *Secret Missions*, p. 155.
39. McPherson, *Battle Cry*, p. 661; Carhart, *Lost Triumph*, pp. xii, 2–5.
40. McPherson, *Battle Cry*, pp. 661–64; Stevens, pp. 278–88; Catton, pp. 186–91.
41. Carhart, pp. xii–xiii, 6.
42. McPherson, *Battle Cry*, pp. 661–64; Stevens, pp. 278–88; Catton, pp. 186–91.
43. McPherson, *Battle Cry*, pp. 661–64; Stevens, pp. 278–88.
44. Strong, p. 328; McCague, *Second Rebellion*, pp. 4–5.
45. *Daily News*, July 6, 1863.
46. Stevens, p. 108.
47. Wall, p. 28; Bernstein, pp. 7–8.
48. Lincoln quoted in Richard Posner, "Desperate Times, Desperate Measures," *New York Times*, August 24, 2003.
49. Stevens, pp. 108–11.
50. Burrows and Wallace, p. 888; Bernstein, p. 10; Wall, pp. 32–33. Provost Marshal General James Fry later acknowledged that New York's quota did not give the state credit for the full number of volunteers it had raised: Fry, *New York and the Conscription of 1863*, p. 9.

51. Stevens, pp. 109–11.
52. Quoted in McJimsey, *Genteel Partisan,* pp. 47–48.
53. Stevens, pp. 110–11.
54. McJimsey, pp. 46–48; Mushkat, *Fernando Wood,* p. 137; *World,* June 15, 1863.
55. McJimsey, pp. 46–48; *World,* June 9, 1863.
56. *Daily News,* June 16, 1863.
57. Ibid.
58. Ibid., July 6, 1863.
59. This paragraph and the following account of Lee's retreat: Wingate, pp. 33–38; Stevens, pp. 291–93; Sears, pp. 477–85.

2. THE BATTLE LINES ARE DRAWN: RACE, CLASS, AND RELIGION

1. McJimsey, p. 49; McCague, pp. 12 and 44; *Herald,* July 13, 1863.
2. McCague, pp. 44–46; *Tribune,* July 7, 1863; John Jay to Stanton, *War of the Rebellion,* ser. 3, 3:540.
3. *World,* July 11, 1863; Wall, pp. 35–36; Andrew Jackson Downing quoted in Burrows and Wallace, p. 790.
4. Burrows and Wallace, p. 862; Stevens, pp. 123–29.
5. McPherson, *Battle Cry,* pp. 11–15; Schlesinger, pp. 8–9; Bernstein, pp. 77–81.
6. McPherson, *Battle Cry,* pp. 23–24; Schlesinger, pp. 8–10. Jefferson quoted in Schlesinger, p. 8.
7. McPherson, *Battle Cry,* pp. 25–27; Schlesinger, pp. 30–33 and 90–92; Burrows and Wallace, pp. 571–73.
8. McPherson, *Ordeal,* pp. 32–33, 498 and *Battle Cry,* pp. 31 and 88; Ignatiev, *Irish Became White,* p. 100.
9. Gilje, *Mobocracy,* pp. 92, 100, 118–19, 128, 133, 135, 140–41, 176–78, 187–88, 201–2, 277, 286.
10. Headley, *Great Riots,* p. 149; O'Donnell, *1001 Things,* pp. 23–26.
11. Gibson, *New York Irish,* p. 70; Cogan, "The Irish-American Press," pp. 34–35; Gilje, pp. 129–36; O'Donnell, pp. 24–25.
12. Burrows and Wallace, pp. 542–44.
13. Ibid., p. 544; McPherson, *Battle Cry,* p. 8.
14. Burrows and Wallace, pp. 544–46.
15. Ignatiev, pp. v, 69, 76, 87, 100–101, 109–12, 117, 120–21.
16. Burrows and Wallace, p. 554; Gilje, pp. 159–60; Harris, pp. 5, 97, 118–19; second footnote: Harris, p. 119.
17. Burrows and Wallace, pp. 553–56; Strong, p. 335; Ignatiev, p. 41.
18. Burrows and Wallace, pp. 547–48; no black ghettoes: Harris, pp. 7, 75–76 and Freeman, *The Free Negro,* pp. 165–66.
19. Burrows and Wallace, pp. 554–55; Five Points and footnote: Anbinder, *Five Points,* p. 4 and maps.
20. Quoted in Gibson, p. 15.
21. Quoted in Freeman, p. 97.
22. Quoted in Burrows and Wallace, p. 547.

23. Including footnote: Hewitt, *Protest and Progress,* preface and pp. xv–xvii and Harris, pp. 34–35, 84.
24. Burrows and Wallace, p. 543.
25. Conyngham, *Irish Brigade,* pp. xiii–xiv; Gilje, p. 146; Harris, pp. 3, 7; footnote: Harris, pp. 3, 7.
26. Du Bois, p. 18; Harris, p. 174.
27. Burrows and Wallace, pp. 549–52; Harris, pp. 171–72, 192–95; footnote: Woodson, *Negro Migration,* p. 2.
28. *Freedom's Journal,* October 26, 1827; footnote: Quigley, p. 17.
29. Burrows and Wallace, pp. 434, 551; Harris, pp. 170, 174–75, 187–88.
30. Burrows and Wallace, p. 551; Mayer, *All on Fire,* pp. 313, 327, 445; Harris, pp. 175, 194–97.
31. Burrows and Wallace, pp. 551–52; Harris, pp. 194–95.
32. Burrows and Wallace, pp. 571–73; Schlesinger, pp. 126, 143, 90–92.
33. Burrows and Wallace, pp. 572–73; Schlesinger, pp. 76–79.
34. Burrows and Wallace, pp. 573–74; Hale, pp. 38–39; *Encyclopedia of New York City,* p. 164.
35. Burrows and Wallace, pp. 573–74.
36. Ibid., pp. 574–75; Schlesinger, pp. 97–98, 100–102.
37. Burrows and Wallace, pp. 556–57; Harris, pp. 191–97.
38. Burrows and Wallace, pp. 557–58; Harris, pp. 197–98; Gilje, pp. 162–70.
39. Burrows and Wallace, pp. 558–59.
40. Hale, pp. 38–39.
41. Harris, pp. 198–202; Burrows and Wallace, p. 559.
42. Burrows and Wallace, pp. 434, 559–60.
43. Harris, pp. 135–37, 145–54.
44. Freeman, p. 177; Harris, pp. 145–47.
45. Freeman, p. 177; Harris, pp. 145–47.
46. Harris, p. 154, 167; Freeman, pp. 178–79.
47. Association for the Benefit of Colored Orphans, *Seventh Annual Report,* pp. 8–9.
48. Freeman, p. 178; Harris, p. 157; Stauffer, *The Black Hearts of Men,* pp. 123–24.
49. Association for the Benefit of Colored Orphans, *Seventh Annual Report,* p. 6; Harris, p. 157.
50. Freeman, p. 152.
51. Stauffer, p. 219.
52. Ibid., pp. 218–24 and 188.
53. Schlesinger, pp. 169–70, 192–93, 424–26.

3. HORACE GREELEY AND THE BIRTH OF THE REPUBLICAN PARTY

1. Hale, pp. 40–41; Greeley, *Recollections,* p. 144.
2. Burrows and Wallace, pp. 611–15.
3. Greeley, *Recollections,* p. 145.
4. Ibid., pp. 145–50; Hale, pp. 37–39; Burrows and Wallace, pp. 768–69.
5. Greeley, *Recollections,* pp. 285–87.

6. Burrows and Wallace, pp. 620 and 629.

7. Ibid., pp. 629–31; O'Donnell, p. 32.

8. Burrows and Wallace, pp. 631–33.

9. Ibid., pp. 612 and 616.

10. Ibid., pp. 784–85; Homberger, pp. 44–47. Griscorn quoted in Burrows and Wallace, p. 785.

11. Burrows and Wallace, pp. 633–34 and 637.

12. Ibid., pp. 633–35.

13. Ibid., pp. 636–37.

14. Ibid., p. 636.

15. Leland, *The First Hundred Years*, pp. 3–5.

16. Burrows and Wallace, pp. 636–38.

17. McPherson, *Battle Cry*, p. 130; O'Donnell, pp. 32–43.

18. O'Donnell, pp. 38, 127–28; Conyngham, pp. xviii–xix.

19. Burrows and Wallace, pp. 769–73.

20. McCague, p. 13; Burrows and Wallace, pp. 650–51.

21. Burn, *Three Years Among the Working-Classes*, pp. 14 and 120.

22. Burrows and Wallace, pp. 659, 567–69; Bernstein, p. 168.

23. McCague, p. 20.

24. Judson, *Mysteries and Miseries of New York*, pp. 9–12.

25. Burrows and Wallace, pp. 761–65; Asbury, pp. 39–41; Gibson, pp. 30–34.

26. Gibson, pp. 28–29.

27. Hale, pp. 56–62, 131–33.

28. Ibid., pp. 132–33; McPherson, *Battle Cry*, pp. 115–16; Lossing, *Our Country*, 2:1629–30.

29. Greeley, "Why I Am A Whig," pp. 1–5; Greeley, *Recollections*, p. 286; Hale, p. 47.

30. McPherson, *Battle Cry*, pp. 52–54.

31. Greeley, *Recollections*, p. 285.

32. Hale, pp. 140–42.

33. McPherson, *Battle Cry*, pp. 70–77.

34. Hale, pp. 143–44 and 156–59.

35. McPherson, *Battle Cry*, pp. 118–19; Hale, p. 159.

36. Hale, pp. 159–64. Greeley did not come up with the name on his own. George Henry Evans had spoken of a "Great Republican Party of Progress" eight years earlier, and Alvan Bovay had tried to form a "Republican" party in the West earlier in 1854, appealing for help to Greeley, who turned him down; Greeley asserted, apparently with great acumen, that the moment was not yet ripe (Hale, pp. 164–65).

37. McPherson, *Battle Cry*, p. 126; Hale, p. 170.

38. McPherson, *Battle Cry*, pp. 126–29; Hale, pp. 169–73.

39. McPherson, *Battle Cry*, pp. 129–31, 133–36.

40. Ibid., p. 132.

41. Ibid., pp. 136–44; Hale, pp. 171–73.

42. Hale, pp. 169–70.

43. Atchison and Seward quoted in McPherson, *Battle Cry*, p. 145.

4. FERNANDO WOOD, THE "SOUTHERN" MAYOR OF NEW YORK

1. Schlesinger, pp. 490–91. "Southern" Mayor: Mushkat, *Fernando Wood*, p. 98.
2. Burrows and Wallace, p. 553.
3. Ibid., pp. 785, 790.
4. Ibid., pp. 770–73.
5. Ibid., pp. 774, 821, 829–30.
6. Ibid., pp. 825–30; *Encyclopedia of New York City*, pp. 267–68; Bernstein, pp. 92–93.
7. Burrows and Wallace, pp. 825–30; *Encyclopedia of New York City*, p. 977; Bernstein, pp. 92–93.
8. Burrows and Wallace, pp. 825–30; Bernstein, p. 200.
9. Burrows and Wallace, p. 823.
10. Ibid., pp. 823, 827.
11. Ibid., pp. 827, 830.
12. Ibid., pp. 830–31.
13. Mushkat, *Fernando Wood*, pp. 28–37; footnote: Schlesinger, pp. 191–92.
14. Homberger, p. 151.
15. Mushkat, *Fernando Wood*, p. 11.
16. Ibid., pp. 15–18.
17. Ibid., pp. 22–23.
18. Ibid., pp. 40–51.
19. Quoted in McPherson, *Battle Cry*, p. 159.
20. Quoted in ibid., pp. 159, 161.
21. Mushkat, *Fernando Wood*, pp. 54–59.
22. Macleod, *Hon. Fernando Wood*, pp. 14–15. Paris as context: Burrows and Wallace, pp. 821–22, 831.
23. Burrows and Wallace, p. 832.
24. Mushkat, *Fernando Wood*, pp. 58–59.
25. Rioters quoted in Mushkat, *Fernando Wood*, p. 74; Strong quoted in Burrows and Wallace, p. 839.
26. Mushkat, *Fernando Wood*, pp. 69–70; Burrows and Wallace, p. 838.
27. Mushkat, *Fernando Wood*, pp. 68–71; Burrows and Wallace, p. 840; Anbinder, pp. 278–79.
28. Quoted in Mushkat, *Fernando Wood*, p. 72.
29. Ibid., pp. 74–75; Burrows and Wallace, p. 839.
30. Anbinder, pp. 280–84; Burrows and Wallace, pp. 839–40; footnote: *Encyclopedia of New York City*, p. 639.
31. Burrows and Wallace, pp. 840–41; McCague, p. 20.
32. Quoted in Mushkat, *Fernando Wood*, pp. 74–75.
33. Ruffin, *Diary*, 1:83.
34. Burrows and Wallace, pp. 842–46.
35. Ruffin, *Diary*, 1:122.
36. Burrows and Wallace, pp. 847–51.
37. Ruffin, *Diary*, 1:124.
38. Mushkat, *Fernando Wood*, pp. 77–81.

39. Burrows and Wallace, pp. 789–90.
40. Ruffin, *Diary,* 1:229.
41. Mushkat, *Fernando Wood,* p. 85.
42. Ibid., p. 91.
43. Ibid., p. 93.
44. Mushkat, *Fernando Wood,* pp. 93–94.
45. Quoted in Gibson, pp. 104–5.
46. McPherson, *Battle Cry,* pp. 53–54, 135, 162–67; Hale, pp. 202–3; Donald, *Lincoln,* pp. 203–4.
47. Donald, pp. 187–95, 236.
48. Ibid., pp. 206–9.
49. Ibid., pp. 207–8; *American Negro Reference Book,* pp. 484–86.
50. Ibid., pp. 209, 231–32.
51. Ibid., pp. 233–35.
52. Ibid., pp. 234, 245.
53. Ibid., pp. 237–39.
54. Ibid., pp. 236, 243.
55. McPherson, *Battle Cry,* pp. 215–16, 220–22.
56. Ibid., pp. 223–24.
57. Mushkat, *Fernando Wood,* pp. 113–14; Spann, *Gotham at War,* pp. 5, 8; newspapers quoted in Burrows and Wallace, p. 865.
58. McPherson, *Battle Cry,* pp. 228–30.
59. Ibid., p. 232.
60. McPherson, *Battle Cry,* pp. 232–33.
61. Foner, p. 502; McPherson, *Ordeal,* p. 569.
62. Ruffin, *Diary,* 1:504.
63. Quoted in Lee, *Discontent in New York,* p. 2.
64. Mushkat, *Fernando Wood,* pp. 111–13; Spann, *Gotham at War,* p. 6; Burrows and Wallace, pp. 867–68.
65. Lee, *Discontent in New York,* p. 2; McPherson, *Battle Cry,* pp. 234–35.
66. McPherson, *Battle Cry,* pp. 115–16.
67. Ibid.; McCague, pp. 51–52; Lossing, 2:1629–30.
68. Mushkat, *Fernando Wood,* pp. 113–14; footnote: Burrows and Wallace, pp. 872–73.

5. "SLAVERY MUST DIE THAT THE NATION MIGHT LIVE"

1. Mushkat, *Fernando Wood,* p. 114.
2. Ibid.
3. McPherson, *Ordeal,* pp. 144–45; Spann, *Gotham at War,* p. 8; Ruffin, *Diary,* 1:588.
4. Mushkat, *Fernando Wood,* pp. 114 and 119.
5. Strong, p. 121.
6. Spann, "Union Green," p. 194; Cogan, "Irish-American Press," pp. 37–38; Conyngham, p. xv.
7. Spann, "Union Green," p. 194; Cogan, *Irish-American Press,* pp. 37–38; Conyngham, p. xv.
8. Spann, "Union Green," p. 193; Strong quoted in Cogan, p. 33; Conyngham, p. xv.

9. Conyngham, p. xv.

10. McPherson, *Ordeal*, p. 149; Lowitt, *Merchant Prince*, p. 212; Spann, *Gotham at War*, pp. 14–15; Mushkat, *Fernando Wood*, pp. 116–17.

11. Lee, *Discontent in New York*, p. 2.

12. Spann, "Union Green," p. 194.

13. Jones, *Irish Brigade*, p. 7; Conyngham, p. xii; Spann, "Union Green," pp. 197–98; O'Donnell, pp. 128, 204–208; footnote: O'Donnell, p. 208.

14. Conyngham, p. xvi; Halpine quoted in Spann, "Union Green," p. 194.

15. McPherson, *Battle Cry*, pp. 333, 347, 354; Geary, p. 6.

16. McPherson, *Battle Cry*, p. 354.

17. Conyngham, p. xvi; Gibson, p. 144.

18. McPherson, *Battle Cry*, pp. 355–56, 358.

19. Ibid., pp. 350–56.

20. Ibid., pp. 356–58.

21. Mushkat, *The Reconstruction*, pp. 27–31; Klement, *Copperheads*, p. 2.

22. Mushkat, *The Reconstruction*, pp. 27–31.

23. Ibid., p. 32.

24. McPherson, *Battle Cry*, pp. 367–68; Donald, p. 330.

25. McPherson, *Battle Cry*, pp. 413–15, 418–22.

26. Ibid., p. 437; Geary, p. 8.

27. McPherson, *Battle Cry*, pp. 495–96.

28. Ibid., pp. 496–99.

29. Ibid., pp. 494–99.

30. Ibid., p. 499; Mushkat, *The Reconstruction*, pp. 32–34; Donald, p. 363.

31. McPherson, *Battle Cry*, pp. 497–99; Donald, p. 355.

32. Mushkat, *The Reconstruction*, pp. 32–34, and *Fernando Wood*, p. 128.

33. McPherson, *Battle Cry*, pp. 491, 499–500; Donald, p. 362.

34. Donald, pp. 187–95, 236, 362.

35. Ibid., p. 363.

36. Ibid., pp. 363–64.

37. McPherson, *Battle Cry*, pp. 490–91, 499–500; Donald, pp. 364–65.

38. McPherson, *Battle Cry*, pp. 491–92; Geary, p. 10.

39. McPherson, *Battle Cry*, pp. 491–92.

40. Geary, p. xiv; McPherson, *Ordeal*, p. 163.

41. McPherson, *Battle Cry*, pp. 491–92, 500; Murdock, *One Million Men*, p. 6; Geary, pp. xv, 12.

42. McPherson, *Battle Cry*, pp. 492–93; Geary, pp. 34–35.

43. McPherson, *Battle Cry*, p. 493; Geary, p. 44.

44. McPherson, *Battle Cry*, p. 493.

45. Ibid., pp. 504–6.

46. Ibid.; Donald, pp. 364–66.

47. McPherson, *Battle Cry*, pp. 506–9.

48. Ibid.

49. The following account of Gilmore as liaison between Lincoln and Greeley: Hale, pp. 255–65.

50. McPherson, *Battle Cry*, pp. 524–33.

51. Ibid., pp. 532–45 and *Ordeal*, p. 285.

52. Hale, p. 264; Donald, pp. 374–76.

53. Seward quoted in "Africans in America," PBS Web site, under Historical Documents: Emancipation Proclamation.

54. Hale, p. 265.

55. Foner, pp. xxv, 585. Slavery was abolished in New York State in 1827.

56. See, for example, Wood, *The Proceedings of Censure,* or the various essays published by the Society for the Diffusion of Political Knowledge, for biblical justifications of racism and slavery.

57. Daly, p. 179.

58. Ibid., pp. 160–61, 177; Spann, *Gotham at War,* p. 61.

59. Daly, pp. 182–83.

60. Spann, "Union Green," pp. 197, 202.

61. Mushkat, *The Reconstruction,* p. 34.

62. McJimsey, p. 17.

63. McJimsey, pp. 31, 37–39; Mushkat, *Fernando Wood,* p. 126.

64. Bernstein, p. 201; Mushkat, *The Reconstruction,* pp. 34–35 and *Fernando Wood,* p. 92.

65. McJimsey, pp. 39–43; Mushkat, *Fernando Wood,* p. 126.

66. McJimsey, pp. 41–42.

67. Mushkat, *The Reconstruction,* pp. 34–35; McJimsey, p. 39.

68. McJimsey, p. 42.

69. Mushkat, *The Reconstruction,* pp. 35–37; Wall, pp. 20–21.

70. Mushkat, *Fernando Wood,* p. 130; Spann, *Gotham at War* p. 90.

71. Mitchell, *Horatio Seymour,* p. 254; Strong, p. 264; Mushkat, *The Reconstruction,* pp. 36–37.

72. Daly, pp. 194–95; Strong, p. 271.

73. Ruffin, *Diary,* 2:496.

74. Strong, p. 284.

6. EMANCIPATION AND ITS ENEMIES

1. Gibbons Morse, "Personal Recollections of the Draft Riot of 1863," p. 1. Lucy Gibbons Morse wrote these recollections after she was married, but I refer to her in the text by her maiden name to avoid confusion; Emerson, ed., *Abby Gibbons,* 1:243–44; McPherson, *Battle Cry,* p. 491.

2. Emerson, 1:385.

3. Ibid., 1:229–30.

4. Ibid., 1:192.

5. Ibid., 1:210–11.

6. Ibid., 1:238.

7. Howland, *My Heart Toward Home,* pp. xv–xviii.

8. Quarles, *The Negro in the Civil War,* p. 173.

9. Pasternak, "Rise Now and Fly to Arms," p. 187; Geary, p. 52.

10. Pasternak, p. 187.

11. Garnet, p. 55; Harris, p. 226.

12. Schor, *Henry Highland Garnet,* p. 4; Garnet, p. 54; Pasternak, pp. 12–13 and 21–22.

13. Pasternak, pp. 187–88.
14. Ibid., pp. 189–90.
15. Quarles, p. 184; Spann, *Gotham at War,* p. 128.
16. Conyngham, p. xvi; Spann, "Union Green," p. 203; Gibson, p. 142.
17. Conyngham, p. xvi; Gibson, p. 144; Spann, "Union Green," p. 203, 207.
18. Spann, *Gotham at War,* p. 114; Burrows and Wallace, pp. 885–86.
19. *Irish-American,* Jan. 17, 1863.
20. Mitchell, pp. 284–85.
21. Wall, pp. 5–20; Mitchell, pp. 12, 16–17, 19–20, 22–23, 33–35, 44–45, 57–58, 63–64, 95, 111, 131.
22. Burrows and Wallace, p. 886; Bernstein, pp. 146–47.
23. McJimsey, p. 46; Burrows and Wallace, p. 886.
24. McPherson, *Battle Cry,* p. 599; Fredrickson, *Inner Civil War,* pp. 130–31; Burrows and Wallace, p. 887.
25. Bernstein, pp. 152–59.
26. Lowitt, pp. 219–20; Fredrickson, p. 131; Bernstein, pp. 159–60.
27. Geary, pp. 48–51.
28. McPherson, *Battle Cry,* pp. 430–31.
29. Ibid., p. 432.
30. Geary, pp. 50–52, 82, 98; Bernstein, pp. 7–8; Spann, *Gotham at War,* pp. 58, 62.
31. Burrows and Wallace, p. 883; Bernstein, p. 9; Spann, *Gotham at War,* p. 60 and "Union Green," p. 203.
32. Gibson, p. 143.
33. Welsh, *Irish Green and Union Blue,* p. 78; Geary, pp. 50–51, 57–64.
34. Bernstein, pp. 7–8; Geary, p. 52.
35. Welsh, p. 78.
36. Ibid., p. 70.
37. Ibid., p. 65.
38. Ibid., pp. 3–4 (introduction).
39. Ibid., pp. 113–14.
40. Quoted in Spann, "Union Green," p. 204.
41. Wall, pp. 31–32; *World,* March 13, 1863.
42. The following account of the Detroit riot, including footnote: Yacovone, pp. 67–71.
43. Quoted in Gibson, p. 143.
44. Spann, *Gotham at War,* pp. 112–13 and "Union Green," p. 202.
45. Burrows and Wallace, p. 883.
46. Smith, *The City That Was,* p. 58; Bernstein, p. 105.
47. Smith, p. 59.
48. Cook, pp. 9–11; Whitman, *New York Dissected,* p. 92.
49. Smith, pp. 76 and 81.
50. Quoted in ibid., p. 62.
51. Quoted in ibid., pp. 65–69; Cook, pp. 11–12.
52. Quoted in Smith, pp. 65–69.
53. Ibid., pp. 71–76.
54. Ibid., pp. 81–88.
55. Burrows and Wallace, pp. 873–76.

56. Ibid., p. 877; Burn, p. 14.
57. Burrows and Wallace, pp. 877–79.
58. Ibid., p. 888.
59. Spann, "Union Green," p. 203; Gibson, p. 144.
60. Kinchen, pp. 15–16 and 19–20.
61. Ibid., pp. 20–23; Stevenson, pp. 300 and 311; Klement, pp. 123–25.
62. Kinchen, pp. 20–23; Stevenson, pp. 300 and 311; Klement, pp. 123–25.

7. "A HIGHWAYMAN'S CALL ON EVERY AMERICAN CITIZEN FOR '$300 OR YOUR LIFE'"

1. Ruffin, *Diary,* 2:664.
2. Stevens, p. 301; Schor, p. 196.
3. Mitchell, p. 322; *War of the Rebellion,* ser. 3, 3:467; Fry, p. 20.
4. *World,* July 8, 1863.
5. *Daily News,* July 10, 1863.
6. McCague, pp. 46–47; *Tribune,* July 9, 1863.
7. *Herald,* July 11, 1863.
8. Governor Seymour's "Second Annual Message," Fairchild Collection, N-YHS, typescript.
9. Wall, p. 31.
10. Ibid., pp. 36–37; William Kidd to Henry S. Miller, Feb. 3, 1912, Fairchild Collection, N-YHS.
11. *Daily News,* July 11, 1863; *Herald,* July 11, 1863.
12. *War of the Rebellion,* ser. 3, 3:467.
13. Bernstein, p. 13.
14. Benjamin and Benjamin, "New York in the Civil War," pp. 549–50; Cook, p. 6; footnote: *Encyclopedia of New York City,* p. 1127.
15. Jones, p. 15; O'Donnell, pp. 127–28; recruiting poster reproduced in Conyngham.
16. Sifakis, *Who Was Who,* p. 472; Nugent, "The Sixty-ninth Regiment at Fredericksburg"; Conyngham, p. 548.
17. *Evening Post,* July 23, 1863.
18. McCague, pp. 51–52; Horan, pp. 16–18.
19. McCague, pp. 51–52; Horan, pp. 16–18.
20. McCague, pp. 51–52; *Tribune,* July 11, 1863.
21. *Herald,* July 12, 1863; *Banquet . . . Union League Club,* p. 41.
22. *Tribune,* July 11 and 13, 1863; *Daily News,* July 11, 1863; *Herald,* July 12, 1863.
23. News of the draft in other cities reprinted in the *Herald,* July 12, 1863.
24. Ibid., July 14, 1863.
25. Gilmore, *Personal Recollections,* pp. 168–69.
26. Strong, p. 333.
27. Headley, *Great Riots,* p. 149.
28. *World,* July 14, 1863.
29. *Herald,* July 13, 1863.
30. Burrows and Wallace, p. 889; Bernstein, p. 18; Cook, p. 56.
31. Kirk, p. 105; Costello, *Our Firemen,* p. 174.
32. Costello, p. 521.

33. Ibid., pp. 174–75.

34. Ibid., pp. 611–12.

35. Stoddard, *The Volcano,* p. 38.

36. Ibid.; Bernstein, p. 18.

37. McCague, pp. 55–56.

38. Stoddard, pp. 24–26.

39. Walling, *Personal Recollections,* p. 78; Bernstein, pp. 13–14.

40. *Tribune,* July 15, 1863; *World,* July 13, 1863.

41. *Daily News,* July 13, 1863.

42. *Evening Post,* July 23, 1863. On Aug. 1, 1863, the *Irish-American* angrily ridiculed a similar accusation by the *Tribune* that Irish domestics were part of a plot. See also Spann, "Union Green," p. 205.

43. Gilmore, pp. 169–70.

8. "DOWN WITH THE RICH MEN!": THE NEW YORK CITY DRAFT RIOTS BEGIN

1. Daly, p. 250.

2. Bernstein, p. 18; Headley, *Great Riots,* p. 152; *Evening Post,* July 23, 1863.

3. Stoddard, p. 31.

4. Grand Jury Dismissals, the case of Thomas Fitzsimmons, testimony of Charles Clinch and James Jackson, Aug. 18 and 28, 1863, MACNY; Bernstein, p. 18; Stoddard, p. 30; Burrows and Wallace, p. 889.

5. Grand Jury Dismissals, the case of Thomas Fitzsimmons, MACNY; Stoddard, p. 31; Asbury, p. 115.

6. Grand Jury Dismissals, the case of Thomas Fitzsimmons, testimony of Charles Clinch and James Jackson, Aug. 18 and 28, 1863, MACNY.

7. Headley, *Great Riots,* pp. 152–53.

8. Grand Jury Dismissals, Aug. 3, 4, 10, 13, 14, 1863, MACNY.

9. Bernstein, pp. 20–21.

10. Headley, *Great Riots,* p. 153.

11. Stoddard, p. 33.

12. *War of the Rebellion,* ser. 1, 27: pt. 2:899, 905.

13. Crowley's action: Stoddard, pp. 34–35; Headley, p. 159; *World,* July 14, 1863. (Headley quotes the rioters, and Stoddard quotes Crowley's response.)

14. Stoddard, p. 35.

15. Headley, *Great Riots,* pp. 150, 158–59; Stoddard, pp. 34–36; Chapin, "Recollections," pp. 12–13. Chapin's "Recollections" (1890), written decades after the riots, contains entire passages lifted from Headley's *Great Riots* (1873) and is not an authoritative source for most topics. However, since Chapin was a police telegrapher, I cite him for matters relating to the police telegraph system, of which he had firsthand knowledge.

16. Headley, *Great Riots,* pp. 151, 154–55.

17. Strong, p. 335.

18. Stoddard, p. 34.

19. Strong, p. 335.

20. Attack on Kennedy: Grand Jury Dismissals, 1863, MACNY (Cusick is quoted in the testimony of Officer William Kimball, the clerk who accompanied Kennedy);

Tribune, July 14, 1863; *Evening Post,* July 23, 1863; *Banquet . . . of the Union League Club,* pp. 41–42 (and pp. 38–39 for footnote about Kennedy); Headley, *Great Riots,* pp. 154–56; Stoddard, pp. 36–37; Bernstein, p. 18; Cook, pp. 58–59; McCague, prologue.

21. *Evening Post,* July 23, 1863.
22. Opdyke, pp. 265–67; Bernstein, p. 45; Mushkat, *Fernando Wood,* p. 69.
23. Bernstein, pp. 46–49.
24. Choate, *The Life of Joseph H. Choate,* p. 258.
25. *War of the Rebellion,* ser. 1, 27:pt. 2:905–6; *Times,* July 14, 1863; Stoddard, p. 41.
26. Stoddard, pp. 41–43.
27. Grand Jury Dismissal, Aug. 13, 1863, MACNY.
28. Strong, p. 336.
29. Stoddard, p. 50; *War of the Rebellion,* ser. 1, 27:pt. 2:900.
30. Headley, *Great Riots,* pp. 161–62; McCague, pp. 68–69.
31. McCague, p. 72.
32. Headley, *Great Riots,* pp. 156–57; Stoddard, p. 37.
33. McCague, p. 76.
34. Headley, *Great Riots,* p. 157.
35. McCague, pp. 76–77.
36. Chapin, p. 23; McCague, p. 77.
37. McCague, p. 78.
38. Ibid., pp. 78–79.
39. Howland, pp. 319–20.
40. Headley, *Great Riots,* p. 164.
41. Stoddard, p. 43.
42. McCague, pp. 55–56; Stoddard, p. 44. However, no evidence was found to implicate Andrews as a Confederate agent sent to instigate the riots (Neely, *Fate of Liberty,* pp. 132–33).
43. "The Bloody Week," p. 4.
44. Stoddard, pp. 45–46; Bernstein, pp. 18–19.
45. Stoddard, pp. 46–47.
46. New York County District Attorney's Indictments, Aug. 4 to 11, 1863, MACNY.
47. Headley, *Great Riots,* p. 165.
48. McCague, p. 79.
49. Ibid.
50. Stoddard, p. 52.
51. Ibid., p. 53.
52. McCague, pp. 79–80.
53. Stoddard, pp. 53–54.
54. McCague, p. 72.
55. Including footnote: Ackerman, pp. 17, 19–20, 24–25.
56. Chapin, p. 50.
57. *Times,* July 14, 1863.
58. Bernstein, p. 46.
59. Cook, pp. 84, 290 note 24.
60. Cook, pp. 84–85; Bernstein, p. 54.

61. Opdyke, p. 268; Bernstein, p. 45.
62. Cook, pp. 85–86; "Report of Lieutenant McElrath," July 28, 1863, in Headley, *Great Riots,* pp. 328–31.
63. Cook, p. 86.
64. Headley, *Great Riots,* pp. 265–66.
65. Stoddard, p. 79.
66. Chapin, pp. 13–14.
67. Stoddard, pp. 54–58; McCague, pp. 79–81. Burrows and Wallace, p. 890, say ten people died in the fire. See also Cook, p. 70 for death toll.
68. Cook, p. 85.
69. Ibid., p. 78; Bernstein, pp. 24–25.
70. *World,* July 14, 1863.
71. Lord, *The Fremantle Diary,* pp. 240–41.

9. "CHASED, STONED, AND BEATEN": "A CRUSADE AGAINST NEGROES"

1. *New York Age,* Jan. 9, 1896. Williamson Collection, Schomburg Center, NYPL.
2. A business card for the outfitting store advertises its other services. Williamson Collection.
3. Lyons, "Memories of Yesterdays," p. 1. Williamson Collection.
4. Ibid., p. 8.
5. Powell to Garrison, July 18, 1863, in Yacovone, pp. 72–74.
6. Forbes, *African American Women During the Civil War,* p. 157.
7. Association for the Benefit of Colored Orphans, *Twenty-seventh Annual Report,* 1864, p. 5.
8. Association for the Benefit of Colored Orphans, *Seventh Annual Report,* 1844, pp. 7–8.
9. Harris, pp. 148–49; Freeman, p. 177.
10. Forbes, pp. 74–75.
11. Association for the Benefit of Colored Orphans, *Twenty-seventh Annual Report,* 1864, pp. 5–14, for Shotwell's narrative of the first day, July 13.
12. Quoted in Burrows and Wallace, p. 890.
13. Cook, pp. 78 and 85.
14. Quoted in *African-American History in the Press,* 1:302; Spann, *Gotham at War,* p. 100.
15. Association for the Benefit of Colored Orphans, *Twenty-seventh Annual Report,* 1864, pp. 5–14, for Shotwell's narrative of the first day, July 13; Cook, pp. 83–84.
16. New York County District Attorney's indictments, Aug. 4 to Aug. 11, 1863, MACNY. The incident and the dialogue are from Long's testimony.
17. Chapin, pp. 36–37.
18. Quoted in Dannett, *Noble Women of the North,* p. 264.
19. Gibbons Morse, pp. 1–3; Emerson, 1:248.
20. Stoddard, pp. 75–76; Bernstein, p. 47.
21. Stoddard, p. 79; Headley, *Great Riots,* p. 171.
22. Asbury, p. 126.
23. Headley, *Great Riots,* p. 172.
24. Stoddard, pp. 79–80.

25. Headley, *Great Riots,* p. 172.
26. Ibid.
27. Stoddard, p. 80.
28. Headley, *Great Riots,* pp. 172–73.
29. Ibid., pp. 173–74.
30. Parton's account is in Gilmore, pp. 171–73; Hale, pp. 272–73.
31. Rioters' song: Seitz, *Horace Greeley,* p. 209.
32. Garnet, p. 58; Brewer, "Henry Highland Garnet," p. 48.
33. Schor, p. 198; Massie, *America,* pp. 345–46.
34. Stauffer, pp. 112–13.
35. This paragraph and the following account are from: Gilmore, pp. 169–70; Hale, pp. 77–78 and 272–73; Bishop, *Notes and Anecdotes,* pp. 11–13; Congdon, *Reminiscences,* pp. 248–51.
36. *Tribune,* July 18, 1863, quoted in Massie, p. 445.
37. Gilmore, pp. 170–73.
38. Ibid., pp. 173–74.
39. Ibid., pp. 181–82.

10. MONDAY NIGHT: "THE FIERY NUCLEUS OF THE ENTIRE RIOT"

1. Cook, p. 82
2. *Harper's Weekly,* Aug. 1, 1863, p. 494, reprinted in *African-American History in the Press,* p. 302.
3. Stoddard, pp. 99–102.
4. Parton's account is in Gilmore, pp. 173–74.
5. Police sergeant: Barnes, *The Draft Riots,* pp. 34–35.
6. Gay's account is in Gilmore, pp. 175–80.
7. Lyons, p. 8.
8. Powell to Garrison, July 18, 1863, in Yacovone, pp. 72–74; Cook, p. 80.
9. Stoddard, p. 110.
10. Cook, pp. 84–86.
11. Ibid., pp. 83–84; Stoddard, pp. 100–103 and 107.
12. *World,* July 14, 1863.
13. Asbury, pp. 129–30.
14. Quoted in Kirk, pp. 110–11.
15. "Report of Lieutenant McElrath," July 28, 1863, in Headley, *Great Riots,* pp. 328–31.
16. Bernstein, pp. 48–49.
17. Strong, pp. 336–37.
18. Bernstein, p. 49.
19. Opdyke, p. 273.
20. Bernstein, p. 49; Cook, pp. 94–95.
21. Strong, p. 337.
22. Emerson, 2:47; Gibbons Morse, pp. 1–3.
23. Emerson, 2:47–48.
24. The following account is from Gilmore, pp. 181–84.

25. Smalley, *Anglo-American Memories,* p. 162.
26. Paragraphs on telegraphers: Barnes, pp. 25–29; Headley, *Great Riots,* pp. 185–88.
27. Paragraphs on detectives: Barnes, pp. 29–31; Headley, *Great Riots,* pp. 188–90.
28. Costello, p. 521; Bernstein, pp. 21–22.
29. Bernstein, p. 22.
30. Ibid., pp. 23–24.
31. Ibid., pp. 19–21, 24.
32. Stoddard, pp. 112–113; Cook, pp. 93–94.
33. "Report of Lieutenant McElrath," July 28, 1863, in Headley, *Great Riots,* pp. 328–31.
34. Franklin's account: "Report of Captain Franklin," July 20, 1863, in ibid., pp. 326–28.
35. "Report of Lieutenant McElrath," July 28, 1863, in ibid., pp. 328–31.

II. "GOVERNMENT IN THE HANDS OF THE WHITE RACE ALONE"

1. Lyons, p. 8.
2. Ibid., pp. 8–9.
3. New York County District Attorney's Indictments, Aug. 4 to Aug. 11, 1863, MACNY. The following account of the assault on a black man on Leroy Street and all of the quotes in it are drawn from the testimony of Edward Ray and others in the case. Ray mentions two different liquor stores in the same vicinity. *To the Memory of the Martyrs,* a pamphlet, mentions that the black man carried a basket on his arm.
4. Ibid. The police captain John Dickson's testimony contradicts this, saying that there were no people around the body when he arrived, except some firemen who were helpful in loading the victim onto a cart.
5. Ibid.
6. Headley, *Great Riots,* pp. 206–9.
7. Cook, pp. 99–100.
8. Headley, *Great Riots,* pp. 206–7.
9. *World,* July 14, 1863.
10. Ibid., July 15, 1863.
11. Ibid., July 14, 1863.
12. Ibid.
13. McJimsey, p. 49; *Evening Post,* July 14, 1863.
14. *World,* July 14, 1863.
15. Cook, pp. 86–87, 102–3.
16. Spann, *Gotham at War,* p. 100.
17. Kirk, p. 112.
18. Headley, *Great Riots,* pp. 192–94.
19. Cook, p. 100.
20. Headley, *Great Riots,* pp. 195–96; *Tribune,* July 15, 1863.
21. *Tribune,* July 15, 1863; Headley, *Great Riots,* pp. 195–96; Cook, pp. 100–101; Stoddard, p. 139.
22. Stoddard, p. 123; *Tribune,* July 16, 1863.
23. *Tribune,* July 15, 1863; Cook, p. 101; Stoddard, pp. 140–41; Headley, *Great Riots,* pp. 196–97.

24. "Report of Lieutenant McElrath," July 28, 1863, in Headley, *Great Riots,* pp. 328–31.

25. "Report of Lieutenant Wood," July 20, 1863, in ibid., pp. 322–23.

26. Cook, pp. 102–3; "Report of Captain Franklin," July 23, 1863, in Headley, *Great Riots,* pp. 313–17.

27. Gilmore, pp. 189–92.

28. Hale, pp. 273–274; *Tribune,* July 18, 1863, quoted in Massie, p. 445.

29. Gilmore, pp. 192–93; Bishop, pp. 11–12; Congdon, pp. 248–51.

30. Hale, pp. 273–74; *Tribune,* July 18, 1863, quoted in Massie, p. 445.

31. Gilmore, pp. 192–93; Bishop, pp. 11–12; Congdon, pp. 248–51.

32. Stoddard, pp. 169–70; *Tribune,* July 15, 1863; *World,* July 15, 1863.

33. Cook, p. 101; Stoddard, pp. 169–70; *Tribune,* July 15, 1863.

34. *Times,* July 15, 1863; Stoddard, pp. 169–72; Cook, p. 101; Headley, *Great Riots,* pp. 200–201.

35. Barnes, p. 61; Headley, *Great Riots,* pp. 200–201; *World,* July 15, 1863.

36. *Tribune,* July 15, 1863; Stoddard, pp. 169–72; Cook, p. 101; Headley, *Great Riots,* pp. 200–201.

37. *World,* July 15, 1863; *Times,* July 15, 1863.

38. Stoddard, pp. 171–72; Cook, pp. 101–2.

39. *War of the Rebellion,* ser. 3, 3:488–494.

40. Ruffin, *Diary,* 3:70.

12. "THE POLICE CANNOT MUCH LONGER SUSTAIN THE CONTEST"

1. Wingate, p. 40.

2. Stevens, p. 293; Wingate, p. 40.

3. Lockwood, pp. 144–45.

4. Wingate, pp. 42–43.

5. Opdyke, p. 274; *War of the Rebellion,* ser. 1, 27: pt. 2:916; Stoddard, pp. 257, 265.

6. *World,* July 15, 1863.

7. Ackerman, p. 13; *World,* July 16, 1863 quoted in Wall, p. 39.

8. Ackerman, pp. 15–17, 20; Bernstein, p. 50.

9. *World,* July 15, 1863.

10. Ibid.; Bernstein, pp. 50–51, 54; Ackerman, pp. 20–21; Cook, p. 106.

11. *World,* July 15, 1863; Bernstein, pp. 50–51, 54; Ackerman, pp. 20–21.

12. Bernstein, pp. 51–52.

13. Dupree and Fishel, eds., "An Eyewitness Account," p. 476; Cook, p. 72.

14. Daly, p. 251.

15. Cook, pp. 116–17.

16. Spann, *Gotham at War,* p. 100.

17. *Tribune,* July 15, 1863; Bernstein, p. 55.

18. Lowitt, p. 220.

19. *Tribune,* July 16, 1863; *Evening Post,* July 15, 1863.

20. "Report of Captain Putnam," July 21, 1863, in Headley, *Great Riots,* pp. 307–08.

21. Stoddard, pp. 262–64.

22. "Report of Captain Putnam," July 21, 1863, in Headley, *Great Riots,* pp. 307–13; Headley, *Great Riots,* pp. 211–12; Walling, p. 80; Cook, p. 120.

23. "Report of Captain Putnam," July 21, 1863, in Headley, *Great Riots,* pp. 307–13; *World,* July 15, 1863; *Tribune,* July 15, 1863; footnote on Jews' Hospital: *Encyclopedia of New York City,* pp. 560–61 and Mount Sinai Hospital Web site.

24. The following account is from: *Tribune,* July 15, 1863; *World,* July 15, 1863; "Report of Captain Franklin," July 23, 1863, in Headley, *Great Riots,* pp. 313–17; Headley, *Great Riots,* pp. 202–3; Barnes, pp. 86–88.

25. The following account is from the *World,* July 15, 1863.

26. Headley, *Great Riots,* pp. 223–24.

27. "Report of Captain Franklin," July 23, 1863, in Headley, *Great Riots,* pp. 313–17; Supreme Court Cases, Grand Jury Dismissals, 1863, MACNY; Cook, p. 123.

28. The following account is from: Gibbons Morse, pp. 4–5.

29. James Gibbons quoted in Emerson, 2:46–47.

30. Barnes, pp. 79–80, 84–85; "Report of Captain Franklin," July 23, 1863, in Headley, *Great Riots,* pp. 313–17.

31. Gibbons Morse, pp. 6–7.

32. Emerson, 2:50–51.

33. Gibbons Morse, p. 7; Choate, pp. 255–57.

34. Choate, pp. 255–57.

35. Headley, *Great Riots,* p. 225; Bernstein, pp. 38–39; Walling, pp. 81–82; Chapin, p. 88; Cook, pp. 126–28.

36. Headley, *Great Riots,* pp. 224–25; Cook, p. 128.

37. Walling, pp. 81–82; "Report of Captain Wilkins," July 21, 1863, in Headley, *Great Riots,* pp. 317–19.

38. Headley, *Great Riots,* pp. 224–25.

39. "Report of Captain Wilkins," July 21, 1863, in Headley, *Great Riots,* pp. 317–19.

40. Gilmore, pp. 194–95.

41. Cook, pp. 133–34.

42. Ibid., pp. 135–36.

43. Ibid., p. 129.

44. Leonard, "Three Days of Terror," p. 227.

45. Strong, pp. 338–39.

46. Powell to Garrison, July 18, 1863, in Yacovone, pp. 72–74.

47. Cook, p. 128; Walling, pp. 82–84; Barnes, p. 70; Headley, *Great Riots,* p. 226.

48. Headley, *Great Riots;* p. 226.

49. Bernstein, pp. 50–51.

50. Headley, pp. 226–27; Mitchell, pp. 284–85.

51. Daly, pp. 246–50.

52. Gibbons Morse, p. 8.

53. Dupree and Fishel, eds., "An Eyewitness Account," pp. 476–78.

54. *Report of the Committee of Merchants,* p. 26.

55. Emerson, 2:47, 49–50; Gibbons Morse, p. 8.

56. *War of the Rebellion,* ser. 1, 27:pt. 2:888–89.

13. DOOM OR DELIVERANCE: WEDNESDAY, JULY 15— DAY THREE

1. Opdyke, p. 274; *War of the Rebellion,* ser. 1, 27:pt. 2:916.
2. *Times,* July 14, 1863.
3. Stevens, pp. 301, 311.
4. *Tribune,* July 15, 1863.
5. Strong, p. 341.
6. *Times,* July 17, 1863; *Boston Courier,* July 15, 1863, reprinted in the *Times,* July 18, 1863.
7. Ibid.
8. *Times,* July 16, 1863; Cook, p. 139; McCague, pp. 135–36.
9. Cook, p. 139.
10. Asbury, p. 148; Headley, *Great Riots,* pp. 206–8, 210.
11. Quoted in Cook, p. 140.
12. *Report of the Committee of Merchants,* pp. 17–18; Cook, pp. 140–41, 298n; *Tribune,* July 16, 1863; New York County District Attorney's Indictments, Aug. 11 to Oct. 17, 1863, MACNY.
13. *Tribune,* July 16, 1863; Cook, pp. 141–42.
14. "Report of Lieutenant Ryer," July 20, 1863, printed in Headley, *Great Riots,* pp. 323–26; *Times,* July 16, 1863.
15. Cook, pp. 142–43.
16. Pasternak, p. 192.
17. New York County District Attorney's Indictments, Aug. 11 to Oct. 17, 1863, *The People v. Joseph Marshall,* MACNY.
18. Account of Franklin's murder: *To the Memory of the Martyrs;* Grand Jury Dismissals, July 27, 1863; New York County District Attorney's Indictments, Aug. 4 to Aug. 11, 1863, MACNY.
19. Strong, pp. 339–40.
20. Cook, p. 106; Choate, pp. 260–61; Headley, *Great Riots,* pp. 256–57; *Herald,* July 15, 1863.
21. *Herald,* July 15, 1863; *Tribune,* July 14 and 16, 1863; Cook, p. 106.
22. *Herald,* July 15, 1863.
23. Cook, pp. 139–40; *Times,* July 15, 1863.
24. Choate, pp. 256–57.
25. Gibbons Morse, p. 8.
26. Emerson, 2:43.
27. Ibid., 44–45.
28. Gibbons Morse, pp. 8–9.
29. This account is from New York County District Attorney's Indictments, Aug. 4 to Aug. 11, 1863, MACNY. The quotes are from the testimony of Josiah and Ellen Porter.
30. Ibid. For Doherty's act of vengeance, see Cook, p. 145.
31. Bernstein, pp. 52–53; Cook, p. 149.
32. Ruffin, *Diary,* 3:74–75.
33. Opdyke, p. 277.

34. Headley, *Great Riots,* p. 245.

35. *Times,* July 15, 1863.

36. Bernstein, pp. 38–39, 61–62.

37. *World,* July 15, 1863; Bernstein, p. 51.

38. Bernstein, p. 55 and notes 77–78 on p. 306; quoted in Bernstein, p. 54.

39. *Times,* July 16, 1863.

40. Quoted in Bernstein, pp. 55–56.

41. Ibid.

42. Quoted in ibid., p. 59.

14. "HELLISH PASSIONS CULMINATING IN RIOTS, ARSON, AND MURDER"

1. Bernstein, p. 61.

2. *World,* July 15, 1863.

3. *Daily News,* July 15, 1863.

4. Quoted in Kirk, p. 114.

5. Gilmore, p. 195.

6. *Tribune,* July 18, 1863, quoted in Massie, p. 445.

7. Headley, *Great Riots,* p. 21.

8. *Times,* July 15, 1863.

9. Gilmore, pp. 195–96.

10. Mayor Opdyke's proclamation printed in Stoddard, appendix, pp. 347–48.

11. *Cook,* pp. 148–49; *War of the Rebellion,* ser. 1, 27:pt. 2:895–96.

12. *War of the Rebellion,* ser. 1, 27:pt. 2:898.

13. Bernstein, pp. 60–61.

14. The following account is from "Report of Lieutenant Ryer," in Headley, *Great Riots,* pp. 324–25; Cook, pp. 149–50.

15. Cook, p. 150; Headley, *Great Riots,* pp. 252–53; Bernstein, pp. 39, 51, 59.

16. Cook, pp. 152–53.

17. Leonard, p. 229.

18. *Times,* July 16, 1863.

19. Ibid.; *Tribune,* July 17, 1863; Cook, p. 153; Leonard, p. 229.

20. *Times,* July 16, 1863; Cook, p. 153; "Report of Captain Putnam" and "Report of Captain Shelley" in Headley, *Great Riots,* pp. 309–10, 333; Headley, *Great Riots,* p. 242.

21. The following account is from Leonard, pp. 229–31; Cook, pp. 154–55.

22. *Times,* July 16, 1863; Cook, p. 151.

23. Cook, p. 126.

24. Chapin, pp. 55–56.

25. Stoddard, p. 256.

26. Chapin, pp. 24–25; McCague, p. 53.

27. *War of the Rebellion,* ser. 1, 27:pt. 2:920.

28. Stoddard, pp. 257, 265; Cook, pp. 155, 157; Quigley, p. 5; Swinton, pp. 350–53.

29. Headley, *Great Riots,* p. 243; Stoddard, p. 257; Leonard, p. 233.

15. THE FINAL DAYS: THURSDAY AND FRIDAY

1. Lyons, p. 9.
2. Stoddard, pp. 266–71; Cook, pp. 157–58.
3. Cook, p. 160.
4. Ibid., pp. 160–61; Barnes, pp. 56–57; Bernstein, p. 39.
5. Opdyke, p. 279.
6. McCague, pp. 160–62; Cook, pp. 184–87; Neely, p. 133; *World,* July 17, 1863; *Tribune,* July 16, 1863.
7. Cook, p. 157.
8. Choate, pp. 257–58.
9. *War of the Rebellion,* ser. 1, 27:pt. 2:902.
10. *World,* July 16, 1863.
11. The following account is from the *Times,* July 16, 1863.
12. Cook, p. 162; *Banquet . . . of the Union League Club,* pp. 43–44.
13. Cook, pp. 160–61; Bernstein, p. 39.
14. Stoddard, p. 273; Cook, pp. 162–63; Headley, *Great Riots,* p. 249 and Putnam's account on pp. 310–13.
15. The following account is from Stoddard, pp. 272–74; Cook, pp. 163–64; Headley, *Great Riots,* pp. 249–50 and Putnam's account on pp. 310–13; McCague, p. 164.
16. Dispersal of mobs and flushing out snipers: Bernstein, pp. 38–39, 60–61; McCague, p. 164; Henry Congdon to Charles Congdon, July 17, 1863, N-YHS, MSS; Cook, p. 164.
17. Emerson, 2:45–47.
18. Ibid., 1:4.
19. Ibid., 2:51–52.
20. Ibid., 2:57–58.
21. Ibid., 2:53–54.
22. Smalley, *Anglo-American Memories,* p. 161.
23. Cook, p. 188.
24. Choate, p. 259.
25. Cook, p. 165; Bernstein, p. 62; Headley, *Great Riots,* pp. 256–58.
26. Hughes's speech: *Irish-American,* July 25, 1863.
27. Bernstein, p. 62; Cook, p. 165.
28. Choate, pp. 260–61.
29. Welsh, p. 110.
30. Ibid., p. 113.
31. Ibid., p. 115.
32. *Times,* July 29, 1863; *Encyclopedia of New York City,* p. 860.
33. Brownson, *Brownson's Quarterly Review,* Oct. 1863, pp. 385–89; Wittke, *The Irish in America* pp. 41–42, 122; Schlesinger, p. 495; *Encyclopedia of New York City,* p. 162.
34. Strong, p. 343; *Tribune,* July 18, 1863; Bernstein, pp. 24–25; footnote: Anbinder, pp. 167–70.
35. *Harper's Weekly,* Aug. 1, 1863, quoted in Gibson, p. 158.
36. Gibson, p. 158; Spann, *Gotham at War,* p. 102.
37. Clarence Eytinge to "My dear Admiral" July 16, 1863, N-YHS, MSS.

38. Bernstein, p. 62.
39. Daly, pp. 251–52.
40. Bernstein, pp. 62–63.
41. Choate, p. 258.
42. Cook, pp. 165–66; Headley, *Great Riots*, p. 263.

16. A PLOT TO "MAKE THE NORTHERN STATES A BATTLE-FIELD"

1. *Richmond Enquirer,* July 18, 1863, quoted in *Tribune,* July 22, 1863.
2. Ruffin, *Diary*, 3:83.
3. Stevenson, pp. 311–12.
4. Wingate, p. 46.
5. McPherson, *Battle Cry,* pp. 667–70.
6. Yacovone, p. 71.
7. Quoted in Quigley, pp. 10–11.
8. McPherson, *Battle Cry,* pp. 686–87.
9. Ruffin, *Diary*, 3:74.
10. Choate, pp. 259–60.
11. *Christian Recorder,* Sept. 1863, quoted in Maynard and Cottman, *Weeksville Then and Now,* p. 20; "Many Thousands Gone: Long Island African-Americans and the Civil War," exhibit at Federal Hall National Memorial, New York, Feb. 2003; *Report of the Committee of Merchants,* pp. 7, 30.
12. Choate, pp. 259–60.
13. Daly, pp. 249–50.
14. Ibid., p. 251.
15. Ibid., p. 252.
16. Jay's letter is in *War of the Rebellion,* ser. 3, 3:541–42.
17. Ibid., ser. 1, 27:pt. 2:903–4.
18. Hale, p. 274.
19. Ibid.
20. Garnet, p. 59; Bernstein, p. 57; *Report of the Committee of Merchants,* pp. 4–10.
21. *Report of the Committee of Merchants,* p. 30.
22. Ibid., pp. 4–6.
23. Ibid., pp. 12 and 27.
24. Bernstein, pp. 56–57.
25. Choate, pp. 259–60.
26. Lyons, pp. 9–10.
27. Ibid., pp. 9–10.
28. Ibid., p. 10.
29. Association for the Benefit of Colored Orphans, *Twenty-seventh Annual Report,* 1864, pp. 9–10.
30. *Report of the Committee of Merchants,* p. 26.
31. Cook, p. 176; Asbury, pp. 154–55; Wall, p. 39. Because construction materials and labor are a more expensive today, replacing and repairing a similar number of buildings would cost much more than $100 million.

32. Cook, pp. 174–75; Spann, *Gotham at War,* p. 101; Vincent Colyer to Matthew Brennan, Feb. 23, 1864, Museum of the City of New York; *Sketch of the Life of the Rev. Charles B. Ray,* pp. 49–50.

33. Cook, pp. 176–77; Asbury, p. 154; future strikes: Bruce, *1877: Year of Violence,* passim.

34. Cook, pp. 115, 194.

35. Cook, p. 64 and footnotes 64–65 on p. 281.

36. Ibid., p. 194.

37. Asbury, p. 154; Quigley, p. 12; *Christian Recorder,* Aug. 1, 1863; *Sketch of the Life of the Rev. Charles B. Ray,* p. 49.

38. Cook, pp. 197–98.

39. Stoddard, p. 274.

40. Asbury, p. 125; Burrows and Wallace, p. 890. See also Cook, p. 70.

41. Spann, *Gotham at War,* p. 101; Cook, pp. 193–94.

42. Cook, p. 195.

43. Blacks driven northward to Harlem: Harris, p. 2; Everett Beanne, a map titled "The Trek Northward: Movement of the Negro Population in N.Y.C.," facing title page in Ottley and Weatherby; Edward O'Donnell, "A Neighborhood of Their Own," *Times,* June 6, 2004. Comparison of draft riots and Ku Klux Klan violence: Thomas Nast, cartoons in *Harper's Weekly,* Sept. 5 and Oct. 10, 1868.

17. AFTERMATH: "SITTING ON TWO VOLCANOES"

1. Gilmore, pp. 198–99. Judge Edmonds's role in Rynders trial: Gibson, p. 34.

2. Gilmore, pp. 198–99.

3. Bernstein, p. 63; Wall, pp. 45, 46–51. The case against the draft never reached the Supreme Court.

4. Ackerman, pp. 24–26; Spann, *Gotham at War,* pp. 103–5; Bernstein, pp. 201–2.

5. Wall, pp. 51–52; Burrows and Wallace p. 896; Headley, Great Riots, p. 157; quoted in Chapin, p. 22.

6. Wall, p. 51; Ackerman, p. 28.

7. Ruffin, *Diary,* 3:118.

8. Ackerman, p. 28; Opdyke, pp. 277, 290; Cook, p. 174; Spann, *Gotham at War,* pp. 103–4; Burrows and Wallace, p. 896; Bernstein, pp. 201–2.

9. Spann, *Gotham at War,* pp. 103–5; Ackerman, pp. 28–29.

10. Spann, *Gotham at War,* p. 104; Murdock, pp. 259–60, 273–74, 283.

11. Welsh, p. 121.

12. Bernstein, pp. 63–64; Cook, p. 180; Ackerman, pp. 28–29; footnote: Ackerman, p. 28.

13. Cook, pp. 177–80.

14. Ibid., p. 180.

15. Ruffin, *Diary,* 3:122.

16. Matthew Powers to Matthew Brennan, Aug. 31, 1863, New York County District Attorney's Indictments, Aug. 4 to Aug. 11, 1863, MACNY. While of a later date, the letter is included on the microfilm with testimony from the indictment of Powers.

17. Costello, p. 521.

18. Cook, pp. 173, 304 note 12.

19. *Times,* July 15, 1863.

20. Bernstein, p. 203.

21. McPherson, *Battle Cry,* pp. 670–71; Ruffin, *Diary,* 3:134–35.

22. McPherson, *Battle Cry,* pp. 670–75; Catton, pp. 246–50, 255–57.

23. McPherson, *Battle Cry,* pp. 676; Catton, p. 258. Draft call: Wall, p. 53.

24. McPherson, *Battle Cry,* pp. 676–81; Catton, pp. 258–59, 261–65, 270–74.

25. McPherson, *Battle Cry,* p. 682; Catton, pp. 235–37.

26. Stevens, pp. 399–401.

27. Mushkat, *The Reconstruction,* pp. 42–43; *Fernando Wood,* p. 139.

28. McPherson, *Battle Cry,* pp. 684–85.

29. Ibid., pp. 685–86.

30. Ibid., pp. 687–88.

31. Daly, pp. 267–68; McPherson, *Battle Cry,* pp. 687–88.

32. Quoted in Mushkat, *The Reconstruction,* p. 43.

33. Mushkat, *Fernando Wood,* pp. 139–45.

34. Mushkat, *The Reconstruction,* pp. 43–44; Gibson, pp. 159–60.

35. Mushkat, *The Reconstruction,* p. 44; Gibson, p. 159.

36. Mushkat, *The Reconstruction,* pp. 42–44; Gibson, p. 160; Quigley, p. 9; Ackerman, p. 21.

37. Homberger, pp. 149–50; Hershkowitz, *Tweed's New York,* p. 149.

38. Homberger, pp. 149–50.

39. Bernstein, pp. 71, 222–23; Mushkat, *The Reconstruction,* pp. 42–43, 59 and *Fernando Wood,* p. 139; Gibson, pp. 160–62.

40. Cook, p. 175.

41. Quigley, pp. 4, 81–82.

42. Lyons, pp. 10–12, 16; Yacovone, p. 75; Quigley, p. 4.

43. *Report of the Committee of Merchants,* p. 12; Bernstein, p. 66; Harris, pp. 118–19.

44. *Sketch of the Life of the Rev. Charles B. Ray,* pp. 48–51.

45. Ibid., pp. 7–18 and 30; Woodson, *History of the Negro Church,* p. 173.

46. Quoted in *Sketch of the Life of the Rev. Charles B. Ray,* pp. 48–51.

47. Quigley, p. 12.

48. Pasternak, pp. 194–95.

49. Garnet, p. 58. Blacks encountered dismal treatment in the Union army and when captured by the Confederates, but they continued to enlist in order to secure the end of slavery. Because they were given dangerous duty and rarely allowed to surrender by the enemy, of all blacks who signed up, an estimated 37 percent were killed (Burrows and Wallace, pp. 898–99).

50. Pasternak, p. 197.

51. Quoted in ibid.

52. Ibid., p. 198.

53. Quoted in ibid., pp. 197–98.

54. Quoted in Quigley, p. 13.

55. Spann, "Union Green," p. 205.

56. Daly, p. 278.

18. "OUR BLEEDING, BANKRUPT, ALMOST DYING COUNTRY"

1. Matthew Powers to Matthew Brennan, Dec. 25, 1863, New York County District Attorney's Indictments, Aug. 4 to Aug. 11, 1863, MACNY. While of a later date, the letter is included on the microfilm with testimony from the indictment of Powers.
2. McPherson, *Battle Cry,* pp. 698–703.
3. Horan, *Confederate Agent,* p. 65.
4. Kinchen, pp. 25–26.
5. McPherson, *Battle Cry,* p. 763; Horan, p. 79; Axelrod, p. 220; Kinchen, pp. 51–52.
6. Horan, p. 68; Axelrod, pp. 220–21.
7. McPherson, *Battle Cry,* pp. 762–64; Horan, p. 68; Axelrod, p. 223.
8. McPherson, *Battle Cry,* pp. 762–64; Horan, p. 68; Axelrod, p. 223.
9. Horan, pp. 72–73; McPherson, *Battle Cry,* p. 763.
10. McPherson, *Battle Cry,* pp. 762–64; Horan, pp. 94–96.
11. Horan, p. 79; Axelrod, p. 223.
12. McPherson, *Battle Cry,* pp. 718–19.
13. Ibid., pp. 719–20.
14. Ibid., p. 720.
15. Quoted in Pullen, *The Twentieth Maine,* p. 154.
16. McPherson, *Battle Cry,* pp. 720–21.
17. Ibid., p. 722.
18. Welsh, p. 155.
19. McPherson, *Battle Cry,* pp. 724–32.
20. Welsh, pp. 102–3, 156–58.
21. Daly, pp. 296–97; McPherson, *Battle Cry,* p. 732.
22. McPherson, *Battle Cry,* p. 732.
23. Catton, p. 378.
24. McPherson, *Battle Cry,* pp. 732–35.
25. Daly, p. 299.
26. McPherson, *Battle Cry,* pp. 735–43.
27. Ibid., p. 742.
28. Ibid., pp. 735–43.
29. Ibid., pp. 743–50.
30. Ibid., pp. 751–58; Catton, pp. 379–80.
31. Strong, p. 474.
32. Hale, pp. 280–81.
33. McPherson, *Battle Cry,* p. 762; Hale, pp. 281–84.
34. McPherson, *Battle Cry,* pp. 762–65.
35. Horan, pp. 89–90.
36. McPherson, *Battle Cry,* pp. 762–65.
37. Ibid.
38. Ibid.; Horan, pp. 121–23, 128.
39. McPherson, *Battle Cry,* pp. 762–65.
40. Ibid., p. 758; Wall, p. 54.
41. Horan, p. 121.

42. McPherson, *Battle Cry,* p. 765; Horan, pp. 121, 127; Axelrod, p. 237.

43. McPherson, *Ordeal,* pp. 407, 497n; Hale, pp. 277–78; Lowitt, pp. 222–23.

44. McPherson, *Battle Cry,* pp. 766–68; Hale, pp. 281–84.

45. McPherson, *Battle Cry,* pp. 766–68.

46. Greeley to Opdyke, Aug. 18, 1864, John A. Stevens Papers, N-YHS, MSS.

47. McPherson, *Battle Cry,* pp. 768–71.

48. Horan, pp. 123, 128–29.

49. Ibid., p. 129.

50. Ibid., pp. 125–26, 129.

51. Ibid., pp. 129–30.

52. Ibid., p. 130.

53. Ibid., pp. 130–31.

54. McPherson, *Battle Cry,* pp. 764–66.

55. Ibid., pp. 771–72.

56. Strong, pp. 480–81.

57. McPherson, *Battle Cry,* pp. 774–75.

58. Ruffin, *Diary,* 3:558–59.

59. McPherson, *Battle Cry,* pp. 778–79.

60. Ruffin, *Diary,* 3:603.

19. "VILLAINOUS THREATS OF LAYING NORTHERN CITIES IN ASHES"

1. Quigley, p. 20.

2. Hewitt, *Protest and Progress,* pp. 128–29.

3. Association for the Benefit of Colored Orphans, *Twenty-seventh Annual Report,* pp. 11–12, 17.

4. Ibid., pp. 5–6.

5. Ibid.

6. Association for the Benefit of Colored Orphans, *Twenty-eighth Annual Report,* p. 6; Harris, p. 285.

7. Pasternak, pp. 198–199; Quigley, pp. 20–21.

8. Schor, pp. 38–43, 47–48; Harris, pp. 174–79.

9. Pasternak, pp. 200–204; Harris, pp. 175, 278; Quigley, p. 18.

10. Pasternak, pp. 200–204; Quigley, p. 18.

11. *Proceedings of the National Convention of Colored Men,* p. 19.

12. Ibid.

13. Ignatiev, pp. 6–31.

14. "Address of the Colored National Convention to the People of the U.S.," in *Proceedings of the National Convention of Colored Men,* p. 54.

15. Pasternak, pp. 201, 203; footnote: introduction by McCune Smith in Garnet, p. 34.

16. McPherson, *Battle Cry,* pp. 779–80.

17. Ibid., pp. 781–82.

18. Ibid., pp. 782–83: "Delays and appeals kept them in prison until after the war, when the Supreme Court invalidated the conviction of one of them—Lambdin P. Milligan—on the ground that civilians could not be tried by military courts in

non-war zones where civil courts were functioning. The alleged conspirators—along with several other convicted by military courts—went free."

19. McPherson, *Battle Cry,* pp. 782–83.
20. Ibid., pp. 783–88.
21. Ibid., pp. 788–90.
22. Ibid., pp. 789–90.
23. Ibid., p. 790.
24. Horan, p. 181.
25. Ibid.
26. Ibid., pp. 181, 183.
27. Ibid., p. 183; Burrows and Wallace, p. 902.
28. Horan, pp. 164–65, 209; Burrows and Wallace, p. 902.
29. Horan, p. 210; Burrows and Wallace, p. 902; McPherson, *Battle Cry,* p. 781.
30. McPherson, *Battle Cry,* pp. 781–82; Horan, pp. 184–98.
31. Quoted in Horan, pp. 208–11.
32. Burrows and Wallace, p. 903; McPherson, *Battle Cry,* p. 805.
33. Spann, "Union Green," p. 208 and *Gotham at War,* p. 119; Gibson, p. 170.
34. Mushkat, *The Reconstruction,* p. 54; Bernstein, pp. 71, 223, 238, 243; Foner, pp. 478–81.
35. Mushkat, *The Reconstruction,* pp. 53–55.
36. Ibid., pp. 19–20, 37, 53–55, 61, 65, 173–74; Foner, pp. 412–21.
37. McPherson, *Battle Cry,* pp. 774, 806–11; Donald, p. 553.

20. WAR'S END: SLAVERY IS DEAD, THE "DEMON OF CASTE" LIVES ON

1. Horan, pp. 211–13; Burrows and Wallace, pp. 902–3.
2. Horan, pp. 213–15; Burrows and Wallace, pp. 902–3.
3. Horan, pp. 213–15.
4. Ibid., pp. 215–19; Burrows and Wallace, pp. 902–3.
5. Horan, pp. 219–23; footnote: Burroughs and Wallace, p. 903.
6. Burrows and Wallace, p. 903; McPherson, *Battle Cry,* pp. 811–25.
7. Geary, pp. 78, 82–84; Sandburg, *Abraham Lincoln: The War Years,* 2:377 (includes footnote).
8. McPherson, *Battle Cry,* pp. 811–25.
9. Ibid., pp. 706, 712–13, 838–40; Donald, p. 553; Pasternak, p. 204.
10. Donald, pp. 553–54; McPherson, *Battle Cry,* p. 839.
11. Donald, pp. 553–54.
12. McPherson, *Battle Cry,* pp. 839–40.
13. Schor, pp. 205–7; Pasternak, pp. 205–7.
14. Garnet, p. 77.
15. Ibid., pp. 85–86.
16. Pasternak, p. 208.
17. Garnet, p. 72.
18. Blight, *Race and Reunion,* p. 4.
19. Foner, p. 232.
20. Hale, pp. 314–16.

21. Ibid.
22. Ibid., pp. 316–17; Foner, p. 460.
23. Hale, p. 317.
24. Foner, p. 467.
25. Homberger, pp. 67–68; Quigley, pp. 34–36.
26. Quigley, pp. 34–35.
27. Inspectors quoted in Citizens' Association, *Report . . . upon the Sanitary Condition,* pp. 64–65.
28. Homberger, pp. 83–85; Foner, p. 470.
29. Cook, p. 190; Burrows and Wallace, pp. 921–922; Foner, p. 470.
30. Foner, p. 470; Cook, pp. 189–90.
31. Quigley, pp. 36–40; Homberger, p. 59; Foner, pp. 488–511.
32. Burrows and Wallace, p. 904; McPherson, *Battle Cry,* pp. 844–47.
33. Ruffin, *Diary,* 3:829–30.
34. *Journal of the American Irish Historical Society,* 9 (1910), pp. 168–70.
35. Nugent, p. 200.
36. Daly, pp. 351–52.
37. Ibid., p. 352; Blight, pp. 1–5.
38. "Mr. Greeley's Record," p. 3; Daly, pp. 352–54.
39. Winik, *April 1865,* pp. 216, 221–29.
40. Hale, p. 321.
41. "Mr. Greeley's Record," pp. 5–6 and passim; Foner, p. 500, analysis of Schurz true for Greeley.
42. *Journal of the American Irish Historical Society,* 9 (1910), pp. 168–70; Joyce, "The New York Draft Riots," p. 26; Spann, "Union Green," pp. 208–9.
43. Ruffin, *Diary,* 3:946–50.

21. "CONDEMNATION AND REVERSAL OF NEGRO SUFFRAGE"

1. McPherson, *Ordeal,* pp. 495–96; Foner, pp. 176–78, 183.
2. McPherson, *Ordeal,* pp. 497–98; Foner, pp. 178–81.
3. McPherson, *Ordeal,* pp. 497–98; Foner, pp. 178–79.
4. McPherson, *Ordeal,* pp. 498–99; Foner, pp. 180–83, 187, 192–93.
5. McPherson, *Ordeal,* p. 500; Foner, p. 184.
6. McPherson, *Ordeal,* pp. 500–503; Foner, pp. 189–90, 196–97.
7. McPherson, *Ordeal,* pp. 511–12; Foner, pp. 198–200; footnote: McPherson, *Ordeal,* p. 467.
8. Ibid., pp. 513–16.
9. Quoted in Hale, pp. 320–21.
10. McPherson, *Ordeal,* pp. 503–5.
11. McPherson, *Ordeal,* pp. 502, 519–20; Foner, pp. 261–63, 265.
12. McPherson, *Ordeal,* pp. 519–20; Foner, pp. 262–63.
13. McPherson, *Ordeal,* p. 520.
14. Burrows and Wallace, p. 559; *World* and *Daily News,* July 15, 1863; Mushkat, *The Reconstruction,* pp. 130, 236.
15. "Mr. Greeley's Record," p. 9.

16. McPherson, *Ordeal,* pp. 513–15; Foner, pp. 239–51.
17. McPherson, *Ordeal,* pp. 516–18; Foner, pp. 251–54, 256.
18. McPherson, *Ordeal,* pp. 517–18; Fourteenth Amendment, section 2; Foner, p. 255.
19. McPherson, *Ordeal,* p. 518; Foner, p. 255.
20. McPherson, *Ordeal,* pp. 517, 521.
21. Ibid., pp. 518–19; Foner, pp. 260–61, 267–68.
22. McPherson, *Ordeal,* p. 519; Foner, p. 267.
23. McPherson, *Ordeal,* pp. 518, 520–22; Foner, pp. 276–77; Trelease, p. 383.
24. McPherson, *Ordeal,* p. 524; Foner, pp. 276–77, 294.
25. McPherson, *Ordeal,* pp. 524–27; Foner, pp. 282–83, 303–4.
26. "Mr. Greeley's Record," pp. 7 and 11.
27. Ibid., pp. 12–17.
28. McPherson, *Ordeal,* pp. 516–18, 535–36; Foner, pp. 316–23, 352–56; *American Negro Reference Book,* pp. 418–20.
29. McPherson, *Ordeal,* pp. 516–18, 535–36; Foner, pp. 314–15.
30. Mushkat, *The Reconstruction,* pp. 117–18, 120–25, 127–28, 130–31, 136; *World,* Apr. 7, 1868.
31. Mushkat, *Fernando Wood,* pp. 159–61.
32. Wood, *The Proceedings of Censure.*
33. *World,* Apr. 3, 1868.
34. McPherson, *Ordeal,* pp. 537, 543–44; *Tribune,* June 14, 1871.
35. *World,* Apr. 7, 1868.
36. McPherson, *Ordeal,* pp. 537–39; Mushkat, *The Reconstruction,* p. 130.
37. *World,* Apr. 14, 1868; Mushkat, *The Reconstruction,* p. 132.
38. Mushkat, *The Reconstruction,* pp. 16, 127–28, 130–31; Spann, "Union Green," p. 209.
39. Spann, "Union Green," p. 209.
40. Mushkat, *The Reconstruction,* pp. 131, 136–37, 146; Gibson, pp. 218–22, 225–26, 229; Ackerman, p. 53.
41. Mitchell, pp. 396, 412–13.
42. Ibid., pp. 414–15; McPherson, *Ordeal,* p. 587.
43. Mitchell, pp. 415–16.
44. Ibid., pp. 423–48.
45. McPherson, *Ordeal,* pp. 542–43; Foner, pp. 340–41.
46. Mitchell, p. 453.
47. *Seymour, Vallandigham, and the Riots of 1863*; McPherson, *Ordeal,* pp. 542–43.
48. *Harper's Weekly,* Oct. 10, 1868; Blight, illustration on p. 115.
49. *Harper's Weekly,* Sept. 5, 1868; Quigley, illustration between pp. 78 and 79.
50. McPherson, *Ordeal,* pp. 543–44; Foner, pp. 342–43.
51. McPherson, *Ordeal,* p. 543.
52. Mushkat, *The Reconstruction,* p. 130; McPherson, *Ordeal,* p. 544.
53. Mushkat, *The Reconstruction,* pp. 117–18.
54. Ibid., pp. 130–31; Quigley, p. 63; McJimsey, pp. 123–24.
55. McPherson, *Ordeal,* pp. 544–45. Foner, p. 343: "Nationally, [Grant] won every state except eight, but received less than 53 percent of the vote. It is more than likely that Seymour carried a majority of the white electorate."

56. Gibson, pp. 229–30.
57. Homberger, p. 175; Hershkowitz, *Tweed's New York,* pp. 135–37, 146–48; Gibson, pp. 229–30.
58. Mushkat, *The Reconstruction,* pp. 143–44; Quigley, pp. 64–65.
59. McJimsey, pp. 76–77; footnote: McPherson, *Ordeal,* p. 553.
60. Mushkat, *The Reconstruction,* p. 143; Quigley, pp. 64–65.
61. Hale, pp. 326–27.
62. Foner, p. 470; Hershkowitz, p. 141.
63. Foner, pp. 446–447; Quigley, p. 81.
64. Hershkowitz, pp. 146–47.
65. Quigley, pp. 64–65.
66. Mushkat, *The Reconstruction,* pp. 124–25, 156; Bernstein, pp. 225–26.
67. Bernstein, pp. 224–26.
68. Foner, pp. 478–81.
69. Bernstein, pp. 223–24.
70. Ibid., pp. 71, 224; Burrows and Wallace, pp. 770–73.
71. Bernstein, pp. 225–26.
72. Ibid.; Mushkat, *The Reconstruction,* p. 156.
73. Hershkowitz, pp. 147–48; *Herald,* Oct. 28, 1869.
74. Bernstein, p. 219.

22. STRANGE BEDFELLOWS: HORACE GREELEY AND THE LIBERAL REPUBLICANS

1. Foner, p. 444; Trelease, p. 384.
2. Foner, pp. 439–40, 457; Trelease, pp. 382–84; McPherson, *Ordeal,* pp. 565–66.
3. McPherson, *Ordeal,* pp. 545–46.
4. *World,* Mar. 6, 1871, quoted in Gillette, *Retreat,* p. 42.
5. Foner, pp. 446–47.
6. Ibid., p. 449.
7. Mushkat, *The Reconstruction,* pp. 172–73; McPherson *Ordeal,* pp. 565–67; Trelease, pp. 385–89; Foner, pp. 454–57.
8. Foner, p. 455; Trelease, pp. 389–90.
9. *Tribune,* May 17, 1871.
10. Foner, pp. 456–57; Trelease, pp. 389–95.
11. McPherson, *Ordeal,* p. 567; Foner, pp. 457–59, 528; Gillette, pp. 42–45; Trelease, p. 391.
12. McPherson, *Ordeal,* p. 567.
13. Bernstein, p. 60; Quigley, pp. xiii–xiv, 95–96.
14. Bernstein, p. 35.
15. Ibid., pp. 235–36.
16. Ibid., pp. 207–9; Mushkat, *The Reconstruction,* pp. 158–60; Homberger, pp. 181–82.
17. Bernstein, pp. 200–201.
18. Ibid., pp. 201–2.
19. Ibid., pp. 227–28, 198–99.

20. Ibid., p. 199.
21. Ibid.
22. Mushkat, *The Reconstruction,* pp. 175–76; Quigley, pp. 94–95.
23. Homberger, pp. 181–82; Quigley, pp. 94–95; Mushkat, *The Reconstruction,* p. 176.
24. Homberger, pp. 177–78.
25. Ibid.
26. Ackerman, pp. 2–3.
27. Bernstein, pp. 228–29; Mushkat, *The Reconstruction,* pp. 178–79; Homberger, pp. 202–4.
28. Bernstein, p. 229; Mushkat, *The Reconstruction,* pp. 177–78.
29. Bernstein, pp. 230–31; Homberger, p. 195.
30. Quigley, pp. xiii–xiv, 95–96; Bernstein, p. 230.
31. Bernstein, pp. 230–32.
32. Quigley, pp. 97–98; Hershkowitz, p. 176.
33. Quigley, pp. 36–37.
34. Ibid., pp. 97–99; Homberger, p. 178.
35. Mushkat, *The Reconstruction,* pp. 176–78; Quigley, p. 97.
36. Homberger, pp. 198, 205; Mushkat, *The Reconstruction,* pp. 180–84.
37. Homberger, pp. 198, 294–99; Bernstein, p. 246.
38. Mushkat, *The Reconstruction,* pp. 181–84.
39. Homberger, p. 149; Mushkat, *The Reconstruction,* p. 189.
40. Homberger, pp. 202–3.
41. Bernstein, pp. 233–34.
42. Homberger, pp. 204–5.
43. Ibid., p. 206.
44. *Tribune,* Sept. 30, 1863.
45. Homberger, pp. 200–201.
46. Quigley, p. 100; Mushkat, *The Reconstruction,* pp. 187–88.
47. Homberger, pp. 206–9.
48. Ibid., pp. 207–11; Mushkat, *The Reconstruction,* pp. 178–89; McJimsey, pp. 148–52; Quigley, pp. 98–99.
49. Mushkat, *The Reconstruction,* pp. 189–90.
50. *Tribune,* June 13, 1871.
51. Foner, pp. 488–92, 498–99.
52. Ibid.
53. *Tribune,* June 13, 1871.
54. Foner, pp. 488–92, 498–500; McPherson, *Ordeal,* p. 563.
55. McPherson, *Ordeal,* p. 553; Foner, pp. 484–87.
56. McPherson, *Ordeal,* p. 553; Foner, pp. 444–45.
57. McPherson, *Ordeal,* p. 553; Foner, pp. 488–92, 499–500.
58. Hale, pp. 324–27; Mushkat, *The Reconstruction,* p. 190.
59. Foner, p. 500.
60. Ibid., pp. 500–501.
61. McPherson, *Ordeal,* pp. 569–70; Foner, pp. 501–2; Hale, pp. 334–37.
62. Foner, p. 503; Hale, p. 337; McPherson, *Ordeal,* p. 570.
63. Mushkat, *Fernando Wood,* p. 194; Quigley, p. 101.

64. Mushkat, *Fernando Wood*, p. 194; Foner, pp. 505–6; McPherson, *Ordeal*, p. 570.
65. Mushkat, *Fernando Wood*, p. 194; Foner, pp. 505–6.
66. McPherson, *Ordeal*, p. 571.
67. Foner, p. 507.
68. Ibid., pp. 502–4, 509; McPherson, *Ordeal*, p. 571.
69. Mushkat, *The Reconstruction*, pp. 201–5; Foner, pp. 502–3; McPherson, *Ordeal*, p. 571.
70. Quigley, pp. 101–3; Foner, p. 503.
71. Bernstein, pp. 237–39, 247; Foner, pp. 488–91.
72. Hale, pp. 339–43.
73. Mushkat, *The Reconstruction*, p. 205; Foner, pp. 507–8; McPherson, *Ordeal*, p. 571.
74. Hale, pp. 344–45.
75. Ibid., pp. 345–53.
76. Foner, p. 508; McPherson, *Ordeal*, p. 571.
77. Hale, pp. 347–49.
78. Ibid., pp. 350–53.
79. *World*, Nov. 30, 1863; *Evening Post*, Nov. 30, 1863.
80. *Evening Post*, Dec. 4, 1863.

23. A FINAL DEVIL'S BARGAIN: THE END OF RECONSTRUCTION

1. Foner, p. 510.
2. McJimsey, p. 162; Foner, p. 510.
3. McJimsey, p. 162.
4. Ibid.; Foner, p. 510; McPherson, *Ordeal*, p. 571.
5. Foner, p. 512; footnote: Foner, p. 512.
6. McPherson, *Ordeal*, pp. 582–85; Foner, pp. 461, 464.
7. Foner, pp. 461–63.
8. McPherson, *Ordeal*, pp. 582–86.
9. Foner, pp. 512–13; McPherson, *Ordeal*, pp. 585–86.
10. Foner, pp. 461, 512–13.
11. Ibid., p. 512; McPherson, *Ordeal*, pp. 593–94.
12. McPherson, *Ordeal*, pp. 590–91; footnote: McPherson, *Ordeal*, p. 585.
13. McPherson, *Ordeal*, pp. 591–92; Foner, p. 550.
14. McPherson, *Ordeal*, pp. 591–92; Foner, pp. 550–51.
15. McPherson, *Ordeal*, p. 592; Foner, pp. 554–55; Gillette, p. 123.
16. Foner, pp. 554–55; Gillette, pp. 124–31; McPherson, *Ordeal*, pp. 592–93.
17. Foner, p. 554.
18. Gillette, pp. 126–27.
19. Foner, p. 554; Gillette, p. 124; McPherson, *Ordeal*, pp. 591–92.
20. Americans more upset by federal troops . . . than Klan violence: Foner, pp. 554–55; Trelease, p. 420.
21. Gilmore, pp. 198–99.
22. McPherson, *Ordeal*, pp. 565–66.
23. Foner, pp. 554–55.

24. McPherson, *Ordeal,* p. 593; Foner, p. 555.

25. McPherson, *Ordeal,* p. 593; Foner, pp. 539, 549–50.

26. McPherson, *Ordeal,* pp. 593–94.

27. Ibid.; Foner, pp. 559–63.

28. McPherson, *Ordeal,* pp. 569 and 590–91; Foner, pp. 510–11.

29. Trelease, p. 420; Foner, pp. 525–26; McPherson, *Ordeal,* p. 593.

30. Federal arrests declined, Klan violence increased: Trelease, p. 420.

31. McJimsey, pp. 165–66.

32. Ibid., pp. 166–67.

33. Ibid., pp. 178–80.

34. Ibid., pp. 180–81.

35. Ibid., pp. 177–78.

36. Ibid., pp. 181–83.

37. Ibid., pp. 180–83.

38. Foner, pp. 507–508.

39. McPherson, *Ordeal,* pp. 567n, 592, and 595.

40. Ibid., pp. 596–97.

41. Boatner, *Civil War Dictionary,* p. 389; Foner, pp. 557–58, 567; Morris, *Fraud,* pp. 59–66.

42. McPherson, *Ordeal,* pp. 597–98; Foner, p. 567.

43. McPherson, *Ordeal,* p. 598.

44. Ibid., pp. 598–99; Foner, p. 575.

45. McPherson, *Ordeal,* pp. 598–99.

46. McJimsey, pp. 190–91.

47. Ibid., pp. 190–95.

48. Ibid., pp. 195–97.

49. Mushkat, *Fernando Wood,* pp. 215–17; McPherson, *Ordeal,* pp. 600–601.

50. McPherson, *Ordeal,* p. 601; Mushkat, *Fernando Wood,* p. 216.

51. McJimsey, pp. 196–200; Mushkat, *Fernando Wood,* pp. 215–17; McPherson, *Ordeal,* pp. 600–601; Woodward, pp. 150–51.

52. Mushkat, *Fernando Wood,* p. 219.

53. Ibid., pp. 219–20.

54. Ibid.

55. Ibid., pp. 220–21.

56. Ibid., p. 221.

57. McPherson, *Ordeal,* pp. 603–4.

58. Foner, p. 582.

59. McPherson, *Ordeal,* pp. 603–4; Foner, p. 582.

60. Foner, p. 582.

61. Foner, p. 582; McPherson, *Ordeal,* pp. 603–4.

62. Foner, pp. 583–86; McPherson, *Ordeal,* p. 587.

63. Foner, pp. 583–86.

64. McPherson, *Ordeal,* pp. 586–87.

65. Foner, pp. 479–80.

66. Woodson, pp. 126–46.

67. Foner, pp. 479–80.

68. Ibid., pp. 513–14.
69. Ibid., pp. 514–15.
70. Ibid., p. 515.
71. Ibid.
72. Ibid., pp. 515, 519; McPherson, *Ordeal,* p. 587.
73. Foner, p. 583.
74. Ibid., pp. 583–84.
75. Ibid., pp. 583–84; McPherson, *Ordeal,* pp. 587–88.
76. Bruce, pp. 222–23.
77. Foner, pp. 583–84; McPherson, *Ordeal,* pp. 587–88.
78. McPherson, *Ordeal,* pp. 587–88; Foner, p. 585; Bruce, *1877,* p. 185 and passim.
79. Quigley, p. xiv; Foner, p. 585.
80. Foner, p. 586; Bernstein, illustration facing p. 125.
81. Opdyke, p. 290.
82. Foner, p. 585.
83. Stoddard, pp. 112–14.
84. Foner, pp. 477, 585.
85. Ibid., pp. 478, 515–18, 585.
86. Foner, p. 585: Interracial cooperation in the Great Strike of 1877 prefigured African American membership in the Knights of Labor in the 1880s.

APPENDIX: A WALKING TOUR
OF CIVIL WAR NEW YORK

1. Sources for the walking tour in Manhattan include: Gerard Wolfe, *New York: A Guide to the Metropolis,* New York: McGraw-Hill, 1994; Anbinder; "Points of Contention," an interview with Kevin Baker, author of *Paradise Alley,* in *Time Out New York,* Dec. 12–26, 2002, p. 17. Web site sources include http://www.nyc.govparks.org; http://www.nps.gov; and http://www.lowermanhattan.info.

2. Sources for the walking tour in Brooklyn include four booklets titled *Neighborhood History Guide,* published in 2000–2003 by the Brooklyn Historical Society: DUMBO/Fulton Ferry Landing/Vinegar Hill, Red Hook/Gowanus, Williamsburg, and Bay Ridge/Fort Hamilton; Jeffrey Richman, *Brooklyn's Green-Wood Cemetery,* Brooklyn: Green-Wood Cemetery, 1998; Glenn Collins, "Stories of the Civil War Carved on Headstones," *New York Times,* July 4, 2003 (about Green-Wood Cemetery). Web site sources include http://www.weeksvillesociety.org.

3. Sources for the walking tour in the Bronx include Edward Bergman, *Woodlawn Remembers: Cemetery of American History,* Utica, NY: North Country Books, 1988.

4. Sources for the walking tour in Staten Island include Ian Urbina, "A Bastion of Black History Amid Staten Island Development," *New York Times,* Nov. 4, 2003 (about Sandy Ground).

5. Sources for the walking tour in Queens and Nassau Counties include John Hanc, "There's a Riot Going On," *Newsday,* Aug. 7, 2003 (about the reenactment at Old Bethpage Village Restoration).

Bibliography

❧

ABBREVIATIONS

MACNY   Municipal Archives of the City of New York
N-YHS, MSS   New-York Historical Society, Manuscripts Division
NYPL   New York Public Library

Ackerman, Kenneth. *Boss Tweed.* New York: Caroll and Graf, 2005.
African-American History in the Press, 1851–1899. New York: Gale, 1996.
Allen, Oliver E. *The Tiger: The Rise and Fall of Tammany Hall.* New York: Addison-Wesley, 1993.
Anbinder, Tyler. *Five Points.* New York: Penguin, 2002.
Andrews, Charles C. *History of the New-York African Free-Schools.* New York: Printed by M. Day, 1830.
Anti-Negro Riots in the North, 1863. Introduction by James M. McPherson. New York: Arno Press, 1969. Reprint of two reports on riots in Detroit and New York.
Asbury, Herbert. *The Gangs of New York: An Informal History of the Underworld.* New York: Thunder's Mouth Press, 2001.
Association for the Benefit of Colored Orphans. *Annual Report of the Association for the Benefit of Colored Orphans.* New York, 1837–83. Schomburg Center, NYPL.
Axelrod, Alan. *The War Between the Spies: A History of Espionage During the Civil War.* New York: Atlantic Monthly Press, 1992.
Baker, Kevin. *Paradise Alley.* New York: HarperCollins, 2002.
Baker, La Fayette C. *History of the United States Secret Service.* Philadelphia: L. C. Baker, 1867.
Banquet given by the members of the Union League Club of 1863 and 1864, to commemorate the departure for the seat of war of the 20th Regiment of United States Colored Troops, raised by the Club. New York, 1886. Includes police commissioner Thomas Acton's recollections of the riots.

Barnes, David M. *The Draft Riots in New York, July, 1863: The Metropolitan Police, Their Services During Riot Week, Their Honorable Record.* New York: Baker and Godwin, 1863. Based on a series of articles in the *New York Times.*

Bayor, Ronald, and Timothy Meagher, eds. *The New York Irish.* Baltimore: Johns Hopkins University Press, 1996.

Benjamin, Walter R., and Mary A. Benjamin, "New York in the Civil War." *The Collector: A Magazine for Autograph and Historical Collectors* 41, no. 4 (Feb. 1928), pp. 549–50. Clipping in Seymour Papers in the Fairchild Collection, N-YHS.

Bernstein, Iver. *The New York City Draft Riots: Their Significance for American Society and Politics in the Age of the Civil War.* New York: Oxford, 1990.

Bishop, Joseph Bucklin. *Notes and Anecdotes of Many Years.* New York: Charles Scribner's Sons, 1925.

Blight, David. *Race and Reunion: The Civil War in American Memory.* Cambridge, MA: Harvard University Press, 2001.

The Bloody Week: Riot murder and arson, containing a full account of this wholesale outrage on life and property, accurately prepared from the official sources/ by eye witnesses, with portraits of "Andrews," the leader and "Rosa," his Eleventh street mistress. New York: Coutant and Baker, 1863.

Brandt, Nat. *The Man Who Tried to Burn New York.* Syracuse: Syracuse University Press, 1986.

Brewer, W. M. "Henry Highland Garnet." *Journal of Negro History* 13, issue 1 (Jan. 1928), pp. 36–52.

Bruce, Robert. *1877: Year of Violence.* New York: Bobbs-Merrill, 1959.

Burn, James. *Three Years Among the Working-Classes in the United States During the War.* London: Smith, Elder, 1865.

Burrows, Edwin and Mike Wallace. *Gotham: A History of New York City to 1898.* New York: Oxford University Press, 1998.

Cahill, Thomas. *How the Irish Saved Civilization.* New York: Nan A. Talese/ Doubleday, 1995.

Carhart, Tom. *Lost Triumph: Lee's Real Plan at Gettysburg and Why It Failed.* Introduction by James McPherson. New York: Putnam, 2005.

Cashin, Joan, ed. *The War Was You and Me: Civilians in the American Civil War.* Princeton: Princeton University Press, 2002.

Catton, Bruce. *Never Call Retreat.* Garden City, NY: Doubleday, 1965.

Chapin, Charles Loring. "Personal Recollections of the Draft Riots of New York City, 1863." N-YHS, MSS.

Choate, Joseph Hodges. *The Life of Joseph Hodges Choate.* New York: Charles Scribner's Sons, 1921.

Citizens' Association. *Report of the Council of Hygiene and Public Health of the Citizens' Association of New York upon the Sanitary Condition of the City.* New York, 1865.

Cogan, Brian. "The Irish-American Press as an Agent of Change: The Transformation of the New York Irish 1850–1880." *New York Irish History,* 14 (2000), pp. 29–46.

Committee of Merchants for the Relief of Colored People, Suffering from the Late Riots in the City of New York. Letter to New York City comptroller M. C. Brennan, re: blacks should not accept draft riot damage awards smaller than those given to whites. Museum of the City of New York.

Congdon, Charles. *Reminiscences of a Journalist.* Boston: J. K. Osgood, 1880.

Congdon, Henry. Letter to his father, Charles Congdon, July 17, 1863. N-YHS, MSS.

Cook, Adrian. *The Armies of the Streets: The New York City Draft Riots of 1863.* Lexington: University Press of Kentucky, 1974.

Costello, Augustine E. *Our Firemen: A History of the New York Fire Departments from 1609 to 1887.* New York: Knickerbocker Press, 1997.

Coyningham, D. P. *The Irish Brigade and Its Campaigns.* Edited, with an Introduction, by Lawrence Frederick Kohl. New York: Fordham University Press, 1994.

Curtis, Nancy C., *Black Heritage Sites: The North.* New York: New Press, 1996.

Daly, Maria Lydig. *Diary of a Union Lady, 1861–1865.* Lincoln: University of Nebraska Press, 2000.

Dannett, Sylvia, ed. *Noble Women of the North.* New York: Thomas Yoseloff, Sagamore Press, 1959.

Davenport, John I. *The Election and Naturalization Frauds in New York City, 1860–1870.* New York, 1894.

Dayton, Abram C. *Last Days of Knickerbocker Life in New York.* New York: G. P. Putnam's Sons, 1897.

De Costa, B. F. *Three Score and Ten. The Story of St. Philip's Church, New York City. A discourse delivered in the new church. West Twenty-fifth St., at its opening, Sunday morning, February 17, 1889, by the Rev. B.F. De Costa.* New York, 1889.

Delafield, Richard. Letterpress Copybook, 1862–64. N-YHS.

Dickenson, Richard B., ed. *Holden's Staten Island: The History of Richmond County.* New York: Center for Migration Studies, 2003.

Diner, Hasia. *Erin's Daughters in America: Irish Immigrant Women in the Nineteenth Century.* Baltimore: Johns Hopkins University Press, 1983.

Donald, David Herbert. *Lincoln.* New York: Simon and Schuster, 1995.

Du Bois, W. E. B. *Black Reconstruction in America, 1860–1880.* Cleveland: World, 1967.

Dupree, A. H., and Leslie Fishel, eds. "An Eyewitness Account of the New York Draft Riots, July 1863." *Mississippi Valley Historical Review,* vol. 47, No. 3, Dec. 1960, pp. 472–79.

Emerson, Sarah Hopper, ed. *Life of Abby Hopper Gibbons.* 2 vols. New York: G. P. Putnam's Sons, 1897.

Ernst, Robert. *Immigrant Life in New York City, 1825–1863.* New York: King's Crown Press, 1949.

Famous Adventures and Prison Escapes of the Civil War. New York: Century, 1915.

Fletcher, George P. *Our Secret Constitution: How Lincoln Redefined American Democracy.* New York: Oxford University Press, 2001.

Foner, Eric. *Reconstruction: America's Unfinished Revolution, 1863–1877.* New York: Perennial, 1989.

Forbes, Ella. *African American Women During the Civil War.* New York: Garland, 1998.

Fredrickson, George M. *The Inner Civil War: Northern Intellectuals and the Crisis of the Union.* New York: Harper and Row, 1965.

Freeman, Rhoda Golden. *The Free Negro in New York City in the Era Before the Civil War.* New York: Garland, 1994.

Frothingham, O. B. *Recollections and Impressions, 1822–1890.* New York: G. P. Putnam's Sons, 1891.

Fry, James Barnet. *New York and the Conscription of 1863.* New York: G. P. Putnam's Sons, 1885.

Gallman, J. Matthew. *The North Fights the Civil War: The Home Front.* Chicago: Ivan R. Dee, 1994.

Garner, Stanton. *The Civil War World of Herman Melville.* Lawrence: University Press of Kansas, 1993.

Garnet, Henry Highland. *A Memorial Discourse/by Henry Highland Garnet, delivered in the Hall of the House of Representatives, Washington City, D.C., on Sabbath, February 12, 1865; with an introduction by James McCune Smith.* Philadelphia: J. M. Wilson, 1865.

Geary, James. *We Need Men: The Union Draft and the Civil War.* Dekalb: Northern Illinois University Press, 1991.

Gellman, David, and David Quigley, eds. *Jim Crow New York: A Documentary History of Race and Citizenship, 1777–1877.* New York: New York University Press, 2003.

Gibbons Morse, Lucy. "Recollections of the Draft Riots of 1863 in New York City." August 1927. N-YHS, MSS.

Gibson, Florence. *The Attitudes of the New York Irish Toward State and National Affairs, 1848–1892.* New York: Columbia University Press, 1951.

Gilje, Paul. *The Road to Mobocracy: Popular Disorder in New York City, 1763–1834.* Chapel Hill: University of North Carolina Press, 1987.

Gillette, William. *Retreat from Reconstruction, 1869–1879.* Baton Rouge: Louisiana State University Press, 1979.

Gilmore, James R. *Personal Recollections of Abraham Lincoln and the Civil War.* Boston: L. C. Page, 1898.

Grand Jury Dismissals, 1863. MACNY.

Gray, Wood. *The Hidden Civil War: The Story of the Copperheads.* New York: Viking, 1942.

Greeley, Horace. Papers in the N-YHS, MSS.

———. *Recollections of a Busy Life.* New York: J. B. Ford, 1868.

———. "Why I Am a Whig." 1852. NYPL, microfilm.

———. "Mr. Greeley's Record on the Questions of Amnesty and Reconstruction from the Hour of Gen. Lee's Surrender." 1872. NYPL, microfilm. A compilation from the New York *Tribune.*

Hale, William Harlan. *Horace Greeley, Voice of the People.* New York: Harper and Brothers, 1950.

Hammond, Harold. *A Commoner's Judge: The Life and Times of Charles Patrick Daly.* Boston: Christopher, 1954.

Harris, Leslie. *In the Shadow of Slavery.* Chicago: University of Chicago Press, 2003.

Headley, Joel Tyler. *The Great Riots of New York, 1712 to 1873; including a full and complete account of the four days' draft riot of 1863.* New York: Dover, 1971.

Headley, John William. *Confederate Operations in New York and Canada.* New York: Neale, 1906.

Hershkowitz, Leo. *Tweed's New York: Another Look.* Garden City, NY: Anchor/Doubleday, 1977.

Hewitt, John H. "New York's Black Episcopalians: In the Beginning, 1704–1722." In *African Americans in New York Life and History.* Jan. 1979. Schomburg Center, NYPL.

———. *Protest and Progress: New York's First Black Episcopal Church Fights Racism.* New York: Garland, 2000.

Hirsch, Leo H., Jr. "The Slave in New York." *Journal of Negro History,* 16, issue 4 (Oct. 1931), pp. 383–414.

Hodges, Graham Russell. *Root and Branch: African-Americans in New York and New Jersey, 1613–1863.* Chapel Hill: University of North Carolina Press, 1999.

Homberger, Eric. *Scenes from the Life of a City: Corruption and Conscience in Old New York.* New Haven: Yale University Press, 1994.

Horan, James. *Confederate Agent: A Discovery in History.* New York: Crown, 1954.

Howland, Eliza Woolsey. *My Heart Toward Home: Letters of a Family During the Civil War.* Roseville, MN: Edinborough Press, 2001.

Hyman, Harold M. "New Yorkers and the Civil War Draft." *New York History,* Apr. 1955.

Ignatiev, Noel. *How the Irish Became White.* New York: Routledge, 1995.

Jackson, Kenneth, ed. *The Encyclopedia of New York City.* New Haven: Yale University Press, 1995.

Jones, Paul. *The Irish Brigade.* Washington: Robert B. Luce, 1969.

Journal of the Irish Historical Society, 9 (1910).

Joyce, Toby. "The New York Draft Riots of 1863: An Irish Civil War?" *History Ireland,* Summer 2003, pp. 22–27.

Judson, E. Z. C. The *Mysteries and Miseries of New York: A Story of Real Life, by Ned Buntline [pseud.].* Dublin: James M'Glashan, 1849.

Keneally, Thomas. *The Great Shame and the Triumph of the Irish in the English-speaking World.* New York: Nan A. Talese, 1999.

Kinchen, Oscar. *Confederate Operations in Canada and the North.* North Quincy, MA: Christopher, 1970.

Kirk, Highland C. *Heavy Guns and Light: A History of the 4th New York Heavy Artillery.* New York: C. T. Dillingham, 1890.

Klement, Frank L. *The Copperheads in the Middle West.* Gloucester, MA: Peter Smith, 1972.
———. *Dark Lanterns: Secret Political Societies, Conspiracies, and Treason Trials in the Civil War.* Baton Rouge: Louisiana State University Press, 1984.

Klingaman, William K. *Abraham Lincoln and the Road to Emancipation.* New York: Viking, 2001.

Kohn, Stephen M. *Jailed for Peace. The History of American Draft Law Violators, 1658–1985.* Westport, CT: Greenwood Press, 1986.

Lee, Basil Leo. *Discontent in New York City, 1861–1865.* Washington, DC: Catholic University of America Press, 1943.

Lee, Robert E. *The Wartime Papers of Robert E. Lee.* Boston: Little, Brown, 1961.

Leland, Claude. *The First Hundred Years: Records and Reminiscences of a Century of Company I, Seventh Regiment, N.G.N.Y., 1839–1938.* New York, 1838. New York Society Library.

Levine, Peter. "Draft Evasion in the North during the Civil War, 1863–1865." *Journal of American History,* 67 (Mar., 1981), pp. 816–34.

Leonard, Ellen. "Three Days of Terror." *Harpers New Monthly Magazine,* Jan. 1867, pp. 225–33.

Lincoln, Abraham. "Emancipation Proclamation." Printed in the *New York Tribune,* Jan. 3, 1863. Gilder Lehrman Collection, N-YHS.

———. "Printed Draft Call for Troops from New York," Signed by Lincoln on July 7, 1863. Gilder Lehrman Collection, N-YHS.

———. "President Lincoln on Vallandigham And 'Arbitrary Arrests.' " 1863. NYPL, microfilm.

———. "President Lincoln's Views: An Important Letter On the Principles Involved In the Vallandigham Case." 1929. NYPL, microfilm.

Litwack, Leon, and August Meier, eds. *Black Leaders of the Nineteenth Century.* Urbana: University of Illinois Press, 1988.

Livingston, E. A. *President Lincoln's Third Largest City: Brooklyn and the Civil War.* Glendale, NY: Budd Press, 1994.

Lord, Walter, ed. *The Fremantle Diary.* Boston: Little, Brown, 1954.

Lossing, Benson John. *Our Country.* New York: Johnson and Wilson, 1875–78.

Lowenfels, Walter. *Walt Whitman's Civil War.* New York: Da Capo, 1989.

Lowitt, Richard. *A Merchant Prince of the Nineteenth Century, William E. Dodge.* New York: Columbia University Press, 1954.

Lockwood, John. *Our Campaign Around Gettysburg.* Brooklyn: A. H. Rome and Brothers, 1864.

Lunde, Erik S. *Horace Greeley.* Boston: Twayne, 1981.

Lyons, Maritcha Remond. "Memories of Yesterdays: All of Which I Saw and Part of Which I Was." Unpublished typescript, 1928. Henry Albro Williamson Collection. Schomburg Center, NYPL.

Macleod, Donald. *Biography of Hon. Fernando Wood, Mayor of the City of New-York.* New York: O. F. Parsons, 1856.

Man, Albon P. Jr. "Labor Competition and the New York Draft Riots of 1863." *Journal of Negro History,* Oct. 1951, pp. 375–405.

Massie, James. *America: The Origin of her Present Conflict.* London: J. Snow, 1864.

Mayer, Henry. *All on Fire: William Lloyd Garrison and the Abolition of Slavery.* New York: St. Martin's Press, 1998.

Maynard, Joan, and Gwen Cottman. *Weeksville Then and Now: The Search to Discover The Efforts to Preserve Memories of Self in Brooklyn, New York.* Brooklyn: Society for the Preservation of Weeksville and Bedford-Stuyvesant History, 1988.

McCague, James. *The Second Rebellion: The Story of the New York City Draft Riots of 1863.* New York: Dial Press, 1968.

McJimsey, George T. *Genteel Partisan: Manton Marble, 1834–1917.* Ames: Iowa State University Press, 1971.

McKay, Ernest A. *The Civil War and New York City.* Syracuse: Syracuse University Press, 1990.

McPherson, James M. *Battle Cry of Freedom: The Civil War Era.* New York: Oxford University Press, 1988.

———. *Ordeal by Fire: The Civil War and Reconstruction.* New York: Knopf, 1982.

———. *The Negro's Civil War.* New York: Ballantine, 1991.

Miller, Kerby. *Emigrants and Exiles: Ireland and the Irish Exodus to North America.* New York: Oxford University Press, 1985.

Milton, G. F. *Abraham Lincoln and the Fifth Column.* New York: Vanguard, 1942.

Mitchell, Stewart. *Horatio Seymour of New York.* Cambridge, MA: Harvard University Press, 1938.

Morris, Roy, Jr. *Fraud of the Century: Rutherford B. Hayes, Samuel Tilden, and the Stolen Election of 1876.* New York: Simon and Schuster, 2003.

Morse, Lucy Gibbons. *See* Gibbons Morse, Lucy.

Murdock, Eugene. *One Million Men: The Civil War Draft in the North.* Madison: State Historical Society of Wisconsin, 1971.

Mushkat, Jerome. *Fernando Wood: A Political Biography.* Kent, Ohio: Kent State University Press, 1990.

———. *The Reconstruction of the New York Democracy, 1861–1874.* Rutherford, NJ: Fairleigh Dickinson University Press, 1981.

Neely, Mark. *The Fate of Liberty: Abraham Lincoln and Civil Liberties.* New York: Oxford University Press, 1991

Nelson, Larry. *Bullets, Ballots, and Rhetoric: Confederate Policy for the United States Presidential Contest of 1864.* Tuscaloosa: University of Alabama Press, 1980.

Nevins, Alan. *War for the Union, 1862–1863: War Becomes Revolution.* New York: Scribner, 1960.

New York County District Attorney. Indictment Records. MACNY, microfilm.

Nugent, Robert. "The Sixty-Ninth Regiment at Fredericksburg," *Supplement to the Journal of the American Irish Historical Society,* Jan. 1917.

O'Doherty, Cahir. "Common Ground: Yale Project Examines the Links Between Irish, African Americans." *Irish Echo,* July 23–29, 2003.

O'Donnell, Edward. *1001 Things Everyone Should Know About Irish American History.* New York: Broadway Books, 2002.

Opdyke, George. *Official documents, addresses, etc., of George Opdyke, mayor of the city of New York during the years 1862 and 1863.* New York: Hurd and Houghton, 1866.

Ottley, Roi, and William J. Weatherby, eds. *The Negro in New York: An Informal Social History.* Edited from manuscripts in the Schomburg Collection, with a preface by James Baldwin. New York: NYPL, 1967; Dobbs Ferry: Oceana, 1967.

Padgett, James A. "Ministers to Liberia and their Diplomacy." *Journal of Negro History,* 22, issue 1 (Jan. 1937), pp. 50–92.

Pasternak, Martin B. "Risk Now and Fly to Arms: The Life of Henry Highland Garnet." Ph.D. diss. University of Massachusetts, 1981.

Peterson, Jon A. *The Birth of City Planning in the United States, 1840–1917.* Baltimore: Johns Hopkins, 2003.

Proceedings of the National Convention of Colored Men: Held in the city of Syracuse, N. Y., October 4, 5, 6, and 7, 1864; with the bill of wrongs and rights, and the address to the American people. Boston: Printed for and by order of the convention by G. C. Avery, 1864.

Pullen, John J. *The Twentieth Maine: A Volunteer Regiment in the Civil War.* Philadelphia: Lippincott, 1957.

Quarles, Benjamin. *The Negro in the Civil War.* Boston: Little, Brown, 1953.

Quigley, David. *Second Founding: New York City, Reconstruction, and the Making of American Democracy.* New York: Hill and Wang, 2004.

Quinn, Peter. *Banished Children of Eve: A Novel of Civil War New York.* New York: Viking, 1994.

Rable, George. *But There Was No Peace: The Role of Violence in the Politics of Reconstruction.* Athens: University of Georgia Press, 1984.

Report of the Committee of Merchants for the Relief of Colored People, Suffering from the Late Riots in the City of New York. New York: George A Whitehorn, steam printer, 1863.

Riddle, Albert. *Recollections of War Times.* New York: G. P. Putnam's Sons, 1895.

Ruffin, Edmund. *Anticipations of The Future,* Richmond: J. W. Randolph, 1861.

———. *The Diary of Edmund Ruffin.* 3 vols. Baton Rouge: Louisiana State University Press, 1989.

Sandburg, Carl. *Abraham Lincoln: The Prairie Years and the War Years.* one-vol. edition. New York: Harcourt Brace, 1954.

———. *Abraham Lincoln: The War Years.* 4 vols. New York: Harcourt Brace and World, 1939.

Schlegel, Jacob. " 'A Time of Terror': Letters from a German Immigrant in Civil War New York." *American History Illustrated,* May 1976.

Schlesinger, Arthur Jr. *The Age of Jackson.* Old Saybrook, CT: Konecky and Konecky, 1971.

Schor, Joel. *Henry Highland Garnet: A voice of black radicalism in the nineteenth century.* Westport, CT: Greenwood Press, 1977.

Sears, Stephen. *Gettysburg.* Boston: Houghton Mifflin, 2003.

Seitz, Don C. *Horace Greeley, Founder of the New York Tribune.* Indianapolis: Bobbs-Merrill, 1926.

Seraile, William. *New York's Black Regiments during the Civil War.* New York: Routledge, 2001.

Seymour, Horatio. Seymour Papers in the Fairchild Collection. N-YHS, MSS.

Seymour, Vallandingham, and The Riots of 1863. London, 1867. In *U.S. Civil War and Reconstruction: A Collection of Pamphlets, in the NYPL.* Microfilm. Republican campaign literature from 1867, attacking Horatio Seymour.

Sifakis, Stewart. *Who Was Who in the Civil War.* New York: Facts on File, 1988.

Sketch of the life of the Rev. Charles B. Ray. New York: Press of J. J. Little, 1887.

Smalley, George. *Anglo-American Memories.* New York: G. P. Putnam's Sons, 1911.

Smith, David. *Who Only Stand and Wait: Civil War Letters of David and Ann Smith, 1863–1865.* Interlaken, NY: Heart of the Lakes, 1990.

Smith, Henry B. *Between the Lines: Secret Service Stories Told Fifty Years After.* New York: Booz Brothers, 1911.

Smith, Stephen. *The City That Was.* New York: F. Allaben, 1911.

Spann, Edward K. *Gotham at War: New York City, 1860–1865.* Wilmington, DE: Scholarly Resources, Inc., 2002.

———. "Union Green: The Irish Community in the Civil War." In *The New York Irish,* ed. Ronald Bayor and Timothy Meager. Baltimore: Johns Hopkins University Press, 1996.

Stauffer, John. *The Black Hearts of Men: Radical Abolitionists and the Transformation of Race.* Cambridge, MA: Harvard University Press, 2002.

Stern, Philip Van Doren. *Secret Missions of the Civil War.* New York: Bonanza, 1990.

Stevens, Joseph E. *1863: The Rebirth of a Nation.* New York: Bantam Books, 1999.

Stidger, Felix. *Treason History of the Order of Sons of Liberty.* Chicago, 1903.

Stoddard, William Osborn. *The Volcano Under the City.* New York: Fords, Howard and Hulbert, 1887.

Stone, Geoffrey. *Perilous Times: Free Speech in War Time from the Sedition Act of 1798 to the War on Terrorism.* New York: Norton, 2004.

Stott, Richard. *Workers in the Metropolis: Class, Ethnicity, and Youth in Antebellum New York City.* Ithaca, NY: Cornell University Press, 1990.

Strong, George Templeton. *Diary of the Civil War, 1860–1865.* New York: Macmillan, 1962.

Swinton, William. *History of the Seventh Regiment, National Guard, State of New York, During the War of the Rebellion.* New York: Fields, Osgood, 1870.

Thomas, Herman Edward. *James W.C. Pennington: African American Churchman and Abolitionist.* New York: Garland, 1995.

To the Memory of the Martyrs, Funeral Services held in Shiloh Church, N.Y., Sunday Evening, September 20th, 1863. New York: Vincent Colyer, 1863.

Trelease, Allen. *White Terror: The Ku Klux Klan Conspiracy and Southern Reconstruction.* New York: Harper and Row, 1971.

Van Deusen, Glyndon G. *Horace Greeley, Nineteenth-Century Crusader.* Philadelphia: University of Pennsylvania Press, 1967.

Wall, Alexander J. *Sketch of the Life of Horatio Seymour, 1810–1886, with a Detailed Account of his Administration as Governor of the State of New York during the War of 1861–1865.* New York, 1929.

Walling, George W. *Personal Recollections of a New York Chief of Police.* Montclair, NJ: Patterson Smith, 1972.

The War of the Rebellion: A Compilation of Official Records of the Union and Confederate Armies/Prepared Under the Direction of the Secretary of War by Robert N. Scott. 130 vols. Pasadena, CA: Broadfoot, 1985.

Washington, S. A. M. *George Thomas Downing; sketch of his life and times.* Newport, RI: Milne Printery, 1910.

Welsh, Peter. *Irish Green and Union Blue: The Civil War Letters of Peter Welsh.* Edited by Lawrence Frederick Kohl with Margaret Cosse Richard. New York: Fordham University Press, 1986.

Whitman, Walt. *New York Dissected.* New York: Rufus Rockwell Wilson, 1936.

Williamson, Henry Albro. Henry Albro Williamson Collection. Schomburg Center, NYPL.

Wingate, George. *Last Campaign of the Twenty-second Regiment, N.G.S.N.Y.* New York: C. S. Westcott, 1864.

Winik, Jay. *April 1865: The Month That Saved America.* New York: HarperCollins, 2001.

Wittke, Carl. *The Irish in America.* Baton Rouge: Louisiana State University Press, 1956.

Women's Prison Association and Home. *150 Years in the Forefront: The Women's Prison Association and Home.* New York: Women's Prison Association and Home, 1995.

Wood, Fernando. *The Proceedings of Censure and Suppressed Speech of Hon. Fernando Wood of New York.* Washington: F. and J. Rives and G. A. Bailey, 1868.

Wood, Forrest G. *Black Scare: The Racist Response to Emancipation and Reconstruction.* Berkeley: University of California Press, 1968.

Woodson, Carter G. *A Century of Negro Migration.* Mineola, NY: Dover, 2002.

Wool, John E. to George Opdyke, July 7, 1863. Gilder Lehrman Collection, N-YHS.

Woodward, C. Vann. *Reunion and Reaction: The Compromise of 1877 and the End of Reconstruction.* New York: Oxford University Press, 1991.

Yacovone, Donald, ed. *Freedom's Journey: African American Voices of the Civil War.* Chicago: Lawrence Hill Books, 2004.

Index

abolition:
  in British colonies, 38, 78
  and Civil War, 80, 81, 83, 85, 91
  and draft riots, 154, 199, 293
  and Emancipation Proclamation, 5, 7,
    89–92, 97, 99, 100, 359
  and Greeley, 4, 47, 54, 55, 58, 87–88, 90,
    93, 347, 350, 352
  newspapers and pamphlets of, 4, 38, 40–42
  and political parties, 54–57, 59, 72–74,
    81, 93, 102, 261, 262, 282
  and racial strife, 37–39, 40–42, 47,
    57–58, 142, 144, 288
  and radical Republicans, 5, 8, 81, 87
  and Reconstruction, 296, 314
  and social issues, 59–60, 90
  Thirteenth Amendment, 6, 300–302, 311
  waning public interest in, 356–57
  and white supremacy, 44–45, 90, 104
Acton, Thomas, 100
  and draft riots, 129, 133–34, 138,
    140–41, 151, 152, 162, 168, 170,
    175–76, 178, 192, 199, 203, 214, 222,
    225, 227, 229, 231, 306
  and Metropolitan police, 129, 133–34,
    162, 175, 199, 222, 227
Adams, Charles Francis, 261, 347, 354
Adams, Henry, 261
African Americans:
  "amalgamation," 38–39, 40, 75, 106, 293
  civil rights for, 5, 6, 8, 35, 36–39, 72, 74,
    81, 90, 262, 265, 270, 286, 288, 296,
    301–3, 306, 310–17, 320, 324, 329,
    333–34, 359, 362–63, 370
  clergymen, 246–47, 266–67, 286–91,
    301–2
  colonization, 38–39, 40, 42, 47, 87, 288
  convention movement of, 288–91
  elected public officials, 349
  and Emancipation Proclamation, 5, 6, 7,
    89–90, 97, 262, 286, 291, 315
  and end of war, 307
  and Fifteenth Amendment, 6, 329, 330,
    333, 334, 342, 348, 361
  flight from New York, 3, 243, 265–66,
    286, 304, 328
  and Fourteenth Amendment, 6, 313–15,
    320, 329, 333, 334, 361
  Freedmen's Bureau, 313, 360–61, 367
  and Irish, see Irish immigrants
  and job competition, 5, 6, 37, 44, 60, 87,
    99, 106, 113, 262, 366
  and labor movement, 342, 366–67
  racial violence against, 4, 6, 8, 37, 40, 41,
    47, 57–58, 87, 95, 106–7, 252, 262,
    302, 324, 325, 358–59; see also draft
    riots
  and Reconstruction, 5, 6, 8, 302, 310–15,
    332–36, 355
  slavery vs. freedom, 4, 6, 35, 44, 288; see
    also abolition
  and Thirteenth Amendment, 6, 300–302,
    311, 329
  in Union army, 86, 88, 97, 99, 102, 198,
    242, 262, 267–68
  white supremacists vs., 8, 32, 44–45,
    74–75, 90, 317–19, 324, 342, 360–61
Akerman, Amos, 334
Alcock, John, 131–32
American Anti-Slavery Society, 38, 40,
  41–42, 144
Andrews, John, 123, 126, 135, 137, 155,
  212, 226
Anthony, Susan B., 321

Astor, John Jacob Jr., 304
Astor, William B., 303, 304
Atchison, David, 58

Banks, Nathaniel, 274
Bank War, 31–32, 39–40, 63
Barlow, Samuel, 81, 83, 92, 187, 212, 263, 276, 360
Barnard, George, 92, 151, 163, 187, 212, 328, 343
Barnes, David, 191, 198, 226
Barnett, James, 147
Beecher, Henry Ward, 179
Bell, John, 74
Bellows, Henry, 102
Belmont, August, 81, 83, 92, 102, 212, 263, 304, 320–21, 324, 338, 341, 347
Benjamin, Judah, 282
Bennett, James Gordon, 29, 74, 115
Berens, William, 225–26, 229
Bickley, George, 76, 119
Black Friday (1869), 346
Black Joke engine company, 122, 131, 169, 259
Blair, Francis, 322, 360
Blunt, Orison, 255, 256
Booth, John Wilkes, 307–8
Boston:
    abolitionists in, 38, 41, 54, 97, 356
    draft enrollment in, 120
    mobs in, 202–3, 232, 323
Bradley, John, 229
Brady, James, 237
Bragg, Braxton, 21, 110, 228, 259, 260, 269
Breckenridge, John, 74
Brennan, Matthew T., 237, 250, 258–59, 263, 269
Brooks, James, 212
Brown, B. Gratz, 347
Brown, Harvey, 140, 162, 163, 175, 177, 178, 189, 195, 198, 199, 204–5, 212, 214, 219, 225, 227, 229–30, 233, 239
Brown, John, 70, 73, 74
Brown, William Wells, 145
Brownson, Orestes, 237
Bruce, Blanche, 349n
Bryant, William Cullen, 39, 40–41, 56, 73, 175, 215, 281, 322, 347, 352
Buchanan, James, 64, 71, 72, 239
Buford, John, 15
Burke, Patrick, 192
Burnside, Ambrose, 11, 21, 112, 241, 259
Burr, Chauncey, 115
Butler, Benjamin, 212, 213, 238, 274, 277, 295, 298

Calhoun, John C., 53, 63, 129n
Cameron, Simon, 84
Canary, Patrick, 126
Canby, E. R. S., 239
Canfield, Edward, 172
Carnegie, Andrew, 31
Carpenter, Daniel, 152–54, 162, 167–68, 176
Cassidy, James, 204
Castleman, John, 283
Chairman, Adam, 126
Channing, Rev. William Henry, 301
Chapin, Charles Loring, 140, 195, 255
Chase, Salmon, 56, 110
Chicago, social unrest in, 254, 271, 279–81, 283–84, *369*
Child, Lydia Maria, 348
Chinese immigrants, 314, 333, 354–55, 366, 368
Choate, Joseph, 5, 131, 194, 199, 208–9, 227, 231, 233, 235, 239, 243, 246, 247, 333, 341
Christensen, Christian, 162–63
Cincinnati, racial strife in, 37, 87, 201
Civil War:
    Antietam, 89
    Atlanta, 284, 285, 296
    Bull Run, 80, 89, 190
    Chancellorsville, 12, 17, 110
    Charleston, 229, 242, 259
    Chattanooga, 242, 259, 260, 269
    Chickamauga, 260
    and conscription law, 10–11, 12, 18–19, 23, 25–26
    control of Mississippi River in, 10, 19, 110, 242, 269
    death tolls in, 22, 273, 275, 277–78
    and deserters, 11, 12, 27, 103, 259, 267, 272, 273–74
    and elections, 276–79
    and emancipation, 80, 83, 85, 87, 89–90, 91, 99, 207, 228, 242, 262, 282
    end of, 6, 307
    European support sought in, 12, 22, 78, 89, 213, 232–33, 261
    Fort Sumter, 11, 12, 77, 78, 79, 338
    Fredericksburg, 11, 99, 119
    Gettysburg, 1, 15, *16*, 17, 19–20, 21–23, 27, 29, 30, 112, 201, 236, 241–42, 277
    habeas corpus suspended in, 23–24, 26, 86
    Harpers Ferry, 70, 89
    Kennesaw Mountain, 278
    and Missouri guerrillas, 292–93
    Northwest Conspiracy, 271–72

objectives of, 80, 89–90

opponents of, 25–27, 29

peace negotiations in, 10, 22, 25, 81, 89, 279, 281–82

Port Hudson, 228, 236, 242, 262, 269, 282

reunification after, 10, 86, 281, 316

Richmond, 11, 12, 83, 202, 306

Savannah, 299

Seven Days' Battles, 17, 84, 85, 86

Sherman's march to the sea, 297

Shiloh, 82

social issues of, 4–5, 6, 8

Spotsylvania, 275, 276

Vicksburg, 1, 10, 12, 29, 82, 228, 236, 242

war profiteering in, 8, 110, 151, 208

Wilderness, 275

Clancy, John, 212, 263

Clay, Clement, 272, 279, 281

Colfax, Schuyler "Smiler," 351

Colored Orphan Asylum, 42–43, 44, 146–50, *147*, *149*, 151, 236–37, 238, 249, 262, 286–87, 324

Committee of Merchants for the Relief of Colored People, 246–47, 249, 250

Compromise of 1820, 55

Compromise of 1850, 54

Compromise of 1877, 8, 365–66

Confederate States of America:

carpetbaggers in, 315, 333, 345, 346, 355, 357, 358, 361

draft law in, 103, 272

and elections, 262, 284

formation of, 76

home rule in, 5, 6, 296, 311, 321, 351, 353, 355

martial law in, 315, 318, 324, 334, 363

and Northwest Conspiracy, 192–93, 271–72, 283–84, 294–95, 298–99

racial issues in, *see* African Americans; slavery

readmission of, 310, 311, 324, 326, 333

Reconstruction in, *see* Reconstruction

riots supported by, 3–4, 212, 232, 236, 240, 245, 254, 295, 298–300

scalawags in, 315

and secession, 12, 74–76, 90, 105, 110, 212, 244

at war, *see* Civil War

Confiscation Acts, 80, 81, 82–83, 85, 88

Congdon, Charles, 155

Congdon, Henry, 231

Congress, U.S.:

draft law passed by, 23, 104

and election of 1876, 364–65

federal vs. state powers, 25, 334, 361

Fifteenth Amendment, 329, 333, 334

Fourteenth Amendment, 313–15, 333, 334

habeas corpus suspended by, 23–24

and Homestead Act, 303–4

and labor law, 330

and liberal reform, 346

militia law passed by, 85–86, 104

and Reconstruction, 212–13, 270, 311, 315, 317, 332–33

and slavery, 54, 83, 84–85

Thirteenth Amendment, 300–302, 312n

Connolly, Michael, 218, 229

Connolly, Richard, 264, 327, 339, 342–44

Conroy, Daniel, 132

conscription law, 103

beginning in New York, 115–20, 213

class bias in, 18, 26, 30–31, 120–21

court action suggested against, 114–15, 151, 186, 188, 208, 210–11, 254–55

enforcement of, 212, 215, 217, 239, 255–56, 260

enrollment for, 18–19, 30, 104, 113–14, 117

evaders of, 18–19, 273

lottery for, 18, 30, 113, 120, 255

opposition to, 11, 19, 23–27, 114–15, 175, 181–82; *see also* draft riots

passage of, 23, 104

resumption of, 255–56, 259

soldiers drafted under, 260, 273–74, 280–81, 299–300

state quotas in, 13, 18, 116, 255, 285

state vs. federal powers in, 4, 23–25, 104, 213

substitute relief fund, 210–11, 255, 256, 338

substitutes/exemptions in, 3, 11, 18, 30–31, 32, 104, 106, 121, 199, 207, 221, 250, 256, 261, 300

Union soldiers replaced in, 10–11, 273, 291

Cooke, Jay, 355

Cooper, Peter, 48, 61, 62, 304, 339, 341

Copperheads, *30*

Confederate sympathies of, 5, 9–10, 20, 29–30, 81, 113, 302

and Knights of the Golden Circle, 10, 102, 119, 292

newspapers of, 26, 111, 272, 293

riots fomented by, 29, 121, 164, 180, 244, 247, 253, 254, 270–72, 280–81, 283–84, 292–93, 294, 295, 299, 364

and Vallandigham, 24, 111, 262, 348

Corcoran, Michael, 79

Cornish, Samuel, 37–38, 144

Corrigan, John, 192
Costello, James, 203–4, 205
Cox, S. S., 334
Cram, Thomas, 163
Crédit Mobilier, 355, 359
Crittenden, John, 74–75
Crowley, James, 127, 128
Crummell, Alexander, 288
Curtin, Andrew, 12, 17, 19
Cusick, Francis, 126, 128, 180
Custer, George Armstrong, 22

Daly, Charles Patrick, 52, 90, 277
Daly, Maria, 7–8, 90–91, 104, 125, 188,
    199, 239, 243–45, 268, 276, 277, 307
Davis, David, 347
Davis, Jefferson, 9–11, 58, 260, 271, 279,
    282, 296, 307, 308, 316
Davis, William, 148
Decker, John, 135, 136, 147–48
Delafield, Richard, 14
Democrats:
    Civil War split of, 81, 83, 91, 214, 263,
        296, 317
    Congressional power of, 361
    conscription law opposed by, 11, 25–27
    Copperheads, *see* Copperheads
    and debt financing, 211, 330
    and economic depression, 355, 360
    and election of 1860, 74–75
    and election of 1863, 261–63
    and election of 1864, 279–84, 293,
        294–96
    and election of 1868, 320–24, 326, *327*
    and election of 1872, 348–50
    and election of 1876, 359, 360–66
    and Irish immigrants, 7, 39, 63, 102, 237,
        261, 263–65, 279–80, 295, 321,
        338–40, 343
    Jacksonian, 31–32, 39–40, 44, 63, 296,
        310, 340, 344
    and liberals, 345, 354
    newspapers of, 4, 7, 25–27, 39, 74, 78,
        92, 216, 272, 326
    in New York, 5, 6, 7, 8, 24, 35, 50, 62,
        66, 75, 94, 102, 186, 199, 212, 239,
        254, 270, 306, 315, 321, 328–29, 340
    Peace, 9–10, 24, 25, 81, 83, 89, 106,
        114, 119, 215, 261, 265, 272, 284,
        294, 317, 338
    racism of, 32, 34–36, 63, 64, 74, 81, 87,
        92–94, 114, 216, 242, 262, 293, 302,
        310, 317, 321, 322, 326, 327, 334,
        342, 348, 359, 360, 362, 365
    and Reconstruction, 6, 296, 302, 324,
        328, 353, 358
    and slavery, 5, 7, 54, 55, 71, 102, 114, 284
    social unrest fomented by, 52-54, 87,
        113-15, 133, 164, 211, 212, 217, 228,
        237, 245, 254, 261, 281, 283–84, 294,
        313, 315, 317, 324, 326, 358, 361
    Swallowtails, 25, 83, 92, 329
    and Tammany, *see* Tammany Hall
    War, 81, 83, 90, 91, 238–39, 257, 263,
        317, 338
    and working class, 5, 26, 93, 113, 217,
        261, 263, 306, 329–31
Denison, Samuel, 249
Derrickson family, 196–97, 258
Detroit, unrest in, 106, 181–82
Devlin, John, 237
Dilks, George, 180, 181, 190, 191
Dix, John A., 202, 238–39, 255, 257, 267,
    294, 299, 341, 359
Dodge, William, 61, 102, 188–89, 246, 281
Douglas, Stephen, 55, 56, 71–72, 73–74, 84
Douglass, Frederick, 80, 87, 288, 291, 310,
    366
Dowling, Joseph, 237
Downing, Thomas, 35n
draft riots:
    aftermath of, 252, 253–68, 296, 304–6,
        314–15, 326, 328, 337, 359
    attempted beyond New York City, 3–4,
        182, 203, 241, 254, 271, 279, 283–84,
        291, 343, 350
    barricades in, 194–95, 211, 214, 231
    beginning of, 3, 19, 125–29, 131
    blacks targeted in, 141–42, 143–50, 151,
        154, 157–58, 160–61, 162, 171–74,
        181, 188, 196–97, 199–200, 202–6,
        215, 224–25, 227, 242, 243, 246–48,
        250, 251, 252, 258, 266–67, 289–90,
        304, *325*
    blame assigned in, 214–16, 227–28, 237,
        245, 263, 340
    civilian patrols in, 175–76, 188, 190,
        216, 218
    clearing the streets, 177–78, 180, 195,
        211, 214, 218, 230–31
    communications cut in, 127, 128, 134,
        137, 168–69, 200, 221–22
    conspiracy theories of, 3, 8, 116, 138,
        212, 232, 243–45, 254, 261, 272, 296,
        322–23
    death toll in, 3, 218, 251–52
    and draft law, *see* conscription law
    draft offices targeted in, 127, 128, 131,
        132, 135, 148
    and elections, 261–63, 322–24, *325*
    federal intervention forestalled in, 186,
        198–99, 211–13, 217, 252, 328

fires set in, 135–36, 141, 148, *149*, 162, 176, 189–90, 194, 197, 200, 210, 211, 217, 250, 252

incitement by newspapers, 4, 24, 26, 29, 106, 114–15, 123–24, 174–75, 215–16, 228, 294, 318

incitement by politicians, 4, 26-27, 113, 121, 133, 164, 180, 186n, 194, 217, 237, 317, 326

investigation of, 212, 253–54, 270, 315, 357

liability for destruction in, 247–48, 250, 266, 286, 287

looting and street crime in, 132–33, 137, 148, 150, 153, 178, 188, 193–94, 216, 217, 250

martial law sought for, 5, 6–7, 8, 163–64, 186, 188, 212, 235, 238, 253–54, 295, 333, 357

mob leaders, 126, 135, 136, 155, 159, 169, 180, 192, 212, 226, 231, 259

mobs in, 123, 125–27, 129–33, *130*, 134, 135, 136–37, 147, 150, 152–53, 158, 160, 166–68, *167*, 174, 176–78, 180–81, *181*, *187*, 190–97, 200, 204–5, 211, 217–21, 225–28, 229–31, 252

New York as example for nation, 181–83, 213, 232, 241, 252

police activity in, 128, 129, 131, 132–33, 134, 137, 141, 151–53, 159, 162, 168, 176–77, 180, 190–92, 251, 252

refugees from, 203, 243, 248–49, 252, 265–66, 304

rumors about, 119–20, 124, 243–45, 254

social issues in, 4–5, 6, 7–8, 121–22, 133, 134, 153, 250, 254, 336–37, 340, 369–70

trials and punishments for, 257–59

troops requested in, 127, 129, 134, 138–39, 161–62, 163–64, 170, 178, 184–85, 189–90, 195, 199, 201, 218–19, *222*, 227, 229–30, 233, 252

wealthy Protestants as targets of, 4, 188, 189, 206, 326

Dunn, Michael, 209

Eagan, John, 129

Early, Jubal, 278, 285, 291

Edmonds, John W., 52–53, 253

Elliot, Robert, 349n

Emancipation Proclamation, 5, 6, 7, 89–92, 95, 96, 97, 99, 100, 262, 286, 291, 315, 317, 324, 359, 366

Emmet, Thomas Addis, 33

Europe, riots in, 51, 195, 251, 336–37, 340, 350

Evans, George Henry, 39

Evarts, William, 368

Everett, Edward, 74

Ewell, Richard, 15, 20, 21

Eytinge, Clarence, 238

Fagan, Barney, 209–10

Farley, Terence, 138

Farragut, David, 82

Federalist party, 31–32, 35

Fenian Brotherhood, 51, 79, 119, 317–18

Fenton, Reuben, 295, 305, 306, 326, 328, 329, 347

Fessenden, William, 313

Fifteenth Amendment, 6, 329, 330, 333, 334, 342, 348, 361

Fifty-fourth Massachusetts (black) regiment, 99, 242

Finney, Charles, 38

Fish, Hamilton, 304

Fisk, Jim, 346

Fisk, Theophilus, 44–45

Fitzsimmons, Thomas, 126, 169

Five Points slum, 36, 37, 40, 49, 108, 237, 324

Forrest, Nathan Bedford, 319, 324

Fourier, Charles, 47

Fourteenth Amendment, 6, 313–15, 320, 329, 333, 334, 361

Franklin, Abraham, 205–6

Franklin, Walter, 170, 191, 192, 193

Freedom's Journal, 37–38

Freeman's Journal, 78, 106, 294

Free Soil party, 54, 55, 56, 58, 71

Frémont, John C., 64, 80–81, 83, 84

Frothingham, Octavius B., 246

Fry, James, 104, 114, 116–17, 182, 216–17, 227, 245

Garfield, James, 333, 345

Garnet, Rev. Henry Highland, 6, 97–99, 154, 205, 246, 267–68, 287–91, *289*, 301–2

Garrison, William Lloyd, 38, 144, 198, 348, 354, 357

Gay, Sidney, 88, 124, 155, 159–60, 166, 178–79, 253, 254

German immigrants, 60, 66, 67–68, 86, 135, 261, 314, 329–30, 333, 367

Gibbons, Abby Hopper, 96–97, 208–9, 231, 247, 321

Gibbons, James, 85, 96–97, 192, 193, 208, 231–32

Gibbons, Julia, 151, 192–94, 199, 200, 208–9, 231, 247–48

Gibbons, Lucy, 96, 151, 164, 192–94, 199, 200, 208–9, 231, 247–48
Gilded Age, 7, 328, 337, 350, 351, 370
Gilmore, James, 87–88, 121, 155–56, 158, 165–67, 178–79, 196, 216, 253–54, 270, 282
Godkin, E. L., 306, 345, 347
Gould, Jay, 346, 351
Governors Island, 132, 139, 156, 158, 165
Grant, Ulysses S., 307, *335*, 352
  in Civil War battles, 10, 12, 29, 82, 260, 272–79, 285, 291, 297, 306, 332
  and elections, 321, 326, 346, 348, 350–51, 353, 354, 359, 360, 364
  and Ku Klux Klan, 334–36, 357–58
  opponents of, 346, 359
  as president, 8, 332, 334, 345, 346, 357–58, 360, 362, 366
  and scandals, 346, 355, 357, 361
Greeley, Horace, *55*, 306
  and abolition, 4, 47, 54, 55, 58, 87–88, 90, 93, 347, 350, 352
  and compromise, 75, 316–17, 334, 344–45
  death of, 351–52
  and draft riots, 123, 136, 153, 155–56, 179, 196, 207, 209, 212, 216, 237, 245–46
  and elections, 281, 282, 329, 346–51, 353, 360
  and liberal reform, 345, 346–50
  and *New-Yorker,* 40, 46, 53
  political shifts of, 350
  and Republican party, 56–57, 66, 73, 87
  and social unrest, 41, 46–47, 52, 53–54, 71, 87, 303, 308, 312, 313
  and *Tribune,* 40n, 47; *see also* New York *Tribune*
  on war, 279, 307, 308
  and Whig party, 53, 54–55
Greeley, Mary, 245–46, 321, 351
Green, Andrew Haswell, 342–43
Griffin, Allen, 149
Griscom, John H., 48–49, 69, 305
Gunther, C. Godfrey, 265, 304, 330

Hall, A. Oakey, 5, 23, 163, 186, 257–58, 327, 328–29, 331, 338–39, 340, 341–44
Halleck, Henry, 88, 202, 272
Halpine, Charles, 79, 268
Hamilton, Alexander, 31, 39
Hammens, Frederick, 209
Harper, James, 48
Harper's Weekly, 102, 157, 237–38, 242, 267, 324

Harris, Elisha, 304
Havemeyer, William, 341, 342
Hawley, Seth, 199
Hay, John, 281
Hayes, Rutherford B., 6, 361–62, 364–66, 368
Headley, Joel Tyler, 32, 121, 126, 133, 135, 152–53, 173, 176, 211, 223, 239, 252, 340
Headley, John, 294, 295, 298, 299
Helme, John, 190–91
Hill, Benjamin, 364
Hillhouse, Thomas, 368
Hines, Thomas, 261, 271–72, 279–81, 283–84, 292, 294–95
Hoffman, John, 5, 257–58, 327, 328, 329, 330, 337, 339, 340, 341, 347
Holcomb, James, 279, 281
Homestead Act, 303–4
Hood, John Bell, 296–97, 299
Hooker, "Fighting Joe," 11, 14–15, 260
Hopper, John, 247
Houston, Sam, 47
Howland, Eliza Woolsey, 134–35
Hughes, Archbishop John, 57, 78, 91, 100, 105, *234*, 269n
  as "Dagger John," 47–48
  and draft riots, 186, 206–8, 233–35, 244
Hunter, David, 83, 84

immigrants:
  civil rights for, 36–37, 314, 333, 340
  and industrialization, 354–55
  jobs for, 51, 303
  nativists vs., 35, 40, 48, 49, 56–57, 72, 78, 208, 216, 236, 247, 314, 329, 333, 340
  naturalization mills, 328–29
  and political parties, 63, 65, 68, 133, 263–65, 329–31, 338
  poverty of, 47–48, 50–51, 59, 69, 108
  in riots and strikes, 60, 67–68, 71, 216
Irish-American, 52, 53, 70–71, 78, 100, 104, 238, 329, 341
Irish Brigade, 79, 99, 104, 105, 110, 235, 269n, 276, 308
Irish immigrants:
  and Battle of the Boyne, 33, 210, 340
  Catholic vs. Protestant, 32–34, 57, 209–10, 251, 339–41
  and draft resistance, 19, 86
  and draft riots, 7, 125, 132, 136, 157, 173, 177, 192, 204, 209–10, 233–38, 242, 247, 251
  fighting in Civil War, 11, 32–34, 78, 79–80, 91, 99–100, 104, 110, 119, 207, 238, 307, 321

in gangs, 49
incitement to riot, 53, 71, 236, 237–38
and Irish famines, 48, 50–51, 52, 107, 119
and jobs, 37, 99, 107, 207–8
nativists vs., 48, 49, 78, 216, 236, 238, 247, 314, 333, 340, 341
and politicians, 7, 39, 63, 66, 102, 237, 261, 263–65, 279–80, 295, 317–18, 321, 333, 338–40, 342–43
and poverty, 47–48, 51
and racial issues, 32, 34–36, 37, 40, 87, 99–100, 104, 107, 173, 238, 289, 290
Irish Legion, 79, 308
Irish Sixty-ninth Regiment of Volunteers, 11, 79, 119, 307

Jackson, Andrew, 31–32, 39, 42
Jackson, Charles, 205, 258
Jackson, James, 126, 169, 225–26, 229
Jackson, Stonewall, 260
Jaquess, James, 282
Jardine, Edward, 218–20, 229
Jay, John, 24, 244–45
Jefferson, Thomas, 31, 35
Jenkins, Charles, 131
Johns, Francis, 323
Johnson, Andrew, 281, 307, 310–15, *312*, 322
Johnson, Samuel, 225
Johnston, Joseph E., 10, 260, 274, 278, 296
Jones, William, 157, 170
Joyce, Robert, 205
Judson, Edward, 52
Julian, George, 56, 82, 301, 313, 347, 354

Kansas, Lecompton Constitution for, 71
Kansas-Missouri border wars, 292–93
Kansas-Nebraska Act (1854), 55, 57–58
Kellogg, William, 356–58
Kelly, John, 263, 265, 342, 344
Kennedy, John, 100, 119–20, 123, 128–29, 132, 133, 134, 144, 180, 255, 299
Kennedy, Robert Cobb, 294, 299n
Kidd, William, 116, 296
Kiernan, Patrick, 209
Kiernan, Thomas, 132
Kilpatrick, Hugh, 233
King, Charles, 188, 268
Kingston, New York, draft opposed in, 182
Knights of the Golden Circle, 10, 76, 102, 119, 271
Know Nothings, 56, 57, 69, 238
Ku Klux Klan, 6, 8, 319–20, 324–26, 332–36, 350, 357–58, 359

labor movement:
associations of, 47, 49, 60, 321, 330, 366, 367
and eight-hour day, 60, 296, 321, 330, 342, 350, 367, 368
and equal opportunity, 30–32, 303–4
European radicals in, 51, 60
and factory system, 7, 31, 49, 303
fragmentation of, 367
and immigration, 51, 303
and job competition, 5, 6, 7, 37, 44, 60, 87, 99, 106, 107, 113, 207–8, 221, 262, 366
and job safety, 370
and Molly Maguires, 367
and poverty, 7, 32, 46–47, 59–61
and race, 4, 5, 32, 35, 37, 44, 87, 104, 330, 342, 366–67, 368
repressive responses to, 7, 350, 368
and riots, 60, 126, 169, 221, 343, 367–69, *369*
strikes, 26, 41, 50, 60, 87, 104, 106, 126, 169, 221, 306, 330, 342, 350, 366–70
and Tammany, 40, 296, 329–31, 342
and unemployment, 367, 368
and wages, 37, 41, 60, 61, 303, 367, 368, 370
and wealth gap, 7, 31, 303
and women, 60, 321–22, 366
Lamb, James, 172
Lee, Robert E.:
in Civil War battles, 9–12, 15, 17, 21–22, 89, 260, 273, 274, 275, 276–78, 291, 299, 306
in retreat, 22, 27–28, 184, 185, 201, 202, 206, 228, 242, 274
invasion of Pennsylvania, 1, 3, 8, 9–11, 12–15, 17, 20, 32
surrender of, 307
Lefferts, Marshall, 14
Leonard, Ellen, 197, 218–21, 223
Lincoln, Abraham, *98*
assassination of, 307–8, 311
civil rights curbed by, 4, 23–24, 25–27, 86, 100, 261, 272, 284
and Civil War, 12, 14–15, 77, 78, 82, 84–85, 86–87, 89, 184, 242, 259, 260, 277–78, 280, 297, 299
and conscription law, 3, 18, 29, 213, 232, 255, 256, 280
and Douglas, 56, 71–72, 73–74, 84
and draft riots, 5, 6–7, 8, 86, 164, 212, 213, 235, 238–39, 253–54, 256, 303, 315, 328
and election of 1860, 71–75
and election of 1863, 262

Lincoln, Abraham (*continued*)
  and election of 1864, 263, 276, 278, 279,
    281–82, 291, 293, 294–96, 300, 306
  Emancipation Proclamation of, 5, 7,
    89–90, 262, 286
  executive powers expanded by, 86, 270
  political attacks on, 4, 8, 23, 26–27, 29,
    88, 92, 174–75
  political strategy of, 24–25, 72–73, 77,
    81, 82, 83, 84–85, 87–88, 238–39,
    253–54, 262, 269, 270, 281–82,
    300–301, 357, 362
  and racial issues, 72–73, 80–81, 83,
    84–85, 87, 95, 96
  and Reconstruction, 270, 286
  and Republican party, 8, 56, 72–75, 84,
    262, 282, 291, 315
  and Thirteenth Amendment, 300–301
Lockwood, John, 12, 13, 19–20, 185
Long, Jacob, 150
Longstreet, James, 17, 21–22, 27, 260
Longuemare, Captain, 271
Los Angeles, riots in, 251n
Louisiana, corruption in, 356–58, 361
Lovejoy, Elijah P., 47
Lynch, Richard, 150
Lyons, Albro, 143, *144*, 145, 160–61, 171,
  224, 248, 265–66
Lyons, Maritcha, 143, 161, 171, 224, 248,
  249, 265
Lyons, Mary, 145, *145*, 160–61, 171, 224,
  248, 265–66

MacCool, Finn, 51
MacNeven, William James, 33
Macready, William, 52
Maguire, Thomas, 132
Marble, Manton, 91–93, *93*, 328, 352
  and Democratic party, 92–93, 102,
    214–15, 227–28, 263, 317, 326, 348,
    353, 359–60, 363–64
  draft denounced by, 25–26, 106, 114,
    257
  and elections, 263, 348, 353, 360, 363–64
  Reconstruction undermined by, 6, 333,
    357, 359
  and Republican party, 92, 93, 215, 227,
    353
  violence defended by, 4, 24, 106, 174
  and *World, see* New York *World*
Martin, Robert, 294, 298, 299
Massie, Rev. James, 154
Masterson, John and William, 122, 259
Masterson, Peter, 122–23, *123*, 131, 135,
  169, 259
Matthews, Richard, 330

M'Caffrey, Paddy, 148
McClellan, George, 82, 86–87, 187
  and Civil War, 11, 15, 17, 83, 84, 85, 86,
    88, 89, 260
  as presidential candidate, 86-87, 102,
    263, 276, 284, 293-94, 295, 312n
McCredie, Robert, 132–33
McCune Smith, James, 4, 43-45, *45*, 143,
  268, 287, 291n, 302
McCunn, John H., 208, 244, 328
McDowell, Irvin, 11
McElrath, T. P., 140, 162–63, 170, 177
McGee, Thomas D'Arcy, 53
McKeon, John, 265
McMasters, James, 78, 106, 119, 294, 295,
  299
McMullen, Edgar, 246
Meade, George, 15, 17, 20, 21, 22, 27–28,
  30, 79, 184, 201, 202, 242, 260, 272,
  274, 277
Meagher, Thomas Francis, 79, 99–100, 110,
  235
Mealy, William, 203
Mellon, James, 31
Merry, Patrick, 126
Mexican laborers, 354–55
Moore, Ely, 44
Moran, Martin, 231
Morgan, John Hunt, 3, 20–21, 111–12, *111*,
  113, 201–2, 241, 261, 271, 294, 361
Morgan, J. Pierpont, 31
Morse, Samuel F. B., 34n
Morton, Oliver, 314–15
Muhlenberg, Rev. Dr. William, 134–35
Murray, Mary, 42, *43*

Nast, Thomas, 237, 324, 325, 327, 340,
  348–50
Nation, 53, 53n, 102, 306, 345, 347, 370
National Convention of Colored Men,
  288–91
Newark, New Jersey, riots in, 182, 203
New York Anti-Slavery Society, 38
New York City:
  Astor Place riots, 52, 60, 67, 138, 139, 253
  Board of Health, 305
  Board of Supervisors, 250, 255, 256, 304
  bounty jumpers in, 257, 273
  Citizens' Association, 304, 306, 341, 345
  and Civil War, 78–79
  as commercial center, 3, 40, 41, 51–52,
    68, 75, 76, 92, 109–10, 212, 251
  Common Council, 61–62, 138, 210–11,
    236, 244, 255, 266
  Confederate sympathies in, 5, 68, 70,
    75–76, 77–78, 294

Council for Political Reform, 341, 343
debt financing in, 330, 337–40
Democrats in power, 5, 6, 7, 8, 24, 35,
    50, 62, 66, 75, 94, 102, 186, 199, 212,
    239, 254, 270, 306, 315, 321, 328–29,
    340
draft brokers in, 256–57
draft law in, *see* conscription law
draft riots in, *see* draft riots
gangs in, 49–50, 62, 67, 119
labor unrest in, 4, 50, 60, 107, 306, 330,
    350
metropolitan area, 66
militia called away from, 3, 13–14, 17,
    27–28, 32, 116, 296
militia on riot duty in, 50, 52, 129,
    222–23, 225–27, 241
Mozart Hall in, 69, 92, 94
Orange riot in, 33, 339–41, 342, 347, 350
police in, 49, 50, 62, 65–68, 100, 129
political corruption in, 61–66; *see also*
    Tammany Hall
racial issues in, 35–39, 40–45, 83, 87,
    252, 287–91, 306
refugees from, 203, 243, 248–49, 252,
    265–66
Seventh Regiment, 13, 14, 40n, 52, 67,
    185, 201, 222–23, 231
slums and poverty in, 4, 7, 8, 11, 35–37,
    40, 46, 48–49, 51, 59–60, 61, 69,
    107–9, 250–51, 266, 303–6
social unrest in, 32, 33, 39–40, 48–50,
    52–53, 67–69, 77–78, 222, 230, 250,
    254, 261, 340–44
soldiers recruited from, 11, 12–14, 24,
    78–79, 86, 90, 256
substitute relief fund in, 210–11, 255,
    256, 338
supervision of elections in, 329
Tammany in, *see* Tammany Hall
transportation system of, 61–62, 108,
    134, 192, 203, 216
volunteer fire companies in, 49, 62,
    122–23, 131, 169, 198, 259,
    305–6
walking tour of, 371–75
war profiteers in, 8, 17, 151
wealth gap in, 7, 8, 47–48, 50–51, 68,
    306, 337, 370
New York Daily News, 26, 69–70, 74, 78,
    116, 124, 215, 272
New-Yorker, 40, 46, 53
New York *Evening Post,* 39, 40–41, 125–26,
    175, 215–16, 228, 322, 347, 352
New York Herald, 29, 49, 52, 74, 104, 115,
    116, 206, 268, 366

New York State:
    Albany Regency in, 25, 83, 328, 360
    housing code of, 69, 305
    and Metropolitan police, 100, 129
    militia of, *see* Sandford, Charles
    National Guard, 12, 40
    reform movement in, 329
    Republicans in, 66, 68, 69, 100
New York Times, 3, 68, 106, 179, 201–2,
    216, 219, 228, 259, 336–37, 370
New York *Tribune:*
    on conscription law, 106, 115
    and elections, 346–51
    ownership of, 40n, 47, 351
    on politics, 4, 63, 87–88
    on social issues, 4, 52, 53–54, 55, 58, 65,
        87, 107, 215, 226, 228, 303–4, 319
    as target of riots, 4, 136, 153–54,
        155–56, 158–60, 165–67, *167,*
        178–79, 185, 196, 216, 258
    war news in, 9–10, 29–30, 202, 267
New York *World:*
    anti-emancipation campaigns in, 92, 93,
        102, 114, 359
    central government attacked in, 24,
        25–26, 123, 357
    Democratic party views in, 92–93, 226,
        293, 348, 353
    draft denounced in, 25–26, 106, 124,
        174, 257
    on draft riots, 162, 173–75, 191–92, 211
    Marble as editor of, 4, 92, 328, 359–60
    sale of, 360
    on white supremacy, 114, 226, 228, 293,
        319, 320, 324, 326, 333, 359
Northwest Conspiracy, 271–72, 283–84,
    291–93, 294–95, 298–99
Nugent, Robert, *118*
    and draft lottery, 117, 216–17, 245
    and draft riots, 127, 131, 132, 162, 170,
        175, 227, 245, 250
    and Irish Brigade, 308
    and Irish Sixty-Ninth, 11, 119, 307

O'Brien, H. T., 177, 189, 191, 219
O'Brien, James, 339
O'Connell, Daniel, 33, 51, 290
O'Conor, Charles, 236, 304, 342
O'Gorman, Richard, 237
Olmsted, Frederick Law, 5, 102, 212, 270
Opdyke, George, 17–18, 32, 81, *139,* 341
    and draft riots, 4, 129, 131, 134, 137–39,
        151, 155, 156, 163, 175, 186, 201,
        211, 216–17, 222, 225, 226–27, 233,
        255, 258, 369
    and substitute relief fund, 256

Order of American Knights, 292–93
Orton, William, 351

Panic of 1837, 46–48, 49, 303
Panic of 1857, 68, 138
Panic of 1873, 354–55, 360, 366, 367
Paris Commune (1871), 336–37, 340, 350
Parton, James, 153–54, 155–56, 158–60
Paulding, Hiram, 178, 179
Pemberton, John, 29
Pendleton, George, 119, 284
Pennsylvania, Lee's invasion of, 1, 3, 8,
    9–11, 12–15, 17, 20, 32
Philadelphia, 37, 40, 48, 182, 240
Phillips, Wendell, 356
Pickett, George, 22
Pierce, Franklin, 54
Plains Indians, 354
Polk, James K., 53, 175
Pollard, Edward, 76
Pope, John, 11, 89
Porter, Josiah and Ellen, 209–10, 258
Powell, Sarah, 193
Powell, William, 144–45, 161, 197–98, 266
Powers, Matthew, 210, 258–59, 269
Price, Sterling, 292–93
Protestants:
    and abolition, 100
    Catholics vs., 32–34, 57, 100, 209–10,
        251, 339–41
    dominant culture of, 33
    and Republican party, 4, 7, 57, 59, 247,
        251, 333
    Second Great Awakening, 34, 37, 57, 97
Purdy, Elijah, 84
Putnam, H. R., 189–90, 219, 221, 229–30,
    252
Putnam, Israel, 190

Randall, Samuel, 365
Ray, Rev. Charles, 246, 251, 266–67
Ray, Edward, 172
Raymond, Henry, 216, 228, 246
Reconstruction, 310–17, 362
    amendments passed in, 6, 329, 333, 334,
        361, 366
    and Emancipation Proclamation, 5, 89,
        90, 95, 366
    end of, 333, 358
    Freedmen's Bureau in, 313, 360–61, 367
    and industrialization, 354–55
    in Louisiana, 356–58, 361
    martial law in, 6, 315, 318, 320, 324,
        332, 356, 358, 362–63, 366
    opponents of, 6, 90, 322, 328, 336, 345,
        348, 353, 359

    and racial violence, 6, 302, 310, 313, 317,
        324, 332–36, 358–59, 361, 362
    as social revolution, 5, 8, 90, 212–13, 296
    and state powers, 270, 311, 314, 324,
        326, 332, 334, 346, 357, 361
    undermined, 6, 296, 349, 355, 358–59,
        362
    waving the bloody shirt, 314, 322, 362
Reid, Whitelaw, 347, 351
Republicans:
    birth of party, 56–57, 66, 316
    Congressional power of, 81, 87, 94, 265,
        296, 317, 333–34, 349, 351
    and election of 1860, 72–75
    and election of 1863, 261–63
    and election of 1864, 281–82, 291, 294–96
    and election of 1868, 321–22, 326
    and election of 1872, 346–51
    and election of 1876, 358, 362–65
    Liberal, 345–51, 353–54
    nativism of, 216, 247, 333
    newspapers of, 4, 87, 216, 237
    in New York State, 66, 68, 69, 100
    Protestants as, 4, 7, 57, 59, 247, 251, 333
    on racial equality, 5, 8, 30, 57–58, 64,
        74–75, 81, 84, 87, 91, 311, 359
    radical, 4, 5, 6, 8, 81, 87, 235, 311, 313,
        321, 326, 346, 353, 357, 361
    and Reconstruction, 270, 296, 313, 326,
        358–59
    Stalwarts, 346, 353
    and tariffs, 303, 347, 348
Reynolds, Whitney, 106–7
Richmond, H. E., 216
Rockefeller, John D., 31
Roosevelt, Robert, 341
Rosecrans, William, 12, 21, 242, 259, 260
Rothschild family, 92, 338
Ruffin, Edmund, 2, 75
    and Civil War, 77, 242, 284, 306
    on the draft, 256, 259, 284–85
    novel by, 1–2, 3
    riots applauded by, 1–2, 68–69, 71, 94,
        113, 182–83, 211, 240, 245, 258, 272
    suicide of, 308–9
Ruggles, Samuel, 341
Russell, William, 75, 79
Russwurm, John, 37
Ryer, B. Franklin, 204–5, 217–18
Rynders, Isaiah, 52–53, 133, 144, 163, 253

Sampson, William, 33
Sandford, Charles:
    and Astor Place riots, 52, 139
    and draft riots, 129, 131, 138–39, 140,
        141, 148, 161–62, 163, 170, 175, 178,

195, 198, 199, 204, 217–19, 225, 227, 229, 239

and state arsenal, 138–39, 141, 163, 175, 198, 204

and state militia, 13, 17, 52, 129, 138–39, 227

Schurz, Carl, 334, 345, 346–47, 356

Scott, Dred, 72

Scott, Thomas, 360

Scott, Winfield, 54, 300

Seamen's Home, 143, 160–61, 171

Seddon, James, 271

Seward, William, 56, 58, 72, 73, 74, 84, 85, 87, 89–90, 182, 262, 307–8

Seymour, Horatio, *101*, 121
  and black regiment, 99, 100–102, 247, 267, 268
  and conscription law, 24, 115–16, 216–17, 254–55
  and Democratic party, 23, 25, 26, 92, 93, 102, 139, 199
  during draft riots, 138, 139, 185–87, *187*, 188, 194, 198–99, 206, 211, 212, 213, 216–17, 219, 225, 229, 233, 235, 239, 244–45, 322
  and elections, 93, 94, 295, 321, 322–24, 360
  as governor, 101–2
  incendiary speeches by, 4, 23, 26–27, 194
  and state militia, 12, 13, 14, 17, 19, 32, 116, 138, 244–45

Shamrock, 33–34, 342

Sheridan, Philip, 79, 278, 285, 291, 298, 356–58, 361

Sherman, William Tecumseh, 206, 260, 272, 274, 278, 284, 297, 298, 299, 306

Shotwell, Anna, 42–43, *43*, 146–49, 249, 287

Shotwell, Hannah, *43*

Sigel, Franz, 274

Simmons, Robert, 242

Sinclair, Samuel, 155, 351

slavery:
  abolition of, *see* abolition
  and Brown's raid, 70, 73, 74
  caste system in lieu of, 6, 90
  and Constitution, 80, 86, 291
  de facto, 311–12
  as dividing issue, 64, 71, 72, 75, 76, 78, 80, 82–83, 84, 96, 262, 281
  and Emancipation Proclamation, 5, 89–90, 95, 100, 324
  free blacks vs., 4, 6, 35, 44, 288
  fugitive laws, 54, 72, 74, 83, 143
  and political goals, 5, 7–8, 53–56, 57–58, 71–73

and Supreme Court, 72

and Thirteenth Amendment, 6, 300–302, 329

Underground Railroad, 96, 143

and white supremacy, 32, 64, 90, 114

see also African Americans

Smalley, George, 232

Smalls, Robert, 349n

Smith, Andrew, 126

Smith, Gerrit, 93

Smith, Stephen, 304

social Darwinism, 370

Sons of Liberty, 271, 283–84, 291–92, 294, 295, 298

South, *see* Confederate States of America

Spencer, Herbert, 370

Sprague, John, 116, 139

Spring, Lindley, 114

Stanton, Edwin, 13, 14, 82, 86, 102–3, 104, 138, 201, 226, 256, 267

Stanton, Elizabeth Cady, 321

Steinway, Theodore, 341

Stephens, Alexander, 10, 22, 311

Stevens, Thaddeus, 81, 303, 311, 313, 361

Stewart, A. T., 110

Stoddard, William, 161, 176, 181, 223, 225, 369

Strong, George Templeton, 23, *207*
  and draft riots, 5, 7, 128, 132, 163, 164, 197, 202, 206, 270
  nativism of, 197, 202
  Republican views of, 5, 66, 78, 95, 121, 212, 237, 342
  and Union League, 102, 163, 212
  on the war, 278, 284

Stuart, Augustus, 205

Stuart, J.E.B., 21, 22, 27–28

Sumner, Charles, 56, 84, 303, 311, 313, 353

Supreme Court, U.S., 72, 255, 361, 366

Sweeny, Peter B., 263, 264, 327, 329, 330–31, 339, 342–44

Tammany Hall, 49, 53, 69
  and Bank War, 39–40
  and conscription law, 255–56
  and corruption, 61–63, 92, 137–38, 337–44, 345
  debt financing by, 211, 337–40
  and Democratic party, 23, 39–40, 62, 64, 83, 94, 163, 211, 238, 257, 263–65, 320, 326–31
  and draft riots, 137–38, 163, 218, 229
  and elections, 69, 237, 294, 296, 318, 320, 321, 326, 328–29, 331, 343
  investigation of, 341–42, 344

Tammany Hall (*continued*)
  and labor movement, 40, 296, 329–31, 342
  and Orange riot, 340–41, 342
  rise to power, 23, 263
  and show trials, 257–59
  and Tweed, 23, 62, 263–65, 320, 321, 326–31, 337–44, 345, 359, 360
  and white supremacy, 342
Taney, Roger, 72
Tappan, Arthur, 38, 40, 41, 42, 144
Tappan, Lewis, 38, 40, 41, 42, 144
Taylor, Zachary, 54
Texas, 47, 53, 175
Thirteenth Amendment, 6, 300-302, 311, 312n, 329
Thomas, George, 260, 299
Thompson, Jacob, 272, 279, 281, 292, 294
Thompson, Richard, 368
Tilden, Samuel, 6, 81, 83, 92, 254, 317, 319, 322, 326, 329, 341–44, 359, 360, 361–64, *363*
Tilton, Henry, 126
Torrey, John, 188, 199–200
transcontinental railroad, 354–55
Trobriand, Phillippe de, 358
Trumbull, Lyman, 313, 334, 347, 354
Tulsa, Oklahoma, riots in, 251n
Turner, Benjamin, 349n
Tweed, William "Boss," 7, *264*, 347
  and Board of Supervisors, 250, 255, 256
  and draft riots, 5, 137–38, 163, 186, 250
  and home rule, 137–38, 163
  and Tammany Hall, 23, 62, 263–65, 320, 321, 326–31, 337–44, 345, 359, 360
Tweed Ring, 337–44, 345

Union forces:
  Army of the Potomac, 14, 22, 104, 272, 273, 308
  battles of, *see* Civil War
  blacks in, 86, 88, 97, 99, 102, 198, 242, 247, 262, 267–68, 282
  losses of, 11–12, 22, 85, 267, 276, 277
  political divisions in, 23
  units of, 13, 18, 85–86, 102–3
Union League Club, 102, 133, 163, 164, 188, 206, 212–13, 244, 247, 267–68, 315, 316–17, 326, 329, 341, 357
Union Steam Works, 137, 179–81, *181*, 190, 197

Vallandigham, Clement, 24–25, 81, 111, 119, 194, 262, 271, 279, *280*, 281, 284, 291–92, 322–23, 348
Vaux, Calvert, 102

Wade, Ben, 303
Wade, Henry, 126
Wadsworth, James, 93
Walker, Norman S., 323
Walling, George W., 67, 123, 190, 195, 198
Walsh, Charles, 279, 283, 294, 295
Walsh, Mike, 59
Warburton, A. F., 236
Warren, John, 106–7
Weed, Thurlow, 17n
Welles, Gideon, 84, 262
Welsh, Peter, 104–6, *105*, 235–36, 257, 274–76
Whig party, 32, 39–40, 44, 47, 53, 54–55, 59, 62, 74, 263, 270, 303
White League, 356–57
Whitman, Walt, 7, 8, 108
Whitney, Stephen, 61
Whitten, James, 126, 136, 155
Wilkins, John, 195
William of Orange, 33, 210n
Williams, Rev. Peter Jr., 36, 37, 38, 40, 41, 43, 144
Wilmot, David, 53–54
Wilmot Proviso, 53–54, 64
Wingate, George, 13, 27–28, 184–85, 241
Winslow, Cleveland, 218–19, 225
Women's Suffrage Association of America, 321–22
Wood, Ben, 26, 69, 70, 76, 81, 94, 124, 212, 215, 295
Wood, Fernando, 6, *65*, 79, 92
  on class warfare, 5, 94, 133, 340
  Confederate sympathies of, 4, 76, 77
  and *Daily News*, 26, 69–70, 124, 272
  and elections, 62–64, 94, 261–63, 295, 348, 364–65
  and McClellan, 86–87
  as Peace Democrat, 25, 81, 119, 265, 272, 338
  and police, 65–68, 100
  and racial hatred, 5, 94, 302, 317–18, 334, 365
  and riots, 65–67, 69, 70, 78, 133, 194, 212, 244, 261, 263
  and Tammany, 62–64, 69, 84, 318, 331, 339
Wood, Thomas, 177–78
Woodward, George, 262
Wool, John, 14, 129, 138, 139–40, 156, 159–60, 162–63, 170, 175, 190, 212, 227, 238, 239, 299
Woolsey, Caroline, 150–51
Wright, Rev. Theodore, 38, 98, 144